A Textbook of
Remedial Mathematics
Third Edition

P. Seshagiri Rao
M.Sc., M.Phil
Associate Professor
Department of Mathematics
Vignan Pharmacy College
Vadlamudi, Guntur Dist. (A.P)

PharmaMed Press
An imprint of BSP Book Pvt. Ltd.
4-4-309/316, Giriraj Lane,
Sultan Bazar, Hyderabad - 500 095.

A Textbook of Remedial Mathematics 3rd Edition by *P. Seshagiri Rao*

Third Edition 2018

Fourth Reprint 2024

Published by :

PharmaMed Press

An imprint of BSP Books Pvt. Ltd.

4-4-309/316, Giriraj Lane, Sultan Bazar, Hyderabad - 500 095.

Phone: 040-23445600, 23445688; Fax: 91+40-23445611

E-mail: info@pharmamedpress.com

www.pharmamedpress.com/pharmamedpress.net

Printed at

Aditya Offset Process (I) Pvt. Ltd.

Hyderabad.

Price: Rs. 895.00

ISBN: 978-93-86819-49-9 (Paperback)

A Textbook of
Remedial Mathematics
Third Edition

Dedicated to

My Beloved Parents

Foreword

This book 'A Textbook of Remedial Mathematics' is a unique attempt, which tries to meet almost all the requirements of the pharmacy students. This book has fulfilled the requirements of all universities. The book can be recommended as a very useful reference book for the students and pharmacy professionals.

I congratulate the author for his sincere efforts and hard work put in for the benefit of the students.

Lastly I wish all the success for his future endeavours.

Dr. P. Srinivasa Babu
M.Pharm., Ph.D.
Professor & Principal
Vignan Pharmacy College,
Vadlamudi Post,
Chebrolu Mandal,
Guntur Dist – 522 213.

Preface to Third Edition

This 3rd edition is completely updated with totally new chapters and content in order to comply with the revised regulations for the B. Pharmacy(CBCS) and Pharm.D programs of the Pharmacy Council of India, New Delhi. This book completely meets all the specific requirements of the new PCI syllabus and I hope this book will be extremely useful to all the Pharmacy students of various universities across the country to secure 100% marks in Remedial Mathematics. This book can also be easily followed by the students of Bio-technology, food technology and various other technical and paramedical programs throughout the country.

The subject matter has been presented in detail in a simple form with clarity so as to enable students of varied background to understand the subject with less effort. An attempt has been made to explain the theory through illustrations, diagrams and examples for understanding the concepts involved, keeping in mind the different levels of intelligence. The book contains a good number of solved examples along with a large number of graded problems for practice in the exercises, provided under each topic and at the end of each chapter.

The author is extremely grateful to many individuals and organizations that have helped in various ways in bringing out this book. The author takes the opportunity to express his sincere thanks to the publisher, for their untiring efforts in bringing out this book adequately with a pleasant getup.

The author hopes that the students and teachers of Mathematics at Pharmacy Colleges will appreciate our attempt and receive the book with enthusiasm.

Any shortcomings or errors that have crept in unnoticed may kindly be brought to our notice for rectification in the next edition.

Suggestions for the improvement and enhancing the utility of this book will be gratefully acknowledged.

-Author

Preface to First Edition

This book on Remedial Mathematics has been specially written for the students of Pharmacy Colleges affiliated to various universities and has entirely covered the revised syllabus in Mathematics.

The subject matter has been presented in detail in a simple form with clarity so as to enable students of varied background to understand the subject with less effort. An attempt has been made to explain the theory through illustrations, diagrams and examples for understanding the concepts involved, keeping in mind the different levels of intelligence. The book contains a good number of solved examples along with a large number of graded problems for practice in the exercises, provided under each topic and at the end of each chapter.

The author is extremely grateful to many individuals and organizations that have helped in various ways in bringing out this book. The author takes the opportunity to express his sincere thanks to the publisher, for their untiring efforts in bringing out this book adequately with a pleasant getup.

The author hopes that the students and teachers of Mathematics at Pharmacy Colleges will appreciate our attempt and receive the book with enthusiasm.

Any shortcomings or errors that have crept in unnoticed may kindly be brought to our notice for rectification in the next edition.

Suggestions for the improvement and enhancing the utility of this book will be gratefully acknowledged.

-Author

Acknowledgement

It gives me deep and profound pleasure to express my deep sense of gratitude and indebtedness to my Principal, Dr. P. Srinivasa Babu, Vignan Pharmacy College, Vadlamudi, for his dense and dynamic interest and guidance and also providing facilities for carrying out part of the work in Vignan Pharmacy College, Vadlamudi.

The author expresses his heartfelt thanks to Vignan Educational Institutions for giving me the opportunity and for providing facilities.

The author wishes to express his gratitude to Dr. L. Rathaiah, Chairman and Executive Director, Sri.P. Koteswara Rao and other members of Vignan Educational Institutions for their encouragement and constant support.

The author express his special thanks to Principal, Dr. N. Srinivasu, Vignan Junior College, Vadlamudi, and all staff members for their encouragement and constant support.

Lastly author extends his gratefulness to all his family members for their moral support.

- Author

Contents

UNIT - I
ALGEBRA

Chapter - 2
Partial Fractions

Chapter - 3
Matrices

Chapter - 4
Binomial Theorem

UNIT - II

TRIGONOMETRY

Chapter - 8

Trigonometric Ratios

Chapter - 9

Compound Angles

Chapter - 10

Multiple and Sub-Multiple Angles

Chapter - 11

Heights and Distances

UNIT - III
GEOMETRY

Chapter - 15
Circles

Chapter - 16
Parabola

UNIT - IV
DIFFERENTIAL CALCULUS

Chapter - 17
Limits

UNIT - V
INTEGRAL CALCULUS

UNIT - VI
DIFFERENTIAL EQUATIONS

Chapter - 26
Differential Equations

UNIT - VII
LAPLACE TRANSFORMS

Chapter - 27
Laplace Transforms

UNIT - VIII

Chapter - 28

Applications of Differential Equations of First Order and First Degree

Chapter - 29

Linear Differential Equations of Second and Higher Order

UNIT - I

ALGEBRA

UNIT - I

ALGEBRA

$$\therefore S_n = \frac{n}{2}[2a + (n-1)d] = \frac{n}{2}[2.(6) + (n-1)4]$$

$$= n(6 + (n-1)2)$$

$$= 6n + 2n^2 - 2n$$

$$= 2n^2 + 4n$$

5. The sum of p terms of A.P is $3p^2 + 4p$ find the nth term.

Sol. Given $S_p = 3p^2 + 4p$

$$\therefore \text{Sum of } (p-1) \text{ terms} = S_{p-1} = 3(P-1)^2 + 4(P-1)$$

$$= 3(P^2 + 1 - 2P) + 4P - 4$$

$$= 3P^2 + 3 - 6P + 4P - 4$$

$$= 3P^2 - 2P - 1$$

$$\therefore T_p = S_p - S_{p-1} = (3P^2 + 4P) - (3P^2 - 2P - 1) = 6P + 1$$

$$\therefore \text{nth term} = T_n = 6n + 1$$

6. An A.P consists of 25 terms. The middle term is 20 find the sum of all terms.

Sol. Given A.P consists 25 terms

$\therefore$ its middle term is 13th term.

$$\therefore T_{13} = a + 12d = 20$$

$$\therefore S_{25} = \frac{25}{2}[2a + (25-1)d]$$

$$= \frac{25}{2}[2a + 24d] = 25[a + 12d]$$

$$= 25(20)$$

$$= \mathbf{500}$$

7. The sum of n terms of two arithmetic progressions are in the ratio $5n + 4 : 9n + 6$. Find the ratio of their 18th terms.

Sol. Let a_1, a_2 and d_1, d_2 be first terms and common difference of the first and second A.P's, respectively.

$\therefore$ by given condition we have

$$\frac{\text{Sum of n terms of first A.P}}{\text{Sum of n terms of second A.P}} = \frac{5n+4}{9n+6}$$

1

Progressions

1.1 Sequence (Progression)

An arrangement of numbers in a definite order according to some rule is called sequence of the numbers.

The sequence $\{t_1, t_2 \ldots\ldots\ldots\ldots\}$ is denoted by $\{t_n\}$. The various numbers occurring in a sequence are called its terms. So in above sequence $t_1, t_2 \ldots\ldots\ldots t_n \ldots\ldots\ldots$ are terms of the sequence t_n is n^{th} term of the sequence. That is the nth term is the number at the nth position of the sequence.

A sequence which contains a finite number of terms is called finite sequence and a sequence which contains an infinite number of terms is called an infinite sequence.

Examples :

1. 2, 10, 50, 250, 1250 is a finite sequence
2. $\frac{1}{9}, \frac{1}{81}, \frac{1}{789}, \ldots\ldots\ldots$ is the infinite sequence $\left\{\frac{1}{9^n}\right\}$

1.2 Arithmetic Progression (A.P.)

Definition: A sequence of numbers $t_1, t_2, t_3, t_4 \ldots\ldots\ldots\ldots$ is called an A.P if $t_n - t_{n-1}$ is constant for all n.

i.e. $t_2 - t_1 = t_3 - t_2 = t_4 - t_3 = \ldots\ldots\ldots\ldots\ldots\ldots = \text{constant.}$

This constant is called common difference and is generally denoted by d.

Ex :

1. 1, 3, 5, 7 .... is an A.P.

here $t_1 = 1, t_2 = 3, t_3 = 5, t_4 = 7$ ....

$\Rightarrow \quad t_2 - t_1 = 3 - 1 = 2, t_3 - t_2 = 5 - 3 = 2$ ....

$\therefore \quad t_2 - t_1 = t_3 - t_2 = t_4 - t_3 = t_5 - t_4 =$ .... = constant = 2

$\therefore \quad$ 1, 2, 5, 7,............ is an A.P. with common difference 2. In this progression the first terms is $t_1 = 1$

Ex : 10, 15, 20, 25, 30, 35 .... is an A.P

here $t_1 = 10, t_2 = 15, t_3 = 20, t_4 = 25$............

$\therefore \quad t_2 - t_1 = 15 - 10 = 5, t_3 - t_2 = 20 - 15 = 5$..........

$\therefore \quad t_2 - t_1 = t_3 - t_2 = t_4 - t_3 =$ .... = constant = 5

$\therefore \quad$ 10, 15, 20 .... is an A.P with common difference 5. Here the first term is $t_1 = 10$.

Note: The A.P with first term a and common difference d is a, a + d, a + 2d, a + 3d, ... here the nth term $t_n = a + (n - 1)\,d$.

since, $t_1 = a = a + (1 - 1)\,d$

$t_2 = a + d = a + (2 - 1)d$

$t_3 = a + 2d = a + (3 - 1)d$

$t_n = a + (n - 1)\,d$

So nth term of an AP = first term + (n – 1) common difference

Ex : Suppose in an A.P with first term 2, and common difference 4 then its nth term

$t_n = a + (n - 1)d$

$= 2 + (n - 1) . 4$

$= 2 + 4n - 4$ ($\because$ first term a = 2, common difference is 4)

$= 4n - 2$

If we have first term a and common difference d of an AP then we can find the term which is in any position. Also we can from the sequence.

Ex : If a = 2, d = 3 then find t_{10} also form the corresponding A.P.

Sol. given first term a = 2, common difference d = 3.

We have $t_n = a + (n - 1)d$

$t_{10} = a + (10 - 1)\,d = a + 9d = 2 + 9.(3)$

$= 2 + 27 = 29$

also the corresponding sequence is

$$a, \quad a + d \quad a + 2d \text{ ....}$$

i.e. $\quad 2, 5, 8, 11, \text{ ....}$

Properties of an A.P.

1. If a constant is added to each term of an A.P the resulting sequence is also an A.P.

Ex: 2, 4, 6, ... is a sequence of an A.P with first term 2 and common difference 2.

Now forming another A.P. by adding some constant '3' to above sequence we get

$$2 + 3, \; 4 + 3, \; 6 + 3, \text{ ....}$$

i.e. $\quad 5, 7, 9, \text{............}$ is also an A.P.

since $\quad t_2 - t_1 = 7 - 5 = 2$

$$t_3 - t_2 = 9 - 7 = 2$$

....

....

$$\therefore t_2 - t_1 = t_3 - t_2 = \text{.............} = \text{constant} = 2.$$

2. If a constant is subtracted from each of an A.P, the resulting sequence is also an A.P.

Ex: Take the above example

2, 4, 6, 8 .... is an A.P

Consider 2 – 3, 4 – 3, 6 – 3, 8 – 3, ...

(by subtracting 3 from each of term of the sequence)

i.e. $\quad -1, 1, 3, 5 \text{................}$

it is also an A.P. since

$$t_1 = -1, t_2 = 1, t_3 = 3, t_4 = 5 \text{..............}$$

$$t_2 - t_1 = 1 - (-1) = 2$$

$$t_3 - t_2 = 3 - 1 = 2$$

$$t_4 - t_3 = 5 - 3 = 2$$

....

....

$$\therefore t_2 - t_1 = t_3 - t_2 = \text{ ....} = \text{constant} = 2.$$

$\therefore$ a constat is subtracted from each of an A.P; the resulting sequence is also an A.P.

3. If each term of an A.P is multiplied by a constant, then the resulting sequence is also an A.P.

Ex: Consider an A.P, 2, 4, 6, 8, ...

multiplying each with 5, we get

10, 20, 30, 40 ....

clearly it is also an A.P

$$\because t_2 - t_1 = 20 - 10 = 10,$$

$$t_3 - t_2 = 30 - 20 = 10$$

....

....

$$\therefore t_2 - t_1 = t_3 - t_2 = ... = \text{constat} = 10.$$

4. If each term of an A.P is divided by non zero constant then the resulting sequence is also an A.P.

Ex: Consider an A.P, 2, 4, 6, 8...............

obtain a new sequence by dividing each of above by 4,

we get $\frac{2}{4}, \frac{4}{4}, \frac{6}{4}, \frac{8}{4}$ ....

i.e. $\frac{1}{2}, 1, \frac{3}{2}, 2,$ .... is also an A.P

since $t_2 - t_1 = 1 - \frac{1}{2} = \frac{1}{2}$

$$t_3 - t_2 = \frac{3}{2} - 1 = \frac{1}{2}$$

$$t_4 - t_3 = 2 - \frac{3}{2} = \frac{1}{2}$$

$$\therefore \quad t_2 - t_1 = t_3 - t_2 = t_4 - t_3 = ... = \text{constant} = \frac{1}{2}$$

5. Suppose the three given numbers are in A.P then let them taken as a – d, a, a + d

6. Suppose the four given numbers are in A.P then let them taken as a – 3d, a – d, a + d, and a + 3d,

7. The three given numbers a, b, c are in A.P

then $2b = a + c$

since $c - b = b - a$ (i.e common difference is same)

$\Rightarrow$ $2b = a + c$

8. $(n + 1)^{th}$ term of an A.P is obtained by adding the common difference to its nth term

i.e. $t_{n+1} = t_n + d$ $(\because t_{n+1} - t_n = d)$

Solved Examples

1. Find the common difference and write the next 4 term of each of the following arithmetic progressions.

(i) 3, 6, 9, 12, ...

(ii) $\frac{1}{6}, \frac{1}{3}, \frac{1}{2}, \ldots$

(iii) $x + y, x - y, x - 3y$..............

(iv) −1, −2, −3, −4, ...

Sol. (i) The given sequence is 3, 6, 9, 12, ...

$\therefore t_1 = 3, t_2 = 6, t_3 = 9, t_4 = 12$

$\therefore$ common difference $= t_2 - t_1 = 6 - 3 = 3.$

$\therefore t_5 = t_4 + 3 = 12 + 3 = 15$ ($\because$ by property (8))

$t_6 = t_5 + 3 = 15 + 3 = 18$

$t_7 = t_6 + 3 = 18 + 3 = 21$

$t_8 = t_7 + 3 = 21 + 3 = 24$

$\therefore$ the next 4 terms are 15, 18, 21, 24.

(ii) The given sequence is $\frac{1}{6}, \frac{1}{3}, \frac{1}{2}$ ....

$\therefore t_1 = \frac{1}{6}, \; t_2 = \frac{1}{3}, \; t_3 = \frac{1}{2}$

$\therefore$ Common difference $= d = t_2 - t_1 = \frac{1}{3} - \frac{1}{6} = \frac{2-1}{6} = \frac{1}{6}$

$$\therefore\ t_4 = t_3 + d = \frac{1}{2} + \frac{1}{6} = \frac{4}{6} = \frac{2}{3}$$

$$t_5 = t_4 + d = \frac{2}{3} + \frac{1}{6} = \frac{4+1}{6} = \frac{5}{6}$$

$$t_6 = t_5 + d = \frac{5}{6} + \frac{1}{6} = \frac{6}{6} = 1$$

$$t_7 = t_6 + d = 1 + \frac{1}{6} = \frac{7}{6}$$

$\therefore$ the next 4 terms are $\frac{2}{3}, \frac{5}{6}, 1, \frac{7}{6}$.

(iii) The given sequence is $x + y, x - y, x - 3y$ ....

$t_1 = x + y,\ t_2 = x - y,\ t_3 = x - 3y$

$\therefore$ common difference $= d = t_2 - t_1$

$= (x - y) - (x + y) = x - y - x - y$

$= -2y$

$\therefore\ t_4 = t_3 + d = (x - 3y) + (-2y) = x - 5y$

$t_5 = t_4 + d = (x - 5y) + (-2y) = x - 7y$

$t_6 = t_5 + d = (x - 7y) + (-2y) = x - 9y$

$t_7 + t_6 + d = (x - 9y) + (-2y) = x - 11y$

$\therefore$ the next 4 terms are $x - 5y, x - 7y, x - 9y, x - 11y$

2. Find the idential terms in each of the following arithmetic progressions.

(i) 21, 16, 11, 6, 1, –4, –9 ....; t_{20}, t_{25}, t_n

(ii) n – 1, n – 2, n – 3 ....; t_n

Sol. (i) We know that nth term of an arithmetic progression $t_n = a + (n - 1)d$

here $a = 21,\ d = 16 - 21 = -5$

$\therefore\quad t_{20} = (21) + (20 - 1)\ (-5)$

$= 21 + (19)(-5) = 21 - 95 = -74$

and $t_{25} = a + (25 - 1)d$

$= 21 + (24)(-5) = 21 - 120 = -99$

also $t_n = a + (n-1)d$

$= 21 + (n-1)(-5)$

$= \mathbf{26 - 5n}$

(ii) $n-1, n-2, n-3$ ....

here $a = n-1$, $d = (n-2) - (n-1)$

$= -1$

$\therefore$ $t_n = a + (n-1)d$

$= \mathbf{(n-1) + (n-1).(-1) = 0}$

3. (i) The first term of an A.P is – 4 and 10th term is 14. Determine 30th term.

(ii) The first term of an A.P is y + p and common difference is 2p. Determine n^{th} term.

Sol. (i) given $a = -4$, $t_{10} = 14$

we know that nth term of an A.P is

$t_n = a + (n-1)d$

Since $t_{10} = 14 \Rightarrow a + (10-1).d = 14$

$\Rightarrow -4 + (9)d = 14$

$\Rightarrow 9d = 14 + 4 = 18$

$\Rightarrow 9d = 18 \Rightarrow d = 2$

$\therefore$ $d = 2$, we have $a = -4$

$\therefore$ $t_{30} = a + (30-1)d$

$= -4 + (29)(2)$

$= \mathbf{-4 + 58 = 54}$

(ii) given $a = y + p$; $d = 2p$.

$\therefore$ $t_n = a + (n-1)d$

$= (y + p) + (n-1).2p$

$= \mathbf{(2n + 1)p + y - 2p}$

4. (i) Which term of the A.P 5, 2, –1, ... is –22

(ii) Which term of the A.P 1, 6, 11, 16 .... is 301

Sol. (i) Given A.P is 5, 2, –1, ...

$\therefore$ $a = 5, d = 2 - 5 = -3$

Suppose nth term = $t_n = -22$

$\therefore \quad t_n = a + (n - 1)\, d = -22$

$\Rightarrow 5 + (n - 1) . (-3) = -22$

$\Rightarrow 5 - 3n + 3 = -22$

$\Rightarrow \mathbf{8 - 3n = -22 \Rightarrow -3n = -30 \Rightarrow n = 10}$

$\therefore$ 10th term is -22

(ii) Given A.P is 1, 6, 11, 16, ...

$\therefore \quad a = 1, \quad d = 6 - 1 = 5$

Suppose n^{th} term = $t_n = 301$

$\therefore \quad a + (n - 1)d = 301$

$\Rightarrow \quad 1 + (n - 1)\, 5 = 301 \quad \Rightarrow (n - 1)\, 5 = 300$

$\Rightarrow \quad n - 1 = 60$

$\Rightarrow \quad \mathbf{n = 61.}$

$\therefore$ 61st term is 301.

5. (i) The 6th term of an A.P is 12 and 8th term is 22 then find 2nd term and r^{th} term

(ii) The 10th term of an A.P is 52, and 16th term is 82.

Find the 32nd term.

Sol. (i) Given $t_6 = 12, \; t_8 = 22$

Let a be first term and d be the common difference of the sequence

$\therefore \quad t_6 = a + (6 - 1)d = 12 \Rightarrow a + 5d = 12$ .....(1)

$t_8 = a + (8 - 1)d = 22$

$\Rightarrow \quad a + 7d = 22$ .....(2)

$(2) - (1) \Rightarrow 2d = 10 \Rightarrow d = 5$

Substitute d = 5 in (1) we get

i.e. in $a + 5d = 12 \Rightarrow \quad a + 5(5) = 12$

$\Rightarrow \quad a = 12 - 25 = -13.$

$\therefore \quad a = -13, \; d = 5$

now $t_2 = a + (2 - 1)\, d = a + d = -13 + 5 = -8$

$t_r = a + (r - 1)\, d = -13 + (r - 1)\, 5 = -13 + 5r - 5$

$= \mathbf{5r - 18}$

(ii) Given that $t_{10} = 52$, and $t_{16} = 82$

$\therefore$ $a + (10 - 1)d = 52 \Rightarrow a + 9d = 52$ .....(1)

$a + (16 - 1)d = 82 \Rightarrow a + 15d = 82$ .....(2)

$(2) - (1) \Rightarrow 15d - 9d = 30 \Rightarrow 6d = 30 \Rightarrow d = 5$

Substitute $d = 5$ in (1) i.e. in $a + 9d = 52$

$\therefore a + 9(5) = 52$

$\Rightarrow a + 45 = 52$

$\Rightarrow a = 7$

$\therefore$ $a = 7,\ d = 5$

Hence $t_{32} = a + (32 - 1)d$

$= 7 + (31) . 5$

$= 7 + 155 = 162$

$\therefore$ **32nd term = 162**

6. Split 69 into 3 parts such that they are in A.P and the product of two small parts is 483.

Sol. Let the three numbers be $a - d, a, a + d$

$\therefore$ $a - d + a + a + d = 69$

$\Rightarrow 3a = 69 \Rightarrow a = 23$

also product of two small parts = 483

$\Rightarrow a(a - d) = 483$

$\Rightarrow 23(23 - d) = 483 \Rightarrow 23 - d = 21$

$\Rightarrow d = 2$

$\therefore$ **$a - d = 23 - 2 = 21,\ a + d = 23 + 2 = 25$**

$\therefore$ three numbers are 21, 23, 25.

7. Find three numbers in A.P whose sum is 21 and product is 315.

Sol. Let the three numbers be $a - d, a, a + d$

$\therefore$ $a - d + a + a + d = 21$

$\Rightarrow$ $3a = 21$

$\Rightarrow$ $a = 7$ and $(a - d)a(a + d) = 315 \Rightarrow 7(a - d)(a + d) = 315$

$\Rightarrow \quad a^2 - d^2 = 45 \Rightarrow \quad d^2 = 4 \quad \Rightarrow \quad d = \pm 2$

when $a = 7, d = -2 \quad \Rightarrow \quad a - d, a, a + d$ are 9, 7, 5

a = 7, d = 2 then a –d, a a + d as 5, 7, 9.

8. The pth, q^{th}, r^{th} terms of an A.P are a, b, c respectively show that

$$(q - r)\, a + (r - p)\, b + (p - q)\, c = 0$$

Sol. Let t be first term, d be common difference of the A.P.

$\therefore \quad T_p = t + (p - 1)\, d = a; \qquad T_q = t + (q - 1)\, d; \qquad T_r = t + (r - 1)d$

$\therefore \quad \Sigma(q - r)\, a = \Sigma(q - r)\,(t + (p - 1)d)$

$= \Sigma(q - r)\, t + \Sigma(q - r)\,(p - 1)d$

$= t\,\Sigma(q - r) + d\,\Sigma(p - 1)\,(q - r)$

$= t(0) + d\,[\Sigma\, p(q - r) - \Sigma(q - r)]$

$= t(0) + d\,[0 \quad - \quad 0]$

$\mathbf{= 0 + d(0) = 0}$

Exercise - 1.1

1. Find the common difference and write next four terms of each of the following arithmetic progressions.

   (i) 0, 2, 4, 6 .... (ii) 1, 3, 5, 7, ...

   (iii) 2, 0, –2, –4 (iv) 10, 7, 4, ...

2. Find the

   (i) 15th term of 1, 5, 9, 13........... (ii) 6th term of 5, 8, 11, 14, ...

   (iii) 11th term of 3, 0, –3, –6 .... (iv) 7th term of 0.2, 1, 1.8, 2.6, ...

3. (i) Which term of an A.P 4, 11, 18, ... is 144

   (ii) Find 4th, 6th, 10th terms of an A.P whose n^{th} term is $3n + 2$

   (iii) which term of the A.P $\frac{1}{5}, \frac{7}{10}, \frac{12}{10}$, ... is 4.7

   (iv) Find the common difference and 10th term of A.P

   Whose first term is 10, and 5th term is 2.

   (v) Determine t so that $\frac{3}{4}$, t, $\frac{2}{3}$t are three consecutive terms of A.P.

4. (i) The first term of an A.P is 5 and common difference is 2 find 20th term.

   (ii) The 8th term of an A.P is –10, 10th term of A.P is –16 find 15th term.

   (iii) The third term of an A.P is 25 and 10th term is –3 then find the common difference and 4th term.

   (iv) If p times the pth term of an A.P is q times the qth term of an A.P then find the (p + q)th term of this A.P.

5. (i) If mth term of an A.P is n and nth term is m then show that (m + n)th term is 0.

   (ii) If 10th term of an A.P is 20 and 20th term is 10 then find 30th term ?

6. If t_n denotes the nth term of an A.P and $t_3 : t_5 = 2 : 3$ then find $t_4 : t_6$

Answers

1. (i) Common difference = 2, next four terms are 8, 10, 12, 14

   (ii) Common difference = 2, next four terms are 9, 11, 13, 15

   (iii) Common difference = –2, next four terms are –6, –8, –10, –12

   (iv) Common difference = –3, next four terms are +1, –2, –5, –8

2. (i) 57 (ii) 20 (iii) –27 (iv) 5

3. (i) 21 (ii) 14, 20, 32 (iii) 10 (iv) –2, –8 (v) $\frac{9}{16}$

4. (i) 43 (ii) – 31 (iii) –4, 21 (iv) 0

5. (ii) 0

6. 5 : 7

1.3 Sum of the First n Terms of an Arithmetic Progression

Consider the arithmetic progression,

$$a,\ a + d,\ a + 2d,\ \ldots\ldots\ldots$$

$\therefore$ its nth term is $t_n = a + (n - 1)d$

Let S_n is the sun of first n terms of A.P

$$\therefore \quad S_n = a + (a + d) + (a + 2d) + \ldots\ldots\ldots + a + (n - 1)d \qquad \ldots..(1)$$

$$\therefore \quad S_n = (a + (n - 1)d) + (a + (n - 2)d + (a + (n - 3)d) + \ldots\ldots + (a+d) + a \qquad \ldots..(2)$$

(writing from last to first of the sequence)

adding (1) and (2)

$$\Rightarrow \quad 2S_n = [a + (a + (n-1))] + [(a+d) + (a + (n-2)d)] + \dots\dots + [(a + (n-1)d) + a]$$

$$= [2a + (n-1)d] + [2a + (n-1)d] + \dots\dots + [2a + (n-1)d] \text{ (n times)}$$

$$\Rightarrow \quad 2S_n = n[2a + (n-1)d]$$

$$\Rightarrow \quad S_n = \frac{n}{2}[2a + (n-1)d]$$

$\therefore$ Sum of first n terms of A.P with first term a and common difference d is

$$\frac{n}{2}[2a + (n-1)d]$$

Note:

$$S_n = \frac{n}{2}[2a + (n-1)d]$$

$$= \frac{n}{2}[a + (a + (n-1)d)] = \frac{n}{2}[\text{first term} + \text{nth term}] = \frac{n}{2}[F + L]$$

F = first term

L = n^{th} term

Solved Examples

1. Find the sum of terms of an A.P 2, 4, 6, 8, ... 100 terms

Sol. Given progression is 2, 4, 6, 8,............

$\therefore$ first term a = 2

common difference d = 2

hence, we have sum of n term of an A.P is

$$S_n = \frac{n}{2}[2a + (n-1)d]$$

$$\therefore S_{100} = \frac{100}{2}[2(2) + (100-1)(2)]$$

$$= \mathbf{100\ (2 + 99) = 100 \times 101 = 10100}$$

2. Find the sum of all natural numbers between 100 and 1000 which are multiple of 5.

Sol. The numbers between 100 and 1000 which are multiple of 5 are 105, 110, 115....... 995

$\therefore$ a = 105, l = nth term = a + (n – 1)d = 995 $\Rightarrow$ 105 + (n – 1) 5 = 995

$(n-1)5 = 890$

$n - 1 = 178$

$n = 179$

$\therefore$ The number of numbers between 100 and 1000 which are multiple of 5 is 179

$\therefore$ Sum of the numbers $S_n = \frac{n}{2}[a + l]$

$$\therefore \quad S_{179} = \frac{179}{2}[105+995]$$

$$= \frac{179}{2}\ \mathbf{[1100] = 98450}$$

3. Determine the sum of first 35 terms of an A.P, if second term is 2 and seventh term is 22.

Sol. Let a be the first term and d be common difference of the sequence

given 2nd term = 2 $\Rightarrow a + d = 2$ .....(1)

also given seventh term = 22 $\Rightarrow a + 6d = 22$ .....(2)

$(2) - (1) \Rightarrow 5d = 20 \Rightarrow d = 4$

Substitute $d = 4$ in (1) $\Rightarrow a + 4 = 2$

$\Rightarrow a = -2$

$\therefore a = -2,\ d = 4$

$\therefore$ Sum of first 35 terms of sequence =

$$S_{35} = \frac{35}{2}[2(-2)+(35-1)(4)] \qquad \left(\because S_n = \frac{n}{2}(2a + (n-1)d)\right)$$

$$\mathbf{= 35\ [-2 + (34)\ (2)] = 35\ (66) = 2310}$$

4. Find the sum of n terms of an A.P whose 7th term if 30 and 13th term is 54

Sol. Given $T_7 = 30,\ T_{13} = 54$

$\Rightarrow a + 6d = 30,$ .....(1)

$a + 12d = 54$ .....(2)

$(2) - (1) \Rightarrow 6d = 24 \Rightarrow d = 4$

Substitute $d = 4$ in (1) $\Rightarrow a + 24 = 30 \Rightarrow a = 6$

$$\therefore S_n = \frac{n}{2}[2a + (n-1)d] = \frac{n}{2}[2.(6) + (n-1)4]$$
$$= n(6 + (n-1)2)$$
$$= 6n + 2n^2 - 2n$$
$$= \mathbf{2n^2 + 4n}$$

5. The sum of p terms of A.P is $3p^2 + 4p$ find the nth term.

Sol. Given $S_p = 3p^2 + 4p$

$$\therefore \text{Sum of } (p-1) \text{ terms} = S_{p-1} = 3(P-1)^2 + 4(P-1)$$
$$= 3(P^2 + 1 - 2P) + 4P - 4$$
$$= 3P^2 + 3 - 6P + 4P - 4$$
$$= 3P^2 - 2P - 1$$
$$\therefore T_P = S_P - S_{P-1} = (3P^2 + 4P) - (3P^2 - 2P - 1) = 6P + 1$$
$$\therefore \textbf{nth term} = \mathbf{T_n = 6n + 1}$$

6. An A.P consists of 25 terms. The middle term is 20 find the sum of all terms.

Sol. Given A.P consists 25 terms

∴ its middle term is 13th term.

$$\therefore T_{13} = a + 12d = 20$$
$$\therefore S_{25} = \frac{25}{2}[2a + (25-1)d]$$
$$= \frac{25}{2}[2a + 24d] = 25[a + 12d]$$
$$= 25(20)$$
$$= \mathbf{500}$$

7. The sum of n terms of two arithmetic progressions are in the ratio $5n + 4 : 9n + 6$. Find the ratio of their 18th terms.

Sol. Let a_1, a_2 and d_1, d_2 be first terms and common difference of the first and second A.P's, respectively.

∴ by given condition we have

$$\frac{\text{Sum of n terms of first A.P}}{\text{Sum of n terms of second A.P}} = \frac{5n+4}{9n+6}$$

$$\Rightarrow \quad \frac{\frac{n}{2}[2a_1 + (n-1)d_1]}{\frac{n}{2}[2a_2 + (n-1)d_2]} = \frac{5n+4}{9n+6}$$

$$\Rightarrow \quad \frac{2a_1 + (n-1)d_1}{2a_2 + (n-1)d_2} = \frac{5n+4}{9n+6} \qquad .....(1)$$

Now $\dfrac{\text{18th term of first A.P}}{\text{18th term of second A.P}} = \dfrac{a_1 + 17d_1}{a_2 + 17d_2}$

$$= \frac{2a_1 + 34d_1}{2a_2 + 34d_2} = \frac{5 \times 35 + 4}{9 \times 35 + 6} \qquad \text{[by putting } n = 35 \text{ in (1)]}$$

$$= \mathbf{\frac{179}{321}}$$

hence the required ratio is $\dfrac{179}{321}$

8. Find the three numbers which are in A.P whose sum is 12 and the sum of their cubes is 408.

Sol. Let the three numbers of an A.P be $a - d, a, a + d$

$\therefore$ by given condition that $a - d + a + a + d = 12$

$\Rightarrow 3a = 12 \Rightarrow a = 4$

and $(a - d)^3 + a^3 + (a + d)^3 = 408$

$\therefore (a - d)^3 + (a + d)^3 + a^3 = 408$

$\Rightarrow 2(a^3 + 3ad^2) + a^3 = 408 \qquad (\because (a + b)^3 + (a - b)^3 = 2(a^3 + 3ab^2))$

$\Rightarrow 2(64 + 12d^2) + 64 = 408 \qquad (\because a = 4)$

$\Rightarrow 192 + 24d^2 = 408$

$\Rightarrow 24d^2 = 216 \qquad \Rightarrow d^2 = 9 \qquad \Rightarrow d = \pm 3$

If $a = 4$, $d = 3$, then the required numbers are 1, 4, 7

If $a = 4$, $d = -3$, the required numbers are 7, 4, 1

1.4 Arithmetic-Means

The numbers a, A_1, A_2 .... A_n, b are in A.P then we say that the numbers A_1, A_2 .... A_n are 'n' arithmetic means between a and b.

If a, A, b are in A.P then A is arithmetic mean of a and b.

Now a, A, b in A.P $\Rightarrow$ 2A = a + b

$$\therefore A = \frac{a+b}{2}$$

$\therefore$ The arithmetic mean of a and b is $\frac{a+b}{2}$

Note: We can insert any number of arithmetic means between given two numbers.

Ex :

Consider 1, 3, 5 these are in A.P $\therefore$ 3 is A.M of 1, 5

Similarly 1, 2, 3, 4, 5 are in A.P 2, 3, 4 are A.Ms of 1, 5.

Consider two numbers a, b and suppose there are n A.Ms between them.

Say A_1, A_2 .... A_n.

$\therefore$ a_1 A_1 A_2 .... A_n b are in A.P.

Let d be the common difference of the sequence

$$\therefore A_1 = a + d, \qquad A_2 = a + 2d .... \qquad A_n = a + nd$$

$\therefore b = a + (n+1)d$ ($\because$ b is (n + 2)th term of an A.P)

$$\therefore d = \left(\frac{b-a}{n+1}\right), \text{ where n is number of A.Ms}$$

Again $A_1 + A_2$ .... $+ A_n$

$= (a + d) + (a + 2d) + ... + (a + nd)$

$= na + (1 + 2 + 3 + ... n)\, d$

$$= na + \frac{n(n+1)}{2}\cdot\left(\frac{b-a}{n+1}\right) = na + \frac{n(b-a)}{2}$$

$$= n\left[a + \frac{b-a}{2}\right] = \left[\frac{a+b}{2}\right]$$

$$\therefore A_1 + A_2 .... + A_n = n\left[\frac{a+b}{2}\right]$$

$\therefore$ Sum of n A.M's between a, b = n [A.M's between a, b]

Solved Examples

1. **Insert five arithmetic means between 8, 26.**

Sol. Let A_1, A_2, A_3, A_4, A_5, be five A.M's between 8, 26.

$\therefore$ 8, A_1, A_2, A_3, A_4, A_5, 26 in A.P.

Let d be the common differnece of this A.P

$$\therefore d = \frac{b-a}{n+1} = \frac{26-8}{5+1} = \frac{18}{6} = 3$$

$$\therefore A_1 = a + d = 8 + 3 = 11, \quad A_2 = 11 + 3 = 14, \quad A_3 = 14 + 3 = 17$$

$$A_4 = 17 + 3 = 20 \quad A_5 = 20 + 3 = 23$$

$\therefore$ the five A.Ms are 11, 14, 17, 20, 23

2. **Between 1 and 31, m arithmetic means have been inserted in such a way that the ratio of 7th and (m – 1) th A.M's ratio is 5 : 9. Find the value of m.**

Sol. Let d be the common difference of the

$$7\text{th A.M} = a + 7d = 1 + 7d$$

$$(m-1)\text{th A.M} = a + (m-1)d = 1 + (m-1)d$$

$$\therefore \frac{1+7d}{1+(m-1)d} = \frac{5}{9} \text{ (given)}$$

$$9 + 63d = 5 + 5(m-1)d \quad \text{.....(1)}$$

also $$d = \frac{b-a}{n+1} = \frac{31-1}{m+1} = \frac{30}{m+1}$$

$$\therefore d = \frac{30}{m+1}$$

Substitute $d = \frac{30}{m+1}$ in (1) we get

$$9 + \frac{(63)(30)}{m+1} = 5 + \frac{5(m-1)}{m+1}(30) \Rightarrow 146m = 2044 \Rightarrow m = 14$$

Exercise - 1.2

1. Find the sum of the indicated number of terms in each of the following arithmetic progressions.
   (i) 2, 4, 6, 8, ...; 200 terms.
   (ii) 16, 11, 6, ...; 23 terms
   (iii) $-1, \frac{1}{4}, \frac{3}{2}$ ....; 81 terms
   (iv) $-0.5, -1.0, -1.5$..........; 10 terms
   (v) $x + y, x - y, x - 3y$ ....; 22 terms
2. How many terms of A.P. $-6, \frac{-11}{2}, -5$........ are needed to give the sum -25?
3. In an A.P; 18, 16, 14.........., How many terms should be taken so that their sum is zero.
4. In an A.P of the 5th and 12th terms are 30 and 65 respectively, what is the sum of first 20 terms?
5. In an A.P the 12th term is -13 and sum of first 4 terms is 24. What is the sum of the first 10 terms?
6. In an A.P the first term is 22, the common difference is -4 and sum of n terms is 64. Find n?
7. In an A.P the first term is 2 and the sum of first 5 terms is one forth of the sum of the next five terms. Show that the 20th term is -112.
8. Find the sum of all numbers between 100 and 1000 which are divisible by 13.
9. Find the sum of all integers between 50 and 500 which are divisible by 7.
10. If S_1, S_2, S_3 are the sum of n, 2n, 3n terms respectively of an A.P. Show that $S_3 = 3(S_2 - S_1)$
11. A Person pays Rs.975/- in monthly installments. Each instalment being less than the formar by Rs.5/-, amount of first instalment is 100. In what time will the entire amount be paid.
12. Find the sum of all even inegers from 92 to 768.
13. In an A.P if the pth term is $\frac{1}{q}$ and qth term is $\frac{1}{p}$. Prove that the sum of the first pq terms must be $\frac{1}{2}(pq + 1)$
14. Sum of the first p, q, and r terms of A.P are a, b, c respectively. Prove that $\frac{a}{p}(q-r)+\frac{b}{q}(r-p)+\frac{c}{r}(r-q)=0$.

15. The ratio of the sum of m and n terms of an A.P is $m^2 : n^2$. Show that the ratio of mth and nth terms is 2m – 1:2n – 1.

16. Insert 6 arithmetic means between 3 and 24.

Answers

1. (i) 40200 (ii) – 897 (iii) 3969 (iv) –27.5 (v) 22 (x – 20y)

2. 5 or 20 3. 19 4. 1150 5. 0 6. 4 or 8

8. 37, 674 9. 17696 11. 15 months 12. 145770 16. 6, 9, 12, 15, 18, 21

1.5 Geometric Progression (G. P.)

Definition: A sequence a_1, a_2, ... a_n .... is called geometric progression (G.P) if each term is non zero and $\frac{a_{K+1}}{a_K} = r$ (constant) for every $k \geq 1$ (r is called common ratio of the sequence) by taking $a_1 = a$ we obtain the geometric progression a, ar, ar^2 ....

here first term = $a_1 = a$,

second term = $a_2 = ar = ar^{2-1}$

third term = $a_3 = ar^2 = ar^{3-1}$

....

....

nth term = $a_n = ar^{n-1}$

$\therefore$ nth term of G.P is ar^{n-1} and is denoted by T_n.

Ex :

1. The sequence 1, 2, 4, 8, 16............ is in G.P

Since $\frac{2}{1} = \frac{4}{2} = \frac{8}{4} = \frac{16}{8} = \ldots\ldots\ldots = 2$ is a constant

$\therefore$ the sequence is in GP with common ratio 2

2. The sequence 1, $\frac{1}{2}, \frac{1}{4}, \frac{1}{8}, \frac{1}{16}$ .... is in G.P

Since $\frac{\frac{1}{2}}{1} = \frac{\frac{1}{4}}{\frac{1}{2}} = \frac{\frac{1}{8}}{\frac{1}{4}} = \ldots\ldots\ldots = \frac{1}{2}$ is a constant

$\therefore$ the sequence is in G.P with common ratio $\frac{1}{2}$

Note: 1. If three numbers are in G.P then we may take them as $\frac{a}{r}$, a, ar its common ratio is r.

2. If each term of G.P is multiplied by a non zero constant then its resultant sequence is also in G.P having same common ratio.

Ex: 1, 3, 3^2, 3^3................ G.P then 5, 5.3, 5.3^2, 5.3^3 ..... also G.P.

1.6 Sum of n Terms for Geometric Progression

Consider the geometric progression a, ar, ar^2...............ar^{n-1}.

Let S_n be the sum of the elements of the G.P.

i.e. $S_n = a + a.r + a.r^2 + ... + ar^{n-1}$ .....(1)

$\Rightarrow r.S_n = a.r + ar^2 + ... + ar^{n-1} + ar^n$ .....(2)

$(1) - (2) \Rightarrow S_n - r.S_n = a - ar^n = a(1 - r^n)$

$\therefore S_n (1 - r) = a(1 - r^n)$

$$\Rightarrow S_n = \frac{a(1-r^n)}{1-r} \quad \text{or} \quad S_n = \frac{a(r^n-1)}{r-1}$$

Thus, if a is a first term and r is the common ratio of the G.P, then the sum of n terms is

$$S_n = \frac{a(r^n-1)}{r-1} \quad \text{for } r > 1$$

$$= \frac{a(1-r^n)}{1-r} \quad \text{for } r < 1$$

1.7 Sum of Infinite Terms of Geometric Progression

If $|r| < 1$ then we can find the sum of infinite terms of G.P; a, ar, ar^2, ar^3 .... it is denoted by S_∞.

We know that $S_n = \frac{a(1-r^n)}{1-r}$

as $n \to \infty$ $\quad r^n \to 0 \quad$ (since $|r| < 1$)

$$\therefore S_\infty = \frac{a(1-0)}{1-r} = \frac{a}{1-r}$$

$\therefore$ Sum of infinite term of G.P with first term a and common ratio r is $\frac{a}{1-r}$.

1.8 Geometric Means

If a, G_1, G_2, G_3, ... G_n, b are in geometric progression then G_1, G_2.......... G_n are called 'n' geometric means between a and b.

Note: We can insert any number of geometric means between two given numbers.

Let r be the common ratio of above G.P.

here b is (n + 2)th term, we have

$$b = ar^{n+1} \Rightarrow r^{n+1} = \frac{b}{a} \Rightarrow r = \left(\frac{b}{a}\right)^{\frac{1}{n+1}}$$

Hence $\quad G_1 = ar = a\left(\frac{b}{a}\right)^{\frac{1}{n+1}}$

$$G_2 = ar^2 = a\left(\frac{b}{a}\right)^{\frac{2}{n+1}}$$

....

....

$$G_n = ar^n = a\left(\frac{b}{a}\right)^{\frac{n}{n+1}}$$

Ex : Find two geometric means between 3 and 81.

Sol. Let G_1, G_2 be two geometric means between 3 and 81

Thus 3, G_1, G_2, 81 is a G.P

$\therefore\ 81 = 3r^3 \Rightarrow r^3 = 27 \Rightarrow r = 3$

Thus $G_1 = ar = 3 \,.\, 3 = 9$

$G_2 = ar^2 = 3 \,.\, 3^2 = 27$

Hence, 9 and 27 are two Geometric means between 3 and 81.

Note: Geometric mean of two numbers a, b is $\sqrt{ab}$

Solved Examples

1. Find the 10th term of Geometric progression 5, 5^2, 5^3....... also find the nth term?

Sol. Given progression is 5, 5^2, 5^3..............

$$\therefore a = 5, \quad r = \frac{5^2}{5} = 5$$

We know that nth term of G.P = ar^{n-1}

$\therefore$ $T_{10} = ar^{10-1} = ar^9 = 5.(5)^9 = 5^{10}$

and $T_n = ar^{n-1} = 5.(5)^{n-1} = 5^n$

2. The 5th, 8th, 11th terms of G.P are p, q and r respectively show that $q^2 = ps$

Sol. Let a be first term r be the common ratio of the progression

$$\therefore T_5 = ar^4, \quad T_8 = ar^7, \quad T_{11} = ar^{10}$$

$$\therefore P = ar^4, \quad q = ar^7, \quad s = ar^{10} \text{ (given)}$$

now $\text{LHS} = q^2 = (ar^7)^2 = a^2 r^{14}$

$\text{RHS} = ps = (ar^4)(ar^{10}) = a^2 r^{14}$

$\therefore$ LHS = RHS

Hence proved.

3. If the 4th term of G.P is square of its 2nd term and first term is –3. Determine its 7th term.

Sol. Given first term of the G.P is –3. $\therefore a = -3$

Let r be the common ratio of the sequence

$$\therefore T_2 = ar, \quad T_4 = ar^3$$

Given $T_4 = (T_2)^2 \Rightarrow ar^3 = (ar)^2 \Rightarrow ar^3 = a^2r^2 \Rightarrow r = a$

$$\therefore r = a = -3$$

now the 7th term = $T_7 = ar^6 = r.r^6 = r^7 = (-3)^7 = -2187$

4. Which term of the Geometric sequence

(i) $2, 2\sqrt{2}, 4$ .... is 128

(ii) $\frac{1}{3}, \frac{1}{9}, \frac{1}{27}$, ... is $\frac{1}{19683}$

Sol. (i) Here $a = 2$, $r = \frac{2\sqrt{2}}{2} = \sqrt{2}$

Let nth term of the sequence be 128

$$\therefore ar^{n-1} = 128$$

$$\Rightarrow 2.(\sqrt{2})^{n-1} = 128$$

$$\Rightarrow (\sqrt{2})^{n-1} = 64 \Rightarrow 2^{\frac{n-1}{2}} = 2^6 \Rightarrow \frac{n-1}{2} = 6 \Rightarrow n = 13$$

(ii) Here first term = a = $\frac{1}{3}$, common ratio r = $\frac{\frac{1}{9}}{\frac{1}{3}} = \frac{1}{3}$

Let nth term of the sequence be $\frac{1}{19683}$

$$\therefore ar^{n-1} = \frac{1}{19683}$$

$$\Rightarrow \frac{1}{3}\cdot\left(\frac{1}{3}\right)^{n-1} = \frac{1}{19683} \Rightarrow \left(\frac{1}{3}\right)^{n} = \frac{1}{19683}$$

$$\Rightarrow \left(\frac{1}{3}\right)^{n} = \left(\frac{1}{3}\right)^{9}$$

$$\therefore n = 9$$

5. For what value of x the numbers $\frac{-2}{7}, x, \frac{-7}{2}$ are in G.P

Sol. We know that a, b, c are in G.P then $b^2 = ac$

$\therefore$ $\frac{-2}{7}, x, \frac{-7}{2}$ are in G.P then

$$x^2 = \left(\frac{-2}{7}\right)\left(\frac{-7}{2}\right) = 1 \Rightarrow x^2 = 1$$

$$\therefore x = \pm 1$$

6. The sum of the First three terms of G.P is $\frac{39}{10}$ and their product is 1. Find the first term and common ratio of the terms.

Sol. Let $\frac{a}{r}$, *a*, *ar* be the first three terms of G.P

Then $\frac{a}{r} + a + ar = \frac{39}{10}$ .....(1)

and $\left(\frac{a}{r}\right).a(ar) = 1$ .....(2)

from (2) we get $a^3 = 1$ i.e. $a = 1$

Substituting a = 1 in (1), we get

$$\frac{1}{r}+1+r=\frac{39}{10}$$

$$\Rightarrow \frac{1+r+r^2}{r}=\frac{39}{10}$$

$$\Rightarrow 10r^2 + 10r + 10 = 39r$$

$$\Rightarrow 10r^2 - 29r + 10 = 0$$

$$\therefore r=\frac{29\pm\sqrt{(29)^2-4\times10\times10}}{2\times10}=\frac{29\pm21}{20}=\frac{5}{2}\text{ or }\frac{2}{5}$$

Thus the three terms in G.P are

$\frac{2}{5}, 1, \frac{5}{2}$ for $r=\frac{5}{2}$

and $\frac{5}{2}, 1, \frac{2}{5}$ for $r=\frac{2}{5}$

7. The sum of first 3 terms of G.P is 16 and the sum of next three terms is 128. Determine the first term, common ratio, and the sum of n terms of G.P.

Sol. Consider G.P with first term a and common ratio r

i.e.a, ar, ar^2 ....

$\therefore$ by given condition that $a + ar + ar^2 = 16 \Rightarrow a(1 + r + r^2) = 16$ .....(1)

and $ar^3 + ar^4 + ar^5 = 128$

$ar^3 (1 + r + r^2) = 128$ .....(2)

$$\Rightarrow \frac{ar^3(1+r+r^2)}{a(1+r+r^2)}=\frac{128}{16}=8$$

$$\therefore r^3 = 8 \Rightarrow r = 2 > 1$$

we have $a (1 + r + r^2) = 16$

$$\Rightarrow a(1 + 2 + 4) = 16 \Rightarrow a = \frac{16}{7}$$

also the sum of n terms $=\frac{a\left(r^n-1\right)}{r-1}=\frac{16}{7}\frac{\left(2^n-1\right)}{2-1}=\frac{16}{7}(2^n-1)$

$$\therefore a=\frac{16}{7},\quad r=2,\quad S_n=\frac{16}{7}(2^n-1)$$

8. Find four numbers forming a geometric progression in which the third term is greater than the first by 9 and the second term is greater than the fourth by 18.

Sol: Let a, ar, ar^2, ar^3 are four terms of G.P satisfying given conditions.

$\therefore\ ar^2 = a + 9$ .....(1)

$ar = ar^3 + 18$ .....(2)

from (1) & (2) $\Rightarrow ar^2 - a = 9$ i.e. $a(r^2 - 1) = 9$

$ar - ar^3 = 18$ $ar(1 - r^2) = 18$

$$\therefore \frac{a(r^2-1)}{ar(1-r^2)} = \frac{9}{18} \Rightarrow \frac{1}{r} = \frac{-1}{2} \Rightarrow r = -2$$

Substitute r = –2 in (1) $\Rightarrow a(-2)^2 = a + 9$

$\Rightarrow 4a = a + 9$

$\Rightarrow 3a = 9$

$\Rightarrow a = 3$

$\therefore$ the four numbers are 3, (3) (–2), (3) $(-2)^2$, (3) $(-2)^3$

i.e. 3, – 6, 12, – 24

9. Find the sum of n terms of sequence 7, 77, 777, ...

Sol: Given sequence is 7, 77, 777..........

This is not a G.P, Hower, we can relate it is to a G.P by writing the terms as

$$7 = \frac{7}{9}(10-1),\ 77 = \frac{7}{9}(10^2-1),\ 777 = \frac{7}{9}(10^3-1).......$$

$\therefore\ S_n = 7 + 77 + 777 +$ .... n terms

$$= \frac{7}{9}(10-1) + \frac{7}{9}(10^2-1) + ... + \frac{7}{9}(10^n-1)$$

$$= \frac{7}{9}\left[(10-1) + (10^2-1) + ... + 10^n - 1\right]$$

$$= \frac{7}{9}\left[(10 + 10^2 + ... + 10^n) - n\right]$$

$$= \frac{7}{9}\left[10\frac{(10^n-1)}{10-1} - n\right]$$

$$= \frac{7}{9}\left[\frac{10}{9}(10^n-1) - n\right] = \frac{70}{81}(10^n-1) - \frac{7n}{9}$$

10. The sum of the three numbers in a geometrical progression is 7 and sum of their square is 21. Find the geometric progression.

Sol. Consider a, ar, ar^2 these are in A.P such that

$$a + ar + ar^2 = 7 \quad .....(1)$$

$$a^2 + (ar)^2 + (ar^2)^2 = 21 \Rightarrow a^2 + a^2r^2 + a^2r^4 = 21$$

$$\Rightarrow a^2 (1 + r^2 + r^4) = 21 \quad .....(2)$$

Squaring (1) on both sides we get

$$a^2 (1 + r + r^2)^2 = 49$$

$$\Rightarrow a^2 (1 + r^2 + r^4 + 2r + 2r^3 + 2r^2) = 49$$

$$\Rightarrow a^2 (1 + r^2 + r^4) + 2r.a^2 (1 + r + r^2) = 49$$

$$\Rightarrow 21 + 2r.\ a (7) = 49$$

$$\Rightarrow 21 + 2ar\ 7 = 49$$

$$\Rightarrow 3 + 2ar = 7 \Rightarrow 2ar = 4$$

$$\Rightarrow ar = 2$$

Substitute $r = \frac{2}{a}$ in (1) we get

$$a + a.\frac{2}{a} + a.\frac{4}{a^2} = 7$$

$$\Rightarrow a + 2 + \frac{4}{a} = 7$$

$$\Rightarrow a^2 + 2a + 4 = 7a$$

$$\Rightarrow a^2 - 5a + 4 = 0$$

$$\Rightarrow a^2 - 4a - a + 4 = 0 \quad \Rightarrow a(a-4) - 1(a-4) = 0$$

$$\Rightarrow a = 1, \text{ or } a = 4$$

when $a = 1 \Rightarrow r = \frac{2}{a} = \frac{2}{4} = \frac{1}{2}$

∴ when a = 1, r = 2 than the sequence is 1, 1(2), $1(2)^2 \rightarrow 1, 2, 4$ when a = 1, r = $\frac{1}{2}$, then the sequence is 4, $4.\frac{1}{2}$, $4\left(\frac{1}{2}\right)^2 \rightarrow 4, 2, 1$.

11. Find sum of infinite G.P $\frac{-3}{4}, \frac{3}{16}, \frac{-3}{64}$ ....

Sol. Here $a = \frac{-3}{4}, r = \frac{-1}{4}$ also $|r| < 1$

$$\therefore S_\infty = \frac{a}{1-r} = \frac{\frac{-3}{4}}{1-\left(\frac{-1}{4}\right)} = \frac{\frac{-3}{4}}{\frac{5}{4}} = \frac{-3}{5}$$

12. Prove that $3^{\frac{1}{2}} \times 3^{\frac{1}{4}} \times 3^{\frac{1}{8}}$ .... $= 3$.

Sol. LHS $= 3^{\frac{1}{2}} \times 3^{\frac{1}{4}} \times 3^{\frac{1}{8}}$ ....

$$= 3^{\frac{1}{2}} \times 3^{\frac{1}{4}} \times 3^{\frac{1}{8}} \ldots\ldots\ldots\ldots = 3^{\frac{1}{2}+\frac{1}{4}+\frac{1}{8}+\ldots} = 3^{\frac{1}{2}+\left(\frac{1}{2}\right)^2+\left(\frac{1}{2}\right)^3+\ldots\ldots} = 3^{\frac{\frac{1}{2}}{1-\frac{1}{2}}} = 3^{\frac{1}{1}} = 3$$

13. Find a rational number which when expressed as a decimal will have $0.23\overline{4}$ as its expansion.

Sol. We write $0.23\overline{4} = 0.2344924$

$$= 0.23 + [0.004 + 0.0004 + \ldots\ldots\ldots\ldots]$$

$$= 0.23 + \frac{0.004}{1-0.1} \qquad \left(\because s_\infty = \frac{a}{1-r}\right)$$

$$= 0.23 + \frac{4}{900} = \frac{211}{900}$$

14. Let $x = 1 + a + a^2 +$ .... and $y = 1 + b + b^2 +$ ....

when $|a| < 1$ and $|b| < 1$, prove that $1 + ab + a^2 b^2 + \ldots\ldots\ldots = \frac{xy}{x+y-1}$

Sol. Given $x = 1 + a + a^2 + \ldots\ldots\ldots\ldots = \frac{1}{1-a}$

$$y = 1 + b + b^2 + \ldots\ldots\ldots\ldots = \frac{1}{1-b}$$

$$\therefore x = \frac{1}{1-a} \Rightarrow 1 - a = \frac{1}{x} \Rightarrow a = 1 - \frac{1}{x} = \frac{x-1}{x}$$

$$y = \frac{1}{1-b} \Rightarrow 1 - b = \frac{1}{y} \Rightarrow b = 1 - \frac{1}{y} = \frac{y-1}{y}$$

now consider $1 + ab + a^2 b^2 + \ldots\ldots\ldots = \frac{1}{1-ab} = \frac{1}{1-\left(\frac{x-1}{x}\right)\left(\frac{y-1}{y}\right)}$

$$= \frac{xy}{(xy)-(xy-x-y+1)}$$

$$= \frac{xy}{x+y-1}$$

$$\therefore 1 + ab + a^2 b^2 + \ldots\ldots\ldots = \frac{xy}{x+y-1}$$

15. Find the geometric progression whose sum of infinity is $4\frac{1}{2}$ and whose second term is -2

Sol. Let a be first term, r be common ratio of the G.P

$$\therefore \quad S_\infty = \frac{a}{1-r} = 4\frac{1}{2} = \frac{9}{2} \text{ and } ar = -2$$

$$\frac{a}{1-r} = \frac{9}{2}$$

$\Rightarrow 2a = 9 - 9r$ .....(1)

also $ar = -2$

$\Rightarrow a = \frac{-2}{r}$ ..... (2)

now substitute (2) in (1) we get

$$2\left(\frac{-2}{r}\right) = 9 - 9r \Rightarrow -4 = 9r - 9r^2$$

$$\Rightarrow 9r^2 - 9r - 4 = 0$$

$$\Rightarrow 9r^2 - 12r + 3r - 4 = 0$$

$\Rightarrow 3r(3r-4) + 1(3r-4) = 0$ i.e. $(3r+1)(3r-4) = 0$

$$\Rightarrow r = \frac{4}{3} \text{ or } r = \frac{-1}{3}$$

when $r = \frac{4}{3} \Rightarrow a = \frac{-2}{r} = \frac{-2}{\left(\frac{4}{3}\right)} = \frac{-3}{2}$

∴ the progressioning

$$\frac{-3}{2}, \frac{-3}{2}\left(\frac{4}{3}\right), \frac{-3}{2}\left(\frac{4}{3}\right)^2 \ldots\ldots\ldots\ldots$$

when $r = \frac{-1}{3} \Rightarrow a = \frac{-2}{r} = \frac{-2}{\left(\frac{-1}{3}\right)} = 6$

∴ The progressioning

$$6, 6.\left(\frac{-1}{3}\right), 6.\left(\frac{-1}{3}\right)^2 \ldots\ldots\ldots$$

16. **A person.is entitled a monthly payment which in each month is less by one-tenth than it was a month is before. If he receives Rs.5000 in the first month, show that he can not receive more than Rs.50000 in his life.**

Sol. The amount received in the first month is Rs.5000

The amount received in the second month = Rs.5000 – $\frac{1}{10}$ (5000)

= 4500

The amount received in the third month = 4500 – $\frac{1}{10}$ (4500)

= 4050

and so on.........

Thus we obtain the sequence of monthly payment (in Rs.)
as 5000, 4500, 4050, 3045, ...

which is a G.P with first term a = 5000, and common ratio $r = \frac{4500}{5000} = \frac{9}{10} < 1$

Consider the sum of infinity which is given by

$$S_\infty = \frac{a}{1-r} = \frac{5000}{1-\frac{9}{10}} = 50000$$

This implies that however long, the person may live but cannot get more than 50000.

Exercise - 1.3

1. Find the 20th and nth terms of the G.P

$\frac{5}{2}, \frac{5}{4}, \frac{5}{8}$ ....

2. Find the 12th term of G.P whose 8th term is 192 and common ratio is 2

3. Which term of the geometric sequence

(i) $\sqrt{3}, 3, 3\sqrt{3}$ .... is 729

(ii) 2, 8, 32, ... is 131072

4. For what value of x, the numbers $\frac{7}{-2}, x, \frac{-2}{7}$ are in G.P

5. Find the sum of the indicated terms of each of the following geometric progressions

(i) $1, \frac{2}{3}, \frac{4}{9}$, ...; 10 terms

(ii) x^3, x^5, x^7, ...; n terms $(x \neq \pm 1)$

(iii) $1, -a, a^2, -a^3$ .... n terms $(a \neq -1)$

6. The sum of the first three terms of G.P is $\frac{13}{12}$ and their product is –1. Find the terms.

7. (i) How many terms of G.P $3, 3^2, 3^3$....... are needed to give sum 120

(ii) How many terms of G.P $3, \frac{3}{2}, \frac{3}{4}$ .... are needed to give the sum $\frac{3069}{512}$

8. (i) Given in a G.P the third terms is 24 and 6th term is 192. Find the 10th term.

(ii) Given in a G.P first term is 729 and 7th term is 64. Determine S_7

9. Find the sum of the following sequence to n terms

9, 99, 999, 9999.............

10. If the first and nth terms of a G.P are a and b respectively and if p is product of first n terms, prove that $P^2 = (ab)^n$

11. If a, b, c are in G.P, prove the following are also in G.P

(i) a^2, b^2, c^2 (ii) a^3, b^3, c^3 (iii) $a^2 + b^2, ab + bc, b^2 + c^2$

12. Insert three geometric means between 1 and 256.

13. Show that the product of n geometric means between given numbers is equal to the nth power of the single geometric mean between them.

14. Find the sum to infinity in each of the following geometric progressions.

(i) $1, \frac{1}{3}, \frac{1}{9}$ .... (ii) 50, 42.5, 36.125........

(iii) 10, –9, 8.1........... (iv) $(\sqrt{2}+1), 1, (\sqrt{2}-1)$ ....

15. The first term of G.P is 2 and sum to infinity is 6. Find the common ratio.

16. The common ratio of G.P is $\frac{-4}{5}$ and sum to infinity is $\frac{80}{9}$. Find the first term.

17. If the sum of an infinite geometric series is 15 and the sum of the squares of them is 45, find the sequence.

18. The sum of the first two terms of an infinite geometric series is 15 and each term is equal to the sum of all the terms following it, then find the sequence

19. Find the sum to infinity of series

$$\frac{2}{5}+\frac{3}{5^2}+\frac{2}{5^3}+\frac{3}{5^4}+\ldots\ldots.$$

20. The three numbers whose sum is 18 are in A.P. If 2, 4 and 11 are added to them respectively, the resulting numbers are in A.P. Find the numbers.

Answers

1. $\frac{5}{2^{20}}, \frac{5}{2^n}$
2. 3072
3. (i) 12th term (ii) 9th term
4. $x = \pm 1$
5. (i) $3\left[1-\left(\frac{2}{3}\right)^{10}\right]$ (ii) $\frac{x^3(1-x^{2n})}{1-x^2}$ (iii) $\frac{[1-(-a)^n]}{1+a}$
6. $\frac{4}{3}, -1, \frac{3}{4}$ (or) $\frac{3}{4}, -1, \frac{4}{3}$
7. (i) 4 terms (ii) 10 terms
8. (i) 3072 (ii) 2059

9. $\frac{10}{9}(10^n - 1) - n$

12. 4, 16, 64

14. (i)1.5 (ii) $\frac{1000}{3}$ (iii) $\frac{100}{9}$ (iv) $\frac{4+3\sqrt{2}}{2}$

15. $\frac{2}{3}$

16. 16

17. $5, \frac{10}{3}, \frac{20}{9}, \ldots\ldots\ldots$

18. $10, 5, \frac{5}{2}, \frac{5}{4}, \frac{5}{8}, \ldots\ldots\ldots$

19. $\frac{13}{24}$

20. 3, 6, 9

2

Partial Fractions

2.1 Rational Fractions

Polynomial : An expression $a_0 x^n + a_1 x^{n-1} + a_2 x^{n-2} \dots + a_n$ where $a_i \in R, 0 \le i \le n$ is called a polynomial in x with real coefficients and is denoted by $f(x)$, $g(x)$ ... etc., and a_i is called the coefficient of x_i in the polynomial.

Ex : $x^3 + 3x^2 + 2x + 4, \quad x^2 + 6x - 5$, etc

Degree of a polynomial : If $f(x) = a_0 x^n + a_1 x^{n-1} + \dots + a_n$ and $a_0 \neq 0$ then n is called the degree of $f(x)$. Here a_0 is called leading coefficient of the polynomial.

Two polynomials $f(x) = a_0 x^n + a_1 x^{n-1} + \dots + a_n$ and $g(x) = b_0 x^n + b_1 x^n + \dots + b_m$ of degree n and m are said to be equal if n = m and ai = bi for $0 \le i \le n$.

Ex : The degree of polynomial $x^3 + 2x + 1$ is 3.

Rational fraction : If $f(x)$, $g(x)$ are two polynomials and $g(x)$ is non zero polynomial then $\frac{f(x)}{g(x)}$ is called a rational fraction or simply a fraction.

Ex: (i) $\frac{x+2}{x^2+3x+2}$ is a rational fraction

(ii) $\frac{x^3+6x^2+3x+1}{x+1}$ is a rational fraction

Proper and improper fraction : A rational fraction $\frac{f(x)}{g(x)}$ is called a proper fraction if the degree of f(x) is less than the degree of *g(x)*.

Example (i) $\frac{2x+1}{x^2 3x+2}$ is a proper fraction

(ii) $\frac{x^3}{x^4+3x^2+2}$ is a proper fraction

A rational fraction $\frac{f(x)}{g(x)}$ is called an improper fraction if the degree if *f(x)* is greater than or equal to degree of g(x).

Example (i) $\frac{x^3}{(x-a)(x-b)(x-c)}$ is an improper fraction

(ii) $\frac{x^4}{(x+2)(x-2)}$ is an improper fraction

Irreduceble Polynomial of Degree 2 : A polynomial of degree 2 is of the form $ax^2 + bx + c$ is said to be irreduceble if $b^2 - 4ac < 0$.

Example (i) $x^2 + 1$ is an irrreduceble polynomial of degree 2 since

$b^2 - 4ac = 0 - 4 (1) \quad (1) < 0.$

(ii) $x^2 + x + 1$ is an irreduceble polynomial of degree 2

$\therefore b^2 - 4ac = 1 - 4 . 1 . 1 = -3 < 0.$

Division Algorithm for Polynomials

If $f(x)$ and $g(x)$ are two polynomials with $g(x) \neq 0$ then there exists unique polynomials $q(x)$ and $r(x)$ such that

$$f(x) = q(x)\, g(x) + r(x)$$

where either $r(x) = 0$ or the degree of $r(x)$ less than the degree of $g(x)$.

Partial Fraction

In lower classes we know that how to add two proper fractions to get another proper fraction.

For example $\frac{1}{x+2}+\frac{2}{x+3}=\frac{3x+7}{x^2+5x+6}$

Now conversely we are intereseted to learn using some of the rules to express the given proper fraction $\frac{3x+7}{x^2+5x+6}$ as sum of two proper fractions $\frac{1}{x+2}$ and $\frac{2}{x+3}$. This process is known as resolving into partial fractions.

So a proper fraction is expressed as the sum of two or more proper fractions where in the denominators are powers of irreducible polynomials, then each such proper fraction is called a partial fraction of the given fraction.

2.2 Type (1)

Partial fractions of proper fraction $\frac{f(x)}{g(x)}$, where $g(x)$ contains non repeated linear factors.

$\frac{f(x)}{g(x)}$ is given proper fraction and ax + b, a $\neq$ 0 is a non repeated linear factor of $g(x)$.

Then there will be a partial fraction of the form $\frac{A}{ax+b}$. Corresponding to the factor ax + b, where A is non zero real number, to be determined.

Solved Problems

1. Resolve $\frac{2x+3}{(x+1)(x-3)}$ into partial fractions

Sol. Let $\frac{2x+3}{(x+1)(x-3)}=\frac{A}{x+1}+\frac{B}{x-3}$

$$\frac{2x+3}{(x+1)(x-3)}=\frac{A(x-3)+B(x+1)}{(x+1)(x-3)}$$

$$2x+3=A(x-3)+B(x+1) \qquad \text{.....(i)}$$

Put $x = 3$ in (i) we get

$$2(3) + 3 = A(3 - 3) + B(3 + 1)$$

$$9 = B(4) \qquad B = \frac{9}{4}$$

Put $x = -1$ in (i) we get

$$2(-1) + 3 = A(-1 - 3) + B(-1 + 1)$$

$$1 = -4A \qquad A = -\frac{1}{4}$$

$$\therefore \quad \frac{2x+3}{(x+1)(x-)} = \frac{-\frac{1}{4}}{(x+1)} + \frac{\frac{9}{4}}{(x-3)}$$

2. Resolve $\dfrac{x+4}{(x^2-4)(x+1)}$ in to partial factors

Sol. $$\frac{x+4}{(x^2-4)(x+1)} = \frac{x+4}{(x+2)(x-2)(x+1)} = \frac{A}{x+2} + \frac{B}{x-2} + \frac{C}{x+1}$$

$$\therefore \quad \frac{x+4}{(x^2-4)(x+1)} = \frac{A(x-2)(x+1) + B(x+2)(x+1) + C(x+2)(x-2)}{(x^2-4)(x+1)}$$

$$\Rightarrow x + 4 = A(x-2)(x+1) + B(x+2)(x+1) + C(x+2)(x-2) \qquad \text{.....(i)}$$

Put $x = 2$ in (i) we get

$$6 = A(0) + B(2 + 2)(2 + 1) + C(0)$$

$$\Rightarrow \quad 6 = 12B \quad \Rightarrow \quad B = \frac{1}{2}$$

Put $x = -2$ in (i) we get

$$2 = A(-2 - 2)(-2 + 1) + B(0) + C(0)$$

$$\Rightarrow \quad 2 = 4A \quad \Rightarrow \quad A = \frac{1}{2}$$

Put $x = -1$ (i) in we get

$$3 = C(1)(-3) \Rightarrow \quad C = -1$$

$$\therefore \quad \frac{x+4}{(x^2-4)(x+1)} = \frac{\frac{1}{2}}{x+2} + \frac{\frac{1}{2}}{x-2} + \frac{-1}{x+1}$$

3. Resolve $\frac{3x+2}{2-x-x^2}$ in to partial fractions.

Sol. $\frac{3x+2}{2-x-x^2} = \frac{3x+2}{2-2x+x-x^2} = \frac{3x+2}{2(1-x)+x(1-x)} = \frac{3x+2}{(2+x)(1-x)}$

$\therefore$ Let $\frac{3x+2}{(2+x)(1-x)} = \frac{A}{2+x} + \frac{B}{1-x}$

$\Rightarrow$ $3x+2 = A(1-x) + B(2+x)$ .....(i)

Put $x = 1$ (i) in we get

$3+2 = A(0) + B(2+1)$

$\Rightarrow$ $5 = 3B \Rightarrow B = 5/3$

Put $x = -2$ in (i) we get

$3(-2) + 2 = A(1-(-2)) + 0$

$\Rightarrow$ $-4 = 3A \Rightarrow A = -4/3$

$\therefore$ $\frac{3x+2}{(2+x)(1-x)} = \frac{-4/3}{2+x} + \frac{5/3}{1-x}$

2.3 Type (2)

Partial Fractions of proper fractions $\frac{f(x)}{g(x)}$, where $g(x)$ contains repeated and non repeated linear factors.

Let $\frac{f(x)}{g(x)}$ be a proper fraction and $(ax+b)^n$, $a \neq 0$ (n is largest index t (> 1)) is a factor of $g(x)$ then there will be n partial fractions of the form $\frac{A_1}{ax+b} + \frac{A_2}{(ax+b)^2} + \ldots + \frac{A_n}{(ax+b)^n}$.

where $A_1, A_2, \ldots A_n$ are real numbers to be determined.

Solved Examples

1. Resolve $\frac{9}{(x-1)(x+2)^2}$ in to partial fractions

Sol. Let $\frac{9}{(x-1)(x+2)^2} = \frac{A}{x-1} + \frac{B}{x+2} + \frac{C}{(x+2)^2}$

$$\frac{9}{(x-1)(x+2)^2} = \frac{A(x+2)^2 + B(x-1)(x+2) + C(x-1)}{(x-1)(x+2)^2}$$

$\Rightarrow \quad 9 = A(x + 2)^2 + B(x - 1)(x + 2) + C(x - 1)$ ..... (i)

Put $x = 1$ in (i) we get

$9 = A(1 + 2)^2 + B(0) + C(0)$

$9A = 9 \quad \Rightarrow \quad A = 1$

Put $x = -2$ (i) in we get

$9 = A(0) + B(0) + C(-2 - 1)$

$\Rightarrow \quad -3C = 9 \quad \Rightarrow \quad C = -3$

and comparing constant terms on both side of (i) we get

$9 = A(4) + B(-2) - C$

$\Rightarrow \quad 9 = (1)(4) + B(-2) + 3$ (by substituting A and C)

$9 = 4 - 2B + 3$

$-2B = 2 \quad \Rightarrow \quad B = -1$

$$\therefore \quad \frac{9}{(x-1)(x+2)^2} = \frac{1}{x-1} + \frac{-1}{x+2} + \frac{-3}{(x+2)^2}$$

2. Resolve $\frac{2x^2+2x+1}{x^3+x^2}$ in to partial fractions

Sol. $\frac{2x^2+2x+1}{x^3+x^2} = \frac{2x^2+2x+1}{x^2(x+1)} = \frac{A}{x} + \frac{B}{x^2} + \frac{C}{x+1}$

$$\therefore \quad \frac{2x^2+2x+1}{x^2(x+1)} = \frac{Ax(x+1)+B(x+1)+C(x^2)}{x^2(x+1)}$$

$\Rightarrow \quad 2x^2 + 2x + 1 = Ax(x + 1)\ B(x + 1) + C(x^2)$ .....(i)

Put $x = 0$ in (i) we get

$$1 = A(0) + B(0+1) + C(0)$$

$\Rightarrow$ $B = 1$

Put $x = -1$ (i) in we get

$$2(1) + 2(-1) + 1 = A(0) + B(0) + C(-1)^2$$

$\Rightarrow$ $= 1 = C \Rightarrow C = 1$

again, comparing x^2 coefficient as both sides we get

$$2 = A + C \Rightarrow 2 = A + 1 \quad (\because C = 1)$$

$$\Rightarrow A = 1$$

$$\therefore \quad \frac{2x^2+2x+1}{x^3+x^2} = \frac{1}{x} + \frac{1}{x^2} + \frac{1}{x+1}$$

3. Resolve $\dfrac{x^2+5x+7}{(x-3)^3}$ into partial fractions

Sol. Method : 1

Let $$\frac{x^2+5x+7}{(x-3)^3} = \frac{A}{x-3} + \frac{B}{(x-3)^2} + \frac{C}{(x-3)^3}$$

$$\frac{x^2+5x+7}{(x-3)^3} = \frac{A(x-3)^2 + B(x-3) + C}{(x-3)^3}$$

$$x^2 + 5x + 7 = A(x-3)^2 + B(x-3) + C \qquad .....(i)$$

Put $x = 3$ in (i) we get

$$9 + 15 + 7 = A(0) + B(0) + C$$

$\Rightarrow$ $C = 31$

Comparing x^2 coefficients on both sides of (i) we get

$$1 = A \qquad \Rightarrow \qquad A = 1$$

Comparing x coefficients on both sides of (i) we get

$$5 = A(-6) + B$$

$\Rightarrow$ $5 = (1)(-6) + B \Rightarrow B = 11 \qquad (\because A = 1)$

$$\therefore \quad \frac{x^2+5x+7}{(x-3)^3} = \frac{1}{x-3} + \frac{11}{(x-3)^2} + \frac{31}{(x-3)^3}$$

Method : 2

Consider $\dfrac{x^2+5x+7}{(x-3)^3}$

Put $x-3=y \quad \Rightarrow x=y+3$

$$\therefore \quad \frac{x^2+5x+7}{(x-3)^3} = \frac{(y+3)^2+5(y+3)+7}{y3}$$

$$= \frac{y^2+6y+9+5y+15+7}{y3}$$

$$= \frac{y^2+11y+31}{y3}$$

$$= \frac{1}{y}+\frac{11}{y^2}+\frac{31}{y^3} = \frac{1}{(x-3)}+\frac{11}{(x-3)^2}+\frac{31}{(x-3)^3}$$

Exercise - 2.1

Resolve the following fractions is to partial fractions

1. (i) $\dfrac{5x+1}{(x+2)(x-1)}$ (ii) $\dfrac{5x+6}{(2+x)(1-x)}$ (iii) $\dfrac{3x+7}{x^2-3x+2}$

   (iv) $\dfrac{2x-1}{(2x+3)(x-1)}$ (v) $\dfrac{3x}{(x-6)(x+3)}$

2. (i) $\dfrac{2x+3}{(x-1)^3}$ (ii) $\dfrac{3x^3-8x^2+10}{(x-1)^4}$ (iii) $\dfrac{2x^3+3x^2+5x+7}{(x+1)^5}$

3. (i) $\dfrac{1}{(x-1)^2(x-2)}$ (ii) $\dfrac{x-1}{(x+1)(x-2)^2}$ (iii) $\dfrac{1}{(1-2x)^2(1-3x)}$

   (iv) $\dfrac{1}{x^3(x+2)}$ (v) $\dfrac{3x-18}{x^3(x+3)}$

4. (i) if $\dfrac{3x-4}{(x-3)(x+a)} = \dfrac{1}{x-3} + \dfrac{2}{x+a}$ then find the value of a .

(ii) If $\dfrac{ax+b}{(2x+3)^2} = \dfrac{1}{2x+3} - \dfrac{2}{(2x+3)^2}$ then find the value of a + b.

(iii) Find the number of partial fractions of $\dfrac{x+2}{x^2(x^2-1)}$

Answers

1. (i) $\dfrac{3}{x+2} + \dfrac{2}{x-1}$ (ii) $\dfrac{11}{3(1-x)} - \dfrac{4}{3(2+x)}$

(iii) $\dfrac{-10}{x-1} + \dfrac{13}{x-2}$ (iv) $\dfrac{-1}{5(x-1)} + \dfrac{8}{5(2x+3)}$

(v) $\dfrac{2}{x-6} + \dfrac{1}{x+3}$

2. (i) $\dfrac{2}{(x-1)^2} + \dfrac{5}{(x-1)^3}$ (ii) $\dfrac{3}{x-1} + \dfrac{1}{(x-1)^2} - \dfrac{7}{(x-1)^3} + \dfrac{5}{(x-1)^4}$

(iii) $\dfrac{2}{(x+1)^2} - \dfrac{3}{(x+1)^3} + \dfrac{5}{(x+1)^4} + \dfrac{3}{(x+1)^5}$

3. (i) $\dfrac{1}{x-1} - \dfrac{1}{(x-1)^2} - \dfrac{2}{(x-2)}$ (ii) $\dfrac{\left(\frac{-2}{9}\right)}{(x+1)} + \dfrac{\left(\frac{2}{9}\right)}{x-2} + \dfrac{(1/3)}{(x-2)^2}$

(iii) $\dfrac{9}{1-3x} - \dfrac{6}{1-2x} - \dfrac{2}{(1-2x)^2}$ (iv) $\dfrac{1}{8x} - \dfrac{1}{9x^2} + \dfrac{1}{2x^3} - \dfrac{1}{8(x+2)}$

(v) $\dfrac{-1}{x} + \dfrac{3}{x^2} - \dfrac{6}{x^3} + \dfrac{1}{x+3}$

4. (i) 2 (ii) 3 (iii) 4

2.4 Type (3)

Partial fractions of $\frac{f(x)}{g(x)}$ (proper), when g(x) contains non repeated irreduceble factor of degree 2.

Let $\frac{f(x)}{g(x)}$ be a proper fraction and $ax^2 + bx + c$, $a \neq 0$, is a non repeated irreducible factor of degree 2 of $g(x)$.

With respect to this factor there will be a partial fraction of the form $\frac{Ax+B}{ax^2+bx+c}$ in the expression of $\frac{f(x)}{g(x)}$, where A and B are real numbers to be determined.

Solved Problems

1. Resolve $\frac{x^2-3}{(x+2)(x^2+1)}$ in to partial fractions

Sol. Let
$$\frac{x^2-3}{(x+2)(x^2+1)} = \frac{A}{x+2} + \frac{Bx+C}{x^2+1}$$

where A, B, C are real numbers to be determined

$$\frac{x^2-3}{(x+2)(x^2+1)} = \frac{A(x^2+1)+(Bx+C)\,(x+2)}{(x+2)(x^2+1)}$$

$$x^2 - 3 = A(x^2 + 1) + (Bx + C)\,(x + 2) \quad .....(i)$$

Put $x = -2$ in (i) we get

$$4 - 3 = A\,(4 + 1) \Rightarrow A = 1/5$$

Comparing x^2 coefficients on both sides of (i) we get

$$1 = A + B \Rightarrow B = 1 - A = 1 - 1/5 = 4/5$$

$$\therefore \quad B = 4/5$$

Comparing constant terms on both sides of (i) we get

$$-3 = A + 2C$$

$$\Rightarrow \quad -3 = \frac{1}{5} + 2c$$

$$2c = -3 - \frac{1}{5}$$

$$= \frac{-16}{5}$$

$$\Rightarrow \quad c = \frac{-8}{5}$$

$$\therefore \quad \frac{x^2-3}{(x+2)(x^2+1)} = \frac{1/5}{x+2} + \frac{4/5\,x - 8/5}{x^2+1}$$

2. Resolve $\frac{x+3}{(1-x)^2(1+x^2)}$ in to partial fractions

Sol. $\frac{x+3}{(1-x)^2(1+x^2)} = \frac{A}{1-x} + \frac{B}{(1-x)^2} + \frac{Cx+D}{1+x^2}$.

$$\frac{x+3}{(1-x)^2(x^2+1)} = \frac{A(1-x)(1+x^2)+B(1+x^2)+(Cx+D)(1-x)^2}{(1-x)^2(1+x^2)}$$

$x + 3 = A(x - 1)(1 + x^2) + B(1 + x^2) + (Cx + D)(1 - x)^2$ ..... (I)

Put $x = 1$ in (I) we get

$4 = 0 + B(1 + 1) + 0 \qquad B = 2$

Comparing x^3 coefficients of both sides, of (I) we get

$0 = A + C$ .....(i)

Comparing x^2 coefficients as both sides of (I) we get

$0 = -A + B - 2C + D$ .....(ii)

Comparing x coefficients as both sides of (I) we get

$1 = A + C - 2D$ .....(iii)

Comparing constant terms on both sides of (I) we get

$3 = -A + B + D$ .....(iv)

$\because \quad B = 2 \quad \Rightarrow \quad 3 = -A + 2 + D \quad \Rightarrow \quad -A + D = 1$ .....(v)

Put $A + C = 0$ in (iii) we get

$$1 = 0 - 2D \Rightarrow D = -\tfrac{1}{2}$$

Put $D = -\tfrac{1}{2}$ in (v)

$$-A - \tfrac{1}{2} = 1 \Rightarrow A = -\tfrac{3}{2}$$

$$\Rightarrow C = \tfrac{3}{2} \quad (\because A + C = 0)$$

$$\therefore \quad \frac{x+3}{(1-x)^2(1+x^2)} = \frac{-\tfrac{3}{2}}{1-x} + \frac{2}{(1-x)^2} + \frac{\tfrac{3}{2}x - \tfrac{1}{2}}{1+x^2}$$

3. Resolve $\dfrac{2x^2+1}{x^3-1}$ in to partial fractions.

Sol. $$\frac{2x^2+1}{x^3-1} = \frac{2x^2+1}{(x-1)(x^2+x+1)} = \frac{A}{x-1} + \frac{Bx+C}{(x^2+x+1)}$$

$$= \frac{A(x^2+x+1)+(Bx+C)(x-1)}{(x-1)(x^2+x+1)}$$

$$\therefore \quad 2x^2 + 1 = A(x^2 + x + 1) + (Bx + C)(x - 1) \qquad \text{.....(i)}$$

Put $x = 1$ in (i) we get

$$3 = A(1 + 1 + 1) + 0 \Rightarrow 3A = 3 \Rightarrow A = 1$$

Comparing x^2 coefficients on both sides

$$2 = A + B \Rightarrow 2 = 1 + B \Rightarrow B = 1$$

Comparing constant terms on both sides of (i) we get

$$1 = A - C \Rightarrow C = A - 1$$

$$\therefore \quad \frac{2x^2+1}{x^3-1} = \frac{1}{x-1} + \frac{x}{x^2+x+1}$$

2.5 Type (4)

Partial fractions of $\dfrac{f(x)}{g(x)}$ (proper fraction) where $g(x)$ contains repeated or non repeated irreducible factors of degree 2.

w.r.t every irreducible factor $(ax^2 + bx + c)^n$ there will be n partial fractions such that

$$\therefore \quad \frac{A_1}{ax^2+bx+c} + \frac{A_2}{(ax^2+bx+c)^2} + \ldots + \frac{A_n}{(ax^2+bx+c)^n}$$

Solved Examples

1. Resolve $\dfrac{x^2+1}{(x^2+x+1)^2}$ in to partial fractions

Sol. Let $\dfrac{x^2+1}{(x^2+x+1)^2} = \dfrac{Ax+B}{(x^2+x+1)} + \dfrac{Cx+D}{(x^2+x+1)^2}$

$$\Rightarrow \quad \frac{x^2+1}{(x^2+x+1)^2} = \frac{(Ax+B)(x^2+x+1)+(Cx+D)}{(x^2+x+1)^2}$$

$$\Rightarrow \quad x^2 + 1 = (Ax + B)(x^2 + x + 1) + (Cx + D) \qquad \text{..... (i)}$$

Comparing x^3 coefficients, on both sides of (i) we get $0 = A \quad \Rightarrow \quad A = 0$

Comparing x^2 coefficients, on both sides of (i) we get $1 = A + B \Rightarrow \quad B = 1$

Comparing x coefficients, we get $0 = A + B + C$

$$0 = 1 + C \quad \Rightarrow \quad C = -1$$

Comparing constant terms on both sides of (i) we get

$$1 = B + D \quad \Rightarrow \quad 1 = 1 + D \quad \Rightarrow \quad D = 0$$

$$\therefore \quad \frac{x^2+1}{(x^2+x+1)^2} = \frac{1}{x^2+x+1} + \frac{-x}{(x^2+x+1)^2}$$

2. Resolve $\dfrac{x^3}{(x^2+1)^2}$ in to partial fractions

Sol. Let $\dfrac{x^3}{(x^2+1)^2} = \dfrac{Ax+B}{(x^2+1)} + \dfrac{Cx+D}{(x^2+1)^2}$

$$\frac{x^3}{(x^2+1)^2} = \frac{(Ax+B)(x^2+1)+)(Cx+D)}{(x^2+1)^2}$$

$$\Rightarrow \quad x^3 = (Ax+B)(x^2+1)+(Cx+D) \qquad \text{..... (i)}$$

Comparing x^3 coefficients on both sides, of (i) we get

$$1 = A \quad \Rightarrow \quad A = 1$$

Comparing x^2 coefficients on both sides, of (i), we get

$$0 = B \quad \Rightarrow \quad B = 0$$

Comparing x coefficients on both sides, of (i), we get,

$$0 = A + C \quad \Rightarrow \quad C = -A = -1$$

Comparing constant terms on both sides of (i).we get

$$0 = B + D \quad \Rightarrow \quad D = -B = 0$$

$$\therefore \quad \frac{x^3}{(x^2+1)^2} = \frac{1.x+0}{(x^2+1)} + \frac{-1.x+0}{(x^2+1)^2} = \frac{x}{x^2+1} - \frac{x}{(x^2+1)^2}$$

Exercise - 2.2

Resolve the following into partial fractions

1. (i) $\dfrac{x^2+1}{(x^2+4)(x-2)}$ (ii) $\dfrac{3x-1}{(1-x+x^2)(x+2)}$

   (iii) $\dfrac{2x^2+3x+4}{(x-1)(x^2+2)}$

2. (i) $\dfrac{x^3+x^2+1}{(x-1)(x^3-1)}$ (ii) $\dfrac{x^3+x^2+1}{(x^2+2)(x^2+3)}$

3. (i) $\dfrac{3x^3-2x^2-1}{x^4+x^2+1}$ (ii) $\dfrac{x^4-24x^2+28}{(x^2+1)^3}$

Answers

1. (i) $\frac{3x+6}{8(x^2+4)}+\frac{5}{8(x-2)}$ (ii) $\frac{x}{1-x+x^2}-\frac{1}{x+2}$

(iii) $\frac{3}{x-1}+\frac{2-x}{x^2+2}$

2. (i) $\frac{2}{3(x-1)}+\frac{1}{(x-1)^2}+\frac{x+2}{3(x^2+x+1)}$ (ii) $\frac{3x+2}{x^2+3}-\frac{2x+1}{x^2+2}$

3. (i) $\frac{2x+1}{x^2+x+1}+\frac{x-2}{x^2-x+1}$ (ii) $\frac{1}{x^2+1}+\frac{22}{(x^2+1)^2}+\frac{5}{(x^2+1)^3}$

2.6 Applications of Partial Fractions in Chemical Kinetics and Pharmacokinetics

1. In first order absorption (Infusion methods) for a drug that enters the body by an apparent first order absorption process is eliminated by first order process and distribute in the body by one compartment model is given by equation.

$$\frac{dx}{dt}=k_a x_a - kx$$

by applying laplace tranformation we get $\bar{x}=\frac{k_a F x_0}{(s+k)(s+k_a)}$

to find the value of x we have to find the partical fraction of the expression

$$\frac{1}{(s+k)(s+k_a)}$$

Let $$\frac{1}{(s+k)(s+k_a)}=\frac{A}{s+k}+\frac{B}{s+k_a}$$

$$\frac{1}{(s+k)(s+k_a)}=\frac{A(s+k_a)+B(s+k)}{(s+k)\ (s+k_a)}$$

$\therefore$ $1 = A(s + k_a) + B(s + k)$ .....(i)

Put $S = -k_a$ in (i) we get

$$1 = 0 + B(-k_a + k) \quad \Rightarrow \quad B = \frac{1}{-k_a + k}$$

Similarly put s = –k we get

$$1 = A(-k + k_a) \qquad \therefore \qquad A = \frac{-1}{k - k_a}$$

$$\frac{1}{(s+k)(s+k_a)} = \frac{\left(\frac{-1}{k-k_a}\right)}{s+k} + \frac{\frac{1}{(k-k_a)}}{s+k_a}$$

$$= \frac{1}{k_a - k}\left[\frac{1}{s+k} + \frac{1}{s+k_a}\right]$$

2. In second order kinetics, the rate expression is given by the equation

$$r = \frac{dx}{dt} = k_2\,(a - x)\,(b - x)$$

$$\Rightarrow \qquad \frac{dx}{(a-x)(b-x)} = k_2 dt$$

To solve x we need to partial fractions the expression $\frac{1}{(a-x)(b-x)}$

Consider $$\frac{1}{(a-x)(b-x)} = \frac{A}{a-x} + \frac{B}{b-x}$$

$$\frac{1}{(a-x)(b-x)} = \frac{A(b-x) + B(a-x)}{(a-x)(b-x)}$$

$$\Rightarrow \qquad 1 = A(b - x) + B(a - x) \qquad .....(i)$$

Put $x = b$ in (i) we get

$1 = 0 + B(a - b)$

$$\Rightarrow \qquad B = \frac{1}{a-b}$$

Put x = a in (i) we get

$1 = A(b - a) + 0$

$$\therefore \qquad A = \frac{1}{b-a}$$

$$\therefore \quad \frac{1}{(a-x)(b-x)} = \frac{\left(\frac{1}{b-a}\right)}{a-x} + \frac{\left(\frac{1}{a-b}\right)}{b-x}$$

$$= \frac{1}{b-a}\left[\frac{1}{a-x} - \frac{1}{b-x}\right]$$

3. The rate of change of drug in the body with respect to time when the drug is administrated intravenously, we can obtain the linear differential equations.

$$\frac{dx}{dt} = k_0 - kx$$

Where k_0 is rate of drug infusion
by applying laplace transformations and simplifying we get

$$\bar{x} = \frac{k_0}{s(s+k)}$$

to calculate x (total amount of drug in the body) the expression $\frac{k_0}{s(s+k)}$ has to be resolved in to partial fractions.
so consider

$$\frac{1}{s(s+k)} = \frac{A}{s} + \frac{B}{s+k}$$

$$\Rightarrow \quad \frac{1}{s(s+k)} = \frac{A(s+k)+Bs}{s(s+k)}$$

$$\Rightarrow \quad 1 = A(s+k) + BS \qquad .....(i)$$

Put s = 0 (i) we get
$1 = A(0 + k)$

$$\Rightarrow \quad A = \frac{1}{k}$$

put s = –k in (i) we get
$1 = B(-k)$

$$\Rightarrow \quad B = \frac{-1}{k}$$

$$\therefore \quad \frac{1}{s(s+k)} = \frac{\frac{1}{k}}{s} + \frac{-\frac{1}{k}}{s+k}$$

$$= \frac{1}{k}\left[\frac{1}{s} - \frac{1}{s+k}\right]$$

$$\therefore \quad \frac{k_0}{s(s+k)} = \frac{k_0}{k}\left[\frac{1}{s} - \frac{1}{s+k}\right]$$

4. The rapid intravenous injection of a drug that distribute in the body according to two compartment model system with elimination occuring from the central compartment is as shown in model and the amount of drug in the central compartment a_{ac} is given by

$$a_{ac} = x_0 \frac{(s+E_2)}{(s+\mu_1)(s+\mu_2)}$$

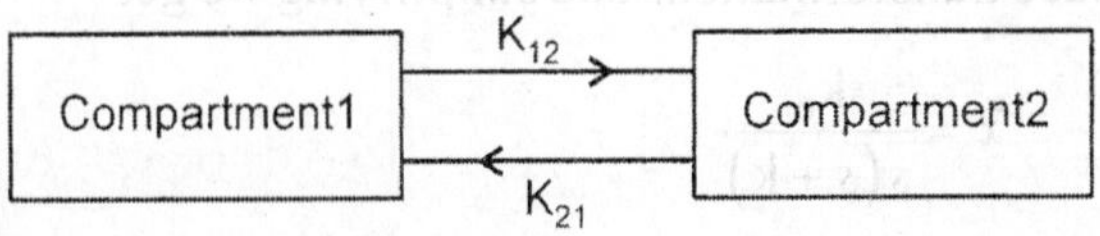

to calculate the concentration of drug in the central compartment, $\dfrac{s+E_2}{(s+\mu_1)(s+\mu_2)}$ has to resolve in to partial fractions.

$$\therefore \quad \frac{s+E_2}{(s+\mu_1)(s+\mu_2)} = \frac{A}{s+\mu_1} + \frac{B}{s+\mu_2}$$

$\therefore \quad s + E_2 = A(s + \mu_2) + B(s + \mu_1)$

Put $s = -\mu_2$ we get

$-\mu_2 + E_2 = 0 + B(-\mu_2 + \mu_1)$

$$\therefore \quad B = \frac{E_2 - \mu_2}{\mu_1 - \mu_2}$$

Put $s = -\mu_1$ we get

$-\mu_1 + E_2 = A(-\mu_1 + \mu_2)$

$$\therefore A = \frac{E_2 - \mu_1}{\mu_2 - \mu_1}$$

$$\therefore \quad \frac{s+E_2}{(s+\mu_1)(s+\mu_2)} = \frac{E_2-\mu_1}{\mu_2-\mu_1}\frac{1}{s+\mu_1} + \frac{E_2-\mu_1}{\mu_1-\mu_2}\frac{1}{s+\mu_2}$$

$$= \frac{1}{\mu_2-\mu_1}\left[\frac{E_2-\mu_1}{s+\mu_1} - \frac{E_2-\mu_2}{s+\mu_2}\right]$$

Partial fractions of $\frac{f(x)}{g(x)}$, when $\frac{f(x)}{g(x)}$ is an improper fraction

Here $\frac{f(x)}{g(x)}$ is an improper fraction

$\therefore$ degree of f(x) $\geq$ degree of g(x)

To find the partial fractions of $\frac{f(x)}{g(x)}$, there will be two cases.

Case (i) : Degree of $f(x)$ = deg of $g(x)$

Then by division algorithm there exists unique K and $r(x)$ such that

$$f(x) = Kg(x) + r(x) \text{ where deg } r(x) < \text{deg } g(x)$$

$$\therefore \quad \frac{f(x)}{g(x)} = K + \frac{r(x)}{g(x)}$$

Now $\frac{r(x)}{g(x)}$ is proper fraction which can be solved in to partial fractions using the above types.

Case (ii) : If $\frac{f(x)}{g(x)}$ is an improper fraction of degree of $f(x)$ > the degree of $g(x)$ then

$$f(x) = q(x)\, g(x) + r(x) \qquad \text{(by division algorithm)}$$

$$\frac{f(x)}{g(x)} = = q(x) + \frac{r(x)}{g(x)}$$

here $\frac{r(x)}{g(x)}$ is proper fraction, this can be resolved in to partial fractions by using above types.

Solved Problems

1. Resolve $\frac{x^3}{(x-a)(x-b)(x-c)}$ in to partial fractions.

Sol. Given $\frac{f(x)}{g(x)} = \frac{x^3}{(x-a)(x-b)(x-c)}$

$\therefore$ degree of f(x) = degree of g(x) = 3

$$\therefore \quad \frac{x^3}{(x-a)(x-b)(x-c)} = K + \frac{r(x)}{(x-a)(x-b)(x-c)}$$

(proper fraction)

$$\frac{x^3}{(x-a)(x-b)(x-c)} = K + \frac{A}{x-a} + \frac{B}{x-b} + \frac{C}{x-c}$$

$$\Rightarrow \quad x^3 = K(x-a)(x-b)(x-c) + A(x-b)(x-c)$$

$$+ B(x-a)(x-c) + C(x-a)(x-b) \quad .....(i)$$

Put $x = a$ in (i) we get

$$a^3 = A(a-b)(a-c) \Rightarrow A = \frac{a^3}{(a-b)(b-c)}$$

Put $x = b$ in (i) we get

$$b^3 = B(b-a)(b-c) \Rightarrow B = \frac{b^3}{(b-a)(b-c)}$$

Put $x = c$ in we get

$$c^3 = C(c-a)(c-b)$$

$$\Rightarrow \quad C = \frac{c^3}{(c-a)(c-b)}$$

again, comparing x^3 coefficient on both sides, of (i) we get

$$1 = K \Rightarrow K = 1$$

$$\therefore \quad \frac{x^3}{(x-a)(x-b)(x-c)} = 1 + \frac{\frac{a^3}{(a-b)(a-c)}}{(x-a)} + \frac{\frac{b^3}{(b-a)(b-c)}}{(x-b)} + \frac{\frac{c^3}{(c-a)(a-b)}}{(x-c)}$$

$$\frac{x^3}{(x-a)(x-b)(x-c)} = 1 + \frac{a^3}{(a-b)(a-c)(x-a)}$$

$$+ \frac{b^3}{(b-a)(b-c)(x-b)} + \frac{c^3}{(c-a)(c-b)(x-c)}$$

2. Resolve $\frac{x^4}{(x-1)(x-2)}$ in to partial fractions

Sol. Here, $\frac{f(x)}{g(x)} = \frac{x^4}{(x-1)(x-2)} = \frac{x^4}{x^2-3x+2}$

$\therefore$ degree $f(x) = 4$, deg $g(x) = 2$ $\quad\therefore$ degree $f(x) >$ degree $g(x)$

$$\therefore \frac{f(x)}{g(x)} = Q(x) + \frac{r(x)}{g(x)}$$

where Q (x), r(x), are obtained as follows

$$\begin{array}{r l}
x^2 - 3x + 2 \,)\, x^4 & (x^2 + 3x + 7 \\
x^4 - 3x^3 + 2x^2 & [\text{(dividing } x^4 \text{ with } x^2 - 3x + 12)] \\
\hline
3x^3 - 2x^2 & \\
3x^3 - 9x^2 + 6x & \\
\hline
7x^2 - 6x & \\
7x^2 - 21x + 14 & \\
\hline
15x - 14 & \\
\hline
\end{array}$$

$\therefore$ $Q(x) = x^2 + 3x + 7$; $\quad R(x) = 15x - 14$

$$\therefore \frac{f(x)}{g(x)} = (x^2 + 3x + 7) + \frac{15x-14}{x^2-3x+2}$$

$$= x^2 + 3x + 7 + \frac{15x-14}{(x-1)(x-2)}$$

now the partial fractions of $\frac{15x-14}{(x-1)(x-2)}$ is $\frac{-1}{x-1} + \frac{16}{x-2}$

$$\therefore \frac{x^4}{(x-1)(x-2)} = (x^2 + 3x + 7) - \frac{1}{x-1} + \frac{16}{x-2}$$

Exercise - 2.3

1. Resolve the following fractions in to partial fractions

(i) $\frac{x^2}{(x-1)(x-2)}$ (ii) $\frac{x^3}{(2x-1)(x-1)^2}$

(iii) $\frac{x^3}{(x-1)(x+2)}$

2. (i) $\dfrac{x^3}{(2x-1)(x+2)(x-3}$ (ii) $\dfrac{x^4+1}{x^3+x}$

Answers

1. (i) $1-\dfrac{1}{x-1}+\dfrac{4}{x-2}$ (ii) $\dfrac{1}{2}+\dfrac{1}{2(2x-1)}+\dfrac{1}{(x-1)}+\dfrac{1}{(x-1)^2}$

(iii) $(x-1)+\dfrac{1}{3(x-1)}+\dfrac{8}{3(x+2)}$

2. (i) $\dfrac{1}{2}-\dfrac{1}{50(2x+1)}-\dfrac{8}{25(x+2)}+\dfrac{27}{25(x-3)}$

(ii) $x+\dfrac{1}{x}-\dfrac{2x}{x^2+1}$

3

Matrices

3.1 Matrices

Definition : An ordered rectangular array of elements is called a matrix. We confine to matrices whose elements are real or complex numbers.

Matrices are generally enclosed by brackets and we denote by capital letters A, B, C.....

Ex : (i) $A = \begin{bmatrix} 1 & 2 \\ 3 & 4 \end{bmatrix}$

(ii) $B = \begin{bmatrix} 4 & 7 & 8 \\ -1 & 2 & 3 \end{bmatrix}$

(iii) $\begin{bmatrix} x+1 & \sin x & \cos x \\ \tan x & 2+\sec x & 3 \\ 1 & 2 & 0 \end{bmatrix}$ $\begin{matrix} \longrightarrow \text{1st row} \\ \longrightarrow \text{2nd row} \\ \longrightarrow \text{3rd row} \end{matrix}$

$\downarrow$ 1st column $\quad$ $\downarrow$ 2nd column $\quad$ $\downarrow$ 3rd column

So, the horizontal lines of elements in the matrix are called rows of the matrix and the vertical lines of elements of the matrix are called columns of the matrix.

So, matrix is an arrangement of numbers (real or complex) in the form of rows and columns with in brackets.

If a matrix A has 'm' rows and 'n' columns then A is called the matrix of order m x n (read as m by n matrix)

In the above examples order of A is 2×2, order of B is 2×3 order of C is 3×3.

In general, a matrix having m rows and n columns is represented as follows.

$$A = \begin{bmatrix} a_{11} & a_{12} & a_{13} & .. & a_{1j} & .. & a_{1n} \\ a_{21} & a_{22} & a_{23} & .. & a_{2j} & .. & a_{2n} \\ .. & .. & .. & .. & .. & .. & .. \\ a_{i1} & a_{i2} & a_{i3} & .. & a_{ij} & .. & a_{in} \\ .. & .. & .. & .. & .. & .. & .. \\ a_{m1} & a_{m2} & a_{m3} & .. & a_{mj} & .. & a_{mn} \end{bmatrix}$$

So, in the above matrix every element is specified by its position in terms of the row and column in which the element is present. The first and second suffixes of an element indicate respectively the row and column in which the element is present.

For example, a_{32} is the element present in the third row and the second column.

In simplest form of the above matrix is denoted by $A = [a_{ij}]_{m \times n}$ where $1 \leq i \leq m, 1 \leq j \leq n$.

3.2 Types of Matrices

1. *Null matrix (or) zero matrix*

A matrix in which each element is zero is called null matrix or zero matrix and is denoted by O.

Ex : (i) $\begin{pmatrix} 0 & 0 & 0 \\ 0 & 0 & 0 \\ 0 & 0 & 0 \end{pmatrix}$ is null matrix of order 3×3

(ii) $\begin{pmatrix} 0 & 0 & 0 \\ 0 & 0 & 0 \end{pmatrix}$ is null matrix of order 2×3.

2. *Row matrix*

A matrix having only one row is called a row matrix.

Ex : (i) $(1\ 2\ 3)_{1 \times 3}$

(ii) $(1\ 0\ 0\ 0\ 0)_{1 \times 5}$ are row matrices of orders 1×3, 1×5 respectively.

3. *Column matrix*

A matrix having only one column is called a column matrix.

Ex : (i) $\begin{pmatrix} 1 \\ 3 \end{pmatrix}_{2\times1}$ (ii) $\begin{pmatrix} a \\ b \\ c \\ d \end{pmatrix}_{4\times1}$

are column matrices of orders 2 × 1, 4 × 1 respectively.

4. *Square matrix*

A matrix in which the number of rows equal to number of columns is called a square matrix. A square matrix having n rows and n columns is called a square matrix of order n.

Ex : (i) $\begin{pmatrix} 2 & 3 \\ 5 & 7 \end{pmatrix}_{2\times2}$ (ii) $\begin{pmatrix} a & b & c \\ b & c & a \\ c & a & b \end{pmatrix}_{3\times3}$

are square matrices of orders 2 and 3 respectively.

In a square matrix the elements along the diagonal which runs from left top to right bottom called diagonal elements.

In the above example (i) 2, 7 are diagonal elements, (not 3, 5) and in example (ii) a, c, b are diagonal elements (not c, c, c).

5. *Trace of a matrix*

The sum of the diagonal elements of a square matrix is called trace of matrix.

Ex : If $A = \begin{bmatrix} 1 & 2 \\ 3 & 4 \end{bmatrix}$ then trace of A = 1 + 4 = 5

6. *Rectangular matrix*

A matrix in which number of rows is not equal to number of columns is called rectangular matrix.

Ex : (i) $\begin{pmatrix} 1 & 2 & 3 \\ 5 & 7 & 8 \end{pmatrix}_{2\times3}$ (ii) $\begin{pmatrix} 2 & 3 \\ 6 & 8 \\ 5 & 7 \end{pmatrix}_{3\times2}$

are rectangular matrices

7. ***Diagonal matrix***

A square matrix in which the elements except the diagonal elements are zero is called a diagonal matrix

Ex : (i) $\begin{pmatrix} 2 & 0 \\ 0 & 7 \end{pmatrix}$ (ii) $\begin{pmatrix} a & 0 & 0 \\ 0 & b & 0 \\ 0 & 0 & c \end{pmatrix}$ are diagonal matrices

8. ***Scalar matrix***

A diagonal matrix in which all the diagonal elements are equal is called a scalar matrix.

Ex : (i) $\begin{pmatrix} 3 & 0 \\ 0 & 3 \end{pmatrix}$ (ii) $\begin{pmatrix} -2 & 0 & 0 \\ 0 & -2 & 0 \\ 0 & 0 & -2 \end{pmatrix}$ are scalar matrices

9. ***Unit matrix***

A diagonal matrix in which each diagonal entry is unity is called unit matrix or identity matrix.

The unit matrix of order n is denoted by I_n

Ex : (i) $I_2 = \begin{pmatrix} 1 & 0 \\ 0 & 1 \end{pmatrix}$ (ii) $I_4 = \begin{pmatrix} 1 & 0 & 0 & 0 \\ 0 & 1 & 0 & 0 \\ 0 & 0 & 1 & 0 \\ 0 & 0 & 0 & 1 \end{pmatrix}$

Algebraic Properties of Matrices

3.3 Equality of Two Matrices

Matrices A and B are said to be equal if

(i) A and B are same order

(ii) The corresponding elements of Aand B are the same

Thus $A = \begin{bmatrix} a_{11} & a_{12} \\ a_{21} & a_{22} \\ a_{31} & a_{32} \end{bmatrix}$ $B = \begin{bmatrix} b_{11} & b_{12} \\ b_{21} & b_{22} \\ b_{31} & b_{32} \end{bmatrix}$ are equal if $a_{ij} = b_{ij}$ for i = 1, 2, 3, j = 1, 2

Ex. If $\begin{bmatrix} x-1 & 2 & y-4 \\ z & 0 & 2 \\ 1 & -1 & 1+a \end{bmatrix} = \begin{bmatrix} 1-x & 2 & -y \\ 2 & 0 & 2 \\ 1 & -1 & 1 \end{bmatrix}$

then find the values of x, y, z, a

Sol. From the above property i.e equality of matrices we have $x-1=1-x$; $y-4=-y$, $z=2$, p + a = 1

Hence $2x = 2 \Rightarrow x = 1$; $2y = 4 \Rightarrow$ y = 2 ; z = 2, a = 0

$\therefore x = 1, y = 2, z = 2$ and a = 0

3.4 Additon of Two Matrices

Let A and B be two matrices of same order, then addition (sum) of A and B denoed by A + B and is defined as the matrix of same order in which each element is the sum of corresponding elements of A and B.

Ex : If. $A = \begin{bmatrix} 1 & 2 & 3 \\ 7 & 8 & -2 \end{bmatrix}$ $B = \begin{bmatrix} 4 & 6 & 2 \\ 3 & -4 & 7 \end{bmatrix}$

then $A + B = \begin{bmatrix} 1+4 & 2+6 & 3+2 \\ 7+3 & 8+(-4) & (-2)+7 \end{bmatrix} = \begin{bmatrix} 5 & 8 & 5 \\ 10 & 4 & 5 \end{bmatrix}$

Properties of addition of matrices

Let A, B, C be matrices of same order. Then the addition of matrices satisfies the following properties.

(i) *Commatative property :*

A + B = B + A

(ii) *Associative property :*

A + (B + C) = (A + B) + C

(iii) *Additive identity :*

Let A be m × n matrix and O is the m × n null matrix then

A + O = O + A = A

Here O is called the additive identity in the set of all m × n matrices.

(iv) *Additive inverse :*

Let A is a $(m \times n)$ matrix then there exists unique matrix B of order $m \times n$ such that $A + B = B + A = 0$ where 0 is $m \times n$ null matrix then B is called additive inverse of A.

Ex : If $A = \begin{bmatrix} 1 & 2 & 3 \\ 7 & -2 & 1 \\ -3 & 4 & 6 \end{bmatrix}$ then

additive inverse of A is $\begin{bmatrix} -1 & -2 & -3 \\ -7 & 2 & -1 \\ 3 & -4 & -6 \end{bmatrix}$

3.5 Scalar Multiple of Matrix

Let A be a matrix of order $m \times n$ and k be a scalar. Then the matrix of order $m \times n$ obtained by multiplying each element of A by k is called scalar multiple of A and is denoted by kA.

Ex : If $k = 3$ $A = \begin{bmatrix} 5 & 2 \\ 3 & 1 \\ -2 & 4 \end{bmatrix}$ then

$$kA = \begin{bmatrix} 3\times 5 & 3\times 2 \\ 3\times 3 & 3\times 1 \\ 3\times -2 & 3\times 4 \end{bmatrix} = \begin{bmatrix} 15 & 6 \\ 9 & 3 \\ -6 & 12 \end{bmatrix}$$

Note that $-A = (-1)A$ since $A + (-1)A = 0$

Properties of Scalar multiple of matrix

Let A and B be matrices of same order and α, β be scalars then

(i) $\alpha(\beta A) = (\alpha\beta)A = \beta(\alpha A)$ (ii) $(\alpha + \beta)A = \alpha A + \beta A$

(ii) $oA = O$ (iv) $\alpha O = O$

(v) $\alpha(A + B) = \alpha A + \alpha B$

Solved Problems (on 3.3, 3.4, 3.5)

1. Find the sum (addition) of the following pair of matrices

(i) $\begin{bmatrix}1 & 2 & 3\end{bmatrix}, \begin{bmatrix}3 & 2 & 1\end{bmatrix}$ (ii) $\begin{bmatrix}5\\6\\7\end{bmatrix}, \begin{bmatrix}-5\\3\\2\end{bmatrix}$

(iii) $\begin{bmatrix}a & 0 & 0\\0 & b & 0\\0 & 0 & c\end{bmatrix}, \begin{bmatrix}0 & 0 & x\\0 & y & 0\\z & 0 & a\end{bmatrix}$ (iv) $\begin{bmatrix}1 & 2 & 4\\-4 & 3 & -5\\7 & 9 & 6\end{bmatrix}, \begin{bmatrix}4 & 1 & 0\\-2 & 3 & 5\\6 & 7 & -6\end{bmatrix}$

Sol. (i) $\begin{bmatrix}1 & 2 & 3\end{bmatrix} + \begin{bmatrix}3 & 2 & 1\end{bmatrix} = \begin{bmatrix}1+3 & 2+2 & 3+1\end{bmatrix} = \begin{bmatrix}4 & 4 & 4\end{bmatrix}$

(ii) $\begin{bmatrix}5\\6\\7\end{bmatrix} + \begin{bmatrix}-5\\3\\2\end{bmatrix} = \begin{bmatrix}0\\9\\9\end{bmatrix}$

(iii) $\begin{bmatrix}a & 0 & 0\\0 & b & 0\\0 & 0 & c\end{bmatrix} + \begin{bmatrix}0 & 0 & x\\0 & y & 0\\z & 0 & a\end{bmatrix} = \begin{bmatrix}a & 0 & x\\0 & b+y & 0\\z & 0 & a+c\end{bmatrix}$

(iv) $\begin{bmatrix}1 & 2 & 4\\-4 & 3 & -5\\7 & 9 & 6\end{bmatrix} + \begin{bmatrix}4 & 1 & 0\\-2 & 3 & 5\\6 & 7 & -6\end{bmatrix} = \begin{bmatrix}5 & 3 & 4\\-6 & 6 & 0\\13 & 16 & 0\end{bmatrix}$

2. If $A = \begin{bmatrix}-1 & -2 & 3\\1 & 2 & 4\\2 & -1 & 3\end{bmatrix}$, $B = \begin{bmatrix}1 & -2 & 5\\0 & -2 & 2\\1 & 2 & -3\end{bmatrix}$, $C = \begin{bmatrix}-2 & 1 & 2\\1 & 1 & 2\\2 & 0 & 1\end{bmatrix}$, then find A + B + C.

Sol. $A + B + C = \begin{bmatrix}-1+1+(-2) & -2+(-2)+1 & 3+5+2\\1+0+1 & 2+(-2)+1 & 4+2+2\\2+1+2 & -1+2+0 & 3+-3+1\end{bmatrix}$

$= \begin{bmatrix}-2 & -3 & 10\\2 & 1 & 8\\5 & 1 & 1\end{bmatrix}$

3. If $A=\begin{bmatrix}3 & 2 & -1\\ 2 & -2 & 0\\ 1 & 3 & 1\end{bmatrix}$, $B=\begin{bmatrix}-3 & -1 & 0\\ 2 & 1 & 3\\ 4 & -1 & 2\end{bmatrix}$ and $X=\begin{bmatrix}x_1 & x_2 & x_3\\ x_4 & x_5 & x_6\\ x_7 & x_8 & x_9\end{bmatrix}$ such that $X = A + B$ then find the value of $x_1 + x_5 + x_9$.

Sol. $A+B=\begin{bmatrix}3+(-3) & 2-1 & -1+0\\ 2+2 & -2+1 & 0+3\\ 1+4 & 3-1 & 1+2\end{bmatrix}=\begin{bmatrix}0 & 1 & -1\\ 4 & -1 & 3\\ 5 & 2 & 3\end{bmatrix}$

and $X=\begin{bmatrix}x_1 & x_2 & x_3\\ x_4 & x_5 & x_6\\ x_7 & x_8 & x_9\end{bmatrix}$

Given A + B = X i.e, X = A + B

$$\Rightarrow \begin{bmatrix}x_1 & x_2 & x_3\\ x_4 & x_5 & x_6\\ x_7 & x_8 & x_9\end{bmatrix}=\begin{bmatrix}0 & 1 & -1\\ 4 & -1 & 3\\ 5 & 2 & 3\end{bmatrix}$$

$\therefore$ We have $x_1 = 0, x_5 = -1, x_9 = 3$

$\Rightarrow x_1 + x_5 + x_9 = 0 + (-1) + 3 = 2$

4. If $\begin{bmatrix}x-1 & 2 & 5-y\\ 0 & z-1 & 7\\ 1 & 0 & a-5\end{bmatrix}=\begin{bmatrix}1 & 2 & 3\\ 0 & 4 & 7\\ 1 & 0 & 0\end{bmatrix}$ then find the value of $x - y + z - a$

Sol. Given $\begin{bmatrix}x-1 & 2 & 5-y\\ 0 & z-1 & 7\\ 1 & 0 & a-5\end{bmatrix}=\begin{bmatrix}1 & 2 & 3\\ 0 & 4 & 7\\ 1 & 0 & 0\end{bmatrix}$

by definition of equality of two matrices we have

$x - 1 = 1, 5 - y = 3, z - 1 = 4, a - 5 = 0$

i.e., $x = 2, \quad y = 2, \quad z = 5, \quad a = 5$

$\therefore \quad x - y + z - a = 2 - 2 + 5 - 5 = 0$

5. Find the trace of $\begin{bmatrix} 1 & 3 & -5 \\ 2 & -1 & 5 \\ 2 & 0 & 1 \end{bmatrix}$

Sol. The trace of a square matrix is sum of the diagonal elements of the matrix.

$\therefore$ trace = 1 + (–1) + 1 = 1

6. If $A = \begin{bmatrix} 0 & 1 & 2 \\ 2 & 3 & 4 \\ 4 & 5 & -6 \end{bmatrix}$ and $B = \begin{bmatrix} -1 & 2 & 3 \\ 0 & 1 & 0 \\ 0 & 0 & -1 \end{bmatrix}$ then find B – A and 4A – 5B.

Given $A = \begin{bmatrix} 0 & 1 & 2 \\ 2 & 3 & 4 \\ 4 & 5 & -6 \end{bmatrix}$, $B = \begin{bmatrix} -1 & 2 & 3 \\ 0 & 1 & 0 \\ 0 & 0 & -1 \end{bmatrix}$

(i) $$B - A = \begin{bmatrix} -1-0 & 2-1 & 3-2 \\ 0-2 & 1-3 & 0-4 \\ 0-4 & 0-5 & -1-(-6) \end{bmatrix} = \begin{bmatrix} -1 & 1 & 1 \\ -2 & -2 & -4 \\ -4 & -5 & 5 \end{bmatrix}.$$

also $$4A = \begin{bmatrix} 4\times 0 & 4\times 1 & 4\times 2 \\ 4\times 2 & 4\times 3 & 4\times 4 \\ 4\times 4 & 4\times 5 & 4\times -6 \end{bmatrix} = \begin{bmatrix} 0 & 4 & 8 \\ 8 & 12 & 16 \\ 16 & 20 & -24 \end{bmatrix}$$

$$5B = \begin{bmatrix} 5\times -1 & 5\times 2 & 5\times 3 \\ 5\times 0 & 5\times 1 & 5\times 0 \\ 5\times 0 & 5\times 0 & 5\times -1 \end{bmatrix} = \begin{bmatrix} -5 & 10 & 15 \\ 0 & 5 & 0 \\ 0 & 0 & -5 \end{bmatrix}$$

(ii) $$4A - 5B = \begin{bmatrix} 0-(-5) & 4-10 & 8-15 \\ 8-0 & 12-5 & 16-0 \\ 16-0 & 20-0 & -24-(-5) \end{bmatrix}$$

$$= \begin{bmatrix} 5 & -6 & -7 \\ 8 & 7 & 16 \\ 16 & 20 & 19 \end{bmatrix}$$

Excercise - 3.1

1. Find the sum of the following pair of matrices

(i) $\begin{bmatrix} 2 & 3 & -1 \\ 7 & 8 & 5 \end{bmatrix}, \begin{bmatrix} 1 & 0 & 1 \\ 2 & -4 & -1 \end{bmatrix}$ (ii) $\begin{bmatrix} 2 & 3 & 1 \\ 6 & -1 & 5 \end{bmatrix}, \begin{bmatrix} 1 & 2 & -1 \\ 0 & -1 & 3 \end{bmatrix}$

2. Find the additive inverse of A, where

(i) $A = \begin{bmatrix} i & 0 & 1 \\ 0 & -i & 2 \\ -1 & 1 & 5 \end{bmatrix}$ (ii) $A = \begin{bmatrix} 1 & 2 & -\frac{1}{2} \\ 0 & -1 & 2 \\ -\frac{1}{2} & 2 & 1 \end{bmatrix}$

3. Find the trace of the following matrices

(i) $\begin{bmatrix} 1 & -2 & 0 \\ 0 & 1 & -1 \\ -1 & 0 & 3 \end{bmatrix}$ (ii) $\begin{bmatrix} 0 & 1 & 2 \\ 2 & 3 & 4 \\ 4 & 5 & 6 \end{bmatrix}$

(iii) $\begin{bmatrix} 1 & 2 & -\frac{1}{2} \\ 0 & -1 & 2 \\ -\frac{1}{2} & 2 & 1 \end{bmatrix}$

4. If $A = \begin{bmatrix} 4 & -5 \\ -2 & 3 \end{bmatrix}$ then find 5A, –5A

5. If $\begin{bmatrix} x-3 & 2y-8 \\ z+2 & 6 \end{bmatrix} = \begin{bmatrix} 3 & 2 \\ -2 & a-4 \end{bmatrix}$ then find the x, y, z, a.

6. If $A = \begin{bmatrix} -1 & 3 \\ 4 & 2 \end{bmatrix}$ $B = \begin{bmatrix} 2 & 1 \\ 3 & -5 \end{bmatrix}$, and $A + B - X = 0$ then find the values of x_1, x_2, x_3, x_4. where $X = \begin{bmatrix} x_1 & x_2 \\ x_3 & x_4 \end{bmatrix}$

7. If $A = \begin{pmatrix} 3 & 2 & -1 \\ 2 & -1 & 0 \\ 1 & 3 & 1 \end{pmatrix}$, $B = \begin{pmatrix} -3 & -1 & 0 \\ 2 & 1 & 3 \\ 4 & -1 & 2 \end{pmatrix}$ and $X - A = B$ then find X.

8. If $A = \begin{pmatrix} 1 & 2 & 3 \\ 3 & 2 & 1 \end{pmatrix}$ and $B = \begin{pmatrix} 3 & 2 & 1 \\ 1 & 2 & 3 \end{pmatrix}$ then find 3B – 2A.

9. If $A=\begin{bmatrix}1 & 2\\ 3 & 4\end{bmatrix}$, $B=\begin{bmatrix}3 & 8\\ 7 & 2\end{bmatrix}$ and $2X+A=B$ then find X.

10. If $A=\begin{bmatrix}0 & 1 & 2\\ 2 & 3 & 4\\ 4 & 5 & 6\end{bmatrix}$ and $B=\begin{bmatrix}1 & -2 & 0\\ 0 & 1 & -1\\ -1 & 0 & 3\end{bmatrix}$ then find $A-B$ and $4B-3A$.

Answers

1. (i) $\begin{bmatrix}3 & 3 & 0\\ 9 & 4 & 4\end{bmatrix}$ (ii) $\begin{bmatrix}3 & 5 & 0\\ 6 & -2 & 8\end{bmatrix}$

2. (i) $\begin{bmatrix}-i & 0 & -1\\ 0 & i & -2\\ 1 & -1 & -5\end{bmatrix}$ (ii) $\begin{bmatrix}-1 & -2 & \frac{1}{2}\\ 0 & 1 & -2\\ \frac{1}{2} & -2 & -1\end{bmatrix}$

3. (i) 5 (ii) 9 (iii) 1

4. (i) $\begin{bmatrix}20 & -25\\ -10 & 15\end{bmatrix}$ (ii) $\begin{bmatrix}-20 & 25\\ 10 & -15\end{bmatrix}$

5. $x=6, y=5, z=-4, a=10$

6. $x_1=1, x_2=4, x_3=7, x_4=-3$

7. $\begin{pmatrix}0 & 1 & -1\\ 4 & 0 & 3\\ 5 & 2 & 3\end{pmatrix}$

8. $\begin{pmatrix}7 & 2 & -3\\ -3 & 2 & 7\end{pmatrix}$

9. $\begin{pmatrix}1 & 3\\ 2 & -1\end{pmatrix}$

10. (i) $\begin{bmatrix}-1 & 3 & 2\\ 2 & 2 & 5\\ 5 & 5 & 3\end{bmatrix}$ (ii) $\begin{bmatrix}4 & -11 & -6\\ -6 & -5 & -16\\ -16 & -15 & -6\end{bmatrix}$

3.6 Multiplication (product) of Two Matrices

Let A and B are two matrices then the product AB is exists if the number of columns of A is equal to the number of rows of B, and the product BA is exists if the number of columns of B is equal to number of rows of A.

Example : Let A is matrix of order 2 × 3 and B matrix of order 3 × 5 then product AB exist and product BA does not exists.

Since by above rule that number of columns of A = number of rows of B = 3.

∴ Product AB exists and

number of columns of B = 5 and number of rows of A = 2 these are not equal.

∴ Product BA does not exisits

i.e., product of two matrices A, B is exists in given order of the number of columns of first matrix (A) is equal to number of rows of the second matrix (B). Now let us see how to multiply the two matrices if the multiplication is exists.

Consider two matrices A and B where A is of order m × n and B is of order n × p. So the number of columns of A is equal to number of rows of B. Therefore product AB is exists.

Its ith row, j[th] column element is given by the sum of the product of elements of ith row elements of A with corresponding j[th] column elements of B.

i.e., If $A = (a_{ij})_{m\times n}$, $B = (b_{ij})_{n\times p}$

then $AB = (c_{ij})_{m\times p}$ where $a_{ij} \sum_{r=1}^{n} a_{ir}b_{rj}$

Consider two matrices $A = \begin{pmatrix} x_1 & x_2 & x_3 \\ x_4 & x_5 & x_6 \end{pmatrix}_{2\times 3}$ and $B = \begin{pmatrix} y_1 & y_4 \\ y_2 & y_5 \\ y_3 & y_6 \end{pmatrix}_{3\times 2}$

here the number of columns of A = 3 = number of rows of B.

Now the product matrix AB is of order 2 × 2. To get the elements of AB we follow the procedure.

To get first row first column element of AB, we have to multiply the elements of the first row of A with corresponding elements of first column of B and add, that is

$$x_1 \times y_1 + x_2 \times y_2 + x_3 \times y_3$$

$$\begin{bmatrix} x_1 & x_2 & x_3 \\ x & x & x \end{bmatrix} \begin{bmatrix} y_1 & x \\ y_2 & x \\ y_3 & x \end{bmatrix}$$

Suppose we required to the second row first column element of AB, we multiply second row elements of A with corresponding elements of first column elements of B and add, that is

$$\begin{pmatrix} x_4 & x_5 & x_6 \end{pmatrix} \begin{pmatrix} y_1 \\ y_2 \\ y_3 \end{pmatrix}$$

$$= x_4 y_1 + x_5 y_2 + x_6 y_3$$

Ex : If $A = \begin{pmatrix} 2 & 3 & -1 \\ 1 & -2 & 4 \end{pmatrix}$, $B = \begin{pmatrix} 1 & 1 \\ 2 & -1 \\ 4 & 2 \end{pmatrix}$ then find AB

Here A is 2×3 matrix and B is 3×2 matrix.

$\therefore$ AB is of order 2×2. Now we find AB as follows

$$AB = \begin{pmatrix} 2 & 3 & -1 \\ 1 & -2 & 4 \end{pmatrix} \begin{pmatrix} 1 & 1 \\ 2 & -1 \\ 4 & 2 \end{pmatrix}$$

$$= \begin{pmatrix} (2)\times(1)+(3)\times(2)+(-1)(4) & (2)\times(1)+(3)(-1)+(-1)(2) \\ (1)\times(1)+(-2)\times(2)+(4)\times(4) & (1)\times(1)+(-2)(-1)+(4)(2) \end{pmatrix}$$

$$= \begin{pmatrix} 2+6-4 & 2+-3-2 \\ 1-4+16 & 1+2+8 \end{pmatrix} = \begin{pmatrix} 4 & -3 \\ 13 & 11 \end{pmatrix}$$

Properties of Multiplication of Matrices

(i) *Associative law* : If A, B, C are three matrices whose orders respectively are $m \times n$, $n \times p$, $p \times q$ respectively then A . (B . C) = (A . B) . C.

(ii) *Distributive law* : If A is a matrix of order $m \times n$ and B, C are matrices of order $n \times p$ then

A. (B + C) = A . B + A . C (left distributive law)

(A + B) . C = A . C + B. C (right distributive law)

(iii) If A is $m \times n$ matrix then $A . I_n = A$, and $I_m . A = A$.

(iv) *Commutative law :*

If A and B are two matrices

such that AB = BA then

A, B are said to be commutative

Note : Matrix multiplication is not commutative, for example

Let $A=\begin{pmatrix}1 & 2\\ 3 & 4\end{pmatrix} \quad B=\begin{pmatrix}3 & 2\\ -1 & 4\end{pmatrix}$

$$AB=\begin{pmatrix}1 & 2\\ 3 & 4\end{pmatrix}\begin{pmatrix}3 & 2\\ -1 & 4\end{pmatrix}=\begin{pmatrix}1\times 3+2\times -1 & 1\times 2+2\times 4\\ 3\times 3+4\times -1 & 3\times 2+4\times 4\end{pmatrix}=\begin{pmatrix}1 & 10\\ 5 & 22\end{pmatrix}$$

$$BA=\begin{pmatrix}3 & 2\\ -1 & 4\end{pmatrix}\begin{pmatrix}1 & 2\\ 3 & 4\end{pmatrix}=\begin{pmatrix}3\times 1+2\times 3 & 3\times 2+2\times 4\\ -1\times 1+4\times 3 & -1\times 2+4\times 4\end{pmatrix}=\begin{pmatrix}9 & 14\\ 11 & 14\end{pmatrix}$$

$\therefore$ AB $\neq$ BA

3.7 Transpose of a Matrix

Let $A = [a_{ij}]_{m\times n}$ is a matrix of order m × n then matrix obtained by interchanging the rows and columns of A is called the transpose of A. Transpose of the matrix A is denoted by A^T or A^1.

Ex : If $A=\begin{bmatrix}1 & 2 & 3\\ 4 & 5 & 6\end{bmatrix}_{2\times 3}$ then $A^T=\begin{bmatrix}1 & 4\\ 2 & 5\\ 3 & 6\end{bmatrix}_{3\times 2}$

Properties of Transpose of Matrices

(i) $(A^T)^T = A$

(ii) $(KA)^T = KA^T$

(iii) $(A + B)^T = A^T + B^T$

(iv) $(AB)^T = B^T A^T$

Symmetric matrix : A square matrix A is said to be symmetric if $A^T = A$

Ex : $\begin{bmatrix}a & h & g\\ h & b & f\\ g & f & c\end{bmatrix}$ is a symmetric matrix since its transpose is itself.

Skew Symmetric matrix : A square matrix A is said to be skew symmetric matrix if $A^T = -A$.

Ex : $\begin{bmatrix} 0 & -a & -b \\ a & 0 & -c \\ b & c & 0 \end{bmatrix}$ is a skew symmetric matrix

Note :

1. If A is symmetric matrix then $A + A^T$ is symmetric.
2. If A is skew symmetric matrix then $A - A^T$ is skew symmetric matrix
3. Every square matrix can be usually expressed as sum of symmetric and skew symmetric matrices.

i.e., $A = \left(\frac{A + A^T}{2}\right) + \left(\frac{A - A^T}{2}\right)$

Solved Examples (on 3.6 and 3.7)

1. Find the following products of matrices (if possible)

(i) $\begin{bmatrix} 5 & 1 & 3 \end{bmatrix} \begin{bmatrix} -1 \\ 4 \\ 2 \end{bmatrix}$ (ii) $\begin{bmatrix} 2 & 1 & 4 \\ 6 & -2 & 3 \end{bmatrix} \begin{bmatrix} 1 \\ 2 \\ 1 \end{bmatrix}$

(iii) $\begin{bmatrix} 3 & 4 & 9 \\ 0 & -1 & 5 \\ 2 & 6 & 12 \end{bmatrix} \begin{bmatrix} 13 & -2 & 0 \\ 0 & 4 & 1 \end{bmatrix}$ (iv) $\begin{bmatrix} 0 & c & -b \\ -c & 0 & a \\ b & -a & 0 \end{bmatrix} \begin{bmatrix} a^2 & ab & ac \\ ab & b^2 & bc \\ ac & bc & c^2 \end{bmatrix}$

Sol. (i) Let $A = \begin{bmatrix} 5 & 1 & 3 \end{bmatrix}_{1\times 3}$, $B = \begin{bmatrix} -1 \\ 4 \\ 2 \end{bmatrix}_{3\times 1}$

$$AB = \begin{bmatrix} 5 & 1 & 3 \end{bmatrix}_{1\times 3} \begin{bmatrix} -1 \\ 4 \\ 2 \end{bmatrix}_{3\times 1}$$

$$= [5 \times -1 + 1 \times 4 + 3 \times 2]_{1\times 1}$$

$$= [-5 + 4 + 6]_{1\times 1} = [5]_{1\times 1}$$

(ii) Let $A = \begin{bmatrix} 2 & 1 & 4 \\ 6 & -2 & 3 \end{bmatrix}_{2\times3}$, $B = \begin{bmatrix} 1 \\ 2 \\ 1 \end{bmatrix}_{3\times1}$

$$AB = \begin{bmatrix} 2 & 1 & 4 \\ 6 & -2 & 3 \end{bmatrix}_{2\times3} \begin{bmatrix} 1 \\ 2 \\ 1 \end{bmatrix}_{3\times1}$$

$$= \begin{bmatrix} 2\times1 & + & 1\times2 & + & 4\times1 \\ 6\times1 & + & -2\times2 & + & 3\times1 \end{bmatrix}$$

$$= \begin{bmatrix} 2 & + & 2 & + & 4 \\ 6 & - & 4 & + & 3 \end{bmatrix} = \begin{bmatrix} 8 \\ 5 \end{bmatrix}_{2\times1}$$

(iii) $\begin{bmatrix} 3 & 4 & 9 \\ 0 & -1 & 5 \\ 2 & 6 & 12 \end{bmatrix}_{3\times3} \cdot \begin{bmatrix} 13 & -2 & 0 \\ 0 & 4 & 1 \end{bmatrix}_{2\times3}$

Let $A = \begin{bmatrix} 3 & 4 & 9 \\ 0 & -1 & 5 \\ 2 & 6 & 12 \end{bmatrix}_{3\times3}$, $B = \begin{bmatrix} 13 & -2 & 0 \\ 0 & 4 & 1 \end{bmatrix}_{2\times3}$

The no.of row s of Matrix B is not equal to the no. of columns of Matrix A. Hence Matrix multiplication is not possible.

(iv) $\begin{bmatrix} 0 & c & -b \\ -c & 0 & a \\ b & -a & 0 \end{bmatrix}_{3\times3} \begin{bmatrix} a^2 & ab & ac \\ ab & b^2 & bc \\ ac & bc & c^2 \end{bmatrix}_{3\times3}$

Let $A = \begin{bmatrix} 0 & c & -b \\ -c & 0 & a \\ b & -a & 0 \end{bmatrix}_{3\times3}$, $B = \begin{bmatrix} a^2 & ab & ac \\ ab & b^2 & bc \\ ac & bc & c^2 \end{bmatrix}_{3\times3}$

$$AB = \begin{bmatrix} 0\times a^2 + c\times ab + -b\times ac & 0\times ab + b^2\times c + -b\times bc & 0\times ac + c\times bc + -b\times c^2 \\ c\times a^2 + 0\times ab + a\times ac & -c\times ab + 0\times b^2 + a\times bc & -c\times ac + 0\times bc + a\times c^2 \\ b\times a^2 - a\times ab + 0\times ac & b\times ab + a\times b^2 + 0\times bc & b\times ac - 1 - a\times bc + 0\times c^2 \end{bmatrix}$$

$$\begin{bmatrix} 0 & 0 & 0 \\ 0 & 0 & 0 \\ 0 & 0 & 0 \end{bmatrix}_{3\times3} = \text{Null Matrix}$$

2. If $A = \begin{bmatrix} 1 & -2 & 3 \\ 2 & 3 & -1 \\ -3 & 1 & 2 \end{bmatrix}$, $B = \begin{bmatrix} 1 & 0 & 2 \\ 0 & 1 & 2 \\ 1 & 2 & 0 \end{bmatrix}$ then find AB, BA and verify the cummutative property (AB = BA)

$$AB = \begin{bmatrix} 1 & -2 & 3 \\ 2 & 3 & -1 \\ -3 & 1 & 2 \end{bmatrix}_{3\times3} \begin{bmatrix} 1 & 0 & 2 \\ 0 & 1 & 2 \\ 1 & 2 & 0 \end{bmatrix}_{3\times3}$$

$$= \begin{bmatrix} 1\times1 - 2\times0 + 3\times1 & 1\times0 + -2\times1 + 3\times2 & 1\times2 + -2\times2 + 3\times0 \\ 2\times1 + 3\times0 - 1\times1 & 2\times0 + 3\times1 + -1\times2 & 2\times2 + 3\times2 + -1\times0 \\ -3\times1 + 1\times0 + 2\times1 & -3\times0 + 1\times1 + 2\times2 & -3\times2 + 1\times2 + 2\times0 \end{bmatrix}$$

$$= \begin{bmatrix} 4 & 4 & -2 \\ 1 & 1 & 10 \\ -1 & 5 & -4 \end{bmatrix}_{3\times3}$$

$$BA = \begin{bmatrix} 1 & 0 & 2 \\ 0 & 1 & 2 \\ 1 & 2 & 0 \end{bmatrix} \begin{bmatrix} 1 & -2 & 3 \\ 2 & 3 & -1 \\ -3 & 1 & 2 \end{bmatrix}$$

$$= \begin{bmatrix} 1\times1 + 0\times2 + 2\times-3 & 1\times-2 + 0\times3 + 2\times1 & 1\times3 + 0\times-1 + 2\times2 \\ 0\times1 + 1\times2 + 2\times-3 & 0\times-2 + 1\times3 + 2\times1 & 0\times3 + 1\times-1 + 2\times2 \\ 1\times1 + 2\times2 + 0\times-3 & 1\times-2 + 2\times3 + 0\times1 & 1\times3 + 2\times-1 + 0\times2 \end{bmatrix} = \begin{bmatrix} -5 & 0 & 7 \\ -4 & 5 & 3 \\ 5 & 4 & 1 \end{bmatrix}$$

$AB \neq BA$

∴ Matrix Multiplication does not obey commutative law

3. If $A = \begin{bmatrix} i & 0 \\ 0 & -i \end{bmatrix}, B = \begin{bmatrix} 0 & -1 \\ 1 & 0 \end{bmatrix}$ and $C = \begin{bmatrix} 0 & i \\ i & 0 \end{bmatrix}$ and I is unit matrix of order 2 then show that

(i) $A^2 = B^2 = C^2 = -I$

(ii) $AB = BA = -C$

(i) $A^2 = A \times A = \begin{bmatrix} i & 0 \\ 0 & -i \end{bmatrix}\begin{bmatrix} i & 0 \\ 0 & -i \end{bmatrix} = \begin{bmatrix} i\times i+0\times 0 & i\times 0+0\times -i \\ 0\times i+-1\times 0 & 0\times 0+\times i\times i \end{bmatrix} = \begin{bmatrix} -1 & 0 \\ 0 & -1 \end{bmatrix}$

$= -I$ $\qquad (\because I^2 = -1)$

Similarly $B^2 = -I \qquad C^2 = -I$

(ii) $AB = \begin{bmatrix} i & 0 \\ 0 & -i \end{bmatrix}\begin{bmatrix} 0 & -1 \\ 1 & 0 \end{bmatrix} = \begin{bmatrix} i\times 0+0\times 1 & i\times -1+0\times 0 \\ 0\times 0+-i\times 1 & 0\times -1+-i\times 0 \end{bmatrix}$

$= \begin{bmatrix} 0 & -i \\ -i & 0 \end{bmatrix}$

Similarly $\quad BA = \begin{bmatrix} 0 & -i \\ -i & 0 \end{bmatrix}$

$\therefore AB = -BA = -C$

4. If $A = \begin{bmatrix} 3 & 0 & 0 \\ 0 & 3 & 0 \\ 0 & 0 & 3 \end{bmatrix}$ then find A^4.

Sol. $A^4 = A^2 \times A^2 \qquad \Rightarrow \qquad A^2 = A \times A$

$\therefore \quad A^2 = \begin{bmatrix} 3 & 0 & 0 \\ 0 & 3 & 0 \\ 0 & 0 & 3 \end{bmatrix}\begin{bmatrix} 3 & 0 & 0 \\ 0 & 3 & 0 \\ 0 & 0 & 3 \end{bmatrix}$

$= \begin{bmatrix} 3\times 3+0\times 0+0\times 0 & 3\times 0+0\times 3+0\times 0 & 3\times 0+0\times 0+0\times 3 \\ 0\times 3+3\times 0+0\times 0 & 0\times 0+3\times 3+0\times 0 & 0\times 0+3\times 0\times 3\times 0 \\ 0\times 3+0\times 0+3\times 0 & 0\times 0+0\times 3+3\times 0 & 0\times 0+0\times 0+3\times 3 \end{bmatrix}$

$= \begin{bmatrix} 9 & 0 & 0 \\ 0 & 9 & 0 \\ 0 & 0 & 9 \end{bmatrix}$

$$\therefore\ A^4 = A^2 \times A^2 = \begin{bmatrix} 9 & 0 & 0 \\ 0 & 9 & 0 \\ 0 & 0 & 9 \end{bmatrix}\begin{bmatrix} 9 & 0 & 0 \\ 0 & 9 & 0 \\ 0 & 0 & 9 \end{bmatrix} = \begin{bmatrix} 81 & 0 & 0 \\ 0 & 81 & 0 \\ 0 & 0 & 81 \end{bmatrix}$$

5. If $A = \begin{bmatrix} 1 & -2 & 1 \\ 0 & 1 & -1 \\ 3 & -1 & 1 \end{bmatrix}$ then find $A^3 - 3A^2 - A - 3I$

Sol. $A^3 - 3A^2 - A - 3I$

$$A^2 = A\,.\,A = \begin{bmatrix} 1 & -2 & 1 \\ 0 & 1 & -1 \\ 3 & -1 & 1 \end{bmatrix}\begin{bmatrix} 1 & -2 & 1 \\ 0 & 1 & -1 \\ 3 & -1 & 1 \end{bmatrix}$$

$$= \begin{bmatrix} 1\times1+-2\times0+1\times3 & 1\times-2+-2\times1+1\times-1 & 1\times1+-2\times-1+1\times1 \\ 0\times1+1\times0+-1\times3 & 0\times-2+1\times1+-1\times-1 & 0\times1+1\times-1+-1\times1 \\ 3\times1+-1\times0+1\times3 & 3\times-2+-1\times1+1\times-1 & 3\times1+-1\times-1+1\times1 \end{bmatrix}$$

$$= \begin{bmatrix} 4 & -5 & 4 \\ -3 & 2 & -2 \\ 6 & -8 & 5 \end{bmatrix}$$

$$\Rightarrow \quad 3A^2 = 3\begin{bmatrix} 4 & -5 & 4 \\ -3 & 2 & -2 \\ 6 & -8 & 5 \end{bmatrix} = \begin{bmatrix} 12 & -15 & 12 \\ -9 & 6 & -6 \\ 18 & -24 & 15 \end{bmatrix}$$

$$A^3 = A^2 \times A = \begin{bmatrix} 4 & -5 & 4 \\ -3 & 2 & -2 \\ 6 & -8 & 5 \end{bmatrix}\begin{bmatrix} 1 & -2 & 1 \\ 0 & 1 & -1 \\ 3 & -1 & 1 \end{bmatrix}$$

$$= \begin{bmatrix} 4-0+12 & -8-5-4 & 4+5+4 \\ -3+0-6 & +6+2+2 & -3-2-2 \\ 6+0+15 & -12-8-5 & 6+8+5 \end{bmatrix} = \begin{bmatrix} +16 & -17 & 13 \\ -9 & 10 & -7 \\ 21 & -25 & 19 \end{bmatrix}$$

$\therefore\ A^3 - 3A^2 - A - 3I$

$$= \begin{bmatrix} 16 & -17 & 13 \\ -9 & 10 & -7 \\ 21 & -25 & 19 \end{bmatrix} + \begin{bmatrix} -12 & 15 & -12 \\ 9 & -6 & 6 \\ -18 & 24 & -15 \end{bmatrix} + \begin{bmatrix} -1 & 2 & -1 \\ 0 & -1 & 1 \\ -3 & 1 & -1 \end{bmatrix} + \begin{bmatrix} -3 & 0 & 0 \\ 0 & -3 & 0 \\ 0 & 0 & -3 \end{bmatrix}$$

$$= \begin{bmatrix} 16-12-1-3 & -17+15+2+0 & 13-12-1+0 \\ -9+9+10+0 & 10-6-1-3 & -7+6+1+0 \\ 21-18-3+0 & -25+24+1+0 & 19-15-1-3 \end{bmatrix} = \begin{bmatrix} 0 & 0 & 0 \\ 0 & 0 & 0 \\ 0 & 0 & 0 \end{bmatrix}$$

6. If $I = \begin{bmatrix} 1 & 0 \\ 0 & 1 \end{bmatrix}$ and $E = \begin{bmatrix} 0 & 1 \\ 0 & 0 \end{bmatrix}$ then show that $(aI + bE)^3 = a^3I + 3a^2\,bE$

Sol. $aI = \begin{pmatrix} a & 0 \\ 0 & a \end{pmatrix}$, $\quad bE = \begin{pmatrix} 0 & b \\ 0 & 0 \end{pmatrix}$

$(aI + bE) = \begin{pmatrix} a & b \\ 0 & a \end{pmatrix}$ $\quad (aI + bE)^2 = \begin{pmatrix} a & b \\ 0 & a \end{pmatrix}\begin{pmatrix} a & b \\ 0 & a \end{pmatrix}$

$$\therefore\ (aI + bE)^3 = \begin{pmatrix} a & b \\ 0 & a \end{pmatrix}\begin{pmatrix} a^2 & 2ab \\ 0 & a^2 \end{pmatrix}$$

$$= \begin{pmatrix} a^3 + 0 & 3a^2b \\ 0 & a^3 \end{pmatrix} = \begin{pmatrix} a^3 & 3a^2b \\ 0 & a^3 \end{pmatrix}$$

$$a^3I = \begin{bmatrix} a^3 & 0 \\ 0 & a^3 \end{bmatrix};\quad 3a^2bE = \begin{bmatrix} o & 3a^2b \\ 0 & 0 \end{bmatrix}$$

$$a^3I + 3a^2bE = \begin{bmatrix} a^3 & 0 \\ 0 & a^3 \end{bmatrix} + \begin{bmatrix} 0 & 3a^2b \\ 0 & 0 \end{bmatrix} = \begin{bmatrix} a^3 + 0 & 3a^2b \\ 0 & a^3 \end{bmatrix} = \begin{pmatrix} a^3 & 3a^2b \\ 0 & a^3 \end{pmatrix}$$

Hence $(aI + bE)^3 = a^3I + 3a^2\,bE$

7. If $\theta - \phi = \dfrac{\pi}{2}$ then show that $\begin{bmatrix} \cos^2\theta & \cos\theta\sin\theta \\ \cos\theta\sin\theta & \sin^2\theta \end{bmatrix}\begin{bmatrix} \cos^2\phi & \cos\phi\sin\phi \\ \cos\phi\sin\phi & \sin^2\phi \end{bmatrix} = 0$

Sol. $\begin{bmatrix} \cos^2\theta\times\cos^2\phi + \cos\theta\sin\theta\times\cos\phi\sin\phi & \cos^2\theta\times\cos\phi\sin\phi + \sin^2\phi(\cos\theta\sin\theta) \\ \cos\theta\sin\theta\times\cos^2\phi + \sin^2\theta\times\cos\phi\sin\phi & \cos\theta\times\sin\theta\times\cos\phi\sin\phi + \sin^2\theta\times\sin^2\phi \end{bmatrix}$

$$= \begin{bmatrix} \cos\theta\cos\phi(\cos\theta\cos\phi + \sin\theta\sin\phi) & \cos\theta\sin\phi(\cos\theta\cos\phi + \sin\theta\sin\phi) \\ \sin\theta\times\cos\phi(\cos\theta\cos\phi + \sin\theta\sin\phi & \sin\theta\times\sin\phi(\cos\theta\cos\phi + \sin\theta\sin\phi) \end{bmatrix}$$

$$= \begin{bmatrix} \cos\theta\cos\phi(\cos(\theta-\phi)) & \cos\theta\sin\phi\cos(\theta-\phi) \\ \sin\theta\cos\phi(\cos(\theta-\phi)) & \sin\theta\sin\phi(\cos(\theta-\phi) \end{bmatrix}$$

$(\because \cos A + B = \cos A\cos B - \sin A\sin B)$

But $\theta - \phi = \dfrac{\pi}{2} \quad \Rightarrow \quad \cos(\theta - \phi) = \cos\dfrac{\pi}{2} = 0$

$$\therefore \; = \begin{bmatrix} 0 & 0 \\ 0 & 0 \end{bmatrix}$$

Hence the problem

8. If $A = \begin{bmatrix} 0 & -\tan\dfrac{\alpha}{2} \\ \tan\dfrac{\alpha}{2} & 0 \end{bmatrix}$, show that $I + A = (I - A)\begin{bmatrix} \cos\alpha & -\sin\alpha \\ \sin\alpha & \cos\alpha \end{bmatrix}$

Sol. LHS $I + A = \begin{bmatrix} 1 & 0 \\ 0 & 1 \end{bmatrix} + \begin{bmatrix} 0 & -\tan\frac{\alpha}{2} \\ \tan\frac{\alpha}{2} & 0 \end{bmatrix} = \begin{bmatrix} 1 & -\tan\frac{\alpha}{2} \\ \tan\frac{\alpha}{2} & 1 \end{bmatrix}$

$$I - A = \begin{bmatrix} 1 & 0 \\ 0 & 1 \end{bmatrix} - \begin{bmatrix} 0 & -\tan\frac{\alpha}{2} \\ \tan\frac{\alpha}{2} & 0 \end{bmatrix} = \begin{bmatrix} 1 & \tan\frac{\alpha}{2} \\ -\tan\frac{\alpha}{2} & 1 \end{bmatrix}$$

$$\text{RHS} = \begin{pmatrix} 1 & \tan\frac{\alpha}{2} \\ -\tan\frac{\alpha}{2} & 1 \end{pmatrix} \begin{pmatrix} \dfrac{1-\tan^2\frac{\alpha}{2}}{1+\tan^2\frac{\alpha}{2}} & \dfrac{-2\tan\frac{\alpha}{2}}{1+\tan^2\frac{\alpha}{2}} \\ \dfrac{2\tan\frac{\alpha}{2}}{1+\tan^2\frac{\alpha}{2}} & \dfrac{1-\tan^2\frac{\alpha}{2}}{1+\tan^2\frac{\alpha}{2}} \end{pmatrix}$$

$$= \begin{pmatrix} \dfrac{1+\tan^2\frac{\alpha}{2}}{1+\tan^2\frac{\alpha}{2}} & \dfrac{-\tan\frac{\alpha}{2}-\tan^3\frac{\alpha}{2}}{1+\tan^2\frac{\alpha}{2}} \\ \dfrac{-\tan\frac{\alpha}{2}+\tan^3\frac{\alpha}{2}+2\tan\frac{\alpha}{2}}{1+\tan^2\frac{\alpha}{2}} & \dfrac{\tan^2\frac{\alpha}{2}+1}{1+\tan^2\frac{\alpha}{2}} \end{pmatrix}$$

$$= \begin{pmatrix} 1 & -\tan\frac{\alpha}{2} \\ \tan\frac{\alpha}{2} & 1 \end{pmatrix} = \text{LHS}$$

9. If $F(x) = \begin{bmatrix} \cos x & -\sin x & 0 \\ \sin x & \cos x & 0 \\ 0 & 0 & 1 \end{bmatrix}$ then show that

$F(x)\,F(y) = F(x+y)$ $\quad F(y) = \begin{bmatrix} \cos y & -\sin y & 0 \\ \sin y & \cos y & 0 \\ 0 & 0 & 1 \end{bmatrix}$

Sol. LHS $F(x)F(y) = \begin{bmatrix} \cos x & -\sin x & 0 \\ \sin x & \cos x & 0 \\ 0 & 0 & 1 \end{bmatrix} \begin{bmatrix} \cos y & -\sin y & 0 \\ \sin y & \cos y & 0 \\ 0 & 0 & 1 \end{bmatrix}$

$$= \begin{bmatrix} \cos x\cos y - \sin x\sin y + 0 & \cos x \times -\sin y + -\sin x \times \cos y + 0\times 0 & 0+0+0 \\ \sin x\cos y + \cos x\sin y + 0 & \sin x - \sin y + \cos x \times \cos y + 0 & 0+0+0 \\ 0+0+0 & 0+0+0 & 0+0+1 \end{bmatrix}$$

$$= \begin{bmatrix} \cos(x+y) & -\sin(x+y) & 0 \\ \sin(x+y) & \cos(x+y) & 0 \\ 0 & 0 & 1 \end{bmatrix}$$

RHS F(x + y) i.e., Replace x with (x + y)

$$= \begin{bmatrix} \cos(x+y) & -\sin(x+y) & 0 \\ \sin(x+y) & \cos(x+y) & 0 \\ 0 & 0 & 1 \end{bmatrix}$$

$\therefore$ LHS = RHS Hence proved

10. If $A = \begin{bmatrix} 3 & -4 \\ 1 & -1 \end{bmatrix}$ then for any integer n > 1 show that $A^n = \begin{bmatrix} 1+2n & -4n \\ n & 1-2n \end{bmatrix}$

Sol. we prove this by principle of mathematical induction

Consider statement $A^n = \begin{bmatrix} 1+2n & -4n \\ n & 1-2n \end{bmatrix}$

for n = 1 then LHS = $A^1 = \begin{pmatrix} 3 & -4 \\ 1 & -1 \end{pmatrix}$

$$\text{RHS} = \begin{bmatrix} 1+2(1) & -4(1) \\ 1 & 1-2(1) \end{bmatrix}$$

$$= \begin{bmatrix} 3 & -4 \\ 1 & -1 \end{bmatrix}$$

$\therefore$ LHS = RHS

$\therefore$ the statement is true for n = 1

Suppose it is true for n = k i.e $A^k = \begin{bmatrix} 1+2k & -4k \\ k & 1-2k \end{bmatrix}$

we prove that the statement is true

For n = k + 1 for this consider $A^{k+1} = A^k . A$

$$= \begin{bmatrix} 1+2k & -4k \\ k & 1-2k \end{bmatrix} \begin{bmatrix} 3 & -4 \\ 1 & -1 \end{bmatrix}$$

$$= \begin{bmatrix} 3+6k-4k & -4-8k+4k \\ 3k+1-2k & -4k-1+2k \end{bmatrix}$$

$$= \begin{bmatrix} 2(k+1)+1 & -4(k+1) \\ k+1 & 1-2(k+1) \end{bmatrix}$$

so statement is true for n = k + 1

Hence the result.

11. If $A = \begin{bmatrix} 2 & 0 & 1 \\ -1 & 1 & 5 \end{bmatrix}$ and $B = \begin{bmatrix} -1 & 1 & 0 \\ 0 & 1 & -2 \end{bmatrix}$ then find $(A(B)^T)^T$

Sol. $(A(B)^T)^T = (B^T)^T (A^T) = \begin{pmatrix} -1 & 1 & 0 \\ 0 & 1 & -2 \end{pmatrix}_{2\times3} \begin{pmatrix} 2 & -1 \\ 0 & 1 \\ 1 & 5 \end{pmatrix}_{3\times2}$

$$= \begin{pmatrix} -2+0+0 & 1+1+0 \\ 0+0-2 & 0+1-10 \end{pmatrix}$$

$$= \begin{pmatrix} -2 & 2 \\ -2 & -9 \end{pmatrix}$$

12. If A = [1 2 3] and $B = \begin{bmatrix} 3 \\ 2 \\ 1 \end{bmatrix}$ then find $A + B^T$

Sol. $A + B^T = [1\ 2\ 3] + [3\ 2\ 1] = [4\ 4\ 4]$

13. If $A = \begin{bmatrix} 1 & 4 & 7 \\ 2 & 5 & 8 \end{bmatrix}$ and $B = \begin{bmatrix} -3 & 4 & 0 \\ 4 & -2 & -1 \end{bmatrix}$ verify that

(i) $(A^T)^T = A$ (ii) $(A + B)^T = A^T + B^T$ (iii) $(5B)^T = 5\,B^T$

Sol. (i) $A = \begin{bmatrix} 1 & 4 & 7 \\ 2 & 5 & 8 \end{bmatrix}$

$$A^T = \begin{bmatrix} 1 & 2 \\ 4 & 5 \\ 7 & 8 \end{bmatrix}$$

$$(A^T)^T = \begin{bmatrix} 1 & 4 & 7 \\ 2 & 5 & 8 \end{bmatrix}$$

$\therefore\ (A^T)^T = A$

(ii) $A + B = \begin{pmatrix} 1-3 & 4+4 & 7+0 \\ 2+4 & 5-2 & 8-1 \end{pmatrix}$

$$= \begin{pmatrix} -2 & 8 & 7 \\ 6 & 3 & 7 \end{pmatrix}$$

$$(A + B)^T = \begin{pmatrix} -2 & 6 \\ 8 & 3 \\ 7 & 7 \end{pmatrix}$$

$$A^T = \begin{pmatrix} 1 & 2 \\ 4 & 5 \\ 7 & 8 \end{pmatrix} \quad B^T = \begin{pmatrix} -3 & 4 \\ 4 & -2 \\ 0 & -1 \end{pmatrix}$$

$$A^T + B^T = \begin{pmatrix} -2 & 6 \\ 8 & 3 \\ 7 & 7 \end{pmatrix}$$

$\therefore\ (A + B)^T = A^T + B^T$

(iii) $B = \begin{bmatrix} -3 & 4 & 0 \\ 4 & -2 & -1 \end{bmatrix}$

$$5B = 5\begin{bmatrix} -3 & 4 & 0 \\ 4 & -2 & -1 \end{bmatrix}$$

$$= \begin{bmatrix} -15 & 20 & 0 \\ 20 & -10 & -5 \end{bmatrix}$$

$$\Rightarrow \quad (5B)^T = \begin{pmatrix} -15 & 20 \\ 20 & -10 \\ 0 & -5 \end{pmatrix}$$

$$\text{also } 5B^T = 5\begin{pmatrix} -3 & 4 \\ 4 & -2 \\ 0 & -1 \end{pmatrix} = \begin{pmatrix} -15 & 20 \\ 20 & -10 \\ 0 & -5 \end{pmatrix}$$

$\therefore \quad (5B)^T = 5\ B^T$

14. If $A = \begin{bmatrix} 2 & -1 & 2 \\ 1 & 3 & -4 \end{bmatrix}$ and $B = \begin{bmatrix} 1 & -2 \\ -3 & 0 \\ 5 & 4 \end{bmatrix}$ then verify that $(AB)^T = B^T A^T$.

Sol. $$AB = \begin{pmatrix} 2 & -1 & 2 \\ 1 & 3 & -4 \end{pmatrix}\begin{pmatrix} 1 & -2 \\ -3 & 0 \\ 5 & 4 \end{pmatrix}$$

$$= \begin{pmatrix} 2+(3)+10 & -4-0+8 \\ 1-9-20 & -2+0-16 \end{pmatrix}$$

$$\therefore \ AB = \begin{pmatrix} 15 & 4 \\ -28 & -18 \end{pmatrix} \quad \Rightarrow \quad (AB)^T = \begin{pmatrix} 15 & -28 \\ 4 & -18 \end{pmatrix}$$

$$A^T = \begin{pmatrix} 2 & 1 \\ -1 & 3 \\ 2 & -4 \end{pmatrix} \quad B^T = \begin{pmatrix} 1 & -3 & 5 \\ -2 & 0 & 4 \end{pmatrix}$$

$$B^T A^T = \begin{pmatrix} 1 & -3 & 5 \\ -2 & 0 & 4 \end{pmatrix}\begin{pmatrix} 2 & 1 \\ -1 & 3 \\ 2 & -4 \end{pmatrix} = \begin{pmatrix} 2+3+10 & 1-9-20 \\ -4+0+8 & -2+0-16 \end{pmatrix} = \begin{pmatrix} 15 & -28 \\ 4 & -18 \end{pmatrix}$$

$\therefore \ (AB)^T = B^T A^T$

15. If $A = \begin{bmatrix} 1 & 5 & 3 \\ 2 & 4 & 0 \\ 3 & -1 & -5 \end{bmatrix}$ and $B = \begin{bmatrix} 2 & -1 & 0 \\ 0 & -2 & 5 \\ 1 & 2 & 0 \end{bmatrix}$ then find $3A - 4\ B^T$

Sol. $3A = \begin{pmatrix} 3 & 15 & 9 \\ 6 & 12 & 0 \\ 9 & -3 & -15 \end{pmatrix}$; $B^T = \begin{pmatrix} 2 & 0 & 1 \\ -1 & -2 & 2 \\ 0 & 5 & 0 \end{pmatrix}$

$$4B^T = \begin{pmatrix} 8 & 0 & 4 \\ -4 & -8 & 8 \\ 0 & 20 & 0 \end{pmatrix}$$

$$3A - 4B^T = \begin{pmatrix} 3 & 15 & 9 \\ 6 & 12 & 0 \\ 9 & -3 & -15 \end{pmatrix} - \begin{pmatrix} 8 & 0 & 4 \\ -4 & -8 & 8 \\ 0 & 20 & 0 \end{pmatrix}$$

$$= \begin{pmatrix} -5 & 15 & 5 \\ 10 & 20 & -8 \\ 9 & -23 & -15 \end{pmatrix}$$

16. **If** $A = \begin{bmatrix} 0 & 2 & 1 \\ -2 & 0 & -2 \\ -1 & x & 0 \end{bmatrix}$ **is skew symmetric then find** x.

A is skew symmetric $\Rightarrow$ $A^T = -A$

$$\therefore \begin{pmatrix} 0 & -2 & -1 \\ 2 & 0 & x \\ 1 & -2 & 0 \end{pmatrix} = -\begin{pmatrix} 0 & 2 & 1 \\ -2 & 0 & -2 \\ -1 & x & 0 \end{pmatrix} = \begin{pmatrix} 0 & -2 & -1 \\ +2 & 0 & 2 \\ 1 & -x & 0 \end{pmatrix}$$

$\therefore -2 = -x \Rightarrow x = 2$

Excercise - 3.2

1. **Find the following products of matrices (if possible)**

(i) $\begin{bmatrix} 3 & -2 \\ 1 & 6 \end{bmatrix}\begin{bmatrix} 4 & -1 \\ 2 & 5 \end{bmatrix}$ (ii) $\begin{bmatrix} 1 & 2 & 3 \end{bmatrix}\begin{bmatrix} 4 \\ 5 \\ 6 \end{bmatrix}$

(iii) $\begin{bmatrix} 4 \\ 5 \\ -6 \end{bmatrix}\begin{bmatrix} 1 & 2 & 3 \end{bmatrix}$ (iv) $\begin{bmatrix} 3 & 4 & 9 \\ 0 & -1 & 5 \\ 2 & 6 & 12 \end{bmatrix}\begin{bmatrix} 13 & -2 & 0 \\ 0 & 4 & 1 \end{bmatrix}$

2. If $A = \begin{bmatrix} 1 & -2 & 3 \\ 2 & 3 & -1 \\ -3 & 1 & 2 \end{bmatrix}$ and $B = \begin{bmatrix} 1 & 0 & 2 \\ 0 & 1 & 2 \\ 1 & 2 & 0 \end{bmatrix}$ then find AB, BA and verify AB = BA or not.

3. If $A = \begin{bmatrix} i & 0 \\ 0 & i \end{bmatrix}$, find A^2

4. If $A = \begin{bmatrix} 2 & 4 \\ -1 & k \end{bmatrix}$ and $A^2 = 0$, find the value of k.

5. If $A = \begin{bmatrix} 1 & 1 & 3 \\ 5 & 2 & 6 \\ -2 & -1 & -3 \end{bmatrix}$ then find A^3

6. If $A = \begin{bmatrix} 1 & 2 & 2 \\ 2 & 1 & 2 \\ 2 & 2 & 1 \end{bmatrix}$ then show that $A^2 - 4A - 5I = 0$

7. If $A = \begin{bmatrix} \cos\theta & \sin\theta \\ -\sin\theta & \cos\theta \end{bmatrix}$ then show that for all positive integers 'n'

$$A^n = \begin{bmatrix} \cos n\theta & \sin n\theta \\ -\sin n\theta & \cos n\theta \end{bmatrix}$$

8. If $A = \begin{bmatrix} -2 & 1 & 0 \\ 3 & 4 & -5 \end{bmatrix}$ and $B = \begin{bmatrix} 1 & 2 \\ 4 & 3 \\ -1 & 5 \end{bmatrix}$ then find $A + B^T$

9. If $A = \begin{bmatrix} 2 & -4 \\ -5 & 3 \end{bmatrix}$ then find $A + A^T$ and $A A^T$

10. If $A = \begin{bmatrix} -1 & 2 & 3 \\ 2 & 5 & 6 \\ 3 & x & 7 \end{bmatrix}$ is a symmetric matrix, then find x.

11. If $A=\begin{bmatrix}7 & -2\\ -1 & 2\\ 5 & 3\end{bmatrix}$ and $B=\begin{bmatrix}-2 & -1\\ 4 & 2\\ -1 & 0\end{bmatrix}$ then find AB^T and BA^T.

12. If $A=\begin{bmatrix}1 & -1 & 0\\ 2 & 1 & 3\\ 4 & 1 & 3\end{bmatrix}$ and $B=\begin{bmatrix}4 & 1 & 0\\ 2 & -3 & 0\\ 1 & 1 & -1\end{bmatrix}$ then verify

(i) $(A+B)^T = A^T + B^T$ (ii) $(AB)^T = B^T A^T$

Answers

1. (i) $\begin{pmatrix}8 & -13\\ 16 & 29\end{pmatrix}$ (ii) (32)

(iii) $\begin{pmatrix}4 & 8 & 12\\ 5 & 10 & 15\\ -6 & -12 & -18\end{pmatrix}$ (iv) Product not possible

2. $\begin{pmatrix}4 & 4 & -2\\ 1 & 1 & 10\\ -1 & 5 & -4\end{pmatrix},\begin{pmatrix}-5 & 0 & 7\\ -4 & 5 & 3\\ 5 & 4 & 1\end{pmatrix}$ and $AB \neq BA$

3. $\begin{pmatrix}-1 & 0\\ 0 & -1\end{pmatrix}$

4. -2

5. $0_{3\times 3}$

8. $\begin{pmatrix}-1 & 5 & -1\\ 5 & 7 & 0\end{pmatrix}$

9. $\begin{pmatrix}4 & -9\\ -9 & 6\end{pmatrix},\begin{pmatrix}20 & -22\\ -22 & 34\end{pmatrix}$

10. $x=6$

11. $\begin{pmatrix}-12 & 24 & -7\\ 0 & 0 & 1\\ -13 & 26 & -5\end{pmatrix},\begin{pmatrix}-12 & 0 & -13\\ 24 & 0 & 26\\ -7 & 1 & -5\end{pmatrix}$

3.8 Determinants

Determinents are define for square matrices. Determinant of matrix A is denoted by det A or $|A|$.

Determinent of 1 × 1 matrix : If A is a square matrix of order 1, then the determinant of A is defined as the element of A.

Ex : If $A = [5]_{1\times1}$ then $|A| = 5$

$A = [-4]_{1\times1}$ then $|A| = -4$

Determinant of 2 × 2 matrix

If $A = \begin{bmatrix} a & b \\ c & d \end{bmatrix}$ then the determinant of A is defined as the number ad – bc.

$\therefore \quad |A| = ad - bc$

Ex : (i) If $A = \begin{bmatrix} 1 & 2 \\ 3 & 7 \end{bmatrix}$ then $|A| = 1 . 7 - 3 . 2 = 7 - 6 = 1$

(ii) If $B = \begin{bmatrix} 3 & x \\ 4 & y \end{bmatrix}$ then $|B| = 3y - 4x$

To find the determinants of order 3 or more we see some definitions.

Minor

Definition : If a_{ij} is an element which is in ith row, jth column of square matrix, then the minor of the element a_{ij} is defined as the determinant of matrix obtained by deleting the ith row and and jth column of A.

Ex : (i) If $A = \begin{bmatrix} 1 & 2 \\ 3 & 4 \end{bmatrix}$ then minor of 1 is obtained by deleting i^{th} row and j^{th} column

i.e., the first row and the first column

Here $A = \begin{bmatrix} 1 & 2 \\ 3 & 4 \end{bmatrix}$

$\therefore$ minor of $1 = |4| = 4$

(ii) If $B = \begin{bmatrix} 1 & 2 & 3 \\ 5 & -1 & 4 \\ 8 & 6 & 9 \end{bmatrix}$ then find minors of 5, 8.

Sol. To find minor of 5.

Here, 5 is in the 2nd row, first column.

∴ Minor of 5 is obtained by the determinent of matrix obtained by deleting the 2nd row and 1st column.

$$\therefore \text{Minor of } 5 = \begin{vmatrix} 2 & 3 \\ 6 & 9 \end{vmatrix} = 18 - 18 = 0$$

$$\text{Similarly minor of } 8 = \begin{vmatrix} 2 & 3 \\ -1 & 4 \end{vmatrix} = 8 - (-3) = 8 + 3 = 11$$

Cofactor

Definition : If a_{ij} is an element which is in the ith row and jth column of square matrix A, then the cofactor of a_{ij} is defined as the product of $(-1)^{i+j}$ and the minor of aij i.e., cofactor of an element is obtained by just multiplying the minor of element with $(-1)^{i+j}$. (a_{ij} isthe number present in ith row j_{th} column).

Ex : (i) If $A = \begin{bmatrix} 1 & 2 & 3 \\ 4 & 7 & 8 \\ 9 & 5 & 6 \end{bmatrix}$ then find cofactor of 2.

Sol. Here 2 is in the 1st row 2nd column.

$$A = \begin{bmatrix} 1 & 2 & 3 \\ 4 & 7 & 8 \\ 9 & 5 & 6 \end{bmatrix}$$

$$\therefore \text{ minor of } 2 = \begin{vmatrix} 4 & 8 \\ 9 & 6 \end{vmatrix} = 24 - 72 = -48$$

$$\therefore \text{ Cofactor of } 2 = \text{minor of } 2 \times (-1)^{1+2}$$

$$= -48 \times (-1)^3 = -48 \times -1 = 48$$

(ii) Find the cofactor of 6 in above A

$$\text{Minor of } 6 = \begin{vmatrix} 1 & 2 \\ 4 & 7 \end{vmatrix} = 7 - 8 = -1$$

$$\therefore \text{ cofactor of } 6 = (\text{minor of } 6) \times (-1)^{3+3}$$ [6 is in 3rd row, 3rd column]

$$= -1 \times (-1)^6 = -1 \times 1 = -1$$

Determinant of a Square matrix

Definition : The sum of the product of the elements, of the first row of square matrix A, with their corresponding cofactors is called determinant of the matrix.

Suppose $A = \begin{bmatrix} a_1 & b_1 & c_1 \\ a_2 & b_2 & c_2 \\ a_3 & b_3 & c_3 \end{bmatrix}_{3\times 3}$ is a square matrix of order 3 and A_1, B_1, C_1 are cofactors of a, b, c respectively then

$$|A| = a_1 A_1 + b_1 B_1 + c_1 C_1$$

$$= a_1\left((-1)^{1+1}\begin{vmatrix} b_2 & c_2 \\ b_3 & c_3 \end{vmatrix}\right) + b_1\left((-1)^{1+2}\begin{vmatrix} a_2 & c_2 \\ a_3 & c_3 \end{vmatrix}\right) + c_1\left((-1)^{1+3}\begin{vmatrix} a_2 & b_2 \\ a_3 & b_3 \end{vmatrix}\right)$$

$$= a_1\begin{vmatrix} b_2 & c_2 \\ b_3 & c_3 \end{vmatrix} - b_1\begin{vmatrix} a_2 & c_2 \\ a_3 & c_3 \end{vmatrix} + c_1\begin{vmatrix} a_2 & b_2 \\ a_3 & b_3 \end{vmatrix}$$

$|A| = a_1$ (minor of a_1) $- b_1$ (minor of b_1) $+ c_1$ (minor of c_1)

Ex : If $A = \begin{bmatrix} 1 & 4 & 7 \\ 2 & 3 & -1 \\ 1 & 8 & 9 \end{bmatrix}$ then find | A |.

Sol. | A | = 1(cofactor 1) + 4 (cofactor of 4) + 7 (cofactor of 7)

$$= 1(-1)^{1+1}\begin{vmatrix} 3 & -1 \\ 8 & 9 \end{vmatrix} + 4(-1)^{1+2}\begin{vmatrix} 2 & -1 \\ 1 & 9 \end{vmatrix} + 7(-1)^{1+3}\begin{vmatrix} 2 & 3 \\ 1 & 8 \end{vmatrix}$$

$$= 1(27 + 8) - 4(18 + 1) + 7(16 - 3)$$

$$= 35 - 4(19) + 7(13)$$

$$= 35 - 76 + 91 = 50$$

Since $|A| = a_1 A_1 + b_1 B_1 + c_1 C_1$

Note : The determinant of a square matrix A is equal to the sum of the products of the elements any row (or column) of a with their corresponding cofactors.

Let $\begin{bmatrix} a_1 & b_1 & c_1 \\ a_2 & b_2 & c_2 \\ a_3 & b_3 & c_3 \end{bmatrix}$ is a square matrix of order 3 and A_1, B_1, C_1 ; A_2, B_2, C_2 ; A_3, B_3, C_3 are cofactors of a_1, b_1, c_1, ; a_2, b_2, c_2 ; a_3, b_3, c_3 respectively then

$$|A| = a_1 A_1 + b_1 B_1 + c_1 C_1$$

$$= a_2 A_2 + b_2 B_2 + c_2 C_2$$

$$= a_3 A_3 + b_3 B_3 + c_3 C_3$$

$$= a_1 A_1 + a_2 A_2 + a_3 A_3$$

$$= b_1 B_1 + b_2 B_2 + b_3 B_3$$

$$= c_1 C_1 + c_2 C_2 + c_3 C_3$$

Since $|A| = a_1 A_1 + b_1 B_1 + c_1 C_1$

$$= a_1(b_2 c_3 - b_3 c_2) - b_1 (a_2 c_3 - a_3 c_2) + c_1 (a_3 b_3 - a_3 b_2)$$

Properties of Determinants

1. If each element of a row (or column) of square matrix is zero then the determinant of the matrix is 0.

Proof : Let $A = \begin{bmatrix} 0 & 0 & 0 \\ a_2 & b_2 & c_2 \\ a_3 & b_3 & c_3 \end{bmatrix}$

then $|A| = 0 (b_2 c_3 - b_3 c_2) - 0 (a_2 c_3 - a_3 c_2) + 0 (a_2 b_3 - a_3 b_2)$

$= 0$

2. If two rows (or columns) of a square matrix are identical, then the determinant of matrix is zero

Proof : Let $A = \begin{bmatrix} a_1 & b_1 & c_1 \\ a_2 & b_2 & c_2 \\ a_2 & b_2 & c_2 \end{bmatrix}$

(second and third rows are identical)

$|A| = a_1(b_2 c_2 - b_2 c_2) - b_1 (a_2 c_2 - a_2 c_2) + c1(a_2 b_2 - a_2 b_2)$

$= 0 - 0 + 0 = 0$

3. If any two rows (or columns) in the matrix are interchanged then the sign of determinant changes.

Proof : Let $A = \begin{bmatrix} a_1 & b_1 & c_1 \\ a_2 & b_2 & c_2 \\ a_3 & b_3 & c_3 \end{bmatrix}$ and $B = \begin{bmatrix} a_1 & b_1 & c_1 \\ a_3 & b_3 & c_3 \\ a_2 & b_2 & c_2 \end{bmatrix}$

(second and third rows are interchanged)

$$|B| = a_1(b_3 c_2 - b_2 c_3) - a_2 (a_3 c_2 - a_2 c_3) + a_3 (a_3 b_2 - a_2 b_3)$$

$$= -[a_1 (b_2 c_3 - b_3 c_2) - a_2 (a_2 c_3 - a_3 c_2) + a_3(a_2 b_3 - a_3 b_2)$$

$$= -|A|$$

$$\therefore |B| = -|A|$$

$$= a_2 \text{ (cofactor of } a_2) + b_2 \text{ (cofactor of } b_2) + c_2 \text{ (cofactor of } c_2)$$

$$= a_2 A_2 + b_2 B_2 + c_2 C_2$$

Similarly we can prove remaining.

Note 2 : If $A = \begin{bmatrix} a_1 & b_1 & c_1 \\ a_2 & b_2 & c_2 \\ a_3 & b_3 & c_3 \end{bmatrix}$

then $|A| = a_1 \text{ (minor } a_1) - b_1 \text{ (minor of } b_1) + c_1 \text{ (minor of } c_1)$

If $A = \begin{bmatrix} a_1 & b_1 & c_1 & d_1 \\ a_2 & b_2 & c_2 & d_2 \\ a_3 & b_3 & c_3 & d_3 \\ a_4 & b_4 & c_4 & d_4 \end{bmatrix}$ then

$$|A| = a_1 \text{ (minor of } a_1) - b_1 \text{ (minor of } b_1) + c_1 \text{ (minor of } c_1) + d_1 \text{ (minor of } d_1)$$

4. If each element of a row (or column) of a square matrix is multiplied by a non zero number k, then the determinant of the matrix obtained is k times the determinant of given matrix.

Proof : Let $A = \begin{bmatrix} a_1 & b_1 & c_1 \\ a_2 & b_2 & c_2 \\ a_3 & b_3 & c_3 \end{bmatrix}$ $B = \begin{bmatrix} ka_1 & kb_1 & kc_1 \\ a_2 & b_2 & c_2 \\ a_3 & b_3 & c_3 \end{bmatrix}$

(Elements of the first row are multiplied by k)

$|B| = ka_1(b_2 c_3 - b_3 c_2) - kb_1 (a_2 c_3 - a_3 c_2) + kc_1(a_2 b_3 - a_3 b_2)$

$= k [a_1 (b_2c_3 - b_3 c_2) - b_1 (a_2 c_3 - a_3 c_2) + c_1 (a_2 b_3 - a_3 b_2)]$

$= k |A|$

$\therefore |B| = k |A|$

Note : A is square matrix of order n, then $|KA| = k^n |A|$.

5. **If the corresponding elements of two rows (or columns) of a square matrix are in the same ratio, then the determinant of the matrix is zero.**

Proof : Let $A = \begin{bmatrix} a_1 & b_1 & c_1 \\ ka_1 & kb_1 & kc_1 \\ a_3 & b_3 & c_3 \end{bmatrix}$

$$\text{then } |A| = \begin{vmatrix} a_1 & b_1 & c_1 \\ ka_1 & kb_1 & kc_1 \\ a_3 & b_3 & c_3 \end{vmatrix} = k\begin{vmatrix} a_1 & b_1 & c_1 \\ a_1 & b_1 & c_1 \\ a_3 & b_3 & c_3 \end{vmatrix} \quad \text{(by property 4)}$$

$$= k\,(0) \quad \text{(by property 2)}$$

$$= 0$$

6. **If each element in a row (or column) of square matrix is the sum of two numbers, then its determinant can be expressed as the sum of determinants of two square matrices.**

Proof : Let $A = \begin{bmatrix} a_1 + x_1 & b_1 + x_2 & c_1 + x_3 \\ a_2 & b_2 & c_2 \\ a_3 & b_3 & c_3 \end{bmatrix}$; $B = \begin{bmatrix} a_1 & b_1 & c_1 \\ a_2 & b_2 & c_2 \\ a_3 & b_3 & c_3 \end{bmatrix}$;

$$C = \begin{bmatrix} x_1 & x_2 & x_3 \\ a_2 & b_2 & c_2 \\ a_3 & b_3 & c_3 \end{bmatrix}$$

then $|A| = (a_1 + x_1)(b_2 c_3 - b_3 c_2) - (b_1 + x_2)(a_2 c_3 - a_3 c_2)$

$+ (c_1 + x_3)(a_2 b_3 - a_3 b_2)$

$= (a_1(b_2 c_3 - b_3 c_2) - b_1 (a_2 c_3 - a_3 c_2) + c_1 (a_2 b_3 - a_3 b_2))$

$+ (x_1(b_2 c_3 - b_3 c_2) - x_2 (a_2 c_3 - a_3 c_2) + x_3(a_2 b_3 - a_3 b_2)$

$= |B| + |C|$

$\therefore |A| = |B| + |C|$

7. If each element of a row (or column) of a square matrix are added with k times the corresponding elements of another row (or column), then the value of the determinant of resulting matrix is equal to value of the determinant of the given matrix.

Proof : Let $A = \begin{bmatrix} a_1 & b_1 & c_1 \\ a_2 & b_2 & c_2 \\ a_3 & b_3 & c_3 \end{bmatrix}$; $B = \begin{bmatrix} a_1 + ka_2 & b_1 + kb_2 & c_1 + kc_2 \\ a_2 & b_2 & c_2 \\ a_3 & b_3 & c_3 \end{bmatrix}$

(B is obtained from A by multiplying each element of 2nd row of A by k and added them to the corresponding elements of the 1st row of A).

$$|B| = \begin{bmatrix} a_1 + ka_2 & b_1 + kb_2 & c_1 + kc_2 \\ a_2 & b_2 & c_2 \\ a_3 & b_3 & c_3 \end{bmatrix}$$

$$= \begin{vmatrix} a_1 & b_1 & c_1 \\ a_2 & b_2 & c_2 \\ a_3 & b_3 & c_3 \end{vmatrix} + \begin{vmatrix} ka_2 & kb_2 & kc_2 \\ a_2 & b_2 & c_2 \\ a_3 & b_3 & c_3 \end{vmatrix} \qquad \text{(by property 6)}$$

$$= \begin{vmatrix} a_1 & b_1 & c_1 \\ a_2 & b_2 & c_2 \\ a_3 & b_3 & c_3 \end{vmatrix} + k\begin{vmatrix} a_2 & b_2 & c_2 \\ a_2 & b_2 & c_2 \\ a_3 & b_3 & c_3 \end{vmatrix} \qquad \text{(by property 4)}$$

$$= \begin{vmatrix} a_1 & b_1 & c_1 \\ a_2 & b_2 & c_2 \\ a_3 & b_3 & c_3 \end{vmatrix} + k(0) \qquad \text{(by property 2)}$$

$$= \begin{vmatrix} a_1 & b_1 & c_1 \\ a_2 & b_2 & c_2 \\ a_3 & b_3 & c_3 \end{vmatrix}$$

$$= |A|$$

8. The sum of the product of the elements of any row (or column) of a square matrix with the cofactors of a the corresponding elements of another row (or column) of the matrix is zero.

Proof : Let $A = \begin{bmatrix} a_1 & b_1 & c_1 \\ a_2 & b_2 & c_2 \\ a_3 & b_3 & c_3 \end{bmatrix}$

Consider the sum of the products the elements of first row with the corresponding cofactors of second row i.e.,

$$a_1 A_2 + b_1 B_2 + c_1 C_2$$

$$= a_1\left((-1)^{2+1}\begin{vmatrix} b_1 & c_1 \\ b_3 & c_3 \end{vmatrix} + b_1(-1)^{2+2}\begin{vmatrix} a_1 & c_1 \\ a_3 & c_3 \end{vmatrix} + c_1(-1)^{2+3}\begin{vmatrix} a_1 & b_1 \\ a_3 & b_3 \end{vmatrix}\right)$$

$$= -a_1(-b_3 c_1 + b_1 c_3) + b_1(a_1 c_3 - a_3 c_1) - c_1 (a_1 b_3 - a_3 b_1)$$

$$= 0$$

9. For any square matrix A, $|A| = |A^T|$

Proof : Let $A = \begin{bmatrix} a_1 & b_1 & c_1 \\ a_2 & b_2 & c_2 \\ a_3 & b_3 & c_3 \end{bmatrix}$ then $A^T = \begin{bmatrix} a_1 & a_2 & a_3 \\ b_1 & b_2 & b_3 \\ c_1 & c_2 & c_3 \end{bmatrix}$

$$|A| = a_1(b_2 c_3 - b_3 c_2) - b_1(a_2 c_3 - a_3 c_2) + c_1(a_2 b_3 - a_3 b_2)$$

($\because$ by expanding the determinant along 1st row)

$$|A^T| = a_1 (b_2 c_3 - b_3 c_2) - b_1 (a_2 c_3 - a_3 c_2) + c_1(a_2 b_3 - a_3 b_2)$$

($\because$ by expanding the determinant along 1st column)

$$\therefore |A| = |A^T|$$

10. If the elements of square matrix are polynomials in x and its determinant is zero when $x = a$, then $x - a$ is factor of determinant of the matrix.

Let $A(x) = \begin{bmatrix} f_1(x) & g_1(x) & h_1(x) \\ f_2(x) & g_2(x) & h_2(x) \\ f_3(x) & g_3(x) & h_3(x) \end{bmatrix}$

$$A(a) = \begin{bmatrix} f_1(a) & g_1(a) & h_1(a) \\ f_2(a) & g_2(a) & h_2(a) \\ f_3(a) & g_3(a) & h_3(a) \end{bmatrix} = 0$$

$\therefore$ by remainder theorem $(x - a)$ is factor of $A(x)$.

Note :

(i) $|AB| = |A|\,|B|$

(ii) If A is triangular matrix (upper or lower) then the determinant of A is the product of diagonal matrix.

Notation : While evaluating determinants, we use the following notation.

(i) $R_1 \to R_1 + kR_2$ to mean that the elements of R_1 are added with k times the corresponding elements of R_2.

(ii) $C_1 \to C_1 + kC_2$ to mean that the elements of C_1 are added with k times the corresponding elements of C_2.

Similar notation is used for other rows and columns.

Solved Examples

1. Find the determinants of following matrices.

(i) $\begin{bmatrix} 1 & 2 \\ 3 & 4 \end{bmatrix}$ (ii) $\begin{bmatrix} 0 & 1 & 1 \\ 1 & 0 & 1 \\ 1 & 1 & 0 \end{bmatrix}$

(iii) $\begin{bmatrix} 1 & 2 & -3 \\ 4 & -1 & 7 \\ 2 & 4 & -6 \end{bmatrix}$ (iv) $\begin{bmatrix} a & b & c \\ b & c & a \\ c & a & b \end{bmatrix}$

Sol. (i) Let $A = \begin{bmatrix} 1 & 2 \\ 3 & 4 \end{bmatrix}$

$\therefore \ |A| = (1)(4) - (3)(2)$ $\left(\because \begin{vmatrix} a & b \\ c & d \end{vmatrix} = ad - bc \right)$

$= 4 - 6$

$= -2$

(ii) Let $A = \begin{bmatrix} 0 & 1 & 1 \\ 1 & 0 & 1 \\ 1 & 1 & 0 \end{bmatrix}$

$\therefore \ |A| = \begin{vmatrix} 0 & 1 & 1 \\ 1 & 0 & 1 \\ 1 & 1 & 0 \end{vmatrix}$

$= 0(0-1) - 1(0-1) + 1(1-0)$ (expanding the determinant along R_1)

$= 0 + 1 + 1 = 2$

(iii) Let $A = \begin{bmatrix} 1 & 2 & -3 \\ 4 & -1 & 7 \\ 2 & 4 & -6 \end{bmatrix}$

$$|A| = \begin{vmatrix} 1 & 2 & -3 \\ 4 & -1 & 7 \\ 2 & 4 & -6 \end{vmatrix}$$

$$= 1(6 - 28) - 2(-24 - 14) - 3(16 + 2)$$

$$= -22 + 76 - 54 = 0$$

(iv) Let $A = \begin{bmatrix} a & b & c \\ b & c & a \\ c & a & b \end{bmatrix}$

$$\therefore \ |A| = \begin{vmatrix} a & b & c \\ b & c & a \\ c & a & b \end{vmatrix}$$

$$= a(bc - a^2) - b(b^2 - ac) + c(ab - c^2) = 3abc - a^3 - b^3 - c^3$$

2. Find the determinant of following matrices

(i) $\begin{bmatrix} i & 0 \\ 0 & -i \end{bmatrix}$ (where $i^2 = -1$) (ii) $\begin{bmatrix} 1 & w & w^2 \\ w & w^2 & 1 \\ w^2 & 1 & w \end{bmatrix}$

(w is cube root of unity)

(iii) $\begin{bmatrix} 2008 & 2007 \\ 2007 & 2006 \end{bmatrix}$ (iv) $\begin{bmatrix} 1^2 & 2^2 & 3^2 \\ 2^2 & 3^2 & 4^2 \\ 3^2 & 4^2 & 5^2 \end{bmatrix}$

Sol. (i) Let $A = \begin{bmatrix} i & 0 \\ 0 & -i \end{bmatrix}$ $\therefore |A| = \begin{vmatrix} i & 0 \\ 0 & -i \end{vmatrix} = -i^2 - 0 = -(-1) - 0 = 1$

(ii) Let $A = \begin{bmatrix} 1 & w & w^2 \\ w & w^2 & 1 \\ w^2 & 1 & w \end{bmatrix}$

$\therefore \quad |A| = \begin{vmatrix} 1 & w & w^2 \\ w & w^2 & 1 \\ w^2 & 1 & w \end{vmatrix} \quad R_1 \to R_1 + R_2 + R_3$

$= \begin{vmatrix} 1+w+w^2 & 1+w+w^2 & 1+w+w^2 \\ w & w^2 & 1 \\ w^2 & 1 & w \end{vmatrix}$

$= \begin{vmatrix} 0 & 0 & 0 \\ w & w^2 & 1 \\ w^2 & 1 & w \end{vmatrix} = 0$ ($\because$ sum of cube rutes of unity = 0)

(iii) Let $A = \begin{bmatrix} 2008 & 2007 \\ 2007 & 2006 \end{bmatrix}$

$\therefore \quad |A| = \begin{vmatrix} 2008 & 2007 \\ 2007 & 2006 \end{vmatrix}$

$= \begin{vmatrix} 2008 & 2007 \\ -1 & -1 \end{vmatrix}$ applying $R_2 \to R_2 - R_1$

$= -2008 + 2007$

$= -1$

(iv) Let $A = \begin{bmatrix} 1^2 & 2^2 & 3^2 \\ 2^2 & 3^2 & 4^2 \\ 3^2 & 4^2 & 5^2 \end{bmatrix}$

$\therefore \quad A = \begin{bmatrix} 1^2 & 2^2 & 3^2 \\ 2^2 & 3^2 & 4^2 \\ 3^2 & 4^2 & 5^2 \end{bmatrix} = \begin{vmatrix} 1 & 4 & 9 \\ 4 & 9 & 16 \\ 9 & 16 & 25 \end{vmatrix}$

applying $R_2 \rightarrow R_2 - R_1, R_3 \rightarrow R_3 - R_2$

$$= \begin{vmatrix} 1 & 4 & 9 \\ 3 & 5 & 7 \\ 5 & 7 & 9 \end{vmatrix}$$

applying $R_2 \rightarrow R_2 - R_1, R_3 \rightarrow R_3 - R_2$

$$= \begin{vmatrix} 1 & 4 & 9 \\ 2 & 1 & -2 \\ 2 & 2 & 2 \end{vmatrix}$$

on expanding the determinant along R_1 we get

$$1(2+4) - 4(4+4) + 9(4-2)$$
$$= 6 - 32 + 18$$
$$= 24 - 32$$
$$= -8$$

3. If $A = \begin{bmatrix} 1 & 0 & 0 \\ 2 & 3 & 4 \\ 5 & -6 & x \end{bmatrix}$ and det A = 45, find the value of x

Sol. Given $|A| = 45 \Rightarrow \begin{vmatrix} 1 & 0 & 0 \\ 2 & 3 & 4 \\ 5 & -6 & x \end{vmatrix} = 45$

$$\Rightarrow \quad 1(3x + 24) = 45$$
$$3x = 45 - 24 = 21$$
$$\Rightarrow \quad x = 7$$

4. Show that $\begin{vmatrix} 1 & a & a^2 \\ 1 & b & b^2 \\ 1 & c & c^2 \end{vmatrix} = (a-b)(b-c)(c-a)$

Sol. LHS $= \begin{vmatrix} 1 & a & a^2 \\ 1 & b & b^2 \\ 1 & c & c^2 \end{vmatrix}$

on applying $R_2 \to R_2 - R_1$, $R_3 \to R_3 - R_2$

$$\text{LHS} = \begin{vmatrix} 1 & a & a^2 \\ 0 & b-a & b^2-a^2 \\ 0 & c-b & c^2-b^2 \end{vmatrix}$$

on taking common b–a, c–b from R_2, R_3 respectively

$$= (b-a)(c-b)\begin{vmatrix} 1 & a & a^2 \\ 0 & 1 & b+a \\ 0 & 1 & c+b \end{vmatrix}$$

on expanding the det along c_1 we get

$$= (b-a)(c-b)(1)\begin{vmatrix} 1 & b+a \\ 1 & c+b \end{vmatrix}$$

$$(b-a)(c-b)(c+b-b-a) = (b-a)(c-b)(c-a)$$

$$= (a-b)(b-c)(c-a)$$

5. Show that $\begin{vmatrix} 1 & a^2 & a^3 \\ 1 & b^2 & b^3 \\ 1 & c^2 & c^3 \end{vmatrix} = (a-b)(b-c)(c-a)(ab+bc+ca)$

Sol. $\text{LHS} = \begin{vmatrix} 1 & a^2 & a^3 \\ 1 & b^2 & b^3 \\ 1 & c^2 & c^3 \end{vmatrix}$

on applying $R_2 \to R_2 - R_1$, $R_3 \to R_3 - R_2$

$$= \begin{vmatrix} 1 & a^2 & a^3 \\ 0 & b^2-a^2 & b^3-a^3 \\ 0 & c^2-b^2 & c^3-b^3 \end{vmatrix}$$

on taking common (b – a), (c – b) from R_2, R_3 respectively

$$= (b-a)(c-b)\begin{vmatrix} 1 & a^2 & a^3 \\ 0 & b+a & b^2+a^2+ab \\ 0 & c+b & c^2+b^2+bc \end{vmatrix}$$

on applying $R_3 \to R_3 - R_2$ we get

$$= (b-a)(c-b)\begin{vmatrix} 1 & a^2 & a^3 \\ 0 & b+a & b^2+a^2+ab \\ 0 & c-a & (c^2-a^2)+(bc-ab) \end{vmatrix}$$

on taking (c – a) common from R_3 we get

$$(b-a)(c-b)(c-a)\begin{vmatrix} 1 & a^2 & a^3 \\ 0 & b+a & b^2+a^2+ab \\ 0 & 1 & c+a+b \end{vmatrix}$$

$$= (a-b)(b-c)(c-a)\begin{vmatrix} 1 & a^2 & a^3 \\ 0 & b+a & b^2+a^2+ab \\ 0 & 1 & c+a+b \end{vmatrix}$$

on expanding the det. along c_1 we get

$$= (a-b)(b-c)(c-a)\begin{vmatrix} b+a & b^2+a^2+ab \\ 1 & c+a+b \end{vmatrix}$$

$= (a-b)(b-c)(c-a)\{(a+b)(a+b+c) - (b^2+a^2+ab)\}$

$= (a-b)(b-c)(c-a)\{(a+b)^2 + c(a+b) - b^2 - a^2 - ab\}$

$= (a-b)\, b-c)(c-a)\{a^2 + b^2 + 2ab + ac + bc - b^2 - a^2 - ab\}$

$= (a-b)(b-c)(c-a)(ab+bc+ca)$

6. If $\begin{vmatrix} a & a^2 & 1+a^3 \\ b & b^2 & 1+b^3 \\ c & c^2 & 1+c^3 \end{vmatrix} = 0$ and a, b, c are different and non zero then show that

abc = –1.

Sol. Given $\begin{vmatrix} a & a^2 & 1+a^3 \\ b & b^2 & 1+b^3 \\ c & c^2 & 1+c^3 \end{vmatrix} = 0$

$$\Rightarrow \begin{vmatrix} a & a^2 & 1 \\ b & b^2 & 1 \\ c & c^2 & 1 \end{vmatrix} + \begin{vmatrix} a & a^2 & a^3 \\ b & b^2 & b^3 \\ c & c^2 & c^3 \end{vmatrix} = 0$$ (∵ by property 6)

$$\Rightarrow \begin{vmatrix} a & a^2 & 1 \\ b & b^2 & 1 \\ c & c^2 & 1 \end{vmatrix} + abc\begin{vmatrix} 1 & a & a^2 \\ 1 & b & b^2 \\ 1 & c & c^2 \end{vmatrix} = 0$$

(taking a, b, c from 1st, 2nd, 3rd row of 2nd det)

$$\Rightarrow \begin{vmatrix} 1 & a & a^2 \\ 1 & b & b^2 \\ 1 & c & c^2 \end{vmatrix} + abc\begin{vmatrix} 1 & a & a^2 \\ 1 & b & b^2 \\ 1 & c & c^2 \end{vmatrix} = 0$$

$$\Rightarrow \begin{vmatrix} 1 & a & a^2 \\ 1 & b & b^2 \\ 1 & c & c^2 \end{vmatrix} (1 + abc) = 0$$

⇒ (a – b) (b – c) (c – b) (1 + abc) = 0 (∵ by property (4))

∵ a, b, c are non zero distinct numbers

(a – b) (b – c) (c – a) ≠ 0

⇒ (1 + abc) = 0

⇒ abc = –1

7. Show that $\begin{vmatrix} y+z & x & x \\ y & z+x & y \\ z & z & x+y \end{vmatrix} = 4xyz$

Sol. LHS = $\begin{vmatrix} 0 & -2z & -2y \\ y & z+x & y \\ z & z & x+y \end{vmatrix}$

on applying $R_1 \to R_1 - (R_2 + R_3)$ we get

$$\begin{vmatrix} 0 & -2z & -2y \\ y & z+x & y \\ z & z & x+y \end{vmatrix}$$

on taking '–2' common from R_1, we get

$$-2\begin{vmatrix} 0 & z & y \\ y & z+x & y \\ z & z & x+y \end{vmatrix}$$

on applying $R_2 \to R_2 - R_1$ we get

$$-2\begin{vmatrix} 0 & z & y \\ y & x & 0 \\ z & z & x+y \end{vmatrix}$$

now expanding the det along R_1 we get

$$-2\{0(x(y+z)-0) - z(y(x+y)-0) + y(yz - zx)\}$$

$$= -2\{-zxy - zy^2 + zy^2 - yzx\}$$

$$= -2\{-2xyz\} = 4xyz$$

8. Show that $\begin{vmatrix} bc & b+c & 1 \\ ca & c+a & 1 \\ ab & a+b & 1 \end{vmatrix} = (a-b)(b-c)(c-a)$

Sol. LHS = $\begin{vmatrix} bc & b+c & 1 \\ ca & c+a & 1 \\ ab & a+b & 1 \end{vmatrix}$

on applying $R_2 \to R_2 - R_1$, $R_3 \to R_3 - R_2$ we get

$$\begin{vmatrix} bc & b+c & 1 \\ c(a-b) & a-b & 0 \\ a(b-c) & b-c & 0 \end{vmatrix}$$

on taking common (a – b), (b – c) from 2nd and 3rd rows respectively we get

$$= (a-b)(b-c)\begin{vmatrix} bc & b+c & 1 \\ c & 1 & 0 \\ a & 1 & 0 \end{vmatrix}$$

expanding the det along c_3 we get

$$= (a-b)(b-c)\, 1\begin{vmatrix} c & 1 \\ a & 1 \end{vmatrix}$$

$$= (a-b)(b-c)(c-a)$$

9. Without expanding, with any row or column of the determinant show that

(i) $\begin{vmatrix} 1 & a & a^2-bc \\ 1 & b & b^2-ca \\ 1 & c & c^2-ab \end{vmatrix} = 0$ (ii) $\begin{vmatrix} b+c & c+a & a+b \\ c+a & a+b & b+c \\ a+b & b+c & c+a \end{vmatrix} = 2\begin{vmatrix} a & b & c \\ b & c & a \\ c & a & b \end{vmatrix}$

Sol. (i) LHS $= \begin{vmatrix} 1 & a & a^2-bc \\ 1 & b & b^2-ca \\ 1 & c & c^2-ab \end{vmatrix}$

$$= \begin{vmatrix} 1 & a & a^2 \\ 1 & b & b^2 \\ 1 & c & c^2 \end{vmatrix} - \begin{vmatrix} 1 & a & bc \\ 1 & b & ca \\ 1 & c & ab \end{vmatrix}$$

$$= \begin{vmatrix} 1 & a & a^2 \\ 1 & b & b^2 \\ 1 & c & c^2 \end{vmatrix} - \frac{1}{abc}\begin{vmatrix} a & a^2 & abc \\ b & b^2 & abc \\ c & c^2 & abc \end{vmatrix}$$

$$= \begin{vmatrix} 1 & a & a^2 \\ 1 & b & b^2 \\ 1 & c & c^2 \end{vmatrix} - \frac{abc}{abc}\begin{vmatrix} a & a^2 & 1 \\ b & b^2 & 1 \\ c & c^2 & 1 \end{vmatrix}$$

$$= \begin{vmatrix} 1 & a & a^2 \\ 1 & b & b^2 \\ 1 & c & c^2 \end{vmatrix} - \begin{vmatrix} 1 & a & a^2 \\ 1 & b & b^2 \\ 1 & c & c^2 \end{vmatrix}$$

$$= 0 = \text{RHS}$$

(ii) $\text{LHS} = \begin{vmatrix} b+c & c+a & a+b \\ c+a & a+b & b+c \\ a+b & b+c & c+a \end{vmatrix}$

on applying $R_1 \rightarrow R_1 + R_2 + R_3$ we get

$$= \begin{vmatrix} 2(a+b+c) & 2(a+b+c) & 2(a+b+c) \\ c+a & a+b & b+c \\ a+b & b+c & c+a \end{vmatrix}$$

$$= 2\begin{vmatrix} a+b+c & a+b+c & a+b+c \\ c+a & a+b & b+c \\ a+b & b+c & c+a \end{vmatrix}$$

on applying $R_1 \rightarrow R_1 - R_2$ we get

$$= 2\begin{vmatrix} b & c & a \\ c+a & a+b & b+c \\ a+b & b+c & c+a \end{vmatrix}$$

on applying $R_3 \rightarrow R_3 - R_1$ we get

$$= 2\begin{vmatrix} b & c & a \\ c+a & a+b & b+c \\ a & b & c \end{vmatrix}$$

on applying $R_2 \rightarrow R_2 - R_3$ we get

$$= 2\begin{vmatrix} b & c & a \\ c & a & b \\ a & b & c \end{vmatrix}$$

$$= 2(-1)\begin{vmatrix} a & b & c \\ c & a & b \\ b & c & a \end{vmatrix} \qquad (\because R_1 \leftrightarrow R_3)$$

$$= 2(-1)(-1)\begin{vmatrix} a & b & c \\ b & c & a \\ c & a & b \end{vmatrix} \quad (\because R_2 \leftrightarrow R_3)$$

$$= 2\begin{vmatrix} a & b & c \\ b & c & a \\ c & a & b \end{vmatrix}$$

10. Show that $\begin{vmatrix} a-b-c & 2a & 2a \\ 2b & b-c-a & 2b \\ 2c & 2c & c-a-b \end{vmatrix} = (a+b+c)^3$

Sol. LHS $= \begin{vmatrix} a-b-c & 2a & 2a \\ 2b & b-c-a & 2b \\ 2c & 2c & c-a-b \end{vmatrix}$

applying $R_1 \to R_1 + R_2 + R_3$ we get

$$= \begin{vmatrix} a+b+c & a+b+c & a+b+c \\ 2b & b-c-a & 2b \\ 2c & 2c & c-a-b \end{vmatrix}$$

$$= (a+b+c)\begin{vmatrix} 1 & 1 & 1 \\ 2b & b-c-a & 2b \\ 2c & 2c & c-a-b \end{vmatrix}$$

on applying $c_2 \to c_2 - c_1$, $c_3 \to c_3 - c_2$ we get

$$= (a+b+c)\begin{vmatrix} 1 & 0 & 0 \\ 2b & -b-c-a & b+a+c \\ 2c & 2c-2c & -c-a-b \end{vmatrix}$$

$$= (a+b+c)^2\begin{vmatrix} 1 & 0 & 0 \\ 2b & -(a+b+c) & 1 \\ 2c & 0 & -1 \end{vmatrix}$$

($\because$ by taking a + b + c common from c_3)

$$= (a+b+c)^2(1)\begin{vmatrix} -(a+b+c) & 1 \\ 0 & -1 \end{vmatrix}$$

$$= (a+b+c)^2 \{ (a+b+c) \}$$

$$= (a+b+c)^3 = \text{RHS}$$

11. Show that $\begin{vmatrix} a & b & c \\ b & c & a \\ c & a & b \end{vmatrix}^2 = \begin{vmatrix} 2bc-a^2 & c^2 & b^2 \\ c^2 & 2ac-b^2 & a^2 \\ b^2 & a^2 & 2ab-c^2 \end{vmatrix} = (a^3+b^3+c^3-3abc)^2$

Sol. $\begin{vmatrix} a & b & c \\ b & c & a \\ c & a & b \end{vmatrix} = a(bc-a^2) - b(b^2-ac) + c(ab-c^2)$

$$= abc - a^3 - b^3 + abc + abc - c^3$$

$$= 3abc - a^3 - b^3 - c^3$$

$$\therefore \begin{vmatrix} a & b & c \\ b & c & a \\ c & a & b \end{vmatrix}^2 = (3abc - a^2 - b^3 - c^3)^2 = (a^3+b^3+c^3-3abc)^2 \quad \text{..... (i)}$$

again consider

$$\begin{vmatrix} a & b & c \\ b & c & a \\ c & a & b \end{vmatrix}^2 = \begin{vmatrix} a & b & c \\ b & c & a \\ c & a & b \end{vmatrix} \times \begin{vmatrix} a & b & c \\ b & c & a \\ c & a & b \end{vmatrix}$$

$$= \begin{vmatrix} a & b & c \\ b & c & a \\ c & a & b \end{vmatrix} \times (-1) \begin{vmatrix} a & b & c \\ c & a & b \\ b & c & a \end{vmatrix} \qquad (\because R_2 \leftrightarrow R_3)$$

$$= \begin{vmatrix} a & b & c \\ b & c & a \\ c & a & b \end{vmatrix} \times \begin{vmatrix} -a & -b & -c \\ c & a & b \\ b & c & a \end{vmatrix}$$

$$= \begin{vmatrix} -a^2+bc+bc & -ab+ab+c^2 & -ac+b^2+ac \\ -ab+c^2+ab & -b^2+ac+ac & bc+bc+a^2 \\ -ac+ac+b^2 & -bc+a^2+bc & -c^2+ab+ab \end{vmatrix}$$

$$\therefore \quad \begin{vmatrix} a & b & c \\ b & c & a \\ c & a & b \end{vmatrix}^2 = \begin{vmatrix} 2bc-a^2 & c^2 & b^2 \\ c^2 & 2ac-b^2 & a^2 \\ b^2 & a^2 & 2ab-c^2 \end{vmatrix} \qquad \text{..... (2)}$$

Hence from (1) and (2) we get

$$\begin{vmatrix} a & b & c \\ b & c & a \\ c & a & b \end{vmatrix}^2 = \begin{vmatrix} 2bc-a^2 & c^2 & b^2 \\ c^2 & 2ac-b^2 & a^2 \\ b^2 & a^2 & 2ab-c^2 \end{vmatrix} = (a^3+b^3+c^3-3abc)^2$$

12. If a + b + c = 0 and $\begin{vmatrix} a-x & c & b \\ c & b-x & a \\ b & a & c-x \end{vmatrix} = 0$ then find the value of x

Sol. Given a + b + c = 0 and $\begin{vmatrix} a-x & c & b \\ c & b-x & a \\ b & a & c-x \end{vmatrix} = 0$

on applying $R_1 \to R_1 + R_2 + R_3$ we get

$$\Rightarrow \begin{vmatrix} a+b+c-x & a+b+c-x & a+b+c-x \\ c & b-x & a \\ b & a & c-x \end{vmatrix} = 0$$

$$\Rightarrow \quad (a+b+c-x)\begin{vmatrix} 1 & 1 & 1 \\ c & b-x & a \\ b & a & c-x \end{vmatrix} = 0$$

$$\Rightarrow \quad a+b+c-x = 0 \text{ or } \begin{vmatrix} 1 & 1 & 1 \\ c & b-x & a \\ b & a & c-x \end{vmatrix} = 0$$

$$\therefore \quad a+b+c-x = 0$$

$$\Rightarrow \quad 0 - x = 0 \quad (\because a+b+c=0) \text{ or } \begin{vmatrix} 1 & 1 & 1 \\ c & b-x & a \\ b & a & c-x \end{vmatrix} = 0$$

$$\Rightarrow \quad x = 0$$

again, take $\begin{vmatrix} 1 & 1 & 1 \\ c & b-x & a \\ b & a & c-x \end{vmatrix} = 0$

on applying $c_2 \to c_2 - c_1$, $c_3 \to c_3 - c_2$ we get

$$\begin{vmatrix} 1 & 0 & 0 \\ c & b-x-c & a-b+x \\ b & a-b & c-x-a \end{vmatrix} = 0$$

on expanding det along R_1 we get

$$(b - x - c)(c - x - a) - (a - b)(a - b + x) = 0$$

$\Rightarrow \quad bc - bx - ab - cx + x^2 + ax - c^2 + cx + ac$

$\quad -(a^2 - ab + ax - ab + b^2 - bx) = 0$

$\Rightarrow \quad bc - ab + x^2 - c^2 + ac + ab + ab - b^2 - a^2 = 0$

$\Rightarrow \quad x^2 + ab + bc + ca - a^2 - b^2 - c^2 = 0$

$\Rightarrow \quad x^2 = a^2 + b^2 + c^2 - ab - bc - ca$

Given $a + b + c = 0$

$\Rightarrow \quad (a + b + c)^2 = 0 \quad \Rightarrow \quad a^2 + b^2 + c^2 = -2(ab + bc + ca)$

$$\Rightarrow \quad -(ab + bc + ca) = \frac{a + b^2 + c^2}{2}$$

$\therefore \quad x^2 = (a^2 + b^2 + c^2) - (ab + bc + ca)$

$$= a^2 + b^2 + c^2 + \frac{a^2 + b^2 + c^2}{2} = \frac{3}{2}\left(a^2 + b^2 + c^2\right)$$

$\therefore \quad x = \pm\sqrt{\frac{3}{2}\left(a^2 + b^2 + c^2\right)}$

$\therefore \quad x = 0 \text{ or } x = \pm\sqrt{\frac{3}{2}\left(a^2 + b^2 + c^2\right)}$

Exercise - 3.3

1. Find the determinant of the following matrices.

(i) $\begin{bmatrix} 2 & 2 \\ 2 & 2 \end{bmatrix}$ (ii) $\begin{bmatrix} 4 & 5 \\ 6 & 2 \end{bmatrix}$ (iii) $\begin{bmatrix} -i & 0 \\ 0 & i \end{bmatrix}$

(iv) $\begin{bmatrix} a & h & g \\ h & b & f \\ g & f & c \end{bmatrix}$ (v) $\begin{bmatrix} 1 & 2 & 3 \\ 4 & -1 & 7 \\ 2 & 4 & -6 \end{bmatrix}$

2. Find the determinant of the following matrices

(i) $\begin{bmatrix} 111 & 222 \\ 110 & 221 \end{bmatrix}$ (ii) $\begin{bmatrix} 1^3 & 2^3 & 3^3 \\ 2^3 & 3^3 & 4^3 \\ 3^3 & 4^3 & 5^3 \end{bmatrix}$

3. If $A = \begin{bmatrix} 1 & 2 & 6 \\ 0 & 3 & 5 \\ 0 & 4 & x \end{bmatrix}$ and det A = 10 then find x.

4. Show that $\begin{vmatrix} a & b & c \\ a^2 & b^2 & c^2 \\ a^3 & b^3 & c^3 \end{vmatrix} = (abc)(a-b)(b-c)(c-a).$

5. Show that $\begin{vmatrix} b+c & c+a & a+b \\ a+b & b+c & c+a \\ a & b & c \end{vmatrix} = a^3 + b^3 + c^3 - 3abc$

6. Show that $\begin{vmatrix} b+c & a & a \\ b & c+a & b \\ c & c & a+b \end{vmatrix} = 4abc$

7. Show that $\begin{vmatrix} a^2+2a & 2a+1 & 1 \\ 2a+1 & a+2 & 1 \\ 3 & 3 & 1 \end{vmatrix} = (a-1)^3$

8. Show that $\begin{vmatrix} a+b+2c & a & b \\ c & b+c+2a & b \\ c & a & c+a+2b \end{vmatrix} = 2(a+b+c)^3$

9. Without expanding the determinant along any row or column show that

(i) $\begin{vmatrix} a-b & b-c & c-a \\ b-c & c-a & a-b \\ c-a & a-b & b-c \end{vmatrix} = 0$

(ii) $\begin{vmatrix} 1 & bc & a(b+c) \\ 1 & ca & b(c+a) \\ 1 & ab & c(a+b) \end{vmatrix} = 0$

10. Show that

(i) $\begin{vmatrix} 1+a & b & c \\ a & 1+b & c \\ a & b & 1+c \end{vmatrix} = 1+a+b+c$

(ii) $\begin{vmatrix} 1+a & 1 & 1 & 1 \\ 1 & 1+b & 1 & 1 \\ 1 & 1 & 1+c & 1 \\ 1 & 1 & 1 & 1+d \end{vmatrix} = abcd\left(1+\frac{1}{a}+\frac{1}{b}+\frac{1}{c}+\frac{1}{d}\right)$

11. Show that

(i) $\begin{vmatrix} -a^2 & ab & ac \\ ab & -b^2 & bc \\ ac & bc & -c^2 \end{vmatrix} = 4a^2b^2c^2$

(ii) $\begin{vmatrix} a^2 & bc & ac+c^2 \\ a^2+ab & b^2 & ac \\ ab & b^2+bc & c^2 \end{vmatrix} = 4a^2b^2c^2$

12. Find the value of x if $\begin{vmatrix} 15-x & 11 & 10 \\ 11-3x & 17 & 16 \\ 7-x & 14 & 13 \end{vmatrix} = 0$

13. Find the value of x if $\begin{vmatrix} 3x-8 & 3 & 3 \\ 3 & 3x-8 & 3 \\ 3 & 3 & 3x-8 \end{vmatrix} = 0$

14. Find the value of x if $\begin{vmatrix} x-2 & 2x-3 & 3x-4 \\ x-4 & 2x-9 & 3x-16 \\ x-8 & 2x-27 & 3x-64 \end{vmatrix} = 0$

15. Show that $\begin{vmatrix} 1 & a & a^2 & a^3+bcd \\ 1 & b & b^2 & b^3+cda \\ 1 & c & c^2 & c^3+dab \\ 1 & d & d^2 & d^3+abc \end{vmatrix} = 0$

16. Evaluate $\begin{vmatrix} a & b & c & d \\ -a & b & c & d \\ -a & -b & c & d \\ -a & -b & -c & d \end{vmatrix}$

17. Show that $\begin{vmatrix} x & a & a \\ a & x & x \\ a & a & x \end{vmatrix} = (x+2a)(x-a)^2$

18. Show that $\begin{vmatrix} -2a & a+b & c+a \\ a+b & -2b & b+c \\ c+a & c+b & -2c \end{vmatrix} = 4(a+b)(b+c)(c+a)$

Answers

1. (i) 0 (ii) −22 (iii) 1

 (iv) $abc + 2fgh - af^2 - bg^2 - ch^2$

 (v) 108

2. (i) 111 (ii) −756

3. $x = 10$

12. $x = 6$

13. $x = \frac{2}{3}$ or $\frac{11}{3}$

14. $x = 4$

16. 8 abcd

3.9 Product of Two Determinants

We know that the value of determinant is not altered when its row and columns are interchanged. Hence to find the product of two determinants, we can use row by column or row by row or column by column multiplication method.

Consider,

Let $A = \begin{bmatrix} a_1 & b_1 \\ c_1 & d_1 \end{bmatrix} B = \begin{bmatrix} a_2 & b_2 \\ c_2 & d_2 \end{bmatrix}$

then $AB = \begin{bmatrix} a_1 & b_1 \\ c_1 & d_1 \end{bmatrix}\begin{bmatrix} a_2 & b_2 \\ c_2 & d_2 \end{bmatrix}$

$$= \begin{bmatrix} a_1a_2 + b_1c_2 & a_1b_2 + b_1d_2 \\ c_1a_2 + d_1c_2 & c_1b_2 + d_1d_2 \end{bmatrix}$$

$$|AB| = \begin{vmatrix} a_1a_2 + b_1c_2 & a_1b_2 + b_1d_2 \\ c_1a_2 + d_1c_2 & c_1b_2 + d_1d_2 \end{vmatrix}$$

$$= (a_1\, a_2 + b_1\, c_2)\,(c_1\, b_2 + d_1d_2) - (c_1\, a_2 + d_1\, c_2)\,(a_1\, b_2 + b_1\, d_2)$$

$$= a_1\, a_2\, c_1\, b_2 + a_1\, a_2\, d_1\, d_2 + b_1\, c_2\, c_1\, b_2 + b_1\, c_2\, d_1\, d_2 - c_1\, a_2\, a_1\, b_2 - c_1\, a_2\, b_1\, d_2 - d_1\, c_2\, a_1\, b_2 - d_1\, c_2\, b_1\, d_2$$

$$|A| = \begin{vmatrix} a_1 & b_1 \\ c_1 & d_1 \end{vmatrix} = a_1\, d_1 - c_1\, b_1$$

$$|B| = \begin{vmatrix} a_2 & b_2 \\ c_2 & d_2 \end{vmatrix} = a_2\, d_2 - c_2\, b_2$$

$$|A|\,|B| = (a_1 d_1 - c_1 b_1)(a_2 d_2 - c_2 b_2)$$
$$= a_1 d_1 a_2 d_2 - a_1 d_1 c_2 b_2 - c_1 b_1 a_2 d_2 + c_1 b_1 c_2 b_2$$
$$\therefore \quad |AB| = |A|\,|B|$$

So A and B are two square matrices of same order then |AB| = |A| |B|

Consider

$$\begin{vmatrix} a & b \\ c & d \end{vmatrix}^2$$

$$= \begin{vmatrix} a & b \\ c & d \end{vmatrix}\begin{vmatrix} a & b \\ c & d \end{vmatrix}$$

$$= \begin{vmatrix} a^2+bc & ab+bd \\ ca+dc & cb+d^2 \end{vmatrix} \quad \text{(by multiplying row-column method)}$$

again $\begin{vmatrix} a & b \\ c & d \end{vmatrix}\begin{vmatrix} a & b \\ c & d \end{vmatrix}$

$$= \begin{vmatrix} a^2+b^2 & ac+bd \\ ca+db & c^2+d^2 \end{vmatrix} \quad \text{(by multiply row-row method)}$$

also $\begin{vmatrix} a & b \\ c & d \end{vmatrix}\begin{vmatrix} a & b \\ c & d \end{vmatrix}$

$$= \begin{vmatrix} a^2+c^2 & ab+cd \\ ba+cd & b^2+d^2 \end{vmatrix} \quad \text{(by multiply column-column method)}$$

Ex 1: Prove that $\begin{vmatrix} xy \\ zt \end{vmatrix}^2 = \begin{vmatrix} x^2+z^2 & xy+zt \\ xy+zt & y^2+t^2 \end{vmatrix}$

Consider $\begin{vmatrix} xy \\ zt \end{vmatrix}^2 = \begin{vmatrix} x & y \\ z & t \end{vmatrix}\begin{vmatrix} x & y \\ z & t \end{vmatrix}$

$$= \begin{vmatrix} x^2+z^2 & xy+zt \\ yx+tz & y^2+t^2 \end{vmatrix} \quad \text{(by using column-column method)}$$

Ex 2: Prove that $\begin{vmatrix} 3 & a+b+c & a^2+b^2+c^2 \\ a+b+c & a^2+b^2+c^2 & a^3+b^3+c^3 \\ a^2+b^2+c^2 & a^3+b^3+c^3 & a^4+b^4+c^4 \end{vmatrix} = ((a-b)(b-c)(c-a))^2$

We have $\begin{vmatrix} 1 & 1 & 1 \\ a & b & c \\ a^2 & b^2 & c^2 \end{vmatrix} = (a-b)(b-c)(c-a)$

Squaring on both sides we get

$$\begin{vmatrix} 1 & 1 & 1 \\ a & b & c \\ a^2 & b^2 & c^2 \end{vmatrix}^2 = [(a-b)(b-c)(c-a)]^2$$

$$\text{LHS} = \begin{vmatrix} 1 & 1 & 1 \\ a & b & c \\ a^2 & b^2 & c^2 \end{vmatrix}^2 = \begin{vmatrix} 1 & 1 & 1 \\ a & b & c \\ a^2 & b^2 & c^2 \end{vmatrix}\begin{vmatrix} 1 & 1 & 1 \\ a & b & c \\ a^2 & b^2 & c^2 \end{vmatrix}$$

$$= \begin{vmatrix} 1+1+1 & a+b+c & a^2+b^2+c^2 \\ a+b+c & a^2+b^2+c^2 & a^3+b^3+c^3 \\ a^2+b^2+c^2 & a^3+b^3+c^3 & a^4+b^4+c^4 \end{vmatrix}$$

(by using row-row multiplication)

hence LHS = RHS

Exercise - 3.4

1. If $A\begin{pmatrix} a & ib \\ ib & a \end{pmatrix} B = \begin{pmatrix} c & id \\ id & c \end{pmatrix}$ prove that $(a^2 + b^2)(c^2 + d^2)$ $= (ac - bd)^2 + (ad + bc)^2$.

2. If $A = \begin{pmatrix} 1 & 2 \\ 3 & 4 \end{pmatrix}$ $B = \begin{pmatrix} 4 & 2 \\ 3 & 1 \end{pmatrix}$ prove that $|AB| = |A|\,|B|$

3. If $A = \begin{vmatrix} \sin\theta & -\cos\theta \\ \cos\theta & \sin\theta \end{vmatrix}$ find $|A|^2$

4. Prove that $2\begin{vmatrix} 1 & a & a^2 \\ 1 & b & b^2 \\ 1 & c & c^2 \end{vmatrix}^2 = \begin{vmatrix} 0 & (a-b)^2 & (a-c)^2 \\ (b-a)^2 & 0 & (b-c)^2 \\ (c-a)^2 & (c-b)^2 & 0 \end{vmatrix}$

3.10 Adjoint and Inverse of a Matrix

Singular Matrix

A square matrix is said to be singular if its determinant is zero otherwise it is said to be non singular matrix.

Ex : $\begin{bmatrix} 1 & 2 \\ 2 & 4 \end{bmatrix}$ is singular ; $\begin{bmatrix} 1 & 2 \\ 3 & 4 \end{bmatrix}$ is non singular

Cofactor Matrix

Let A be a square matrix. The matrix B be obtained by replacing the elements of A by its cofactors. Then the matrix B is called cofactor matrix of A.

Adjoint of a Matrix

Let A be a square matrix then the transpose of cofactor matrix of A is called Adjoint of A. It is denoted by 'AdjA'.

Let $A = \begin{bmatrix} a_1 & b_1 & c_1 \\ a_2 & b_2 & c_2 \\ a_3 & b_3 & c_3 \end{bmatrix}$ and Ai, Bi, Ci are cofactors of ai, bi, ci respectively then

$$\text{Adj}\,A = \begin{bmatrix} A_1 & B_1 & C_1 \\ A_2 & B_2 & C_2 \\ A_3 & B_3 & C_3 \end{bmatrix}^T = \begin{bmatrix} A_1 & A_2 & A_3 \\ B_1 & B_2 & B_3 \\ C_1 & C_2 & C_3 \end{bmatrix}$$

Inverse of a matrix

Let A be a square matrix. We say that A is invertible if a matrix B exists such that AB = BA = I where I is unit matrix.

Theorem If $A = \begin{bmatrix} a_1 & b_1 & c_1 \\ a_2 & b_2 & c_2 \\ a_3 & b_3 & c_3 \end{bmatrix}$ is non singular matix then A is invertible and

$$A^{-1} = \frac{\text{Adj}A}{|A|}$$

Proof Let A_i, B_i, C_i are cofactors of a_i, b_i c_i then $\text{Adj}\,A = \begin{bmatrix} A_1 & A_2 & A_3 \\ B_1 & B_2 & B_3 \\ C_1 & C_2 & C_3 \end{bmatrix}$

$$\text{Now } A.\text{Adj}A = \begin{bmatrix} a_1 & b_1 & c_1 \\ a_2 & b_2 & c_2 \\ a_3 & b_3 & c_3 \end{bmatrix}\begin{bmatrix} A_1 & A_2 & A_3 \\ B_2 & B_2 & B_3 \\ C_1 & C_2 & C_3 \end{bmatrix}$$

$$= \begin{bmatrix} a_1A_1 + b_1B_1 + c_1C_1 & a_2A_2 + b_1B_2 + c_1C_2 & a_1A_3 + b_1B_3 + c_3C_3 \\ a_2A_1 + b_2B_1 + c_2C_1 & a_2A_2 + b_2B_2 + c_2C_2 & a_2A_3 + b_2B_3 + c_2C_3 \\ a_3A_1 + b_3B_1 + c_3C_1 & a_3A_2 + b_3B_2 + c_3C_2 & a_3A_3 + b_3B_3 + c_3C_3 \end{bmatrix}$$

$$= \begin{bmatrix} \det A & 0 & 0 \\ 0 & \det A & 0 \\ 0 & 0 & \det A \end{bmatrix}$$

$$= (\det A)\begin{bmatrix} 1 & 0 & 0 \\ 0 & 1 & 0 \\ 0 & 0 & 1 \end{bmatrix} = (\det A)\, I$$

Similarly we can show that Adj A . A = (detA) I

$\therefore$ A. (Adj A) = (adj A) A = (det A) I

since det A $\neq$ 0

$$\Rightarrow \quad A\frac{\text{Adj}A}{\det A} = \frac{(\text{Adj}A)}{\det A}A = I$$

$$\text{Let } B = \frac{\text{Adj}A}{\det A} \qquad \therefore \quad AB = BA = I$$

$$\Rightarrow \quad A^{-1} = B$$

$$\Rightarrow \quad A^{-1} = \frac{\text{Adj}A}{\det A}$$

Note 1

(i) If A is invertible $\Leftrightarrow$ A is non singular

(ii) If A is invertible then its inverse is unique

(iii) If A, B are invertable then $(AB)^{-1} = B^{-1}A^{-1}$

(iv) If $A = \begin{bmatrix} a & b \\ c & d \end{bmatrix}$ is non singular matrix then its inverse is

$$A^{-1} = \frac{1}{ad-bd}\begin{bmatrix} d & -b \\ -c & a \end{bmatrix} \quad \text{here} \quad \text{Adj } A = \begin{bmatrix} d & -b \\ -c & a \end{bmatrix}$$

Solved Examples

1. Find the Adjoint and the inverse of the matrix $A = \begin{bmatrix} 1 & 2 \\ 3 & 4 \end{bmatrix}$

Sol. Let $A = \begin{bmatrix} 1 & 2 \\ 3 & 4 \end{bmatrix} = \begin{bmatrix} a & b \\ c & d \end{bmatrix}$

$|A| = ad - bc = 4 - 6 = -2$

$$\text{Adj } A = \begin{bmatrix} d & -b \\ -c & a \end{bmatrix} = \begin{bmatrix} 4 & -2 \\ -3 & 1 \end{bmatrix}$$

$$\therefore \quad A^{-1} = \frac{\text{Adj}A}{|A|} = \frac{\begin{bmatrix} 4 & -2 \\ -3 & 1 \end{bmatrix}}{-2} = \frac{-1}{2}\begin{bmatrix} 4 & -2 \\ -3 & 1 \end{bmatrix}$$

2. Find Adjoint and inverse of the matrix $\begin{bmatrix} 2 & 1 & 2 \\ 1 & 0 & 1 \\ 2 & 2 & 1 \end{bmatrix}$

Sol. Let $A = \begin{bmatrix} 2 & 1 & 2 \\ 1 & 0 & 1 \\ 2 & 2 & 1 \end{bmatrix}$

$$|A| = 2(0-2) - 1(1-2) + 2(2)$$
$$= -4 + 1 + 4 = 1$$

$\therefore \quad |A| = 1 \neq 0$

$\therefore \quad A^{-1}$ exists

$$\text{Now Adj } A = \begin{bmatrix} +(-2) & -(-1) & +(2) \\ -(-3) & +(-2) & -(2) \\ +(1) & -(0) & +(-1) \end{bmatrix}^T$$

$$= \begin{bmatrix} -2 & 1 & 2 \\ 3 & -2 & -2 \\ 1 & 0 & -1 \end{bmatrix}^T = \begin{bmatrix} -2 & 3 & 1 \\ 1 & -2 & 0 \\ 2 & -2 & -1 \end{bmatrix}$$

$$\therefore \quad A^{-1} = \frac{\text{Adj}A}{|A|} = \frac{1}{1}\begin{bmatrix} -2 & 3 & 1 \\ 1 & -2 & 0 \\ 2 & -2 & -1 \end{bmatrix} = \begin{bmatrix} -2 & 3 & 1 \\ 1 & -2 & 0 \\ 2 & -2 & -1 \end{bmatrix}$$

3. If a b c $\neq$ 0, find the Inverse of $\begin{bmatrix} a & 0 & 0 \\ 0 & b & 0 \\ 0 & 0 & c \end{bmatrix}$

Sol. Let $A = \begin{bmatrix} a & 0 & 0 \\ 0 & b & 0 \\ 0 & 0 & c \end{bmatrix}$

$\therefore \quad |A| = a(bc - 0) - 0 + 0 = abc$

$$\text{cofactor matrix of } A = \begin{bmatrix} +(bc) & -(0) & +(0) \\ -(0) & +(ac) & -(0) \\ +(0) & -(0) & +(ab) \end{bmatrix} = \begin{bmatrix} bc & 0 & 0 \\ 0 & ac & 0 \\ 0 & 0 & ab \end{bmatrix}$$

$$\therefore \quad \text{Adj } A = (\text{Cofactor matrix of } A)^T = \begin{pmatrix} bc & 0 & 0 \\ 0 & ac & 0 \\ 0 & 0 & ab \end{pmatrix}$$

$$\therefore \quad A^{-1} = \frac{\text{Adj}A}{|A|} = \frac{1}{abc}\begin{pmatrix} bc & 0 & 0 \\ 0 & ac & 0 \\ 0 & 0 & ab \end{pmatrix} = \begin{pmatrix} \frac{1}{a} & 0 & 0 \\ 0 & \frac{1}{b} & 0 \\ 0 & 0 & \frac{1}{c} \end{pmatrix}$$

4. If $A = \begin{bmatrix} -1 & -2 & -2 \\ 2 & 1 & -2 \\ 2 & -2 & 1 \end{bmatrix}$ then show that $\text{Adj}(A) = 3A^T$ and find A^{-1}.

Sol. Given $A = \begin{bmatrix} -1 & -2 & -2 \\ 2 & 1 & -2 \\ 2 & -2 & 1 \end{bmatrix}$

$$\text{Cofactor of } A = \begin{bmatrix} +(-3) & -(6) & +(-6) \\ -(-6) & +(3) & -(6) \\ +(6) & -(6) & +(3) \end{bmatrix}$$

$$= \begin{bmatrix} -3 & -6 & -6 \\ 6 & 3 & -6 \\ 6 & -6 & 3 \end{bmatrix}$$

$$\therefore \quad \text{Adj } A = (\text{cofactor of } A)^T = \begin{bmatrix} -3 & 6 & 6 \\ -6 & 3 & -6 \\ -6 & -6 & 3. \end{bmatrix}$$

also $A^T = \begin{bmatrix} -1 & 2 & 2 \\ -2 & 1 & -2 \\ -2 & -2 & 1 \end{bmatrix}$

$$3A^T = \begin{bmatrix} -3 & 6 & 6 \\ -6 & 3 & -6 \\ -6 & -6 & 3 \end{bmatrix} = \text{Adj } A$$

$\therefore$ Adj $A = 3A^T$

also $|A| = -1(1-4) + 2(2+4) - 2(-4-2)$

$= 3 + 12 + 12 = 27$

$$\therefore \quad A^{-1} = \frac{\text{Adj}A}{|A|} = \frac{1}{27}\begin{bmatrix} -3 & 6 & 6 \\ -6 & 3 & -6 \\ -6 & -6 & 3 \end{bmatrix}$$

$$= \frac{1}{9}\begin{bmatrix} -1 & 2 & 2 \\ -2 & 1 & -2 \\ -2 & -2 & 1 \end{bmatrix}$$

5. If $3A = \begin{bmatrix} 1 & 2 & 2 \\ 2 & 1 & -2 \\ -2 & 2 & -1 \end{bmatrix}$ then show that $A^{-1} = A^T$

Sol. Given $$3A = \begin{bmatrix} 1 & 2 & 2 \\ 2 & 1 & -2 \\ -2 & 2 & -1 \end{bmatrix}$$

$$\therefore \quad A = \begin{bmatrix} \frac{1}{3} & \frac{2}{3} & \frac{2}{3} \\ \frac{2}{3} & \frac{1}{3} & \frac{-2}{3} \\ \frac{-2}{3} & \frac{2}{3} & \frac{-1}{3} \end{bmatrix}$$

We have to show that $A^{-1} = A^T$, it is enough to show that $AA^T = A^TA$

now $$A^T = \begin{bmatrix} \frac{1}{3} & \frac{2}{3} & \frac{-2}{3} \\ \frac{2}{3} & \frac{1}{3} & \frac{2}{3} \\ \frac{2}{3} & \frac{-2}{3} & \frac{-1}{3} \end{bmatrix}$$

$$A.A^T = \begin{bmatrix} \frac{1}{3} & \frac{2}{3} & \frac{2}{3} \\ \frac{2}{3} & \frac{1}{3} & \frac{-2}{3} \\ \frac{-2}{3} & \frac{2}{3} & \frac{-1}{3} \end{bmatrix} \begin{bmatrix} \frac{1}{3} & \frac{2}{3} & \frac{-2}{3} \\ \frac{2}{3} & \frac{1}{3} & \frac{2}{3} \\ \frac{2}{3} & \frac{-2}{3} & \frac{-1}{3} \end{bmatrix}$$

$$= \begin{bmatrix} \frac{1}{9}+\frac{4}{9}+\frac{4}{9} & \frac{2}{9}+\frac{2}{9}-\frac{4}{9} & \frac{-2}{9}+\frac{4}{9}-\frac{2}{9} \\ \frac{2}{9}+\frac{2}{9}-\frac{4}{9} & \frac{4}{9}+\frac{1}{9}+\frac{4}{9} & \frac{-4}{9}+\frac{2}{9}+\frac{2}{9} \\ \frac{-2}{9}+\frac{4}{9}-\frac{2}{9} & \frac{-4}{9}+\frac{2}{9}+\frac{2}{9} & \frac{4}{9}+\frac{4}{9}+\frac{1}{9} \end{bmatrix}$$

$$= \begin{bmatrix} \frac{9}{9} & 0 & 0 \\ 0 & \frac{9}{9} & 0 \\ 0 & 0 & \frac{9}{9} \end{bmatrix} = \begin{bmatrix} 1 & 0 & 0 \\ 0 & 1 & 0 \\ 0 & 0 & 1 \end{bmatrix}$$

Similarly we can show that $A^TA = I$

$\therefore \quad AA^T = A^TA = I$

$\therefore \quad A^{-1} = A$

Exercise - 3.5

1. Find the Adjoint and Inverse of the following matrices

(i) $\begin{bmatrix} 1 & 2 \\ 3 & -5 \end{bmatrix}$ (ii) $\begin{bmatrix} \cos\alpha & -\sin\alpha \\ \sin\alpha & \cos\alpha \end{bmatrix}$

(iii) $\begin{bmatrix} 1 & 3 & 3 \\ 1 & 4 & 3 \\ 1 & 3 & 4 \end{bmatrix}$ (iv) $\begin{bmatrix} 1 & 0 & 2 \\ 2 & 1 & 0 \\ 3 & 2 & 1 \end{bmatrix}$

2. If $A = \begin{bmatrix} 3 & -3 & 4 \\ 2 & -3 & 4 \\ 0 & -1 & 1 \end{bmatrix}$ then show that $A^{-1} = A^3$.

3. If $A = \begin{bmatrix} 1 & -2 & 3 \\ 0 & -1 & 4 \\ -2 & 2 & 1 \end{bmatrix}$ then show that $(A^T)^{-1} = \begin{bmatrix} -9 & -8 & -2 \\ 8 & 7 & 2 \\ -5 & -4 & -1 \end{bmatrix}$

4. If $A = \begin{bmatrix} 0 & 1 & 1 \\ 1 & 0 & 1 \\ 1 & 1 & 0 \end{bmatrix}$ and $B = \frac{1}{2}\begin{bmatrix} b+c & c-a & b-a \\ c-b & c+a & a-b \\ b-c & a-c & a+b \end{bmatrix}$ then show that ABA^{-1} is a diagonal matrix.

5. If $A = \begin{bmatrix} 5 & 0 & 0 \\ 0 & 6 & 0 \\ 0 & 0 & 7 \end{bmatrix}$ then show that $A^{-1} = \begin{bmatrix} \frac{1}{5} & 0 & 0 \\ 0 & \frac{1}{6} & 0 \\ 0 & 0 & \frac{1}{7} \end{bmatrix}$

Answers

1. (i) $\begin{bmatrix} -5 & -2 \\ -3 & 1 \end{bmatrix}, \begin{bmatrix} \frac{5}{11} & \frac{2}{11} \\ \frac{3}{11} & \frac{-1}{11} \end{bmatrix}$ (ii) $\begin{bmatrix} \cos\alpha & \sin\alpha \\ -\sin\alpha & \cos\alpha \end{bmatrix}, \begin{bmatrix} \cos\alpha & \sin\alpha \\ -\sin\alpha & \cos\alpha \end{bmatrix}$

(iii) $\begin{bmatrix} 7 & -3 & -3 \\ -1 & 1 & 0 \\ -1 & 0 & 1 \end{bmatrix}, \begin{bmatrix} 7 & -3 & -3 \\ -1 & 1 & 0 \\ -1 & 0 & 1 \end{bmatrix}$

(iv) $\begin{bmatrix} 1 & 4 & -2 \\ -2 & -5 & 4 \\ 1 & -2 & 1 \end{bmatrix}, \frac{1}{3}\begin{bmatrix} 1 & 4 & -2 \\ -2 & -5 & 4 \\ 1 & -2 & 1 \end{bmatrix}$

3.11 Characteristic Equation and Cayley-Hamilton Theorem

Characteristic Equation: If A is any square matrix and I is the identity matrix of the same order of A, then $|A - \lambda I| = 0$ where λ is constant is called the characteristic equation of matrix A. The roots of the equation $|A - \lambda I| = 0$ are called the characteristic roots or eigen values of the equation.

Solved Examples

1. If $A = \begin{bmatrix} 1 & 2 \\ 3 & 4 \end{bmatrix}$ then find characteristic equation and its eigen values.

Sol. Consider $A = \begin{bmatrix} 1 & 2 \\ 3 & 4 \end{bmatrix}$ take $I = \begin{bmatrix} 1 & 0 \\ 0 & 1 \end{bmatrix}$

$\therefore$ Characteristic equation is $|A - \lambda I| = 0$

take $A - \lambda I = \begin{bmatrix} 1 & 2 \\ 3 & 4 \end{bmatrix} - \lambda \begin{bmatrix} 1 & 0 \\ 0 & 1 \end{bmatrix}$

$$= \begin{bmatrix} 1 & 2 \\ 3 & 4 \end{bmatrix} - \begin{bmatrix} \lambda & 0 \\ 0 & \lambda \end{bmatrix}$$

$$\begin{bmatrix} 1-\lambda & 2 \\ 3 & 4-\lambda \end{bmatrix}$$

$$\therefore \quad |A-\lambda I| = \begin{vmatrix} 1-\lambda & 2 \\ 3 & 4-\lambda \end{vmatrix} = 0$$

$$\Rightarrow \quad (1-\lambda)(4-\lambda) - 6 = 0$$

$$\Rightarrow \quad 4 - \lambda - 4\lambda + \lambda^2 - 6 = 0$$

$$\lambda^2 - 5\lambda - 2 = 0$$

$$\lambda = \frac{5 \pm \sqrt{25+8}}{2} = \frac{5 \pm \sqrt{33}}{2}$$

$\therefore$ **eigen values are** $\dfrac{5+\sqrt{33}}{2}, \dfrac{5-\sqrt{33}}{2}$

2. **If** $A = \begin{bmatrix} 2 & 2 & 3 \\ 1 & 0 & -1 \\ 1 & 2 & 1 \end{bmatrix}$ **then find the characteristic equation.**

Sol. Consider $A = \begin{bmatrix} 2 & 2 & 3 \\ 1 & 0 & -1 \\ 1 & 2 & 1 \end{bmatrix}$

take $I = \begin{bmatrix} 1 & 0 & 0 \\ 0 & 1 & 0 \\ 0 & 0 & 1 \end{bmatrix}$

Consider $A - \lambda I = \begin{bmatrix} 2 & 2 & 3 \\ 1 & 0 & -1 \\ 1 & 2 & 1 \end{bmatrix} - \lambda \begin{bmatrix} 1 & 0 & 0 \\ 0 & 1 & 0 \\ 0 & 0 & 1 \end{bmatrix}$

$$= \begin{bmatrix} 2 & 2 & 3 \\ 1 & 0 & -1 \\ 1 & 2 & 1 \end{bmatrix} - \begin{bmatrix} \lambda & 0 & 0 \\ 0 & \lambda & 0 \\ 0 & 0 & \lambda \end{bmatrix}$$

$$= \begin{bmatrix} 2-\lambda & 2 & 3 \\ 1 & -\lambda & -1 \\ 1 & 2 & 1-\lambda \end{bmatrix}$$

Characteristic equation is $|A - \lambda I| = 0$

$$\Rightarrow \begin{vmatrix} 2-\lambda & 2 & 3 \\ 1 & -\lambda & -1 \\ 1 & 2 & 1-\lambda \end{vmatrix} = 0$$

$$(2-\lambda)(-\lambda+\lambda^2) - 2(1-\lambda+1) + 3(2+\lambda) = 0$$

$$\Rightarrow \quad -2\lambda + 2\lambda^2 + \lambda^2 - \lambda^3 - 4 + 2\lambda + 6 + 3\lambda = 0$$

$$\Rightarrow \quad -\lambda^3 + 3\lambda^2 + 3\lambda + 2 = 0 \quad \Rightarrow \quad \lambda^3 - 3\lambda^2 - 3\lambda - 2 = 0$$

3. Find the characteristic equation and the roots of matrix

$$A = \begin{bmatrix} 1 & 0 & -1 \\ 1 & 2 & 1 \\ 2 & 2 & 3 \end{bmatrix}$$

Sol. Consider $|A - \lambda I| = 0$

$$\Rightarrow \begin{bmatrix} 1-\lambda & 0 & -1 \\ 1 & 2-\lambda & 1 \\ 2 & 2 & 3-\lambda \end{bmatrix} = 0$$

$$\Rightarrow (1-\lambda)\{(2-\lambda)(3-\lambda)-2\} - 0 - 1\{2 - 2(2-\lambda)\} = 0$$

$$\Rightarrow \lambda^3 - 6\lambda^2 + 11\lambda - 6 = 0$$

by trail and error method we get $\lambda = 1$ and using by synthetic division

$$\lambda = 1 \left| \begin{array}{cccc} 1 & -6 & 11 & -6 \\ 0 & 1 & -5 & 6 \\ 1 & -5 & 6 & 0 \end{array} \right.$$

$$\lambda^3 - 6\lambda^2 + 11\lambda - 6 = (\lambda-1)(\lambda^2 - 5\lambda + 6) = 0$$

$$\Rightarrow (\lambda-1)(\lambda-2)(\lambda-3) = 0 \Rightarrow \quad \lambda = 1, 2, 3$$

Cayley-Hamilton Theorem

Every square matrix satisfies its characteristic equation.

Solved Examples

1. Verify the Cayley-Hamilton theorem for the square matrix $\begin{bmatrix}1 & 2\\3 & 4\end{bmatrix}$ and hence find its inverse also.

Sol. Let $A = \begin{bmatrix}1 & 2\\3 & 4\end{bmatrix}$

Consider $|A - \lambda I| = 0$

$$\Rightarrow \quad \left[\begin{pmatrix}1 & 2\\3 & 4\end{pmatrix} - \lambda\begin{pmatrix}1 & 0\\0 & 1\end{pmatrix}\right] = 0$$

$$\begin{vmatrix}1-\lambda & 2\\3 & 4-\lambda\end{vmatrix} = 0$$

$$\Rightarrow \quad (1-\lambda)(4-\lambda) - 6 = 0$$

$$4 - \lambda - 4\lambda + \lambda^2 - 6 = 0$$

$$\lambda^2 - 5\lambda - 2 = 0$$

To prove

$\therefore \quad A^2 - 5A - 2I = 0$

$$A^2 = \begin{bmatrix}1 & 2\\3 & 4\end{bmatrix}\begin{bmatrix}1 & 2\\3 & 4\end{bmatrix} = \begin{bmatrix}1+6 & 2+8\\3+12 & 6+16\end{bmatrix} = \begin{bmatrix}7 & 10\\15 & 22\end{bmatrix}$$

$$5A = \begin{bmatrix}5 & 10\\15 & 20\end{bmatrix} \qquad 2I = \begin{bmatrix}20\\02\end{bmatrix}$$

$$A^2 - 5A + 2I = \begin{bmatrix}7 & 10\\15 & 22\end{bmatrix} - \begin{bmatrix}5 & 10\\15 & 20\end{bmatrix} - \begin{bmatrix}20\\02\end{bmatrix}$$

$$= \begin{bmatrix}7 & 10\\15 & 22\end{bmatrix} - \begin{bmatrix}7 & 10\\15 & 22\end{bmatrix} = \begin{bmatrix}0 & 0\\0 & 0\end{bmatrix}$$

so the Cayley Hamilton theorem is verified

again consider $\quad A^2 - 5A - 2I = 0$

$\Rightarrow \quad A^{-1}(A^2 - 5A - 2I) = 0$

$\quad A - 5I - 2A^{-1} = 0$

$\Rightarrow \quad 2A^{-1} = A - 5I$

$$A^{-1} = \frac{1}{2}(A - 5I)$$

$$= \frac{1}{2}\left(\begin{pmatrix} 1 & 2 \\ 3 & 4 \end{pmatrix} - \begin{pmatrix} 5 & 0 \\ 0 & 5 \end{pmatrix}\right)$$

$$= \frac{1}{2}\left(\begin{pmatrix} -4 & 2 \\ 3 & -1 \end{pmatrix} = \begin{pmatrix} -2 & 1 \\ 3/2 & -1/2 \end{pmatrix}\right)$$

$$\therefore \quad A^{-1} = \begin{pmatrix} -2 & 1 \\ 3/2 & -1/2 \end{pmatrix}$$

2. If $A = \begin{bmatrix} 2 & 1 \\ -2 & -1 \end{bmatrix}$ find A^8 using Cayley Hamilton Theorem.

Sol. Given $A = \begin{bmatrix} 2 & 1 \\ -2 & -1 \end{bmatrix}$

Characteristic equation is $|A - \lambda I| = 0$

$$\left|\begin{pmatrix} 2 & 1 \\ -2 & -1 \end{pmatrix} - \begin{pmatrix} \lambda & 0 \\ 0 & \lambda \end{pmatrix}\right| = 0$$

$$= \begin{vmatrix} 2-\lambda & 1 \\ -2 & -1-\lambda \end{vmatrix} = 0$$

$\Rightarrow (2 - \lambda)(-1 - \lambda) + 2 = 0$

$-2 - 2\lambda + \lambda + \lambda^2 + 2 = 0$

$\Rightarrow \quad \lambda^2 - \lambda = 0$

$\Rightarrow \quad \lambda^2 = \lambda$

A satisfies this equation

$\therefore \quad A^2 = A$

$\therefore \quad A^6 = A^3 = A^2 . A = A . A = A^2 = A$

$$\therefore \quad A^6 = A = \begin{pmatrix} 2 & 1 \\ -2 & -1 \end{pmatrix}$$

3. If $A = \begin{bmatrix} 1 & 2 \\ 3 & 4 \end{bmatrix}$ thus show that $A^5 - 5A^4 - 10A^2 - 4A = 0$.

Sol. Given $A = \begin{bmatrix} 1 & 2 \\ 3 & 4 \end{bmatrix}$

Characteristic equations $\begin{vmatrix} 1-\lambda & 2 \\ 3 & 4-\lambda \end{vmatrix} = 0$

$$\Rightarrow \quad (1-\lambda)(4-\lambda) - 6 = 0$$
$$4 - 5\lambda + \lambda^2 - 6 = 0$$
$$\lambda^2 - 5\lambda - 2 = 0$$
$$\Rightarrow \quad A^2 - 5A - 2I = 0 \quad \text{(by Cayley Hamilton Theorem)}$$

Consider

$$A^5 - 5A^4 - 10A^2 - 4A$$
$$= A^3(A^2 - 5A) - 10\,A^2 - 4A$$
$$= A^3(2I) - 10A^2 - 4A$$
$$= 2A^3 - 10A^2 - 4A$$
$$= 2A(A^2 - 5A - 2I) = 2A(0) = 0$$

Exercise - 3.6

1. Find the eigen values of the matrix $\begin{bmatrix} 1 & 3 \\ 2 & -4 \end{bmatrix}$

2. Find the eigen values of matrix $\begin{bmatrix} 1 & 4 \\ 3 & 2 \end{bmatrix}$

3. Verify the Caley Hamilton Theorem for $A = \begin{pmatrix} 1 & -1 \\ 2 & 1 \end{pmatrix}$ and hence show that $A^6 - A^4 + A^3 + 5A^2 - 4A + 6I = 0$.

4. Verify the Caley Hamilton Theorem for $A = \begin{bmatrix} 1 & 2 & 2 \\ 2 & 1 & 2 \\ 2 & 2 & 1 \end{bmatrix}$

5. Find inverse of $A = \begin{bmatrix} 2 & 2 \\ 3 & 5 \end{bmatrix}$ by using Cayley Hamilton Theorem.

Answers

1. (i) 2, –5 (ii) –2, 5

3.12 Solving the Simultaneous Linear Equations by Crammers Rule

Consider the system of equations

$a_1x + b_1y + c_1z = d_1$

$a_2x + b_2y + c_2z = d_2$

$a_3x + b_3y + c_3z = d_3$

Where $A = \begin{bmatrix} a_1 & b_1 & c_1 \\ a_2 & b_2 & c_2 \\ a_3 & b_3 & c_3 \end{bmatrix}$ is non singular i.e., $|A| \neq 0$.

Let $X = \begin{bmatrix} x \\ y \\ z \end{bmatrix}$ be the solution of AX = D where $D = \begin{bmatrix} d_1 \\ d_2 \\ d_3 \end{bmatrix}$

Let $\Delta = \begin{vmatrix} a_1 & b_1 & c_1 \\ a_2 & b_2 & c_2 \\ a_3 & b_3 & c_3 \end{vmatrix}$

$$\Delta_1 = \begin{vmatrix} d_1 & b_1 & c_1 \\ d_2 & b_2 & c_2 \\ d_3 & b_3 & d_3 \end{vmatrix} \quad ; \quad \Delta_2 = \begin{vmatrix} a_1 & d_1 & c_1 \\ a_2 & d_2 & c_2 \\ a_3 & d_3 & c_3 \end{vmatrix}$$

$$\Delta_3 = \begin{vmatrix} a_1 & b_1 & d_1 \\ a_2 & b_2 & d_2 \\ a_3 & b_3 & d_3 \end{vmatrix}$$

then $x = \dfrac{\Delta_1}{\Delta}$, $y = \dfrac{\Delta_2}{\Delta}$, $z = \dfrac{\Delta_3}{\Delta}$

This known as cramer's rule.

Ex :Solve the following simultaneous equations by using Crammer's rule

$3x + 4y + 5z = 18$

$2x - y + 8z = 13$

$5x - 2y + 7z = 20$

Let $A=\begin{bmatrix}3 & 4 & 5\\ 2 & -1 & 8\\ 5 & -2 & 7\end{bmatrix}$; $X=\begin{bmatrix}x\\ y\\ z\end{bmatrix}$ and $D=\begin{bmatrix}18\\ 13\\ 20\end{bmatrix}$

Then we write the given equations in the form of matrix equation A X = D

Let $\Delta=|A|=\begin{vmatrix}3 & 4 & 5\\ 2 & -1 & 8\\ 5 & -2 & 7\end{vmatrix}$

$= 3(-7 + 16) -4 (14 -40) +5(-4+5)$

$= 27 + 104 + 5 = 136 \neq 0$

and $\Delta_1=\begin{vmatrix}18 & 4 & 5\\ 13 & -1 & 8\\ 20 & -2 & 7\end{vmatrix}=408$

$\Delta_2=\begin{vmatrix}3 & 18 & 5\\ 2 & 13 & 8\\ 5 & 20 & 7\end{vmatrix}=136$

$\Delta_3=\begin{vmatrix}3 & 4 & 18\\ 2 & -1 & 13\\ 5 & -2 & 20\end{vmatrix}=136$

Hence by Crammers rule

$$x=\frac{\Delta_1}{\Delta}=\frac{408}{136}=3,\quad y=\frac{\Delta_2}{\Delta}=\frac{136}{136}=1,\quad z=\frac{\Delta_3}{\Delta}=\frac{136}{136}=1$$

Exercise - 3.7

1. Solve the following simultaneous linear equation by Cramers rule

(i) $x + y + z = 6$
$x - y + z = 2$
$2x - y + 3z = 9$

(ii) $x + y + z = 9$
$2x + 5y + 7z = 52$
$2x + y - z = 0$

(iii) $x + y + z = 6$
$2x + 2y + 3z = 10$
$x + 2y + 4z = 1$

(iv) $2x + 3y + z = 9$
$x + 2y + 3z = 6$
$3x + y + 2z = 8$

(v) $x + y + 4z = 6$
$3x + 2y - 2z = 9$
$5x + y + 2z = 13$

Answers

(i) $x = 1, y = 2, z = 3$ (ii) $x = 1, y = 3, z = 5$ (iii) $x = -7, y = 22, z = -9$

(iv) $x = \frac{35}{18}, y = \frac{29}{18}, z = \frac{5}{18}$ (v) $x = 2, y = 2, z = \frac{1}{2}$

3.13 Applications of Matrices in Solving Pharmacokinetics Equations

Applications on Crammers Rule

1. There are two families P and Q and there are 6 men, 4 women, 2 children in family P, 2 men, 2 women, 3 children in family Q. The recommended daily allowance for calories is: man 2500, woman 2000, child 1750 and proteins for man 60 gm, woman 50 grams, children 30 grams. Represent the above information by matrix using matrix multiplication. Calculate the total requirement of calories and proteins for each of the two families.

Sol. The members of two families can be represented by the 2 × 3 matrix

$$A = \begin{pmatrix} M & W & C \\ 6 & 4 & 2 \\ 2 & 2 & 3 \end{pmatrix}$$

Calories and proteins recommended for each member can be written as 3 × 2 matrices

$$B = \begin{pmatrix} 2500 & 60 \\ 2000 & 50 \\ 1750 & 30 \end{pmatrix}$$

Now multiply matrix A and B to calculate required amount of calories and proteins for each family.

$$\begin{pmatrix} 6 & 4 & 2 \\ 2 & 2 & 3 \end{pmatrix}_{2\times3} \begin{pmatrix} 2500 & 60 \\ 2000 & 50 \\ 1750 & 30 \end{pmatrix}_{3\times2}$$

$$= \begin{pmatrix} 6\times2500+4\times2000+2\times1750 & 6\times60+4\times50+2\times30 \\ 2\times2500+2\times2000+3\times1750 & 2\times60+2\times50+3\times30 \end{pmatrix}$$

$$= \begin{pmatrix} 15000+8000+3500 & 360+200+60 \\ 5000+4000+5250 & 120+100+90 \end{pmatrix}$$

$$= \begin{pmatrix} 26500 & 720 \\ 14250 & 310 \end{pmatrix}$$

2. **The total weight of ingredient present in drug P = 500 mg, drug Q = 400 mg and drug R = 300 mg. The amount of ingredient that present are given in a matrix as shown below. Calculate the individual amount of ingredient present in each drug.**

$$\begin{bmatrix} A & B & C \\ 2 & 1 & 1 \\ 1 & 1 & 1 \\ 2 & 2 & 1 \end{bmatrix}$$

Sol. Let x, y, z be price of ingredients A, B, C the above data can be written as

$$\begin{bmatrix} 2 & 1 & 1 \\ 1 & 1 & 1 \\ 2 & 2 & 1 \end{bmatrix}\begin{bmatrix} x \\ y \\ z \end{bmatrix} = \begin{bmatrix} 500 \\ 400 \\ 300 \end{bmatrix}$$

$2x + y + z = 500$
$x + y + z = 400$
$2x + 2y + z = 300$

the above equations can be solved by using Crammers Rule

$$A = \begin{bmatrix} 2 & 1 & 1 \\ 1 & 1 & 1 \\ 2 & 2 & 1 \end{bmatrix} \qquad B = \begin{bmatrix} 500 \\ 400 \\ 600 \end{bmatrix}$$

$$\Delta = |A| = \begin{bmatrix} 2 & 1 & 1 \\ 1 & 1 & 1 \\ 2 & 2 & 1 \end{bmatrix}$$

$= 2(1 - 2) - 1(1 - 2) + 1(2 - 2)$
$= 2(-1) - (-1) + 0 = -2 + 1 = -1$

$$\Delta_x = \begin{vmatrix} 500 & 1 & 1 \\ 400 & 2 & 1 \\ 600 & 1 & 1 \end{vmatrix}$$

$= 500(2-1) - 400(1-1) + 600(1-2)$
$= -500 + 0 - 600 = -1100$

$$\Delta_y = \begin{vmatrix} 2 & 500 & 1 \\ 1 & 400 & 1 \\ 2 & 600 & 1 \end{vmatrix}$$

$= -500(1-2) + 400(2-2) - 600(2-1)$
$= 500 + 0 - 600 = -100$

$$\Delta_z = \begin{vmatrix} 2 & 1 & 500 \\ 1 & 1 & 400 \\ 2 & 2 & 600 \end{vmatrix}$$

$= 2(-200) - 1(-200) + 500(2-2)$
$= -400 + 200 = -200$

$$x = \frac{\Delta x}{\Delta} = 100, y = \frac{\Delta y}{\Delta} = \frac{-100}{2} = 100, z = \frac{\Delta_z}{2} = \frac{-200}{-1} = 200$$

3. The stability of pharmaceutical formulation obtained by 2 × 2 factorial design is as listed below. Calculate coefficient of each factor by applying matrix method and form a polynomial or linear or regression equation.

Levels	Factor	Low	High
1	Concentration	2 gms	4 gms
2	Temperature	4°C	8°C

Combination	**x_1**	**x_2**	**y(Stability)**
1	2	4	5
a	4	4	10
b	2	8	8
Ab	4	8	6

Sol. The four combinations can be written in the form of matrix as

$$x = \begin{pmatrix} 1 & 2 & 4 \\ 1 & 4 & 4 \\ 1 & 2 & 8 \\ 1 & 4 & 8 \end{pmatrix} \qquad B = \begin{pmatrix} b \\ b_1 \\ b_2 \\ b_3 \end{pmatrix} \qquad y = \begin{pmatrix} 5 \\ 10 \\ 8 \\ 6 \end{pmatrix}$$

$$\text{now } x^T = \begin{pmatrix} 1 & 1 & 1 & 1 \\ 2 & 4 & 2 & 4 \\ 4 & 4 & 8 & 8 \end{pmatrix}$$

$$\text{now } x^Tx = \begin{pmatrix} 1 & 1 & 1 & 1 \\ 2 & 4 & 2 & 4 \\ 4 & 4 & 8 & 8 \end{pmatrix}\begin{pmatrix} 1 & 2 & 4 \\ 1 & 4 & 4 \\ 1 & 2 & 8 \\ 1 & 4 & 8 \end{pmatrix}$$

$$= \begin{pmatrix} 4 & 2+4+2+4 & 4+4+8+8 \\ 2+4+2+4 & 4+16+4+16 & 8+16+16+32 \\ 4+4+8+8 & 8+16+16+32 & 16+16+64+64 \end{pmatrix}$$

$$= \begin{pmatrix} 4 & 12 & 24 \\ 12 & 40 & 72 \\ 24 & 72 & 160 \end{pmatrix} = P \quad \text{say}$$

$$\text{Cofactor (P)} = \begin{pmatrix} +(1256) & -(192) & +(-96) \\ -(192) & +(64) & -(0) \\ +(-96) & -(0) & +(16) \end{pmatrix}$$

$$\text{Adj } P = \begin{pmatrix} 1256 & -192 & -96 \\ -192 & 64 & 0 \\ -96 & 0 & 16 \end{pmatrix}$$

$$|P| = \begin{vmatrix} 4 & 12 & 24 \\ 12 & 40 & 72 \\ 24 & 72 & 160 \end{vmatrix}$$

$$= 4(1256) - 12(-192) + 24(-96)$$
$$= 5024 + 2304 - 2304$$
$$= 5024$$

$$P^{-1} = \frac{\text{Adj}P}{|P|} = \frac{1}{5024}\begin{pmatrix} 1256 & -192 & -96 \\ -192 & 64 & 0 \\ -96 & 0 & 16 \end{pmatrix}$$

$$\text{again } x^T y = \begin{pmatrix} 1 & 1 & 1 & 1 \\ 2 & 4 & 2 & 4 \\ 4 & 4 & 8 & 8 \end{pmatrix}\begin{pmatrix} 5 \\ 10 \\ 8 \\ 6 \end{pmatrix}$$

$$= \begin{pmatrix} 5+10+8+6 \\ 10+40+16+24 \\ 20+40+64+48 \end{pmatrix} = \begin{pmatrix} 29 \\ 88 \\ 172 \end{pmatrix}$$

$\therefore$ least square estimate of β is

$$\begin{pmatrix} b \\ b_1 \\ b_2 \\ b_3 \end{pmatrix} = P^{-1}x^T y$$

$$= \frac{1}{5024}\begin{pmatrix} 1256 & -192 & -96 \\ -192 & 64 & 0 \\ -96 & 0 & 16 \end{pmatrix}\begin{pmatrix} 29 \\ 88 \\ 172 \end{pmatrix}$$

$$= \begin{pmatrix} 0.25 & -0.038 & -0.019 \\ -0.038 & 0.0127 & 0 \\ -0.019 & 0 & 0.003 \end{pmatrix}\begin{pmatrix} 19 \\ 88 \\ 172 \end{pmatrix}$$

$$= \begin{pmatrix} -1.862 \\ 0.3956 \\ 4.799 \end{pmatrix}$$

the least square fit is

$\therefore y = -1.862 + 0.3956\, x_1 + 4.799 x_2$

4

Binomial Theorem

4.1 Factorial Notation

It n is a positive integer, we define n! (read as n factorial) as

$$n! = (n)(n-1)(n-2) \quad .....3 \,.\, 2 \,.\, 1$$

for example $1! = 1$, $2! = 2 \,.\, 1 = 2$, $3! = 3 \,.\, 2 \,.\, 1 = 6$

$4! = 4 \,.\, 3 \,.\, 2 \,.\, 1 = 24$, $5! = 5 \,.\, 4 \,.\, 3 \,.\, 2 \,.\, 1 = 120$ etc

by convention we define $0! = 1$

We can observe that $n! = n(n-1)!$

Note : Throughout this chapter the letters n, r denote the non negative integers.

4.2 n_{c_r}

Suppose n and r are non negative integers such that $n \geq r$ then n_{cr} is defined as

$$n_{c_r} = \frac{n!}{r!(n-r)!}$$

Ex: 1. $$5_{c_2} = \frac{5!}{2!(5-2)!} = \frac{5!}{2!3!} = \frac{5\times4\times3\times2\times1}{(2\times1)(3\times2\times1)} = \frac{20}{2} = 10$$

2. $$6_{c_3} = \frac{6!}{3!(6-3)!} = \frac{6!}{3!\,3!} = \frac{6.5.4.3.2.1}{3.2.1.3.2.1} = \frac{120}{6} = 20$$

4.3 Binomial Theorem

Let n be a positive integer and x, y be real numbers then

$$(x+y)^n = n_{c_0}\, x^n y^0 + n_{c_1}\, x^{n-1} y^1 + n_{c_2}\, x^{n-2} y^2 + \ldots + n_{c_r}\, x^{n-1} y^r + \ldots + n_{c_n}\, x^0 . y^n$$

Note : 1 $n_{c_0}, n_{c_1}, n_{c_2} \ldots n_{c_n}$ are called binomial coefficients

Note : 2 $(x+y)^n = \sum_{r=0}^{n} n_{c_r}\, x^{n-r} . y^r$

Note : 3 $(x+y)^n$ = contains $(n+1)$ terms

Note : 4 $(r+1)^{th}$ term in the expansion is called general term of the expansion

$\therefore \quad T_{r+1} = n_{cr}\, x^{n-r} y^r \qquad$ for $0 \le r \le n$

on replacing y by $-y$ in the expansion of $(x+y)^n$ given in Note : 3 we get

$$(x-y)^n = n_{c_o}\, x^n (-y)^0 + n_{c_1}\, x^{n-1} (-y)^1 + n_{c_2}\, x^{n-2} (-y)^2 + \ldots + n_{cr}\, x^{n-r} (-y)^r + \ldots + n_{c_n}\, x^0 (-y)^n$$

$$= n_{c_o}\, x^n y^0 - n_{c_1}\, x^{n-1} y + n_{c_2}\, x^{n-2} (y)^2 \ldots + (-1)^r . n_{cr}\, x^{n-r} y^r + \ldots + (-1)^n . n_{c_n}\, x^0 y^n$$

Solved Examples

1. Write the expansion of $\left(x+\frac{1}{x}\right)^6$

Sol. We have $(x+y)^n = n_{co}\, x^n y^0 + n_{c1}\, x^{n-1} y^1 + n_{c2}\, x^{n-2} y^2 + \ldots + n_{cr}\, x^{n-r} y^r + \ldots + n_{cn}\, x^0 y^n$

$\therefore$ in $\left(x+\frac{1}{x}\right)^6$ 'x' $= x$, $y = \frac{1}{x}$, $n = 6$

$$\therefore \left(x+\frac{1}{x}\right)^6 = 6_{c0}\, x^6 \left(\frac{1}{x}\right)^o + 6_{c1}\, x^5 \left(\frac{1}{x}\right)^1 + 6_{c2}\, x^4 \left(\frac{1}{x}\right)^2 + 6_{c3}\, x^3 \left(\frac{1}{x}\right)^3 + 6_{c_4}\, x^2 \left(\frac{1}{x}\right)^4 + 6_{c_5}\, x^1 \left(\frac{1}{x}\right)^5 + 6_{c_6}\, x^0 \left(\frac{1}{x}\right)^6$$

$$\Rightarrow \left(x+\frac{1}{x}\right)^6 = 6_{c_0}\, x^6 + 6_{c_1}\, x^4 + 6_{c_2}\, x^2 + 6_{c_3} + 6_{c_4} \frac{1}{x^2} + 6_{c_5} \frac{1}{x^4} + 6_{c_6} \frac{1}{x^6}$$

$$= x^6 + 6x^4 + 15x^2 + 20 + \frac{15}{x^2} + \frac{6}{x^4} + \frac{1}{x^6}$$

2. Write the expansion of $(3x - 4y)^7$

Sol. Here 'x' = $3x$, 'y' = $4y$, $n = 7$

$$\therefore \quad (x - y)^n = n_{c_0}\, x^7 - n_{c_1} \cdot x^6 \cdot y^1 + n_{c_2}\, x^5\, y^2 \ldots + (-1)^n \cdot n_{c_n} \cdot x^0\, y^n$$

$$\therefore \quad (3x - 4y)^7 = 7_{c_0}\,(3x)^7\,(4y)^0 - 7_{c_1}\,(3x)^6\,(4y)^1 + 7_{c_2}(3x)^5\,(4y)^2$$
$$- 7_{c_3}(3x)^4\,(4y)^3 + 7_{c_4}(3x)^3\,(4y)^4 - 7_{c_5}(3x)^2\,(4y)^5$$
$$+ 7_{c_6}\,(3x)^1\,(4y)^6 - 7_{c_7}\,(3x)^0\,(4y)^7$$

3. Write the fifth term in the expansion of $(2a + 3b)^6$

given binomial expressions is $(2a + 3b)^6$.

Sol. We know that T_{r+1} in $(x + y)^n$ is $n_{c_r} . x^{n-r} . y^r$

$$\therefore \quad T_{r+1} \text{ in } (2a + 3b)^6 \text{ is } 6_{cr}\,(2a)^{6-r}\,(3b)^r$$

To get 5th term take $r = 4$

$$\therefore \quad T_5 = 6_{c_4}\,(2a)^{6-4}\,(3b)^4$$
$$= 6_{c_4}\,(2a)^2\,(3b)^4$$
$$= 15 \times 4 \times a^2 \times 81 \times b^4$$
$$= 4860\, a^2\, b^4$$

4. Find the 5th term from the end of the expansion of $(2a + 5b)^8$.

Sol. Given, $(2a + 5b)^8$

The fifth term from the end of the expansion of $(2a + 5b)^8$ is the fifth term from the begining of the expanbsion of $(5b + 2a)^8$

$$\therefore \quad T_5 = T_{4+1} = 8_{c_4}\,(5b)^{8-4} \,.\, (2a)^4$$
$$= 8_{c_4}\,(5b)^4 \,.\, (2a)^4$$
$$= 8_{c_4}\; 5^4 \,.\, 2^4 \,.\, (ab)^4$$

5. Write the number of terms in the expansion of $(a + b + c)^n$.

Sol. $(a + b + c)^n = (a + (b + c))^n = \sum_{r=0}^{n} n_{cr}\, a^{n-r}\,(b + c)^r$

Now for $0 < r < n$, the expansion of $(b + c)^r$ contains $r + 1$ terms. Hence the number of terms in the expansion of $(a + b + c)^n$ is

$$\sum_{r=0}^{n} (r + 1) = \frac{(n+1)(n+2)}{2}$$

$$\therefore \text{ The number of terms} = \frac{(n+1)(n+2)}{2}$$

4.4 Middle Term(s) of Binomial Expansion

(i) If n is even then the expansion of $(x + y)^n$ has (n + 1) number (odd number of terms) hence there is only one middle form which is is $\left(\frac{n}{2}+1\right)$ th term and is given by

$$T_{\frac{n}{2}+1} = n_{c_{n/2}} x^{n/2} . y^{n/2}$$

(ii) If n is odd, then the expansion of $(x + y)^n$ has (n + 1) (even) number of terms. In this case there are two middle terms. They are $\left(\frac{n+1}{2}\right)$ th and $\left(\frac{n+1}{2}+1\right)$ th, terms. These terms are given by

$$T_{\frac{n+1}{2}} = n_{c_{\frac{n-1}{2}}} x^{\frac{n+1}{2}} . y^{\frac{n-1}{2}} \text{ and}$$

$$T_{\frac{n+3}{2}} = n_{c_{\frac{n+1}{2}}} x^{\frac{n-1}{2}} . y^{\frac{n+1}{2}}$$

Solved Examples

1. Find the middle term (s) in the expansion of $(4x^2 + 5x^3)^{18}$

Sol. Given, $(4x^2 + 5x^3)^{18}$

here n = 18 is even

∴ the number of terms in the expansion is 19 (odd)

∴ there will be one middle term that is

$T_{\frac{n}{2}+1}$ th term i.e., $T_{\frac{18}{2}+1}$ th term i.e. T_{9+1} th term

$$\therefore \quad T_{10} = T_{9+1} = 18_{c_9} . (4x^2)^{18-9} (5x^3)^9$$

$$= 18_{c_9} . 4^9 . (x^2)^9 (5x^3)^9$$

$$= 18_{c_9} . 4^9 . 5^9 . x^{18} . x^{27}$$

$$= 18_{c_9} . (20)^9 . x^{18} . x^{29}$$

2. Find the middle terms(s) of the expansion of $\left(\frac{3x}{7}-2y\right)^{11}$

Sol. Given, $\left(\frac{3x}{7}-2y\right)^{11}$

Here n = 11 (odd)

$\therefore$ the expansion contains n + 1 = 12 terms (even)

$\therefore$ There exists two middle terms

They are $T_{\frac{n+1}{2}}, T_{\frac{n+3}{2}}$, i.e., $T_{\frac{11+1}{2}}, T_{\frac{11+3}{2}}$ i.e., T_6, T_7 th

$$\therefore \quad T_6 = T_{5+1} = 11_{c5}\left(\frac{3x}{7}\right)^{11-5}(-2y)^5$$

$$= 11_{c_5}\cdot\left(\frac{3}{7}\right)^6 x^6(-2)^5 . y^5$$

$$= -11_{c_5}\cdot\frac{3^6}{7^6}.2^5 . x^6 . y^5$$

and $$T_7 = T_{6+1} = 11_{c6}\left(\frac{3x}{7}\right)^{11-6}.(-2y)^6$$

$$= 11_{c_6}\cdot\left(\frac{3}{7}\right)^5 . x^5 . (-2)^6 . y^6$$

$$= 11_{c_6}\cdot\left(\frac{3}{7}\right)^5 . 2^6 . x^5 . y^6$$

$\therefore$ the two middle terms are

$$-11_{c_5}\frac{3^6 . 2^5}{7^6}. x^6 . y^5, 11_{c6}\cdot\left(\frac{3}{7}\right)^5 . 2^6 . x^5 . y^6$$

4.5 Finding the Term Independent of x or term contains x^m

To get the term independent of *x* in given expansion, follow two steps

Step 1 : Write the general term i.e., T_{r+1} of given binomial expansion

Step 2 : Equalte its power of x to zero and find r if r is a positive integer less than n then it will be exists other wise it will not not exists.

Similarly to get the term which contains x^m, write general term T_{r+1} and equate power of x to m and then find r, through this r, write T_m, it contains the term x^m.

Note : If r is negative or fraction or more than n then we say that type of term does not exists in the expansion.

Solved Problems

1. Find the term independent of x in the expansion of $\left(\frac{3}{\sqrt[3]{x}}+5\sqrt{x}\right)^{25}$

Sol. Given $\left(\frac{3}{\sqrt[3]{x}}+5\sqrt{x}\right)^{25}$, here n = 25

now general tern $T_{r+1} = 25_{c_r}\left(\frac{3}{\sqrt[3]{x}}\right)^{25-r}\left(5\sqrt{x}\right)^r$

$$= 25_{c_r}\cdot\frac{3^{25-r}}{(x)^{\frac{25-r}{3}}}.5^r.x^{r/2}$$

$$= 25_{c_r}.3^{25-r}.5^r.x^{\left(\frac{r}{2}\right)-\left(\frac{25-r}{3}\right)} \quad .....(i)$$

to get the independent of x, take

$$\frac{r}{2}-\left(\frac{25-r}{3}\right)=0 \Rightarrow \frac{3r-50+2r}{6}=0$$

$$\Rightarrow 5r = 50$$

$$\Rightarrow r = 10$$

$\therefore$ the term indepent of x is T_{10+1} and it is equal to

$$T_{10+1} = 25_{c_{10}}.3^{25-10}.5^{10}.x^0 \quad \text{by (i)}$$

$$= 25_{c_{10}}.3^{15}.5^{10}$$

2. Find the coefficnets of x^9 and x^{10} in the expansion $\left(2x^2-\frac{1}{x}\right)^{20}$

Sol. Given, $\left(2x^2-\frac{1}{x}\right)^{20}$

Here $n = 20$, take $x = 2x^2, y = \frac{-1}{x}$

$\therefore$ general term $T_{r+1} = 20_{c_r} x^{20-r} y^r$

$$= 20_{c_r} (2x^2)^{20-r} . \left(\frac{-1}{x}\right)^r$$

$$= 20_{c_r} . (2)^{20-r} . \left(\frac{-1}{x}\right)^r . x^{2(20-r)}$$

$$= (-1)^r . 20_{c_r} . (2)^{20-r} . x^{2(20-r)} . (x)^{-r}$$

$$= (-1)^r . 20_{c_r} . (2)^{20-r} . x^{40-2r} . x^{-r}$$

$$= (-1)^r . 20_{c_r} . (2)^{20-r} . x^{40-3r} \quad .....(i)$$

to get x^9th coefficent take $40 - 3r = 9$

$\Rightarrow \quad 3r = 31$

$r = \frac{31}{3}$ is fractional

$\therefore$ the term contain x^9 in the expansion does not exists

again, to get x^{10} th coefficient take $40 - 3r = 10$

$\Rightarrow \quad 3r = 30$

$r = 10$

$\therefore \quad T_{10+1} = (-1)^{10} . 20_{c_{10}} . 2^{20-10} . x^{10} \quad (\because$ by (i))

$$= 20_{c_{10}} . 2^{10} . x^{10}$$

$\therefore$ coefficient of x^{10} is $20_{c_{10}} . 2^{10}$

Results

1. if $n_{c_r} = n_{c_s} \Rightarrow n = r + s$ or $r = s$

2. $\frac{n_{c_r}}{n_{c_{r-1}}} = \frac{n - r + 1}{r}$

3. $n_{c_r} + n_{c_{r-1}} = (n + 1)_{c_r}$

3. If the coefficients of (2r + 4) th and (r – 2) th terms in the expansion of $(1+x)^{18}$ are equal. Find r.

Sol. Given, $(1+x)^{18}$

$$T_{2r+4} = T_{(2r+3)+1} = 18_{c_{(2r+3)}} (1)^{18-(2r+3)} \cdot x^{(2r+3)}$$
$$= 18_{c_{2r+3}} \, x^{2r+3}$$

$\therefore$ coefficient of $T_{2r+4} = 18_{c_{2r+3}}$

Similarly coefficient of T_{r-2} is $18_{c_{r-3}}$

given that these two coefficients are equal

$\therefore \quad 18_{c_{(2r+3)}} = 18_{c_{(r-3)}} \qquad (\because n_{c_r} = n_{c_s} \Rightarrow r = s \text{ or } n = r + s)$

$\Rightarrow \quad 2r + 3 = r - 3$ or

$18 = (2r + 3) + (r - 3)$

$\Rightarrow \quad r = 6$

4. If the coefficients of rth, (r + 1)th and (r + 2) th terms in the expansion of $(1+x)^n$ are in A.P., then show that $n^2 - (4r+1)n - 4r^2 - 2 = 0$.

Sol. We have $(1+x)^n = n_{c_0}(1)^n x^0 + n_{c_1}(1)^{n-1} x^1 = n_{c_2}(1)^{n-2} x^2 + \ldots$

$+ n_{c_r} (1)^{n-r} x^r + \ldots + n_{c_n} x^n$

$= n_{c_0} + n_{c_1} x + n_{c_2} x^2 + n_{c_3} x^3 + \ldots + n_{c_r} x^r + \ldots + n_{c_n} x^n$

$\therefore \quad T_r = T_{(r-1)+1} = n_{c_{r-1}} x^{r-1}$

$T_{r+1} = T_{r+1} = n_{c_r} x^r$

$T_{r+2} = T_{(r+1)+1} = n_{c_{r+1}} x^{r+1}$

$\therefore$ coefficients of T_r, T_{r+1}, T_{r+2} are $n_{c_{r-1}}, n_{c_r}, n_{c_{r+1}}$

Given these are in A.P

$\therefore \quad 2 \cdot n_{c_r} = n_{c_{r-1}} + n_{c_{r+1}}$

$$\Rightarrow \quad 2 \cdot \frac{n!}{r!(n-r)!} = \frac{n!}{(r-1)!(n-r+1)!} + \frac{n!}{(r+1)!(n-r-1)!}$$

$$\Rightarrow \quad \frac{2}{r(n-r)} = \frac{1}{(n-r+1)(n-r)} + \frac{1}{(r+1)r}$$

$$\Rightarrow \quad \frac{2}{r(n-r)} - \frac{1}{(n-r+1)(n-r)} = \frac{1}{r(r+1)}$$

$$\Rightarrow \quad \frac{1}{n-r}\left[\frac{2}{r}-\frac{1}{n-r+1}\right]=\frac{1}{r(r+1)}$$

$$\Rightarrow \quad \frac{1}{n-r}\left[\frac{2n-2r+2-r}{r(n-r+1)}\right]=\frac{1}{r(r+1)}$$

$$\Rightarrow \quad \frac{(2n-3r+2)}{(n-r)(n-r+1)}=\frac{1}{(r+1)}$$

$$\Rightarrow \quad (2n-3r+2)(r+1)=(n-r)(n-r+1)$$

$$\Rightarrow \quad 2nr+2n-3r^2-3r+2r+2=(n-r)^2+(n-r)$$

$$\Rightarrow \quad 2nr+2n-3r^2-3r+2r+2=n^2+r^2-2nr+n-r$$

$$\Rightarrow \quad 2nr+2n-3r^2-r+2=n^2+r^2-2nr+n-r$$

$$\Rightarrow \quad n^2-4nr-n+4r^2-2=0$$

$$\Rightarrow \quad n^2-(4r+1)n+4r^2-2=0$$

5. **Using bionomial theorem prove that $50^n - 49n - 1$ is divisible by 49^2 for all positive integers n.**

Sol. Given, $(50)^n - 49n - 1$

$= (1+49)^n - 49n - 1$

$= n_{c_0} + n_{c_1}(49) + n_{c_2}(49)^2 + ... + n_{c_n} - 49n - 1$

$= 1 + 49n + (49)^2 . n_{c_2} + ... + n_{c_n} . (49)^n - (49)n - 1$

$= n_{c_2} . (49)^2 + ... + n_{c_n} . (49)^n$

$= (49)^2 \{n_{c_2} + ... n_{c_n} (49)^{n-2}\}$

$= (49)^2 \times$ (some integer)

$\therefore$ which is divisible by $(49)^2$

$50^n - 49n - 1$ is divisible by $(49)^2$

6. **If $(1+x+x^2)^n = a_0 + a_1 x + a_2 x^2 + ... + a_{2n} x^{2n}$ then prove that**

(i) $a_0 + a_1 + a_2 + ... + a_{2n} = 3^n$

(ii) $a_0 + a_2 + a_4 + ... + a_{2n} = \frac{3^n+1}{2}$

(iii) $a_1 + a_3 + a_5 + ... + a_{2n-1} = \frac{3^n-1}{2}$

Sol. Given $(1+x+x^2)^n = a_0 + a_1 x + a_2 x^2 + \dots + a_{2n} \cdot x^{2n}$ ..... (1)

(i) Put $x = 1$ in (i) we get

$$(1+1+1)^n = a_0 + a_1(1) + a_2(1)^2 + \dots + a_{2n} \quad \text{..... (2)}$$

$$3^n = a_0 + a_1 + a_2 + \dots + a_{2n}$$

(ii) Put $x = -1$ in (i) we get

$$(1-1+1)^n = a_0 - a_1 + a_2 \dots + a_{2n}$$

$$\Rightarrow \quad a_0 - a_1 + a_2 + \dots + a_{2n} = 1^n = 1 \quad \text{..... (3)}$$

$$(2)+(3) \Rightarrow \quad 2[a_0 + a_2 + \dots a_{2n}] = 3^n + 1$$

$$\Rightarrow \quad a_0 + a_2 + \dots a_{2n} = \frac{3^n + 1}{2}$$

(iii) $(2)-(3) \Rightarrow 2a_1 + 2a_3 + \dots 2a_{n-1} = 3^n - 1$

$$2(a_1 + a_3 + \dots + a_{2n-1}) = 3^n - 1$$

$$a_1 + a_3 + \dots + a_{2n-1} = \frac{3^n - 1}{2}$$

7. If 22_{c_r} is largest binomial coefficient in the expansion of $(1+x)^{22}$, find the value of 13_{cr}..

Sol. Here n = 22 is an even integer, therefore there is only one largest binomial coefficient and it is $n_{c_{(n/2)}} = 22_{c_{11}} = 22_{c_r}$ (given)

$$\Rightarrow \quad r = 11$$

Now $\quad 13_{cr} = 13_{c11} = 13_{c2} = \dfrac{13 \times 12}{1 \times 2} = 78$

[binomial coefficient of middle term is the largest binomial coefficient in the expansion]

4.6 Numarically Greatest Term in the Expansion of (1 + x)^n

To get the numarically greatest term in the expansion of $(1+x)^n$ follow the below steps.

Step 1 : Find $\dfrac{(n+1)|x|}{1+|x|}$ for given x.

(Suppose given problem is in the form $(x+y)^n$ convert it in to $x^n(1+X)^n$ by taking x as common where $X = y/x$).

Step 2 : Let $P = \dfrac{(n+1)|x|}{1+|x|}$, if p is an integer then T_p, T_{p+1} are two numarically greatest terms. If p is not an integer then $T_{[p]+1}$ is the numarically greatest term in the expansion. Where [P] is integral part of P. For example p = 7.3 then [P] = 7 and if P = 8.7 then [P] = 8 etc.

Solved Examples

1. Find the numarically greatest term (s) in the expansion of $(3x + 5y)^{12}$ when $x = 1/2, y = 4/3$

Sol. Given $(3x + 5y)^{12} = (3x)^{12}\left[1+\frac{5y}{3x}\right]^{12}$

Take $X = \frac{5y}{3x}$, at $x = 1/2, y = 4/3$

$$x = \frac{5.(4/3)}{3.(1/2)} = \frac{20}{3}\times\frac{2}{3} = \frac{40}{9}$$

Now $$\frac{(n+1)|X|}{1+|X|} = \frac{(13)\left(\frac{40}{9}\right)}{1+\frac{40}{9}} = \frac{13\times 40}{49} = \frac{520}{49} = 10.6.$$

∴ P = 10.6 is not as integer

∴ there exists only one numerically greatest term that is $T_{[p]+1} = T_{10+1} = T_{11}$.

∴ $T_{11} = T_{10+1} = 12_{c_{10}} . (3x)^{12-10} . (5y)^{10}$

$= 12_{c_{10}} . (3 . 1/2)^2 . (5 . 4/3)^{10}$

$= 12_{c_{10}} . (3/2)^2 . \left(\frac{20}{3}\right)^{10}$

2. Find the numarically greatest term (s) in the expansion of $(4a - 6b)^{13}$ when a = 3, b = 5.

Sol. Given expansion is $(4a - 6b)^{13}$

$$= (4a)^{13}\left[1-\frac{6b}{4a}\right]^{13}$$

take $$X = \frac{6b}{4a} = \frac{3b}{2a} = \frac{3}{2}\cdot\frac{5}{3} = \frac{15}{6}$$

now $$\frac{(n+1)|X|}{1+|X|} = \frac{14.\,^{15}\!/_{6}}{1+\,^{15}\!/_{6}} = \frac{14\times 15}{6+15} = \frac{14\times 15}{21} = 10$$

$\therefore$ $$p = \frac{(n+1)|X|}{1+|X|} = 10 \text{ is an integer}$$

$\therefore$ There exists two numarically greatest form for $(4a - 6b)^{13}$ they are T_p, T_{p+1}

$$T_p = T_{10} = T_{9+1} = 13_{c_9} \cdot (4a)^{13-9} \cdot (-6b)^9$$
$$= 13_{c_9} \cdot (4 \,.\, 3)^4 \cdot (6 \,.\, 5)^9$$
$$= -13_{c_9} \cdot (4 \,.\, 3)^4 \cdot (6 \,.\, 5)^9$$
$$= -13_{c_9} \cdot (12)^4 \cdot (30)^9$$
$$T_{p+1} = T_{10+1} = 13_{c_{10}} \cdot (4a)^{13-10} \cdot (-6b)^{10}$$
$$= -13_{c_{10}} \cdot (12)^3 \cdot (30)^{10}$$

Exercise 4.1

1. Expand the following using binomial theorem

(i) $\left(\frac{2}{3}x + \frac{7}{4}y\right)^5$ (ii) $\left(\frac{2p}{5} - \frac{3q}{7}\right)^6$

2. Write down and simplify

(i) 3rd term in the expansion of $(3 - 4x)^6$

(ii) 6th term in the expansion of $\left(\frac{2x}{3} + \frac{3y}{2}\right)^9$

(iii) rth term in the expansion is $\left(\frac{3a}{5} + \frac{5b}{7}\right)^8$ $1 \le r \le 9$

3. Find the number of terms in the expansion of

(i) $(x + 3y)^7$ (ii) $\left(x^2 + \frac{4}{x^3}\right)^{10}$

(iii) $((x + y)(x - y))^{15}$ (iv) $(x + 2y + 3z)^7$

4. Find the coefficient of

(i) x^{-8} in $\left(2x^4 - \frac{1}{3x^2}\right)^5$ (ii) x^3 in $\left(\sqrt{x^5} - \frac{3}{\sqrt{x^3}}\right)^6$

(iii) x^2 in $\left(7x^3 - \frac{2}{x^2}\right)^9$ (iv) x^{-7} in $\left(\frac{2x}{3} - \frac{5}{4x^5}\right)^7$

5. Find the term independent of x in the expansion of

(i) $\left(4x^3 + \frac{7}{x^2}\right)^{14}$ (ii) $\left(\frac{\sqrt{x}}{3} - \frac{4}{x^2}\right)^{10}$

(iii) $\left(\frac{\sqrt{x}}{3} - \frac{4}{x\sqrt{x}}\right)^{11}$

6. Find the middle term (s) in the expansion of

(i) $(3a - 5b)^6$ (ii) $(2x + 3y)^7$

(iii) $\left(4a + \frac{3}{2}b\right)^{11}$ (iv) $\left(\frac{3}{a^3} + 5a^4\right)^{20}$

7. Show that the middle term in the expansion of $(1 + x)^{2n}$ is $\frac{1.3.5....(2n-1)}{n!}(2x)^n$

8. Using binomial theorem prove that $5^{4n} + 52n - 1$ is divisible by 676 for all positive integers n.

9. If n is posivite integer then prove that $81^n + 20n - 1$ is divisible by 100.

10. If the coefficients of $(2r + 4)$ th term and $(3r + 4)$ th term in the expansion of $(1 + x)^{21}$ are equal, find r.

11. If the coefficients of 4 consecutive terms in the expansion of $(1 + x)^n$ are a_1, a_2, a_3, a_4 respectively show that

$$\frac{a_1}{a_1 + a_2} + \frac{a_3}{a_3 + a_4} = \frac{2a_2}{a_2 + a_3}$$

12. If $(1 + 3x - 2x^2)^{10} = a_0 + a_1 x + a_2 x^2 + \ldots + a_{20} x^{20}$ then prove that

(i) $a_0 + a_1 + a_2 + \ldots + a_{20} = 2^{10}$ (ii) $a_0 - a_1 + a_2 + \ldots + a_{20} = 4^{10}$

Answers

1. (i) $5_{c_0}\left(\frac{2}{3}x\right)^5\left(\frac{7}{4}y\right)^0 + 5_{c_1}\left(\frac{2}{3}x\right)^4\left(\frac{7}{4}y\right)^1 + \ldots + 5_{c_5}\left(\frac{2}{3}x\right)^0\left(\frac{7}{4}y\right)^5$

(ii) $6_{c_0}\left(\frac{2p}{5}\right)^6\left(\frac{3q}{7}\right)^0 - 6_{c_1}\left(\frac{2p}{5}\right)^5\left(\frac{3q}{7}\right)^1 + \ldots + 6_{c_6}\left(\frac{2p}{5}\right)^0\left(\frac{3q}{7}\right)^6$

2. (i) $19440\,x^2$ (ii) $189\,x^4\,y^5$ (iii) $8_{c_{r-1}}\left(\frac{3a}{5}\right)^{9-r}\cdot\left(\frac{5b}{7}\right)^{r-1}$

3. (i) 8 (ii) 11 (iii) 16 (iv) 36

4. (i) 0 (ii) 540 (iii) $-126 \,.\, 7^4 \,.\, 2^5$ (iv) $\frac{-4375}{324}$

5. (i) 0 (ii) $T_3 = \frac{80}{729}$ (iii) $T_4 = -12_{c3}\cdot\frac{4^3}{3^9} = \frac{-14080}{19683}$

6. (i) $T_4 = -6_{c_3}\; 3^3.5^3.a^3.b^3$

(ii) $T_4 = 7_{c_3}.2^4.3^3.x^4.y^3$ and $T_5 = 7_{c_4}\, 2^3.3^4\, x^3\, y^4$

(iii) $T_6 = 77 \times 2^8 \times 3^6 \times a^6\, b^5$ and $T_7 = 77 \times 2^5 \times 3^7 \times a^5\, b^6$

(iv) $T_{11} = 20_{c10}\, (15)^{10}\, a^{10}$

10. 0, 3

4.7 Properties of Binomial Coefficients

We know that $(1 + x)^n = n_{c_0} + n_{c_1} x + n_{c_2} x^2 + \ldots + n_{c_r} x^r + \ldots + n_{c_n} x^n$ where $n_{c_0}, n_{c_1}, n_{c_2} \ldots n_{c_r} \ldots n_{c_n}$ are called binomial coeffcient of the expansion of $(1 + x)^n$. Simply these are denoted by $c_0, c_1, c_2 \ldots\ldots\ldots c_r, \ldots\ldots\ldots c_n$

i.e., $c_r = n_{c_r}$ for $0 \le r \le n$

also this expansion $(1 + x)^n = c_0 + c_1 x + c_2 x^2 + \ldots c_2 x^2 + \ldots + c_r x^r + \ldots c_n x^n$ is called standard binomial expansion.

Theorem 1 : With the standard notation, if n is a positive integer then

(i) $c_0 + c_1 + c_2 + ... + c_n = 2^n$

(ii) $c_0 - c_1 + c_2 + ... + (-1)^n c_n = 0$

(iii) $c_0 + c_2 + c_4 + ... = 2^{n-1}$

(iv) $c_1 + c_3 + c_5 + ... = 2^{n-1}$

Proof : We have $(1 + x)^n = c_0 + c_1 x + c_2 x^2 + c_3 x^3 + ... + c_r x^r + ... + c_n x^n$ ..... (1)

(i) Put $x = 1$ in (1) we get

$$(1 + 1)^n = c_0 + c_1 + c_2 + ... + c_n$$

$$c_0 + c_1 + c_2 + ... + c_n = 2^n \quad ..... (2)$$

(ii) Put $x = -1$ in (1) we get

$$(1 - 1)^n = c_0 - c_1 + c_2 + ... + (-1)^n c_n$$

$$c_0 - c_1 + c_2 ... + (-1)^n c_n = 0 \quad ..... (3)$$

(iii) $(2) + (3) \Rightarrow 2[c_0 + c_2 + c_4 + ...] = 2^n + 0$

$$c_0 + c_2 + c_4 ... = \frac{2^n}{2} = 2^{n-1}$$

(iv) $(2) - (3) \Rightarrow 2[c_1 + c_3 + c_5 + ...] = 2^n - 0$

$$c_1 + c_3 + c_5 ... = \frac{2^n}{2} = 2^{n-1}$$

Theorem 2 : Prove that for any real numbers a, d; $ac_0 + (a + d) c_1 + (a + 2d) c_2 + ... + (a + nd) c_n = (2a + nd) 2^{n-1}$

Proof : Let $S = a c_0 + (a + d) c_1 + (a + 2d) c_2 + ... + (a + (n-1)d) c_{n-1} + (a + nd) c_n$ .... (1)

$$S = (a + nd) c_n + (a + (n-1)d) c_{n-1} + ... + a c_0$$

(Writing from last to first)

$$= (a + nd) c_0 + (a + (n-1)d) c_1 + ... + a c_n \quad ..... (2)$$

$(\because n_{c_r} = n_{c_{n-r}})$

$\therefore$ $(1) + (2) \Rightarrow S + S = [a + (a + nd)] c_0 + [(a + d) + (a + (n-1)d)] c_1$

$$+ .... + [(a + nd) + a] c_n$$

$\Rightarrow 2S = (2a + nd)\, c_0 + (2a + nd)\, c_1 + ... + (2a + nd)\, c_n$

$= (2a + nd)(c_0 + c_1 + ... c_n) = (2a + nd)\, 2^n$ $\quad [\because c_0 + c_1 + ... + c_n = 2^n]$

$\Rightarrow 2S = (2a + nd)\, 2^n$

$\Rightarrow S = (2a + nd)\, 2^{n-1}$

Corollary : $\sum_{r=1}^{n} r.c_r = n.2^{n-1}$

$$\sum_{r=1}^{n} r\ c_r = 1.c_1 + 2.c_2 + 3.c_3 + ... + n.c_n$$

$$= 0.c_0 + 1.c_1 + 2.c_2 + ... + nc_n$$

here a = 0, d = 1

$$\therefore \quad \sum_{r=1}^{n} r\ c_r = (2a + nd)\, 2^{n-1} = [2(0) + n(1)^{2n-1}]$$

$$= n.2^{n-1}$$

Ex : $1c_0 + 3c_1 + 5c_2 + ... + (2n + 1)\, c_n = (2n + 2)2^{n-1}$

here a = 1, d = 3 – 1 = 2

$\therefore$ L.H.S $= (2a + nd)\, 2^{n-1} = (2(1) + n(2)).2^{n-1} = (2n + 2)2^{n-1}$

Solved Examples

1. Prove that $c_0 + 3c_1 + 3^2c_2 + ... + 3^n . c_n = 4^n$

Sol. We have $(1 + x)^n = c_0 + c_1\, x + c_2\, x^2 + c_3\, x^3 + ... + c_n . x^n$

Put $x = 3$ we get

$$(1 + 3)^n = c_0 + c_1 . 3 + c_2\, (3)^2 + ... + c_n . 3^n$$

$$\Rightarrow \quad c_0 + 3 . c_1 + 3^2 . c_2 + ... + 3^n . c_n = 4^n$$

2. Prove that $2c_0 + 5c_1 + 8.c_2 + ... + (3n + 2)\, c_n = (3n + 4) . 2^{n-1}$

Sol. we know that

$$ac_0 + (a + d)\, c_1 + (a + 2d)\, c_2 + ... + (a + nd)\, c_n = (2a + nd)\, 2^{n-1}$$

$\therefore$ here a = 2, a + d = 5

$\Rightarrow$ d = 5 – 2 = 3

$\therefore$ $(2a + nd)\, 2^{n-1} = (2.(2) + n.(3))\,.\, 2^{n-1}$

$= (4 + 3n)\, 2^{n-1} = (3n + 4)\, 2^{n-1}$

3. Prove that $C_0 - 3c_1 + 7c_2 - 11c_3 + ... = 0$

Sol. We know that $ac_0 - (a + d)\, c_1 + (a + 2d)\, c_2 + ... = 0$

here a = 1, a = 2

$\therefore C_0 - 3c_1 + 7c_2 - 11c_3 + ... = 0$

4. Prove that $\frac{c_1}{c_0} + 2.\frac{c_2}{c_1} + 3.\frac{c_3}{c_2} + ... + n.\frac{c_n}{c_{n-1}} = \frac{n(n+1)}{2}$

Sol. LHS $= \sum_{r=1}^{n} \frac{cr}{c_{r-1}}.r = \sum_{r=1}^{n} r.\frac{n_{c_r}}{n_{c_{r-1}}}$

$= \sum_{r=-1}^{n} r.\frac{(n-r+1)}{r}$ $\left[\because \frac{n_{c_r}}{n_{c_{r-1}}} = \frac{n-r+1}{r}\right]$

$= \sum_{r=1}^{n} r.(n-r+1)$

$= n+(n - 1) + (n - 2) + ... 3 + 2 + 1$

$= 1 + 2 + 3 + 4 + ... + n$

$= \frac{n(n+1)}{2}$ ($\because$ sum of first n natural numbers is n(n+1))

Exercise - 4.2

1. Prove that $c_0 + 2c_1 + 2^2 . c_2 + 2^3\, c_3 + ... + 2^n . c_n = 3^n$.

2. Prove that $3.c_0 + 5c_1 + 7\, c_2 + ... + (2n + 1)\, c_n = (2n + 6) . 2^{n-1} = (n + 3)\, 2^n$.

3. Prove that $2c_0 + 7\, c_1 + 12\, c_2 + ... + (5n + 2)\, c_n = (4 + 5n)2^n$.

4. Prove that $c_0 - 3c_1 + 5c_2 - 7c_3 .... = 0$.

5. Prove that $c_0 + \frac{3}{2}c_1 + \frac{9}{3}.c_2 + \frac{27}{4}c3 + \dots\dots\dots + \frac{3^n}{n+1}c_n = \frac{4^{n+1}-1}{3(n+1)}$.

6. Prove that $a\,c_0^2 + (a+d)c_1^2 + \dots\dots\dots + (a+nd)\,c_n^2 = \frac{(2a+nd)}{2}.(2n_{c_n})$.

7. Prove that $(2n_{c0})^2 - (2n_{c_1})^2 + (2n_{c_2})^2 \dots\dots + (2n_{c_{2n}})^2 = (-1)^n.2n_{c_n}$

8. Prove that $\frac{15c_1}{15c_0} + 2.\frac{15c_2}{15c_1} + 3.\frac{15c_3}{15c_2} + \dots\dots\dots + 15.\frac{15c_{15}}{15c_{14}} = 120$

9. Prove that $c_0 . c_3 + c_1 . c_4 + c_2\,c_5 + \dots\dots\dots + c_{n-3} . c_n = 2n_{c_{n+3}}$

10. Prove that (i) $\sum_{r=2}^{n} r(r-1).c_r = n.(n-1).2^{n-2}$.

(ii) $\sum_{r=1}^{n} r^2.c_r = n(n+1)\,2^{n-2}$

Binomial theorem for rational index

For $|x| < 1$, p, q are positive integer then we define, $(1-x)^{-p/q} = 1 + p\left(\frac{x}{q}\right) + p\frac{(p+q)}{2!}$

$$\left(\frac{x}{q}\right)^2 + \left(\frac{p(p+q)(p+2q)}{3!}\right)\left(\frac{x}{q}\right)^3 + \dots + \frac{(p(p+q)(p+2q)\dots\dots\dots(p+(r-1)q)}{r!}\left(\frac{x}{q}\right)^r + \dots\dots$$

$$(1+x)^{-p/q} = 1 - p\left(\frac{x}{q}\right) + \frac{p(p+q)}{2!}\left(\frac{x}{q}\right)^2 + \dots\dots\dots(-1)^r\frac{p(p+q)(p+2q)\dots(p+(r-1)q)}{r!}\left(\frac{x}{q}\right)^r + \dots\dots$$

$$(1+x)^{p/q} = 1 + p\left(\frac{x}{q}\right) + \frac{p(p-q)}{2!}\left(\frac{x}{q}\right)^2 + \dots\dots\dots\frac{p(p-q)\dots(p-(r-1)q)}{r!}\left(\frac{x}{q}\right)^r + \dots\dots$$

$$(1+x)^{p/q} = 1 - p\left(\frac{x}{q}\right) + \frac{p(p-q)}{2!}\left(\frac{x}{q}\right)^2 + \dots\dots\dots + (-1)^r\frac{p(p-q)\dots(p-(r-1)q)}{r!}\left(\frac{x}{q}\right)^r + \dots\dots$$

1. Show that $1+\frac{1}{3}+\frac{1.3}{3.6}+\frac{1.3.5}{3.6.9}+.....=\sqrt{3}$

Sol. LHS = $1+1\left(\frac{1}{3}\right)+\frac{1.3}{2!}\left(\frac{1}{3}\right)^2+\frac{1.3.5}{2!}\left(\frac{1}{3}\right)^3+.....$

it is of the form $1+p\left(\frac{x}{q}\right)+\frac{p(p+q)}{2!}\left(\frac{x}{q}\right)^2+.....=(1-x)^{-p/q}$

$\therefore$ $x/q=\frac{1}{3}$, $p=1$, $p+q=3 \Rightarrow q=2$ we have $\frac{x}{q}=\frac{1}{3}\Rightarrow x=\frac{q}{3}=\frac{2}{3}$.

$\therefore$ LHS = $(1-x)^{-p/q}=\left(1-\frac{2}{3}\right)^{-1/2}=\left(\frac{1}{3}\right)^{-1/2}=3^{1/2}=\sqrt{3}$

2. Find the approximate value of $\sqrt[5]{32.16}$

Sol. $\sqrt[5]{32.16}=(32.16)^{\frac{1}{5}}=(32+0.16)^{\frac{1}{5}}=(32)^{\frac{1}{5}}\left(1+\frac{0.16}{32}\right)^{\frac{1}{5}}$

$$=2[1+0.005]^{\frac{1}{5}}=2\left\{1+1.\left(\frac{0.005}{5}\right)+\frac{1.(1-5)}{2!}\left(\frac{0.005}{2!}\right)^2+.......\right\}$$

$$\approx 2\{1+0.001\}=2.002$$

Exercise 4.3

1. Write the first 3 term in the expansion of

(i) $(1+4x)^{-4}$ (ii) $(1-2x)^{\frac{-1}{2}}$ (iii) $(1+4x)^{\frac{-1}{2}}$ (iv) $\left(1-\frac{2x}{3}\right)^{\frac{3}{4}}$

2. Show that $1+\frac{2}{3}\left(\frac{1}{2}\right)+\frac{2.5}{3.6}\left(\frac{1}{2}\right)^2+\frac{2.5.8}{3.6.9}\left(\frac{1}{2}\right)^3+.......=3\sqrt{4}$

3. Show that $\frac{7}{5}\left[1+\frac{1}{10^2}+\frac{1.3}{1.2}\frac{1}{10^4}+\frac{1.3.5}{1.2.3}\frac{1}{10^6}+......\right]=\sqrt{2}$

4. Show that $\frac{5}{6.12}+\frac{5.8}{6.12.18}+\frac{5.8.11}{6.12.18.24}+......=\frac{3\sqrt[3]{4}-4}{6}$

5. Find the values of following corrected to 4 decimal places.

(i) $(627)^{\frac{1}{4}}$ (ii) $\sqrt{199}$

(iii) $\sqrt[7]{127}$ (iv) $\frac{1}{\sqrt[3]{999}}$

Answers

1. (i) $1, -16x, 160x^2$

(ii) $1, x, \frac{3x^2}{2}$

(iii) $1, -2x, 6x^2$

(iv) $1, \frac{-x}{2}, \frac{-x^2}{24}$

5. (i) 5.004

(ii) 14.1067

(iii) 1.9844

(iv) 0.10003

5

Permutations and Combinations

5.1 Fundamental Principle

If a work W_1 can be performed in m different ways and a second work W_2 can be performed (after W_1, has been performed in any one of the 'm' ways) in n different ways, then the two works (one after other) can be performed 'mn' different ways.

Example

If a man has 3 different coloured pants P_1, P_2, P_3 and 4 different coloured shirts S_1, S_2, S_3, S_4 then he can select a, pair (a pant and a shirt) in $3 \times 4 = 12$ different ways as explained bellow.

In this example we take W_1 as selecting a pant which can be performed in 3 ways and W_2 as selecting a shirt which can be performed in 4 ways. Hence by the fundamental principle, he can select a pair in $3 \times 4 = 12$ different ways.

They are

$$\begin{Bmatrix} P_1S_1 & P_1S_2 & P_1S_3 & P_1S_4 \\ P_2S_1 & P_2S_2 & P_2S_3 & P_2S_4 \\ P_3S_1 & P_3S_2 & P_3S_3 & P_3S_4 \end{Bmatrix}$$

Example

If these are 3 different modes of transport available to travel from Hyderabad to Chennai namely bus, car, train (we denote these by B_1, C_1, T_1 respectively) and 4 different modes or transport from Chennai to Bangalore, namely bus, car, train, aeroplane (we denote these by

(B_2, C_2, T_2, A), thus the different modes of transport are available for a person to travel from Hyderabad to Bangalore (via chennai) is $3 \times 4 = 12$. They are

$$\begin{Bmatrix} B_1B_2 & B_1C_2 & B_1T_2 & B_1A \\ C_1B_2 & C_1C_2 & C_1T_2 & C_1A \\ T_1B_2 & T_1C_2 & T_1T_2 & T_1A \end{Bmatrix}$$

5.2 Linear Permutations

Definition: From a given finite set of elements (similar or not) selecting some or all of them and arranging them in a line is called a 'linear permutation' or simply a 'permutation'.

Example

From the letters of the word MILk, 2 letter permutations are MI, ML, MK, IL, IK, LK, IM, LM, KM, LI, KI, KL.

Example

From the letters of the word READING

(i) Permutations with three letters are REA, RED, REI, REN, REG etc.

(ii) Permutations with 4 letters are READ, EADI, ADIN etc.

Example

Using the digits 1, 2, 3, 4, 5

(i) Permutations with two digits are 12, 13, 32, 52 etc.

(ii) Permutations with 4 digits are 1234, 2345 etc.

5.3 Permutations of n Dissimilar Things Taken 'r' at a Time

Theorem : If n, r are positive integers and $r \leq n$ then the number of permutations of n dissimilar things (objects) taken r at a time is n_{p_r}.

Proof: Suppose n dissimilar objects are given, we can observe that the number of required permutations is equal to number of ways of filling r blanks using the given n thing with one object in each blank.

Let us consider r blanks.

To fill the first blank, we can use only one of the given n thing, thus first blank can be filled with n different ways. After filling up the first blank we are left with (n–1) things and (r–1) blanks.

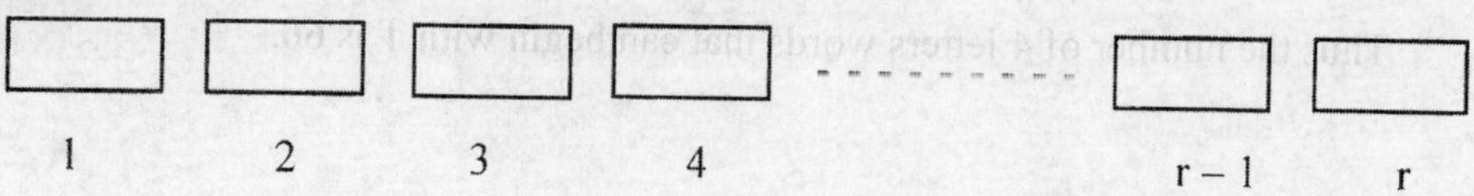

So the second blank can be filled with any one of remaining (n–1) thing in (n–1) ways. So by fundamental principle the first two blanks can be filled with r (r–1) ways. Continuing this process up to r^{th} blanks. The total number of ways is

$$n(n-1)(n-2) \ldots\ldots n-(r-1) \text{ ways.}$$

$\therefore$ the number of way$= n(n-1)(n-2) \ldots.(n-r+1)$

$$= \frac{n(n-1)(n-2)\ldots..(n-r+1)(n-r)\ldots..2.1}{(n-r)(n-r-1)\ldots..1}$$

$$= \frac{n!}{(n-r)!} = n_{p_r}.$$

Note: $n_{p_n} = \frac{n!}{(n-n)!} = \frac{n!}{o!} = n!; \quad n_{p_o} = \frac{n!}{(n-o)!} = \frac{n!}{n!} = 1$

Solved Examples

1. Find the number of 4 letters words that can be formed using the letters of the word TAGORE. How many of these words begin with T? How many end with E? How many begine with T and end with E?

Sol. The word TAGORE has 6 distinct letters we have to fill up 4 blanks using these 6 letters.

This can be done in $6_{p_4} = \frac{6!}{2!} = 6 \times 5 \times 4 \times 3 = 360$ ways.

Hence the number of 4 letter words that can be formed using the letters of the word TAGORE is 360.

Words Beginning with T : Fill the first blank with T shown below.

T			

Now we are left with 5 letters and 3 places they can be filled in $5_{p_3} = \frac{5!}{2!} = 60$ ways.

Thus the number of 4 letters words that can begin with T is 60.

Words Ending with R: This can be done in the same way as above first fill the last place with R as shown below.

			R

Then the remaining 3 places with the remaining 5 letters can be filled in

$$5_{p_3} = \frac{5!}{2!} = 60 \text{ ways.}$$

Hence the number of '4' letter words ending with R is $5_{p_3} = 60$ words beginning with T and ending with R.

T			E

Fill the first blank T and last with R as shown bellow

Now the remaining 2 places can be filled with remaining 4 letters in 4_{p_2} ways.

$\therefore$ The required number of ways is $4_{p_2} = \frac{4!}{2!} = 12$

2. Find the number of ways of arranging 8 boys and 6 girls in a row. In how many of these arrangements

(i) all girls are together

(ii) no two girls sit together

(iii) girls do not sit together

(iv) all boys are together

(v) boys do not sit together

(vi) no two boys sit together

Sol. 8 boys + 6 girls = 14 persons. They can be arranged in a row in (14)! ways.

(i) Treat 6 girls are one unit. Then we have 8 boys + 1 unit of girls

They (9 units) can be arranged in 9! ways. Now 6 girls among themselves can be permuted in 6! ways. Hence by the fundamental principle all girls come together is 9! . 6!

(ii) to get no two girls sit together first we arrange 8 boys in linearly in 8! ways. In each arrangement there are 9 gaps between them.

$$\times B_1 \times B_2 \times B_3 \times B_4 \times B_5 \times B_6 \times B_7 \times B_8 \times$$

if we filling the 9 blanks with girls then no two girls come to gether.

∴ this can be done in 9_{p_6} ways.

∴ by using fundamental principle, the total number of ways of arrangements is $8! \times 9_{p_6}$.

(iii) the number of ways of arrangements of girls do not come together = total number of arrangements – total number of arrangements of girls came together.

$= 14! - 9!\ 6!$

(iv) Take all boys as one unit

∴ 6 girls + 1 units of boys (7 units) can be arranged in a row in 7! and in each arrangement the 8 boys can be permuted themselves in 8! ways.

∴ by using fundamental principal the total number of arrangements since that all the boys came together is 7! . 8!

(v) the number of arrangements of boys don't came together = total number of arrangements – number of arrangements of boys came together

$= 14! - 7!\ .\ 9!$

(vi) first arrange the 6 girls in linearly in 6! ways. There are 7 gaps between them. 8 boys can not be sit in this 7 places. So required arrangement does not possible ∴ the number of arrangements = 0.

3. Find the number of ways of arranging 6 boys and 6 girls in a row so that boys and girls come alternatively.

Sol. Let us take 12 places. The row may begin with a boys or a girl that is two ways. If it begins with a boy, then all odd places (1, 3, 5, 7, 9, 11) will be occupied by boys and even places (2, 4, 6, 8, 10, 12) by girls

B	G	B	G	B	G	B	G	B	G	B	G
1	2	3	4	5	6	7	8	9	10	11	12

the 6 boys can be arranged in the 6 odd places in 6! ways and the 6 girls can be arranged in the 6 even places in 6! ways.

Thus the number of arrangements in which boys and girls came alternatively is

$2 \times 6! \times 6!$

4. Find the number of ways of arranging the letters of the word ORGANIC so that

(i) all vowels come together

(ii) no two vowels come together

(iii) begin with an vowel

(iv) begin and end with vowels

(v) end with a consonant

(vi) the relative positions of vowels and consonants are not disturbed.

Sol. The given word is ORGANIC

it has 3 vowels (O, A, I) and 4 consonants (R, G, N,C)

(i) Treat the three vowels as one unit then we can arrange 4 consonants + 1 unit of vowels in 5! ways. Now the three vowels among themselves can be permuted in 3! ways. Hence the no of ways of required arrangements = 5! . 3!

(ii) First arrange the 4 consonants in 4 ways, these in between the vowels, in the beginning and ending there are 5 gaps as shown below by the letter G.

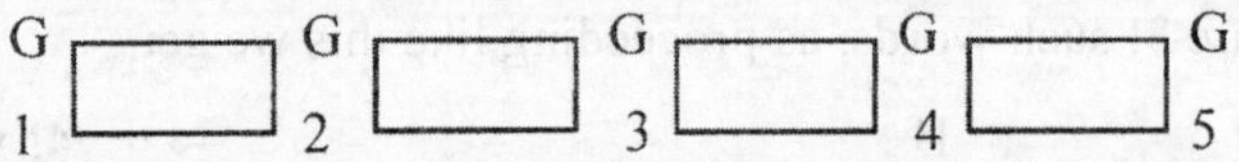

In these 5 places we can arrange the three vowels 5_{p_3} ways. Thus the number of words in which no two vowels come together is $4! \times 5_{p_3} = 24 \times 60 = 1440$.

(iii) We can fill the first place with one of 3 vowels (D, A, I) in 3_{p_1} ways = 3. Now the remaining 6 places can be filled with remaining 6 letters in 6! ways.
$\therefore$ the required number of permutation $= 3 \times 6! = 3 \times 720 = 2160$ ways

(iv) the first and last blank can be filled with 3 vowels in $3_{p_2} = \frac{3!}{1!} = 6$ way. The remaining 5 blanks can be filled with remaining 5 letters (1 vowel + 4 consonants) (remaining) in 5! way.

$\therefore$ the total number of arrangements $= 6 \times 5! = 6 \times 120 = 720$ ways.

(v) Take 7 blanks ; we can fill the last place (blank) with any one of consonant (out of 4) in $4_{p_1} = 4$ ways. The remaining 6 blanks can filled with 6 letters in 6! ways.

$\therefore$ the required number of arrangements $= 4 \times 6! = 4 \times 720 = 2880$ ways.

(vi) The 3 vowels can be arranged themselves in 3! way and 4 consonants can be arranged themselves in 4! ways.

$\therefore$ The number of ways of arrangements relative positions of vowels and consonants are not disturbed is $3! \times 4! = 6 \times 24 = 144$ ways.

5. If the letters of the word 'RUBLE' are permuted in all possible ways and words thus formed are arranged in dictionary order then find the rank of the word 'LUBER'.

Sol. The letters of the given word in dictionary order is

B, E, L, R, U

In the dictionary order, first we write all words that begine with B. If we fill the first place with B then the remaining 4 places can be filled with remaining 4 letters in 4! ways. That is there are 4! words that begin with B. Proceeding like thus, after writing all words that begin with E, we have to write the words that begin with L. Among them first came the words with first two letters L, B, as above there are 3! such words, as proceeding like this we get

B	–	–	–	–	→	4! ways
E	–	–	–	–	→	4! ways
L	B	–	–	–	→	3! ways
L	E	–	–	–	→	3! ways
L	R	–	–	–	→	3! ways
L	U	B	E	R	→	1

Hence the rank the word LUBER is

$$2\,(4!) + 3\,(3!) + 1 = 48 + 18 + 1 = 67$$

6. Find the sum of all 4 digited numbers that can be formed using the digits 1, 2, 4, 5, 6 without repetition.

Sol. We know that the number of 4 digited numbers that can be formed using the given five digits is .... 120 ways.

First we find the sum of the digits in the units place of all these 120 numbers. If we fill the units place with 1 as shown below then

			1

remaining 3 places can be filled with remaining 4 digits in 4_{p_3} ways. This means, the number of 4 digited numbers having 1 in units place is 4_{p_3} . Similarly each of the digit 2, 4, 5, 6 appear $4_{p_3} = 24$ times in units place. By adding all these digits we get the sum of the digits in unit place of all 120 numbers is

$$4_{p_3} \times 1 + 4_{p_3} \times 2 + 4_{p_3} \times 4 + 4_{p_3} \times 5 + 4_{p_3} \times 6 = 4_{p_3} (18)$$

Similarly we get the sum of the digits in 10's place is $4_{p_3} \times (18)$. Since it is in 10's place its value is $4_{p_3} \times 18 \times 10$.

Similarly the values of the sum of the digits in 100's place and 1000's place are 4_{p_3} (18) (100) and 4_{p_3} (18) (1000) respectively. Hence the sum of 4 digited numbers formed by using the digits 1, 2, 4, 5, 6 is

$$4_{p_3} \times 18 \times 1 + 4_{p_3} \times 18 \times 10 + 4_{p_3} (18)(100) + 4_{p_3} (18)(1000)$$

$$= 4_{p_3} (18)(1111)$$

$$= 24 \times 18 \times 1111 = 4,79,952$$

Note

1. The sum of all r digited numbers that can be formed using the given n non zero digits $(1 \le r \le n \le 9)$ is $(n-1)_{p_{(r-1)}} \times$ sum of the given digits × 111 ......1 (r times).

2. In the above if zero ('o') is one digit among the given n digits, then we get that the sum of the r digit number that can be formed using the given n digits (including zero)

$$= \{(n-1)_{p_{r-1}} \times \text{sum of given digits} \times 1111 \text{.......} 1 \text{ (r times)}\}$$

$$- \{(n-2)_{p_{r-2}} \times \text{sum of given digits} \times 1111 \text{.......} 1 \text{ ((r − 1) times)}\}$$

7. Find the number of 4 digited numbers that can be formed using the digits 1, 2, 5, 6, 7. How many of them are divigible by

(i) 2 (ii) 3 (iii) 4 (iv) 5 (v) 25

Sol. The number of 4 digited numbers that can be formed using the 5 digits 1, 2, 5, 6, 7 is $5_{p_4} = 120$.

(i) ***Divisible by 2 :*** For a number to be divisible by 2, the unit place should be filled with an even digit this can be done in 2 ways (2 or 6).

			2 or 6

Now the remaining 3 places can be filled with remaining 4 digits in $4_{P_3} = 24$ way.

Hence the number of 4 digited numbers divisible by 2 is $2 \times 24 = 48$

(ii) ***Divisible by 3*** **:** A number is divisible by 3 if the sum of the digits in it is a multiple of 3. Since the sum of the given 5 digits is 21, we have to leave 6 and use the digits 1, 2, 5, 7 we can permute these digits in 4! ways. Thus the number of 4 digit numbers, divisible by 3 is $1 \times 4! = 24$.

(iii) ***Divisible by 4*****:** A number is divisible by 4 if the number formed by the digits in last two places (tens and unit places) is multiple of 4.

Thus we fill the last two places with

12, 16, 52, 56, 72, 76

that is done by 6 ways. After filling the last two places we can fill remaining two places with remaining 3 digits in $3_{P_2} = 6$ ways.

Thus the number of 4 digited numbers divisible by 4 is $6 \times 6 = 36$.

(iv) ***Divisible by 5*****:** Fill the units place with 5 (one way) and the remaining 3 places can be filled with the remaining 4 digits in $4_{P_3} = 24$ ways. Hence the number of 4 digited numbers divisible by 5 is 24

(v) ***Divisible by 25*** **:** Last two places can be filled with 25, 75 (last two places are multiple of 25)

Now the remaining 2 places can be filled with the remaining 3 digits in $3_{P_2} =$ 6 ways.

Hence the number of 4 digited number divisible by 25 is $2 \times 6 = 12$.

8. (i) If $n_{P_3} = 1320$ find n

(ii) If $n_{P_7} = 42 \ . \ n_{P_5}$, find n

(iii) If $12_{P_5} + 5 \ . \ 12_{P_4} = 13_{P_r}$, find r

(iv) If $(n+1)\,P_5 : nP_6 = 2 : 7$, find n

(v) If $18_{P_{r-1}} : 17_{P_{r-1}} = 9:7$, find r

Sol. (i) given $n_{p_3} = 1320 \Rightarrow \dfrac{n!}{(n-3)!} = 1320$

$$\Rightarrow n(n-1)(n-2) = 1320$$

$$= 12 \times 11 \times 10$$

$$\Rightarrow n = 12$$

$$\begin{array}{r|l} 2 & 1320 \\ \hline 2 & 660 \\ \hline 3 & 330 \\ \hline 11 & 110 \\ \hline & 10 \end{array}$$

$= 12 \times 11 \times 10$

(ii) $n_{p_7} = 42.\ n_{p_5}$

$$\Rightarrow \frac{n!}{(n-7)!} = 42 \cdot \frac{n!}{(n-5)!}$$

$$= \frac{(n-5)!}{(n-7)!} = 42 \quad \Rightarrow (n-5)(n-6) = 42$$

$$\Rightarrow n = 12 (\therefore \text{ take } n-5 = 7, n-6 = 6)$$

(iii) $12_{p_5} + 5 \cdot 12_{p_4} = 13_{p_r}$

$$= \frac{12!}{(12-5)!} + 5 \cdot \frac{12!}{(12-4)!} = 13_{p_r}$$

$$\Rightarrow \frac{12!}{7!} + 5\frac{12!}{8!} = 13_{p_r}$$

$$\Rightarrow 12!\left(\frac{1}{7!} + \frac{5}{8!}\right) = 13_{p_r}$$

$$\Rightarrow 12!\left(\frac{8+5}{8!}\right) = 13_{p_r} \Rightarrow \frac{12!(13)}{8!} = 13_{p_r}$$

$$\Rightarrow \frac{13!}{8!} = \frac{13!}{(13-r)!} \qquad \Rightarrow 8 = 13 - r$$

$$\Rightarrow r = 13 - 8 = 5$$

(iv) $(n + 1)\, P_5 : n_{p6} = 2:7$

$$\Rightarrow \frac{(n+1)!}{(n+1-5)!} \div \frac{n!}{(n-6)!} = \frac{2}{7} \Rightarrow \frac{\frac{(n+1)!}{(n-4)!}}{\frac{n!}{(n-6)!}} = \frac{2}{7}$$

$$\Rightarrow \frac{(n+1)}{(n-4)(n-5)} = \frac{2}{7} \Rightarrow 7n + 7 = 2\,(n^2 - 9n + 20)$$

$$\Rightarrow 2n^2 - 25n + 33 = 0$$

$$\Rightarrow 2n^2 - 22n - 3n + 33 = 0$$

$$= 2n\,(n - 11) - 3\,(n - 11) = 0$$

$$(2n - 3)\,(n - 11) = 0 \quad \Rightarrow n = \frac{3}{2} \text{ or } n = 11$$

but $n = \frac{3}{2}$ is not an integer $\therefore$ $n = 11$

(v) given $18_{p_{r-1}} : 17_{p_{r-1}} = 9 : 7$

$$\Rightarrow \frac{\frac{18!}{[18-(r-1)]!}}{\frac{17!}{[17-(r-1)]!}} = \frac{9}{7}$$

$$\Rightarrow \frac{\frac{18!}{(19-r)!}}{\frac{17!}{(18-r)!}} = \frac{9}{7} \Rightarrow \frac{18}{19-r} = \frac{9}{7} \Rightarrow \frac{2}{19-r} = \frac{1}{7}$$

$$\Rightarrow 14 = 19 - r$$

$$\Rightarrow r = 19 - 14 = 5$$

$$\Rightarrow r = 5.$$

Exercise 5.1

1. (i) If $n_{p_4} = 1680$, find n

   (ii) If $12_{p_r} = 1320$, find r

2. (i) If $56_{p_{r+3}} : 54_{p_{r+3}} = 30800 : 1$, find r

   (ii) If $(n+1)_{p_5} : n_{p_5} = 3 : 2$, find n.

3. Find the number of 4 letters words can be formed using the letters of word MIXTURE which

   (i) contain the letter X

   (ii) do not contain the letter X

4. Find the number of ways of permuting the letters of the word PICTURE so that

   (i) all vowels came together

   (ii) no two vowels came together.

5. Find the number of ways of arranging 5 different mathematic books, 4 different physics books and 3 different chemistry books such that the books of the same subject are together.

6. Find the number of ways of arranging 6 boys and 5 girls in a row so that

   (i) all girls sit together

   (ii) no two girls sit together

   (iii) boys and girls sit alternatively and

   (iv) no two boys sit together

7. Find the number of ways of arranging the letters of word MONDAY so that no vowel occupies even place.

8. If there are 30 railway stations on a railway line, how many types of single second class tickets must be printed so as to enable a passenger to travel from one station to another.

9. In a class there are 25 students, on the new year day every student posts a greeting card to all his/her class mates. Find the total number of greeting cards posted by them.

10. If the letters of the word MASTER are permuted in all possible ways and the words thus formed are arranged in the dictionary order, then find the ranks of the words

(i) REMAST (ii) MASTER

11. If the letters of the word PRISON are permuted in all possible ways and the words thus formed are arranged in dictionary order, find the rank of the word PRISON.

12. Find the sum of all 4-digited numbers that can be formed using the digits 1, 3, 5, 7, 9.

13. Find the number of 4 digit numbers that can be formed using the digits 2, 3, 5, 6, 8 (with out repetition). How many of them are divisible by

(i) 2 (ii) 3 (iii) 4 (iv) 5 (v) 25

14. Find the number of 4 letter words that can be formed using the letters of the word MIRACLE. How many of them

(i) begin with an vowel

(ii) begin and end with vowel

(iii) end with a consonant

15. Find the number of injections of set A with 5 elements to a set B with 7 elements.

Answers

1. (i) $n = 8$ (ii) $r = 3$

2. (i) $r = 41$, (ii) $n = 14$

3. (i) 480, (ii) 360

4. (i) $5!\,.\,3! = 720$ (ii) $4!\,.\,5_{P_3} = 1440$

5. $3!\,.\,5!\,.\,4!.\,3! = 1,03,680$

6. (i) $7! \times 5!$ (ii) $6! \times 7_{P_5}$ (iii) $6! \times 5!$ (iv) $6! \times 5!$

7. $3_{P_2} \times 4! = 144$

8. $30_{P_2} = 870$

9. $25_{P_2} = 600$

10. (i) 391 (ii) 257

11. 438

12. 6, 66, 600

13. 5_{p_4} (i) 72 (ii) 48 (iii) 36 (iv) 24 (v) 6

14. (i) 360 (ii) 120 (iii) 480

15. $7_{p_5} = 2520$

5.4 Permutations when Repetitions are Allowed

Theorem **:** **Let n and r are positive integers. If the repetition of things is allowed then the number of permutations of n dissimilar thing taken r at a time is n^r.**

Proof **:** **The number of required permutations equal to the number of ways of filling up r blank places with the given n things (repetitions allowed).**

The blank 1 can be filled with any one of the given n things in n ways. Now,

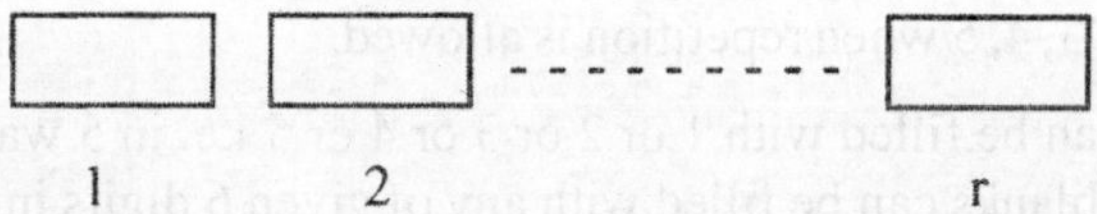

we are left with (r–1) blanks and n things (because repetition is allowed). The second blank can be filled with n thing in n ways. ∴ first and second blanks can be filled in $n \times n = n^2$ ways by fundamental principle. Continuing this process we get, r blanks can be filled in h × n × ..... n (r times) = n^r. ways. Hence the theorem.

Solved Examples

1. **Find the number of permutations of 4 digited numbers that can be formed using 1, 3, 5, 7, 9 when repetition is allowed.**

Sol. **By above theorem the number of 4-digited numbers is $5 \times 5 \times 5 \times 5 = 5^4 = 625$**

2. **Find the number of 4 letter words can be formed using the letters of word 'SIPRON' in which at least one letter is repeated.**

Sol. **the given word has 6 letters. The number of 4 letter words that can be formed using these 6 letters**

(i) when repetition is allowed is 6^4.

(ii) when repetition is not allowed is 6_{p_4}

Hence the number of 4 letter words in which at least one letter repeated is

$$6^4 - 6_{p_4} = 1296 - 360 = 936$$

3. A number lock has 4 rings and each ring has 9 digits 1, 2, 3 ..... 9. Find the maximum number of un successful attempts that can be made by a person who tries to open the lock without knowing the key code.

Sol. Each ring can be rotated in 9 ways. Thus, the total number of different ways in which 4 rings can be rotated in 9^4 $(9 \times 9 \times 9 \times 9)$ ways. Out of these attempts only one attempt is successful. Hence the maximum number of un successful attempts $9^4 - 1$.

4. Find the number of 5 letter words that can be formed using the letters of the word NATURE that begin with N when repetition is allowed.

Sol. we first fill the first blank with N and then remaining 5 blanks can be filled with 6 letters (repeation allowed) in $6 \times 6 \times 6 \times 6 \times 6 = 6^5$ ways.

N					

$\therefore$ the required number of words $= 1 \times 6^5 = 6^5$.

5. Find the number of 5 digited number divigible by 5 that can be formed using the digits 0, 1, 2, 3, 4, 5 when repetition is allowed.

Sol. First blank can be filled with 1 or 2 or 3 or 4 or 5 i.e. in 5 ways and each of remaining 4 blanks can be filled with any of given 6 digits in $6 \times 6 \times 6 \times 2$ ways.

$\therefore$ the required number of numbers is $2 \times 5 \times 6^3$.

6. Find the number of numbers less than 2000 that can be formed using the digits 1, 2, 3, 4 if repetition is allowed.

Sol. (i) one digited numbers are 4

(ii) number of two digited numbers formed by 1, 2, 3, 4 is $4 \times 4 = 16$

(iii) number of 3 digited number formed by 1, 3, 4 is $4 \times 4 \times 4 = 64$

(iv) four digited number less than 2000.

first place can be fill with 1 way remaining 3 places can be filled with the 4 digits in $4 \times 4 \times 4$ way i.e. 4^3 ways.

$\therefore$ the number of numbers formed by 1, 2, 3, 4 which are less than 2000 is

$$4 + 4^2 + 4^3 + 4^3$$

$$= 4 + 16 + 64 + 64$$

$$= 148$$

Exercise - 5.2

1. Find the number of 5 digited numbers that can be formed using the digits 1, 2, 5, 7, 8, 9, when repetitions allowed.

2. Find the number of 4 letter words that can be formed using the letters of the word SIPLA if each letter can be used any number of times.

3. Find the number of 4 digit telephone numbers that can be formed using digits 1, 2, 3, 4, 5, 6 with at least one digit repeated.

4. Find the number of 5 letter words that can be formed using the letters of the word MIXTURE which begin with an vowel when repetitions are allowed.

5. Find the number of 4 digit even numbers can be formed using the digits 0, 2, 5, 7, 8 when repetition is allowed.

Answers

1. 6^5 **2.** 5^4 **3.** $6^4 - 6_{P_4}$

4. 3×7^4 **5.** $3 \times 4 \times 5^2 = 300$

5.5 Circular Permutations

From a given finite set of things (similar or not) choosing some or all of them and arranging them around a circle is called a 'circular permutation'.

Theorem **:** The number of circular permutations on n dissimilar thing (taken all at a time) is (n–1) !.

Proof**:** Let C be the number of circular permutations of n thing taken all at a time. If we take one such permutation as seen in the figure.

This circular permutation gives rise to n linear permutations as given bellow

$a_1, a_2 ------ a_{n-1}\ a_n$

$a_2, a_3 -------- a_n\ a_1$

$a_n\ a_1\ a_2 ------ a_{n-2}\ a_{n-1}$.

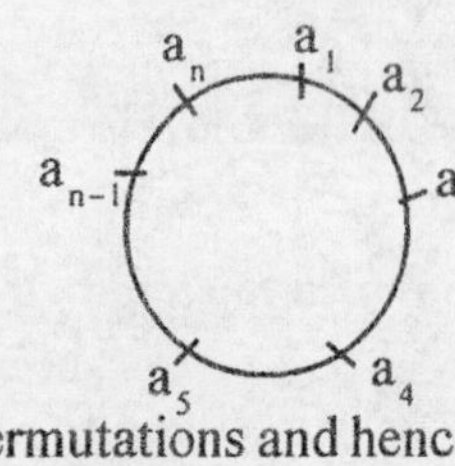

Thus are circular permutation gives rise to n linear permutations and hence C circular permutations gives in C × n linear permutations. But we know that the number of linear permutations of n dissimilar things (taken all at a time) is $n_{P_n} = n!$

Hence, we get $C \times n = n! \Rightarrow C = (n-1)!$

Note: In case of hanging type of circular permutations like garlands of flowers, chains of beads etc. a circular permutation books like clock wise arrangement when seen from one side and anti clock wise arrangement from the other side. Hence, they will be treated as identical. Therefore the number of circular permutations of n things in these case is $\frac{(n-1)!}{2}$.

Solved Examples

1. Find the number of ways of arranging 5 boys and 6 girls around a circle.

Sol. Total number of persons = n = 5 + 6 = 11.

$\therefore$ The number of circular permutations is $(n - 1)! = (11 - 1)! = 10!$

2. Find the number of ways of arranging 8 men and 5 women arround a circular table. In how many of them

(i) all the women came together

(ii) no two woman came together

Sol. Total number of persons = 8 + 5 = 13

$\therefore$ the number of circular permutations is (12)!

(i) treat the 5 woman as one unit then we have 8 men + 1 unit of woman = 9 units (each man can taken as one unit)

They can be arranged a circular in 8! ways. Now the 5 woman among themselves can be arranged in 5! ways. Hence by the fundamental principle the required number of arrangements is $8! \times 5!$

(ii) First we arrange 8 men around the circular table in (8–1) = 7! ways. There are 8 gaps in between them as shown in figure by symbol 'G'.

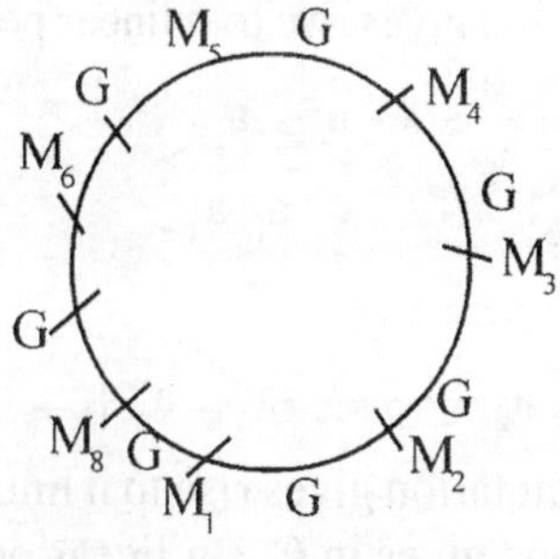

Now we can arrange the 5 women in these places in 8_{p_5} ways thus the number of circular permutations wish no two woman came to gether is

$7! \times 8_{p_5}$

3. A round table conference is attended by 3 Indians, 3 Chinese, 3 Canadians and 2 Americans. Find the number of ways arranging them at the round table so that the delegates belonging to same country sit together.

Sol. Take each of 3 Indians, 3 Chinese, 3 Canadians and 2 Americans as one unit.

$\therefore$ the number of units = 4

These 4 units can be arranged circulary in $(4 - 1)! = 3!$ and in each of the arrangement, the delegates belong to same country sit together arranged themselves in $3! \times 3! \times 3! \times 2!$ ways.

$\therefore$ Total number of arrangement is $3! \times 3! \times 3! \times 3! \times 2!$

$$= 6 \times 6 \times 6 \times 6 \times 2$$

$$= 2 \times 6^4 = 2,592$$

4. Find the number of different ways of preparing garland using 7 distinct red roses and 5 distinct yellow roses such that no two yellow roses came together.

Sol. First we arrange 7 red roses in circular form in $(7-1)! = 6!$. Now there are 7 gaps in between the red roses and we can arrange 5 yellow roses in these 7 gaps in 7_{P_5} ways, then the total number of circular permutations is $6! \times 7_{P_5}$.

But this being the case of garlands, clock wise and anti clock wise arrangements look a like. Hence the required number of ways is $\frac{1}{2}(6! \times 7_{P5})$.

5. Find the number of ways of arranging 7 guests and a host around a circle if 2 particular guests wish to sit on either side of the host.

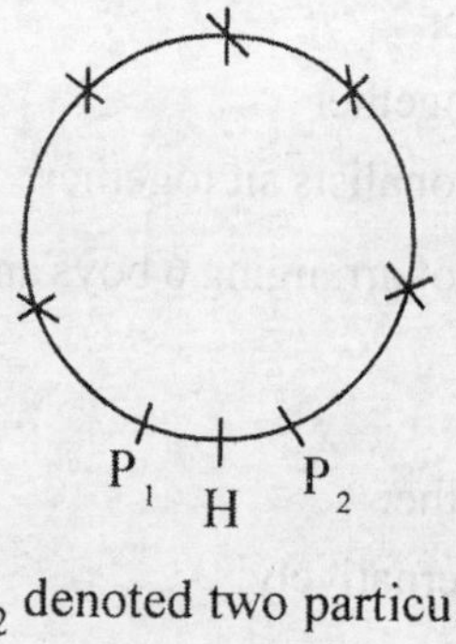

Sol. Let H denote host, P_1, P_2 denoted two particular of seven.

So take $(P_1\ H\ P_2)$ as an unit and remaining 5 persons each one as one unit.

$\therefore$ the six units can be arranged circular by in $(6-1)! = 5!$. In each arrangement P1, P2 be inter changed this can be done in 2! ways. $\therefore$ Total number of arrangements $= 5! \times 2! = 240$.

Exercise - 5.3

1. Find the number of ways of arranging 10 persons around a circle.

2. Find the number of ways of arranging the chief minister and 20 cabinet ministers at curcular table so that chief minister always sit in a particular seat?

3. Find the number of ways of arranging 6 boys and 4 girls around circle so that
   (i) all the girls sit together
   (ii) no two girls sit together

4. Find the number of ways of arranging 10 guests and a host around a circular table if two particular guests wise to sit on either side of the host.

5. Find the number of ways of preparing a garland with 3 yellow, 4 white and 2 red roses of different sizes such that two red roses come to gether.

6. Find the number of ways of arranging 6 red roses and 3 yellow roses of different size in to garland. In how many of them
   (i) all the yellow roses together
   (ii) no two yellow roses together
   (iii) all red, yellows roses came together. (Same type of roses came together)

7. A round table conference is attended by 4 Indians, 5 Chinese, 6 Canadinas and 7 Americans. Find the number of way of arranging them at round table so that the delegates belong to same country sit together.

8. Find the number of ways of seating 5 Indians, 4 Americans and 3 Russians at round table so that
   (i) all Indians sit together.
   (ii) no two russians sit together
   (iii) persons of same nationalists sit together.

9. Find the number of ways of arranging 6 boys and 6 girls around a circular table so that
   (i) all girls sit together
   (ii) no two girls sit together
   (iii) boys and girls sit alternatively

10. A family consists of father, mother, 3 daughters, 2 sons. In how many different ways can they sit at round table if the two daughters wish to sit either side of the father.

Answers

1. 9! 2. 20! 3. (i) 6! . 4! (ii) 5! 6_{p4} 4. 8! × 2!

5. $\frac{7!}{2}\times 2! = 5040!$ 6. (i) $\frac{6!\times 3!}{2!}$ (ii) $\frac{5!\times 6_{p_3}}{2!}$ (iii) $\frac{6!3!}{2}$ 7. 3! × 4! × 5! × 6! × 7!

8. (i) 7! × 5! (ii) $8!\times 9_{p_3}$ (iii) 2! × 5! × 4! × 3! 9. (i) 6! . 6! (ii) 5!6!

(iii) 5! × 6! 10. [3 × 3! × 2!] = 36

5.6 Permutation in which some are a like and rest are different

In the litrature we come across many words whose spelling contains certain repeated letters like MATHEMATICS, EAMCET, PHARMACY, etc and many numbers with repeated digits like 5353, 2008, 177177, etc. In this section we find the number of permutations of such words.

Theorem : The number of linear permutations of n thing in which p things are alike and the rest are different is $\frac{n!}{p!}$

Proof : Let M be the number of permutations of n things in which r things are alike and the rest are different. If we take one such permutation, it contains r things which are alike. If we replace their r like things by r dissimilar things, then we can arrange among themselves (without disturbing the relative positions of the other things) in p! ways. In other words one permutation when P things are a like gives rise to P! permutations when all are different.

Therefore from the M such permutations we get M × (p!) permutations when all n things are different. But we know that the number of permutations of n dissimilar things (taken all at a time) is n!. Hence

$$M \times p! = n! \text{ or } M = \frac{n!}{p!}$$

Hence the proof.

We can extend this result for the case when we have more one set of a like things in given n things.

Note: the number of linear permutations of n things in which there are p like things one kind, q like things of second kind, r like things of third kind and the rest are different is

$$\frac{n!}{p!q!r!}$$

Solve Examples

1. Find the number of ways of arranging the letters of the word

(i) MATHEMATICS (ii) PERMUTATION

(iii) PHARMACY (iv) ENGINEERING

Sol.

(i) The given word has 11 letters in which there are 2 Ms, 2 I's, 2 A's

Hence they can be arranged in $\frac{11!}{2!2!2!}$ ways

(ii) The given word has 11 letters in which there are two T's. Hence they can be arranged in $\frac{11!}{2!}$ ways.

(iii) The given word has 8 letters in which there are 2 A's. Hence they can be arranged in $\frac{8!}{2!}$ ways.

(iv) The word ENGINEERING has 3E's, 3 N's, 2 Gs, 2 I's and one R. Hence they can be arranged in $\frac{11!}{3!3!2!2!}$ ways.

2. Find the number of ways of arranging the letters of the word $a^3 b^4 c^5$ in its expanded form.

Sol. The expanded form of $a^3b^4c^5$ is aaa bbbb ccccc

This word has 12 letters in which there are 3 a's, 4 b's 5c's.

$\therefore$ They can be arranged in $\frac{12!}{3!4!5!}$ ways.

3. There are 3 copies (alike) of 4 different books. Find the number of ways of arranging these 12 books in a shelf in a single row.

Sol. we have 12 books in which 3 books are alike of one kind, 3 books of alike of second kind, 3 books of a like of third kind, 3 books of a like of 4th kind. Hence they can be arranged in a shelf in a row in $\frac{12!}{3!3!3!3!}$ ways

4. In how many ways can the letters of the word CHEESE be arranged so that no two E's came together.

Sol. First we left the three E's and remaining 3 letters C, H, S be arranged in 3! way and there are 4 gaps between the three letters – C – H – S – then the 3E's can be arranged in these 4 places in $\frac{4P_3}{3!}$ ways.

∴ the total no. of ways can the letters of word CHEESE be arranged so that no two E's came together is

$$3! \times \frac{4P_3}{3!} = 4P_3 = 24.$$

5. Find the number of 7 digit numbers can be formed using 2, 2, 2, 3, 3, 4, 4

Sol. the number of given digits is 7 in which there are three 2's, two 3's, two 4's.

∴ the number of seven digited number is $\frac{7!}{3!.2!2!}$

6. Find the numbers of 5 digited numbers that can be formed using all the digits 0, 1, 1, 2, 3.

Sol. The first blank can be filled with 1 or 2 or 3.

Case (i)

If the first blank can be filled with 1 then the remaining 4 balnks can be filled with remaining 4 digits {0, 1, 2, 3} in 4! ways.

Case (ii)

If the first blank can be filled with 2 or 3 then the remaining 4 blanks can be filled with 4 gaps {0, 1, 1, 3 (or) 2} in $\frac{4!}{2!}$ ways.

∴ no. of ways = $2 \times \frac{4!}{2!}$ ways = 4! ways

∴ from case (i) and case (ii) the total number of numbers is 4! + 4! = 2 × 4! = 48.

7. If the letters of the word PHARMA are permited in all possible ways and if the words thus formed are arranged in the dictionary order, find the rank of the word PHARMA.

The dictionary order of the letters of given words

A A H M P R

The number of word which are begine with A is 5!

" " " " H is $\frac{5!}{2!}$

" " " " M is $\frac{5!}{2!}$

" " " " PA is 4!

" " " " PHAA is 2!

" " " " PHAM is 2!

" " " " PHARA is 1!

" " " " PHARMA is 1

$\therefore$ Rank of the word PHARMA is $5! + 2\frac{(5!)}{2!} + 4! + 2\,(2!) + 2$

$= 270$

Exercise - 5.4

1. Find the number of ways of arranging the letters of the word
   (i) MADAM (ii) RAMANA
   (iii) COLLEGE (iv) ASSOCIATION.
2. Find the number of different words that can be formed using 4 A's, 3 B's, 5 C's and 2 D's.
3. How many numbers that can be formed using the digits 1, 2, 3, 4, 5, 3, 2, 1 such that even digits always occupy even places.
4. In a library there are 6 copies of one book, 4 copies each of two different books, 5 copies of each of three different books and 3 copies of each of two different books. Find the number of ways arranging all these books in a shelf in a single row.
5. Find the number of ways of arranging the letters of the word SPECIFIC. In how many of them
   (i) the two C's came together?
   (ii) the two I's donot came together

6. Find the number of 5 digited numbers that can be formed using the digits 1, 1, 2, 2, 3. How many of them are even.

7. Find the number of ways of arranging the letters of the word MISSING so that the two S's are together and two I's are together.

8. Find the number of 4 letter words that can be formed using the letters of the word RAMANA

9. If the letters of the word SIPRON are permited in all possible ways and the words thus formed are arranged in dictionary order, find the rank of the word (i) AJANTA (ii) JANATA.

10. If the letters of the word SIPRON are permited in all possible ways and if the words thus formed are arranged in dictionary order find the rank of the word (i) SIPRON (ii) PRISON.

Answers

1. (i) $\frac{5!}{2!2!}$ (ii) $\frac{6!}{3!}$ (iii) $\frac{7!}{2!2!}$ (iv) $\frac{11!}{(2!)^4}$ 2. $\frac{14!}{4!3!\ 5!2!}$ 3. $\frac{4!}{2!\ 2!} \times \frac{5!}{2!\ 2!}$

4. $\frac{35!}{(3!)^2\ (4!)^2\ (5!)^3\ 6!}$ 5. $\frac{8!}{2!2!}$ (i) $\frac{7!}{2!}$ (ii) $\frac{6!}{2!} \times \frac{{}^7P_2}{2!}$ 6. 30, 12

7. 5! 8. 72 9. (i) 28 (ii) 68 10. (i) 618 (ii) 438

5.7 Combinations

A combination is only a selection of things. There is no importance to the order or arrangement of things in a combination. Thus a combination of n things taken r at a time can be regarged as a subject with r elements of a set containing n elements.

Theorem : The number of combinations of n dissimilar things taken r at a time is

$$\frac{{}^nP_r}{r!} = {}^nC_r \,.$$

Proof : Let A be the set containing the given n dissimilar things. Then the number of combinations (${}^nC_r$) of these n dissimilar things taken r at a time equal to the number of subjects of a containing relevants. If we select one such subject of A containing r elements, these r thing can be arranged in a line in n ways. In other words one combination gives rise to r! permutations. But we know that number of permutations of n thing taken r at a time is ${}^nP_r$.

Hence $n_{c_r} . r! = n_{p_r}$

$$\Rightarrow n_{c_r} = \frac{n_{p_r}}{r!} = \frac{n!}{r!(n-r)!}$$

Note

1. $n_{c_r} = n_{c_{n-r}}$

2. $n_{c_n} = n_{c_0} = 1$ for any positive integers.

3. If $n_{c_r} = n_{c_s} \Rightarrow n = r + s$ or $r = s$.

4. $n_{c_r} + n_{c_{r-1}} = (n+1)_{c_r}$

5. $\frac{n_{c_r}}{n_{c_{r-1}}} = \frac{n-r+1}{r}$

6. $\frac{n_{p_r}}{n_{c_r}} = r!$

Solved Examples

1. (i) If $n_{c_4} = 210$, find n

(ii) If $12_{c_r} = 495$, find possible value of r.

Sol. (i) $n_{c_4} = 210 \Rightarrow \frac{n!}{4!(n-4)!} = 210$

$$= n(n-1)(n-2)(n-3)$$

$$= 210 \times 4!$$

$$= 210 \times 24$$

$$= 10 \times 21 \times 24$$

$$= 5 \times 2 \times 7 \times 3 \times 8 \times 3$$

$$= 10 \times 9 \times 8 \times 7$$

$$\Rightarrow n = 10.$$

(ii) $12_{C_r} = 495$

$$\Rightarrow \frac{12!}{r!(12-r)!} = 495$$

$$\Rightarrow \frac{12\times11\times10\times9!}{r!(12-r)!} = 495$$

$$\Rightarrow \frac{12\times2\times8!}{r!(12-r)!} = 1$$

$$\Rightarrow (24)(8!) = r!\,(12-r)!$$

take r = 8 or 4 ; it is satisfied.

$\therefore$ r = 4 or 8

2. (i) If $n_{c_4} = n_{c_6}$, find n

(ii) If $15_{c_{2r-1}} = 15_{c_{2r+4}}$, find n

(i) We have $n_{c_r} = n_{c_s} \Rightarrow$ n = r + s or r = s

here $n_{c_4} = n_{c_6}$, $4 \neq 6$

$\Rightarrow$ n = 4 + 6 = 10

$\therefore$ n = 10

(ii) $15_{c_{2r-1}} = 15_{c_{2r+4}}$

$\therefore$ 2r – 1 = 2r + 4 ($\because$ r = s) 1

(or)

2r – 1 + 2r + 4 = 15 ($\because$ r + s = n) 2

from (1) $\Rightarrow$ – 1 = 4 (not possible)

from (2) $\Rightarrow$ 4r + 3 = 15 $\Rightarrow$ 4r = 12 $\Rightarrow$ r = 3

3. If $n_{c_5} = n_{c_6}$ then find 13_{c_n}

Sol. Given $n_{c_5} = n_{c_6} \Rightarrow$ n = 5 + 6 = 11 $(\because n_{c_r} = n_{c_s} \Rightarrow n = r + s)$

$\therefore 13_{c_n} = 13_{c_4} = 13_{c_2}$ $(\because n_{c_r} = n_{c_{n-r}})$

$$= \frac{13\times12}{2} = 13\times6 = 78$$

4. Find the number of ways of selecting 6 boys and 4 girls from a group of 9 boys and 5 girls.

Sol. 6 boys can be selected from given 9 boys in 9_{c_6} ways and 4 girls can be selected from 5 girls in 5_{c_4} ways. Hence by fundamental principle, the number of required selections is $9_{c_6} \times 5_{c_4} = 420$

5. Find the number of ways of forming a committee of 5 members out of 7 boys and 6 girls such that there is atleast one girl in the committee.

Sol. The number of ways of forming a committee of 5 members out of 13 members (7 boys + 6 girls) is 13_{c5}. Out of these, the number of committee having no girl is 7_{c_5} (we select all 5 from boys)

$\therefore$ the number of committees having atleast one girl is $13_{c5} - 7_{c5}$

6. Find the number of ways of selecting 11 member cricket team from 7 bats men, 6 bowelers and 2 wicket keepers. So that the team contains atleast 4 bowlers and one wicket keepers.

Sol. The required cricket team can have following compositions

Bowlers (6)	Wicket keepers (2)	Batsmen (7)	Number of ways of selecting team
4	1	6	$6_{c_4} \times 2_{c_1} \times 7_{c_6} = 210$
5	1	5	$6_{c_5} \times 2_{c_1} \times 7_{c_5} = 252$
6	1	4	$6_{c_6} \times 2_{c_1} \times 7_{c_4} = 70$
4	2	5	$6_{c_4} \times 2_{c_2} \times 7_{c_5} = 315$
5	2	4	$6_{c_5} \times 2_{c_2} \times 7_{c_4} = 210$
6	2	3	$6_{c_6} \times 2_{c_2} \times 7_{c_3} = 35$

$\therefore$ The number of ways of selecting the required cricket team

$= 210 + 252 + 70 + 315 + 210 + 35 = 1092$

7. 10 persons sitting around a circle. In how many ways can 2 persons out of them be selected so that they are not adjacent to each other ?

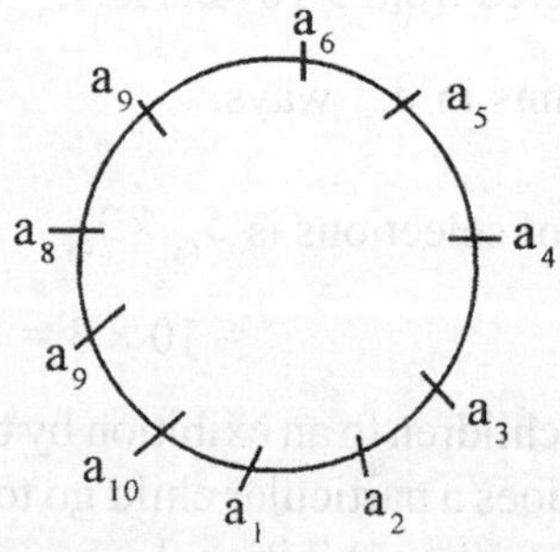

Sol. Let the 10 persons namely $a_1, a_2, a_3 \ldots\ldots a_{10}$ be sit in a round table as shown in the figure. Any two persons can be selected from 10 person in 10_{c_2} way also two persons they are adjacent to each other can be selected from the 10 persons in 10 ways.

They are $a_1\ a_2,\ a_2\ a_3,\ a_3\ a_4,\ a_4\ a_5,\ a_5\ a_6,\ a_6\ a_7,\ a_7\ a_8,\ a_8\ a_9,\ a_1\ a_{10},\ a_{10}\ a_1$

$\therefore$ The required number of selection is $10_{c_2} - 10$

(selected number are not adjacent to each other)

$$= \frac{10 \times 9}{2} - 10 = 45 - 10 = 35$$

8. Find the number of ways of forming a committee of 5 members out of 6 Indians and 5 Americans so that always the Indians will be in majority in the committee.

Sol. The required committee have the following composition.

Indians (6)	Americans (5)	Number of ways of selecting Committee
5	0	$6_{c_5} \times 5_{c_0} = 6$
4	1	$6_{c_4} \times 5_{c_1} = 75$
3	2	$6_{c3} \times 5_{c2} = 200$

$\therefore$ number of ways of selecting the required commitee is $6 + 75 + 200 = 281$

9. Find the number of ways of selecting 3 vowels and 2 consonants from the letters of the word EQUATION.

Sol. The given word is EQUATION

It contains 5 vowels (A E I O U) and 3 consonants (Q, T, N)

$\therefore$ 3 vowels can be selected from 5 vowels is 5_{c_3} ways and 2 consonants can be selected from 3 consonants in 3_{c_2} ways.

$\therefore$ the required number of selections is $5_{c_3} \times 3_{c_2}$

$= 10 \times 3 = 30$

10. A person wants to take 9 children to an exibition by taking 3 at a time in all possible ways. How many times does a particular child go to the exhibition and how many times does the person go to the exhibition ?

(i) To find the number of times a particular child go to exibition, we have to select 2 more students from remaining 8 children, this can be done in 8_{c_2} ways.

Hence each children can go to exibition in $8_{c_2} = \frac{8 \times 7}{2} = 28$ times.

(ii) The number of times the person go to the exibition is equal to

The number of different ways of selecting 3 students out of 9.

$$= 9_{c_3} = \frac{9 \times 8 \times 7}{6} = 84$$

11. Find the number of divisors of 1080

Sol. $1080 = 2^3 \times 5^1 \times 3^3 = 2^3 \times 3^3 \times 5^1$

$\therefore$ The number of positive divisors of

1080 is $(3 + 1)(3 + 1)(1 + 1)$

$= 4 \times 4 \times 2 = 32$

Excercise - 5.5

1. (i) If $n_{p_5} : n_{p_3} = 2:1$ then find n.

(ii) If $(2n + 1)p_{(n-1)} : (2n - 1)p_n = 3 : 5$ then find n

2. (i) If $10 \,.\, n_{c_2} = 3.(n+1)_{c_3}$, find n.

(ii) If $n_{p_r} = 5040$ and $n_{c_r} = 210$, find n and r

3. Prove that

(i) $10_{c_3} + 10_{c_6} = 11_{c_4}$

(ii) $25_{c_4} + \sum_{r=0}^{4} (29-r)_{c_3} = 30_{c_4}$

4. (i) If $12_{c_{(s+1)}} = 12_{c_{(2s-5)}}$, find s

(ii) If $n_{c_{21}} = n_{c_{27}}$, find 50_{c_n}

5. Find the number of ways of selecting 4 boys and 3 girls from a group of 8 boys and 5 girls.

6. Find the number of ways of forming a committee of 4 members out of 6 boys and 4 girls such that there atleast one girl in the committee.

7. Find the number of ways of selecting a cricket team of 11 players from 7 batsmen and 6 bowlers such that there will be atleast 5 bowlers in the team.

8. If a set has 12 elements find the number of subsets of A having (i) 4 elements (ii) Atleast 3 elements (iii) at most 3 elements

9. A Teacher wants to take 10 students to a park. He can take exactly 3 students at a time and he will not take the same group of 3 students more than once. Find the number of times.

(i) each student can go to the park

(ii) the teacher can go to the park

10. A double decker mini bus has 8 seats in the lower and 10 seats in the upper deck. Find the number of ways of arranging 18 persons in the bus if 3 children want to go to the upper deck and 4 old people can not go to the upper deck.

Answers

1. (i) 5 (ii) 4

2. (i) 9 (ii) n = 10, r = 4

4. (i) $s = \frac{16}{3}$ (ii) 1225

5. $8_{c_4} \times 5_{c_3} = 700$

6. $10_{c_4} - 6_{c_4} = 195$

7. $6_{c_5} \times 7_{c_6} + 6_{c_6} \times 7_{c_5} = 63$

8. (i) $12_{c_4} = 495$ (ii) $2^{12} - \{12_{c_0} + 12_{c_1} + 12_{c_2}\} = 4017$

(iii) $12_{c_0} + 12_{c_1} + 12_{c_2} + 12_{c_3} = 299$

9. (i) $9_{c_2} = 36$ (ii) $10_{c_3} = 120$

10. $11_{c_7} \times 10! \times 8!$

6

Functions

6.1 Introduction

We use the mathematics essentially to study the relationship between variables. Function is a special case of relation.

Ordered Pairs: Let A and B be sets. Let $a \in A$ and $b \in B$ then (a, b) is called ordered pair. a is called first component and b is called second component of the ordered pair (a, b).

Note: Two ordered pairs (a_1, b_1), (a_2, b_2) are equal if $a_1 = a_2$; $b_1 = b_2$

Cartesian Product:

Let A and B are any two sets. Then $\{(a,b) / a \in A,\ b \in B\}$ is called the Cartesian product of A and B and is denoted by A × B. (read as A cross B)

Ex: Let A = {1, 2} B = {x, y, z}

$A \times B = \{(1, x), (1, y), (1, z), (2, x), (2, y), (2, z)\}$

$B \times A = \{(x, 1), (x, 2), (y, 1), (y, 2), (z, 1), (z, 2)\}$

$A \times A = \{(1, 1), (1, 2), (2, 1), (2, 2)\}$

$B \times B = \{(x, x), (x, y), (x, z), (y, x), (y, y), (y, z), (z, x), (z, y), (z, z)\}$

Note:

1. If A and B are distinct non empty sets then $A \times B \neq B \times A$
2. If one set of A and B is empty then A × B also empty.
3. Number of elements in A × B = number of elements in A × number of elements in B.

Relation: If A and B are non empty sets and any sub set of $A \times B$ is called a relation from A to B.

Note: Any subset of $A \times A$ is called a binary relation on A.

Ex: Let A = {1, 2, 3} B = {p, q}

$A \times B$ = {(1, p), (1, q), (2, p), (2, q), (3, p), (3, q)}

f : {(1, p), (2, q), (3, q)} is a relation from A to B

g : {(1, p), (1, q), is a relation from A to B

Function: Let A and B be two non empty sets and f be a relation from A to B.

If for each element $a \in A$ there exists a unique $b \in B$ such that $(a, b) \in f$ then f is called a function (mapping) from A to B it is denoted by $f: A \to B$.

The set A is called domain and B is called co domain of f.

A function f can also be seen such way that, which takes in put x and returns an output $f(x)$.

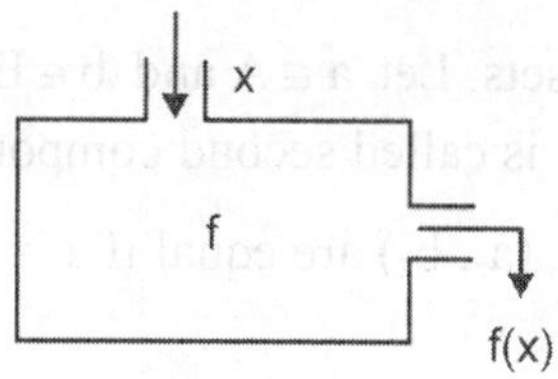

Ex: Let $f: A \to B$ is a function defined as

$f(x) = x + 2$ and A = {1, 2, 3} B = {2, 3, 4, 5, 10, 12} then f(A) = {3, 4, 5}

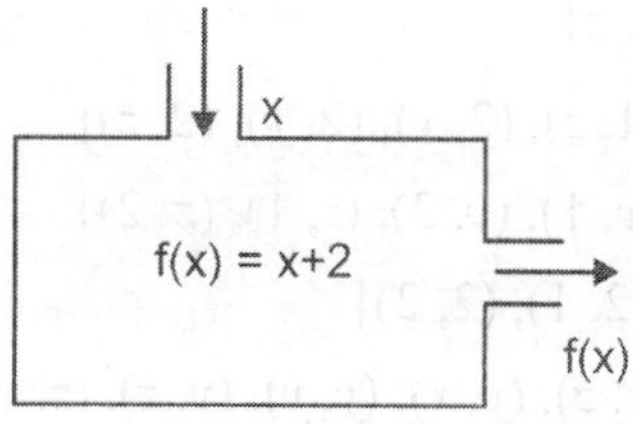

Image, Pre-Image:

If $f: A \to B$ is a function and if f(a) = b then b is called the image of a under f and the element a is called pre image.

Range: If $f: A \rightarrow B$ is a function, then $f(A)$ the set of all f images of elements in A, is called the range of f.

So $\quad f(A) = \{f(a) \,/\, a \in A\} \subseteq B.$

Injection or One-One Function:

A function f is said to be injection function if different elements of A have distinct f images in B.

Note: f is a $A \rightarrow B$ is one-one function

$$\Leftrightarrow \quad a_1, a_2 \in A \quad \text{and} \quad f(a_1) = f(a_2)$$

$$\Rightarrow a_1 = a_2$$

Ex: Let $\quad A = \{x, y, z\} \quad B = \{1, 2, 3, 4\}$

f : $\{(x, 1), (y, 2), (2, 4)\}$ is a one-one function

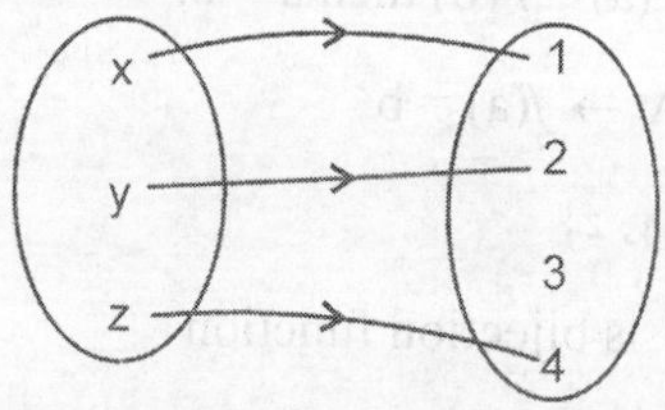

g : $\{(x, 1), (y, 1), (z, 2)\}$ is not one-one function

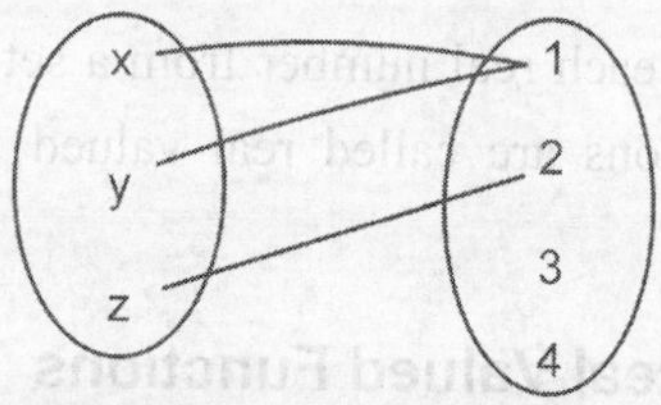

Since $x \neq y \;\Rightarrow\; f(x) = f(y)$

Surjection Function:

A function $f: A \rightarrow B$ is said to be surjection (on to) if the range of f is equal to the co domain of f.

$f: A \rightarrow B$ is a surjection $\Leftrightarrow$ range $f = f(A) = B$

$\Leftrightarrow B = \{f(a) \,/\, a \in A\}$

$\Leftrightarrow$ for every $b \in B$ there exists atleast one $a \in A$ such that $f(a) = b$.

Ex: Let $A = \{1, 2, 3, 4\}$ $B = (x, y, z)$

f : $\{(1, x), (2, y), (3, z), (4, x)\}$ is surjection.

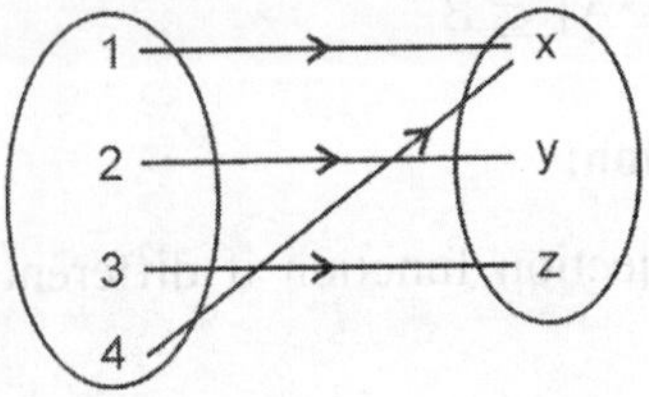

Bijection Function:

If $f: A \rightarrow B$ is both an injection and surjection then f is said to be bijection or one to one from A to B.

$f: A \rightarrow B$ is bijection $\Leftrightarrow$ f is both injection and surjection

$\Leftrightarrow$ (i) If $a, b \in A$ and $f(a) = f(b)$ then $a = b$.

(ii) $\forall b \in B \; \exists \; a \in A \rightarrow f(a) = b$

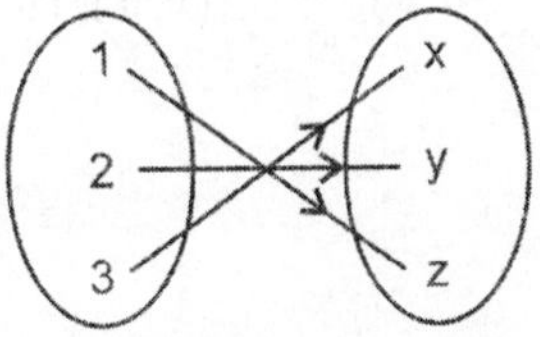

Ex: $A = \{1, 2, 3\}$ $B = \{x, y, z\}$

$f = \{(1, z), (2, y), (3, x)\}$ is bijection function

Real Valued Function

The function that assigned to each real number from a set of real numbers to another set of real numbers, such functions are called real valued functions. So the domain and co-domain are real numbers.

6.2 Classification of Real Valued Functions

1. ***Even and odd function:*** Let A be non empty sub set of R such that $-x \in A$ for all $x \in A$ and $f: A \rightarrow R$

   (i) If $f(-x) = f(x) \; \forall \; x \in A$ then f is called an even function.

   (ii) If $f(-x) = -f(x) \; \forall \; x \in A$ then f is called an odd function.

   Ex: $f(x) = x^2$ is an even function

   $f(x) = x$ is an odd function

2. ***Polynomial function:*** If n is non negative integer, $a_1, a_2, a_3 \ldots . a_n$ are real numbers. Then the function *f* is defined by

$f(x) = a_0 + a_1 x + a_2 x^2 + \ldots . + a_n x^n \ \forall \ x \in R$ is called a polynomial function.

Ex: $f(x) = ax^2 + bx + c$ (a, b, $c \in R$) is a polynomial function.

3. ***Rational function:*** If *f* and g are polynomial functions and $g(x) \neq 0$ for all $x \in R$ then function $\frac{f}{g}$ defined by $\left(\frac{f}{g}\right)(x) = \frac{f(x)}{g(x)}$ is called rational function.

Ex: $F(x) = \frac{3x}{x^2 + 4}$

4. ***Algebraic function:*** Algebraic operations: operations like addition, subtraction, multiplication, division etc., are called algebraic operations.

A function obtained by applying a finite number of algebraic operations on polynomial functions is called a algebraic function.

Ex: 1. $f(x) = x + \sqrt{x}$ $(x \geq 0)$

2. $f(x) = \sqrt{9 - x^2}$ $(x \in [-3, 3])$

5. ***Transdental functions:*** A function which is not algebraic is called a transdental function. They are

(a) Trigonometric functions (b) Exponential functions (c) Logarithmic functions

(a) ***Trigonometric functions:*** The A function of the type $y = \sin x$, $y = \cos x$, $y = \tan x$, $y = \cot x$, $y = \sec x$, $y = \text{cosec } x$ are called trigonometric functions.

(b) ***Exponential functions:*** The function a^x when $1 \neq a > 0$ and x is real is called an exponential function.

Domain of a^x is R and range is R^+

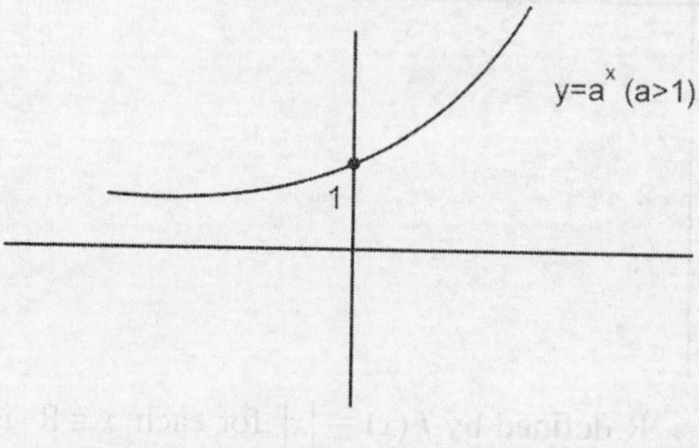

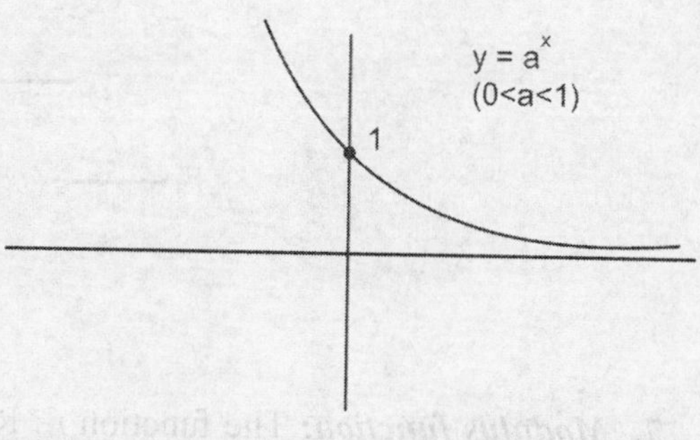

Logarithmic functions: if $a > 0$ $a \neq 1$ given $y > 0$ there exists a unique $x \in R$ such that $a^x = y$ the function defined on R^+ by $f(y) = x$, where $a^x = y$ is called logarithmic function to base a it is denoted by $\log_a$ thus $\log_a^y = x \Leftrightarrow y = a^x$. The logarithmic function to be base e is called the natural logarithmic function and if is denoted by 'ln'. Thus $\ln y = x \Rightarrow y = e^x$.

here Domain is (0, a), Range = R

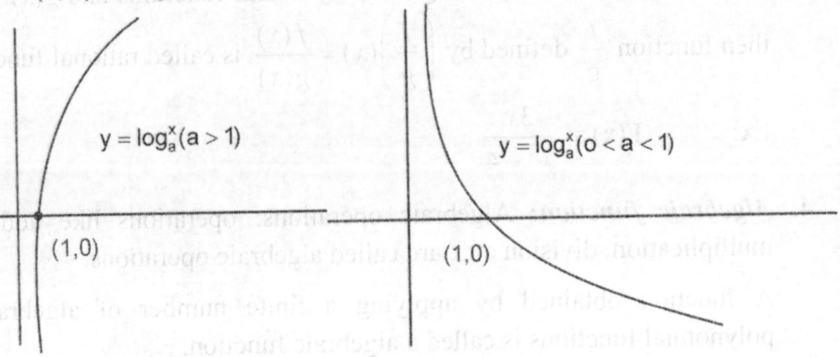

6. ***Greatest integer function:*** For any real number x we denoted by $[x]$ the greatest integer less than or equal to x

   For example: $[1.27] = 1$ $[3.14] = 3$, $[-2.71] = -3$ $[-4.01] = -5$

   here Domain = R, Range = Z

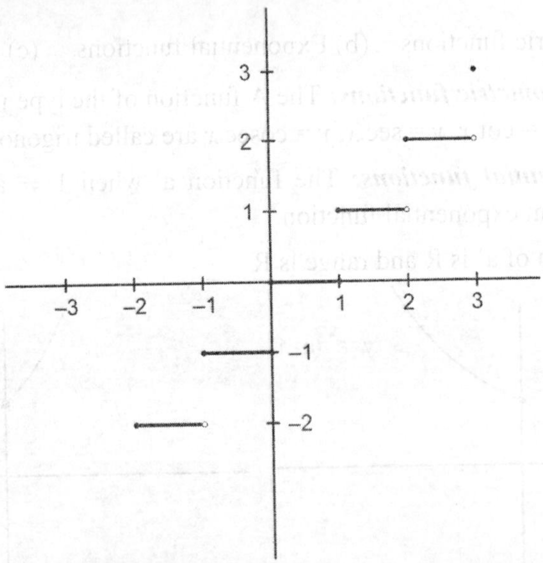

7. ***Modulus function:*** The function $f : R \rightarrow R$ defined by $f(x) = |x|$ for each $x \in R$ is called modulus function.

i.e., $f(x) = \begin{cases} x & x \geq 0 \\ -x & x < 0 \end{cases}$

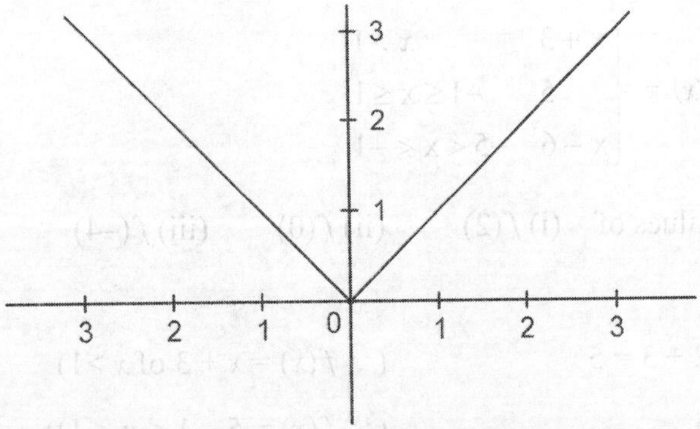

8. *Signum function:* The function $f: R \to R$ defined by sgn $(x) = f(x) = \dfrac{|x|}{x}$

$$= \begin{cases} 1 & x > 0 \\ 0 & x = 0 \\ -1 & x < 0 \end{cases} \quad \text{is called signum function}$$

Here Domain = R: Range = {–1, 0, 1}

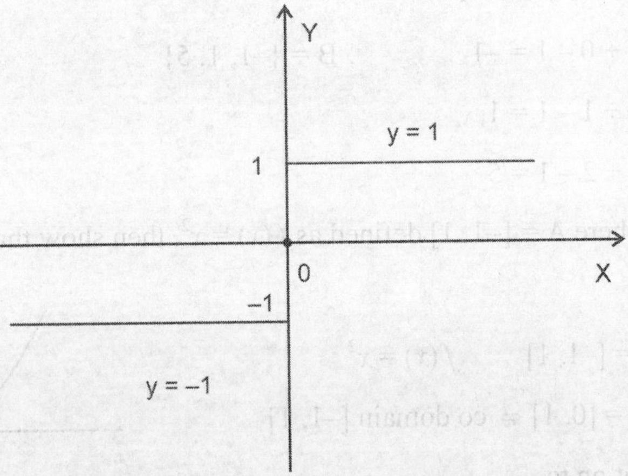

9. *Explicit function:* A function is which the dependent variable y is express uniquely in terms of independent variable x is called as explicit function.

Ex: $y = x^3$ $y = \sin x$ $y = e^x$ $y = \log 2x$

10. *Implicit function:* A function which is not explicit is called as implicit function, here the dependent variable by cannot be expressed unique in terms of x.

Ex: (i) $x^2 + y^2 = 16$ (ii) $y x^2 - y^2 = 9$

Solved Examples

1. If the function $f(x)$ is defined by

$$f(x) = \begin{cases} x+3 & x>1 \\ 5 & -1\le x\le 1 \\ x-6 & -5<x<-1 \end{cases}$$

Then find the values of (i) $f(2)$ (ii) $f(0)$ (iii) $f(-4)$

Sol:

(i) $f(2) = 2 + 3 = 5$ $(\because f(x) = x + 3 \text{ of } x > 1)$

(ii) $f(0) = 5$ $(\because f(x) = 5 \ -1 \le x \le 1))$

(iii) $f(-4) = -4 - 6 = -10$ $(\because f(x) = x - 6 \text{ when } -5 < x < -1)$

2. If A = {– 2, –1, 0, 1, 2} and $f: A \to B$ is surjection by $f(x) = x^2 + x - 1$ then find B.

Sol: $B = \{f(-2), f(-1), f(0), f(1), f(2)\}$

$f(-2) = 4 - 2 - 1 = 1$

$f(-1) = 1 - 1 - 1 = -1$

$f(0) = 0 + 0 - 1 = -1$ $\therefore B = \{-1, 1, 5\}$

$f(1) = 1 + 1 - 1 = 1$

$f(2) = 4 + 2 - 1 = 5$

3. If $f: A \to A$ where $A = [-1, 1]$ defined as $f(x) = x^2$, then show that f is not on to.

Sol:

domain = [–1, 1] $f(x) = x^2$

$\therefore$ range = [0, 1] $\neq$ co domain [–1, 1]

$\therefore f$ is not on to.

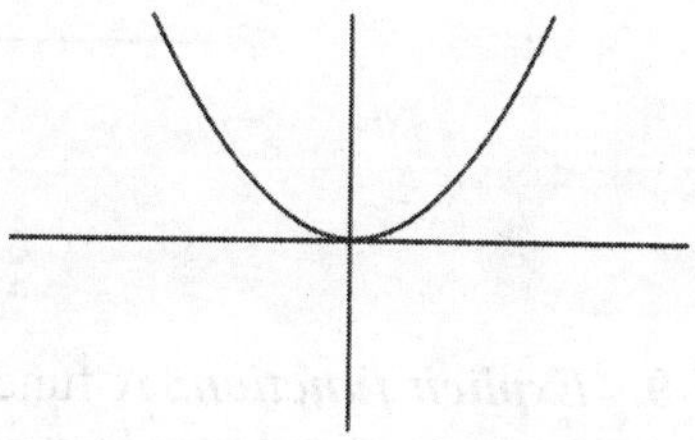

4. If $f: A \rightarrow A$ where $A = [-1, 1]$ defined as $f(x) = x^3$ is on to.

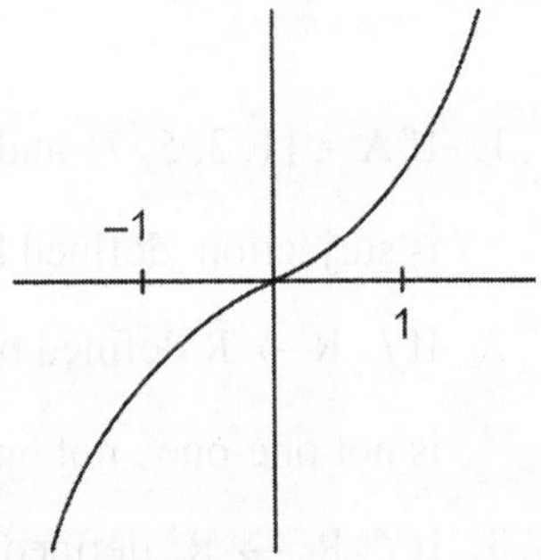

Sol:

co domain = $[-1, 1]$

range = $[-1, 1]$

$\therefore$ co domain = range

$\therefore f$ is on to.

5. If $f = \{(4, 5), (5, 6), (6, -4)\}$ and

$g = \{(4, -4), (6, 5), (8, 5)\}$ then find

(i) $f - g$ (ii) $f + 4$ (iii) $|f|$ (iv) $\frac{f}{g}$ (v) f^2

Sol:

Domain of $f = \{4, 5, 6\}$ domain of $g = \{4, 6, 8\}$

domain of $f + g = \{4, 5, 6\} \cap \{4, 6, 8\}$

$= \{4, 6\}$

(i) $f - g = \{(4, 5 + 4), (6, -4 - 5)\} = \{(4, 9), (6, -9)\}$

(ii) $f + 4 = \{(4, 5 + 4), (5, 6 + 4), (6, -4 + 4)\}$

$= \{(4, 9), (5, 10), (6, 0)\}$

(iii) $|f| = \{(4, |5|), (5, |6|), (6, |-4|)\}$

$= \{(4, 5), (5, 6), (6, 4)\}$

(iv) $\frac{f}{g} = \left\{\left(4, \frac{-5}{4}\right), \left(6, \frac{-4}{5}\right)\right\}$

(v) $f^2 = \{(4, 25), (5, 36), (6, 16)\}$

Exercise

1. If A = {1, 3, 5, 7} and f: A → B

   is surjection defined by $f(x) = x + 3$ then find B.

2. If f: R → R defined by $f(x) = x^2$ then show that f

   is not one-one , not on to.

3. If f: $R^+ \to R^+$ defined by $f(x) = x^2$ then show that f is bijection

4. If f = {(1, 2), (2, –3), (3, –1)} then find

   (i) $2f$ (ii) $2 + f$ (iii) f^2 (iv) $\sqrt{f}$

5. f and g are real valued functions defined by $f(x) = 2x + 1$, $g(x) = x^2$ then find

   (i) $(f + g)(x)$ (ii) $(fg)(x)$ (iii) $f^2(x)$

Answers

1. {4, 6, 8, 10}

4. (i) {(1, 4), (2, –6), (3, –2)} (ii) {(1, 4), (2, –1), (3, 1)}

   (iii) {(1, 4), (2, 9), (3, 1)} (iv) $(1, \sqrt{2})$

5. (i) $x^2 + 2x + 1$ (ii) $2x^3 + x^2$ (iii) $(2x + 1)^2$

7

Logarithms

7.1 Introduction

Logarithms play an important role in calculations. The operations of multiplication and division are replaced by addition and subtraction in logarithms. By using logarithms we can multiply by two large numbers and division with one large number by other.

Definition of logarithms: If a is a positive integer other than 1 such that $a^x = m$ then x is called the logarithm of m to the base a $(m > 0)$ (here x is unique).

Thus $a^x = m \Leftrightarrow x = \log_a m$

Ex: $2^3 = 8 \quad \therefore \quad 3 = \log_3^8$

$4^3 = 64 \quad \therefore \quad 3 = \log_4^{64}$

$10^3 = 1000 \quad \therefore \quad 3 = \log_{10} 1000$

Hence the logarithm of a given number to the given base is the index or power to the base should be raised in order to get the number.

$$\log_a 1 = 0 \quad \left(\because a^0 = 1, a > 0, a \neq 1\right)$$

Note: $\log_a^0 = -\infty$ since $a^{-\infty} \to 0$ the logarithm to the base 10 called common logarithms. The logarithms to the base 'e' are called natural logarithms. Here e is called exponential constant, it lies between 2 and 3.

Graph of $y = \log_{10}^{x}$

where x = 10 $\Rightarrow$ $\log_{10}^{1} = 0$

x = 10 $\Rightarrow$ $\log_{10}^{10} = 1$

x = 100 $\Rightarrow$ $\log_{10}^{100} = 2$ $(\because 100 = 10^2)$

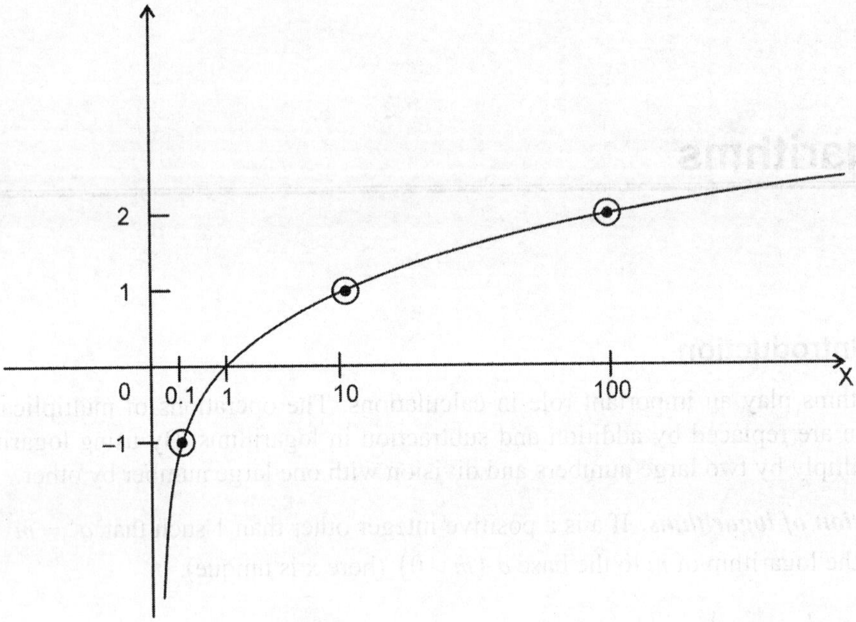

$$\log_{10}^{\frac{1}{10}} = -1 \qquad \because \quad 10^{-1} = \frac{1}{10}$$

The graph of $y = \ln x = \log_{e}^{x}$

x = 1 $\Rightarrow$ $\log_{e}^{e^0} = 0$

x = e^1 $\Rightarrow$ $\log_{e}^{e^1} = 1$

x = e^2 $\Rightarrow$ $\log_{e}^{e^2} = 2$

x = e^3 $\Rightarrow$ $\log_{e}^{e^3} = 3$ $(\because e^3 = e^3)$

where $x = \frac{1}{e} \Rightarrow y = \log_{e}^{\frac{1}{e}} = -1$

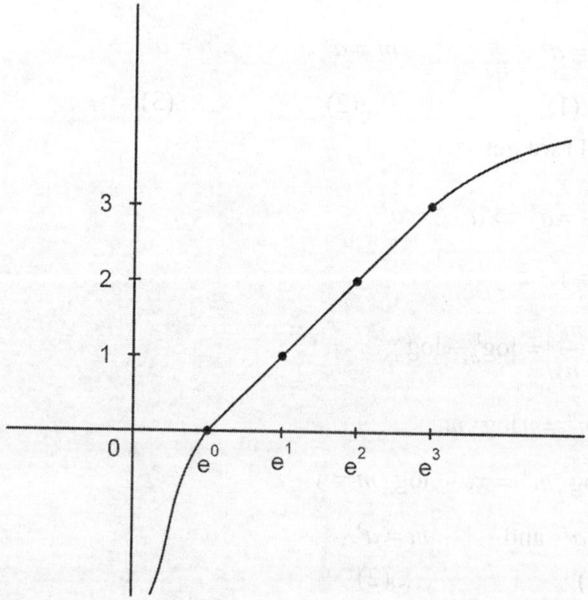

7.2 Theorems on Logarithms

Theorem 1: $\log_a mn = \log_a^m + \log_a^n$

Let $\quad \log_a mn = x, \quad \log_a^m = y, \quad \log_a^n = z$

$\Rightarrow \quad mn = a^x \quad m = a^y \quad n = a^z$

.....(1) .....(2) .....(3)

Sub (2), (3) in (1) we get

$$a^y . a^z = a^x \Rightarrow a^{y+z} = a^x$$

$\therefore \quad x = y + z \qquad (\because a^p = a^q \Rightarrow p = q)$

$\therefore \quad \log_a^{\min} = \log_a^m + \log_a^n$

Similarly we have

$$\log_a(a_1 a_2 .....a_n) = \log_a a_1 + \log_{a^2} a_2 + ...\log_a a_n$$

Theorem 2: $\log_a\left(\frac{m}{n}\right) = \log_a^m - \log_a^n$

Proof: Let $\quad \log_a\left(\frac{m}{n}\right) = x, \quad \log_a m = y, \quad \log_a n = z$

$$\Rightarrow \quad \frac{m}{n} = a^x, \quad m = a^y, \quad n = a^z$$

$$.....(1) \quad .....(2) \quad .....(3)$$

Sub (2), (3) in (1) we get

$$\frac{a^y}{a^z} = a^x \Rightarrow a^{y-z} = a^x$$

$$\Rightarrow \quad x = y - z$$

$$\therefore \quad \log_a\left(\frac{m}{n}\right) = \log_a^m - \log_a^n$$

Theorem 3: $\log_a m^n = n\log_a m$

Proof: Let $\log_a m^n = x, \quad \log_a m = y$

$$\Rightarrow \quad m^n = a^x \text{ and } \quad m = a^y$$

$$.....(1) \quad .....(2)$$

Now substitute (2) in (1) we get

$$\left(a^y\right)^n = a^x$$

$$\Rightarrow \quad a^{ny} = a^x$$

$$\Rightarrow \quad x = ny$$

$$\therefore \quad \log_a m^n = n.\log_a m$$

Note: $a^{\log_a m} = m$

Theorem 4: Change of base theorem

$$\log_b^a = \frac{\log_c^a}{\log_c^b}$$

Proof: Let $\log_b^a = x, \quad \log_c^a = y, \quad \log_c^b = z$

$$\Rightarrow \quad a = b^x \quad a = c^y \quad b = c^z$$

$$.....(1) \quad .....(2) \quad .....(3)$$

Substitute (2), (3) in (1)

$$\Rightarrow \quad c^y = \left(c^z\right)^x$$

$$\therefore \quad c^y = c^{xz}$$

$$\Rightarrow \quad y = xz \text{ or } x = y/z$$

$$\Rightarrow \qquad \log_b^a = \frac{\log_c^a}{\log_c^b}$$

Note: $\log_a^{\left(\frac{1}{x}\right)} = -\log_x^a$

$$\because \qquad \log_a^{\left(\frac{1}{x}\right)} = \log_a^1 - \log_a^x$$

$$= 0 - \log_a^x = -\log_a^x$$

7.3 Characteristics and Mantissa

The integral part of logarithm is called characteristic and fractional part is called mantissa.

To find the characteristic of logarithm of any number greater than 1.

We have $10^0 = 1$, $10^1 = 10$, $10^2 = 100$, $10^3 = 1000$ if it show that number with one digit in its integral part lies between 10^0 and 10^1, a number with two digit in the integral part lies between 10^1 and 10^2 and so on, hence number with a an digit in its integral part lies between 10^{n-1} and 10^n.

So if a number whose integral part contains *n* digits then

$$N = 10^{(n-1)} + \text{ a fraction}$$

$$\Rightarrow \qquad \log_{10}^N = (n-1) + \text{ a fraction}$$

Ex:

1. Characteristic of 32 is 1 $\left(\because 10^1 < 32 < 10^2\right)$
2. Characteristic of 105 is 2 $\left(\because 10^2 < 105 < 10^3\right)$
3. Characteristic of 1123.5 is 3 $\left(\because 10^3 < 1123.5 < 10^4\right)$

to find characteristic of a logarithm of any number less than one.

We have $10^0 = 1$ $\quad 10^{-1} = 0.1$ $\quad 10^{-2} = 0.01$ $\quad 10^{-3} = 0.001$ .... etc

It shows that decimal with no zero immediately after decimal point lies between 10^{-1} and 10^0, a number two zero immediately after the decimal point lies between 10^{-2} and 10^{-1} hence a decimal fraction n zeros immediately after the decimal point lies between $10^{-(n+1)}$ and 10^{-n}

$\therefore$ If D is the decimal fraction with n zeros immediately after the decimal point then

$$D = 10^{-(n+1)} + \text{a fraction}$$

$$\therefore \quad \log_{10}^{D} = -(n+1) + \text{ a fraction}$$

Ex: (i) Characteristic of $\log_{10} 0.0075$ is $(\bar{3})$

(ii) Characteristic of $\log_{10} 0.00016$ is $(\bar{4})$

Relation between natural logarithms and common logarithms

$$(2.303)\log(N) = \ln N$$

Note: In case of logarithm of a decimal fraction the minus is written over the characteristic and not before it.

To indicate that characteristic alone is negative and not the whole expression.

Ex: $\log_{10} 0.002 = -3 + 0.3010$

which is written as $\log_{10} 0.002 = \bar{3}.301$ in working with negative logarithms, some times it is necessary to make mantissa. Positive (mantissa is always positive since it is fractional part of logarithms)

This can be done by adding 1 to mantissa and subtract 1 from characteristic

Ex:
$$-2.3467 = -2 + -0.3467$$
$$= -2 - 1 + 1 - 0.3467$$
$$= -3 + 0.6633$$
$$= \bar{3}.6633$$

To find mantissa: The mantissa are the same for the logarithms of all numbers which have same significant digits (drop decimal point and all zero at the end of whole number)

When using four figure table of logarithms, we use only the first four digits of any whole number. The method of looking at the table is as followed by giving example.

Let the first 4 digits be 1, 2, 3, 4 take the first two digits 12 move along the row 12 to column 3 to find 0899. In the same row 12 move further to column 4 of mean difference table to find 14 add 14 to 0899 to get 0913 which is required mantissa.

Log Table

LOGARTAIM (go ban 10) LOGARITHMS (to base 10)

	0	1	2	3	4	5	6	7	8	9	1	2	3	4	5	6	7	8	9
1·0	·0000	0043	0086	0128	0170	0212	0253	0294	0334	0374	4	8	12	17	21	25	29	33	37
1·1	·0414	0453	0492	0531	0569	0607	0645	0682	0719	0755	4	8	11	15	19	23	26	30	34
1·2	·0792	0828	0864	0899	0934	0969	1004	1038	1072	1106	3	7	10	14	17	21	24	28	31
1·3	·1139	1173	1206	1239	1271	1303	1335	1367	1399	1430	3	6	10	13	16	19	23	26	29
1·4	·1461	1492	1523	1553	1584	1614	1644	1673	1703	1732	3	6	9	12	15	18	21	24	27
1·5	·1761	1790	1818	1847	1875	1903	1931	1959	1987	2014	3	6	8	11	14	17	20	22	25
1·6	·2041	2068	2095	2122	2148	2175	2201	2227	2253	2279	3	5	8	11	13	16	18	21	24
1·7	·2304	2330	2355	2380	2405	2430	2455	2480	2504	2529	2	5	7	10	12	15	17	20	22
1·8	·2553	2577	2601	2625	2648	2672	2695	2718	2742	2765	2	5	7	9	12	14	16	19	21
1·9	·2788	2810	2833	2856	2878	2900	2923	2945	2967	2989	2	4	7	9	11	13	16	18	20
2·0	·3010	3032	3054	3075	3096	3118	3139	3160	3181	3201	2	4	6	8	11	13	15	17	19
2·1	·3222	3243	3263	3284	3304	3324	3345	3365	3385	3404	2	4	6	8	10	12	14	16	18
2·2	·3424	3444	3464	3483	3502	3522	3541	3560	3579	3598	2	4	6	8	10	12	14	15	17
2·3	·3617	3636	3655	3674	3692	3711	3729	3747	3766	3784	2	4	6	7	9	11	13	15	17
2·4	·3802	3820	3838	3856	3874	3892	3909	3927	3945	3962	2	4	5	7	9	11	12	14	16
2·5	·3979	3997	4014	4031	4048	4065	4082	4099	4116	4133	2	3	5	7	9	10	12	14	15
2·6	·4150	4166	4183	4200	4216	4232	4249	4265	4281	4298	2	3	5	7	8	10	11	13	15
2·7	·4314	4330	4346	4362	4378	4393	4409	4425	4440	4456	2	3	5	6	8	9	11	13	14
2·8	·4472	4487	4502	4518	4533	4548	4564	4579	4594	4609	2	3	5	6	8	9	11	12	14
2·9	·4624	4639	4654	4669	4683	4698	4713	4728	4742	4757	1	3	4	6	7	9	10	12	13
3·0	·4771	4786	4800	4814	4829	4843	4857	4871	4886	4900	1	3	4	6	7	9	10	11	13
3·1	·4914	4928	4942	4955	4969	4983	4997	5011	5024	5038	1	3	4	6	7	8	10	11	12
3·2	·5051	5065	5079	5092	5105	5119	5132	5145	5159	5172	1	3	4	5	7	8	9	11	12
3·3	·5185	5198	5211	5224	5237	5250	5263	5276	5289	5302	1	3	4	5	6	8	9	10	12
3·4	·5315	5328	5340	5353	5366	5378	5391	5403	5416	5428	1	3	4	5	6	8	9	10	11
3·5	·5441	5453	5465	5478	5490	5502	5514	5527	5539	5551	1	2	4	5	6	7	9	10	11
3·6	·5563	5575	5587	5599	5611	5623	5635	5647	5658	5670	1	2	4	5	6	7	8	10	11
3·7	·5682	5694	5705	5717	5729	5740	5752	5763	5775	5786	1	2	3	5	6	7	8	9	10
3·8	·5798	5809	5821	5832	5843	5855	5866	5877	5888	5899	1	2	3	5	6	7	8	9	10
3·9	·5911	5922	5933	5944	5955	5966	5977	5988	5999	6010	1	2	3	4	5	7	8	9	10
4·0	·6021	6031	6042	6053	6064	6075	6085	6096	6107	6117	1	2	3	4	5	6	8	9	10
4·1	·6128	6138	6149	6160	6170	6180	6191	6201	6212	6222	1	2	3	4	5	6	7	8	9
4·2	·6232	6243	6253	6263	6274	6284	6294	6304	6314	6325	1	2	3	4	5	6	7	8	9
4·3	·6335	6345	6355	6365	6375	6385	6395	6405	6415	6425	1	2	3	4	5	6	7	8	9
4·4	·6435	6444	6454	6464	6474	6484	6493	6503	6513	6522	1	2	3	4	5	6	7	8	9
4·5	·6532	6542	6551	6561	6571	6580	6590	6599	6609	6618	1	2	3	4	5	6	7	8	9
4·6	·6628	6637	6646	6656	6665	6675	6684	6693	6702	6712	1	2	3	4	5	6	7	7	8
4·7	·6721	6730	6739	6749	6758	6767	6776	6785	6794	6803	1	2	3	4	5	5	6	7	8
4·8	·6812	6821	6830	6839	6848	6857	6866	6875	6884	6893	1	2	3	4	4	5	6	7	8
4·9	·6902	6911	6920	6928	6937	6946	6955	6964	6972	6981	1	2	3	4	4	5	6	7	8
5·0	·6990	6998	7007	7016	7024	7033	7042	7050	7059	7067	1	2	3	3	4	5	6	7	8
5·1	·7076	7084	7093	7101	7110	7118	7126	7135	7143	7152	1	2	3	3	4	5	6	7	8
5·2	·7160	7168	7177	7185	7193	7202	7210	7218	7226	7235	1	2	2	3	4	5	6	7	7
5·3	·7243	7251	7259	7267	7275	7284	7292	7300	7308	7316	1	2	2	3	4	5	6	6	7
5·4	·7324	7332	7340	7348	7356	7364	7372	7380	7388	7396	1	2	2	3	4	5	6	6	7

LOGARTAIM (go ban 10) **LOGARITHMS (to base 10)**

	0	1	2	3	4	5	6	7	8	9	1	2	3	4	5	6	7	8	9
5·5	·7404	7412	7419	7427	7435	7443	7451	7459	7466	7474	1	2	2	3	4	5	5	6	7
5·6	·7482	7490	7497	7505	7513	7520	7528	7536	7543	7551	1	2	2	3	4	5	5	6	7
5·7	·7559	7566	7574	7582	7589	7597	7604	7612	7619	7627	1	2	2	3	4	5	5	6	7
5·8	·7634	7642	7649	7657	7664	7672	7679	7686	7694	7701	1	1	2	3	4	4	5	6	7
5·9	·7709	7716	7723	7731	7738	7745	7752	7760	7767	7774	1	1	2	3	4	4	5	6	7
6·0	·7782	7789	7796	7803	7810	7818	7825	7832	7839	7846	1	1	2	3	4	4	5	6	6
6·1	·7853	7860	7868	7875	7882	7889	7896	7903	7910	7917	1	1	2	3	4	4	5	6	6
6·2	·7924	7931	7938	7945	7952	7959	7966	7973	7980	7987	1	1	2	3	3	4	5	6	6
6·3	·7993	8000	8007	8014	8021	8028	8035	8041	8048	8055	1	1	2	3	3	4	5	5	6
6·4	·8062	8069	8075	8082	8089	8096	8102	8109	8116	8122	1	1	2	3	3	4	5	5	6
6·5	·8129	8136	8142	8149	8156	8162	8169	8176	8182	8189	1	1	2	3	3	4	5	5	6
6·6	·8195	8202	8209	8215	8222	8228	8235	8241	8248	8254	1	1	2	3	3	4	5	5	6
6·7	·8261	8267	8274	8280	8287	8293	8299	8306	8312	8319	1	1	2	3	3	4	5	5	6
6·8	·8325	8331	8338	8344	8351	8357	8363	8370	8376	8382	1	1	2	3	3	4	4	5	6
6·9	·8388	8395	8401	8407	8414	8420	8426	8432	8439	8445	1	1	2	2	3	4	4	5	6
7·0	·8451	8457	8463	8470	8476	8482	8488	8494	8500	8506	1	1	2	2	3	4	4	5	6
7·1	·8513	8519	8525	8531	8537	8543	8549	8555	8561	8567	1	1	2	2	3	4	4	5	5
7·2	·8573	8579	8585	8591	8597	8603	8609	8615	8621	8627	1	1	2	2	3	4	4	5	5
7·3	·8633	8639	8645	8651	8657	8663	8669	8675	8681	8686	1	1	2	2	3	4	4	5	5
7·4	·8692	8698	8704	8710	8716	8722	8727	8733	8739	8745	1	1	2	2	3	4	4	5	5
7·5	·8751	8756	8762	8768	8774	8779	8785	8791	8797	8802	1	1	2	2	3	3	4	5	5
7·6	·8808	8814	8820	8825	8831	8837	8842	8848	8854	8859	1	1	2	2	3	3	4	5	5
7·7	·8865	8871	8876	8882	8887	8893	8899	8904	8910	8915	1	1	2	2	3	3	4	4	5
7·8	·8921	8927	8932	8938	8943	8949	8954	8960	8965	8971	1	1	2	2	3	3	4	4	5
7·9	·8976	8982	8987	8993	8998	9004	9009	9015	9020	9025	1	1	2	2	3	3	4	4	5
8·0	·9031	9036	9042	9047	9053	9058	9063	9069	9074	9079	1	1	2	2	3	3	4	4	5
8·1	·9085	9090	9096	9101	9106	9112	9117	9122	9128	9133	1	1	2	2	3	3	4	4	5
8·2	·9138	9143	9149	9154	9159	9165	9170	9175	9180	9186	1	1	2	2	3	3	4	4	5
8·3	·9191	9196	9201	9206	9212	9217	9222	9227	9232	9238	1	1	2	2	3	3	4	4	5
8·4	·9243	9248	9253	9258	9263	9269	9274	9279	9284	9289	1	1	2	2	3	3	4	4	5
8·5	·9294	9299	9304	9309	9315	9320	9325	9330	9335	9340	1	1	2	2	3	3	4	4	5
8·6	·9345	9350	9355	9360	9365	9370	9375	9380	9385	9390	1	1	1	2	3	3	4	4	5
8·7	·9395	9400	9405	9410	9415	9420	9425	9430	9435	9440	0	1	1	2	2	3	3	4	4
8·8	·9445	9450	9455	9460	9465	9469	9474	9479	9484	9489	0	1	1	2	2	3	3	4	4
8·9	·9494	9499	9504	9509	9513	9518	9523	9528	9533	9538	0	1	1	2	2	3	3	4	4
9·0	·9542	9547	9552	9557	9562	9566	9571	9576	9581	9586	0	1	1	2	2	3	3	4	4
9·1	·9590	9595	9600	9605	9609	9614	9619	9624	9628	9633	0	1	1	2	2	3	3	4	4
9·2	·9638	9643	9647	9652	9657	9661	9666	9671	9675	9680	0	1	1	2	2	3	3	4	4
9·3	·9685	9689	9694	9699	9703	9708	9713	9717	9722	9727	0	1	1	2	2	3	3	4	4
9·4	·9731	9736	9741	9745	9750	9754	9759	9763	9768	9773	0	1	1	2	2	3	3	4	4
9·5	·9777	9782	9786	9791	9795	9800	9305	9809	9814	9818	0	1	1	2	2	3	3	4	4
9·6	·9823	9827	9832	9836	9841	9845	9830	9854	9859	9863	0	1	1	2	2	3	3	4	4
9·7	·9868	9872	9877	9881	9886	9890	9894	9899	9903	9908	0	1	1	2	2	3	3	4	4
9·8	·9912	9917	9921	9926	9930	9934	9939	9943	9948	9952	0	1	1	2	2	3	3	4	4
9·9	·9956	9961	9963	9969	9974	9978	9983	9987	9991	9996	0	1	1	2	2	3	3	3	4

Antilogarithmic tables

Given logarithm of a number (characteristic + mantissa) we can obtain the number itself by looking the antilogarithmic table for the mantissa part in the same way as is explained for finding mantissa of a number. The position of decimal point is fixed depending upon the characteristic part.

If the characteristic is positive or zero and is n then put the decimal point after $(n + 1)$ digits. If the characteristic is negative and is $\bar{n}$ then the decimal point is such way it succeeds by $(n-1)$ zero's.

FRITHLOGARTAIM

ANTI-LOGARITHMS

	0	1	2	3	4	5	6	7	8	9	1	2	3	4	5	6	7	8	9
·00	1000	1002	1005	1007	1009	1012	1014	1016	1019	1021	0	0	1	1	1	1	2	2	2
·01	1023	1026	1028	1030	1033	1035	1038	1040	1042	1045	0	0	1	1	1	1	2	2	2
·02	1047	1050	1052	1054	1057	1059	1062	1064	1067	1069	0	0	1	1	1	1	2	2	2
·03	1072	1074	1076	1079	1081	1084	1086	1089	1091	1094	0	0	1	1	1	1	2	2	2
·04	1096	1099	1102	1104	1107	1109	1112	1114	1117	1119	0	1	1	1	1	2	2	2	2
·05	1122	1125	1127	1130	1132	1135	1138	1140	1143	1146	0	1	1	1	1	2	2	2	2
·06	1148	1151	1153	1156	1159	1161	1164	1167	1169	1172	0	1	1	1	1	1	2	2	2
·07	1175	1178	1180	1183	1186	1189	1191	1194	1197	1199	0	1	1	1	1	2	2	2	2
·08	1202	1205	1208	1211	1213	1216	1219	1222	1225	1227	0	1	1	1	1	2	2	2	3
·09	1230	1233	1236	1239	1242	1245	1247	1250	1253	1256	0	1	1	1	1	2	2	2	3
·10	1259	1262	1265	1268	1271	1274	1276	1279	1282	1285	0	1	1	1	1	2	2	2	3
·11	1288	1291	1294	1297	1300	1303	1306	1309	1312	1315	0	1	1	1	2	2	2	2	3
·12	1318	1321	1324	1327	1330	1334	1337	1340	1343	1346	0	1	1	1	2	2	2	2	3
·13	1349	1352	1355	1358	1361	1365	1368	1371	1374	1377	0	1	1	1	2	2	2	3	3
·14	1380	1384	1387	1390	1393	1396	1400	1403	1406	1409	0	1	1	1	2	2	2	3	3
·15	1413	1416	1419	1422	1426	1429	1432	1435	1439	1442	0	1	1	1	2	2	2	3	3
·16	1445	1449	1452	1455	1459	1462	1466	1469	1472	1476	0	1	1	1	2	2	2	3	3
·17	1479	1483	1486	1489	1493	1496	1500	1503	1507	1510	0	1	1	1	2	2	2	3	3
·18	1514	1517	1521	1524	1528	1531	1535	1538	1542	1545	0	1	1	1	2	2	2	3	3
·19	1549	1552	1556	1560	1563	1567	1570	1574	1578	1581	0	1	1	1	2	2	3	3	3
·20	1585	1589	1592	1596	1600	1603	1607	1611	1614	1618	0	1	1	1	2	2	3	3	3
·21	1622	1626	1629	1633	1637	1641	1644	1648	1652	1656	0	1	1	2	2	2	3	3	3
·22	1660	1663	1667	1671	1675	1679	1683	1687	1690	1694	0	1	1	2	2	2	3	3	3
·23	1698	1702	1706	1710	1714	1718	1722	1726	1730	1734	0	1	1	2	2	2	3	3	4
·24	1738	1742	1746	1750	1754	1758	1762	1766	1770	1774	0	1	1	2	2	2	3	3	4
·25	1778	1782	1786	1791	1795	1799	1803	1807	1811	1816	0	1	1	2	2	2	3	3	4
·26	1820	1824	1828	1832	1837	1841	1845	1849	1854	1858	0	1	1	2	2	3	3	3	4
·27	1862	1866	1871	1875	1879	1884	1888	1892	1897	1901	0	1	1	2	2	3	3	3	4
·28	1905	1910	1914	1919	1923	1928	1932	1936	1941	1945	0	1	1	2	2	3	3	4	4
·29	1950	1954	1959	1963	1968	1972	1977	1982	1986	1991	0	1	1	2	2	3	3	4	4
·30	1995	2000	2004	2009	2014	2018	2023	2028	2032	2037	0	1	1	2	2	3	3	4	4
·31	2042	2046	2051	2056	2061	2065	2070	2075	2080	2084	0	1	1	2	2	3	3	4	4
·32	2089	2094	2099	2104	2109	2113	2118	2123	2128	2133	0	1	1	2	2	3	3	4	4
·33	2138	2143	2148	2153	2158	2163	2168	2173	2178	2183	0	1	1	2	2	3	3	4	4
·34	2188	2193	2198	2203	2208	2213	2218	2223	2228	2234	1	1	2	2	3	3	4	4	5
·35	2239	2244	2249	2254	2259	2265	2270	2275	2280	2286	1	1	2	2	3	3	4	4	5
·36	2291	2296	2301	2307	2312	2317	2323	2328	2333	2339	1	1	2	2	3	3	4	4	5
·37	2344	2350	2355	2360	2366	2371	2377	2382	2388	2393	1	1	2	2	3	3	4	4	5
·38	2399	2404	2410	2415	2421	2427	2432	2438	2443	2449	1	1	2	2	3	3	4	4	5
·39	2455	2460	2466	2472	2477	2483	2489	2495	2500	2506	1	1	2	2	3	3	4	5	5
·40	2512	2518	2523	2529	2535	2541	2547	2553	2559	2564	1	1	2	2	3	4	4	5	5
·41	2570	2576	2582	2588	2594	2600	2606	2612	2618	2624	1	1	2	2	3	4	4	5	5
·42	2630	2636	2642	2649	2655	2661	2667	2673	2679	2685	1	1	2	2	3	4	4	5	6
·43	2692	2698	2704	2710	2716	2723	2729	2735	2742	2748	1	1	2	3	3	4	4	5	6
·44	2754	2761	2767	2773	2780	2786	2793	2799	2805	2812	1	1	2	3	3	4	4	5	6
·45	2818	2825	2831	2838	2844	2851	2858	2864	2871	2877	1	1	2	3	3	4	5	5	6
·46	2884	2891	2897	2904	2911	2917	2924	2931	2938	2944	1	1	2	3	3	4	5	5	6
·47	2951	2958	2965	2972	2970	2985	2992	2999	3006	3013	1	1	2	3	3	4	5	5	6

FRITHLOGARTAIM

ANTI-LOGARITHMS

	0	1	2	3	4	5	6	7	8	9	1	2	3	4	5	6	7	8	9
·50	3162	3170	3177	3184	3192	3199	3206	3214	3221	3228	1	1	2	3	4	4	5	6	7
·51	3236	3243	3251	3258	3266	3273	3281	3289	3296	3304	1	2	2	3	4	5	5	6	7
·52	3311	3319	3327	3334	3342	3350	3357	3365	3373	3381	1	2	2	3	4	5	5	6	7
·53	3388	3396	3404	3412	3420	3428	3436	3443	3451	3459	1	2	2	3	4	5	6	6	7
·54	3467	3475	3483	3491	3499	3508	3516	3524	3532	3540	1	2	2	3	4	5	6	6	7
·55	3548	3556	3565	3573	3581	3589	3597	3606	3614	3622	1	2	2	3	4	5	6	7	7
·56	3631	3639	3648	3656	3664	3673	3681	3690	3698	3707	1	2	3	3	4	5	6	7	8
·57	3715	3724	3733	3741	3750	3758	3767	3776	3784	3793	1	2	3	3	4	5	6	7	8
·58	3802	3811	3819	3828	3837	3846	3855	3864	3873	3882	1	2	3	4	4	5	6	7	8
·59	3890	3899	3908	3917	3926	3936	3945	3954	3963	3972	1	2	3	4	5	5	6	7	8
·60	3981	3990	3999	4009	4018	4027	4036	4046	4055	4064	1	2	3	4	5	6	6	7	8
·61	4074	4083	4093	4102	4111	4121	4130	4140	4150	4159	1	2	3	4	5	6	7	8	9
·62	4169	4178	4188	4198	4207	4217	4227	4236	4246	4256	1	2	3	4	5	6	7	8	9
·63	4266	4276	4285	4295	4305	4315	4325	4335	4345	4355	1	2	3	4	5	6	7	8	9
·64	4365	4375	4385	4395	4406	4416	4426	4436	4446	4457	1	2	3	4	5	6	7	8	9
·65	4467	4477	4487	4498	4508	4519	4529	4539	4550	4560	1	2	3	4	5	6	7	8	9
·66	4571	4581	4592	4603	4613	4624	4634	4645	4656	4667	1	2	3	4	5	6	7	9	10
·67	4677	4688	4699	4710	4721	4732	4742	4753	4764	4775	1	2	3	4	5	7	8	9	10
·68	4786	4797	4808	4819	4831	4842	4853	4864	4875	4887	1	2	3	4	6	7	8	9	10
·69	4898	4909	4920	4932	4943	4955	4966	4977	4989	5000	1	2	3	5	6	7	8	9	10
·70	5012	5023	5035	5047	5058	5070	5082	5093	5105	5117	1	2	4	5	6	7	8	9	11
·71	5129	5140	5152	5164	5176	5188	5200	5212	5224	5236	1	2	4	5	6	7	8	10	11
·72	5248	5260	5272	5284	5297	5309	5321	5333	5346	5358	1	2	4	5	6	7	9	10	11
·73	5370	5383	5395	5408	5420	5433	5445	5458	5470	5483	1	3	4	5	6	8	9	10	11
·74	5495	5508	5521	5534	5546	5559	5572	5585	5598	5610	1	3	4	5	6	8	9	10	12
·75	5623	5636	5649	5662	5675	5689	5702	5715	5728	5741	1	3	4	5	7	8	9	10	12
·76	5754	5768	5781	5794	5808	5821	5834	5848	5861	5875	1	3	4	5	7	8	9	11	12
·77	5888	5902	5916	5929	5943	5957	5970	5984	5998	6012	1	3	4	5	7	8	10	11	12
·78	6026	6039	6053	6067	6081	6095	6109	6124	6138	6152	1	3	4	6	7	8	10	11	13
·79	6166	6180	6194	6209	6223	6237	6252	6266	6281	6295	1	3	4	6	7	9	10	11	13
·80	6310	6324	6339	6353	6368	6383	6397	6412	6427	6442	1	3	4	6	7	9	10	12	13
·81	6457	6471	6486	6501	6516	6531	6546	6561	6577	6592	2	3	5	6	8	9	11	12	14
·82	6607	6622	6637	6653	6668	6683	6699	6714	6730	6745	2	3	5	6	8	9	11	12	14
·83	6761	6776	6792	6808	6823	6839	6855	6871	6887	6902	2	3	5	6	8	9	11	13	14
·84	6918	6934	6950	6966	6982	6998	7015	7031	7047	7063	2	3	5	6	8	10	11	13	15
·85	7079	7096	7112	7129	7145	7161	7178	7194	7211	7228	2	3	5	7	8	10	12	13	15
·86	7244	7261	7278	7295	7311	7328	7345	7362	7379	7396	2	3	5	7	8	10	12	13	15
·87	7413	7430	7447	7464	7482	7499	7516	7534	7551	7568	2	3	5	7	9	10	12	14	16
·88	7586	7603	7621	7638	7656	7674	7691	7709	7727	7745	2	4	5	7	9	11	12	14	16
·89	7762	7780	7798	7816	7834	7852	7870	7889	7907	7925	2	4	5	7	9	11	13	14	16
·90	7943	7962	7980	7998	8017	8035	8054	8072	8091	8110	2	4	6	7	9	11	13	15	17
·91	8128	8147	8166	8185	8204	8222	8241	8260	8279	8299	2	4	6	8	9	11	13	15	17
·92	8318	8337	8356	8375	8395	8414	8433	8453	8472	8492	2	4	6	8	10	12	14	15	17
·93	8511	8531	8551	8570	8590	8610	8630	8650	8670	8690	2	4	6	8	10	12	14	16	18
·94	8710	8730	8750	8770	8790	8810	8831	8851	8872	8892	2	4	6	8	10	12	14	16	18
·95	8913	8933	8954	8974	8995	9016	9036	9057	9078	9099	2	4	6	8	10	12	15	17	19

Anti logarithm table

Solved Examples

1. Find the values of $\log_2^{128}$

Sol. Let $\log_2^{128} = x$

$\Rightarrow \quad 2^x = 128 = 2^7$

$\Rightarrow \quad x = 7$

2. Prove that $\log\left(\frac{a}{b}\right) + \log\left(\frac{b}{c}\right) + \log\left(\frac{c}{d}\right) + \log\left(\frac{d}{a}\right) = 0$

Sol. $\text{LHS} = \log\left(\frac{a}{b}\right) + \log\left(\frac{b}{c}\right) + \log\left(\frac{c}{d}\right) + \log\left(\frac{d}{a}\right)$

$= \log a - \log b + \log b - \log c + \log c - \log d + \log d - \log a$

$= 0$

3. Find the value of ${}_5\log_{25}^{81}$

Sol. ${}_5\log_{25}^{81} = {}_5\log_{5^2}^{9^2} = 5^{\left(\frac{2}{2}\right)}\log_5^9$

${}_5\log_5^9 = 9$

4. Find the value of $\frac{1}{\log_a abc} + \frac{1}{\log_b abc} + \frac{1}{\log_c abc}$

Sol. Consider $\frac{1}{\log_a abc} + \frac{1}{\log_b abc} + \frac{1}{\log_c abc}$

$= \log a_{abc} + \log b_{abc} + \log c_{abc} \qquad \left(\because \log a_b = \frac{1}{\log b_a}\right)$

$= \log_{abc} abc = 1$

5. If $(a+b)^2 = 16ab$ then find $\log(a+b)$

Sol. Given $(a+b)^2 = 16ab$

Taking log on both sides

$\log(a+b)^2 = \log(16\,ab)$

$\Rightarrow \quad 2\log(a+b) = \log 16 + \log a + \log b$

$\therefore \quad \log(a+b) = \frac{1}{2}[\log 16 + \log a + \log b]$

6. If $2\log\left(\frac{a+b}{2}\right) = \log a + \log b$ then show that $a = b$

Sol. $2\log\left(\frac{a+b}{2}\right) = \log a + \log b$

$\Rightarrow \log\left(\frac{a+b}{2}\right)^2 = \log ab \qquad (\because \log m + \log n = \log mn \; n\log m = \log m^n)$

$\Rightarrow \left(\frac{a+b}{2}\right)^2 = ab \Rightarrow (a+b)^2 = 4ab$

$\Rightarrow (a-b)^2 = 0 \Rightarrow a = b \qquad (\because (a+b)^2 - 4ab = (a-b)^2)$

7. If $2\log(x+y) = 3\log 5 + \log x + \log y$ then find the value of $\frac{(x-y)^2}{xy}$

Sol. Given $2\log(x+y) = 3\log 5 + \log x + \log y$

$\Rightarrow \log(x+y)^2 = \log 5^3 + \log xy$

$\log(x+y)^2 = \log(5^3.xy)$

$\Rightarrow (x+y)^2 = 5^3.xy = 125xy$

$x^2 + y^2 = 123xy \qquad \Rightarrow x^2 + y^2 - 2xy = 121xy$

$\Rightarrow \frac{(x-y)^2}{xy} = 121$

8. Simplify $\log\frac{81}{8} - 2\log\left(\frac{3}{2}\right) + 3\log\frac{2}{3} + \log\left(\frac{3}{4}\right)$

Sol. $\log\frac{81}{8} - 2\log\left(\frac{3}{2}\right) + 3\log\frac{2}{3} + \log\left(\frac{3}{4}\right)$

$= \log 81 - \log 8 - 2[\log 3 - \log 2] + 3[\log 2 - \log 3] + \log 3 - \log 4$

$= \log 3^4 - \log 2^3 - 2\log 3 - 2\log 2 + 3\log 2 - 3\log 3 + \log 3 - \log 2^2$

$= 4\log 3 - 3\log 2 - 2\log 3 - 2\log 2 + 3\log 2 - 3\log 3 + \log 3 - 2\log 2$

$= -4\log 2$

9. If $\frac{\log x}{b-c}=\frac{\log y}{c-a}=\frac{\log z}{a-b}$ then find the value of $x^a.y^b.z^c$

Sol. Consider $\frac{\log x}{b-c}=\frac{\log y}{c-a}=\frac{\log z}{a-b}=\lambda$ (say)

$$\log x=\lambda(b-c)$$

$$\log y=\lambda(c-a)$$

$$\log z=\lambda(a-b)$$

Let $p=x^a.y^b.z^c$

$$\log p=a\log x+b\log y+c\log z$$

$$=a(\lambda(b-c))+b(\lambda(c-a))+c(\lambda(a-b))$$

$$=0$$

$$\Rightarrow \log p=0 \qquad \Rightarrow p=1 \qquad \therefore x^a y^b z^c=1$$

10. If $\log_3^x=1+\log_x^9$ then find x

Sol. $\log_3^x=1+\log_x^9$

$$\Rightarrow \quad \log_3^x=1+\log_x^{3^2}$$

$$\Rightarrow \quad \log_3^x=1+2\log_x^3$$

$$\Rightarrow \quad \log_3^x=1+\frac{2}{\log_3^x}$$

Let $\log_3 x=t \qquad \Rightarrow \quad t=1+\frac{2}{t}$

$$\Rightarrow \quad t^2=t+2$$

$$\Rightarrow \quad t^2-t-2=0$$

$$\Rightarrow \quad t^2-2t+t-2=0$$

$$t(t-2)+1(t-2)=0$$

$$t=-1 \ or\ t=2$$

When $t=-1 \Rightarrow \log_3 x = -1 \Rightarrow x = 3^{-1} = \frac{1}{3}$

$t = 2 \Rightarrow \log_3 x = 2 \Rightarrow x = 3^2 = 9$

Problems on Applications of Logarithms in Pharmacy

11. If the first plasma sample is taken at time T_1 and corresponding concentration is C_1 and C_2 is concentration in time T_2 and T is taken as $T_2 - T_1$ the concentration C_2 is given by the equation $C_2 = C_1 e^{-k(T_2 - T_1)}$ prove that.

$$K = \frac{\log C_1 - \log C_2}{T_2 - T_1}$$

Sol. We have $C_2 = C_1 e^{-k(T_2-T_1)}$

Taking natural log on both sides we get

$$\log C_2 = \log\left(C_1 e^{-k(T_2-T_1)}\right)$$

$$\log C_2 = \log C_1 + \log e^{-k(T_2-T_1)}$$

$$\Rightarrow \quad \log C_2 = \log C_1 + \left[-k(T_2 - T_1)\right].\log e$$

$$\Rightarrow \quad \log C_2 = (\log C_1) - k(T_2 - T_1).(1) \qquad (\because \log_e e = 1)$$

$$\Rightarrow \quad \log C_2 = (\log C_1) + (k)(T_1 - T_2)$$

$$\Rightarrow \quad \log C_2 - \log C_1 = k(T_1 - T_2)$$

$$\Rightarrow \quad k = \frac{\log C_2 - \log C_1}{T_1 - T_2} = \frac{\log C_1 - \log C_2}{T_2 - T_1}$$

12. The amount of drug dissolved in a body is given by the equation $d_B = d_B^0\, e^{-kt}$ prove that $\ln d_B = -kt + \ln d_B^0$ also prove that $\log d_B = \frac{-kt}{2.303} + \log d_B^0$

Sol. Consider $d_B = d_B^0\, e^{-kt}$ taking log (natural) on both sides we get

$$\ln d_B = \ln\left(d_B^0 e^{-kt}\right)$$

$$\ln d_B = \ln d_B^0 + \ln e^{-kt}$$

$$\ln d_B = \ln d_B^0 + (-kt)$$

$$\ln d_B = -kt + \ln d_B^0 \qquad .....(1)$$

$$\ln \frac{dB}{2.303} = \frac{-kt}{2.303} + \frac{\ln d_B^0}{2.303} \Rightarrow \log d_B = \frac{-kt}{2.303} + \log d_B^0$$

13. Rate method is used to calculate pharmacokinetics parameter and it is given by the differential equation $\frac{dx_u}{dt} = k\, X_0 e^{-kt}$ Prove that $\log\left(\frac{dx_u}{dt}\right) = \frac{-kt}{2.303} + \log(kx_0)$

Sol. Consider $\frac{dx_u}{dt} = kX_0\, e^{-kt}$

$$\Rightarrow \quad \ln\left(\frac{dx_u}{dt}\right) = \ln\left[kX_0 e^{-kt}\right]$$

$$\Rightarrow \quad \ln\left(\frac{dx_u}{dt}\right) = \ln(kX_0) + \ln e^{-kt}$$

$$\Rightarrow \quad \ln\left(\frac{dx_u}{dt}\right) = \ln(kX_0) + (-kt)$$

$$\Rightarrow \quad 2.303\log\left(\frac{dx_u}{dt}\right) = 2.303\log(kx_0) - kt \qquad (\because \ln X = 2.303\log X)$$

$$\Rightarrow \quad \log\left(\frac{dx_u}{dt}\right) = \log kx_0 \frac{-kt}{2.303}$$

Exercise 7.1

1. Find the value of $\log_3 243$
2. Prove that $\log\left(\frac{m}{n}\right) + \log\left(\frac{n}{m}\right) = 0$
3. If $a^2 + b^2 = 7ab$ show that $\log\left(\frac{a+b}{3}\right) = \frac{1}{2}(\log a + \log b)$
4. Find the characteristic and mantissa of 1.3126
5. Find the number of digits in $(24)^{15}$

6. If $l^2 + m^2 = n^2$ then show that

$$\frac{1}{\log_{m+n} l} + \frac{1}{\log_{m-n} l} = 2$$

7. Simplify with the use of logarithm $\frac{(2.73)^2 \times (3.14)^3}{\sqrt{142.3}}$

8. Find x such that (i) $\log_2 256 = x$ (ii) $\log_{0.5} x = -2$

9. Find the value of $\log_{0.1} 100 + \log_{100} 0.1$

10. Find antilog of 2.4651, $\bar{2}.1432$ by using antilog table.

11. If a drug concentrations is given by the formula $c = a_n e^{-\lambda_n}$ then prove that $\log c = (\log a_n)\left(-\frac{\lambda_n}{2.303}\right)$

12. The rate of the amount of drug extended in the urin is given by $\frac{du}{dt} = k_e d_B^0 e^{-kt}$, k_c is real excretion rate constant d_B^0 is drug in the body at zero hour prove that $\log\left(\frac{dDu}{dt}\right) = \frac{-kt}{2.303} + \log\left(k_e d_B^0\right)$

Answers

1. 5 4. 0, 0.1179 5. 21 7. 19.26 8. (i) 8 (ii) 4

9. $\frac{-5}{2}$ 10. 291.8, 0.01391

Unit - I

Exercise Questions

1. Progressions

1. Sum of the three numbers in a G.P is 7 and sum of their squares is 21. Find the G.P
2. The 7th term of an A.P is 15 and 21st term is 8. Find the sum of the first 13 terms.
3. The sum of 5 terms of an A.P is –5 and 6th term is –13. What is the common difference.
4. If the 9th term of an A.P is 48 and 15th term is 24. Find 31st term.
5. The sum of the second and fifth terms of an A.P is 8 and that of the third and seventh term is 14. Find the progression.
6. Find four numbers forming a G.P in which the sum of the extreme terms is 112 and sum of middle terms is 48.
7. If the sum to first three terms of a G.P is to the sum of the first six terms as 125 : 152, find the common ratio of G . P.
8. If the numbers a, b, c, d are in G.P, show that $(a - d)^2 - (b - d)^2 = (a - c)^2 + (b - c)^2$
9. Insert 5 arithmetic means between 13 and 31.
10. Find the G.P whose sum to infinity is $4\frac{1}{2}$ and whose second term is –2.

2. Partial Fractions

1. Resolve partial fractions of $\dfrac{x^2 - 10 + 13}{(x-1)(x^2 - 5x + 6)}$
2. Resolve in to partial fractions of $\dfrac{7x - 1}{1 - 5x + 6x^2}$
3. Resolve into Partial fractions of $\dfrac{x - 3}{(x^2 + 1)(2x - 1)}$
4. Resolve into partial fractions of $\dfrac{5x - 7}{(x + 8)(x^2 + 2)}$

5. Resolve $\dfrac{x^3}{(2x-1)(x+2)(x-3)}$ into partial fractions

6. Resolve $\dfrac{x^2+15}{(x-1)(x^2+2x+5)}$ into partial fractions.

3. Matrices

1. If $A = \begin{bmatrix} 1 & 2 & 1 \\ 3 & 4 & 1 \\ 1 & 3 & 1 \end{bmatrix}$; $B = \begin{bmatrix} 10 & -4 & -1 \\ -11 & 5 & 0 \\ 9 & -5 & 1 \end{bmatrix}$ then find AB

2. If $A = \dfrac{1}{9}\begin{bmatrix} -8 & 1 & 4 \\ 4 & 4 & 7 \\ 1 & -8 & 4 \end{bmatrix}$ then show that $A^{-1} = A^T$.

3. If $A = \begin{bmatrix} 1 & -2 & 3 \\ 2 & 3 & -1 \\ -3 & 1 & 2 \end{bmatrix}$ and $B = \begin{bmatrix} 1 & 0 & 2 \\ 0 & 1 & 2 \\ 1 & 2 & 0 \end{bmatrix}$ find AB and BA and show that $AB \neq BA$.

4. Prove that $\begin{vmatrix} 1 & a & bc \\ 1 & b & ac \\ 1 & c & ab \end{vmatrix} = (a-b)(b-c)(c-a)$

5. Prove that $\begin{vmatrix} 1 & a & b+c \\ 1 & b & c+a \\ 1 & c & a+b \end{vmatrix} = 0$

6. Prove that $\begin{vmatrix} a+b+2c & a & b \\ c & 2a+b+c & b \\ c & a & a+2b+c \end{vmatrix} = 2(a+b+c)^3$

7. Evaluate $\begin{vmatrix} 1 & a & a^2 & a^3 \\ 1 & b & b^2 & b^3 \\ 1 & c & c^2 & c^3 \\ 1 & d & d^2 & d^3 \end{vmatrix}$

8. Show that $\begin{vmatrix} 1 & a & a^2 & a^3+bcd \\ 1 & b & b^2 & b^3+cda \\ 1 & c & c^2 & c^3+dab \\ 1 & d & d^2 & d^3+abc \end{vmatrix} = 0$

9. Find the value of $\begin{vmatrix} 1 & 15 & 14 & 4 \\ 12 & 6 & 7 & 9 \\ 8 & 10 & 11 & 5 \\ 13 & 3 & 2 & 16 \end{vmatrix}$

10. Evaluate $\begin{vmatrix} a & b & c & d \\ -a & b & c & d \\ -a & -b & c & d \\ -a & -b & -c & d \end{vmatrix}$

11. If $\begin{vmatrix} 15-2x & 11 & 10 \\ 11-3x & 17 & 16 \\ 7-x & 14 & 13 \end{vmatrix} = 0$, find x.

12. Solve the following equations by Crammers rule.

$2x - y - z = 1$

$3x + 2y + 4z = 3$

$x - 5y - 13z = -6$

13. Solve the system of equations by Crammers rule.

$5x + 3y + 7z = 4$

$3x + 26y + 2z = 9$

$7x + 2y + 11z = 5$

14. Solve the system of equations by Crammers rule

$3x + y + 2z = 3$

$2x - 3y - z = -3$

$x + 2y + z = 4$

15. Solve the system of equations by Crammers rule

$2x + y - z = 2$

$x + 2y + z = 7$

$3x + y + z = 10$

4. Binomial Theorem

1. Expand $\left(x + \frac{1}{x}\right)^6$

2. Find the numarically greatest term in the expansion of $(1 + x)^{20}$ when $x = \frac{1}{4}$

3. Find the term independent of x in $\left(\sqrt{x} - \frac{8}{x^2}\right)^9$

4. Write down the middle term (s) in the expansion of $\left(2x - \frac{3}{x}\right)^{15}$

5. Find the coefficient of x^{32} in the expansion of $\left(x^4 - \frac{1}{x^3}\right)^{15}$

6. The coefficients of the 5th, 6th and 7th term of the expansion of $(1 + x)^n$ are in A.P. Find the value of n.

7. Show that $2c_0 + 2^2.\frac{c_1}{2} + 2^3.\frac{c_2}{3} + ... + 2^{n+1}\frac{c_n}{n+1} = \frac{3^{n+1} - 1}{n+1}$ and hence show that

$$2c_0 + \frac{2^2}{2}.c_1 + \frac{2^3}{3}c_2 + ... + \frac{2^{11}}{11}c_{10} = \frac{3^{11} - 1}{11}$$

5. Permutations and Combinations

1. If $4_{p_r} : 3(2_{p_2}) = 4:1$, find r.

2. If $n_{c_6} = n_{c_{12}}$, find $n_{c_{16}}$

3. A committee of 4 is to be selected from amongest 5 boys and 6 girls. In how many ways this can be done so as to include

   (i) Exactly one girl (ii) atleast one girl

4. How many words such contain 3 consonants and 2 vowels can be formed from 6 consonants and 4 vowels.

5. Find the number of ways of arranging 4 boys and 3 girls in a row so that all the girls are together.

6. A candidate has to answer 6 out of 10 questions which are divided into 2 groups, such containing 5 questions, he is not permitted to attempt more than 4 questions from any group. In how many ways can he make his choice ?

7. Find the number of permutations of all the letters of the word 'A C A C I A'.

8. Find the sum of four digited numbers formed by using the digits 1, 2, 3, 5, 9

Unit - I

Answers to Exercise Questions

1. Progressions

1. 1, 2, 4, 8.......
   4, 2, 1 ....

2. 195

3. –4

4. – 40

5. –1, 1, 3, 5, 7 .....

6. $4, 4 \times 3, 4 \times 3^2$ .... $108, 108 \times \frac{1}{3}, 108 \times \frac{1}{9}$ .....

7. $r = \frac{3}{5}$

9. 13, 16, 19, 22, 25, 28, 31

10. $6, 6 \times \frac{-1}{3}, 6 \times \left(\frac{-1}{3}\right)^2 \ldots\ldots \quad \frac{-3}{2}, \frac{-3}{2} \times \frac{4}{3}, \frac{-3}{2} \times \left(\frac{4}{3}\right)^2 \ldots$

2. Partial Fractions

1. $\frac{2}{x-1} + \frac{3}{x-2} + \frac{-4}{x-3}$

2. $\frac{-4}{3x-1} + \frac{5}{2x-1}$

3. $\left(\frac{-2}{2x-1} + \frac{x+1}{x^2+1}\right)$

4. $\frac{\frac{-47}{66}}{x+8} + \frac{\left(\frac{47}{66}\right)x + \left(\frac{-23}{33}\right)}{x^2+2}$

5. $\frac{1}{2} + \frac{\left(\frac{-1}{50}\right)}{(2x-1)} + \frac{\left(\frac{-8}{25}\right)}{(x+2)} + \frac{\frac{27}{25}}{(x-3)}$

6. $\frac{2}{x-1} + \frac{(-x)+(-5)}{x^2+2x+5}$

3. Matrices

1. $B = \begin{bmatrix} -3 & 1 & 0 \\ -5 & 3 & -2 \\ -14 & 6 & 0 \end{bmatrix}$

7. (a – b) (b – c) (c – d) (d – a) (c – a) (d – b)

9. 3308

10. 'Zero'

11. $x = 4$ **12.** $x = \frac{9}{19}, y = \frac{-17}{19}, z = \frac{-44}{19}$

13. $x = \frac{77}{121}, y = \frac{33}{121}, z = 0$ **14.** $x = \frac{7}{5}, y = \frac{16}{5}, z = \frac{-19}{5}$

15. $x = 2, y = 1, z = 3$

4. Binomial Theorem

1. $6_{c_0}(x)^6 + 6_{c_1}(x)^5\left(\frac{1}{x}\right) + 6_{c_2}(x)^4\frac{1}{x^2} + 6_{c_3}(x)^3.\frac{1}{x^3} + 6_{c_4}.x^2.\frac{1}{x^4} + 6_{c_5}.x.\frac{1}{(x^5)} + 6_{c_6}\left(\frac{1}{x^6}\right)$

2. t_{17}, t_{18} **3.** $r = \frac{9}{5}$ does not exist

4. $T_8 = (-1)^7\ 15_{c_7}\ .\ (2)^8\ .(3)^7\ .\ x$ $T_9 = 15_{c_8}\ .\ (2)^7\ .\ (3)^8\ .\ \frac{1}{x}$

5. $15_{c_4} = 1365$ **6.** n = 7 (or) 14.

5. Permatations and Combinations

1. r = 4 (or) r = 3 **2.** $n_{c16} = 153$

3. $6_{c1} \times 5_{c3}$

$6_{c_1} \times 5_{c_3} + 6_{c_2} \times 5_{c_2} + 6_{c_3} + 5_{c_1} + 6_{c_4} \times 5_{c_0}$

4. $6_{c3} \times 4_{c2}$ **5.** 5! 3!

6. $5_{c_4} \times 5_{c_2} + 5_{c_3} \times 5_{c_3} + 5_{c_2} \times 5_{c_4} = 200$ **7.** $\frac{6!}{2!.3!}$

8. 480×1111

Unit - I

Self Test Questions

1. Progressions

1. The sum of four numbers which are in A.P is 32 and product of whose extremes is 55. Find the numbers?
2. Find the 3 numbers which are in A.P whose sum is 12 and the sum of their cubes is 408?
3. Find sum of n terms of an A.P whose 7th term is 30 and 13th term is 54?
4. The sum of 3 numbers in A.P is 54 and product of extremes is 275. Find them?
5. Find the sum of all numbers between 100 and 1000 which are divisible by 13?
6. The third element of a G.P is a square of 1st and 5th element is 64, find G.P?

2. Partial Fractions

1. Resolve $\frac{7x-1}{6x^2-5x+1}$ into Partial fractions
2. Resolve $\frac{2x+1}{(x-1)(x^2+1)}$ into Partial fractions

3. Matrices

1. If $f(x) = x^2 - 5x + 7$ find f(A), where $A = \begin{pmatrix} 3 & 1 \\ -1 & 2 \end{pmatrix}$
2. If $A = \begin{pmatrix} 2 & 3 \\ 1 & 5 \end{pmatrix}$ find x, such that $A - 2x = \begin{pmatrix} 1 & 8 \\ 7 & -6 \end{pmatrix}$
3. Solve using Cramer's rule $2x + 5y + z = -1$, $x + 7y - 6z = -18$, $3y + 6z = 7$
4. Evaluate $\begin{vmatrix} 4 & 2 & -8 \\ 2 & -3 & -6 \\ 0 & -2 & 2 \end{vmatrix}$?
5. Solve using Cramer's rule $4x + y = 7$, $3y + 4z = 5$, $3z + 5x = 2$.

4. Binomial Theorem

1. Find the middle terms in expansion of $\left[\frac{2}{3}x^2 - \frac{3}{2x}\right]^{11}$?

2. Find the term independent of x in expansion of $\left[2x - \frac{1}{x}\right]^{10}$?

3. Find the coefficient of x^7 in the expansion of $\left(x^2 + \frac{2}{x}\right)^{11}$?

4. Find the coefficient of x^{13} in $\left[3x - \frac{1}{6}x^3\right]^7$?

5. Permutations and Combinations

1. Find the value of n if ${}^{n}P_4 = 360$.

2. Prove that $n_{cr} + n_{cr-1} = (n+1)_{cr}$

UNIT - II
TRIGONOMETRY

UNIT - II

TRIGONOMETRY

8

Trigonometric Ratios

8.1 Basic Concepts

Ray : A half line is called a ray. If p^1p is a line and 0 is a point in the line then $\overrightarrow{OP}$ is called a ray and $\overrightarrow{OP'}$ is another ray. The point O is called end point of the ray $\overrightarrow{OP}$.

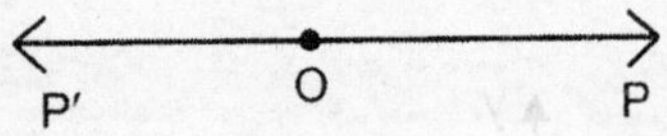

Angle : An angle is union of two rays with common end point 'O' together with the rotation in a plane necessary to bring one ray (the initial side) into the position of the other ray (the terminal side). The end point O is called vertex of the angle.

Note

(i) If A and B are two points such that A lies on the initial side and B lies on the terminal side of an angle θ then the angle is denoted by ∠AOB.

(ii) The angle θ is regarded as positive if it is measured in the anticlockwise direction otherwise negative.

Turn: The angle whose terminal side coincide first with the initial side by rotation is called a 'turn' and onefourth of turn is called a right angle.

Note

(i) If $\overleftrightarrow{P'OP}$ and $\overleftrightarrow{Q'OQ}$ be two intersecting lines then $\angle POQ'$, $\angle POQ$ are called angle between two lines, moreover $\angle POQ^1 - \angle QOP^1$ and $\angle POQ - \angle P^1OQ'$.

(ii) Two lines are side to be perpendicular if an angle between the two lines is right angle.

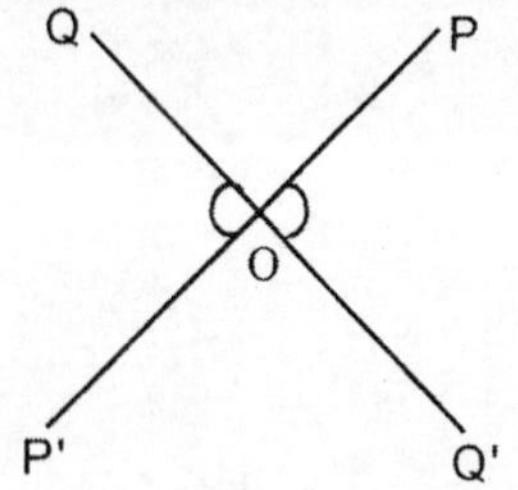

Coordinate System : Let $\overleftrightarrow{x'x}$ and $\overleftrightarrow{yy'}$ be two mutually perpendicular coordinate lines in a plane intersecting at O. The point O is called origin. The line $\overleftrightarrow{x'ox}$ is called *x*-axis. The line $\overleftrightarrow{yoy'}$ is called *y* - axis. Usually we take *x*-axis as horizontal line and y-axis as vertical line.

Let P be any point in the plane. Let L, M be foot of perpendiculars of P from *x*-axis and *y*-axis respectively.

Suppose PM = *x*, PL = *y* then *x* is called *x*-coordinate and *y* is called *y*-coordinate of P. The point P is denoted by (*x*, *y*).

Every point in the plane can determined by two real numbers *x*, *y* (coordinates) and every pair of real numbers determine a point in the plane.

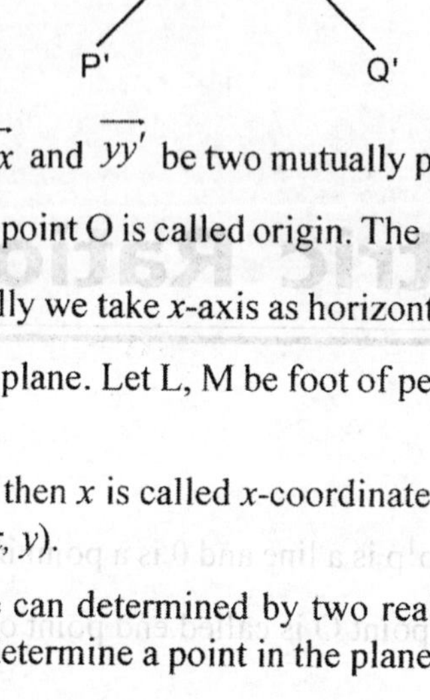

x-axis and *y*-axis are called coordinate axes and the plane is called coordinate plane. The coordinate axes divides the plane into four equal parts. Each part is called quadrant. The region *xoy, yox', x'oy', y'ox* are called I, II, III, and IV quadrants respectively.

Let P(*x*, *y*) be any point in the coordinate plane, then

(i) P lies in I quadrant iff $x > 0$, $y > 0$,

(ii) P lies in II quadrant iff $x < 0$, $y > 0$,

(iii) P lies in III quadrant iff $x < 0,\ y < 0$,

(iv) P lies in IV quadrant iff $x > 0,\ y < 0$,

(v) P lies on x - axis iff $y = 0$,

(vi) P lies on y-axis iff $x = 0$ and

(vii) If P $= 0$ then $x = 0, y = 0$ i.e the coordinate of O are (0, 0).

Definition : An angle θ is said to be in standard position if the vertex of θ is the origin and the initial side of θ is positive x-axis.

Definition : An angle θ is said to be in the rth quadrant if the terminal side of θ lies in the rth quadrant, where r = 1, 2, 3, 4.

Definition : An angle θ is said to be quandrant angle if the terminal side of θ when taken in the standard position of coordinate axis.

Definition : Two angles which are in the standard position are said to be coterminal if they have the same terminal side.

Measurement of angles: The measurement of angles means the measure of the rotation in that angle. An angle is measured in the following systems.

1. ***Sexagesimal measurement (British system):*** In this system $\frac{1}{360}$ of a turn is called a degree (°), $\frac{1}{60}$ of degree is called a minute (') and $\frac{1}{60}$ of a minute is called a second (").

   ∴ Right angle = 90°, $1^\circ = 60'$, $1' = 60''$.

2. ***Centesimal measurement (French system) :*** In this system $\frac{1}{400}$ of turn is called grade (g), $\frac{1}{100}$ of a grade is called a minute (') and $\frac{1}{100}$ of minute is called a second (")

   ∴ right angle = 100 g, 1g = $100'$, $1' = 100''$.

Note

The minutes and seconds in the sexagesimal system are different with the minutes and seconds respectively in the centesimal system.

3. ***Circular measurement (Radian measure) :*** The angle subtendend by an arc of circle whose length is equal to radius of the circle at the centre of circle is called a radian. In this system the unit of measurement is radian (c).

Note

(i) Radian is a constant angle.

(ii) One Right angle = $\frac{\pi}{2}$ radian = 90° = 100 g.

Ex :

(i) Express 120° in circular measure (radians)

$$120° = \frac{\pi}{180} \times 120 = \frac{2\pi}{3}$$

$$\left(\because 90° = \frac{\pi}{2}\text{radians}; 180° = \pi \text{ radians}; \frac{\pi}{180}\text{radians} = 1°\right)$$

(ii) Express 120 g in circular measure

since $100g = \frac{\pi}{2}$ radians $\Rightarrow$ $1g = \frac{\pi}{200}$ radians

$$120g = 120 \times \frac{\pi}{200} = \frac{4\pi}{5} \text{ radians}$$

8.2 Trigonometric Functions (Ratios)

Let θ ε R, take an angle of measure θ radians in standard position. Let P(*x*, *y*) be a point on the terminal side of the angle θ such that OP = r (r > 0).

Then,

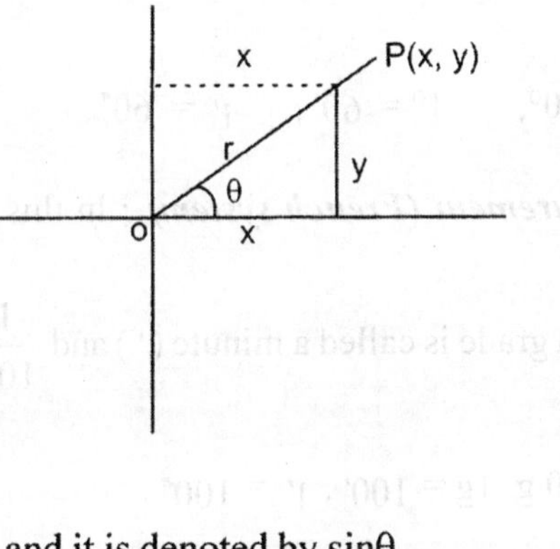

(i) $\frac{y}{r}$ is called sine of θ and it is denoted by sinθ.

(ii) $\frac{x}{r}$ is called cosine of θ and it is denoted by cosθ.

(iii) $\frac{y}{x}$ $(x \neq 0)$ is called tangent of θ and it is denoted by tanθ.

(iv) $\frac{x}{y}$ $(y \neq 0)$ is called cotangent of θ and it is denoted by $\cot\theta$

(v) $\frac{r}{x}$ $(x \neq 0)$ is called secant of θ and it is denoted by $\sec\theta$.

(vi) $\frac{x}{y}$ $(y \neq 0)$ is called cosecant of θ and is denoted by $\text{cosec}\theta$.

The six functions are called trigonometric functions.

Note

If $\angle AOB = \theta$ is acute. Then form right angle triangle, right angle at B and the trigonometric ratios defined as follows.

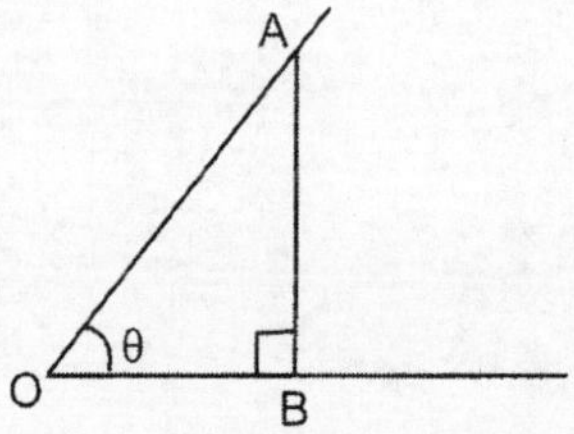

$$\sin\theta = \frac{\text{opposite side}}{\text{Hypotenuse}} = \frac{AB}{OA}$$

$$\cos\theta = \frac{\text{adjacent side}}{\text{Hypotenuse}} = \frac{OB}{OA}$$

$$\tan\theta = \frac{\text{opposite side}}{\text{Adjacent side}} = \frac{AB}{OB}$$

$$\cot\theta = \frac{\text{Adjacent side}}{\text{opposite side}} = \frac{OB}{AB}$$

$$\sec\theta = \frac{\text{Hypotenuse}}{\text{Adjacent side}} = \frac{OA}{OB}$$

$$\text{cosec}\theta = \frac{\text{Hypotenuse}}{\text{opposite side}} = \frac{OA}{AB}$$

8.3 Standard Results

1. $\text{Sin}^2\theta + \cos^2\theta = 1$
2. $1 + \tan^2\theta = \sec^2\theta$ (or) $\sec^2\theta - \tan^2\theta = 1$
3. $1 + \cot^2\theta = \text{cosec}^2$ (or) $\text{cosec}^2\theta - \cot^2\theta = 1$
4. $\sin\theta \,\text{cosec}\theta = 1$
5. $\cos\theta \,.\, \sec\theta = 1$
6. $\tan\theta \,.\, \cot\theta = 1$
7. $\dfrac{\sin\theta}{\cos\theta} = \tan\theta$
8. $\dfrac{\cos\theta}{\sin\theta} = \cot\theta$
9. $\sec\theta + \tan\theta = \dfrac{1}{\sec\theta - \tan\theta}$
10. $\text{cosec}\theta + \cot\theta = \dfrac{1}{\text{cosec}\theta - \cot\theta}$

Proof :- (1)

Let $\theta \in R$, take an angle of measure θ radian in standard position. Let $P(x, y)$ be a point on terminal side of the angle θ such that $OP = r\ (r > 0)$.

$$\therefore \sin\theta = \frac{y}{r},\ \cos\theta = \frac{x}{r}$$

$$\therefore \sin^2\theta + \cos^2\theta = \frac{y^2}{r^2} + \frac{x^2}{r^2} = \frac{x^2 + y^2}{r^2} = 1 \qquad \because OP = r = \sqrt{x^2 + y^2}$$

Alternative method: Consider a right angle triangle right angled at B and $\angle ACB = \theta$.

$\therefore$ by the difinition of trigonometric ratios.

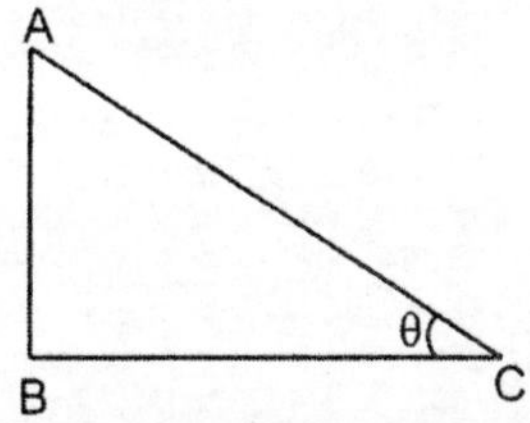

$$\sin\theta = \frac{AB}{AC}, \qquad \cos\theta = \frac{BC}{AC}$$

$$\text{now } \sin^2\theta + \cos^2\theta = \frac{AB^2}{AC^2} + \frac{BC^2}{AC^2} = \frac{AB^2 + BC^2}{AC^2} = 1$$

($\because AB^2 + BC^2 = AC^2$ i.e. by Pythagrous Theorem)

2. $1 + \tan^2\theta = \sec^2\theta$.

From ΔABC, $\tan\theta = \dfrac{AB}{AC}$

$$\therefore\ 1+\tan^2\theta = 1+\frac{AB^2}{BC^2} = \frac{BC^2+AB^2}{BC^2} = \frac{AC^2}{BC^2} = \left(\frac{AC}{BC}\right)^2$$

But $\sec\theta = \dfrac{AC}{BC}$

$$\therefore \left(\frac{AC}{BC}\right)^2 = \sec^2\theta$$

$$\therefore\ 1+\tan^2\theta = \left(\frac{AC}{BC}\right)^2 = \sec^2\theta$$

3. you can prove like **(2)**

4. $\sin\theta\ \text{cosec}\theta = 1$

from ΔABC,

$$\sin\theta = \frac{AB}{AC}$$

$$\text{cosec}\theta = \frac{AC}{AB}$$

$$\therefore\ \sin\theta\ .\ \text{cosec}\theta = \frac{AB}{AC}.\frac{AC}{AB} = 1$$

(5), (6) you can prove like (3)

7. From ΔABC

$$\sin\theta = \frac{AB}{AC},\ \cos\theta = \frac{BC}{AC} \text{ and } \tan\theta = \frac{AB}{BC}$$

$$\text{now } \frac{\sin\theta}{\cos\theta} = \frac{\left(\frac{AB}{AC}\right)}{\left(\frac{BC}{AC}\right)} = \frac{AB}{BC} = \tan\theta$$

8. you can prove like **(7)**

9. we know from **(2)**, $\sec^2\theta - \tan^2\theta = 1$

$$\Rightarrow \quad (\sec\theta + \tan\theta)(\sec\theta - \tan\theta) = 1$$

$$\therefore \quad \sec\theta + \tan\theta = \frac{1}{\sec\theta - \tan\theta}$$

10. we know from **(3)**, $\text{cosec}^2\theta - \cot^2\theta = 1$

$$\Rightarrow (\text{cosec}\theta + \cot\theta)(\text{cosec}\theta - \cot\theta) = 1$$

$$\Rightarrow (\text{cosec}\theta + \cot\theta) = \frac{1}{\text{cosec}\theta - \cot\theta}$$

8.4 Signs of the Trigonometric Functions

(i) If θ is in the I quadrant then $P(x, y)$ lies in the first quadrant, therefore $x > 0$, $y > 0$ and hence the values of all the trigonometric fuctions are positive.

(ii) If θ is in the II quadrant then $P(x, y)$ lies in the II quadrant. Therefore $x < 0, y > 0$ and hence the values of 'sin, cosec' are positive and remaining are negative.

(iii) If θ is in the III quadrant then $P(x, y)$ lies in the III quadrant. Therefore $x < 0$, $y < 0$ and hence the values of 'tan' and 'cot' are positive and remaining are negative.

(iv) If θ is in the IV quadrant $P(x, y)$ lies in the IV quadrant, therefore $x > 0, y < 0$ and hence the values of 'cos', 'sec' are positive and remaining are negative.

Note

$\sin(2n\pi + \theta) = \sin\theta$, $\cos(2n\pi + \theta) = \cot\theta$, $\tan(2n\pi + \theta) = \tan\theta$, $\cot(2n\pi + \theta) = \cot\theta$

$\sec(2n\pi + \theta) = \sec\theta$, $\text{cosec}(2n\pi + \theta) = \text{cosec}\theta$

Values of the trigonometric functions of the given angles

θ	0°	$\frac{\pi}{6} = 30^\circ$	$\frac{\pi}{4} = 45^\circ$	$\frac{\pi}{3} = 60^\circ$	$\frac{\pi}{2} = 90^\circ$	$\pi = 180^\circ$	$\frac{3\pi}{2} = 270^\circ$	$2\pi = 360^\circ$
$\sin\theta$	0	$\frac{1}{2}$	$\frac{1}{\sqrt{2}}$	$\frac{\sqrt{3}}{2}$	1	0	–1	0
cos	1	$\frac{\sqrt{3}}{2}$	$\frac{1}{\sqrt{2}}$	$\frac{1}{2}$	0	–1	0	1
tan	0	$\frac{1}{\sqrt{3}}$	1	$\sqrt{3}$	∞	0	∞	0

Trigonometric functions of 'θ', for all values of θ

Let θ be an angle in the standard position in the I quadrant. Let its terminal side cuts the circle with centre and radius r in P(x, y).

Let $P'(x'y')$ be the point of intersection of terminal side of the angle θ in the standard position with the circle.

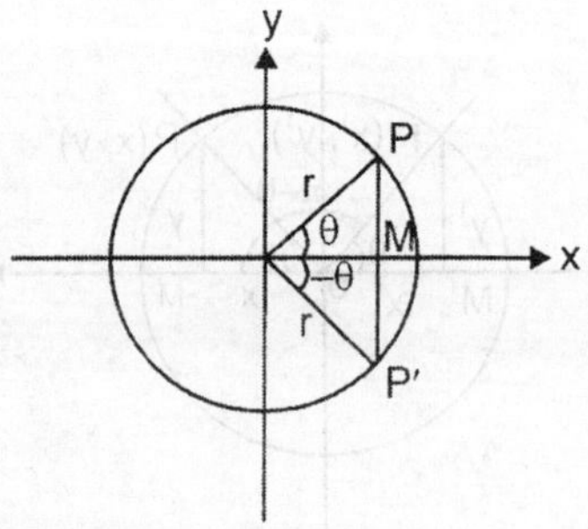

Now, $\angle xop = \angle xop'$ (numerically) and P, P^1 have same projection M in the x-axis.

$\therefore$ ΔOMP = ΔOMP′ $\Rightarrow$ $x = x'$, and $y = -y^1$

$$\therefore \sin(-\theta) = \frac{y'}{r} = \frac{-y}{r} = -\sin\theta \qquad \cot(-\theta) = \frac{x'}{y'} = \frac{x}{-y} = -\cot\theta$$

$$\cos(-\theta) = \frac{x'}{r} = \frac{x}{r} = \cos\theta \qquad \sec(-\theta) = \frac{r}{x'} = \frac{r}{x} = \sec\theta$$

$$\tan(-\theta) = \frac{y'}{x'} = \frac{-y}{x} = -\tan\theta \qquad \mathrm{cosec}(-\theta) = \frac{r}{y'} = \frac{r}{-y} = -\mathrm{cosec}\theta$$

Similarly if θ is in the other quadrant, the above results can also be proved.

Trigonometric functions of π – θ for all values of θ

Let θ be an angle in the standard position in the I quadrant. Let its terminal side cuts the circle with centre O and radius r at P(x, y). Let $P^1(x^1, y^1)$ be the point of intersection of the terminal side of the angle π – θ with the circle. Let M and M^1 be projections (foot of perpendiculars) of P and P^1 respectively on x-axis since Δ $OM^1P^1 \equiv$ Δ OMP.

$$x^1 = -x,\ y^1 = y$$

$$\therefore \sin(\pi - \theta) = \frac{y'}{r} = \frac{y}{r} = \sin\theta \qquad \cot(\pi - \theta) = \frac{x^1}{y^1} = \frac{-x}{y} = -\cot\theta$$

$$\cos(\pi - \theta) = \frac{x^1}{r} = \frac{-x}{y} = -\cos\theta \qquad \sec(\pi - \theta) = \frac{r}{x^1} = \frac{r}{-x} = -\sec\theta$$

$$\tan(\pi - \theta) = \frac{y^1}{x^1} = \frac{y}{-x} = -\tan\theta \qquad \text{cosec}(\pi - \theta) = \frac{r}{y^1} = \frac{r}{y} = \text{cosec}\theta$$

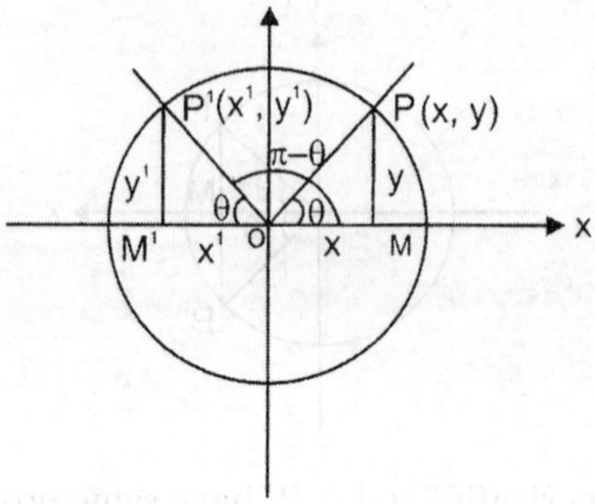

Similarly if θ is in other quadrants then the above results can also be proved.

Similarly we can prove the following results.

1. $\sin\left(\frac{\pi}{2} - \theta\right) = \cos\theta$, $\cos\left(\frac{\pi}{2} - \theta\right) = \sin\theta$, $\tan\left(\frac{\pi}{2} - \theta\right) = \cot\theta$,

   $\cot\left(\frac{\pi}{2} - \theta\right) = \tan\theta$, $\sec\left(\frac{\pi}{2} - \theta\right) = \text{cosec}\,\theta$ $\quad \text{cosec}\left(\frac{\pi}{2} - \theta\right) = \cot\theta$

2. $\sin\left(\frac{\pi}{2} + \theta\right) = \cos\theta$ $\qquad \cot\left(\frac{\pi}{2} + \theta\right) = -\tan\theta$

   $\cos\left(\frac{\pi}{2} + \theta\right) = -\sin\theta$ $\qquad \sec\left(\frac{\pi}{2} + \theta\right) = -\text{cosec}\theta$

   $\tan\left(\frac{\pi}{2} + \theta\right) = -\cot\theta$ $\qquad \text{cosec}\left(\frac{\pi}{2} + \theta\right) = \sec\theta$

3. $\sin(\pi + \theta) = -\sin\theta$ $\qquad \cot(\pi + \theta) = \cot\theta$

   $\cos(\pi + \theta) = -\cos\theta$ $\qquad \sec(\pi + \theta) = -\sec\theta$

   $\tan(\pi + \theta) = \tan\theta$ $\qquad \text{cosec}(\pi + \theta) = -\text{cosec}\,\theta$

4. $\sin\left(\frac{3\pi}{2} - \theta\right) = -\cos\theta$ $\qquad \cot\left(\frac{3\pi}{2} - \theta\right) = \tan\theta$

$$\cos\left(\frac{3\pi}{2}-\theta\right)=-\sin\theta \qquad \sec\left(\frac{3\pi}{2}-\theta\right)=-\operatorname{cosec}\theta$$

$$\tan\left(\frac{3\pi}{2}-\theta\right)=\cot\theta \qquad \operatorname{cosec}\left(\frac{3\pi}{2}-\theta\right)=-\sec\theta$$

5. $$\sin\left(\frac{3\pi}{2}+\theta\right)=-\cos\theta \qquad \cos\left(\frac{3\pi}{2}+\theta\right)=\sin\theta,\ \tan\left(\frac{3\pi}{2}+\theta\right)=-\cot\theta$$

$$\cot\left(\frac{3\pi}{2}+\theta\right)=-\tan\theta \qquad \sec\left(\frac{3\pi}{2}+\theta\right)=\operatorname{cosec}\theta,$$

$$\operatorname{cosec}\left(\frac{3\pi}{2}+\theta\right)=-\sec\theta$$

Note

Let $n\in z$ and $0\leq\theta<\frac{\pi}{2}$ then

(i) $\sin\left(n.\frac{\pi}{2}\pm\theta\right)$ $=\pm\sin\theta$ if n is even

$=\pm\cos\theta$ if n is odd

(ii) $\cos\left(\frac{n\pi}{2}\pm\theta\right)$ $=\pm\cos\theta$ if n is even

$=\pm\sin\theta$ if n is odd

(iii) $\tan\left(\frac{n\pi}{2}\pm\theta\right)$ $=\pm\tan\theta$ if n is even

$=\pm\cot\theta$ if n is odd

(iv) $\cot\left(\frac{n\pi}{2}\pm\theta\right)$ $=\pm\cot\theta$ if n is even

$=\pm\tan\theta$ if n is odd

(v) $\sec\left(\frac{n\pi}{2}\pm\theta\right)$ $=\pm\sec\theta$ if n is even

$=\pm\operatorname{cosec}\theta$ if n is odd

(vi) $\operatorname{cosec}\left(\frac{n\pi}{2}\pm\theta\right)$ $=\pm\operatorname{cosec}\theta$ if n is even

$=\pm\sec\theta$ if n is odd

The sign of R.H.S of above equalities can be decided from the quadrant in which $\frac{n\pi}{2} \pm \theta$ lies.

Solved Examples

1. Find the values of

(i) $\cos 315^o$ (ii) $\sin\left(-17\frac{\pi}{4}\right)$ (iii) $\tan\left(-\frac{2\pi}{3}\right)$

(iv) $\cot(-300^o)$ (v) $\sec(210^o)$ (vi) $\text{cosec}(225^o)$

Sol. (i) $\cos 315^o = \cos(360 - 45^o) = \cos 45^o = \frac{1}{\sqrt{2}}$

(ii) $\sin\left(\frac{-17\pi}{4}\right) = -\sin\left(\frac{17\pi}{4}\right) = -\sin\left(4\pi + \frac{\pi}{4}\right) = -\sin\frac{\pi}{4} = \frac{-1}{\sqrt{2}}$

(iii) $\tan\left(\frac{-2\pi}{3}\right) = -\tan\left(\frac{2\pi}{3}\right) = -\tan\left(\pi - \frac{\pi}{3}\right) = \left(-\tan\frac{\pi}{3}\right) = \sqrt{3}$

(iv) $\cot(-300^o) = -\cot(300^o) = -\cot(270^o + 30^o) = (-\tan 30^o) = \frac{1}{\sqrt{3}}$

(v) $\sec(210^o) = \sec(180^o + 30^o) = -\sec 30^o = \frac{-2}{\sqrt{3}}$

(vi) $\text{cosec}(225^o) = \text{cosec}(180^o + 45^o) = -\text{cosec}(45) = -\sqrt{2}$

2. If $\theta = \frac{\pi}{21}$ show that $\frac{\sin 23\theta - \sin 7\theta}{\sin 2\theta + \sin 14\theta} = -1$

Let $s = \frac{\sin 23\theta - \sin 7\theta}{\sin 2\theta + \sin 14\theta} = \frac{\sin\frac{23\pi}{21} - \sin\frac{7\pi}{21}}{\sin\frac{2.\pi}{21} + \sin\frac{14\pi}{21}}$

$$= \frac{\sin\left(\pi + \frac{2\pi}{21}\right) - \sin\frac{\pi}{3}}{\sin\left(\frac{2\pi}{21}\right) + \sin\left(\frac{2\pi}{3}\right)} = \frac{-\sin\frac{2\pi}{21} - \sin\frac{\pi}{3}}{\sin\frac{2\pi}{21} + \sin\left(\pi - \frac{\pi}{3}\right)}$$

$$= \frac{-\left[\sin\frac{2\pi}{21} + \sin\frac{\pi}{3}\right]}{\sin\frac{2\pi}{21} + \sin\left(\frac{\pi}{3}\right)} = -1$$

3. (i) If $\sin\theta = k$, $0 < k < 1$ and θ does not lies in the first quadrant, find the values of the other trigonometric functions, in terms of k.

(ii) If $\sin^2 A = \frac{1}{5}$ then find remaining trigonometric ratio (A is acute)

Sol. (i) Given $\sin\theta = k$, $0 < k < 1$ and θ does not lies in the first quadrant

$\therefore$ θ in the II quadrant

In second quadrant sin and cosec trigonometric ratios are positive, remaining negative.

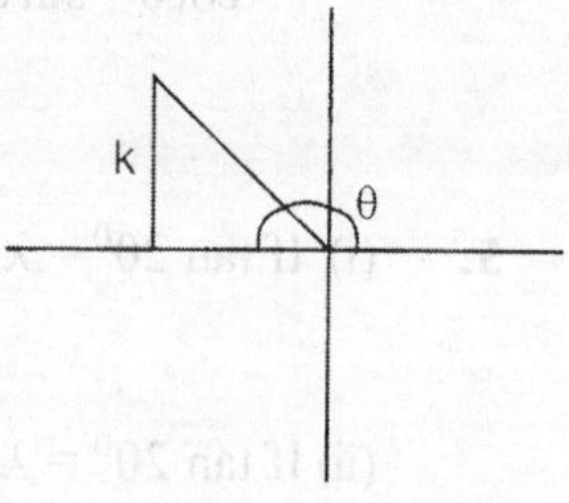

$\cos\theta = -\sqrt{1-k^2}$, $\tan\theta = \frac{\sin\theta}{\cos\theta} = \frac{-k}{\sqrt{1-k^2}}$,

$\cot\theta = \frac{\cos\theta}{\sin\theta} = -\frac{\sqrt{1-k^2}}{k}$, $\sec\theta = \frac{-1}{\sqrt{1-k^2}}$,

$\operatorname{cosec}\theta = \frac{1}{k}$.

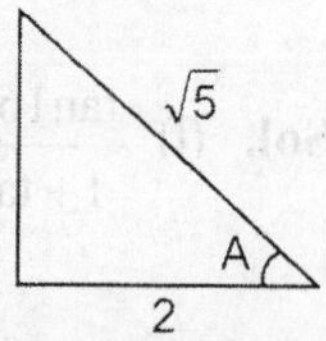

(ii) $\sin^2 A = \frac{1}{5} \Rightarrow \sin A = \frac{1}{\sqrt{5}}$

$\therefore$ $\cos A = \frac{2}{\sqrt{5}}$, $\tan A = \frac{1}{2}$, $\cot A = 2$, $\sec A = \frac{\sqrt{5}}{2}$, $\operatorname{cosec} A = \sqrt{5}$

4. If $\tan\theta = \frac{3}{4}$ and θ not in the first quadrant show that

$$\frac{\sin\left(\frac{\pi}{2}+\theta\right)-\cot(\pi-\theta)}{\tan\left(\frac{3\pi}{2}-\theta\right)-\cos\left(\frac{3\pi}{2}+\theta\right)} = \frac{8}{29}$$

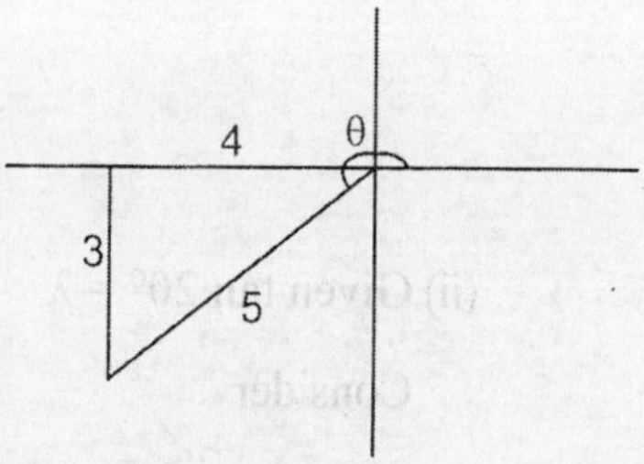

Sol. Since $\tan\theta = \frac{3}{4}$ and θ not in the first quadrant

$\therefore$ θ is in the third quadrant

$\sin\theta = \frac{-3}{5}$ $\cos\theta = \frac{-4}{5}$ $\cot\theta = \frac{4}{3}$

Consider

$$\frac{\sin\left(\frac{\pi}{2}+\theta\right)-\cot(\pi-\theta)}{\tan\left(\frac{3\pi}{2}-\theta\right)-\cos\left(\frac{3\pi}{2}+\theta\right)}$$

$$=\frac{\cos\theta+\cot\theta}{\cot\theta-\sin\theta}=\frac{\frac{-4}{5}+\frac{4}{3}}{\frac{4}{3}+\frac{3}{5}}=\frac{-12+20}{20+9}=\frac{8}{29}$$

5. (i) If $\tan 20^0 = \lambda$, Prove that $\dfrac{\tan 160^\circ - \tan 110^\circ}{1+\tan 160^\circ.\tan 110^\circ}=\dfrac{1-\lambda^2}{2\lambda}$

(ii) If $\tan 20^0 = \lambda$, Show that $\dfrac{\tan 250+\tan 340}{\tan 200-\tan 110^0}=\dfrac{1-\lambda^2}{1+\lambda^2}$

Sol. (i) $\dfrac{\tan 160^\circ - \tan 110^\circ}{1+\tan 160^\circ t 110^\circ}=\dfrac{\tan(180-20^\circ)-\tan(90+20^\circ)}{1+\tan(180-20^\circ)\tan(90+20)}$

$$=\frac{-\tan 20+\cot 20}{1+(-\tan 20)(-\cot 20^\circ)}$$

$$=\frac{\cot 20-\tan 20}{1+\tan 20\cot 20}=\frac{\frac{1}{\lambda}-\lambda}{1+1}\qquad\left(\because \tan 20=\lambda \Rightarrow \cot 20=\frac{1}{\lambda}\right)$$

$$=\frac{1-\lambda^2}{2\lambda}$$

(ii) Given $\tan 20^\circ = \lambda \quad\Rightarrow\quad \cot 20=\dfrac{1}{\lambda}$

Consider

$$\frac{\tan 250+\tan 340^\circ}{\tan 200-\tan 110^\circ}=\frac{\tan(270-20)+\tan(360-20)}{\tan(180+20)-\tan(90+20)}$$

$$=\frac{\cot 20-\tan 20}{\tan 20+\cot 20}$$

$$= \frac{\frac{1}{\lambda} - \lambda}{\lambda + \frac{1}{\lambda}} = \frac{1 - \lambda^2}{\lambda^2 + 1} = \frac{1 - \lambda^2}{1 + \lambda^2}$$

6. Show that $\frac{\cot\theta + \mathrm{cosec}\,\theta - 1}{\cot\theta - \mathrm{cosec}\,\theta + 1} = \frac{1 + \cos\theta}{\sin\theta} = \frac{1 + \cot\theta + \mathrm{cosec}\theta}{1 - \cot\theta + \mathrm{cosec}\theta}$

Sol. Consider $\frac{\cot\theta + \mathrm{cosec}\,\theta - 1}{\cot\theta - \mathrm{cosec}\,\theta + 1}$

$$= \frac{(\cot\theta + \mathrm{cosec}\,\theta) - (\mathrm{cosec}^2\theta - \cot^2\theta)}{(\cot\theta - \mathrm{cosec}\,\theta + 1)} \qquad (\because \mathrm{cosec}^2\theta - \cot^2\theta = 1)$$

$$= \frac{(\cot\theta + \mathrm{cosec}\,\theta) - (\mathrm{cosec}\theta + \cot\theta)(\mathrm{cosec}\theta - \cot\theta)}{(\cot\theta - \mathrm{cosec}\,\theta + 1)}$$

$$= (\cot\theta + \mathrm{cosec}\,\theta)\,\frac{1 - \mathrm{cosec}\theta + \cot\theta}{(1 + \cot\theta - \mathrm{cosec}\theta)}$$

$$= \cot\theta + \mathrm{cosec}\,\theta = \frac{\cos\theta}{\sin\theta} + \frac{1}{\sin\theta}$$

$$= \frac{1 + \cos\theta}{\sin\theta}$$

Again Consider, $\frac{1 + \cot\theta + \mathrm{cosec}\theta}{1 - \cot\theta + \mathrm{cosec}\theta}$

$$= \frac{(\mathrm{cosec}^2\theta - \cot^2\theta) + (\cot\theta + \mathrm{cosec}\theta)}{1 - \cot\theta + \mathrm{cosec}\theta}$$

$$= \frac{(\mathrm{cosec}\theta - \cot\theta)(\mathrm{cosec}\,\theta + \cot\theta) + (\cot\theta + \mathrm{cosec}\theta)}{1 - \cot\theta + \mathrm{cosec}\theta}$$

$$= \frac{(\mathrm{cosec}\theta + \cot\theta)[\mathrm{cosec}\theta - \cot\theta + 1]}{(1 + \mathrm{cosec}\theta - \cot\theta)}$$

$$= \mathrm{cosec}\,\theta + \cot\theta = \frac{1}{\sin\theta} + \frac{\cos\theta}{\sin\theta} = \frac{\cos\theta + 1}{\sin\theta}$$

7. If $\sec\theta + \tan\theta = \frac{1}{5}$, Find the quadrant in which θ lies and the value of $\sin\theta$.

Sol. Given, $\sec\theta + \tan\theta = \frac{1}{5}$ ..... (1)

then $\sec\theta - \tan\theta = 5$ ..... (2)

Adding (1) and (2) we get

$$2\sec\theta = \frac{1}{5} + 5 = \frac{26}{5} \qquad \sec\theta = \frac{13}{5}$$

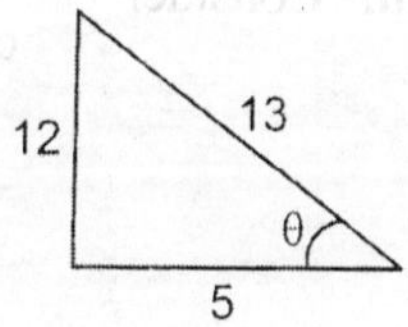

$$\tan\theta = \frac{1}{5} - \frac{13}{5} = \frac{-12}{5}$$

$\sec\theta$ is positive, $\tan\theta$ is negative

∴ θ is in the IV quadrant

$$\sin\theta = \frac{-12}{13}$$

8. If $x = r\cos\alpha\cos\beta$, $y = r\cos\alpha\sin\beta$ and $z = r\sin\alpha$, show that $x^2 + y^2 - z^2 = r^2$.

$$x^2 + y^2 = r^2\cos^2\alpha\cos^2\beta + r^2\cos^2\alpha\sin^2\beta$$

$$= r^2\cos^2\alpha\,[\cos^2\beta + \sin^2\beta] = r^2\cos^2\alpha$$

$$x^2 + y^2 + z^2 = r^2\cos^2\alpha + r^2\sin^2\alpha = r^2(\cos^2\alpha + \sin^2\alpha) = r^2$$

9. If $\frac{x}{a}\sin\theta + \frac{y}{b}\cos\theta = 1$ and $\frac{x}{a}\cos\theta - \frac{y}{b}\sin\theta = 1$ prove that $\frac{x^2}{a^2} + \frac{y^2}{b^2} = 2$

Sol. Let $\frac{x}{a}\sin\theta + \frac{y}{b}\cos\theta = 1 \rightarrow (1)$ $\frac{x}{a}\cos\theta - \frac{y}{b}\sin\theta = 1 \rightarrow (2)$

by squaring and adding (1) and (2), we get

$$\text{i.e., } (1)^2 \Rightarrow \frac{x^2}{a^2}\sin^2\theta + \frac{y^2}{b^2}\cos^2\theta + \frac{2xy}{ab}\sin\theta\cos\theta = 1$$

$$(2)^2 \Rightarrow \frac{x^2}{a^2}\cos^2\theta + \frac{y^2}{b^2}\sin^2\theta - \frac{2xy}{ab}\sin\theta\cos\theta = 1$$

$$\therefore\ (1)^2+(2)^2 \Rightarrow \frac{x^2}{a^2}(\sin^2\theta+\cos^2\theta)+\frac{y^2}{b^2}(\sin^2\theta+\cos^2\theta)=1+1=2$$

$$\Rightarrow \frac{x^2}{a^2}+\frac{y^2}{b^2}=2 \qquad (\because \sin^2\theta+\cos^2\theta=1)$$

Excercise - 8.1

1. Show that $\sin 600^\circ \cos 330^\circ + \cos 120^\circ \sin 150^\circ = -1$

2. Show that $\cot\frac{\pi}{20}.\cot\frac{3\pi}{20}.\cot\frac{5\pi}{20}\cot\frac{7\pi}{20}\cot\frac{9\pi}{20}=1$

3. Prove that $\dfrac{\sin(-\frac{11\pi}{3})\tan\left(\frac{35\pi}{6}\right).\sec\left(-\frac{7\pi}{3}\right)}{\cos\left(\frac{5\pi}{4}\right)\operatorname{cosec}\left(\frac{7\pi}{4}\right)\cos\left(\frac{17\pi}{6}\right)}=\dfrac{2}{\sqrt{3}}$

4. If $\cos\theta = k$, $0 < k < 1$ and θ does not lie in the first quadrant, find the values of the remaining functions in terms of k.

5. (i) If α, β are complementary angles and $q \sin\alpha = P$, find the values of $\sin\alpha\cos\beta - \cos\alpha\sin\beta$.

(ii) If $\cot\theta = \dfrac{2mn}{m^2-n^2} > 0$ and θ is not in the third quadrant, find the values of $\sin\theta$, $\sec\theta$.

(iii) If $\cot\theta = \frac{4}{3}$ and θ lies in the third quadrant find the value of $\cos\theta + \tan\theta$.

6. In ΔABC Prove that

(i) $\sin(A+B) = \sin C$, $\cos(A+B) + \cos C = 0$ and $\tan(A+B) + \tan C = 0$

(ii) $\sin\left(\frac{B+C}{2}\right)=\cos\frac{A}{2}$, $\cos\left(\frac{B+C}{2}\right)=\sin\frac{A}{2}$ and $\tan\left(\frac{B+C}{2}\right)=\cot\frac{A}{2}$.

7. If ABCD is cyclic quadrilataral then prove that

(i) $\sin A + \sin B = \sin C + \sin D$

(ii) $\cos A + \cos B + \cos C + \cos D = 0$.

Answers

4. $\sin\theta = -\sqrt{1-k^2}$, $\tan\theta = -\dfrac{\sqrt{1-k^2}}{k}$, $\cot\theta = \dfrac{-k}{\sqrt{1-k^2}}$, $\sec\theta = \dfrac{1}{k}$,

$\operatorname{cosec}\theta = \dfrac{-1}{\sqrt{1-k^2}}$

5. (i) $\dfrac{2p^2-q^2}{q^2}$ (ii) $\dfrac{m^2-n^2}{m^2+n^2}, \dfrac{m^2+n^2}{2mn}$ (iii) $\dfrac{-1}{20}$

9

Compound Angles

9.1 Compound Angles

Definition : The algebraic sum of two or more angles is called compound angles.

Ex : A + B, A – B, B + C, A + B + C etc are compound angles.

Note: sin (A + B), sin A + sin B need not be equal.

for example if A = 30, B = 60° then A + B = 90

$\sin(A+B) = \sin 90 = 1, \sin A + \sin B = \sin 30 + \sin 60^\circ = \frac{1}{2} + \frac{\sqrt{3}}{2}$

$\therefore \sin(A+B) \neq \sin A + \sin B$

similarly $\cos(A \pm B)$, $\cos A \pm \cos B$ need not be equal.

Theorem If A, B ε R then

(i) $\cos(A+B) = \cos A \cos B - \sin A \sin B$

(ii) $\cos(A-B) = \cos A \cos B + \sin A \sin B$

Proof Consider a unit circle with centre at the origin 'O'. Let the terminal sides of the angle A, A + B, –B in the standard position cuts the circles at Q, R, S respectively. Let OX cuts the circle at P.

$\therefore P = (1, 0), Q = \cos A, \sin A, R = (\cos(A+B), \sin(A+B))$

$S = (\cos(-B), \sin(-B)) = (\cos B, -\sin B)$

$(\because \cos(-\theta) = \cos\theta \ \sin(-\theta) = -\sin\theta)$

$\angle PQR = \angle QOS = A + B$ (numerically)

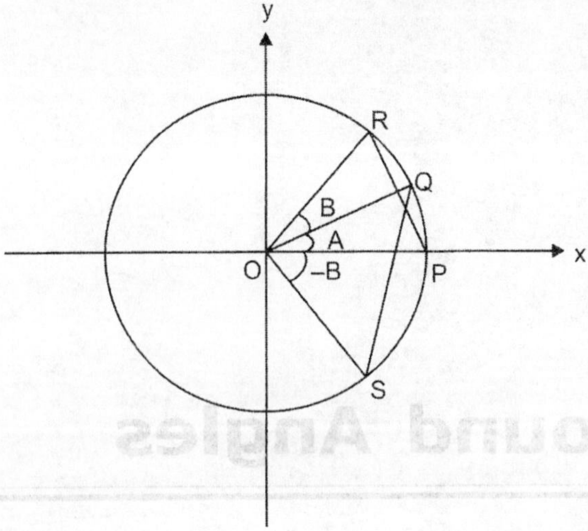

$\Rightarrow$ PR = QS

$\Rightarrow$ $PR^2 = QS^2$

$\Rightarrow$ $(1 - \cos(A + B))^2 + (0 - \sin(A + B)^2) = (\cos A - \cos B)^2 + (\sin A + \sin B)^2$

$\Rightarrow$ $1 + \cos^2 (A + B) - 2\cos(A + B) + \sin^2(A + B) = \cos^2 A + \cos^2 B - 2\cos A \cos B + \sin^2 A + \sin^2 B + 2 \sin A \sin B$

$\Rightarrow$ $1 + 1 - 2 \cos(A + B) = 1 + 1 - 2 [\cos A \cos B - \sin A \sin B]$

$\Rightarrow$ $\cos(A + B) = \cos A \cos B - \sin A \sin B$

(ii) $\cos(A - B) = \cos[(A + (-B)] = \cos A \cos(-B) - \sin A \sin(-B)$

$= \cos A \cos B + \sin A \sin B$

Theorem 2 If A, B ε R then

(i) $\sin(A + B) = \sin A \cos B + \cos A \sin B$

(ii) $\sin(A - B) = \sin A \cos B - \cos A \sin B$

Proof (i) $\sin(A + B) = \cos\left(\frac{\pi}{2} - (A + B)\right)$

$= \cos\left((\frac{\pi}{2} - A) - B\right)$

$= \cos\left(\frac{\pi}{2} - A)\right) \cos B + \sin\left(\frac{\pi}{2} - A)\right) \sin(+B)$

($\because$ by above theorem)

$= \sin A \cos B + \cos A \sin B$

(ii) $\sin(A - B) = \sin(A + (-B))$

$$= \sin A \cos(-B) + \cos A \sin(-B)$$

$$= \sin A \cos B - \cos A \sin B$$

Theorem 3 If $A, B, A + B, A - B \in R - \{(2n + 1)\frac{\pi}{2}, n \in z\}$ then

(i) $\tan(A + B) = \dfrac{\tan A + \tan B}{1 - \tan A \tan B}$

(ii) $\tan(A - B) = \dfrac{\tan A - \tan B}{1 + \tan A \tan B}$

Proof (i) $\tan(A + B) = \dfrac{\sin(A + B)}{\cos(A + B)} = \dfrac{\sin A \cos B + \cos A \sin B}{\cos A \cos B - \sin A \sin B}$

Dividing both numerator and denominator with cos A cos B we get

$$\tan(A + B) = \frac{\tan A + \tan B}{1 - \tan A . \tan B}$$

(ii) $\tan(A - B) = \tan(A + (-B)) = \dfrac{\tan A + \tan(-B)}{1 - \tan A . \tan(-B)} = \dfrac{\tan A - \tan B}{\tan A \tan B}$

Theorem 4 If $A, B, A + B, A - B \in R - \{ n\pi : n \in z \}$ then

(i) $\cot(A + B) = \dfrac{\cot A \cot B - 1}{\cot B + \cot A}$

(ii) $\cot(A - B) = \dfrac{\cot A \cot B + 1}{\cot B - \cot A}$

Proof (i) $\cot(A + B) = \dfrac{\cos(A + B)}{\sin(A + B)} = \dfrac{\cos A \cos B - \sin A \sin B}{\sin A \cos B + \cos A \sin B}$

Dividing Numerator and Denominator with sin A sinB we get

$$\cot(A + B) = \frac{\cos A \cot B - 1}{\cot B + \cot A}$$

(ii) $\cot(A - B) = \cot(A + (-B)) = \dfrac{\cot A \cot(-B) - 1}{\cos(-B) + \cot A} = \dfrac{\cot A \cot B + 1}{\cot B - \cot A}$

Theorem 5 $\sin(A+B)\sin(A-B) = \sin^2 A - \sin^2 B = \cos^2 B - \cos^2 A$

Proof $\sin(A+B)\sin(A-B)$

$= (\sin A\cos B + \cos A\sin B)(\sin A\cos B - \cos A\sin B)$

$= \sin^2 A\cos^2 B - \cos^2 A\sin^2 B$

$= \sin^2 A(1-\sin^2 B) - (1-\sin^2 A)(\sin^2 B)$

$= \sin^2 A - \sin^2 B = (1-\cos^2 A) - (1-\cos^2 B) = \cos^2 B - \cos^2 A$

Theorem 6 $\cos(A+B)\cos(A-B) = \cos^2 B - \sin^2 A = \cos^2 A - \sin^2 B$

Proof $\cos(A+B)\cos(A-B)$

$= (\cos A\cos B - \sin A\sin B)(\cos A\cos B + \sin A\sin B)$

$= \cos^2 A\cos^2 B - \sin^2 A\sin^2 B$

$= \cos^2 A(1-\sin^2 B) - (1-\cos^2 A)\sin^2 B$

$= \cos^2 A - \sin^2 B$

again, $= (1-\sin^2 A) - (1-\cos^2 B) = \cos^2 B - \sin^2 A$

Theorem 7 (i) $\tan\left(\frac{\pi}{4}+A\right) = \frac{1+\tan A}{1-\tan A} = \frac{\cos A+\sin A}{\cos A-\sin A}$

(ii) $\tan\left(\frac{\pi}{4}-A\right) = \frac{1-\tan A}{1+\tan A} = \frac{\cos A-\sin A}{\cos A+\sin A}$

Proof (i) $\tan\left(\frac{\pi}{4}+A\right) = \frac{\tan\frac{\pi}{4}+\tan A}{1-\tan\frac{\pi}{4}\tan A} = \frac{1+\tan A}{1-\tan A}$

$$= \frac{1+\frac{\sin A}{\cos A}}{1-\frac{\sin A}{\cos A}} = \frac{\cos A+\sin A}{\cos A-\sin A}$$

(ii) $\tan\left(\frac{\pi}{4}-A\right) = \frac{\tan\frac{\pi}{4}-\tan A}{1+\tan\frac{\pi}{4}\tan A} = \frac{1-\tan A}{1+\tan A} = \frac{1-\frac{\sin A}{\cos A}}{1+\frac{\sin A}{\cos A}} = \frac{\cos A-\sin A}{\cos A+\sin A}$

Note (i) $\sin(A+B)+\sin(A-B)=2\sin A\cos B$

(ii) $\sin(A+B)-\sin(A-B)=2\cos A\sin B$

(iii) $\cos(A+B)+\cos(A-B)=2\cos A\cos B$

(iv) $\cos(A+B)-\cos(A-B)=-2\sin A\sin B$

Solved Examples

1. Find the values of

(i) sin 15 (ii) cos 15 (iii) tan 15°
(iv) sin 105° (v) cos 105° (vi) tan (105°)

Sol. (i) $\sin 15^o=\sin(45^o-30^o)=\sin 45^o\cos 30^o-\cos 45^o\sin 30^0$

$$=\frac{1}{\sqrt{2}}.\frac{\sqrt{3}}{2}-\frac{1}{\sqrt{2}}.\frac{1}{2}$$

$$=\frac{\sqrt{3}-1}{2\sqrt{2}}$$

(ii) $\cos 15^o=\cos(45^o-30^o)=\cos 45^o\,.\cos 30+\sin 45^o\sin 30^o$

$$=\frac{1}{\sqrt{2}}\frac{\sqrt{3}}{2}+\frac{1}{\sqrt{2}}.\frac{1}{2}=\frac{\sqrt{3}+1}{2\sqrt{2}}$$

(iii) $\tan 15^o=\dfrac{\sin 15^o}{\cos 15^o}=\dfrac{\sqrt{3}-1}{\sqrt{3}+1}=\dfrac{(\sqrt{3}-1)^2}{3-1}=\dfrac{3+1-2\sqrt{3}}{2}=2-\sqrt{3}$

(iv) $\sin 105^o=\sin(90^o+15^o)=\cos 15^o=\dfrac{\sqrt{3}+1}{2\sqrt{2}}$

(v) $\cos(105^o)=\cos(90^o+15^o)=-\sin 15^o=-\left(\dfrac{\sqrt{3}-1}{2\sqrt{2}}\right)$

(vi) $\tan 105^o=\dfrac{\sin 105^o}{\cos 105^o}=\dfrac{\sqrt{3}+1}{-(\sqrt{3}-1)}$

2. Show that

(i) $\sin 20^o\cos 40^o+\cos 20^o\sin 40^o=\dfrac{\sqrt{3}}{2}$

(ii) $\cos 100^o\cos 40^o+\sin 100^o\sin 40^o=\dfrac{1}{2}$

Sol. (i) $\sin 20 \cos 40 + \cos 20^\circ \sin 40^\circ = \sin(20 + 40)$

$(\because \sin A \cos B + \cos A \sin B = \sin(A + B)$

$= \sin 60^\circ = \frac{\sqrt{3}}{2}$

(ii) $\cos 100^\circ \cos 40^\circ + \sin 100^\circ \sin 40^\circ = \cos(100 - 40^\circ) = \cos 60^\circ = \frac{1}{2}$

$(\because \cos A \cos B + \sin A \sin B = \cos(A - B))$

3. Prove that $\tan(\theta + 135^\circ)\tan(\theta - 135^\circ) = -1$

$$\text{LHS} = \frac{\tan\theta + \tan 135^\circ}{1 - \tan\theta an\theta.ta5^\circ} \times \frac{\tan\theta - \tan 135^\circ}{1 + \tan\theta an\theta.ta5^\circ}$$

$$= \left(\frac{\tan\theta - 1}{1 + \tan\theta}\right)\left(\frac{\tan\theta + 1}{1 - \tan\theta}\right) \qquad [\because \tan 135^\circ = -1]$$

$= -1$

4. Prove that

(i) $\sin^2 75^\circ - \sin^2 15^\circ = \frac{\sqrt{3}}{2}$ (ii) $\cos^2 52\left(\frac{1}{2}\right)^\circ - \sin^2 22\left(\frac{1}{2}\right)^\circ = \frac{3-\sqrt{3}}{4\sqrt{2}}$

Sol. (i) $\sin^2 75^\circ - \sin^2 15 = \sin(75^\circ + 15^\circ)\sin(75^\circ - 15^\circ)$

$[\because \sin^2 A - \sin^2 B = \sin(A + B)\sin(A + B)$

$= \sin 90 . \sin 60$

$= 1 \times \frac{\sqrt{3}}{2} = \frac{\sqrt{3}}{2}$

(ii) $$\cos^2 52\left(\frac{1}{2}\right)^\circ - \sin^2 22\left(\frac{1}{2}\right)^\circ = \cos\left[52\left(\frac{1}{2}\right)^\circ + 22\left(\frac{1}{2}\right)^\circ\right]\cos\left[52\left(\frac{1}{2}\right)^\circ - 22\left(\frac{1}{2}\right)^\circ\right]$$

$= \cos(75^\circ)\cos(30^\circ) = \cos(45^\circ + 30^\circ)(\cos 30^\circ)$

$= (\cos 45^\circ \cos 30^\circ - \sin 45^\circ \sin 30^\circ)(\cos 30^\circ)$

$$= \left(\frac{\sqrt{3}-1}{2\sqrt{2}}\right)\frac{\sqrt{3}}{2} = \frac{3-\sqrt{3}}{4\sqrt{2}}$$

5. If tan(A + B) = m, tan (A – B) = n then find tan2A, tan 2B

Sol. tan(2A) = tan ((A + B) + (A – B))

$$= \frac{\tan(A+B)+\tan(A-B)}{1-\tan(A+B)\tan(A-B)} = \frac{m+n}{1-mn}$$

tan(2B) = tan [(A + B) – (A – B)]

$$= \frac{\tan(A+B)+\tan(A-B)}{1+\tan(A+B)\tan(A-B)} = \frac{m-n}{1+mn}$$

6. If sin (θ + α) = cos (θ + α) then express tanθ in terms of α.

Sol. Given sin (θ + α) = cos(θ + α)

$\Rightarrow$ tan (θ + α) = 1

$$\Rightarrow \quad \theta + \alpha = \frac{\pi}{4}$$

$$\theta = \frac{\pi}{4} - \alpha$$

taking tan on both sides we get

$$\tan\theta = \tan\left(\frac{\pi}{4}-\alpha\right) = \frac{\tan\frac{\pi}{4}-\tan\alpha}{1+\tan\alpha.\tan\frac{\pi}{4}} = \frac{1-\tan\alpha}{1+\tan\alpha}$$

7. (i) If A + B = 45° prove that (1 + tan A) (1 + tan B) = 2 and hence deduce that

$$\tan 22\left(\frac{1}{2}\right)^{o} = \sqrt{2}-1$$

(ii) If A + B = 45° prove that (1 + cot A) (1 + cot B) = 2 and hence deduce that

$$\cot 22\left(\frac{1}{2}\right)^{o} = \sqrt{2}+1$$

Sol. (i) A + B = 45°

taking 'tan' on both sides we get

tan(A + B) = tan 45° = 1

$$\frac{\tan A+\tan B}{1-\tan A\tan B} = 1$$

$\Rightarrow \quad \tan A + \tan B = 1 - \tan A . \tan B$

$\Rightarrow \quad \tan A + \tan B + \tan A \tan B = 1$

Adding 1 on both sides we get

$\Rightarrow \quad 1 + \tan A + \tan B + \tan A . \tan B = 1 + 1 = 2$

$\Rightarrow \quad (1 + \tan A) + \tan B (1 + \tan A) = 2$

$\Rightarrow \quad (1 + \tan A)(1 + \tan B) = 2$

Put $A = B = 22\frac{1}{2}^{o}$ we get $A + B = 45^{o}$ again

$$(1+\tan 22\frac{1}{2}^{o})(1+\tan 22\frac{1}{2}^{o}) = 2$$

$$\Rightarrow \quad (1+\tan 22\frac{1}{2}^{o})^2 = 2$$

$$\Rightarrow \quad 1+\tan 22\frac{1}{2}^{o} = \pm\sqrt{2}$$

$$\Rightarrow \quad \tan 22\frac{1}{2}^{o} = \pm\sqrt{2}-1$$

$$\Rightarrow \quad \tan 22\frac{1}{2} = \sqrt{2}-1$$

$(\because \tan 22\left(\frac{1}{2}\right)^{o}$ is positive)

(ii) $A + B = 45^{o}$

taking 'cot' on both sides

$\cot (A + B) = \cot 45^{o} = 1$

$$\frac{\cot A \cot B - 1}{\cot B + \cot A} = 1 \quad \Rightarrow \quad \cot A \cot B - 1 = \cot B + \cot A$$

$$\cot A \cot B - \cot B - \cot A = 1$$

$$\cot A \cot B - \cot B - \cot A + 1 = 1 + 1 = 2$$

$$\cot B (\cot A - 1) - 1 (\cot A - 1) = 2$$

$$(\cot B - 1)(\cot A - 1) = 2$$

take $A = B = 22\left(\frac{1}{2}\right)^{o}$ then $A + B = 45^{o}$

again $(\cot 22\frac{1}{2}^{o} - 1)(\cot 22\frac{1}{2}^{o}) = 2 \Rightarrow \left(\cot 22\frac{1}{2}^{o} - 1\right)^2 = 2$

$\Rightarrow \cot 22\frac{1}{2}^{o} - 1 = \sqrt{2}$

$\cot 22\frac{1}{2}^{o} = \sqrt{2} + 1$

8. Prove that $\tan 70^o - \tan 20^o = 2\tan 40^o + 4\tan 10^o$

Sol. Consider $\tan 50^o = \tan(70^o - 20^o)$

$$= \frac{\tan 70^o - \tan 20^o}{1 + \tan 70^o \tan 20^o} = \frac{\tan 70^o - \tan 20^o}{2}$$

$2\tan 50^o = \tan 70^o - \tan 20^o$ .....(1)

again consider

$$\tan 10^o = \tan(50^o - 40^o) = \frac{\tan 50^o - \tan 40^o}{1 + \tan 50^o \tan 40^o} = \frac{\tan 50^o - \tan 40^o}{1+1}$$

$2\tan 10^o = \tan 50^o - \tan 40^o$

$\tan 50^o = \tan 40^o + 2\tan 10^o$

$\therefore \quad 2\tan 50^o = 2\tan 40^o + 4\tan 10^o$ .....(2)

from (1) and (2) we get

$\tan 70^o - \tan 20^o = 2\tan 40^o + 4\tan 10^o$

9. If $\tan(A - B) = \frac{7}{24}$ and $\tan A = \frac{4}{3}$ where A and B are acute, show that

$A + B = \frac{\pi}{2}$

Sol. $\tan B = \tan(A - (A - B))$

$$= \frac{\tan A - \tan(A - B)}{1 + \tan A . \tan(A - B)} = \frac{\frac{4}{3} - \frac{7}{24}}{1 + \frac{4}{3}.\frac{7}{24}} = \frac{75}{100} = \frac{3}{4}$$

$$\tan(A+B) = \frac{\tan A + \tan B}{1 - \tan A \tan B} = \frac{\frac{4}{3} + \frac{3}{4}}{1 - \frac{4}{3}.\frac{3}{4}} = \frac{\frac{4}{3} + \frac{3}{4}}{0} = \infty$$

$$\therefore \quad A + B = \frac{\pi}{2}$$

10. If $270^\circ < A < 360^\circ$, $90 < B < 180^\circ$, $\cos A = \frac{5}{13}$, $\tan B = \frac{-15}{8}$, find $\sin(A+B)$, $\cos(A+B)$ also find quadrant in which $A + B$ lies.

Sol. A lies in IV quadrant, B in II quadrant

also given $\quad \cos A = \frac{5}{13}, \quad \tan B = \frac{-15}{8}$

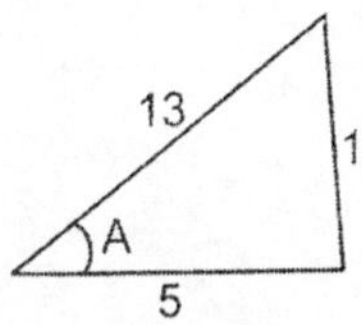

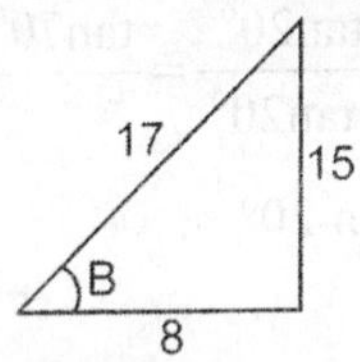

$\sqrt{64 + 225} = \sqrt{289}$

$$\sin A = \frac{-12}{13} \qquad \sin B = \frac{15}{17} \quad \cos B = \frac{-8}{17}$$

$$\sin(A+B) = \sin A \cos B + \cos A \sin B = \frac{-12}{13} \times \frac{-8}{17} + \frac{5}{13} \times \frac{15}{17}$$

$$= \frac{96 + 75}{13 \times 17} = \frac{171}{221}$$

$$\cos(A+B) = \cos A \cos B - \sin A \sin B = \frac{5}{13} \times \frac{-8}{17} - \left(\frac{-12}{13}\right)\left(\frac{15}{17}\right)$$

$$= \frac{-40}{13 \times 17} + \frac{180}{13 \times 17} = \frac{140}{221}$$

both $\sin(A+B)$, $\cos(A+B)$ are positive

$\therefore \quad A + B$ is in first quadrant

10

Multiple and Sub-Multiple Angles

10.1 Multiple Angles

Definition : If A is an angle then 2A, 3A, 4A ... etc are called multiple angles.

10.2 Sub-Multiple Angles

Definition : If A is an angle then $\frac{A}{2}, \frac{A}{3}$ .... etc are called sub-multiple angles.

Theorem 1 If A ε R then $\sin 2A = 2 \sin A \cos A = \frac{2\tan A}{1+\tan^2 A}$

Proof we know that $\sin(A + B) = \sin A \cos B + \cos A \sin B$

now $\sin 2A = \sin (A + A) = \sin A \cos A + \cos A \sin A = 2 \sin A \cos A$

again $2 \sin A \cos A = 2\frac{\sin A}{\cos A} . \cos^2 A = 2 \tan A . \cos^2 A$

$$= \frac{2\tan A}{\sec^2 A} = \frac{2\tan A}{1+\tan^2 A}$$

Hence $\sin 2A = 2 \sin A \cos A = \frac{2\tan A}{1+\tan^2 A}$

Theorem 2 If A ε R then $\cos 2A = \cos^2 A - \sin^2 A = \dfrac{1-\tan^2 A}{1+\tan^2 A}$

Proof we know that

$\cos(A+B) = \cos A \cos B - \sin A \sin B$

$\therefore \cos 2A = \cos(A+A) = \cos A \cos A - \sin A \sin A = \cos^2 A - \sin^2 A$

again $\cos^2 A - \sin^2 A = \cos^2 A \left[1 - \dfrac{\sin^2 A}{\cos^2 A}\right] = \cos^2 A\,[1 - \tan^2 A]$

$$= \frac{1-\tan^2 A}{\sec^2 A} = \frac{1-\tan^2 A}{1+\tan^2 A}$$

$$\therefore \quad \cos 2A = \cos^2 A - \sin^2 A = \frac{1-\tan^2 A}{1+\tan^2 A}$$

Theorem 3 If A ε R then $\tan 2A = \dfrac{2\tan A}{1-\tan^2 A}$

Proof we know that $\tan(A+B) = \dfrac{\tan A + \tan B}{1 - \tan A \tan B}$

$$\tan 2A = \tan(A+A) = \frac{\tan A + \tan A}{1 - \tan A.\tan A} = \frac{2\tan A}{1-\tan^2 A}$$

Corollary

1. $\cos 2A = 2\cos^2 A - 1 \Rightarrow \cos^2 A = \dfrac{1+\cos 2A}{2}$

2. $\cos 2A = 1 - 2\sin^2 A \Rightarrow \sin^2 A = \dfrac{1-\cos 2A}{2}$

3. $\sin A = 2\sin\dfrac{A}{2}\cos\dfrac{A}{2} = \dfrac{2\tan\dfrac{A}{2}}{1+\tan^2\dfrac{A}{2}}$

4. $\cos A = \cos^2\dfrac{A}{2} - \sin^2\dfrac{A}{2} = \dfrac{1-\tan^2\dfrac{A}{2}}{1+\tan^2\dfrac{A}{2}}$

5. $\tan A = \dfrac{2\tan\frac{A}{2}}{1-\tan^2\frac{A}{2}}$

6. $\cos A = \cos^2\frac{A}{2} - \sin^2\frac{A}{2} = 2\cos^2\frac{A}{2} - 1 = 1 - 2\sin^2\frac{A}{2}$

7. $\tan A = \dfrac{2\tan\frac{A}{2}}{1-\tan^2\frac{A}{2}}$

8. $\sin 3A = 3\sin A - 4\sin^3 A$ [for proving take $\sin(3A) = \sin(2A + A)$]

9. $\cos 3A = 4\cos^3 A - 3\cos A$

10. $\tan 3A = \dfrac{3\tan A - \tan^3 A}{1 - 3\tan^2 A}$

Note 1 : $\sin 18^\circ = \dfrac{\sqrt{5}-1}{4}$

Proof : Let $\theta = 18^\circ$ then $5\theta = 90^\circ$

$\therefore \quad 2\theta = 90^0 - 3\theta$

$\Rightarrow \quad \sin 2\theta = \sin(90 - 3\theta) \quad \Rightarrow \quad \sin 2\theta = \cos 3\theta$

$\Rightarrow \quad 2\sin\theta\cos\theta = 4\cos^3\theta - 3\cos\theta \Rightarrow 2\sin\theta\cos\theta$
$= \cos\theta(4\cos^2\theta - 3)$

$\Rightarrow \quad 2\sin\theta = 4\cos^2\theta - 3$

$\Rightarrow \quad 2\sin\theta = 4(1 - \sin^2\theta) - 3$

$\Rightarrow \quad 4\sin^2\theta + 2\sin\theta - 1 = 0$

$\therefore \quad \sin\theta = \dfrac{-2 \pm \sqrt{4 - 4.4(-1)}}{2\times 4} = \dfrac{-2 \pm 2\sqrt{5}}{8} = \dfrac{-1 \pm \sqrt{5}}{4}$

since θ is in the first quadrant

$\therefore \quad \sin\theta = \dfrac{\sqrt{5}-1}{4}$

$\therefore \quad \sin 18^\circ = \dfrac{\sqrt{5}-1}{4}$

Note 2 : $\cos 18^\circ = \dfrac{\sqrt{10+2\sqrt{5}}}{4}$

Proof : we have $\cos^2 18 = 1 - \sin^2 18^\circ = 1 - \left(\dfrac{\sqrt{5}-1}{4}\right)^2$

$$= 1 - \left(\frac{5+1-2\sqrt{5}}{16}\right) = \frac{10+2\sqrt{5}}{16}$$

$$\therefore \cos 18^\circ = \sqrt{\frac{10+2\sqrt{5}}{16}} = \frac{\sqrt{10+2\sqrt{5}}}{4}$$

Note 3 : (i) $\cos 36^\circ = \dfrac{\sqrt{5}+1}{4}$ (ii) $\sin 36^\circ = \sqrt{\dfrac{10+2\sqrt{5}}{4}}$

Proof : (i) $\cos 2\theta = 1 - 2\sin^2\theta = 1 - 2\left(\dfrac{\sqrt{5}-1}{4}\right)^2 = 1 - 2\left(\dfrac{5+1-2\sqrt{5}}{16}\right)$

$$= \frac{4+4\sqrt{5}}{16} = \frac{\sqrt{5}+1}{4}$$

(ii) $\sin^2 36^\circ = 1 - \cos^2 36^\circ$

$$= 1 - \left(\frac{\sqrt{5}+1}{4}\right)^2 = \frac{16-(5+1+2\sqrt{5})}{16} = \frac{10-2\sqrt{5}}{16}$$

$$\therefore \sin 36^\circ = \frac{\sqrt{10-2\sqrt{5}}}{4}$$

Note 4 : $\sin 54^\circ = \sin(90^\circ - 36^\circ) = \cos 36^\circ = \dfrac{\sqrt{5}+1}{4}$

$$\cos 54^\circ = \cos(90^\circ - 36^\circ) = \sin 36^\circ = \frac{\sqrt{10-2\sqrt{5}}}{4}$$

$$\sin 72^\circ = \sin(90^\circ - 18^\circ) = \cos 18^\circ = \frac{\sqrt{10+2\sqrt{5}}}{4}$$

$$\cos 72^\circ = \cos(90^\circ - 18^\circ) = \sin 18^\circ = \frac{\sqrt{5}-1}{4}$$

	18^0	36^0	54^0	72^0
sin	$\frac{\sqrt{5}-1}{4}$	$\frac{\sqrt{10-2\sqrt{5}}}{4}$	$\frac{\sqrt{5}+1}{4}$	$\frac{\sqrt{10+2\sqrt{5}}}{4}$
cos	$\frac{\sqrt{10+2\sqrt{5}}}{4}$	$\frac{\sqrt{5}+1}{4}$	$\frac{\sqrt{10-2\sqrt{5}}}{4}$	$\frac{\sqrt{5}-1}{4}$

Solved Examples

1. Show that

(i) $\frac{\sin 2A}{1-\cos 2A} = \cot A$ (ii) $\frac{1+\sin\theta-\cos\theta}{1+\sin\theta+\cos\theta} = \tan\frac{\theta}{2}$ (iii) $\frac{\sin 3\alpha}{\sin\alpha} - \frac{\cos 3\alpha}{\cos\alpha} = 2$

Sol. (i) LHS $= \frac{\sin 2A}{1-\cos 2A} = \frac{2\sin A\cos A}{1-(1-2\sin^2 A)} = \frac{2\sin A\cos A}{1-1+2\sin^2 A}$

$$= \frac{2\sin A\cos A}{2\sin^2 A} = \frac{\cos A}{\sin A} = \cot A = \text{RHS}$$

(ii) LHS $= \frac{1+\sin\theta-\cos\theta}{1+\sin\theta+\cos\theta} = \frac{1-\cos\theta+\sin\theta}{1+\cos\theta+\sin\theta} = \frac{2\sin^2\frac{\theta}{2}+2\sin\frac{\theta}{2}\cos\frac{\theta}{2}}{2\cos^2\frac{\theta}{2}+2\sin\frac{\theta}{2}\cos\frac{\theta}{2}}$

$$= \frac{2\sin\frac{\theta}{2}(\sin\frac{\theta}{2}+\cos\frac{\theta}{2})}{2\cos\frac{\theta}{2}(\cos\frac{\theta}{2}+\sin\frac{\theta}{2})}$$

$$= \frac{\sin\frac{\theta}{2}}{\cos\frac{\theta}{2}} = \tan\frac{\theta}{2} = \text{RHS}$$

(iii) LHS $= \frac{\sin 3\alpha}{\sin\alpha} - \frac{\cos 3\alpha}{\cos\alpha}$

$$= \left(\frac{3\sin\alpha-4\sin^3\alpha}{\sin\alpha}\right) - \left(\frac{4\cos^3\alpha-3\cos\alpha}{\cos\alpha}\right)$$

$$= (3-4\sin^2\alpha) - (4\cos^2\alpha - 3)$$

$$= 6 - 4(\sin^2\alpha+\cos^2\alpha) = 6 - 4(1) = 6 - 4 = 2$$

2. (i) If $0 < \theta < \frac{\pi}{4}$ then show that $\sqrt{2+\sqrt{2(1+\cos 4\theta}} = 2\cos\theta$

(ii) If $270^0 < \theta < 360^0$ and $\cos\theta = \frac{1}{4}$ find $\tan\frac{\theta}{2}$)

(iii) If $0 < \alpha, \beta < \pi$, $\tan\alpha = \frac{1}{3}$, $\tan\beta = \frac{1}{7}$ prove that $2\alpha + \beta = \frac{\pi}{4}$

Sol. (i) LHS $= \sqrt{2+\sqrt{2(1+\cos 4\theta}} = \sqrt{2+\sqrt{2(2\cos^2\frac{4\theta}{2})}}$

$$= \sqrt{2+2\cos\frac{4\theta}{2}}$$

$$= \sqrt{2+2\cos 2\theta} = \sqrt{2(1+\cos 2\theta)}$$

$$= \sqrt{2(2\cos^2\frac{2\theta}{2})}$$

$$= \sqrt{4\cos^2\theta} = 2\cos\theta$$

$$= \text{RHS}$$

(ii) Given $\cos\theta = \frac{1}{4}$

$$\Rightarrow \quad \frac{1-\tan^2\frac{\theta}{2}}{1+\tan^2\frac{\theta}{2}} = \frac{1}{4} \quad \Rightarrow \quad 4 - 4\tan^2\frac{\theta}{2} = 1 + \tan^2\frac{\theta}{2}$$

$$\Rightarrow \quad 5\tan^2\frac{\theta}{2} = 3 \quad \Rightarrow \quad \tan^2\frac{\theta}{2} = \frac{3}{5}$$

$$\therefore \quad \tan\frac{\theta}{2} = \pm\frac{\sqrt{3}}{\sqrt{5}}$$

but given $270^0 < \theta < 360^0 \quad \Rightarrow \quad 135^0 < \frac{\theta}{2} < 180^0$

$\Rightarrow \quad \frac{\theta}{2}$ lies in II quadrant

$\therefore \quad \tan\frac{\theta}{2}$ is negative

$$\therefore \quad \tan\frac{\theta}{2} = -\sqrt{\frac{3}{5}}$$

(iii) *Hint :* Find $\tan 2\alpha$ from $\tan\alpha$, and show that $\tan(2\alpha+\beta) = 1$

3. (i) show that $\cos^4\theta - \sin^4\theta = \cos 2\theta$

(ii) If $x + \frac{1}{x} = 2\cos\theta$ show that $x^3 + \frac{1}{x^3} = 2\cos 3\theta$

(iii) If $\tan\theta = x$ then prove that $\sin 2\theta + \tan 2\theta = \frac{4x}{1-x^4}$

Sol. (i) LHS $= \cos^4\theta - \sin^4\theta = (\cos^2\theta)^2 - (\sin^2\theta)^2$

$$= (\cos^2\theta - \sin^2\theta)(\cos^2\theta + \sin^2\theta)$$

$$= (\cos^2\theta - \sin^2\theta)(1)$$

$$= \cos 2\theta$$

(ii) Given $x + \frac{1}{x} = 2\cos\theta$

cubing on both sides we get

$$\left(x+\frac{1}{x}\right)^3 = (2\cos\theta)^3 = 8\cos^3\theta$$

$$\therefore \quad x^3 + \frac{1}{x^3} + 3x\frac{1}{x}\left(x+\frac{1}{x}\right) = 8\cos^3\theta$$

$$\Rightarrow \quad x^3 + \frac{1}{x^3} + 3(2\cos\theta) = 8\cos^3\theta$$

$$\Rightarrow \quad x^3 + \frac{1}{x^3} = 8\cos^3\theta - 6\cos\theta$$

$$= 2[4\cos^3\theta - 3\cos\theta]$$

$$\Rightarrow \quad x^3 + \frac{1}{x^3} = 2[\cos 3\theta]$$

Hence $x^3 + \frac{1}{x^3} = 2\cos 3\theta$

(iii) Given $\tan\theta = x$

LHS = $\tan 2\theta + \sin 2\theta$

$$= \frac{2\tan\theta}{1-\tan^2\theta} + \frac{2\tan\theta}{1+\tan^2\theta}$$

$$= 2\tan\theta\left[\frac{1}{1-\tan^2\theta} + \frac{1}{1+\tan^2\theta}\right]$$

$$= 2\tan\theta\left[\frac{1+\tan^2\theta+1-\tan^2\theta}{(1-\tan^2\theta)(1+\tan^2\theta)}\right]$$

$$= 2\tan\theta\left[\frac{2}{1-\tan^4\theta}\right] = \frac{4\tan\theta}{1-\tan^4\theta}$$

but $\tan\theta = x \quad \Rightarrow \quad \frac{4\tan\theta}{1-\tan^4\theta} = \frac{4x}{1-x^4}$ = RHS

4. (i) Show that $\sin^2 42^\circ - \sin^2 12^\circ = \frac{\sqrt{5}+1}{8}$

(ii) $\cos^2 48^\circ - \sin^2 12^\circ = \frac{\sqrt{5}+1}{8}$

(iii) $\frac{1}{\sin 10^\circ} - \frac{\sqrt{3}}{\cos 10^\circ} = 4$

Sol. (i) $\sin^2 42^\circ - \sin^2 12^\circ$

$= \sin(42^\circ + 12^\circ)\sin(42^\circ - 12^\circ)$

[$\because \sin^2 A - \sin^2 B = \sin(A + B)\sin(A - B)$

$= \sin(54^\circ)\sin(30^\circ)$

$$= \cos 36^\circ \frac{1}{2} = \left(\frac{\sqrt{5}+1}{4}\right).\frac{1}{2} = \frac{\sqrt{5}+1}{8}$$

(ii) To show

$$\cos^2 48^\circ - \sin^2 12^\circ = \frac{\sqrt{5}+1}{8}$$

$\cos^2 48^\circ - \sin^2 12^\circ = \cos(48^\circ + 12^\circ)\cos(48^\circ - 12^\circ)$

$= \cos 60^\circ \cos 36^\circ$

$$= \frac{1}{2}.\left(\frac{\sqrt{5}+1}{4}\right) = \frac{\sqrt{5}+1}{8}$$

(iii) $\dfrac{1}{\sin 10^\circ} - \dfrac{\sqrt{3}}{\cos 10^\circ} = 4$

$$\text{LHS} = \frac{\cos 10^\circ - \sqrt{3}\sin 10^\circ}{\cos 10^\circ \sin 10^\circ}$$

$$= \frac{2\left[\frac{1}{2}\cos 10^\circ - \frac{\sqrt{3}}{2}\sin 10^\circ\right]}{\frac{1}{2}[2\cos 10^\circ \sin 10^\circ]}$$

$$= \frac{4[\cos 10\cos 60^\circ - \sin 10\sin 60^\circ]}{\sin 20^\circ}$$

$$= \frac{4.\cos(60^\circ + 10^\circ)}{\sin 20^\circ} = \frac{4\cos 70}{\sin 20} = \frac{4\sin 20^\circ}{\sin 20^\circ} = 4$$

5. Prove that $4(\cos^3 20^\circ + \cos^3 40^\circ) = 3[\cos 20^\circ + \cos 40^\circ]$

$\text{LHS} = 4[\cos^3 20^\circ + \cos^3 40^\circ]$

$$\because \quad \cos 3\theta = 4\cos^3\theta - 3\cos\theta$$

$$\cos^3\theta = \frac{\cos 3\theta + 3\cos\theta}{4}$$

$$= 4\left\{\left[\frac{\cos 60^\circ + 3\cos 20^\circ}{4}\right] + \left[\frac{\cos 120^\circ + 3\cos 40^\circ}{4}\right]\right\}$$

$$= \frac{1}{2} + 3\cos 20 + \left(\frac{-1}{2}\right) + 3\cos 40^\circ$$

$$= 3\,[\cos 20^\circ + \cos 40^\circ]$$

6. Prove that $\tan\alpha + 2\tan 2\alpha + 4\tan 4\alpha + 8\cot 8\alpha = \cot\alpha$

Sol. It is enough to show that

$$\tan\alpha + 2\tan 2\alpha + 4\tan 4\alpha + 8\cot 8\alpha - \cot\alpha = 0$$

Consider $\tan\alpha - \cot\alpha = \tan\alpha - \dfrac{1}{\tan\alpha} = \dfrac{\tan^2\alpha - 1}{\tan\alpha}$

$$= -2\left[\frac{1}{\dfrac{2\tan\alpha}{1-\tan^2\alpha}}\right] = \frac{-2}{\tan 2\alpha} = -2\cot 2\alpha$$

$\therefore\ \tan\alpha - \cot\alpha + 2\tan 2\alpha + 4\tan 4\alpha + 8\cot 8\alpha$

$= -2\cot 2\alpha + 2\tan 2\alpha + 4\tan 4\alpha + 8\cot 8\alpha$

$(\because \tan k\alpha - \cot k\alpha = -2\cot 2k\alpha)$

$= 2[\tan 2\alpha - \cot 2\alpha] + 4\tan 4\alpha + 8\cot 8\alpha$

$= 2[-2\cot 4\alpha] + 4\tan 4\alpha + 8\cot 8\alpha$

$= 4[\tan 4\alpha - \cot 4\alpha] + 8\cot 8\alpha$

$= -8\cot 8\alpha + 8\cot 8\alpha = 0$

7. Prove that

(i) $\cos\theta \cdot \cos(60+\theta) \cdot \cos(60-\theta) = \frac{1}{4}\cos 3\theta$ and hence deduce that

$\cos 10^\circ \cos 30^\circ \cos 50^\circ \cos 70^\circ = \frac{3}{16}$

(ii) $\cos 24^0 \cos 48^\circ \cos 96^\circ \cos 168^\circ = \frac{3}{16}$

Sol. (i) $\cos\theta\cos(60+\theta)\cos(60-\theta)$

$= \cos\theta\,[\cos^2 60^\circ - \sin^2\theta]$

$(\because \cos(A+B)\cos(A-B) = \cos^2 A - \sin^2 B)$

$= \cos\theta\left[\frac{1}{4} - (1-\cos^2\theta)\right]$

$= \cos\theta\left[\cos^2\theta - \frac{3}{4}\right] = \cos\theta\,\frac{(4\cos^2\theta - 3)}{4} = \frac{4\cos^3\theta - 3\cos\theta}{4} = \frac{\cos 3\theta}{4}$

also $\cos 10^\circ \cos 30^\circ \cos 50^\circ \cos 70^\circ$

$= \cos 10^\circ \cos(60o^\circ + 10^\circ)\cos(60^\circ - 10^\circ)\cos 30^\circ$

$= \frac{1}{4}\cos 30^\circ \cdot \cos 30^\circ = \frac{1}{4}\cdot\left(\frac{\sqrt{3}}{2}\right)\left(\frac{\sqrt{3}}{2}\right) = \frac{3}{16}$

(ii) $\cos 24^\circ \cos 48^\circ \cos 96^\circ \cos 168^\circ$

$$= \frac{1}{4} [\, 2 \cos 24 \cos 96^\circ \, 2 \cos 48^\circ \cos 168^\circ \,]$$

$$= \frac{1}{4} [\, (\cos (120) + \cos (72)) (\cos (216^\circ) + \cos (120^\circ) \,]$$

$$= \frac{1}{4} (\frac{-1}{2} + \sin 18^\circ) (\frac{-1}{2} - \cos 36^\circ) = \frac{1}{4} . \frac{3}{4} = \frac{3}{16}$$

8. Prove that (i) $\cos^2 A + \cos^2(120^\circ + A) + \cos^2(120 - A) = \frac{3}{2}$

(ii) $\sin^2\theta + \sin^2(60^\circ + \theta) + \sin^2(60^\circ - \theta) = \frac{3}{2}$

Sol. (i) LHS $= \cos^2 A + \cos^2 (120^\circ + A) + \cos^2(120^\circ - A)$

$$= \frac{1 + \cos 2A}{2} + \frac{1 + \cos 2(120 + A)}{2} + \frac{1 + \cos 2(120 - A)}{2}$$

$$= \frac{3}{2} + \frac{1}{2} [\, \cos 2A + \cos (240^\circ + 2A) + \cos (240^\circ - 2A)]$$

$$= \frac{3}{2} + \frac{1}{2} [\cos 2A + 2 \cos 240^\circ . \cos 2A]$$

$$= \frac{3}{2} + \frac{1}{2} [\, \cos 2A + 2\left(\frac{-1}{2}\right) \cos 2A]$$

$$= \frac{3}{2} + \frac{1}{2}(0) = \frac{3}{2} = \text{RHS}$$

(ii) LHS $= \sin^2 \theta + \sin^2 (60 + \theta) + \sin^2(60 - \theta)$

$$= \frac{1 - \cos 2\theta}{2} + \frac{1 - \cos(120^\circ + 2\theta\theta}{2} + \frac{1 - \cos(120^\circ - 2\theta\theta}{2}$$

$$= \frac{3}{2} - \frac{1}{2} [\cos 2\theta + \cos(120^\circ + 2\theta) + \cos (120^\circ - 2\theta)]$$

$$= \frac{3}{2} - \frac{1}{2} [\, \cos 2\theta + 2\cos 120 \cos 2\theta \,]$$

$$=\frac{3}{2}-\frac{1}{2}\left[\cos 2\theta+2\left(\frac{-1}{2}\right)\cos 2\theta\right]$$

$$=\frac{3}{2}-\frac{1}{2}(0)=\frac{3}{2}=\text{RHS}$$

9. Prove that $\left(1+\cos\frac{\pi}{8}\right)\left(1+\cos\frac{3\pi}{8}\right)\left(1+\cos\frac{5\pi}{8}\right)\left(1+\cos\frac{7\pi}{8}\right)=\frac{1}{8}$

Sol. LHS $=\left(1+\cos\frac{\pi}{8}\right)\left(1+\cos\frac{3\pi}{8}\right)\left(1+\cos(\pi-\frac{3\pi}{8}\right)\left(1+\cos(\pi-\frac{\pi}{8})\right)$

$$=\left(1+\cos\frac{\pi}{8}\right)\left(1+\cos\frac{3\pi}{8}\right)\left(1-\cos\frac{3\pi}{8}\right)\left(1-\cos\frac{\pi}{8}\right)$$

$$=\left(1+\cos\frac{\pi}{8}\right)\left(1-\cos\frac{\pi}{8}\right)\left(1+\cos\frac{3\pi}{8}\right)\left(1-\cos\frac{3\pi}{8}\right)$$

$$=\left(1-\cos^2\frac{\pi}{8}\right)\left(1-\cos^2\frac{3\pi}{8}\right)$$

$$=\sin^2\frac{\pi}{8}\ \sin^2\frac{3\pi}{8}=\frac{(1-\cos\frac{\pi}{4})}{2}\frac{(1-\cos(\frac{3\pi}{4})}{2}$$

$$=\frac{1}{4}(1-\frac{1}{\sqrt{2}})(1+\frac{1}{\sqrt{2}})$$

$$=\frac{1}{4}(1-\frac{1}{2})=\frac{1}{8}$$

10. Prove that

(i) $\cos\frac{2\pi}{7}\cos\frac{4\pi}{7}\cos\frac{6\pi}{7}=\frac{1}{8}$

(ii) $\cos\frac{\pi}{11}\cos\frac{2\pi}{11}\cos\frac{3\pi}{11}\cos\frac{4\pi}{11}\cos\frac{5\pi}{11}=\frac{1}{32}$

Sol. (i) LHS $=\cos\frac{2\pi}{7}\cos\frac{4\pi}{7}\cos\frac{6\pi}{7}$

$$= \frac{1}{2\sin\frac{2\pi}{7}}\, 2\sin\frac{2\pi}{7}\cos\frac{2\pi}{7}\cos\frac{4\pi}{7}\cos\frac{6\pi}{7}$$

$$= \frac{1}{2\sin\frac{2\pi}{7}}\,\sin\frac{4\pi}{7}\cos\frac{4\pi}{7}\cos\frac{6\pi}{7} = \frac{\sin\frac{8\pi}{7}\cos\frac{6\pi}{7}}{4\sin\frac{2\pi}{7}}$$

$$= \frac{\sin(\pi+\frac{\pi}{7})\cos(\pi-\frac{\pi}{7})}{4\sin\frac{2\pi}{7}} = \frac{2\sin\frac{\pi}{7}\cos\frac{\pi}{7}}{8\sin\frac{2\pi}{7}} = \frac{\sin\frac{2\pi}{7}}{8\sin\frac{2\pi}{7}} = \frac{1}{8}$$

(ii) same as above

Exercise - 10.1

1. Prove that $\sin\theta = \frac{\sin 3\theta}{1+2\cos 2\theta}$ and hence deduce the value of sin 15°.

2. Prove that $\cos A = \frac{\cos 3A}{2\cos 2A - 1}$ and hence deduce that $\cos 15° = \frac{\sqrt{3}+1}{2\sqrt{2}}$

3. If 2 tan α = 3 tan β Prove that $\tan(\alpha - \beta) = \frac{\sin 2\beta}{5 - \cos 2\beta}$

4. (i) Prove that $\frac{\cos^3 A - \cos 3A}{\cos A} + \frac{\sin^3 A - \sin 3A}{\sin A} = 3$

   (ii) $4(\cos^3 10° + \sin^3 20°) = 3(\cos 10° + \sin 20°)$

5. Prove that $\sin A \sin(60° + A)\sin(60° - A) = \frac{1}{4}\sin 3A$ and hence deduce that

   $\sin\frac{\pi}{9}\sin\frac{2\pi}{9}\sin\frac{3\pi}{9}\sin\frac{4\pi}{9} = \frac{3}{16}$

6. Prove that $\tan A . \tan(60° + A)\tan(60° - A) = \tan 3A$ and hence deduce that tan6° tan 42° tan 66° tan 78° = 1.

7. If $\alpha = \frac{\pi}{9}$ Prove that 16 sin α sin 2α sin 3 α sin 4 α = 3

8. Prove that cot A + tan A = 2 cosec 2A, cot A – tan A = 2 cot 2A and hence deduce that $\tan 7\frac{1^\circ}{2} = \sqrt{6} - \sqrt{4} - \sqrt{3} + \sqrt{2}$

9. If $xy + yz + zx = 1$ prove that

(i) $\sum \frac{x+y}{1-xy} = \frac{1}{xyz}$

(ii) $\sum \frac{2x}{1-x^2} = \pi\left(\frac{2x}{1-x^2}\right)$

(Hint : x = tan A, *y* = tan B, 2 = tan C]

10. Prove that $\sin^4\frac{\pi}{8} + \sin^4\frac{3\pi}{8} + \sin^4\frac{5\pi}{8} + \sin^4\frac{7\pi}{8} = \frac{3}{2}$

[*Hint :* $\sin^4\frac{\pi}{8} + \sin^4\left(\frac{\pi}{2} - \frac{\pi}{8}\right) + \sin^4\left(\frac{\pi}{2} + \frac{\pi}{8}\right) + \sin^4\left(\pi - \frac{\pi}{8}\right)$

$2[\sin^4\frac{\pi}{8} + \cos^4\frac{\pi}{8}]$

$= 2[\sin^2\frac{\pi}{8} + \cos^2\frac{\pi}{8}]^2 - 2\sin^2\frac{\pi}{8}\cos^2\frac{\pi}{8}]$

$= 2[1 - \frac{1}{2}\sin^2\frac{2\pi}{8}] = 2[1 - \frac{1}{2}.\frac{1}{2}]$

$= [2\left(\frac{3}{4}\right) = \frac{3}{2}]$

11

Heights and Distances

11.1 Angle of Elevation of an Object

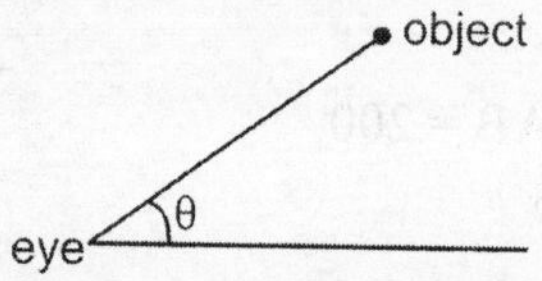

The angle between the horizontal line drawn through the observer's eye and the line joining the eye to the object which is higher level than the eye is called angle of elevation of the object.

11.2 Angle of Depression of an Object

The angle between the horizontal line drawn through the observer's eye and the line joining the eye to any object which is at lower level than the eye is called angle of depression.

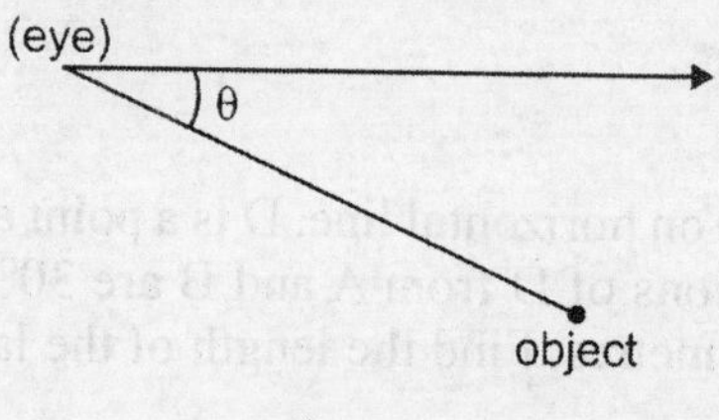

11.3 Sine Rule

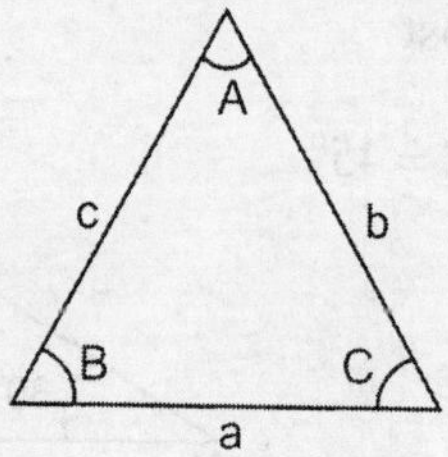

$$\frac{a}{\sin A} = \frac{b}{\sin B} = \frac{C}{\sin c}$$

11.4 m– n rule

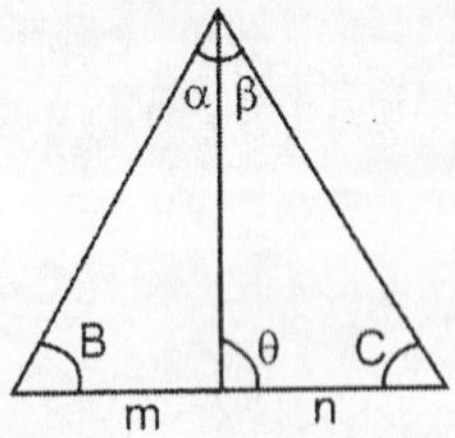

$(m + n) \cot \theta = n \cot B - m \cot A$

$(m + n) \cot \theta = m \cot \alpha - n \cot \beta$

Note :

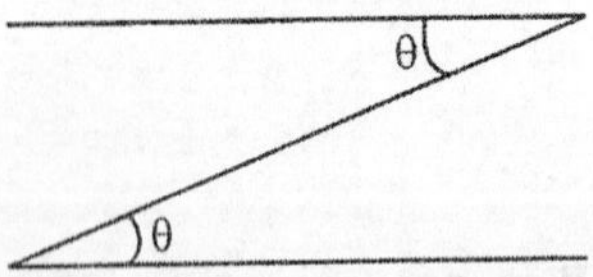

Solved Examples

1. From the top of a light house 200 metres high on the sea-shore, the angle of depression of ship in the sea is 30°. How far is the ship from the sea - shore.

Sol. AB is light house

C is ship

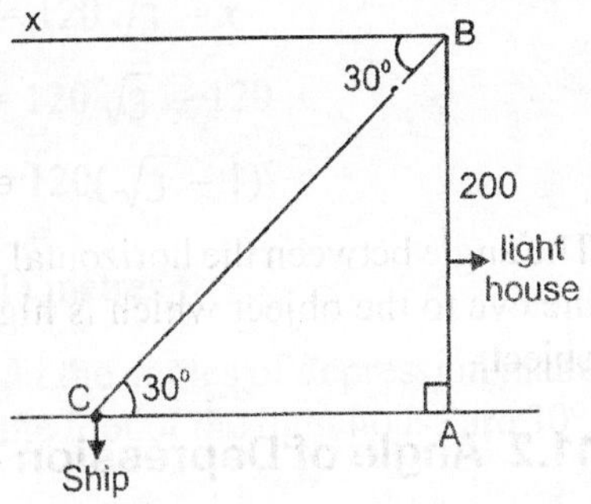

$\therefore$ Given $\angle XBC = 30^o$, $AB = 200$

$\therefore \quad \angle XBC = \angle BCA = 30^o$

from $\triangle$ CAB

$$\tan 30^o = \frac{AB}{AC}$$

$$\tan 30^o = \frac{200}{AC}$$

$$\frac{1}{\sqrt{3}} = \frac{200}{AC}$$

$$AC = 200\sqrt{3}\ m^2$$

2. A, B, C are three points on horizontal line. D is a point at the top of a lamp post at C. The angle of elevations of D from A and B are 30° and 45°. If the distance between A and B is 20 metres. Find the length of the lamp post CD.

Sol. Let CD = x is length of lamp post

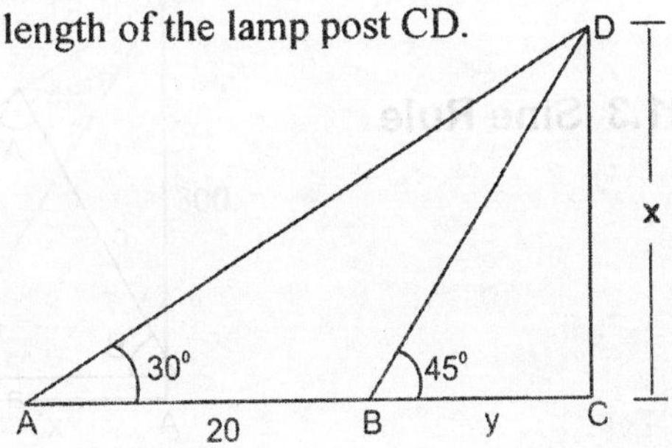

and given $\angle DAC = 30^o, \angle DBC = 45^o$

and AB = 20, BC = y say

from $\triangle$le BCD $\tan 45^\circ = \dfrac{CD}{BC} = \dfrac{x}{y} \Rightarrow \quad 1 = \dfrac{x}{y} \quad \Rightarrow x = y$ ..... (1)

from $\triangle$le ACD $\tan 30^\circ = \dfrac{CD}{AC} = \dfrac{x}{20+y} \Rightarrow \dfrac{1}{\sqrt{3}} = \dfrac{x}{20+y}$

$$\therefore \quad \frac{1}{\sqrt{3}} = \frac{x}{20+x} \qquad (\because x = y)$$

$$\therefore\ 20 + x = \sqrt{3}x$$

$$(\sqrt{3}-1)\ x = 20$$

$$x = \frac{20}{\sqrt{3}-1} = \frac{20(\sqrt{3}+1)}{2} = 10(\sqrt{3}+1)$$

3. From a point on the level ground, the angle of elevation of the top of the hill is α. After moving through a distance of d metres to words the foot of the hill the elevation of its top is to be β. Find the height of the hill.

Sol. Let AB be the hill and it height is h

and $\angle BPA = \alpha, \angle BQA = \beta$, $QA = x$ and PQ = d.

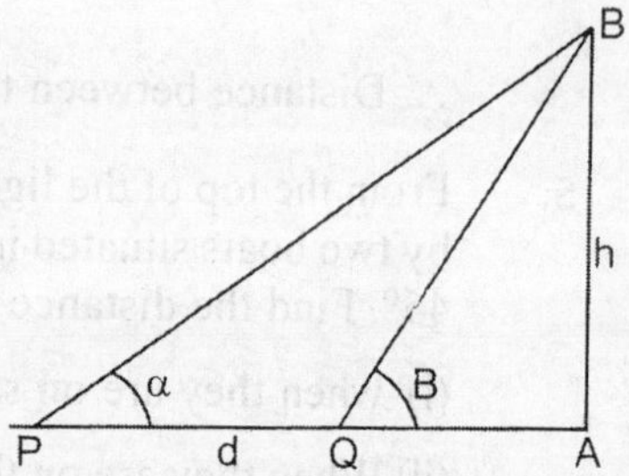

From $\triangle$ PAB $\tan\alpha = \dfrac{h}{d+x}$ ...(1)

From $\triangle$ QAB $\tan\beta = \dfrac{h}{x}$ ....(2)

From (1), $x + d = h \cot\alpha$ ....(3)

From (2), $x = h \cot\beta$ ....(4)

$\therefore$ (3), (4) $\Rightarrow \quad (x + d) - (x) = h\cot\alpha - h\cot\beta$

$$\therefore \quad d = h[\cot\alpha - \cot\beta]$$

$$\therefore \quad h = \frac{d}{\cot\alpha - \cot\beta}$$

4. From the cliff of a mountain 120 metres above the sea level the angle of depression of two boats on the same side of the mountain are 45° and 30° respectively. Find the distance between two boats.

Sol. C, D are two boats

AB is cliff of a mountain

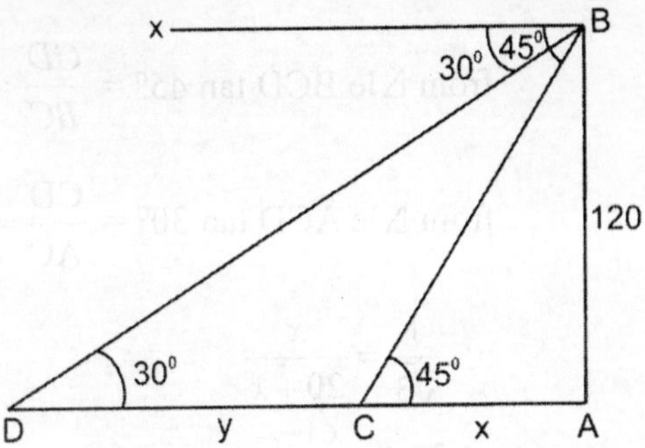

whose height is 120 metres

$\therefore \quad \angle XBC = 45^\circ \Rightarrow \angle BCA = 45^\circ$

$\angle XBD = 30^\circ \Rightarrow \angle BDA = 30^\circ$

Let AC = x, CD = y

from $\triangle$ BAC $\rightarrow$ $\tan 45^\circ = \dfrac{AB}{AC} = \dfrac{120}{x} \Rightarrow 1 = \dfrac{120}{x} \Rightarrow x = 120$ (1)

from $\triangle$ BAD $\rightarrow$ $\tan 30^\circ = \dfrac{120}{x+y} \Rightarrow \dfrac{1}{\sqrt{3}} = \dfrac{120}{x+y}$

$$\Rightarrow x + y = 120\sqrt{3}$$

$$\Rightarrow y = 120\sqrt{3} - x$$

$$= 120\sqrt{3} - 120$$

$$= 120(\sqrt{3} - 1)$$

$\therefore$ Distance between two boats = $120(\sqrt{3} - 1)$ metres

5. From the top of the light house 300 metres height the angles of depression made by two boats situated in a horizontal line along the foot of the light house are 30°, 45°. Find the distance between two boats

(i) when they are on same side

(ii) When they are on the either side of light house.

Sol. (i) Let AB is light house and its height is 300 metres.

C, D are two boats such that

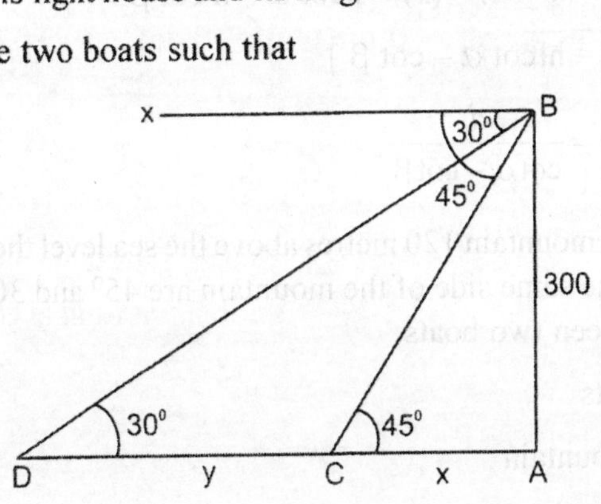

$\angle XBC = 45^\circ \quad \angle XBD = 30^\circ$

$\Rightarrow \angle BCA = 45^\circ \quad , \angle BDA = 30^\circ$

from $\triangle$ BAC $\rightarrow \quad \tan 45^\circ = \dfrac{AB}{AC} = \dfrac{300}{x} \Rightarrow 1 = \dfrac{300}{x} \Rightarrow x = 300$

from $\triangle$ DAB $\rightarrow \quad \tan 30^\circ = \dfrac{BA}{DA} = \dfrac{BA}{DC + CA} = \dfrac{300}{y + x}$

$$\Rightarrow \frac{1}{\sqrt{3}} = \frac{300}{x + y}$$

$$\Rightarrow x + y = 300\sqrt{3}$$

$$y = 300\sqrt{3} - x$$

$$= 300\sqrt{3} - 300$$

$$= 300(\sqrt{3} - 1)$$

$\therefore$ CD $= 300(\sqrt{3} - 1)$

(ii) $\tan 30^\circ = \dfrac{300}{y} \quad \Rightarrow \quad \dfrac{1}{\sqrt{3}} = \dfrac{300}{y}$

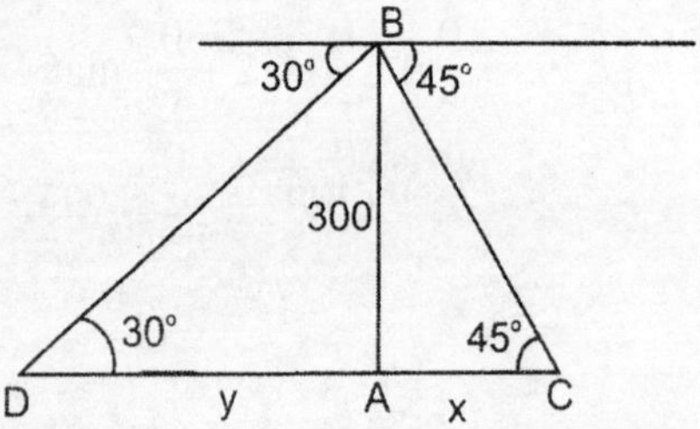

$\Rightarrow \quad y = 300\sqrt{3}$ .....(1)

$\tan 45^\circ = \dfrac{300}{x}$

$\Rightarrow \quad x = 300$

$\therefore$ CD $= x + y = 300 + 300\sqrt{3} = 300(\sqrt{3} + 1)$

6. A piller of 10 metre height is mountend on a spire, from a point on the level ground the anlges of elevation of the top and foot of a pillar are 75° and 45° respectively. Find the height of the spire.

Sol. Let BC is pillar and its height is 10. AB is spire. P is point on ground such that ,

$\angle CPA = 75^\circ \quad \angle BPA = 45^\circ$

from Δ BPA,

$\tan 45^\circ = \dfrac{BA}{PA} = \dfrac{y}{x}$

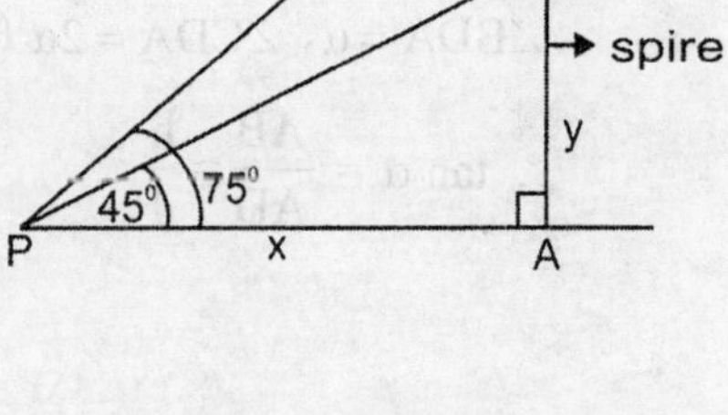

$\Rightarrow \quad 1 = \dfrac{y}{x} \quad \Rightarrow \quad x = y$ ......(1)

$$\text{from } \Delta\text{ CAP } \tan 75^{o} = \frac{AC}{PA} = \frac{CB+BA}{PA} = \frac{10+y}{x}$$

$$\Rightarrow \quad \tan(45+30^{o}) = \frac{10+y}{x} \qquad (\because x = y)$$

$$\therefore \quad \frac{1+\frac{1}{\sqrt{3}}}{1-1.\frac{1}{\sqrt{3}}} = \frac{10+y}{y} \quad \Rightarrow \quad \frac{\sqrt{3}+1}{\sqrt{3}-1} = \frac{10+y}{y}$$

$$\Rightarrow \quad \frac{(\sqrt{3}+1)^2}{2} = \frac{10+y}{y}$$

$$\therefore \quad \frac{4+2\sqrt{3}}{2} = \frac{10+y}{y} \quad \Rightarrow \quad 2+\sqrt{3} = \frac{10+y}{y}$$

$$\Rightarrow \quad (2+\sqrt{3})y = 10+y$$

$$= (\sqrt{3}+1)y = 10$$

$$y = \frac{10}{\sqrt{3}+1} = \frac{10(\sqrt{3}-1)}{2}$$

$$= 5(\sqrt{3}-1)$$

7. Over a tower A B of height h mt, there is a flagstaff BC, AB and BC are making equal angles at a point distance d mts from a foot A of the tower. Show that height of flag staff is $\frac{h(d^2+h^2)}{(d^2-h^2)}$.

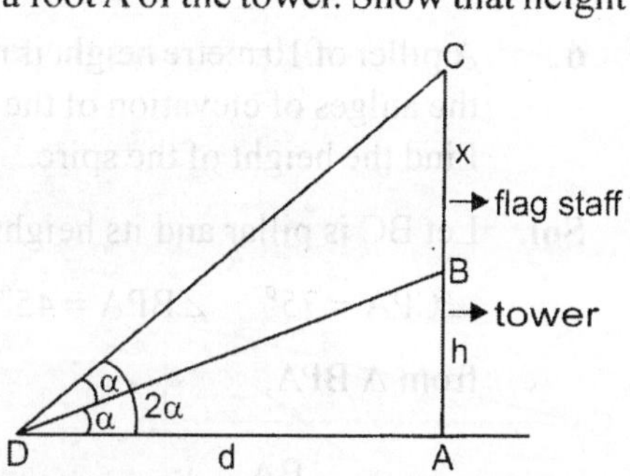

Sol. AB is tower of height h

BC is tower of flag staff of height x say

C is point on level ground.

AD = d

$\angle BDA = \alpha$, $\angle CDA = 2\alpha$ $(\because \angle CDB = \alpha)$

$$\therefore \ \tan\alpha = \frac{AB}{AD} = \frac{h}{d}$$

$$\tan 2\alpha = \frac{x+h}{d} \Rightarrow \frac{2\tan\alpha}{1-\tan^2\alpha} = \frac{x+h}{d} \Rightarrow \frac{2\left(\frac{h}{d}\right)}{1-\left(\frac{h^2}{d^2}\right)} = \frac{x+h}{d}$$

$$\left(\because \tan\alpha = \frac{h}{d}\right)$$

$$\Rightarrow \frac{2hd}{d^2-h^2} = \frac{x+h}{d}$$

$$\Rightarrow x+h = \frac{2hd^2}{d^2-h^2}$$

$$\Rightarrow x = \frac{2hd^2}{d^2-h^2} - h$$

$$= \frac{2hd^2 - hd^2 + h^3}{d^2-h^2}$$

$$= \frac{hd^2+h^3}{d^2-h^2} = \frac{h(d^2+h^2)}{d^2-h^2}$$

8. The angle of elevation of the top of mountain from the top and bottom of a pillar AB of height 5 mts are 30° and 60° respectively. Find the height of the mountain.

Sol. AB is pillar of height 5 mt

CD is mountain of height h mt say

also $\angle DAC = 60^o$, $\angle DBE = 30^o$

Let AC = y

AB = CE = 5

from $\triangle$ ACD

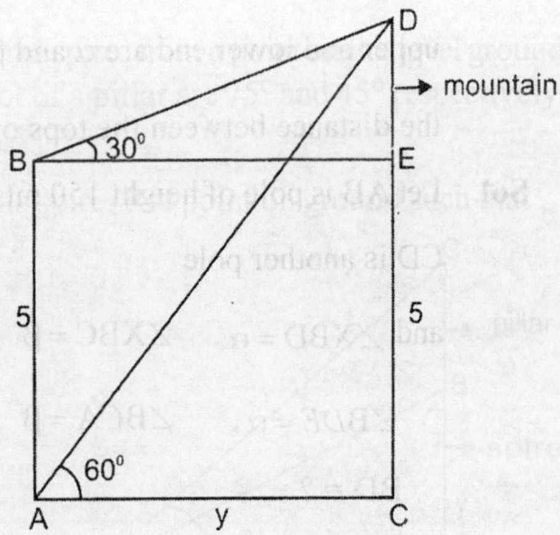

$$\tan 60^0 = \frac{CD}{AC} = \frac{5+ED}{y}$$

$$\Rightarrow \sqrt{3} = \frac{5+ED}{y} \Rightarrow \sqrt{3}y = 5 + ED$$

$$\Rightarrow \quad y = \frac{(5+\text{ED})}{\sqrt{3}}$$

from Δle BED

$$\tan 30^{\circ} = \frac{\text{ED}}{\text{BE}} = \frac{\text{ED}}{\text{AC}} = \frac{\text{ED}}{y}$$

$$\frac{1}{\sqrt{3}} = \frac{\text{ED}}{\text{y}} \quad \Rightarrow \quad \frac{y}{\sqrt{3}} = \text{ED} \qquad \text{..... (i)}$$

Substitute y in (i), we get $\left(\dfrac{\frac{5+\text{ED})}{\sqrt{3}}}{\sqrt{3}}\right) = \text{ED}$

$$5 + \text{ED} = 3\ \text{ED}$$

$$2\text{ED} = 5$$

$$\text{ED} = \frac{5}{2}$$

$$\therefore\ \text{CD} = \text{CE} + \text{ED} = 5 + \frac{5}{2} = \frac{15}{2}\ \text{mt}$$

9. From the top of pole of height 150 mts, the angles of depression of another pole's upper and lower end are α and β respectively. If $\tan\alpha = \frac{4}{3}$, $\tan\beta = \frac{5}{2}$ then find the distance between the tops of two poles.

Sol. Let AB is pole of height 150 mts

CD is another pole

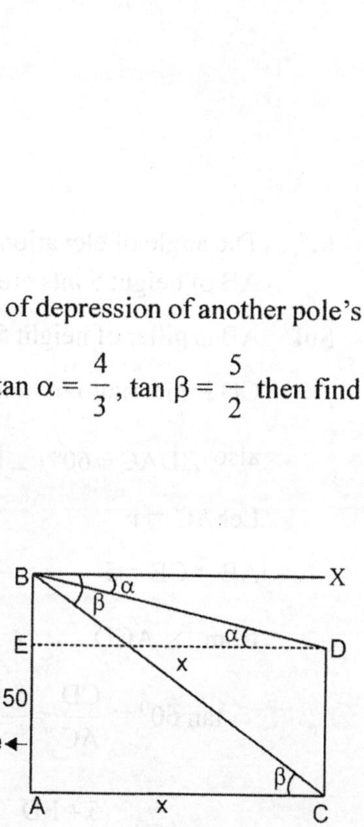

and $\angle XBD = \alpha$, $\angle XBC = \beta$

$\therefore\ \angle BDE = \alpha$, $\angle BCA = \beta$

BD = ?

Let AC = DE = x

from Δ CAB, $\tan\beta = \frac{150}{x} \Rightarrow \frac{5}{2} = \frac{150}{x}$ (Given $\tan\beta = \frac{5}{2}$)

$$\Rightarrow \quad x = \frac{300}{5} = 60$$

from Δ DEB $\cos\alpha = \frac{ED}{BD}$

$$= \frac{x}{BD}$$

given $\tan\alpha = \frac{4}{3}$ $\quad\Rightarrow\quad$ $\cos\alpha = \frac{3}{5}$

$\therefore \frac{3}{5} = \frac{x}{BD} = \frac{60}{BD}$ $\quad\Rightarrow\quad$ $BD = \frac{60\times5}{3} = 100\,mts$

10. B is a point situated vertically upwords on A at a distance of a unit. C is a point at a height 2a units from a horizontal passing through A and the angle of elevation of C from A and B are α and β respectively. Show that cotα . tan β = $\frac{1}{2}$

Sol. Let AB = a units, CD = 2a units

Given $\angle EBC = \beta$, $\angle DAC = \alpha$

Let AD = BE = d, AB = DE = a

∴ CE = a

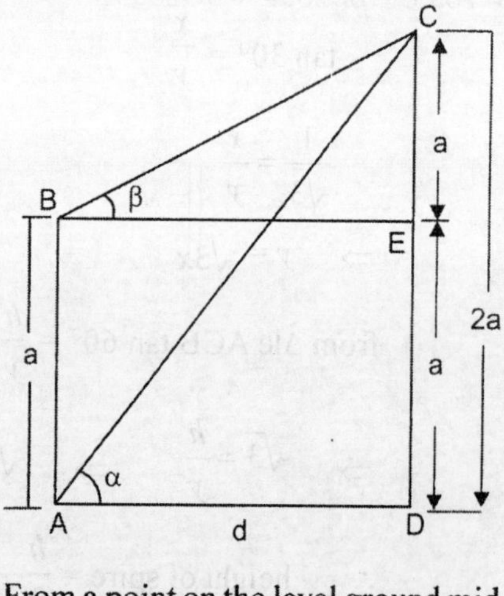

from ⊾le ADC, $\tan\alpha = \frac{2a}{d}$

from ⊾le BEC, $\tan\beta = \frac{a}{d}$

$\therefore \cot\alpha \,.\, \tan\beta = \frac{d}{2a}.\frac{a}{d} = \frac{1}{2}$

11. Two towers are standing on the level ground. From a point on the level ground mid way, between them the angle of elevation are 60° and 30° respectively. The height of the first tower is 100 mt. Find the height of the second tower.

Sol. Let AC, BD are two towers and AC = 100

M is mid point of AB

$\therefore$ AM = MB = x say and $\angle$CMA = 60°, $\angle$DMB = 30°

Let BD = h, from ΔAMC,

$$\tan 60^\circ = \frac{AC}{AM} = \frac{100}{x} \Rightarrow \sqrt{3} = \frac{100}{x} \Rightarrow x = \frac{100}{\sqrt{3}}$$

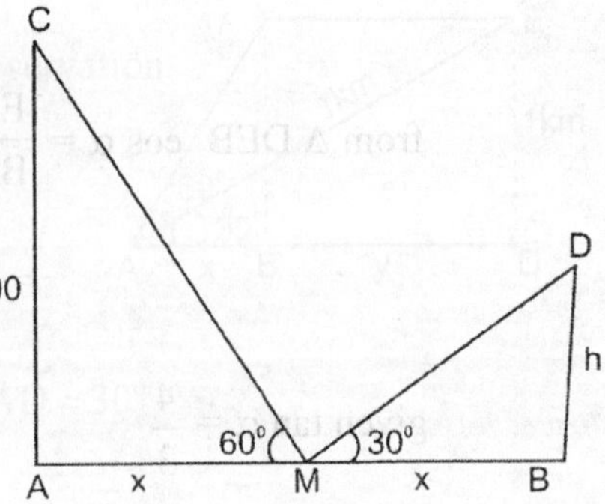

from Δle MBD,

$$\tan 30^\circ = \frac{h}{x} \Rightarrow \frac{1}{\sqrt{3}} = \frac{h}{x}$$

$$\Rightarrow \quad x = h\sqrt{3} \quad \Rightarrow \quad h = \frac{x}{\sqrt{3}}$$

$$= \frac{1}{\sqrt{3}}\left(\frac{100}{\sqrt{3}}\right) = \frac{100}{3} \text{ m}$$

12. From a point A on the level ground away from the foot of spire, the angle of elevation of the top of spire is 30°. From a point at a height of h metres vertically above A the angle of depression of the foot of spire is 60°. Find the height of spire in terms of h.

Sol. CD is spire of height x say

Let AC = y

from $\triangle$ ACD

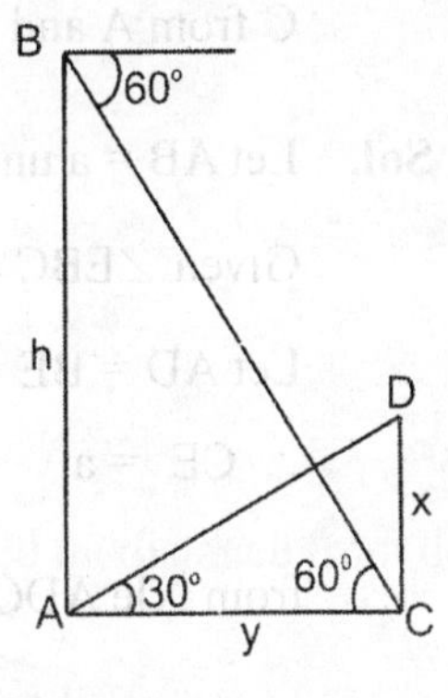

$$\tan 30^\circ = \frac{x}{y}$$

$$\therefore \quad \frac{1}{\sqrt{3}} = \frac{x}{y}$$

$$\Rightarrow \quad y = \sqrt{3}x \qquad \text{......(1)}$$

from Δle ACB $\tan 60^\circ = \dfrac{h}{y}$

$$\Rightarrow \quad \sqrt{3} = \frac{h}{y} \quad \Rightarrow \quad \sqrt{3} = \frac{h}{\sqrt{3}x} \quad \Rightarrow \quad x = \frac{h}{3}$$

$\therefore$ height of spire = $\dfrac{h}{3}$

13. A tree is leaning towards east. Two points due west of tree are at distance a and b from its foot. If α and β are the elevations of the top of the tree from these points, prove that its inclination to its horizon is $\tan^{-1}\left(\dfrac{b-a}{b\cot\alpha - a\cot\beta}\right)$

Sol. PQ is a tree leaning towards east, two points due to west of tree are at distance a and b from its foot also α and β are angles of elevation of the top of tree, from these points.

$\therefore$ AP = a, BP = b $\angle QAP = \alpha$, $\angle QBP = \beta$

QM is perpendicular drawm from Q to $\overrightarrow{BA}$

and Let $\angle QPM = \theta$ and let QM = x, PM = y

from Δ QAM $\tan\alpha = \dfrac{x}{y+a} \Rightarrow x\cot\alpha = y + a$. .....(1)

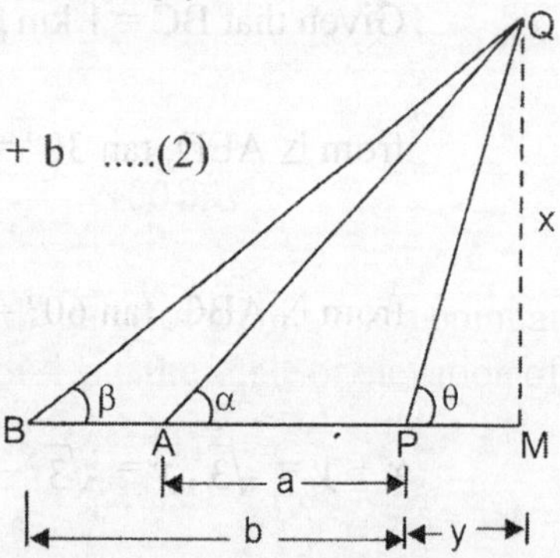

Δle QBM $\tan\beta = \dfrac{x}{b+y} \Rightarrow x\cot\beta = y + b$ .....(2)

$$x\cot\alpha - x\cot\beta = a - b$$

$$x[\cot\beta - \cot\alpha] = b - a$$

$$x = \frac{b-a}{\cot\beta - \cot\alpha}$$

from (1) $y = x\cot\alpha - a \left[\left(\dfrac{b-a}{\cot\beta - \cot\alpha}\right)\cot\alpha\right] - a$

$$y = \frac{(b-a)\cot\alpha - a(\cot\beta - \cot\alpha)}{\cot\beta - \cot\alpha} = \frac{b\cot\alpha - a\cot\beta}{\cot\beta - \cot\alpha}$$

$$\therefore \quad \tan\theta = \frac{x}{y} = \frac{b-a}{b\cot\alpha - a\cot\beta}$$

$$\therefore \quad \theta = \tan^{-1}\left(\frac{b-a}{b\cot\alpha - a\cot\beta}\right)$$

14. An aeroplane is moving one kilometre high from west to east horizontally from a point on the ground. The angle of elevation of the aeroplane is 60° and after 10 seconds the angle of elevation of the aeroplane is observed as 30°. Find the speed of the aeroplane in km/hour.

Sol. Let

A be the point of observation

C = place of the aeroplane at the first observation

E = place of the aeroplane at the second observation

B = foot of C on horizontal

D = foot of E on horizontal

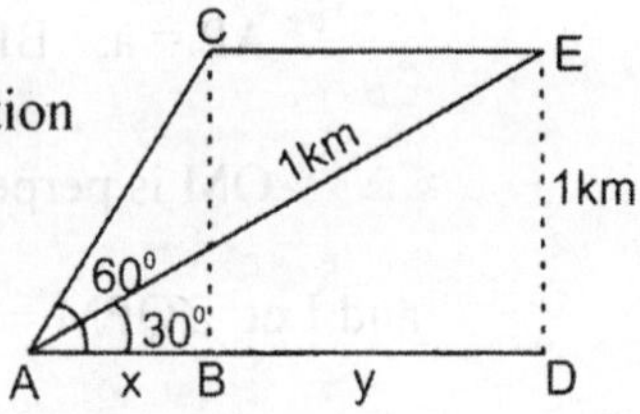

AB = x and BD = y say

Given that BC = 1 km, $\angle CAB = 60°$, $\angle EAD = 30°$

from $\triangle$ AED, $\tan 30° = \frac{1}{x+y} \Rightarrow x + y = \sqrt{3}$

from $\triangle$ ABC, $\tan 60° = \frac{1}{x} \Rightarrow x = \frac{1}{\sqrt{3}}$

$x + y = \sqrt{3}, y = \sqrt{3} - x = \sqrt{3} - \frac{1}{\sqrt{3}} = \frac{3-1}{\sqrt{3}} = \frac{2}{\sqrt{3}}$

speed of aeroplane $= \frac{2}{\sqrt{3}} \times \frac{60 \times 60}{10} = 240\sqrt{3}$ $\quad (\because s = \frac{d}{t})$

Exercise - 11.1

1. The angle of elevation of the top of a tower from a point 20 m, distance from the foot of tower is 60°. Find the height of tower.
2. The angles of depression of two milestones along a road, when viewed from an aeroplane are α, β. Show that the aeroplane is flying at a height of $\frac{\tan\alpha \tan\beta}{\tan\alpha + \tan\beta}$ from the road level taking the two mile stones to be on opposite side.
3. A and B are two opposite points on the either side of a river. C is an external point on the line joining A and B. The angle of elevation of the top of a tree situated at A from the point B is 60°. If BC = 20 metres, and the angle of elevation of the top of the tree from C is 30°, find the height of the tree and the breadth of the river.
4. From the cliff a mountain 120 metres above the sea level, the angles of depression

of two boats on the side of mountain are 45° and 30° respectively. Find the distance between the two boats.

5. From the top of a pillar of height of 80 metres, the angles of depression of the top and foot of another pillar are 30° and 45° respectively. Find the distance between two pillars and height of the second pillar.

6. From the top of a tree on the bank of a lake, an aeroplane in the sky makes an angle of elevation α and its image in the lake an angle of depression β. If the height of the tree from the water surface is 'a' and that of the height of the aeroplane is h, show that $h = \frac{a(\sin(\alpha+\beta)}{\sin(\beta-\alpha)}$

Answers

1. $20\sqrt{3}$

3. 17.32 m, 10 m

4. $120(\sqrt{3}-1)$

5. 80, $\frac{80(\sqrt{3}-1)}{\sqrt{3}}$

Unit - II

Exercise Questions

8. Trigonometric Ratios

9. Compound Angles

10. Multiple and Sub-Multiple Angles

1. If m tan $(\theta - 30^\circ) = $ n tan $(\theta + 120^\circ)$ then show that

$$\cos 2\theta = \frac{m+n}{2(m-n)}$$

2. Prove that $\tan\alpha + 2\tan\alpha + 4\tan 4\alpha + 8\cot 8\alpha = \cot\alpha$

3. Show that

(i) $\tan(A+B) = \dfrac{\tan A + \tan B}{1 - \tan A \tan B}$

(ii) $\cot(A-B) = \dfrac{\cot A \cot B + 1}{\cot B - \cot A}$

4. Find the value of $\dfrac{\sin 2A}{1-\cos 2A}$

5. Compute sin 75°, cos75° and tan 15° from the functions of 30° and 45°.

6. Prove that $\tan\left(\frac{\pi}{4} + \theta/2\right) + \tan\left(\frac{\pi}{4} - \theta/2\right) = 2\sec\theta$

7. If α, β are acute angles and $\sin\alpha = \frac{3}{5}$, $\sin\beta = \frac{8}{17}$ find the value of $\sin(\alpha+\beta)$, $\cos(\alpha+\beta)$ and $\tan(\alpha+\beta)$.

8. If $A + B = 45^\circ$ then find the value of $(1 + \tan A)(1 + \tan B)$

9. Prove that $\cot 2A + \tan A = \operatorname{cosec} 2A$.

10. If $A + B + C = 180^\circ$, prove that $\sin A + \sin B - \sin C = 4\sin A/2 \sin B/2 \sin c/2$

11. Show that $1 + \tan^2 A = \sec^2 A$, $1 + \cot^2 A = \operatorname{cosec}^2 A$

12. Show that $\sin^2 A + \cos^2 A = 1$, $\sin 2A = 2\sin A \cos A$

13. Prove that $(1-\cos^2\theta)(1+\tan^2\theta)=\tan^2\theta$

14. In Δle ABC if $\cot A+\cot B+\cot C=\sqrt{3}$ then show that the triangle is equilataral.

15. If $\tan 20^\circ = k$ show that $\dfrac{\tan 250+\tan 340}{\tan 200-\tan 110^0}=\dfrac{1-k^2}{1+k^2}$

16. Prove that $\sin^2\theta+\sin^2(\theta+60^\circ)+\sin^2(\theta-60^\circ)=\dfrac{3}{2}$

17. Prove that $\cos\dfrac{\pi}{9}\cos\dfrac{2\pi}{9}\cos\dfrac{3\pi}{9}\cos\dfrac{4\pi}{9}=\dfrac{1}{2}$

11. Heights and Distances

1. From the top of cliff 150 feet height the angle of depression of two boats which are due south of the observer are 15° and 75°. Find the distance a part having given cot $15^\circ = 2+\sqrt{3}$ and $\cot 75^\circ = 2-\sqrt{3}$.

2. The angle of elevation of the top of a mountain from the top and bottom of pillar AB of height 5 mts are 30° and 60° respectively. Find the height of the mountain.

3. A flag staff on the top of the tower 80 metres high subtends an angle tan–1 $(\frac{1}{9})$ at a point on the ground 100 metres from the foot of the tower. Find the height of the flag staff.

4. The angle of elevation of top of a tower at a distance of 100 metres from its foot on horizontal plane is found to be 60°. Find the height of the tower ($\tan 60^0 = \sqrt{3}$)

5. The angles of depression of the top and the bottom of a tower are 30° and 45° as seen from the top of the another tower of height 80 m. Find the distance between two towers.

6. A person standing at a distance of 100 meters from the foot of a tower, find the top the tower at an elevation of 60°. Find the height of the tower.

7. A person is walking 20 metres towards a chimney in a horizontal line through its base observes that its angle of elevation changes from 30° to 45°. Find the height of the chimney.

8. A person standing at a distance foot of a tower observes the elevation of the top of the tower is 60°. Find the height of the tower.

Unit - II

Answers to Exercise Questions

8. Trigonometric Ratios

4. cot A

5. $\sin 75 = \frac{\sqrt{3}+1}{2\sqrt{2}}$; $\cos 75 = \frac{\sqrt{3}-1}{2\sqrt{2}}$; $\tan 15 = \frac{\sqrt{3}-1}{\sqrt{3}+1}$

7. $\frac{77}{85}, \frac{36}{85}, \frac{77}{36}$

11. Heights and Distances

1. $300\sqrt{3}$ **2.** 7.5 m/s **3.** 20 m

4. $100\sqrt{3}$ m **5.** 80 m **6.** $100\sqrt{3}$ m

7. $10(\sqrt{3}-1)$ **8.** 60 m

Unit - II

Self Test Questions

Trignometry

1. Prove that $\frac{\sin A + 1 - \cos A}{\sin A - 1 + \cos A} = \frac{1 + \sin A}{\cos A}$

2. Prove the following identities

   (a) $\frac{\operatorname{cosec}\theta + \cot\theta}{\operatorname{cosec}\theta - \cot\theta} = (\operatorname{cosec}\theta + \cot\theta)^2$ (b) $\frac{\tan\alpha + \cot\beta}{\cot\alpha + \tan\beta} = \frac{\tan\alpha}{\tan\beta}$

3. (i) If $\sin\theta = -\frac{5}{13}$ and θ is in the third quadrant, then prove that

   $5\cot^2\theta + 12\tan\theta + 13\operatorname{cosec}\theta = 0$

   (ii) Find x, if $\frac{x \operatorname{cosec}^2 30°.\sec^2 45°}{8\cos 45°.\sin 60°} = \tan^2 60° - \tan^2 30°$

4. Find the value of sin2A, cos2A, tan2A if $\tan A = \frac{3}{4}$?

5. Prove that $\cos A = \frac{\cos 3A}{2\cos 2A - 1}$, hence find the value of cos15.

6. Prove that $\sin(45° + A)\ \sin(45° - A) = \frac{1}{2}\cos 2A$

7. Prove that $\tan(\theta + 135°)\ \tan(\theta - 315°) = -1$

8. If 3A is not an odd multiple of 90°, prove that $\tan A \tan(60° + A)\tan(60° - A) = \tan 3A$.

9. Show that tan70° – tan20° = 2tan40° + 4tan10°.

10. If $x = a\cos\theta$, $y = b\sin\theta$, prove that $\frac{x^2}{a^2} + \frac{y^2}{b^2} = 1$

11. Show that, $\frac{\cos 2A}{1 + \sin 2A} = \tan(45° - A)$.

12. From a point on the ground the angle of elevation of a top of a pole is 60°, if the pole is of height 30 m. Find the distance between the point and foot of the pole.

UNIT - III
GEOMETRY

UNIT - III

GEOMETRY

12

Coordinate System

Coordinate System

Suppose P, Q are two point in a plane. Then generally the distance between P and Q is denoted by PQ. The line segment joining P and Q is denoted by $\overline{PQ}$. The ray from P and passing through Q is denoted by $\overrightarrow{PQ}$. The line passing through P and Q is denoted by $\overleftrightarrow{PQ}$.

12.1 Rectangular Cartesian Coordinate System

Let $\overleftrightarrow{x^{1}ox}$, $\overleftrightarrow{y^{1}oy}$ be two mutually perpendicular lines (coordinate lines) in a plane intersecting at O. The point at O is called origin. The line $\overleftrightarrow{x^{1}ox}$ is called *x*-axis. $\overleftrightarrow{y^{1}oy}$ is called *y*-axis.

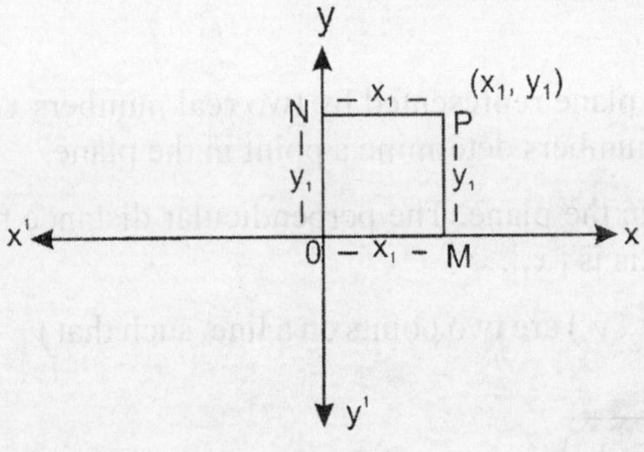

Generally, we take $\overleftrightarrow{x^{1}ox}$ as horizontal line, $\overleftrightarrow{y^{1}oy}$ as vertical line. Let P be any point in the plane. Draw two perpendiculars PM and PN from P to *x*-axis and *y*-axis respectively. (M, N are foot of perpendiculars drawn from P to *x*-axis, *y*-axis respectively).

Let OM = x_1, ON = y_1 then the two distances are fixed. Then the point P is denoted by x_1, here x_1 is called *x*-coordinate (abscissa) of P. y_1 is called *y*-coordinate of P (ordinate).

Here *x*-axis and *y*-axis are called coordinate axes and the plane is called coordinate plane. The coordinate axes divide coordinate plane in four equal parts, each part is called 'quadrant'. The regions xoy, $yox^1, x^1oy^1, y^1 0x$ are called I, II, III, IV quadrants respectively.

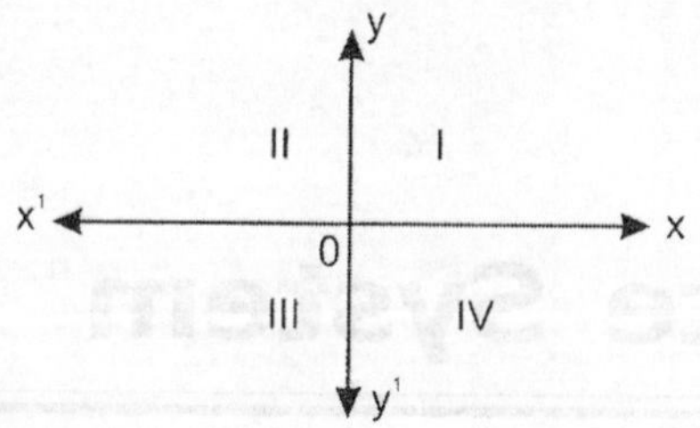

Let P(x_1, y_1) be a point in the coordinate plane. Then

1. P lies in I quadrant if $x_1 > 0,\ y_1 > 0$.
2. P lies in II quadrant if $x_1 < 0,\ y_1 > 0$.
3. P lies in III quadrant if $x_1 < 0,\ y_1 < 0$.
4. P lies in IV quadrant if $x_1 > 0, y_1 < 0$.
5. P lies on *x*-axis if $y_1 = 0$.
6. P lies on *y*-axis if $x_1 = 0$.

∴ The co-ordinates of any point on *x*-axis is of the form $(x_1, 0)$

∴ The coordinates of any point on *y*-axis is of the form $(0, x)$.

Note

1. Every point in the plane represented by two real numbers x_1, y_1 (coordinates), and every pair of real numbers determine a point in the plane.
2. P(x_1, y_1) be point in the plane. The perpendicular distance from P to *x*-axis is $|y_1|$, and from P to *y*-axis is $|x_1|$.
3. If A(x_1, y_1) and B(x_2, y_2) are two points on a line, such that $y_1 = y_2$ then it is horizontal line 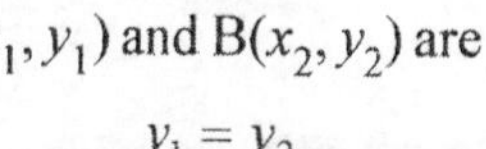

4. If A(x_1, y_1), B(x_2, y_2) are to points on a line such that $x_1 = x_2$ then it is a vertical line.

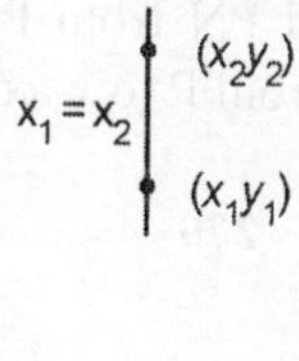

12.2 Distance between Two Points

The distance between two points $P(x_1, y_1)$, $Q(x_2. y_2)$ is

$$PQ = \sqrt{(x_1 - x_2)^2 + (y_1 - y_2)^2}$$

$$\sqrt{(x_2 - x_1)^2 + (y_2 - y_1)^2}$$

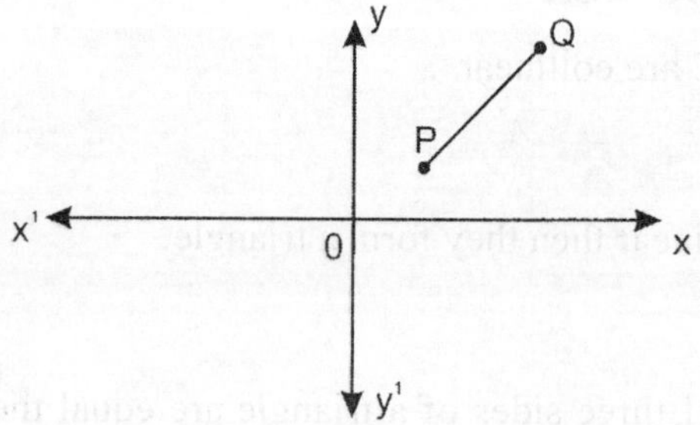

$$= \sqrt{(\textit{difference of x coordinates})^2 + (\textit{difference of y coordinates})^2}$$

Collinear Points : Two or more points lies on a line then the points are said to be collinear.

Note

1. Any two points in a plane are collinear.
2. A, B, C are collinear if

   AB + BC = AC

   (or)

   AC + CB = AB

   (or)

   BA + AC = BC

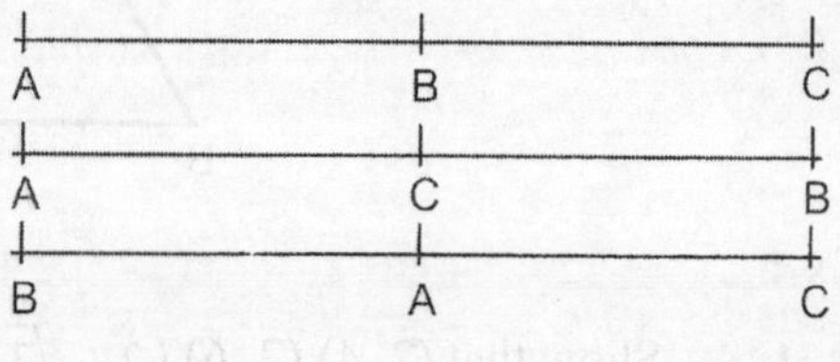

Ex :

1. Find the distance between two point A(2, 3), and B = (1, 1)

Sol. $AB = \sqrt{(2-1)^2 + (3-1)^2} = \sqrt{1+4} = \sqrt{5}$

2. Find the distance between two points.

A = (–1, 4) and B = (2, –3)

Sol. $AB = \sqrt{(-1-2)^2 + (4+3)^2} = \sqrt{9+49} = \sqrt{58}$

3. Show that the three points (0, –2), (–1, 1) (–2, 4) are collinear.

Sol. Let A = (0, –2), B = (–1, 1), C = (–2, 4)

$$AB = \sqrt{(0+1)^2+(-2-1)^2} = \sqrt{1+9} = \sqrt{10}$$

$$BC = \sqrt{(-1+2)^2+(1-4)^2} = \sqrt{1+9} = \sqrt{10}$$

$$CA = \sqrt{(0+2)^2+(-2-4)^2} = \sqrt{4+36} = \sqrt{40} = 2\sqrt{10}$$

$\therefore$ AB + BC = CA

$\therefore$ A, B, C are collinear

12.3 Triangles

If three points are not collinear then they form a triangle.

Types of Triangles

1. ***Equilateral triangle***: If three sides of a triangle are equal then the triangle is called equilateral triangle.

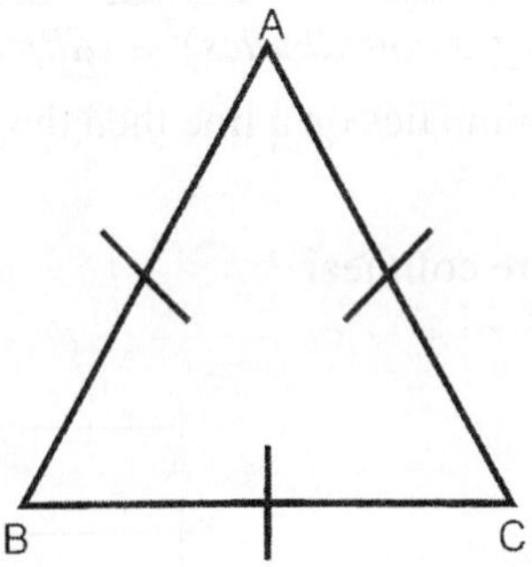

Ex :

1. Show that (2, 4) (2, 6) $(2+\sqrt{3}\ 5)$ form a equilateral traiangle.

Sol. Let A = (2, 4), B = (2, 6), $C = (2+\sqrt{3}, 5)$

$$AB = \sqrt{(2-2)^2+(4-6)^2} = \sqrt{0+(-2)^2} = 2,$$

$$BC = \sqrt{\left(2-(2+\sqrt{3})\right)^2+(6-5)^2} = \sqrt{(\sqrt{3})^2+(1)^2} = \sqrt{3+1} = 2,$$

$$CA = \sqrt{\left(2+\sqrt{3}-2\right)^2+(5-4)^2} = \sqrt{3+1} = 2$$

$\therefore$ AB = BC = CA = 2

2. ***Isosceles triangle***: If any two sides of a triangle are equal then the triangle is said to be an Isosceles triangle.

Show that (0, 0) (1, 2) (2, 1) forms an isosceles traiangle

A = (0, 0) B = (1, 2) C = (2,1)

$\therefore$ AB = $\sqrt{(1-0)^2+(2-0)^2}$

$= \sqrt{1+4} = \sqrt{5}$

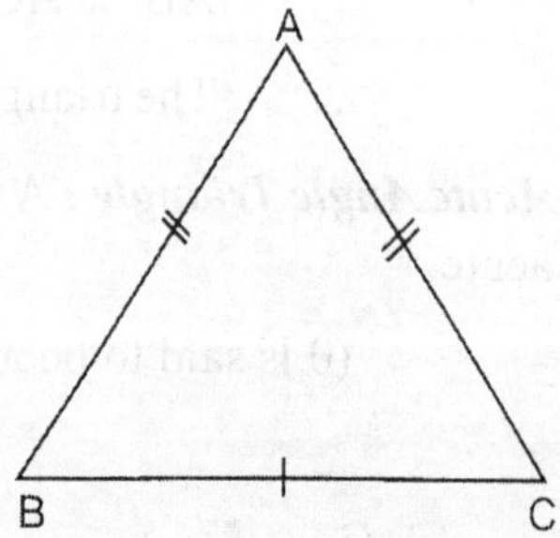

AC = $\sqrt{(2-0)^2+(1-0)^2}$

$= \sqrt{4+1} = \sqrt{5}$

also BC = $\sqrt{(2+1)^2+(1-2)^2} = \sqrt{1+1} = \sqrt{2}$

$\therefore$ ABC is an isosceles traingle

3. ***Right angle triangle***: A triangle is said to be right angled triangle if one angle of the triangle is right angle.

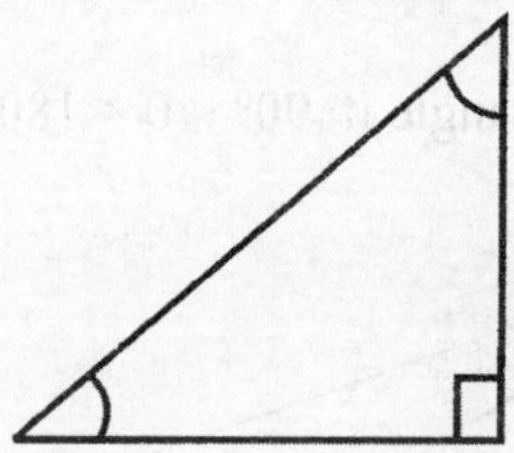

Note

1. Any triangle does not contain two right angles.Since sum of angles in triangle is 180°.
2. A triangle ABC is right angle triangle if $AB^2 + BC^2 = CA^2$ or $AC^2 + CB^2 = AB^2$ or $AB^2 + AC^2 = BC^2$.

Ex:

1. Show that the points (4, 4), (3, 5) and (–1, –1) form a right angled triangle.

Sol. Let A = (4, 4), B = (3, 5), C = (–1, –1)

AB = $\sqrt{(4-3)^2+(4-5)^2} = \sqrt{1^2+(-1)^2} = \sqrt{1+1} = \sqrt{2}$

BC = $\sqrt{(3-(-1))^2+(5-(-1))^2} = \sqrt{16+36} = \sqrt{52}$

CA = $\sqrt{(-1-4)^2+(-1-4)^2} = \sqrt{25+25} = \sqrt{50}$

$AB^2 = 2, \quad BC^2 = 52, \quad CA^2 = 50$

$\therefore \quad AB^2 + AC^2 = BC^2$

$\therefore$ The triangle is right angled triangle, right angled at A.

4. ***Acute Angle Triangle*** **:** A triangle is said to be acute angle triangle if the three angle are acute.

(θ is said to be acute angle if $O < \theta < 90^o$)

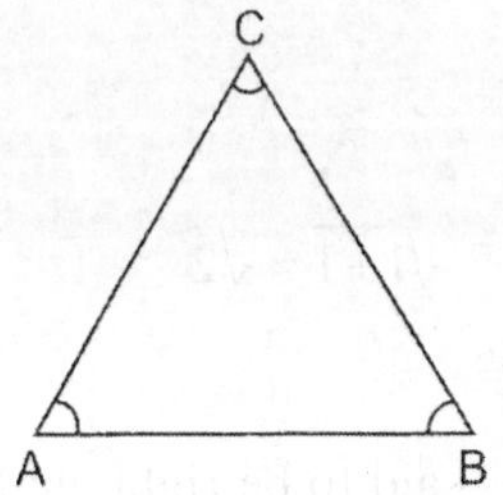

5. ***Obtuse angle triangel*** **:** A triangle is said to be obtuse angle triangle if any one angle of the triangle is obtuse angle.

(θ is said to be obtuse angle if $90^o < \theta < 180^o$)

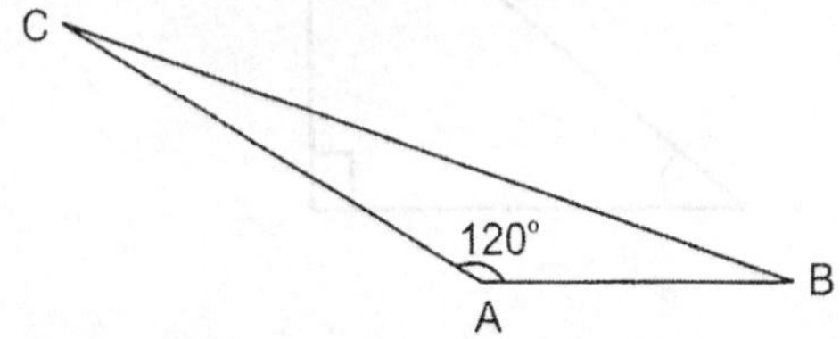

6. ***Right angled Isosceles triangle*** **:** If two sides of right angle triangle are equal then the triangle is called right angled isosceles triangle.

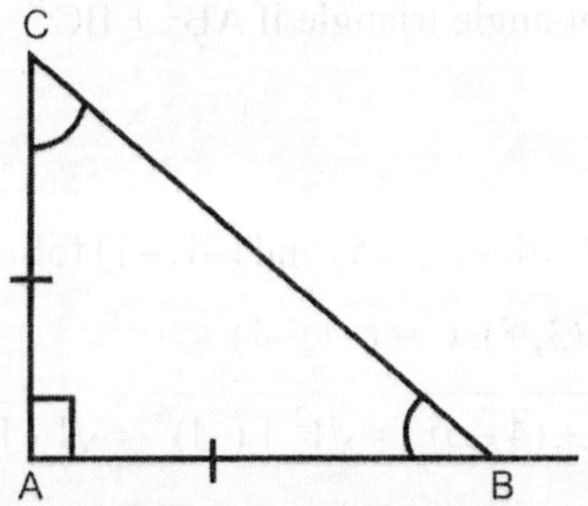

Ex : Show that the points (–2, 5), (3, –4), (7, 10) form a right angled isosceles triangle.

Sol. Let A = (–2, 5), B = (3, –4), C = (7, 10)

$$AB = \sqrt{(-2-3)^2 + (5+4)^2} = \sqrt{25+81} = \sqrt{106}$$

$$BC = \sqrt{(3-7)^2 + (-4-10)^2} = \sqrt{16+196} = \sqrt{212}$$

$$CA = \sqrt{(7+2)^2 + (10-5)^2} = \sqrt{81+25} = \sqrt{106}$$

$\therefore\ AB^2 = 106,\quad BC^2 = 212,\quad CA^2 = 106$

$\therefore\ AB^2 + AC^2 = BC^2$ also $AB = CA = \sqrt{106}$

$\therefore$ The triangle is right angled isosceles triangle

12.4 Quadrilatarals

In given four points if no three are collinear then the four points form a quadrilataral.

Types of Quadrilatarals

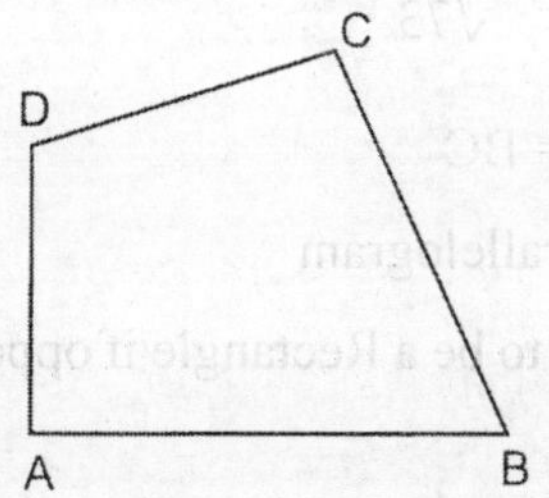

Parallelogram **:** A quadrilataral is said to be 'parallelogram', if opposite sides are parallel and equal.

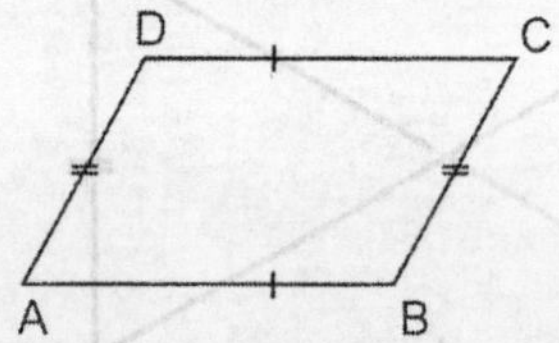

Note

If opposite sides are equal then clearly they are parallel. From figure, ABCD is a parallelogram, here AB = CD; AD = BC.

So the condition that the four points A, B, C, D taken in order form a parallelogram, is AB = CD, AD = BC.

Ex : Show that the points (–3, 1), (–6, –7), (3, –9), (6, –1) taken in order form a Parallelogram.

Let A = (–3, 1), B = (–6, –7) C = (3, –9) D = (6, –1)

$$AB = \sqrt{(-3-(-6))^2 + (1-(-7))^2} = \sqrt{9+64} = \sqrt{73}$$

$$CD = \sqrt{(3-6)^2 + (-9+1)^2} = \sqrt{9+64} = \sqrt{73}$$

$$AD = \sqrt{(-3-6)^2 + (1+1)^2} = \sqrt{81+4} = \sqrt{85}$$

$$BC = \sqrt{(-6-3)^2 + (-7+9)^2} = \sqrt{81+4} = \sqrt{85}$$

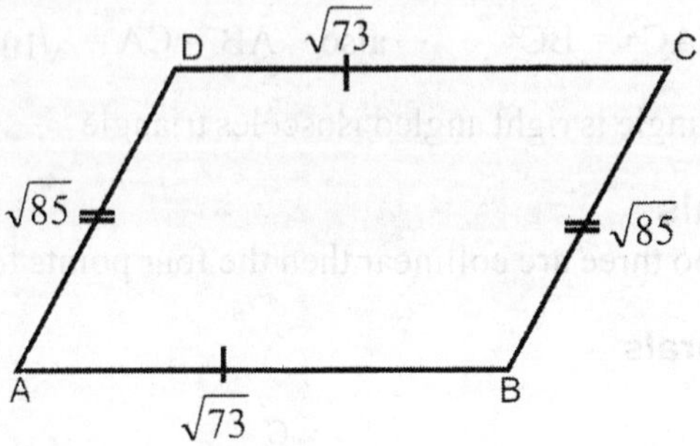

$\therefore$ AB = CD, AD = BC

$\therefore$ A, B, C, D form a parallelogram

Rectangle **:** A quadrilateral is said to be a Rectangle if opposite sides are equal and the two diagonals are equal.

(Diagonal : the line joining of opposite vertices of quadrilateral is called diagonal)

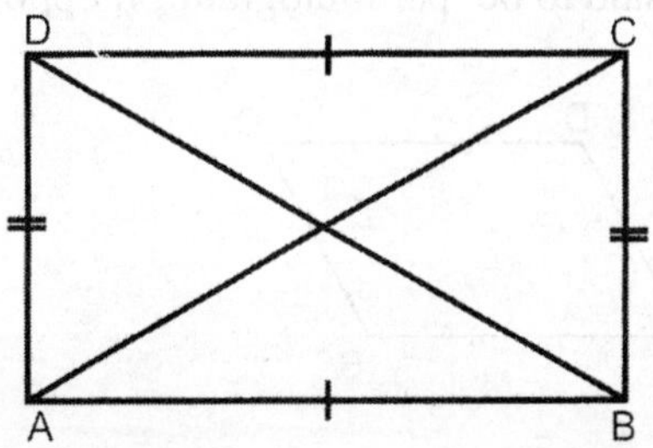

A, B, C, D is Rectangle if AB = CD, AD = BC and AC = BD

Note

(i) In a Parallelogram the two diagonals are equal then it is Rectangle.

$\therefore$ Every rectangle is a parallelogram and every parallelogram need not be rectangle.

(ii) In rectangle opposite sides are parallel and adjacent sides are perpendicular.

Ex : Show that the points (8, 4), (5, 7), (–1, 1), (2, –2) taken in order form a rectangle.

Sol. Let A = (8, 4), B = (5, 7), C = (–1, 1), D = (2, –2)

$AB = \sqrt{(8-5)^2+(4-7)^2} = \sqrt{9+9} = \sqrt{18}$

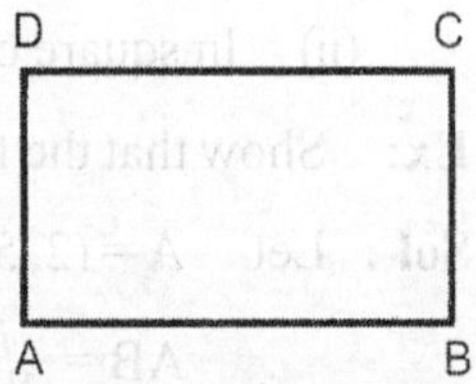

$BC = \sqrt{(5+1)^2+(7-1)^2} = \sqrt{36+36} = \sqrt{72}$

$CD = \sqrt{(-1-2)^2+(1+2)^2} = \sqrt{9+9} = \sqrt{18}$

$AD = \sqrt{(8-2)^2+(4+2)^2} = \sqrt{36+36} = \sqrt{72}$

$AC = \sqrt{(8+1)^2+(4-1)^2} = \sqrt{81+9} = \sqrt{90}$

$BD = \sqrt{(5-2)^2+(7+2)^2} = \sqrt{9+81} = \sqrt{90}$

$\therefore$ AB = CD, AD = BC, AC = BD

$\therefore$ ABCD is a rectangle

***Rhombus*:** A quadrilateral is said to be Rhombus if the four sides are equal.

A, B, C, D is Rhombus if AB = BC = CD = AD

Ex : Show that the Points (3, –2), (7, 6), (–1, 2) and (–5, –6) taken in order form a Rhombus.

Sol : Let A = (3, –2), B = (7, 6), C = (–1, 2), D = (–5, –6)

$AB = \sqrt{(3-7)^2+(-2-6)^2} = \sqrt{16+64} = \sqrt{80}$

$BC = \sqrt{(7+1)^2+(6-2)^2} = \sqrt{64+16} = \sqrt{80}$

$CD = \sqrt{(-1+5)^2+(2+6)^2} = \sqrt{16+64} = \sqrt{80}$

$AD = \sqrt{(3+5)^2+(-2+6)^2} = \sqrt{64+16} = \sqrt{80}$

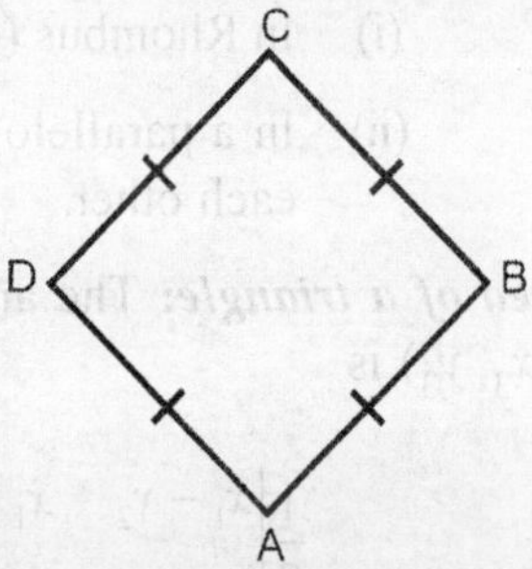

***Square*:** A quadrilateral is said to be square if four sides are equal and the two diagonals are equal.

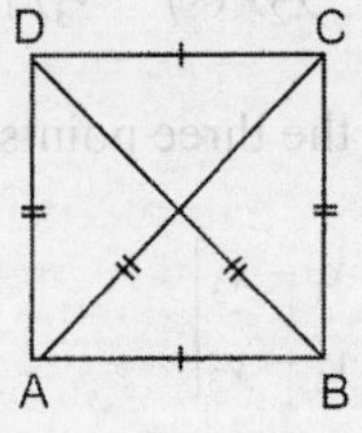

Note

(i) In Rhombus, if two diagonals are equal then it becomes a square.

$\therefore$ Every square is Rhombus but every Rhombus need not be a square.

(ii) In square opposite sides are parallel and adjacent sides are perpendicular.

Ex: Show that the four points (2, 5), (0, 3), (2, 1), (4, 3) taken in order forms a square.

Sol : Let A = (2, 5), B = (0, 3), C = (2, 1), D = (4, 3)

$$AB = \sqrt{(2-0)^2+(5-3)^2} = \sqrt{4+4} = \sqrt{8}$$

$$BC = \sqrt{(0-2)^2+(3-1)^2} = \sqrt{4+4} = \sqrt{8}$$

$$CD = \sqrt{(2-4)^2+(1-3)^2} = \sqrt{4+4} = \sqrt{8}$$

$$AD = \sqrt{(2-4)^2+(5-3)^2} = \sqrt{4+4} = \sqrt{8}$$

$$AC = \sqrt{(2-2)^2+(5-1)^2} = 4, \quad BD = \sqrt{(0-4)^2+(3-3)^2} = 4$$

$\therefore$ AB = BC = CD = AD and AC = BD

$\therefore$ ABCD is a square

Note

(i) In Rhombus (or) Square, the diagonals are perpendicular to each other.

(ii) In a parallelogram or rectangle or rhombus or square the diagonals bisects each other.

Area of a triangle: The area of triangle formed by the three points $P(x_1, y_1)$ $Q(x_2, y_2)$, $R(x_3, y_3)$ is

$$\frac{1}{2}\begin{vmatrix} x_1-x_2 & x_1-x_3 \\ y_1-y_2 & y_1-y_3 \end{vmatrix} \qquad \left(\begin{vmatrix} a & b \\ c & d \end{vmatrix} = ad-bc\right)$$

$$= \frac{1}{2}|(x_1-x_2)(y_1-y_3)-(y_1-y_2)(x_l-x_3)|$$

Ex : Find area of triangle formed by the three points (1, 2), (3, –4) and (–2, 0).

Sol. Area of triangle is $\frac{1}{2}\begin{vmatrix} x_1-x_2 & x_1-x_3 \\ y_1-y_2 & y_1-y_3 \end{vmatrix}$

here $(x_1\, y_1) = (1, 2)$, $(x_2\, y_2) = (3, -4)$, $(x_3, y_3) = (-2, 0)$

$$\text{Area} = \frac{1}{2}\begin{vmatrix} 1-3 & 1-(-2) \\ 2-(-4) & 2-(0) \end{vmatrix}$$

$$= \frac{1}{2}\begin{vmatrix} -2 & 3 \\ 6 & 2 \end{vmatrix}$$

$$= \frac{1}{2}|-4-18|$$

$$= \frac{1}{2}(-22) = -11 \text{ square units}$$

area is always positive

$\therefore$ Area of triangle $= |-11| = 11$ square units

Alternative Method: Area $= \frac{1}{2}\begin{vmatrix} x_1 & x_2 & x_3 & x_1 \\ y_1 & y_2 & y_3 & y_1 \end{vmatrix} = \frac{1}{2}\begin{vmatrix} 1 & 3 & -2 & 1 \\ 2 & -4 & 0 & 2 \end{vmatrix}$

$$= \frac{1}{2}|(-4-6)+(0-8)+(-4-0)|$$

$$= \frac{1}{2}|-10-8-4| = 11 \text{ square units}$$

Note : If area of triangle is zero then the points are collinear.

Area of Quadrilataral: The area of quadrilataral formed by the four points P(x_1, y_1), Q(x_2, y_2), R(x_3, y_3), and S(x_4, y_4) taken in order is $\frac{1}{2}\begin{vmatrix} x_1-x_3 & x_2-x_4 \\ y_1-y_3 & y_2-y_4 \end{vmatrix}$

Ex. Find the area of quadrilataral formed by the points x_1, y_1 (1, 2), x_2, y_2 (2, –3), x_3, y_3 (–2, 4), x_4, y_4 (0, 5) taken in order.

Sol. Area of Quadrilataral is

$$= \frac{1}{2}\begin{vmatrix} x_1-x_3 & x_2-x_4 \\ y_1-y_3 & y_2-y_4 \end{vmatrix}$$

$$= \frac{1}{2}\begin{vmatrix} 1+2 & 2-0 \\ 2-4 & -3-5 \end{vmatrix} = \frac{1}{2}\begin{vmatrix} 3 & 2 \\ -2 & -8 \end{vmatrix} = \frac{1}{2}|-24+4|$$

$$= \frac{1}{2}|-20| = 10 \text{ square units}$$

(or) area of quadrilataral is

$$\frac{1}{2}\begin{vmatrix} x_1 & x_2 & x_3 & x_4 & x_1 \\ y_1 & y_2 & y_3 & y_4 & y_1 \end{vmatrix}$$

$$=\frac{1}{2}\begin{vmatrix} 1 & 2 & -2 & 0 & 1 \\ 2 & -3 & 4 & 5 & 2 \end{vmatrix}$$

$$=\frac{1}{2}\left|(-3-4)+(8-6)+(-10-0)+(0-5)\right|$$

$$=\frac{1}{2}\left|-7+2-10-5\right|=\frac{1}{2}(20)=10 \text{ square units}$$

Some more Solved Examples

1. Find the distance between two points $(at_1^2, 2at_1)(at_2^2, 2at_2)$

Sol. Distance between two points is $\sqrt{(at_1^2 - at_2^2)^2 + (2at_1 - 2at_2)^2}$

$$=\sqrt{a^2(t_1^2-t_2^2)^2+4a^2(t_1-t_2)^2}$$

$$=|a|\sqrt{(t_1+t_2)^2+(t_1-t_2)^2+4(t_1-t_2)^2}$$

$$=|a||t_1-t_2|\sqrt{(t_1+t_2)^2+4}$$ (by taking common $(t_1 - t_2)^2$)

2. Find the distance between two points (a cos θ, a sin θ), (a cos ϕ, a sin ϕ)

Sol. Let A = (a cos θ , b sin θ) B = (a cos ϕ , b sin ϕ)

$$\therefore \text{ AB} = \sqrt{(a\cos\theta - a\cos\phi)^2 + (a\sin\theta - a\sin\phi)^2}$$

$$=\sqrt{a^2(\cos^2\theta+\sin^2\theta)+a^2(\cos^2\phi+\sin^2\phi)-2a^2(\cos\theta\cos\phi+\sin\theta\sin\phi)}$$

$$=a\sqrt{1+1-2(\cos\theta\cos\phi+\sin\theta\sin\phi}$$

$$=a\sqrt{2-2\cos(\theta-\phi)}=a\sqrt{2(1-\cos(\theta-\phi)}$$

$$= a\sqrt{2\left[2\sin^2\left(\frac{\theta-\phi}{2}\right)\right]} \qquad \left[\because 1-\cos\theta = 2\sin^2\frac{\theta}{2}\right]$$

$$= 2a\left|\sin\left(\frac{\theta-\phi}{2}\right)\right|$$

3. Find the point on x-axis which is equi distance from (7, 6) and (-3, 4).

Sol. Let $P(x_1, 0)$ be any point on x-axis and A = (7, 6), B = (–3, 4)

(on x-axis any point y-coordinate is zero)

$\therefore$ PA = PB

$$\Rightarrow (PA)^2 = (PB)^2 \Rightarrow (x_1-7)^2+(0-6)^2 = (x_1+3)^2+(0-4)^2$$

$$\Rightarrow \quad x_1^2 + 49 - 14x_1 + 36 = x_1^2 + 9 + 6x_1 + 16$$

$$\Rightarrow \quad 85 - 14x_1 = 25 + 6x_1$$

$$\Rightarrow \quad 20x_1 = 60$$

$$\Rightarrow \quad x_1 = 3$$

$\therefore$ The point is (3, 0)

4. Find the value of t if the points (t, 2t), (2t, 6t) and (3, 8) are collinear.

Sol. Let A = (t, 2t), B = (2t, 6t), C = (3, 8)

given A, B, C are collinear

$\therefore$ Area of triangle formed A, B, C is zero

$$\therefore \quad \frac{1}{2}\begin{vmatrix} x_1-x_2 & x_1-x_3 \\ y_1-y_2 & y_1-y_3 \end{vmatrix} = 0$$

$$\Rightarrow \quad \frac{1}{2}\begin{vmatrix} t-2t & t-3 \\ 2t-6t & 2t-8 \end{vmatrix} = 0$$

$$\Rightarrow \quad \begin{vmatrix} -t & t-3 \\ -4t & 2t-8 \end{vmatrix} = 0$$

$$\Rightarrow \quad -t(2t-8) - (-4t)(t-3) = 0$$

$$\Rightarrow \quad t[-2t + 8 + 4(t-3)] = 0$$

$$\Rightarrow \quad t = 0 \text{ or } 2t - 4 = 0$$

$$\therefore \quad t = 0 \text{ or } t = 2$$

Exercise - 12.1

1. Find the distance between the points.

   (i) (0, –3) (0, 7) (ii) (0, 0) (–4, 3)

2. Find the value of K if the distance between two points (1, 0), (4, k) is 5.

3. Find the relation between x and y if the point (x, y) is to be equidistant from (6, –1) and (2, 3).

4. Show that the following points are collinear.

5. Show that the three points (2a, 4a), (2a, 6a) (2a + $\sqrt{3}$ a, 5a) form an equilataral triangle.

6. Show that the points (5, 3), (11, –5), (12, 2) form a right angle triangle.

7. Show that the points (1, –3), (8, –2), (9, –9) form a right angled isosceles triangle.

8. Show that the four points (3, –5), (–5, –4), (7, 10), (15, 9) taken in order form a parallelogram.

9. Show that the points (3, 2), (–2, 2), (–2, –1), (3, –1) taken in order form a rectangle.

10. Show that the póints (–2, –3), (5, 1), (6, 9), (–1, 5) taken in order form a Rhombus.

11. Show that the points (2, 5), (0, 3), (2, 1), (4, 3) taken in order form a square.

12. Find the area of triangle formed by the points

    (i) (0, 0), (2, –3), (4, 5) (ii) $\left(a, \frac{1}{a}\right), \left(b, \frac{1}{b}\right) \left(c, \frac{1}{c}\right)$

13. If the area of triangle formed by (1, 2), (2, 3), (x, 4) is 40 square units then find x.

14. Find k if (k, 2k) (2k, 3k) (3, 1) are collinear.

15. If (k, 2 – 2k), (–k + 1, 2k), (–4 –k, 6 –2 k) are collinear find k.

16. Find the area of quadrilataral formed by the points (3, –5), (5, –1), (2, 1), (–3, –2) taken in order.

Answers

1. (i) 10 (ii) 5

2. ± 4

3. $x = y + 3$

4. (i) (1, 4), (3, –2), (–3, 16) (ii) (2, –4), (4, –2), (7, 1)

12. (i) 11 square units (ii) $\left(\frac{(a-b)(b-c)(c-a)}{2abc}\right)$

13. − 77, 83

14. 0 or −2

15. $k = \frac{1}{2}, -1$

16. $\frac{49}{2}$ square units

12.5 Section Formula

- The point P which divides the line segment joining the points $A(x_1, y_1)$, $B(x_2 y_2)$ in the ratio m : n internally is

$$\left(\frac{mx_2 + nx_1}{m+n}, \frac{my_2 + ny_1}{m+n}\right)$$

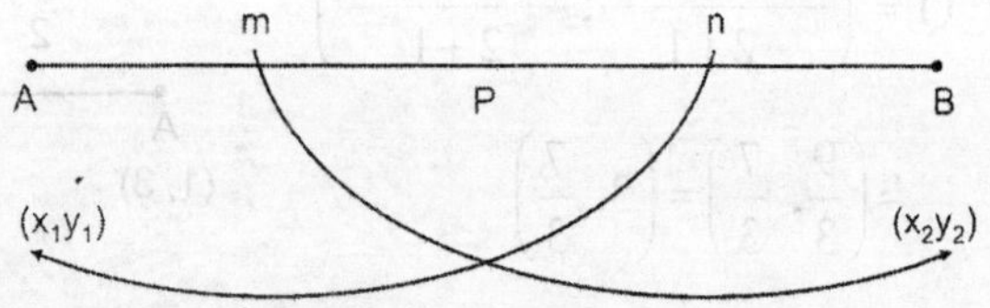

- The point P which divides the line segment joining the points $A(x_1, y_1)$, $B(x_2 y_2)$ in the ratio m : n externally is (m ≠ n).

$$\left(\frac{mx_2 - nx_1}{m-n}, \frac{my_2 - ny_1}{m-n}\right)$$

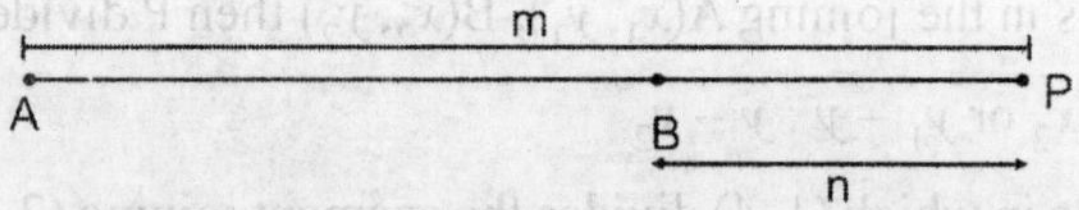

Corollary

1. The mid point of line segment joining $A(x_1, y_1)$ $B(x_2, y_2)$ is

$$\left(\frac{x_1 + x_2}{2}, \frac{y_1 + y_2}{2}\right)$$

Ex : Find the mid point of line joining of the points (1, 2), (3, 8)

$$\text{mid point} = \left(\frac{x_1 + x_2}{2}, \frac{y_1 + y_2}{2}\right) = \left(\frac{1+3}{2}, \frac{2+8}{2}\right) = (2,5)$$

2. ***Trisection Points :*** Let A, B be two points. Then, the points which divides $\overline{AB}$ in the ratio 1 : 2 and 2 : 1 are called points of trisection of $\overline{AB}$.

Ex : Find the points of trisection of line segment joining the points (1, 3), (4, 2).

Sol. Let A = (1, 3), B = (4, 2)

Let P be the point which divides $\overline{AB}$ in the ratio 1 : 2

$$\text{Then } P = \left(\frac{1\times 4+2\times 1}{1+2}, \frac{1\times 2+2\times 3}{1+2}\right)$$

$$= \left(\frac{6}{3}, \frac{8}{3}\right) = \left(2, \frac{8}{3}\right)$$

Let Q be the point which divides $\overline{AB}$ in the ratio 2 : 1 in the ratio then

$$Q = \left(\frac{2\times 4+1\times 1}{2+1}; \frac{2\times 2+1\times 3}{2+1}\right)$$

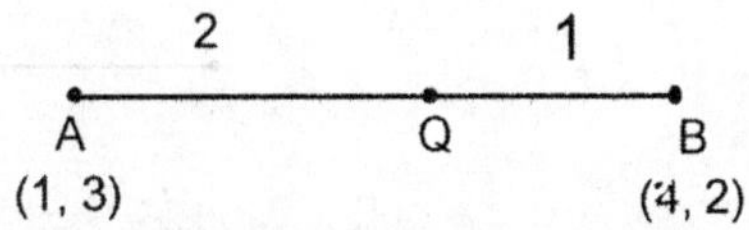

$$= \left(\frac{9}{3}, \frac{7}{3}\right) = \left(3, \frac{7}{3}\right)$$

∴ The trisection points are $P = \left(2, \frac{8}{3}\right)$, $Q = \left(3, \frac{7}{3}\right)$

Note

The mid point of line segment joining of any two points is equal to mid point of line segment joining of their trisection points.

3. If $P(x, y)$ lies in the joining $A(x_1, y_1)$, $B(x_2, y_2)$ then P divides $\overline{AB}$ in the ratio $x_1 - x : x - x_2$ or $y_1 - y : y - y_2$.

Ex : Find the ratio in which (1, 4) divides the segment joining (2, 1), (4, –5).

Sol. Required ratio is 2 – 1 : 1 – 4 = 1 : –3

∴ The point (1, 4) divides line joining (2, 1), (4, –5) in the ratio 1 : 3 externally.

4. x-axis divides the line segment joining (x_1, y_1), (x_2, y_2) in the ratio $-y_1 : y_2$.

Ex : Find the ratio in which x-axis divide the line segment joining the points (1, –3), (5, 7).

Sol. required ratio is $-y_1 : y_2 = -(-3) : 7 = 3 : 7$

5. y-axis divide the line segment joining $(x_1, y_1), (x_2, y_2)$ in the ratio $-x_1 : x_2$.

Ex : Find the ratio in which y-axis divide the line segment joining the points $(-2, 4), (6, -1)$.

Sol. Required ratio is $-(x_1) : x_2 = -(-2) : 6$

$$= 2 : 6$$

$$= 1 : 3$$

Harmonic conjugate of a point with respect to a line segment

Let P be a point on $\overleftrightarrow{AB}$ such that it divides $\overline{AB}$ in the m : n internally (externally). Then the point Q divides $\overline{AB}$ in the ratio m : n externally (internally) is called Harmonic Conjugate of P w.r.t $\overline{AB}$.

Ex : Find the Harmonic Conjugate of (4, –2) w.r.t (2, –4), (7, 1).

Sol. The given point (4, –2) divides (2, –4), (7, 1) in the ratio

$2-4 : 4-7 = -2 : -3 = 2 : 3$ i.e., internally.

∴ The Hormonic conjugate of (4, –2), which divides the segment joining of (2, –4), (7, 1) in the ratio 2 : 3 externally

∴ The Harmonic conjugate is

$$\left(\frac{2\times7-3\times2}{2-3}, \frac{2\times1-3(-4)}{2-3}\right)$$

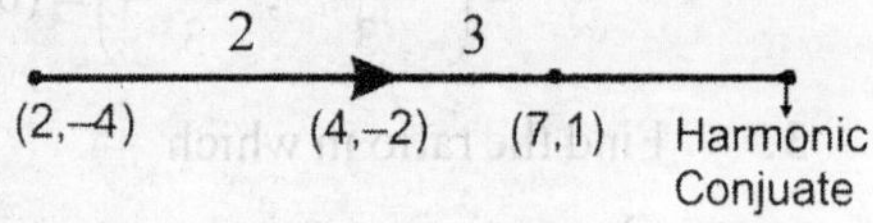

$$= (-8, -14)$$

∴ The Harmonic conjugate of (4, –2) w.r.t (2, –4) (7, 1) is (–8, –14)

Solved Examples

1. Find the points which divides the line segment joining

(i) (–1, 2), (4, –5) in the ratio 3 : 2

(ii) (4, 5) (–3, 4) in the ratio 6 : 5

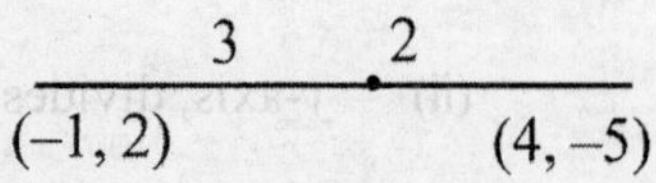

Sol. (i) Let P be the required point

$$\therefore P = \left(\frac{3\times4+2\times-1}{3+2}, \frac{3\times-5+2\times2}{3+2}\right)$$

$$= \left(\frac{10}{5}, \frac{-11}{5}\right) = \left(2, -\frac{11}{5}\right)$$

(ii) Let Q be the required point then

$$Q = \left(\frac{(-6)(-3)+(5)\times(4)}{-6+5}, \frac{(-6)(4)+(5)\times(5)}{-6+5}\right) = (-38, -1)$$

2. Find the points of trisection of the line segment joining (6, –3) (–3, 9).

Sol. Let P, Q be points of trisection of line segment joining A(6, –3), B(–3, 9)

$\therefore$ P divides $\overline{AB}$ in the ratio 1 : 2 internally

$$P = \left(\frac{(1)(-3)+(2)(6)}{1+2}, \frac{(1)(9)+(2)(-3)}{1+2}\right)$$

1 : 2 — (6, –3) ———— (–3, 9)

$$= \left(\frac{-3+12}{3}, \frac{9-6}{3}\right) = (3, 1)$$

Q divides $\overline{AB}$ in the ratio 2 : 1 internally

$$Q = \left(\frac{(2)(-3)+(1)(6)}{2+1}, \frac{2(9)+(1)(-3)}{2+1}\right)$$

$$= \left(\frac{-6+6}{3}, \frac{18-3}{3}\right) = (0, 5)$$

2 : 1 — (6, –3) ———— (–3, 9)

3. Find the ratio in which

(i) x-axis (ii) y-axis (iii) (2, 1)

divides the segment joining the points (1, –2), (4, 7).

Sol. Let A = (1, –2), B = (4, 7)

(i) x-axis divides $\overline{AB}$ in the ratio $-y_1 : y_2$

$$= -(-2) : 7$$
$$= 2 : 7$$

(ii) y-axis, divides $\overline{AB}$ in the ratio $-x_1 : x_2$

$$= -(1) : 4 = -1 : 4$$

i.e. 1 : 4 externally

(iii) (2, 1) divides $\overline{AB}$ in the ratio

$$x_1 - x : x - x_2 = 1 - 2 : 2 - 4$$
$$= -1 : -2 = 1 : 2$$

4. (i) Find the four vertex of the parallelogram whose consecutive vertices are (–2, –1), (1, 0), (4, 3).

(ii) If (2, 6) is one of the extremeties of a diameter of a circle with centre (3, 5). Find the other points.

Sol. (i) Let A = (–2, –1), B = (1, 0), C = (4, 3) are three consecutive vertices of a parallelogram.

Let D(x_1, y_1) be fourth vertex.

We know that in Parallelogram or in Rectangle (or) in Rhombus (or) in square the diagonals bisect each other.

i.e., the mid points of diagonals are equal.

$\therefore$ mid point of AC = mid poin of BD

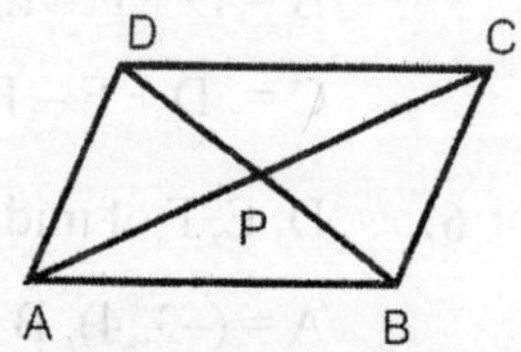

$$\Rightarrow \left(\frac{-2+4}{2}, \frac{-1+3}{2}\right) = \left(\frac{1+x_1}{2}, \frac{0+y_1}{2}\right)$$

$$(\because \text{ mid point} = \left(\frac{x_1+x_2}{2}, \frac{y_1+y_2}{2}\right))$$

$$\Rightarrow (1, 1) = \left(\frac{1+x_1}{2}, \frac{y_1}{2}\right)$$

$$\therefore \quad \frac{1+x_1}{2} = 1, \qquad 1 = \frac{y_1}{2}$$

$$\Rightarrow 1 + x_1 = 2 \qquad y_1 = 2$$

$$\Rightarrow x_1 = 1$$

$$\therefore \quad (x_1, y_1) = (1, 2)$$

(ii) Let A = (2, 6). C = (3, 5) and B = (x_1, y_1) be other extremity of circle

$\therefore$ C is mid point of AB

$$\therefore \quad (3, 5) = \left(\frac{2+x_1}{2}, \frac{6+y_1}{2}\right) \qquad \Rightarrow \quad (x_1, y_1) = (4, 4)$$

5. If the mid points of $\overline{BC}$, $\overline{CA}$, $\overline{AB}$ of ΔABC are (3, –3), (3, –1), (1, 1) respectively then find the vertices A, B, C.

Sol. Let A = $(x_1\ y_1)$, B = $(x_2\ y_2)$ C = $(x_3\ y_3)$ and D = (3, –3), E = (3, –1) F = (1, 1) are mid points of $\overline{BC}$, $\overline{CA}$, $\overline{AB}$ respectively.

Join D, E ; E, F ; F, D

∴ We get the parallelogram B D E F, D C E F, AF D E from B D E F,

mid point of BE = mid point DF.

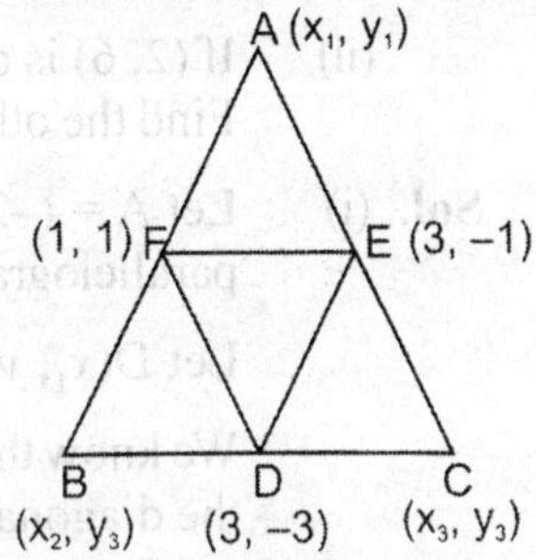

$$\Rightarrow \left(\frac{x_2+3}{2}, \frac{y_2-1}{2}\right) = \left(\frac{3+1}{2}, \frac{-3+1}{2}\right)$$

$$\Rightarrow \frac{x_2+3}{2} = 2 \quad x_2 = 1 \; ; \; \frac{y_2-1}{2} = -1 \quad y_2 = -1$$

∴ B = (1, –1)

Similarly we can find A = (1, 3), C = (5, –5)

(or) A = E + F – D = (3, –1) + (1, 1) – (3, –3) = (1, 3)

B = D + F – E = (3, –3) + (1, 1) – (3, –1) = (1, –1)

C = D + E – F = (3, –3) + (3, –1) – (1, 1) = (5, –5)

6. D, E, F of mid points of sides $\overline{BC}$, $\overline{CA}$, $\overline{AB}$ of Δ ABC where A = (–3, 4), B = (–1, –2), C = (5, 6) then find the area of Δ DEF.

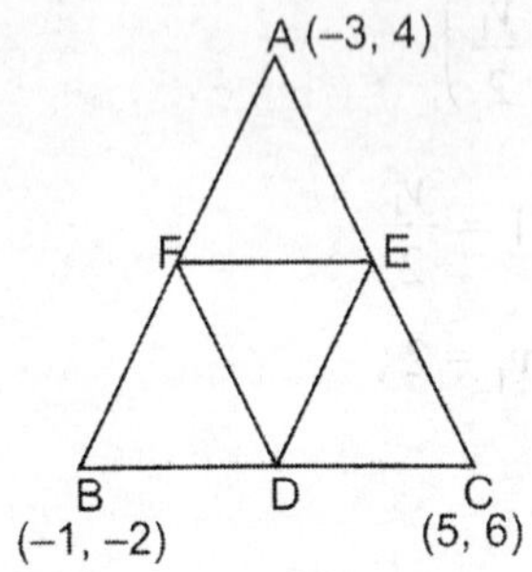

Sol. Area of Δ DEF = $\frac{1}{4}$ (area of Δ ABC)

$$= \frac{1}{4}\frac{1}{2}\begin{vmatrix} -3+1 & -3-5 \\ 4+2 & 4-6 \end{vmatrix} = \frac{1}{8}\begin{vmatrix} -2 & -8 \\ 6 & -2 \end{vmatrix} = \frac{1}{8}(4+48) = \frac{52}{8} = \frac{13}{2}$$

Exercise - 12.2

1. Find the point which divide the line segment joining the points (1, –3), (–3, 9) in the ratio 1 : 3 internally and externally.

2. Find the mid point and the points of trisection of segment joining (2, 3), (11, 6).

3. (i) **Find the ratio in which x-axis and y-axis divides the line segment joining (2, –3), (5, 2).**

(ii) **Find the ratio in which the point (8, 4) divides the line segment joining (5, –2), (9, 6).**

4. **Find the harmonic conjugate of (5, –2) w.r.t (8, 4), (9, 6)**

5. **The three consecutive vertices of rectangle are (4, 1) (7, 4) (13, –2) then find the fourth vertex.**

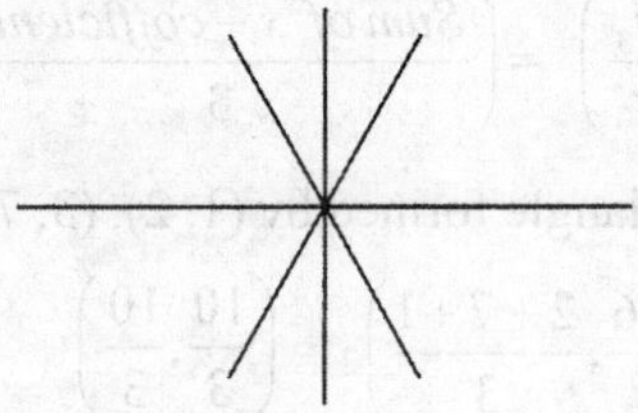

Answers

1. (0, 0), (3, –9)

2. $\left(\left(\frac{13}{2},\frac{9}{2}\right);(5,4'),(8,5)\right)$

3. (i) 3 : 2, –2 : 5 (ii) 3 : 1

4. $\left(\frac{59}{7},\frac{34}{7}\right)$

5. (10, –5)

Concurent lines : If three or more lines meet at a point then we say the lines are concurent at that point.

12.6 Centroid of a Triangle

Median : The line passing through a vertex and mid point of opposite side of triangle is called median.

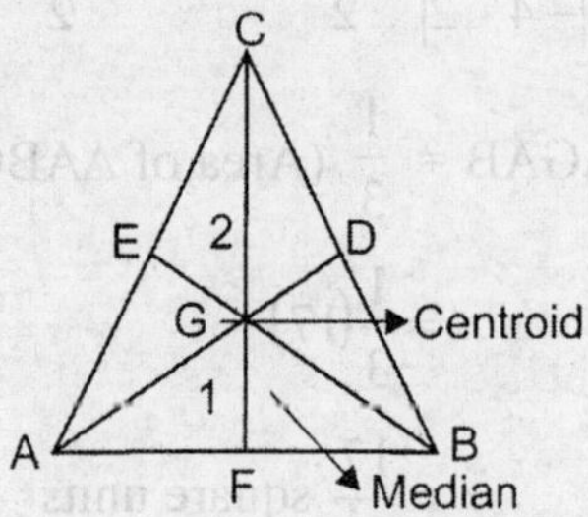

From figure AD, BE, CF are three medians through A, B, C respectively, the three medians of triangle are concurrent.

Centroid : The point of concurence of medians of triangle is called centroid.

It is denoted by G.

The centroid of triangle divides each median in the ratio 2 : 1 (G divides each AD, 1BE, CF in the ratio 2 : 1)

The centroid of triangle formed by the points $(x_1\ y_1)$, $(x_2\ y_2)$, $(x_3\ y_3)$ is

$$\left(\frac{x_1+x_2+x_3}{3}, \frac{y_1+y_2+y_3}{3}\right) = \left(\frac{Sum\ of\ x-cofficients}{3}, \frac{sum\ of\ y-cofficients}{3}\right)$$

Ex : Find the centroid of triangle formed by (1, 2), (3, 7), (6, 1).

Sol. Centroid G $= \left(\frac{1+3+6}{3}, \frac{2+7+1}{3}\right) = \left(\frac{10}{3}, \frac{10}{3}\right)$

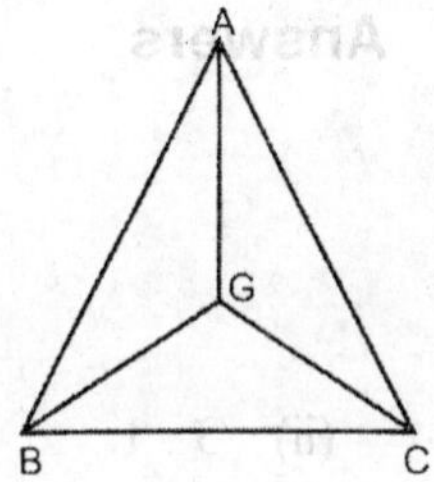

Note

If G is centroid of triangle ABC then area of ΔABC =3GAB= 3ΔGBC = 3ΔGCA

(or) ΔGAB = ΔGBC = ΔGCA = $\frac{1}{3}$ (ΔABC).

Ex : If G centroid of triangle formed by A (6, 1), B (3, 5), C(–1, –1) then find the area of triangle GAB.

Sol. $\because$ Area of ΔABC $= \frac{1}{2}\begin{vmatrix} 6-3 & 6+1 \\ 1-5 & 1+1 \end{vmatrix}$ $\left(\because \text{Area of triangle} = \frac{1}{2}\begin{vmatrix} x_1-x_2 & x_1-x_3 \\ y_1-y_2 & y_1-y_3 \end{vmatrix}\right)$

$$= \frac{1}{2}\begin{vmatrix} 3 & 7 \\ -4 & 2 \end{vmatrix} = \frac{1}{2}(6+28) = \frac{34}{2} = 17$$

$$\therefore \text{Area of } \Delta GAB = \frac{1}{3}\ (\text{Area of } \Delta ABC)$$

$$= \frac{1}{3}(17)$$

$$= \frac{17}{3} \text{ square units}$$

12.7 Circum Centre of Triangle

Perpendicular bisector : If AB is a line segment then the line passing through mid point of AB and perpendicular to AB is called perpendicular bisector.

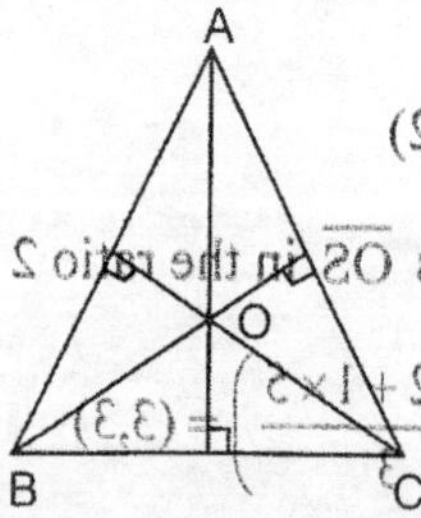

Circum Centre : The point of concurence of perpendicular bisector of sides of a triangle is called circum centre. It is denoted by 'S'.

Note : If S is circum centre of ΔABC then

$$SA = SB = SC$$

We see how to find circum centre of triangle in **straight lines chapter.**

12.8 Orthro Centre of Triangle

Altitude: The lin through a vertex of triangle and perpendicular to the opposite side is called altitude through vertex of triangle.

There exists 3 altitudes to a triangle and these are concurent.

Ortho centre: The point of concurence of altitudes of triangle is called ortho centre of triangle.It is denoted by 'O'.

Note

In right angled triangle the ortho centre is the vertex at which triangle is right angle i.e., it is vertex opposite to hypotenues of triangle.

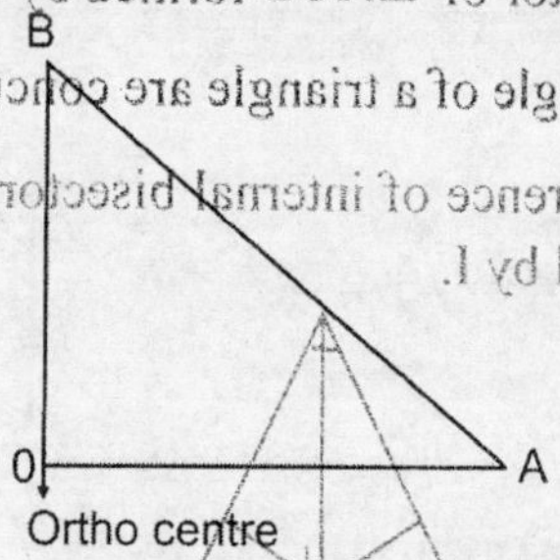

We see how to find the ortho centre of triangle with given vertices in **straight line chapter.**

12.7 Circum Centre of Triangle

Perpendicular bisector : If AB is a line segment then the line passing through mid-point of AB and perpendicular to AB is called perpendicular bisector.

Circum Centre : The point of concurrence of perpendicular bisectors of sides of a triangle is called circum centre. It is denoted by S.

Note : If S is circum centre of ΔABC then

$$SA = SB = SC$$

We see how to find circum centre of triangle in straight lines chapter.

12.8 Ortho Centre of Triangle

Altitude : The line through a vertex of triangle and perpendicular to the opposite side is called altitude through vertex of triangle.

There exists 3 altitudes to a triangle and these are concurrent.

Ortho centre : The point of concurrence of altitudes of triangle is called ortho centre of triangle. It is denoted by 'O'.

Note

In right angled triangle the ortho centre is the vertex at which triangle is right angle i.e., the vertex opposite to hypotenuse of triangle.

Ortho centre

We see how to find the ortho centre of triangle with given vertices in straight line chapter.

$$= \left(\frac{9+35+28}{12}, \frac{6+70+20}{12}\right)$$

$$= (6, 8)$$

$$\text{Ex centre opposite to A} = \left(\frac{-ax_1+bx_2+cx_3}{-a+b+c}, \frac{-ay_1+by_2+cy_3}{-a+b+c}\right)$$

$$= \left(\frac{-9+35+28}{-3+5+4}, \frac{-6+10+20}{-3+5+4}\right) = (9, 4)$$

$$\text{Ex centre opposite to B} = \left(\frac{9-35+28}{3-5+4}, \frac{6-10+20}{3-5+4}\right) = (1, 8)$$

$$\text{Ex centre opposite to C} = \left(\frac{9+35-28}{3+5-4}, \frac{6+10-20}{3+5-4}\right) = (4, -1)$$

Exercise - 12.3

1. Find the centroid of triangle formed by the points

   (i) (6, 1), (3, 5), (−1, −2) (ii) (2, 3), (−2, −5), (−4, −6)

2. The centroid of triangle whose vertices are (2, 4), (3, k) and (4, 2) is (k, 3). Find k.

3. If the centroid of triangle is (1, 4) and two of its vertices are (4, −3), (−9, 7) then find the third vertex and the area of triangle.

4. If two vertices of triangle are (4, 8), (−2, 6) and the centroid is (2, 7) then find the third vertex.

5. The centroid of triangle ABC is (2, 7). The points B, C lie on x, y-axis respectively and A = (4, 8). Find B and C.

   [Hint: Let B = (x, 0), C = (0, y), A = (4, 8)]

   $$\therefore (2, 7) = \left(\frac{x+0+4}{3}, \frac{0+y+8}{3}\right)$$

6. Find the centroid of triangle whose ortho centre is (2, −3) and circum centre is (5, 6).

7. Find the in centre and excentres of triangle formed by the points (2, 3), (−2, −5), (−4, 6).

$$= \left(\frac{9+35+28}{12}, \frac{6+10+20}{12}\right)$$

$$= (6, 3)$$

$$\text{Ex centre opposite to } A = \left(\frac{-ax_1+bx_2+cx_3}{-a+b+c}, \frac{-ay_1+by_2+cy_3}{-a+b+c}\right)$$

$$= \left(\frac{-9+35+28}{-3+5+4}, \frac{-6+10+20}{-3+5+4}\right) = (9, 4)$$

$$\text{Ex centre opposite to } B = \left(\frac{9-35+28}{3-5+4}, \frac{6-10+20}{3-5+4}\right) = (1, 8)$$

$$\text{Ex centre opposite to } C = \left(\frac{9+35-28}{3+5-4}, \frac{6+10-20}{3+5-4}\right) = (4, -1)$$

Exercise - 12.3

1. Find the centroid of triangle formed by the points

   (i) (6, 1), (3, 5), (–1, –2) (ii) (2, 3,) (–2, –5), (–4, –6)

2. The centroid of triangle whose vertices are (2, 4), (3, k) and (4, 2) is (k, 3). Find k.

3. If the centroid of triangle is (1, 4) and two of its vertices are (4, –3), (–9, 7) then find the third vertex and the area of triangle.

4. If two vertices of triangle are (4, 8), (–2, 6) and the centroid is (2, 7) then find the third vertex.

5. The centroid of triangle ABC is (2, 7). The points B, C lie on x, y-axis respectively and A = (4, 8). Find B and C.

   [Hint : Let B = (x, 0) , C=(0,y), A= (4,8)]

   $$(2, 7) = \left(\frac{x+0+4}{3}, \frac{0+y+8}{3}\right)$$

6. Find the centroid of triangle whose ortho centre is (2, –3) and circum centre is (5, 6)

7. Find the in centre and excentres of triangle formed by the points (2, 3), (–2, –5), (–4, 6).

Answers

1. (i) $\left(\frac{8}{3}, \frac{4}{3}\right)$ (ii) $\left(\frac{-4}{3}, \frac{-8}{3}\right)$

2. $k = 3$

3. $(8, 8)$; $\frac{183}{2}$ square units

4. $(4, 7)$

5. $(2, 0), (0, 13)$

6. $(4, 3)$

7. $(-1, 2), (-16, -3)\ (0, 9), (5, -6)$

$\Rightarrow (OP)^2 = 4\ PM$

$\Rightarrow (OP)^2 = 4y_1$

$\Rightarrow (\sqrt{(x_1 - 0)^2 + (y_1 - 0)^2})^2 = 4y_1$

$\Rightarrow x_1^2 + y_1^2 = 4y_1$

locus of (x_1, y_1) is $x^2 + y^2 = 4y$

3. Find the equation of locus of point equidistance from the points $(-3, 2)$, $(0, 4)$.

Sol. Let $A = (-3, 2)$, $B = (0, 4)$

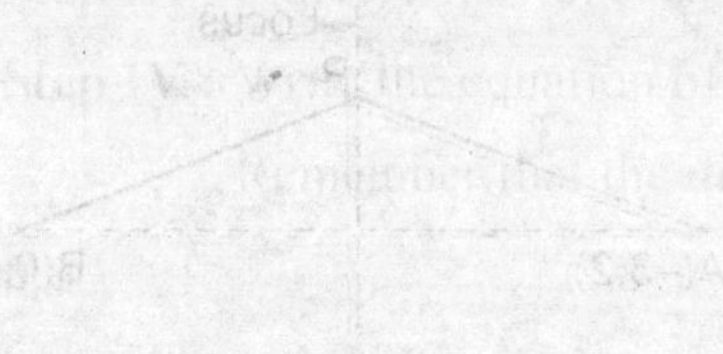

Let $P(x_1, y_1)$ be any point on locus.

$\therefore$ by given condition

$PA = PB$

$$\Rightarrow \sqrt{(x_1 + 3)^2 + (y_1 - 2)^2} = \sqrt{(x_1 - 0)^2 + (y_1 - 4)^2}$$

$\Rightarrow (x_1 + 3)^2 + (y_1 - 2)^2 = (x_1 - 0)^2 + (y_1 - 4)^2$ [by squaring on both sides]

$\Rightarrow x_1^2 + 9 + 6x_1 + y_1^2 + 4 - 4y_1 = x_1^2 + y_1^2 + 16 - 8y_1$

$\Rightarrow 6x_1 + 4y_1 - 3 = 0$

$\therefore$ locus of (x_1, y_1) is $6x + 4y - 3 = 0$.

4. Find the locus of point which is equidistance to the coordinate axes.

Sol. Let $P(x_1, y_1)$ be ay point on the locus.

$\therefore$ by given condition that $PM = PN$

$\Rightarrow |x_1| = |y_1|$

$x_1 = y_1 \Rightarrow x_1 - y_1 = 0$

locus of (x_1, y_1) is $x^2 = y^2$ [illegible]

5. Find the equation to the locus of a point from which the distance to $(3, 0)$ is equal to the distance from the point to y axis.

Sol. Let $P(x_1, y_1)$ be any point on the locus. Let $A = (3, 0)$ the distance from P to y axis is $|x_1|$.

$\therefore\ (OP)^2 = 4\ PM$

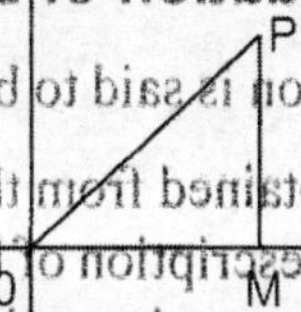

$OP^2 = 4y_1$

$\therefore\ \left(\sqrt{(x_1-0)^2+(y_1-0)^2}\right)^2 = 4y_1$

$\therefore\ x_1^2 + y_1^2 = 4y_1$

$\therefore$ locus of $(x_1\ y_1)$ is $x^2 + y^2 - 4y = 0$

3. Find the equation of locus of point equidistance from the points (–3, 2), (0, 4).

Sol. Let A = (–3, 2), B = (0, 4)

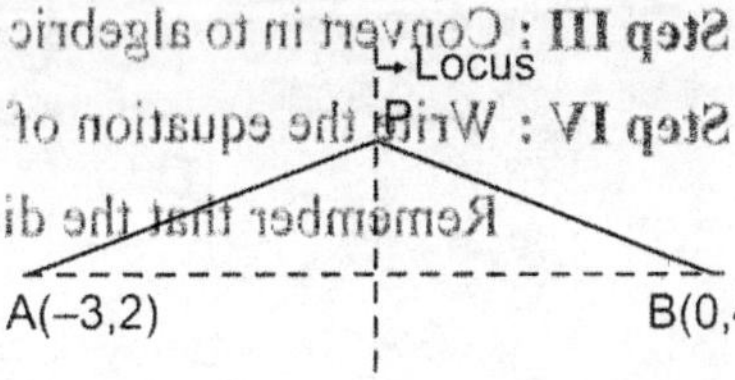

Let $P(x_1, y_1)$ be any point on locus.

$\therefore$ by given condition,

PA = PB

$\Rightarrow\quad \sqrt{(x_1+3)^2+(y_1-2)^2} = \sqrt{(x_1-0)^2+(y_1-4)^2}$

$\Rightarrow\quad (x_1+3)^2 + (y_1-2)^2 = (x_1-0)^2 + (y_1-4)^2$ [by squaring on both sides]

$\Rightarrow\quad x_1^2 + 9 + 6x_1 + y_1^2 + 4 - 4y_1 = x_1^2 + y_1^2 + 16 - 8y_1$

$\Rightarrow\quad 6x_1 + 4y_1 - 3 = 0$

locus of (x_1, y_1) is $6x + 4y - 3 = 0$

4. Find the locus of point which is equidistance to the coordinate axes.

Sol. Let $P(x_1, y_1)$ be ay point on the locus.

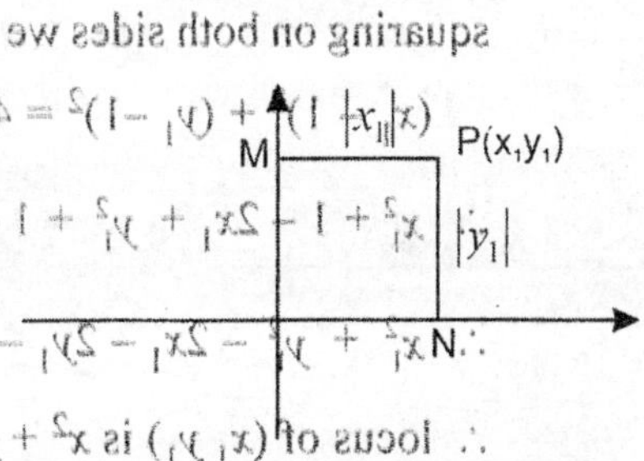

$\therefore$ by given condition that PM = PN

$\Rightarrow\quad |x_1| = |y_1|$

$\Rightarrow\quad x_1^2 = y_1^2 \quad\Rightarrow\quad x_1^2 - y_1^2 = 0$

locus of (x_1, y_1) is $x^2 - y^2 = 0$

5. Find the equation to the locus of a point from which the distance to (3, 0) equal to the distance from the point to y-axis.

Sol. Let $P(x_1, y_1)$ be any point on the locus, Let A = (3, 0) the distance from P to y-axis is $|x_1|$

$\therefore$ by given condition that

$$AP = |x_1|$$

$$\Rightarrow \sqrt{(x_1-3)^2+(y_1-0)^2} = |x_1|$$

$\therefore$ squaring on both sides we get

$$(x_1 - 3)^2 + y_1^2 = x_1^2$$

$$x_1^2 + 9 - 6x_1 + y_1^2 = x_1^2$$

$$\therefore \quad y_1^2 - 6x_1 + 9 = 0$$

$\therefore$ locus of (x_1, y_1) is $y^2 - 6x + 9 = 0$

6. Find the locus of P, if the distance of P from (0, 3) is twice the distance of (0, –3).

Sol. Let A = (0, 3) B = (0, –3)

and Let $P(x_1, y_1)$ be any point on locus by given condition

PA = 2 PB

$$\therefore \quad \sqrt{(x_1-0)^2+(y_1-3)^2} = 2\sqrt{(x_1-0)^2+(y_1+3)^2}$$

$$\therefore \quad x_1^2 + (y_1-3)^2 = 4\left(x_1^2 + (y_1+3)^2\right)$$

$$\therefore \quad 3x^2 + 3y_1^2 + 30y_1 + 27 = 0$$

$$\therefore \quad x_1^2 + y_1^2 + 10y_1 + 9 = 0$$

$\therefore$ locus os $(x_1\ y_1)$ is $x^2 + y^2 + 10y + 9 = 0$

7. If the distance from P to the points (5, –4), (7, 6) are in the ratio 2 : 3 then find the locus of P.

Sol. Let A = (5, –4), B = (7, 6)

Let P = (x_1, y_1) be any point on the locus

by given condition $\dfrac{PA}{PB} = \dfrac{2}{3}$

$$\therefore \quad \frac{\sqrt{(x_1-5)^2+(y_1+4)^2}}{\sqrt{(x_1-7)^2+(y_1-6)^2}} = \frac{2}{3}$$

$\Rightarrow (5x_1 - 2y_1 - 37)(5x_1 - 2y_1 - 1) = 0$

required locus is

$$(5x - 2y - 37)(5x - 2y - 1) = 0$$

$$\Rightarrow \quad 25x^2 - 20xy + 4y^2 - 190x + 76y + 37 = 0$$

12. A = (2, 3), B = (2, −3) are two points. If P is a point such that PA + PB = 6 then find the locus of P.

Sol. Let $P(x_1, y_1)$ be any point on locus

given condition is PA + PB = 6

$$\sqrt{(x_1-2)^2+(y_1-3)^2}+\sqrt{(x_1-2)^2+(y_1+3)^2}=6$$

$$\sqrt{(x_1-2)^2+(y_1-3)^2}=6-\sqrt{(x_1-2)^2+(y_1+3)^2}$$

squaring on both sides, we get

$$(x_1-2)^2+(y_1-3)^2=36+(x_1-2)^2+(y_1+3)^2-12\sqrt{(x_1-2)^2+(y_1+3)^2}$$

$$(y_1-3)^2-(y_1+3)^2=36-12\sqrt{(x_1-2)^2+(y_1+3)^2}$$

$$\Rightarrow \quad -4(3)y_1-36=-12\sqrt{(x_1-2)^2+(y_1+3)^2}$$

$$\Rightarrow \quad 3y_1+9=3\sqrt{(x_1-2)^2+(y_1+3)^2}$$

$$\Rightarrow (y_1+3)^2=(x_1-2)^2+(y_1+3)^2$$

$$\Rightarrow \quad y_1^2+9+6y_1=x_1^2+4-4x_1+y_1^2+9+6y_1$$

$$y_1^2+9-6y_1=x_1^2+4-4x_1+y_1^2+9+6y_1$$

$$\Rightarrow \quad x_1^2-4x_1+4=0$$

locus of (x_1, y_1) is

$$x^2-4x+4=0$$

13. An iron rod of length 2l is sliding on two mutually perpendicular lines. Find the locus of mid point of rod.

Sol. Let the two mutually perpendicular lines be the coordinate axes.

Let A = (a, 0), B = (0, b) be end of rod.

$$5x - 2y = 37 \text{ or } 5x - 2y = 1$$

$\therefore$ required locus is

$$(5x - 2y - 37)(5x - 2y - 1) = 0$$

$$\Rightarrow \quad 25x^2 - 20xy + 4y^2 - 190x + 76y + 37 = 0$$

12. A = (2, 3), B = (2, –3) are two points. If P is a point such that PA + PB = 6 then find the locus of P.

Sol. Let $P(x_1, y_1)$ be any point on locus

given condition is PA + PB = 6

$$\therefore \sqrt{(x_1 - 2)^2 + y_1 - 3)^2} + \sqrt{(x_1 - 2)^2 + (y_1 + 3)^2} = 6$$

$$\therefore \sqrt{(x_1 - 2)^2 + y_1 - 3)^2} = 6 - \sqrt{(x_1 - 2)^2 + (y_1 + 3)^2}$$

squaring on both sides, we get

$$(x_1 - 2)^2 + (y_1 - 3)^2 = 36 + (x_1 - 2)^2 + (y_1 + 3)^2 - 12\sqrt{(x_1 - 2)^2 + (y_1 - 3)^2}$$

$$\Rightarrow \quad (y_1 - 3)^2 - (y_1 + 3)^2 - 36 = -12\sqrt{(x_1 - 2)^2 + (y_1 + 3)^2}$$

$$\Rightarrow \quad -4(3)\, y_1 - 36 = -12\sqrt{(x_1 - 2)^2 + (y_1 + 3)^2}$$

$$\Rightarrow \quad 3y_1 + 9 = 3\sqrt{(x_1 - 2)^2 + (y_1 + 3)^2}$$

$$\Rightarrow (y_1 + 3)^2 = (x_1 - 2)^2 + (y_1 + 3)^2$$

$$\Rightarrow \quad y_1^2 + 9 + 6y_1 = \{x_1^2 + 4 - 4x_1 + y_1^2 + 9 + 6y_1\}$$

$$y_1^2 + 9 - 6y_1 = x_1^2 + 4 - 4x_1 + y_1^2 + 9 + 6y_1$$

$$\Rightarrow \quad x_1^2 - 4x_1 + 4 = 0$$

locus of (x_1, y_1) is

$$x^2 - 4x + 4 = 0$$

13. An iron rod of length 2l is sliding on two mutually perpendicular lines. Find the locus of mid point of rod.

Sol. Let the two mutually perpendicular lines be the coordinate axes.

Let A = (a, 0), B = (0, b) be end of rod.

Let $P(x_1\ y_1)$ be mid point of AB whose length is $2l$

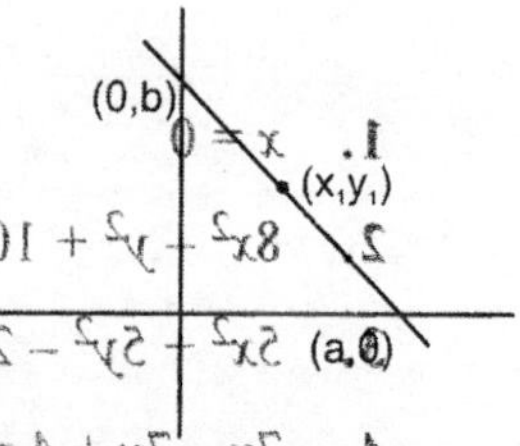

$$\therefore \quad (x_1\ y_1) = \left(\frac{a}{2}, \frac{b}{2}\right)$$

$$\Rightarrow \quad a = 2x_1,\ b = 2y_1$$

$$\therefore \quad A = (2x_1, 0)\ B = (0, 2y_1)$$

$$AB = l \quad \Rightarrow \quad AB^2 = 4l^2$$

$$\Rightarrow \quad 4x^2 + 4y^2 = 4l^2$$

locus is $x^2 + y^2 = l^2$

Exercise - 13.1

1. Find the equation to the locus of the point which is equi-distance from the points (–3, 4), (3, 4)
2. Find the equation of locus of point P from which the distance to (0, 5) is trible the distance from P to y-axis.
3. If the distance from P to the points (2, 3), (2, –3) are in the ratio 2 : 3 then find the locus of P.
4. A = (1, 2), B = (2, –3), C = (–2, 3) are three points. A point P moves such that $(PA)^2 + (PB)^2 = 2(PC)^2$. Find the locus of P.
5. The ends of the hypotenuse of a right angled triangle are (0, 6), (6, 0). Find the locus of the third vertex.
6. Find the locus of P such that the area of ΔPAB is 12 square units where A = (2, 3) and B = (–4, 5)
7. A = (2, 1), B = (1, 2) are two points. If P is a point such that PA = 2PB, then find the locus of P.
8. A = (2, 0), B = (4, 0) are two points. Find the locus of P such that

   $(PA)^2 + (PB)^2 = 10$.
9. Find the locus of point which is at distance 5 units from (–3, 4)
10. A = (2, 0), B = (–2, 0) are two points. Find the locus of P which moves such that PA – PB – 2 .

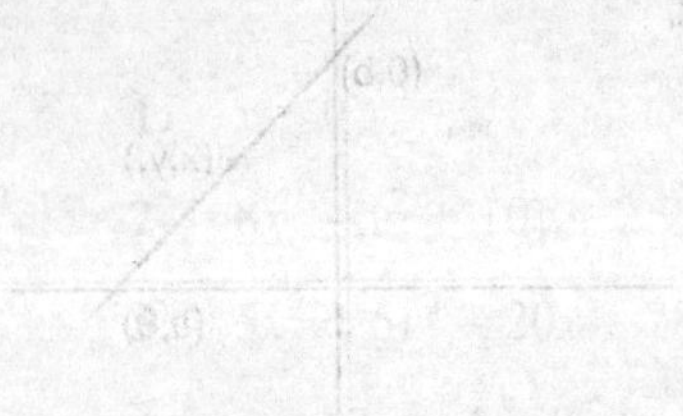

Let $P(x_1, y_1)$ be mid point of AB whose length is 2l.

$$(x_1, y_1) = \left(\frac{a}{2}, \frac{b}{2}\right)$$

$\Rightarrow \quad a = 2x_1, b = 2y_1$

$A = (2x_1, 0)\ B = (0, 2y_1)$

$AB = 2l \quad \Rightarrow \quad AB^2 = 4l^2$

$\Rightarrow \quad 4x_1^2 + 4y_1^2 = 4l^2$

locus is $x^2 + y^2 = l^2$

Exercise - 13.1

1. Find the equation to the locus of the point which is equi-distance from the points (−3, 4), (3, 4)

2. Find the equation of locus of point P from which the distance to (0, 5) is triple the distance from P to y-axis.

3. If the distance from P to the points (2, 3), (2, −3) are in the ratio 2 : 3 then find the locus of P

4. A = (1, 2), B = (2, −3), C = (−2, 3) are three points. A point P moves such that $(PA)^2 + (PB)^2 = 2(PC)^2$. Find the locus of P.

5. The ends of the hypotenuse of a right angled triangle are (0, 6), (6, 0). Find the locus of the third vertex.

6. Find the locus of P such that the area of ΔPAB is 12 square units where A = (2, 3) and B = (−4, 5)

7. A = (2, 1), B = (1, 2) are two points. If P is a point such that PA = 2PB, then find the locus of P

8. A = (2, 0), B = (4, 0) are two points. Find the locus of P such that $(PA)^2 + (PB)^2 = 16$

9. Find the locus of point which is at distance 5 units from (−3, 4)

10. A = (2, 0), B = (−2, 0) are two points. Find the locus of P which moves such that PA − PB = 2.

14

Straight Lines

Remember that: If A, B are any two points ... then

14.1 Inclination of a Line

14.2 Slope of a Line

Note

(i) If slopes of any two non vertical lines are equal then they are parallel.

($\because$ parallel line makes equal angle with x-axis of positive direction)

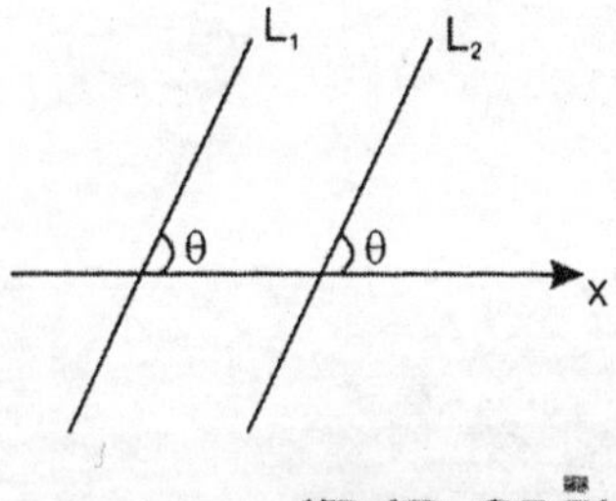

(ii) Two non vertical lines are perpendicular then the product of their slopes is –1.

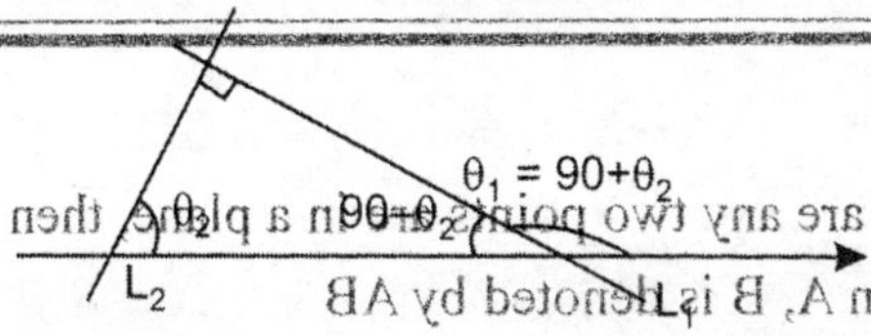

($\because$ suppose θ_1, θ_2, be inclinations and m_1, m_2 be slopes of two non vertical lines respectively.

$\therefore \quad m_1 = \tan\theta_1, \; m_2 = \tan\theta_2$

The lines are perpendicular $\Leftrightarrow \theta_1 = 90 + \theta_2$ (from fig)

$\therefore \quad \tan\theta_1 = \tan(90 + \theta_2) = -\cot\theta_2$

then $\tan\theta_1 \tan\theta_2 = -1$ Or $m_1 m_2 = -1$

$\tan\theta_1 \tan\theta_2 = -1 \;\Rightarrow\; m_1 m_2 = -1$

(iii) Slope of x-axis is 0, y-axis is not defined. (∞)

(iv) Equation of x-axis is $y = 0$

(v) Equation of y-axis is $x = 0$

(vi) Equation of line parallel to x-axis (horizontal line) and passing through (x_1, y_1) is $y = y_1$.

(vii) Equation of line parallel to y-axis and passing through (x_1, y_1) is $x = x_1$.

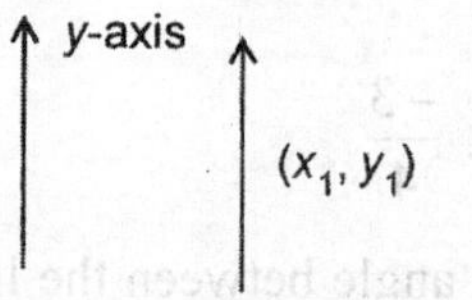

Ex : Find the equation of lines parallel to x and y-axis and passing through (1, 2).

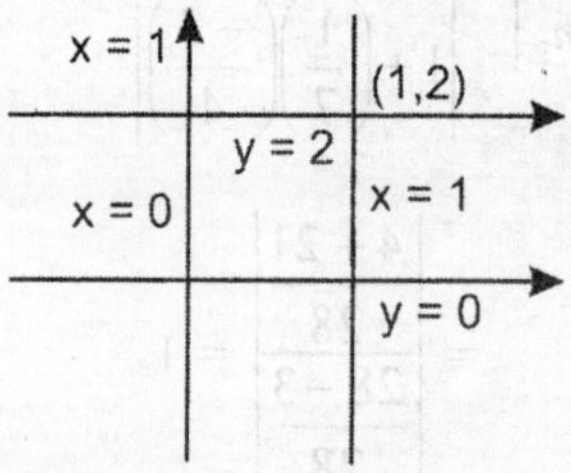

Sol. The equation of line parallel to x-axis and passing through (1, 2) is $y = 2$.

The equation of line parallel to y-axis and passing through (1, 2) is $x = 1$

(viii) Slope of line joining the two points $A = (x_1, y_1)$, $B = (x_2, y_2)$ is $\frac{y_2 - y_1}{x_2 - x_1}$

Ex : Slope of line joining of (1, 2) (3, 4) is $\frac{4-2}{3-1} = \frac{2}{2} = 1$

Theorem If θ is angle between two non vertical lines having slopes m_1, m_2 respectively

then $\tan\theta = \pm\left(\frac{m_1 - m_2}{1 + m_1 m_2}\right)$

Proof Let θ_1, θ_2 be the inclinations of two lines having slopes m_1, m_2 respectively.

$\therefore \tan\theta_1 = m_1 \quad \tan\theta_2 = m_2$

From diagram $\theta_2 + \theta = \theta_1$ (sum of two interior angles of triangle is equal to exterian angle).

$\therefore \theta = \theta_1 - \theta_2$

$\therefore \tan\theta = \tan(\theta_1 - \theta_2)$

$$\tan\theta = \frac{\tan\theta_1 - \tan\theta_2}{1 + \tan\theta_1 \tan\theta_2} = \frac{m_1 - m_2}{1 + m_1 m_2}$$

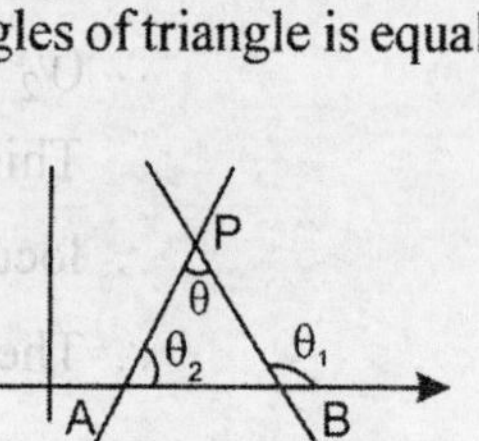

Note If θ is acute angle between lines having slopes m_1, m_2 then

$$\tan\theta = \left|\frac{m_1 - m_2}{1 + m_1 m_2}\right|$$

Ex : Find the acute angle between the lines having slopes $\frac{1}{7}$ and $= \frac{-3}{4}$

Sol. Let $m_1 = \frac{1}{7}$, $m_2 = \frac{-3}{4}$

Let θ be the acute angle between the lines

$$\therefore \tan\theta = \left|\frac{m_1 - m_2}{1 + m_1 m_2}\right| = \left|\frac{\frac{1}{7} - \left(\frac{-3}{4}\right)}{1 + \left(\frac{1}{7}\right)\left(\frac{-3}{4}\right)}\right|$$

$$= \left|\frac{\frac{4+21}{28}}{\frac{28-3}{28}}\right| = 1$$

$\therefore \theta = 45^\circ$

14.3 Equation of Straight Lines in Different Forms

Slope - point form

Theorem The equation of straight line passing through $P(x_1, y_1)$ and having slope m is $y - y_1 = m(x - x_1)$

Proof Let $P(x_2, y_2)$ be any point on line passing through given point $A(x_1, y_1)$

$$\therefore \text{ slope of line} = \frac{y_2 - y_1}{x_2 - x_1}$$

$$= m \quad \text{(given)}$$

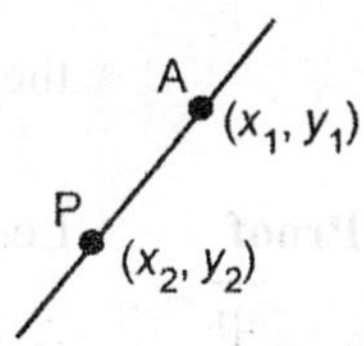

$$\therefore \frac{y_2 - y_1}{x_2 - x_1} = m$$

$$\therefore (y_2 - y_1) = m(x_2 - x_1)$$

This condition is satisfied for any point (x_2, y_2) on the line

$\therefore$ locus of (x_2, y_2) is $(y - y_1) = m(x - x_1)$

$\therefore$ The required equation of straight line is $y - y_1 = m(x - x_1)$

Ex : Find equation of straight line passing through (1, 2) having slope $\frac{1}{2}$

Sol : Given point $= (x_1\ y_1) = (1, 2)$; and slope $m = \frac{1}{2}$

$\therefore$ Required equation

$$y - 2 = \frac{1}{2}(x - 1)$$

$$2(y - 2) = (x - 1) \Rightarrow x - 2y + 3 = 0$$

2. Find the equation of straight line passing through (1, 0) having slope –1.

Sol. Let P = (x_1, y_1) = (1, 0), m = –1

$$y - 0 = -1(x - 1)$$

$$\Rightarrow y = -x + 1 \quad \therefore \quad x + y = 1$$

3. Find the equation of line passing through (0, 0) and having slope m.

Sol. P_1 = (0, 0) = (x_1, y_1) and slope = m

$\therefore y - 0 = m(x - 0) \Rightarrow y = mx$ is equation of required line

Note

The equation of line is of the form $ax + by + c = 0$ where a, b, c are real numbers such that at least one of a, b is non zero.

So, $ax + by + c = 0$ represents an equation of straight line.

2. Two Point form

Theorem The equation of straight line passing through (x_1, y_1), (x_2, y_2) is

$$(y - y_1)(x_2 - x_1) = (x - x_1)(y_2 - y_1)$$

Proof Let A = (x_1, y_1), B = (x_2, y_2)

$$\therefore \text{ Slope of line } \overleftrightarrow{AB} = \frac{y_2 - y_1}{x_2 - x_1} = m$$

$\therefore$ equation of $\overleftrightarrow{AB}$ is $y - y_1 = m(x - x_1)$ ($\because$ by slope point form)

$$\therefore y - y_1 = \frac{y_2 - y_1}{x_2 - x_1}(x - x_1)$$

$$\therefore (y - y_1)(x_2 - x_1) = (y_2 - y_1)(x - x_1)$$

Note : (i) If $x_1 = x_2$ slope of the line is not defined

$\therefore$ it is vertical line and its equation is $x - x_1 = 0$.

(ii) From above two forms, we conclude that to write an equation of line we need one point on it and the slope of line (or) two points on the line. Suppose one point (x_1, y_1) on line, slope m is given use $y - y_1 = m(x - x_1)$.

Suppose two points are given on the line then find m = $\frac{y_2 - y_1}{x_2 - x_1}$ and write equation of line $y - y_1 = m(x - x_1)$

(iii) Parallel lines have same slope (m) and product of perpendicular lines is −1.

(iv) A, B, C are three points on a line (collinear) then

slope of AB = slope of BC = slope of CA.

Solved Examples on Form - 1, Form - 2

(i.e., Slope point form, Two point form)

1. Find the equation of the line passing through the point

(i) (1, 1) having slope 4

(ii) (2, 3) having inclination 135°

(iii) (−1, 4) having inclination 60°

(iv) (1, 2) and parallel to x-axis

(v) (3, −1) and parallel to y-axis

Sol. (i) Let A = (x_1, y_1) = (1, 1) and slope m = 4.

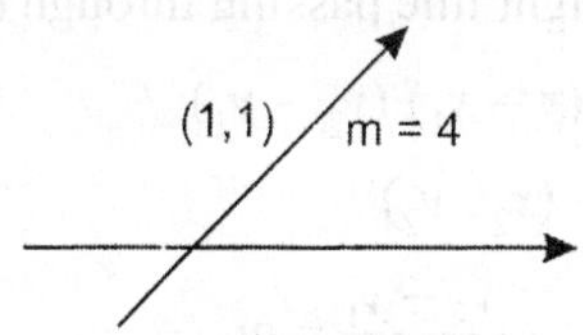

we know that the equation of line passing through (1, 1) and slope m is

$y - y_1 = m(x - x_1)$

$\therefore \quad y - 1 = 4(x - 1) \quad \Rightarrow \quad 4x - y - 3 = 0$

(ii) Inclination of given line is 135°

$\therefore$ slope of line m = tan 135° = −1 $\quad (\because \tan(90 + 45^\circ) = -\cot 45^\circ = -1)$

and a point on line is $(2, 3) = (x_1, y_1)$

$\therefore$ Equation of line is $y - y_1 = m(x - x_1)$

$\therefore y - 3 = -1(x - 2)$

$\Rightarrow x + y = +5 \quad \Rightarrow \quad x + y - 5 = 0$

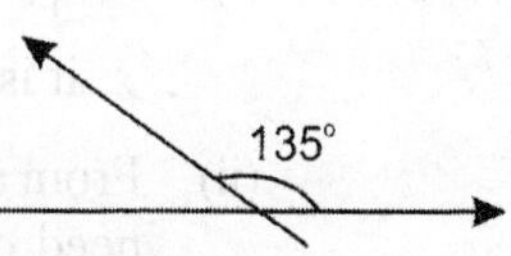

(iii) $m = \tan 60^0 = \sqrt{3} \quad (x_1, y_1) = (-1, 4)$

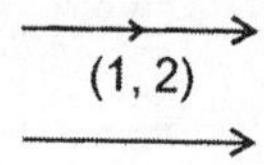

equation of line is $y - 4 = \sqrt{3}\,(x - (-1))$

$$\Rightarrow \quad y - 4 = \sqrt{3}\,x + \sqrt{3}$$

$$\therefore \quad \sqrt{3}x - y + 4 + \sqrt{3} = 0$$

(iv) Here the line parallel to x - axis, also it is passing through the point $(1, 2)$

$\therefore$ its slope $= 0$, also it is passing through the point $(1, 2)$

$\therefore$ Required equation of line is $y - 2 = 0(x - 1)$

$$\therefore y - 2 = 0$$

(v) Here the line parallel to y - axis, its slope is not defined and it is passing through the point $(3, -1) = (x_1\, y_1)$.

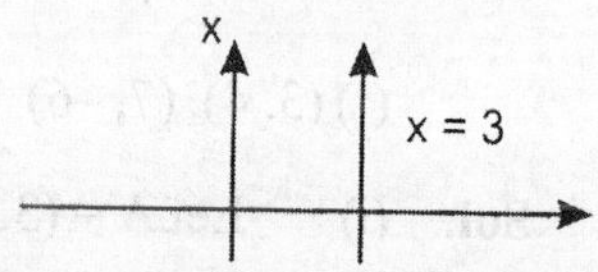

$\therefore$ the equation of line is $x = x_1$ i.e $x = 3$

(or) we can write $y - (-1) = \infty\ (x - 3)$

$$y + 1 = \frac{1}{0}(x - 3) \quad \text{i.e } x = 3$$

2. (a) Find the value of x if the slope of line joining $(2, 5)\ (x, 3)$ is 2.

(b) Find the value of y if the line joining $(3, y)\ (2, 7)$. is parallel to the line joining $(-1, 4), (0, 6)$.

(c) Find the slope of lines (i) parallel to and (ii) perpendicular to the line joining $(6, 3), (-4, 5)$.

Sol. (a) Let $A = (2, 5) = (x_1\, y_1)$, $\quad B = (x, 3) = (x_2\, y_2)$

$\therefore$ Slope of line $\overleftrightarrow{AB}$ is $\dfrac{y_2 - y_1}{x_2 - x_1} = \dfrac{3-5}{x-2} = 2$ (given)

$$\therefore \frac{3-5}{x-2} = 2 \quad \Rightarrow \quad \frac{-2}{x-2} = 2 \quad \Rightarrow \quad -1 = x - 2 \quad \Rightarrow \quad x = 1$$

(b) we know that two lines are parallel if their slopes are equal.

$\therefore$ slope of line joining of $(3, y)\ (2, 7) =$ slope of line joining of $(-1, 4)\ (0, 6)$.

$$\therefore \frac{7-y}{2-3} = \frac{6-4}{0-(-1)} \Rightarrow \frac{7-y}{-1} = \frac{2}{1} \Rightarrow 7 - y = -2$$

$$\Rightarrow \quad y = 9$$

(c) Slope of line joining the two given points A(6, 3), B(–4, 5) is

$$\frac{5-3}{-4-6} = \frac{2}{-10} = \frac{-1}{5} = m$$

$\therefore$ slope of any line parallel to line $\overleftrightarrow{AB}$ is $m = \frac{-1}{5}$ (parallel lines have same slope) again slope of any line perpendicular to line $\overleftrightarrow{AB}$ is $m = \frac{-1}{m} = \frac{-1}{\left(-\frac{1}{5}\right)} = 5$

$(\because mm^1 = -1)$

$\therefore$ the required slopes are $\frac{-1}{5}, 5$

3. Find the equation of line passing through the two points.

(i) (3, 4), (7, –6) (ii) $((at_1^2, 2at_1), (at_2^2, 2at_2))$

Sol. (i) Let A = (3, 4) B = (7, –6)

slope of line $\overleftrightarrow{AB}$ is $\frac{-6-4}{7-3} = \frac{-10}{4} = \frac{-5}{2}$

$\therefore$ equation of $\overleftrightarrow{AB}$ is $y - 4 = \frac{-5}{2}(x-3)$

$\therefore \quad 2(y-4) = -5(x-3)$

$\therefore \quad 5x + 2y - 23 = 0$

(ii) Let $A = (at_1^2, 2at_1) B = (at_2^2, 2at_2)$

$$\text{Slope of } \overleftrightarrow{AB} = \frac{2at_2 - 2at_1}{at_2^2 - at_1^2} = \frac{2a(t_2-t_1)}{a(t_2^2 - t_1^2)} = \frac{2}{t_1+t_2}$$

$\therefore$ Equation of line is $\quad y - 2at_1 = \frac{2}{t_1+t_2}(x - at_1^2)$

$\therefore (y - 2at_1)(t_1 + t_2) = y^2(x - at_1^2)$

$\therefore y(t_1 + t_2) - 2at_1^2 - 2at_1 t_2 = 2x - 2at_1^2$

$\therefore y(t_1 + t_2) = 2(x + at_1 t_2)$

4. Find the equation of straight line passing through A(–1, 3) and (i) Parallel to (ii) Perpendicular to the line passing through the points B(2, –5) and C(4, 6).

Sol. Given A = (–1, 3)

B = (2, –5)

C = (4, 6)

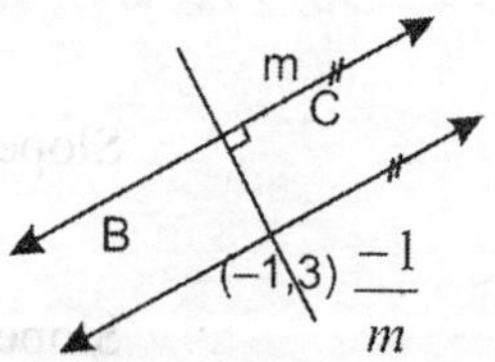

$$\text{Slope of BC} = \frac{6+5}{4-2} = \frac{11}{2} = m$$

(i) The equation of line passing through A(–1, 3) and parallel to $\overleftrightarrow{BC}$ is $y - 3 = m(x + 1)$ ($\because$ parallel lines have same slope)

$$y - 3 = \frac{11}{2}(x+1) \Rightarrow 11x - 2y + 17 = 0$$

(ii) Equation of line passing through A (–1, 3) amd perpendicular to $\overleftrightarrow{BC}$ is

$$y - 3 = \frac{-1}{m}(x+1) \quad (\because \text{product slopes of lines} = -1)$$

$$\therefore \quad y - 3 = \frac{-2}{11}(x+1)$$

$$2x + 11y - 31 = 0$$

5. Show that the points are collinear and find the equation of line through the points.

(i) (–5, 1), (5, 5), (10, 7) (ii) (a, b + c), (b, c + a), (c, a + b)

Sol. (i) Let A = (–5, 1), B = (5, 5), C = (10, 7)

$$\text{Slope of } \overleftrightarrow{AB} = \frac{5-1}{5+5} = \frac{4}{10} = \frac{2}{5}$$

$$\text{Slope of } \overleftrightarrow{BC} = \frac{7-5}{10-5} = \frac{2}{5}$$

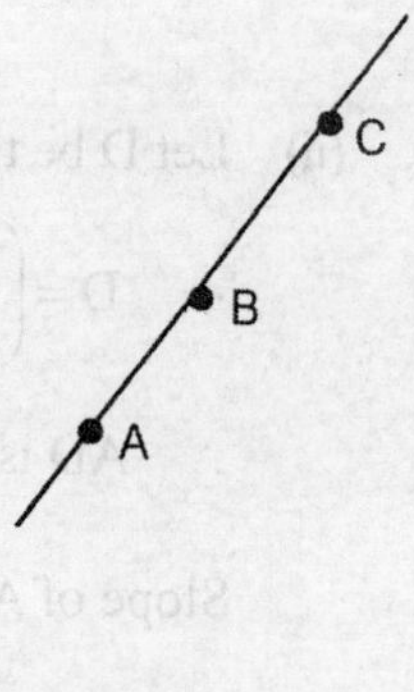

$\therefore$ Slope of $\overleftrightarrow{AB}$ = slope of $\overleftrightarrow{BC}$

$\therefore$ A, B, C are collinear

Also equation of line is $y - 1 = \frac{2}{5}(x+5)$

$$5y - 5 = 2x + 10 \Rightarrow 2x - 5y + 15 = 0$$

(ii) Let A = (a, b + c), B = (b, c + a), = C = (c, a + b)

$$\text{Slope of } \overleftrightarrow{AB} = \frac{(c+a)-(b+c)}{b-a} = \frac{a-b}{b-a} = -1$$

$$\text{Slope of } \overleftrightarrow{BC} = \frac{(a+b)-(c+a)}{c-b} = \frac{b-c}{c-b} = -1$$

∴ Slope of $\overleftrightarrow{AB}$ = Slope of $\overleftrightarrow{BC}$

∴ A, B, C are collinear

Also equation of line is $y-(b+c) = -1\,(x-a)$

$$y-(b+c) = -x+a$$

$$x+y = a+b+c$$

6. A = (10, 4), B = (–4, 9), C = (–2, –1) are the vertices of a triangle. Find the equation of

(i) $\overleftrightarrow{AB}$

(ii) median through A

(iii) the altitude through B

(iv) the perpendicular bisector of the side of the triangle

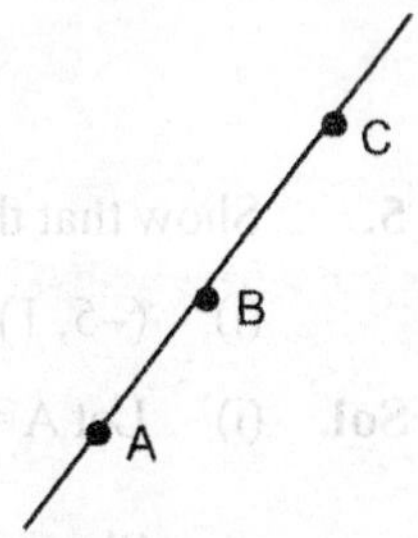

Sol. Given A = (10, 4) B = (–4, 9) C = (–2, –1)

(i) $\text{Slope of } \overleftrightarrow{AB} = \frac{9-4}{-4-10} = \frac{5}{-14}$

equation of $\overleftrightarrow{AB}$ is $y-4 = \frac{-5}{14}(x-10)$

$$14y-56 = -5x+50 \quad \Rightarrow \quad 5x+14y = 106$$

(ii) Let D be the mid point of BC

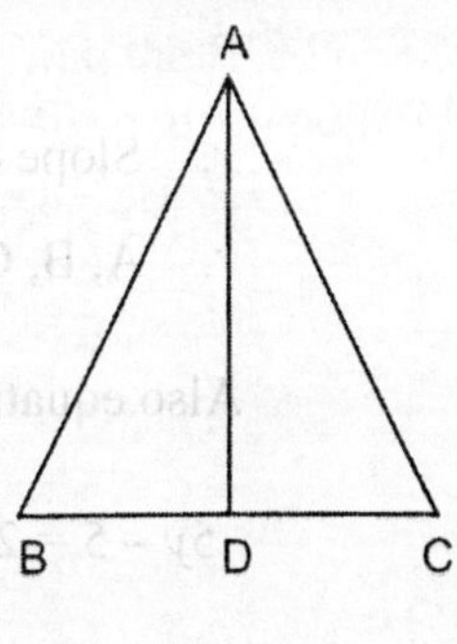

$$\therefore \quad D = \left(\frac{(-4)+(-2)}{2}; \frac{9+(-1)}{2}\right) = (-3,4)$$

∴ AD is median ; A = (10, 4)

$$\text{Slope of AD} = \frac{4-4}{10+3} = 0$$

equation of AD is $y-4 = 0\,(x-10)$

∴ $y = 4$

(iii) Slope of $\overleftrightarrow{AC} = \dfrac{-1-4}{-2-10} = \dfrac{-5}{-12} = \dfrac{5}{12}$

Slope of Altitude $\overleftrightarrow{BE} = \dfrac{-12}{5}$ $\quad\left(\because \overleftrightarrow{AC} \perp r\ \overleftrightarrow{BE}\right)$

$\therefore$ Equation of $\overleftrightarrow{BE}$ is $y-9 = \left(\dfrac{-12}{5}\right)(x+4)$

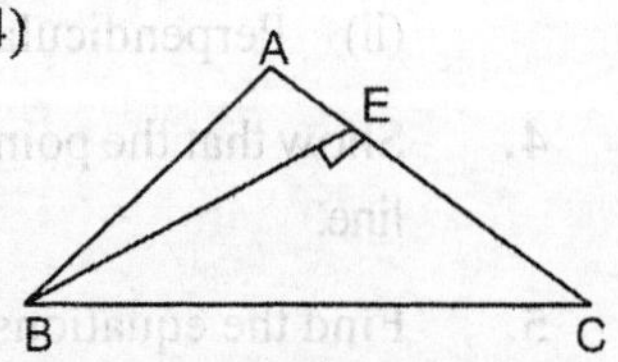

$\therefore \quad 5y - 45 = -12x - 48$

$\therefore \quad 12x + 5y = -3$ (or) $12x + 5y + 3 = 0$

(iv) Slope of $\overleftrightarrow{AB} = \dfrac{9-4}{-4-10} = \dfrac{5}{-14}$

mid point of AB = F = $\left(\dfrac{10-4}{2}, \dfrac{4+9}{2}\right)$

$= \left(3, \dfrac{13}{2}\right)$

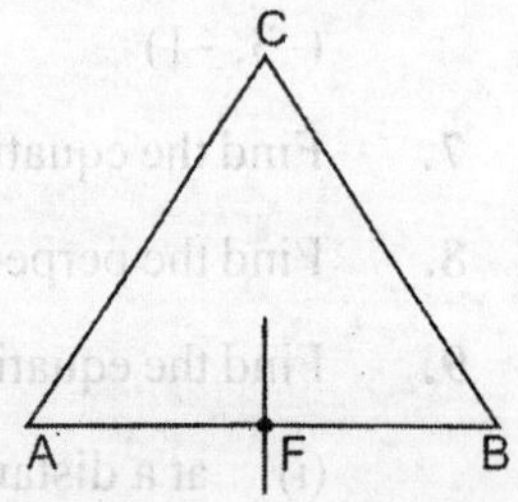

$\therefore$ Equation of perpendicular bisector of AB is

$$y - \frac{13}{2} = \frac{-1}{\left(\frac{-5}{14}\right)}(x-3)$$

$$y - \frac{13}{2} = \frac{14}{5}(x-3)$$

$$\frac{2y-13}{2} = \frac{14(x-2)}{5}$$

$\Rightarrow \quad 10y - 65 = 28x - 84$

$\therefore \quad 28x - 10y - 19 = 0$

Exercise - 14.1

1. Find the slope of line passing through the points.

(i) (1, 2), (3, 4) (ii) (3, 4), (7, –6) (iii) (p, q), (–r, –s)

2. Find the equation of line passing through the point

(i) (1, 2) and having inclination $\dfrac{\pi}{3}$

(ii) (3, –2) and having inclination 135^0

(iii) (–2, –1) and having inclination 150^0

3. Find the equations of straight lines passing through (1, 3).

(i) Parallel to

(ii) Perpendicular to the line passing through the points (3, –5) and (–6, 1)

4. Show that the points (1, 3), (–2, –6), (2, 6) lie on a line and find the equation of the line.

5. Find the equations of sides of the triangle with vertices (2, 1), (–5, 7), (–5, –5).

6. Find the equations of the medians of the triangle with vertices (1, –1), (–1, 2), (–3, –1)

7. Find the equations of altitudes of the triangle with vertices (3, –5), (–5 –4) (7, 10)

8. Find the perpendicular bisector of the line segment joining the points (5, 7), (3, 1)

9. Find the equation of straight line parallel to *y*-axis

(i) at a distance 3 units from *y*-axis to the right of it.

(ii) at a distance 6 units of from *y*-axis to the left of it

Answers

1. (i) 1(ii) $\frac{-5}{2}$ (iii) $\frac{s+q}{p+r}$

2. (i) $x\sqrt{3}-y+(2-\sqrt{3})=0$ (ii) $x + y - 1 = 0$ (iii) $x+\sqrt{3}y+\sqrt{3}+2=0$

3. (i) $2x + 3y - 11 = 0$, $3x - 2y + 3 = 0$

4. $3x - y = 0$

5. $6x + 7y - 19 = 0$, $x = -5$, $6x - 7y = 5$

6. $(x + 2y + 1 = 0, x + 1 = 0, x - 2y + 1 = 0)$

7. $6x + 7y + 17 = 0$, $4x + 15y + 80 = 0$, $8x - y - 46 = 0$

8. $x + 3y - 16 = 0$

9. $x = 3$, $x = -6$

Intercepts of a line: If a line intersects x-axis and y-axis at A(a, 0), B = (0, b) respectively then a, b are called x-intercept and y intercept respectively.

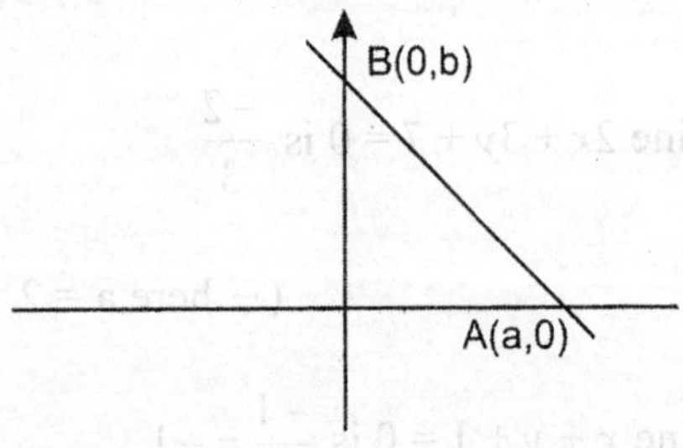

3. Slope-intercept form

Theorem The equation of the line having slope m and y-intercept is $y = mx + c$

Proof Since y intercept of line is c

$\therefore$ the line cuts y-axis at (0, c)

$\therefore$ the line passes through (0, c) and having slop

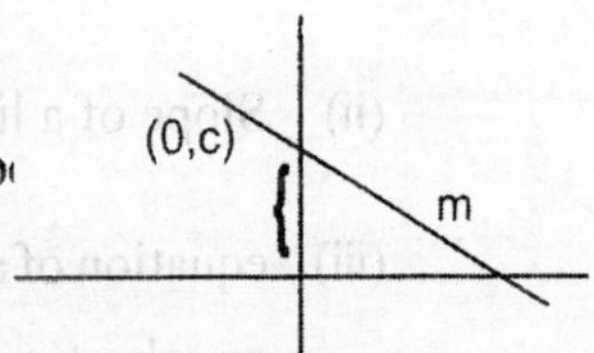

$\therefore$ the equation of line is $y - c = m(x - 0)$

$\therefore$ $y - c = mx$

$\Rightarrow$ $y = mx + c$

Corollaly:

1. Equation of straight line having slope m with x-intercept is $y - 0 = m(x - C)$
$y = m(x - c)$

Ex : (i) The equation of line having slope $\frac{4}{7}$ and with y-intercept 4 is

$$y = \frac{4x}{7} + 4 \Rightarrow 4x - 7y + 28 = 0. \qquad (\because y = m(x + c))$$

(ii) The equation of line having slope 6 and with x-intercept 2 is $y = 6(x - 2)$
$\Rightarrow 6x - y - 12 = 0.$ $\qquad (\because y = m(x + c))$

2. The slope of line $ax + by + c = 0$ is $\frac{-a}{b}$

The equation $ax + by + c = 0$ can be written in slope intercept form as
i.e., $by = -ax - c$

$$y = \left(\frac{-a}{b}\right)x + \left(\frac{-c}{b}\right)$$

It is of the form $y = mx + c$

$\therefore$ slope $m = \frac{-a}{b}$

Ex : (i) Slope of the line $2x + 3y + 7 = 0$ is $\frac{-2}{3}$

($\because$ here a = 2, b = 3 $\therefore$ $m = \frac{-a}{b} = \frac{-2}{3}$)

(ii) Slope of the line $x + y + 1 = 0$ is $\frac{-1}{1} = -1$

Note

(i) Slope of any line parallel to the line $ax + by + c = 0$ is $\frac{-a}{b}$

(ii) Slope of a line perpendicular to the line $ax + by + c = 0$ is $\frac{b}{a}$

(iii) equation of any line parallel to the given line

$ax + by + c = 0$ is $ax + by + k = 0$. (equations are only differ by constant)

(iv) equation of any line perpendicular to the line $ax + by + c = 0$ is

$bx - ay + k = 0$.

4. Intercept form

Theorem The equation of the line having x-intercept a($\neq 0$) and y intercept b($\neq 0$) is

$$\frac{x}{a} + \frac{y}{b} = 1$$

Proof Since x-intercept of line is a then the line intersect x-axis at A(a, 0) and y intercept of line is b then the line intersects y-axis at B(0, b).

Slope of AB $= \frac{b-0}{0-a} = \frac{-b}{a}$

$\therefore$ Equation of line is $y - 0 = \frac{-b}{a}(x - a)$

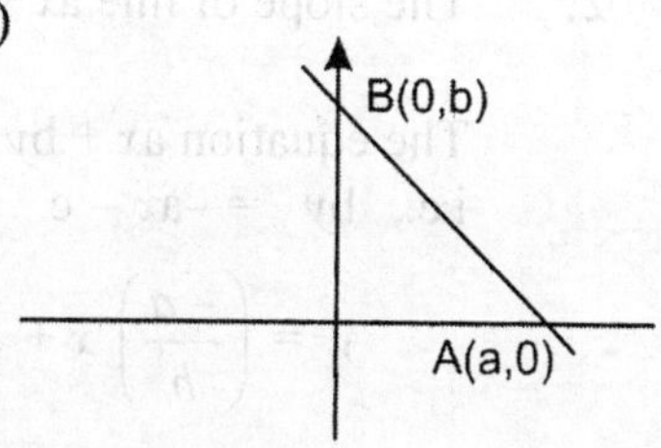

$\Rightarrow \quad y = \frac{-b}{a}(x - a)$

$\Rightarrow \quad \frac{y}{b} = -\frac{1}{a}(x-a) = \frac{-x}{a} + 1$

$$\therefore \quad \frac{x}{a}+\frac{y}{b}=1$$

Note :

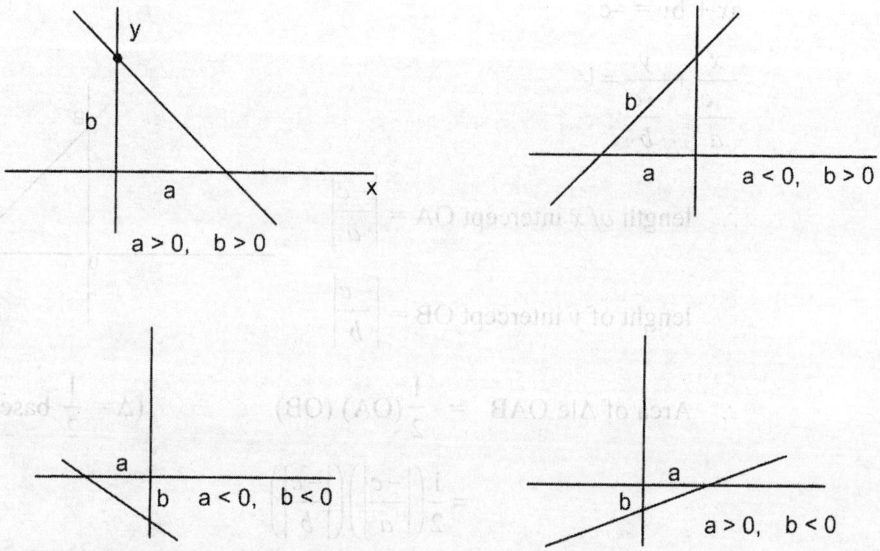

The figure $\frac{x}{a}+\frac{y}{b}=1$ is as follows :

(i)

***Corollary* 1:** The intercept of the line $ax + by + c = 0$ $a \neq 0, b \neq 0$ are $\frac{-c}{a}, \frac{-c}{b}$

The equation $ax + by + c = 0$ can be written as

$$ax + by = -c$$

$$\therefore \quad \frac{x}{\frac{-c}{a}}+\frac{y}{\frac{-c}{b}}=1$$

$\therefore$ x-intercept $= -\frac{c}{a}$, y-intercept $= -\frac{c}{b}$

Ex : Equation of line having x-intercept 3, y - intercepts 5 is $\frac{x}{3}+\frac{y}{5}=1$

$$\Rightarrow 5x + 3y = 15$$

(2). Area of triangle formed by the line ax + by + c = 0 is $\dfrac{c^2}{2|ab|}$

Proof ax + by + c = 0 can be written as

$$ax + by = -c$$

$$\frac{x}{\frac{-c}{a}} + \frac{y}{\frac{-c}{b}} = 1$$

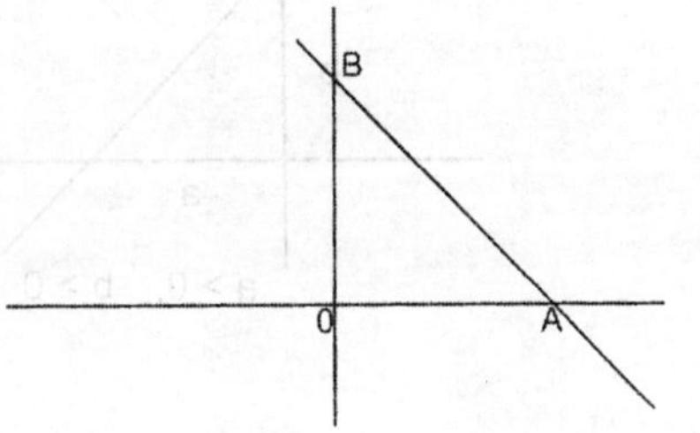

$\therefore$ length of x intercept OA = $\left|\dfrac{-c}{a}\right|$

lenght of y intercept OB = $\left|\dfrac{-c}{b}\right|$

$\therefore$ Area of Δle OAB $= \dfrac{1}{2}$(OA) (OB) $\quad (\Delta = \dfrac{1}{2}$ base × height)

$$= \frac{1}{2}\left(\left|\frac{-c}{a}\right|\right)\left(\left|\frac{-c}{b}\right|\right)$$

$$= \frac{1}{2}\frac{c^2}{|ab|}$$

Ex : (i) Area of triangle formed by the line $\dfrac{x}{2} + \dfrac{y}{3} = 1$ with coordinate axes is $\dfrac{1}{2} x$ $2 \times 3 = 3$ [since area of triangle formed by the line $\dfrac{x}{a} + \dfrac{y}{b} = 1$ with coordinate axes is $\dfrac{1}{2}$ |ab|.]

(ii) Area of the triangle formed by the line $2x + 6y - 4 = 0$ with coordinate axes

$\dfrac{(-4)^2}{2|2.6|} = \dfrac{16}{2.2.6} = \dfrac{4}{6} = \dfrac{2}{3}$ $\quad$ ($\because$ required area $= \dfrac{c^2}{2|ab|}$)

Solved Examples (based on slope intercept form, intercept form)

1. Find the equation of line having inclinations

(i) 45° and y-intercept -2 $\quad$ (ii) $\tan^{-1}\left(\dfrac{2}{3}\right)$ and y-intercept 3

Sol. (i) Slope of line m = tan45° = 1, and y-intercept (–2) equation of line is

$y = mx + c$

$= 1x + (-2)$

$= x - 2$

(ii) Slope of line $m = \tan\left(\tan^{-1}\frac{2}{3}\right) = \frac{2}{3}$ and y-intercept = 3

$\therefore$ equation of line is $y = \frac{2}{3}x + 3 \quad \Rightarrow \quad 2x - 3y + 9 = 0$

2. (i) Find the equation of straight line passing through (5, 4) and parallel to $2x + 3y + 7 = 0$.

(ii) Find the equation of line perpendicular to $5x - 3y + 1 = 0$ and passing through (4, –3).

Sol. **Method 1 :** Slope of given line $= \frac{-2}{3}$

$\therefore$ Slope of any line parallel to the line is $\frac{-2}{3}$

the equation of line parallel to $2x + 3y + 7 = 0$ and passing through (5, 4) is

$y - 4 = \frac{-2}{3}(x - 5)$

$\therefore \quad 3y - 4 . 3 = -2x + 10 \quad \Rightarrow \quad 2x + 3y = 22$

Method 2 : Equation of any line parallel to given line is of the form $2x + 3y + k = 0$ if it is passing through (5, 4) then

$20 + 12 + k = 0 \quad \Rightarrow \quad k = 22$

$\therefore \quad 2x + 3y - 22 = 0$

(ii) **Method 1:** Slope of the given line $-\left(\frac{5}{3}\right) = \frac{5}{3} = m$

$\therefore$ Slope of any line perpendicular to the given line $= \frac{-1}{m} = \frac{-1}{\left(\frac{5}{3}\right)} = -\frac{3}{5}$ the equation of line perpendicular to $5x - 3y + 1 = 0$ and passing throgh (4, –3) is

$y + 3 = \frac{-3}{5}(x - 4) \quad \Rightarrow \quad 5y + 15 = -3x + 12$

$\therefore \ 3x + 5y + 3 = 0$

Method 2 : Equation of any line perpendicular to line $5x - 3y + 1 = 0$ is of the form $-3x - 5y + k = 0$ $\qquad (bx - ay + k = 0)$

if it is passing through (4, –3) then

$$(-3)(4) - 5(-3) + k = 0$$

$$\therefore \quad -12 + 15 + k = 0$$

$$\therefore \quad k = -3$$

$$\therefore \quad -3x - 5y - 3 = 0 \quad \text{(or)} \quad 3x + 5y + 3 = 0$$

3. (i) Find the area of triangle formed by the coordinate axes and the line $2x - 4y - 7 = 0$

(ii) If the area of triangle formed by the straight lines $x = 0$, $y = 0$ (coordinate axes) and $3x + 4y = a$ $(a > 0)$ is 6 square units, find the value of a.

Sol. (i) we know that the area of triangle formed by the line $ax + by + c = 0$ with coordinate axes is $\dfrac{c^2}{2|ab|}$

Here given line is $2x - 4y - 7 = 0 \quad \Rightarrow \quad a = 2, b = -4, c = -7$

$$\therefore \quad \text{Area} = \frac{(-7)^2}{2|2 \times -4|} = \frac{49}{2 \times (-8)} = \frac{49}{16} \text{ sq. units.}$$

(ii) Given $\dfrac{c^2}{2|ab|} = 6$

$$\Rightarrow \quad \frac{(-a)^2}{2|3.4|} = 6$$

$$\Rightarrow \quad \frac{a^2}{24} = 6$$

$$\Rightarrow \quad a^2 = 6 \times 24 = 144$$

$$\therefore \quad a = 12$$

4. Find the equation of line having intercepts a, b on the axes such that $a + b = 5$, $ab = 6$.

Sol. The equation of line having intercepts a, b is $\dfrac{x}{a} + \dfrac{y}{b} = 1$

Given $a + b = 5$ ..... (i)

$$ab = 6$$

$$\Rightarrow \quad a = \frac{6}{b} \qquad \text{..... (ii)}$$

$$\frac{6}{b} + b = 5$$

$$6 + b^2 = 5b \qquad \text{(iii)}$$

$$\Rightarrow \quad b^2 - 5b + 6 = 0$$

$$\Rightarrow \quad b^2 - 3b - 2b + 6 = 0$$

$$\Rightarrow \quad b(b-3) - 2(b-3) = 0$$

$$\Rightarrow \quad b - 3 = 0 \text{ (or) } \quad b - 2 = 0$$

$$\Rightarrow \quad b = 3 \qquad b = 2$$

If $b = 3$ $a = 2$ (or) If $b = 2$ $a = 3$

($\because a + b = 5$) ($\because a + b = 5$)

$\therefore$ by intercept form

$$\frac{x}{2} + \frac{y}{3} = 1 \quad \text{(or)} \quad \frac{x}{3} + \frac{y}{2} = 1$$

$$\Rightarrow \quad 3x + 2y = 6 \Rightarrow \quad 2x + 3y = 6$$

5. Find the equation of straight line passing through the point.

(i) (–4, 5) and having equal intercepts.

(ii) (–2, 4) and having (non zero) intercepts whose sum is zero.

(iii) (3, –4) and having intercepts whose ratios is 2 : 3. Suppose the required equation of line is $\frac{x}{a} + \frac{y}{b} = 1$.

Sol. (i) since the intercepts are equal $a = b$

also the line passing through the point (–4, 5) substitute (–4, 5) in $\frac{x}{a} + \frac{y}{b} = 1$.

$$\therefore \quad \frac{-4}{a} + \frac{5}{b} = 1$$

$$\therefore \quad -4b + 5a = ab$$

$\therefore \quad -4a + 5a = a^2 \qquad (\because a = b)$

$\therefore \quad a^2 = a$

$\therefore \quad a = 1 \qquad (\because a = b)$

$\therefore \quad b = 1$

$\therefore$ Equation of line is $\frac{x}{1} + \frac{y}{1} = 1 \quad \therefore x + y = 1$

(ii) Sum of intercepts = 0

$\therefore a + b = 0 \qquad \therefore \quad a = -b$

also the line $\frac{x}{a} + \frac{y}{b} = 1$ passing through (–2, 4)

$\therefore \quad \frac{-2}{a} + \frac{4}{b} = 1$

$\therefore \quad -2b + 4a = ab$

$\therefore \quad -2(-a) + 4a = a(-a)$

$\therefore \quad 6a = -a^2$

$\therefore \quad a^2 + 6a = 0$

$\therefore \quad a(a + 6) = 0$

$\therefore \quad a = -6 \qquad (\because a \neq 0)$

$\therefore \quad b = 6$

$\therefore \quad \frac{x}{-6} + \frac{y}{6} = 1$

$\therefore \quad -x + y = 6$

$\therefore \quad x - y + 6 = 0$

(iii) Since the intercepts are in the ratio 2 : 3

$\therefore \quad \frac{a}{b} = \frac{2}{3} \qquad \therefore 3a = 2b$

$\Rightarrow \quad b = \frac{3}{2}a \qquad \text{..... (1)}$

and the line passing through the point (+3, –4)

$\therefore \quad \frac{3}{a} - \frac{4}{b} = 1 \qquad \Rightarrow \qquad 3b - 4a = ab$

$\therefore \quad 3\left(\frac{3}{2}a\right) - 4a = a\frac{3}{2}a \qquad \left(\because b = \frac{3}{2}a\right)$

$\therefore \quad \frac{9}{2}a - 4a = \frac{3}{2}a^2$

$\therefore \quad \frac{1}{2}a = \frac{3}{2}a^2 \quad \Rightarrow \quad a = \frac{1}{3}$

$\therefore \quad b = \frac{3}{2}a = \frac{3}{2}\left(\frac{1}{3}\right) = \frac{1}{2}$

$\therefore \quad \frac{x}{\left(\frac{1}{3}\right)} + \frac{y}{\left(\frac{1}{2}\right)} = 1$

$\therefore \quad 3x + 2y = 1$

6. A straight line meets the coordinate axes in A and B. Find the equation of straight line, when.

(i) $\overline{AB}$ is divided in the ratio 1 : 2 at (–5, 4)

(ii) (p, q) bisects $\overline{AB}$

Sol. Suppose the line $\frac{x}{a} + \frac{y}{b} = 1$ intersects coordinate axes at A, B.

$\therefore$ A = (a, 0) B = (0, b)

Let P = (–5, 4) be point on line and divides $\overline{AB}$ in the ratio 1 : 2

$\therefore \quad P = \left(\frac{1\times 0 + 2\times a}{1+2}, \frac{1\times b + 2\times 0}{1+2}\right) = (-5, 4)$

$= \left(\frac{2a}{3}, \frac{b}{3}\right) = (-5, 4)$

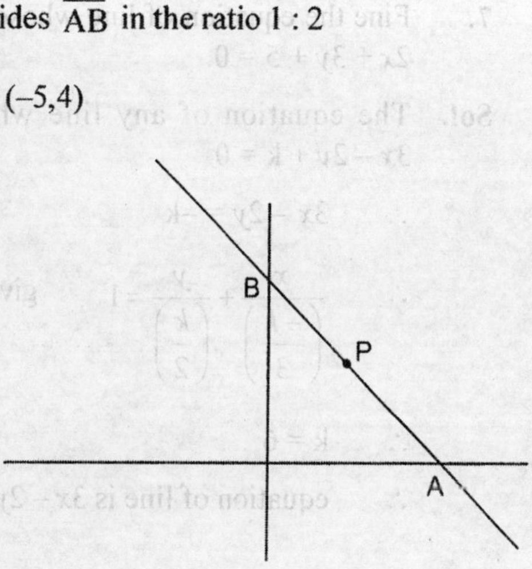

$\therefore \quad \frac{2a}{3} = -5, \qquad \frac{b}{3} = 4$

$\Rightarrow \quad a = \frac{-15}{2}, \qquad b = 12$

$\therefore \quad \frac{x}{a} + \frac{y}{b} = 1$

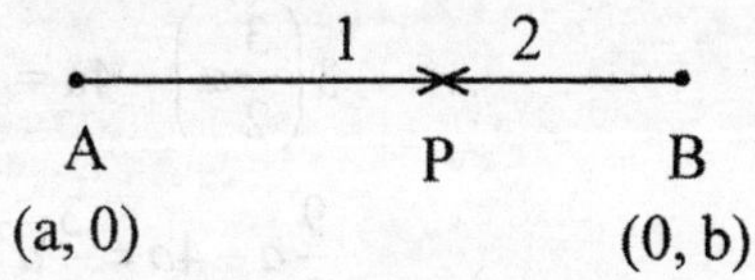

$$\Rightarrow \quad \frac{x}{\left(-\frac{15}{2}\right)} + \frac{y}{12} = 1$$

$$\therefore \quad \frac{2x}{-15} + \frac{y}{12} = 1$$

$$\frac{-8x + 5y}{60} = 1$$

$$\therefore \quad 8x - 5y + 60 = 0$$

(ii) Let P (p, q) be the mid point of AB

$$\therefore \ (p, q) = \left(\frac{a+0}{2}, \frac{0+b}{2}\right)$$

$$\therefore \ P = \frac{a}{2} \quad \Rightarrow \quad a = 2p$$

$$q = \frac{b}{2} \quad \Rightarrow \quad b = 2q$$

$\therefore$ Required equation of line is $\frac{x}{a} + \frac{y}{b} = 1$ i.e., $\frac{x}{2p} + \frac{y}{2q} = 1$

$$\frac{x}{p} + \frac{y}{q} = 2$$

7. Fine the equation of line whose x-intercept is –2 and which is perpendicular to $2x + 3y + 5 = 0$.

Sol. The equation of any line which is perpendicular to $2x + 3y + 5 = 0$ is $3x - 2y + k = 0$

$$\therefore \quad 3x - 2y = -k$$

$$\therefore \quad \frac{x}{\left(\frac{-k}{3}\right)} + \frac{y}{\left(\frac{k}{2}\right)} = 1 \qquad \text{given } \frac{-k}{3} = -2$$

$$\therefore \quad k = 6$$

$\therefore$ equation of line is $3x - 2y + 6 = 0$

8. Transform the equation $x + y + 1 = 0$ into slope intercept form and intercept form.

Sol. Given equation of line is $x + y + 1 = 0$

(i) slope intercept form

$$x + y + 1 = 0 \quad \Rightarrow \quad y = -x - 1$$

$$y = (-1)\,x + (-1) \quad \text{(it is in the form } y = mx + c\text{)}$$

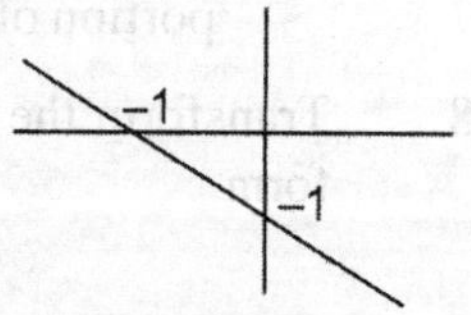

(ii) intercept form

$$x + y + 1 = 0 \quad \Rightarrow \quad x + y = -1$$

$$\frac{x}{-1} + \frac{y}{-1} = 1$$

$$(\therefore \text{ it is in the form } \frac{x}{a} + \frac{y}{b} = 1)$$

Exercise - 14.2

1. Find the equation of line having inclinations

(i) 60° and y intercept 4 (ii) 45° and x intercept 3

2. Find the equation of line parallel to

(i) $2x - 3y + 1 = 0$ and passing through $(2, -5)$

(ii) $2x + 3y = 5$ and passin through $(0, 0)$

3. Find the equation of line perpendicular to the line

(i) $2x + 3y - 4 = 0$ and passing through $(0, 0)$

(ii) $2x + 3y = 5$ and passing through $(1, 1)$

4. Find the area of triangle formed by the coordinate axes and the line

(i) $3x + 5y - 5 = 0$

(ii) passing through the points $(4, 1), (5, -2)$

5. Find the equation of the line having the intercepts a on the axes such that

(i) $a + b = 3, \ ab = \frac{5}{4}$ (ii) $a + b = 5, \ ab = \frac{21}{4}$

6. Find the equation of line passing through the point

(i) $(2, -1)$ and having equal intercepts

(ii) $(-4, 3)$ and having equal intercepts in magnitude but opposite sign

(iii) $(-2, 3)$ and having intercepts whose ratio is $3 : 2$

7. (i) Find the equation of line passing through the point A(1, 2) such that A bisects the part intercepted between the coordinate axes.

(ii) Find the equation of straight line passing through (–4, 3) and is such that portion of it between the axes is divided by the point in the ratio 5 : 3.

8. Transform the equation $2x + 3y - 6 = 0$ into slope intercept form and intercept form.

Answers

1. (i) $y = \sqrt{3}x + 4$ (ii) $y = 1\,(x - 3)$
2. (i) $2x - 3y - 19 = 0$ (ii) $2x + 3y = 0$
3. (i) $3x - 2y = 0$ (ii) $3x - 2y - 1 = 0$
4. (i) $\frac{5}{6}$ square units (ii) $\frac{169}{6}$ square units
5. (i) $2x + 10y - 5 = 0$ and $10x + 2y = 5$

   (ii) $6x + 14y = 21$ and $14x + 6y = 21$
6. (i) $x + y - 1 = 0$ (ii) $x - y + 7 = 0$ (iii) $2x + 3y - 5 = 0$
7. (i) $2x + y - 4 = 0$ (ii) $9x - 20y + 96 = 0$
8. $y = \frac{-2}{3}x + 2,$ $\frac{x}{3} + \frac{y}{2} = 1$

5. Perpendicular form (or) Normal form

Theorem The equation of line whose perpendicular distance from origin is p and the perpendicular makes an angle α ($0 \le \alpha < 360^0$) with positive direction of *x*-axis is $x\cos\alpha + y\sin\alpha = p$ (p is perpendicular distance and is always positive)

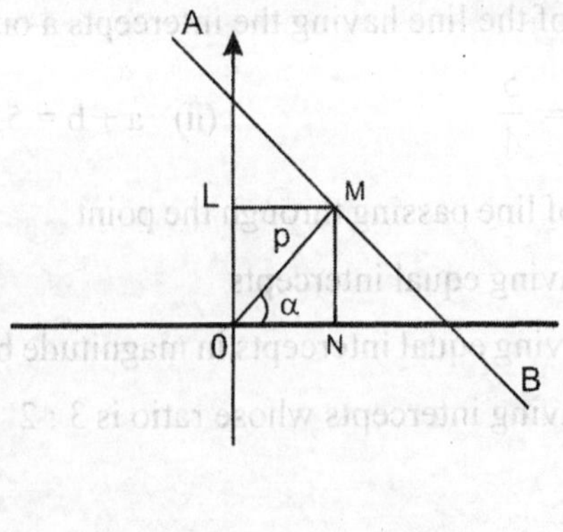

Proof $\overleftrightarrow{AB}$ is required line as shown in the figure .

Draw perpendicular OM from O to $\overleftrightarrow{AB}$

$\therefore$ OM = P

<MOB = α

Draw two $\perp$ MN and ML from M to x and y axis respectively.

from ΔONM, $\cos\alpha = \dfrac{ON}{OM} \Rightarrow ON = OM\cos\alpha = P\cos\alpha$

$\sin\alpha = \dfrac{MN}{OM} \Rightarrow MN = OM\sin\alpha = P\sin\alpha$

$\therefore$ M = (P cos α, P sin α)

slope of $\overleftrightarrow{OM} = \dfrac{p\sin\alpha - 0}{p\cos\alpha - 0} = \tan\alpha$

$\therefore$ slope of $\overleftrightarrow{AB} = \dfrac{-1}{\tan\alpha}$ $\left(\because \overleftrightarrow{OM} \perp \text{ to } \overleftrightarrow{AB}\right)$

$\therefore$ equation of $\overleftrightarrow{AB}$ is

$$y - p\sin\alpha = \frac{-1}{\tan\alpha}(x - p\cos\alpha)$$

$$y - p\sin\alpha = \frac{-\cos\alpha}{\sin\alpha}(x - p\cos\alpha)$$

$\therefore$ $y\sin x - p\sin^2\alpha = -x\cos\alpha + p\cos^2\alpha$

$\therefore$ $x\cos\alpha + y\sin\alpha = p(\sin^2\alpha + \cos^2\alpha) = p$

$\therefore$ $x\cos\alpha + y\sin\alpha = p$

Ex : (i) Equation of line which is at a distance 2 from origin and the perpendicular makes an angle 30° with positive direction of x-axis is $x\cos 30^\circ + y\sin 30^\circ = 2$

i.e., $\dfrac{x\sqrt{3}}{2} + y\dfrac{1}{2} = 2$ i.e., $\sqrt{3}x + y = 4$

(ii) Equation of line which is at a distance 3 from origin and the perpendicular makes a angle 45^0 with positive direction of x-axis is

$$x\cos 45^\circ + y\sin 45^\circ = 3$$

i.e., $x + y = 3\sqrt{2}$

Theorem The equation of the line ax + by + c = 0 into the normal (perpendicular) form is $\frac{a}{\sqrt{a^2+b^2}}x+\frac{b}{\sqrt{a^2+b^2}}y=\frac{-c}{\sqrt{a^2+b^2}}$ if c < 0

$$\frac{-a}{\sqrt{a^2+b^2}}x+\frac{-b}{\sqrt{a^2+b^2}}y=\frac{+c}{\sqrt{a^2+b^2}} \text{ if } c>0$$

Proof case (i) suppose c < 0

Equation of line is ax + by + c = 0 ⇒ ax + by = –c

$$\Rightarrow \frac{a}{\sqrt{a^2+b^2}}x+\frac{b}{\sqrt{a^2+b^2}}y=\frac{-c}{\sqrt{a^2+b^2}} \qquad (\because -c>0)$$

$$\Rightarrow x\cos\alpha + y\sin\alpha = p \quad \text{where}$$

$$\cos\alpha=\frac{-a}{\sqrt{a^2+b^2}},\ \sin\alpha=\frac{b}{\sqrt{a^2+b^2}} \text{ and } p=\frac{-c}{\sqrt{a^2+b^2}}\geq 0$$

case (ii) Suppose c > 0

equation of the line is ax + by + c = 0

$$\Rightarrow -ax-by=c$$

$$\Rightarrow \left(\frac{-a}{\sqrt{a^2+b^2}}\right)x+\left(\frac{-b}{\sqrt{a^2+b^2}}\right)y=\frac{c}{\sqrt{a^2+b^2}}$$

$$\Rightarrow x\cos\alpha + y\sin\alpha = p$$

$$\text{where } \cos\alpha=\frac{-a}{\sqrt{a^2+b^2}},\ \sin\alpha=\frac{-b}{\sqrt{a^2+b^2}},\ \text{and } p=\frac{c}{\sqrt{a^2+b^2}}$$

Ex : (i) Transform the equation $x + y + 2 = 0$ into the normal form.

Sol. $x + y + 2 = 0$

∴ a = 1, b = 1, c = 2 > 0

∴ $-x - y = 2$

Dividing on both sides by $\sqrt{a^2+b^2} \Rightarrow \sqrt{1^2+1^2}=\sqrt{2}$

$$\therefore \frac{-x-y}{\sqrt{2}}=\frac{2}{\sqrt{2}} \Rightarrow \frac{-x}{\sqrt{2}}+\frac{-y}{\sqrt{2}}=\sqrt{2}$$

$$\Rightarrow \left(\frac{-1}{\sqrt{2}}\right)x+\frac{-1}{\sqrt{2}}y=\sqrt{2}$$

$\therefore \quad \cos\alpha = \frac{-1}{\sqrt{2}} \quad \sin\alpha = \frac{-1}{\sqrt{2}}$

$\therefore \quad \alpha \in$ III quadrant

$\therefore \quad \alpha = \pi + \frac{\pi}{4} = \frac{5\pi}{4}$

$\therefore \quad x\cos\frac{5\pi}{4} + y\sin\frac{5\pi}{4} = \sqrt{2}$

Ex : (ii) Transform the equation $x + \sqrt{3}y - 4 = 0$

Sol. $a = 1,\ b = \sqrt{3},\ c = -4 < 0$

$\therefore \quad x + \sqrt{3}y = 4$

Dividing on both sides by $\sqrt{a^2+b^2} = \sqrt{1+3}$

$\therefore \quad \frac{1}{2}x + \frac{\sqrt{3}}{2}y = \frac{4}{2} = 2$

$\therefore \quad \cos\alpha = \frac{1}{2} \quad \sin = \frac{\sqrt{3}}{2}$

$\therefore \quad \alpha = \frac{\pi}{3}$

$\therefore \quad x\cos\frac{\pi}{3} + y\sin\frac{\pi}{3} = 2$

Corollary : The perpendicular distance from the point $P(x_1, y_1)$ to the line $ax + by + c = 0$ is $d = \frac{ax_1 + by_1 + c}{\sqrt{a^2+b^2}}$

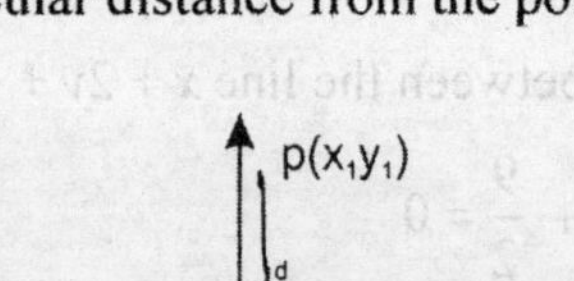

Note : The perpendicular distance from the point (0, 0) to the line $ax + by + c = 0$ is $\frac{|c|}{\sqrt{a^2+b^2}}$

(since $ax + by + c = 0 \quad \Rightarrow \quad \frac{a}{\sqrt{a^2+b^2}}x + \frac{b}{\sqrt{a^2+b^2}}y = \frac{-c}{\sqrt{a^2+b^2}}$)

$\therefore \quad P = \frac{|c|}{\sqrt{a^2+b^2}}$

Ex : (i) Find the perpendicular distant from (1, 2) to the line $3x + 2y - 1 = 0$

Sol. Here point $(x_1\ y_1) = (1, 2)$, a = 3, b = 2, c = –1

$$\therefore \quad \text{Perpendicular distance} = \left|\frac{ax_1 + by_1 + c}{\sqrt{a^2 + b^2}}\right|$$

$$= \left|\frac{(3)(1) + (2)(2) + (-1)}{\sqrt{(3)^2 + (2)^2}}\right|$$

$$= \frac{3 + 4 - 1}{\sqrt{9 + 4}} = \frac{6}{\sqrt{13}} \text{ units}$$

Ex : (ii) Find the perpendicular distance from (0, 0) to the line $x + y - 7 = 0$

Sol. $\text{Perpendicular distance} = \frac{|c|}{\sqrt{a^2 + b^2}} = \frac{|-7|}{\sqrt{1+1}} = \frac{7}{\sqrt{2}}$

Corollarly 2 : The distance betwwen two parallel lines $ax + by + c_1 = 0$, $ax + by + c_2 = 0$ is $\frac{|c_1 - c_2|}{\sqrt{a^2 + b^2}}$

Ex : (i) Find the distance between the two parallel lines $3x + 4y + 3 = 0$, $3x + 4y + 7 = 0$

Sol. a = 3, b = 4, $c_1 = 3$, $c_2 = 7$

$$\therefore \text{ Parallel distance} = \frac{|c_1 - c_2|}{\sqrt{a^2 + b^2}} = \frac{|3 - 7|}{\sqrt{9 + 16}} = \frac{4}{5} \text{ units}$$

Ex : (ii) Find the parallel distance between the line $x + 2y + 4 = 0$, $2x + 4y + 9 = 0$

Sol. $x + 2y + 4 = 0$, $x + 2y + \frac{9}{2} = 0$

$\therefore$ a = 1, b = 2, $c_1 = 4$, $c_2 = \frac{9}{2}$

$$\therefore \quad \text{Parallel distance} = \frac{|c_1 - c_2|}{\sqrt{a^2 + b^2}}$$

$$= \left|\frac{4 - \frac{9}{2}}{\sqrt{1^2 + 2^2}}\right| = \frac{\left|\frac{-1}{2}\right|}{\sqrt{5}} = \frac{1}{2\sqrt{5}} \text{ units}$$

6. Symmetric form

Theorem The equation of line passing through (x_1, y_1) and having inclination θ is

$$\frac{x-x_1}{\cos\theta}=\frac{y-y_1}{\sin\theta} \text{ where } \theta\in\left(0,\frac{\pi}{2}\right)\cup\left(\frac{\pi}{2},\pi\right)$$

Proof Given θ is inclination of the line. Therefore slope of the line is $m = \tan\theta$.

$\therefore$ equation of line passing through (x_1, y_1) and slope

$$y - y_1 = m(x - x_1)$$

$$\therefore \quad y - y_1 = \tan\theta\,(x - x_1)$$

$$\Rightarrow \quad y - y_1 = \frac{\sin\theta}{\cos\theta}(x - x_1)$$

$$\therefore \quad \frac{y-y_1}{\sin\theta}=\frac{x-x_1}{\cos\theta}$$

$\therefore$ The equation of line is $\frac{x-x_1}{\cos\theta}=\frac{y-y_1}{\sin\theta}$

Ex : Find the equation of straight line in the symmetric form having slope $\sqrt{3}$ and passing through the point (2, 3).

Sol. Given point $(x_1, y_1) = (2, 3) \Rightarrow x_1 = 2,\ y_1 = 3$

slope of line $= m = \sqrt{3} \Rightarrow \tan\theta = \sqrt{3} \Rightarrow \theta = 60^0$

$\therefore \sin\theta = \sin 60^0 = \frac{\sqrt{3}}{2},\ \cos\theta = \frac{1}{2}$

$\therefore$ the equation of line in symmetric form is

$$\frac{x-x_1}{\cos\theta}=\frac{y-y_1}{\sin\theta} \Rightarrow \frac{x-2}{\left(\frac{\sqrt{3}}{2}\right)}=\frac{y-3}{\left(\frac{\sqrt{3}}{2}\right)}$$

7. Parametric form

Theorem If $P(x, y)$ is any point on the line passing through the point $A_1(x_1\ y_1)$ and having inclination θ, then $x = x_1 + r\cos\theta$, $y = y_1 + r\sin\theta$ where $|r|$ is the distance from A to P.

Proof Since the line passing through $P_1(x_1\ y_1)$ and having inclination θ.

$\therefore$ its equation in symmetric form

$$\frac{x-x_1}{\cos\theta}=\frac{y-y_1}{\sin\theta}$$

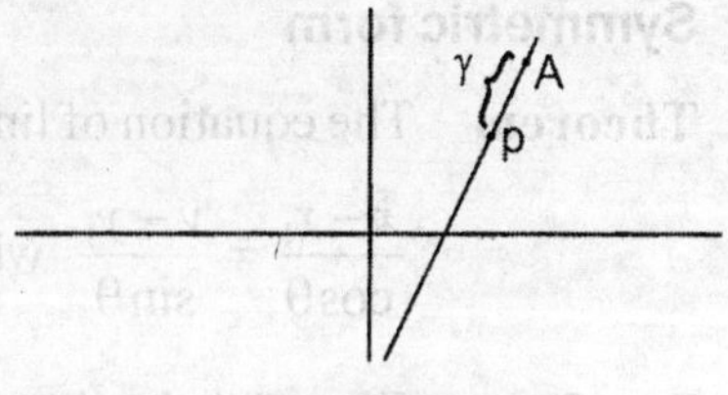

$$\therefore \quad \frac{x-x_1}{\cos\theta}=\frac{y-y_1}{\sin\theta}=t(say)$$

$$\therefore \quad \frac{x-x_1}{\cos\theta}=t \quad \Rightarrow \quad x-x_1=t\cos\theta \Rightarrow \quad x=x_1+t\cos\theta$$

also $\frac{y-y_1}{\sin\theta}=t \quad \Rightarrow \quad y-y_1=t\sin\theta \Rightarrow \quad y=y_1+t\sin\theta$

$\therefore \quad P=(x_1+t\cos\theta, y_1+\sin\theta)$

also given AP = r

$$\therefore \quad AP=\sqrt{(x_1+t\cos\theta-x_1)^2+(y_1+t\sin\theta-y_1)^2}=|r|$$

$$\Rightarrow \quad \sqrt{t^2\cos^2\theta+t^2\sin^2\theta}=|r|$$

$\therefore \quad t=r$

$$\therefore \quad \frac{x-x_1}{\cos\theta}=\frac{y-y_1}{\sin\theta}=r$$

$\therefore \quad x=x_1+r\cos\theta, \quad y=y+r\sin\theta$ are called the parametric equations with parameter r of the line passing through (x_1, y_1) and having incination θ.

Ex : Write the parametric equations of straight line passing through (1, 2) and having inclination 60^0.

Sol. $x=x_1+r\cos\theta, \quad y=y_1+r\sin\theta$

$\Rightarrow \quad x=1+r\frac{1}{2}, \quad y=2+r\frac{\sqrt{3}}{2}$ where r is parametric

Theorem : The ratio in which the line $l=ax+by+c=0$ divide the line segment joining $A(x_1, y_1)$ $B=(x_2, y_2)$ is $L_{11} : L_{22}$ where

$L_{11}=ax_1+by_1+c, L_{22}=ax_2+by_2+c$

Proof : Suppose the line $L=ax+by+c=0$ divide the line segment joining $A(x_1 y_1)$, $B=(x_2, y_2)$ in the ratio λ : 1 at p.

$$\therefore \quad P=\left(\frac{\lambda x_2+1.x_1}{\lambda+1}, \frac{\lambda y_2+1.y_1}{\lambda+1}\right)$$

It lies at the line L = 0

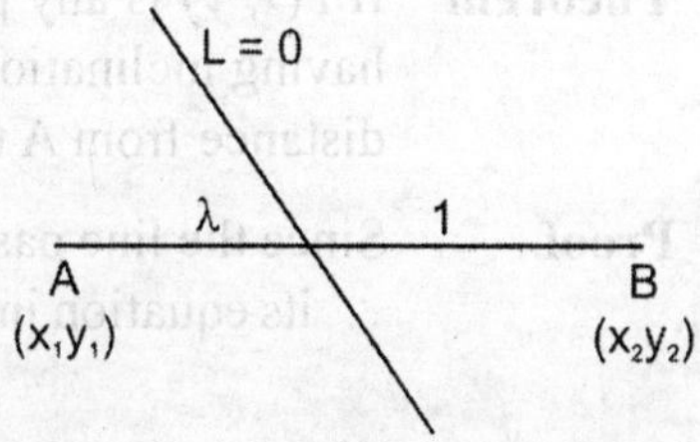

$$\therefore \quad a\left(\frac{\lambda x_2 + x_1}{\lambda+1}\right) + b\left(\frac{\lambda y_2 + y}{\lambda+1}\right) + l = 0$$

$$\therefore \quad a(\lambda x_2 + x_1) + b(\lambda y_2 + y_1) + c(\lambda + 1) = 0$$

$$\therefore \quad (ax_1 + by_1 + c) + \lambda(ax_2 + by_2 + c) = 0$$

$$\therefore \quad (ax_1 + by_1 + c) = \lambda(ax_2 + by_2 + c)$$

$$\therefore \quad \lambda = \frac{-(ax_1 + by_1 + c)}{ax_2 + by_2 + c} = \frac{-L_{11}}{L_{22}}$$

$\therefore$ the ratio is $\lambda : 1$ ie., $-L_{11} : L_{22}$

$$\therefore \quad \lambda = \lambda_{11} : \lambda_{22}$$

Note 1 x-axis divides the line segment joining the points $A(x_1, y_1)$, $B(x_2, y_2)$ is $-y_1 : y_2$.

Note 2 y-axis divides the line segment joining the points $A(x_1, y_1)$, $B(x_2, y_2)$ is $-x_1 : x_2$

two points $A(x_1, y_1)$, $B(x_2, y_2)$ are same side of line if L_{11}, L_{22} have opposite sign.

Ex: Find the ratio in which the line $2x + 3y + 1 = 0$ divides line segment joining the points (1, 4), (3, 2).

Sol. Consider $\dfrac{-l_{11}}{l_{22}} = \dfrac{-(2+12+1)}{(6+12+1)} = \dfrac{-15}{19}$

ratio is $-L_{11} : L_{22} = 15 : 19$

Solved Examples

1. Transform the following equations into normal form

(i) $\sqrt{3}x + y = 4$ (ii) $5x - 2y - 7 = 0$ (iii) $\sqrt{3}x + y + 10 = 0$

Sol. (i) $\sqrt{3}x + y = 4$

$a = \sqrt{3}$, $b = 1$

Dividing on both sides by $\sqrt{a^2 + b^2} = \sqrt{3+1} = 2$

$$\therefore \quad \frac{\sqrt{3}}{2}x + \frac{y}{2} = \frac{4}{2} = 2$$

$$\therefore \quad \frac{\sqrt{3}}{2}x + \frac{1}{2}y = 2$$

$$\therefore \quad x \,.\, \cos\frac{\pi}{6} + y \sin\frac{\pi}{6} = 2$$

(ii) $5x - 2y = 7$ $\quad \sqrt{a^2 + b^2} = \sqrt{25 + 4} = 29$

$$\Rightarrow \quad \frac{5}{\sqrt{29}}x + \frac{-2}{\sqrt{29}}y = \frac{7}{\sqrt{29}}$$

$$x \cos\alpha + y \sin\alpha = p \qquad \text{where } p = \frac{7}{\sqrt{29}},\ \cos\alpha = \frac{5}{\sqrt{29}},\ \sin\alpha = \frac{-2}{\sqrt{29}}$$

(iii) $\sqrt{3}x + y = -10$

Dividing on both sides by $\sqrt{(\sqrt{3})^2 + (1)^2} = \sqrt{3+1} = 2$

$$\frac{\sqrt{3}}{2}x + \frac{y}{2} = \frac{-10}{2} \Rightarrow -\frac{\sqrt{3}}{2}x - \frac{1}{2}y = 5$$

$$x \cos 7 \cos\frac{\pi}{6} + y \sin 7\frac{\pi}{6} = 5$$

2. Show that the distance of the point (6, –2) from the line $4x + 3y - 12 = 0$ is half of the distance of the point (3, 4) from the line $4x - 3y = 12$.

Sol. Let P_1 = Perpendicular distance from (6, –2) to the line $4x + 3y - 12 = 0$

$$\therefore \quad P_1 = \left|\frac{4(6) + 3(-2) - 12}{\sqrt{4^2 + 3^2}}\right| = \left|\frac{24 - 6 - 12}{\sqrt{16 + 9}}\right| = \frac{6}{5}$$

Let P_2 = perpendicular distance from (3, 4) to the line $4x - 3y - 12 = 0$.

$$\therefore \quad P_2 = \left|\frac{4(3) + 3(4) - 12}{\sqrt{16 + 9}}\right| = \left|\frac{12 - 12 - 12}{\sqrt{25}}\right| = \frac{12}{5}$$

$$\therefore \quad P_1 = \frac{1}{2} \,.\, P_2$$

3. If p, q are perpendiculars from the origin to the lines $x \sec\alpha + y \operatorname{cosec}\alpha = a$ and $x \cos\alpha - y \sin\alpha = a \cos 2\alpha$ then show that $4p^2 + q^2 = a^2$.

Sol. Given equations of lines are $x \sec\alpha + y \operatorname{cosec}\alpha = a$ .... (1)

$$x \cos\alpha - y \sin\alpha = a \cos 2\alpha \qquad \text{..... (2)}$$

$\therefore$ P = Perpendicular distance from (0, 0) to 1

$$= \left|\frac{-a}{\sqrt{\sec^2\alpha+\cos^2\alpha}}\right| = \frac{a}{\sqrt{\frac{1}{\cos^2\alpha}+\frac{1}{\sin^2\alpha}}} = \frac{a\sin\alpha\cos\alpha}{\sqrt{\sin^2\alpha+\cos^2\alpha}}$$

q = Perpendicular distance from (0, 0) to (2)

$$= \left|\frac{-a\cos 2\alpha}{\sqrt{\cos^2\alpha+\sin^2\alpha}}\right| = a\cos 2\alpha$$

$\therefore$ $4p^2 + q^2 = 4.(a\sin\alpha\cos\alpha)^2 + a^2\cos^2 2\alpha$

$= 4.a^2 . \sin^2\alpha\cos^2\alpha + a^2\cos^2 2\alpha$

$= a^2\sin^2 2\alpha + a^2\cos^2 2\alpha = a^2(\sin^2 2\alpha + \cos^2 2\alpha)$

$(\because \sin^2 2\alpha + \cos^2 2\alpha = 1)$

$= a^2(1)$

4. Find the distance between the parallel lines

(i) $5x - 3y - 4 = 0, \quad 10x - 6y - 9 = 0$

(ii) $3x + 4y - 3 = 0, \quad 6x + 8y - 1 = 0$

Sol. (i) Given equation of lines are

$5x - 3y - 4 = 0, \quad a = 5, \quad b = -3, \quad c_1 = -4$

$10x - 6y - 9 = 0$ i.e., $5x - 3y - \frac{9}{2} = 0 \quad c_2 = -\frac{9}{2}$

$\therefore$ Distance between the two parallel line is

$$\frac{|c_1 - c_2|}{\sqrt{a^2+b^2}} = \frac{\left|-4-\left(-\frac{9}{2}\right)\right|}{\sqrt{5^2+(-3)^2}} = \left|\frac{\frac{(-8+9)}{2}}{\sqrt{25+9}}\right|$$

$$= \left(\frac{\frac{1}{2}}{\sqrt{34}}\right) = \frac{1}{2\sqrt{34}} \text{ units}$$

(ii) $3x + 4y - 3 = 0 \quad \Rightarrow \quad a = 3, \quad b = 4, \quad c = -3$

$6x + 8y - 1 = 0 \quad \Rightarrow \quad 3x + 4y - \frac{1}{2} = 0 \quad c_2 = \frac{-1}{2}$

$\therefore$ Distance between two parallel lines is

$$\frac{|c_1 - c_2|}{\sqrt{a^2+b^2}} = \frac{\left|-3-(-\frac{1}{2})\right|}{\sqrt{3^2+4^2}} = \frac{\left|-3+\frac{1}{2}\right|}{\sqrt{25}}$$

$$= \left|\frac{-6+1}{2\sqrt{25}}\right|$$

$$= \frac{5}{2\times 5} = \frac{1}{2} \text{ units}$$

5. Find the points on the line $4x - 3y - 10 = 0$ which are at distance 5 from $(1, -2)$.

Sol. Let A = (1, –2), r = 5

Slope of line is $-\left(\frac{4}{-3}\right) = \frac{4}{3}$

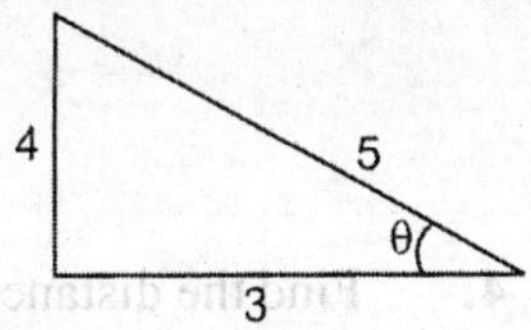

$\therefore$ $\tan\theta = \frac{4}{3}$ (θ is inclination of line)

$\therefore$ $\cos\theta, = \frac{3}{5}, \quad \sin\theta = \frac{4}{5}$

$\therefore$ The required points are $(x_1 \pm r\cos\theta, y_1 \pm r\sin\theta)$

$= (1 \pm 5.\frac{3}{5}, -2 \pm 5.\frac{4}{5})$

$= (1 \pm 3, -2 \pm 4)$

$\therefore$ the points are $(1 + 3, -2 + 4), (1 - 3, -2 - 4)$

i.e., $(4, 2), (-2, -6)$

6. Find the ratio in which the straight lines divide the line joining the given points. State whether the points lie on the same side or on either side of the straight line.

(i) $3x + 4y - 6 = 0$; $(2, -1), (1, 1)$

(ii) $2x + 3y = 5$; $(0, 0), (-2, 1)$

Sol. (i) $L = 3x + 4y - 6 = 0$

$L_{11} = (3x + 4y - 6)_{(2,-1)} = (6 - 4 - 6) = -4$

$L_{22} = (3x + 4y - 6)_{(1,+1)} = 3 + 4 - 6 = 1$

$\therefore$ Required ratio is $L_{11} : L_{22} = -(-4) : 1$

$= 4 : 1$

here $L_{11} < 0, \quad L_{22} > 0$

$\therefore$ The points lies opposite side to each other

(ii) $L = 2x + 3y - 5 = 0$

$L_{11} = 0 + 0 - 5 = -5$

$L_{22} = 2(-2) + 3(1) - 5$

$= -4 + 3 - 5$

$= -5$

Required ratio is $L_{11} : L_{22} = -(-5) : -5 = 5 : -5 = 1 : -1$

Here both L_{11}, L_{22} are -ve (same sign)

$\therefore$ they lie on same side of line

Exercise - 14.3

1. Transform the following equations into normal form.

   (i) $x + y - 2 = 0$ (ii) $4x - 3y + 12 = 0$

2. Find the perpendicular distance from the points.

   (i) $(-2, -3)$ to the line $5x - 2y + 4 = 0$ (ii) $(3, 4)$ to the line $3x - 4y + 10 = 0$

3. If P is length of perpendicular from origin on the straight line making intercepts 3 and 4 on the axes of coordinates then find P.

4. Find the parallel distance between the lines

   (i) $x + y + 4 = 0,\quad 2x + 2y + 5 = 0$

   (ii) $3x + 4y = 12,\quad 3x + 4y + 7 = 0$

5. A straight line passing through A(–2, 1) makes an angle 30^0 with the *x*-axis in the positive direction. Find the points as the straight line whose distance from A is 4 units.

6. Find the ratio in which the straight line $3x - 4y + 5 = 0$ divide the line segment joining the points (2, –4), (–3, 1).

Answers

1. (i) $\frac{x}{\sqrt{2}} + \frac{y}{\sqrt{2}} = \sqrt{2}$ (ii) $-\frac{4}{5}x + \frac{3}{5}y = \frac{12}{5}$

2. (i) 0 (ii) $\frac{3}{5}$

3. $\frac{12}{5}$

4. (i) $\frac{3}{2\sqrt{2}}$ (ii) $\frac{19}{5}$

5. $(-2+2\sqrt{3}, 3)$, $(-2-2\sqrt{3}, -1)$

6. $27:8$

14.4 Point of Intersection of Two Lines

Suppose two lines which are not parallel then they intersect each other at a point, then the point is called point of intersection of the two lines.

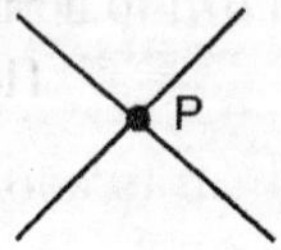

To find the point of intersection of two lines

$$a_1 x + b_1 y + c_1 = 0 \qquad a_2 x + b_2 y + c_2 = 0$$

Since the lines are not parallel

$$\therefore \quad \frac{a_1}{a_2} \neq \frac{b_1}{b_2} \quad \Rightarrow \quad a_1 b_2 - b_2 a_1 \neq 0$$

(If they are parallel then they do not intersect)

Let $P(x_1, y_1)$ be the point of intersection of two lines

$\therefore$ P lies on both the lines

$$\Rightarrow \quad a_1 x_1 + b_1 y_1 + c_1 = 0, \qquad a_2 x_1 + b_2 y_1 + c_2 = 0$$

Point of intersection is obtained by

Step 1 :

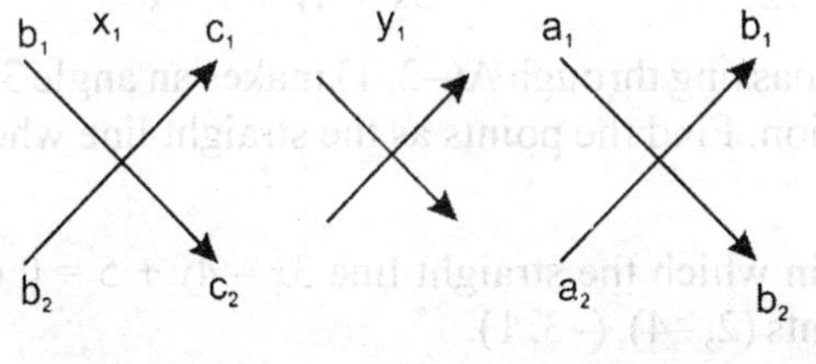

(write coff y_1, constant and coefficient of x_1 and coefficeint of y_1 in order)

(write coff y_2, constant cofficient x_2 and cofficient y_2 in order).

Step 2 : $$\frac{x_1}{b_1c_2 - b_2c_1} = \frac{y_1}{c_1a_2 - a_1c_2} = \frac{1}{a_1b_2 - a_2b_1}$$

Step 3 : $$\frac{x_1}{b_1c_2 - b_2c_1} = \frac{1}{a_1b_2 - a_2b_1}$$

$$\Rightarrow \quad x_1 = \frac{b_1c_2 - b_2c_1}{a_1b_2 - a_2b_1}$$

$$\frac{y_1}{c_1a_2 - a_1c_2} = \frac{1}{a_1b_2 - a_2b_1} \Rightarrow y_1 = \frac{c_1a_2 - a_1c_2}{a_1b_2 - a_2b_1}$$

$$\therefore \quad \text{Point of intersection is } (x_1, y_1) = \left(\frac{b_1c_2 - b_2c_1}{a_1b_2 - a_2b_1}, \frac{c_1a_2 - a_1c_1}{a_1b_2 - a_2b_1}\right)$$

Suppose we have to show that given three lines are concurent it is enough to show that the point of intersection of any two lines satisfies the third line.

(or) it is enough to show that the determinant of coefficient matrix of the three lines is zero.

Ex 1. Find the value of k if the three lines $x - y + 1 = 0$, $x + y + 1 = 0$, $kx + 5y - 7 = 0$ are concurent.

Sol. Let (x_1, y_1) be the point of concurence of the three lines

$\therefore x_1 - y_1 + 1 = 0, \ldots (1) \quad x_1 + y_1 + 1 = 0, \ldots (2) \quad kx_1 + 5y_1 - 7 = 0 \ldots (3)$

Solving (1) and (2)

$$\begin{array}{cccccc} & x_1 & & y_1 & & 1 \\ -1 & & 1 & & 1 & & -1 \\ 1 & & 1 & & 1 & & 1 \end{array}$$

$$\therefore \quad \frac{x_1}{-1-1} = \frac{y_1}{1-1} = \frac{1}{1+1}$$

$$\Rightarrow \quad \frac{x_1}{-2} = \frac{1}{2} \quad \Rightarrow \quad x_1 = -1 \quad ; \quad \frac{y_1}{0} = \frac{1}{2} = 1 \quad \Rightarrow \quad y_1 = 0$$

$\therefore \quad (x_1 y_1) = (-1, 0)$ substitute in (3) we get

$k(-1) + 5(0) - 7 = 0$

$-k - 7 = 0 \qquad \therefore \qquad k = -7$

2. If the lines $2x - ay + 1 = 0$, $3x - by + 1 = 0$, $4x - cy + 1 = 0$ are concurent then show that a, b, c are in A.P.

Sol. Since the given lines are concurent.

$\therefore$ the determinent of cocfficient matrix of lines is zero

$$\therefore \quad \begin{vmatrix} 2 & -a & 1 \\ 3 & -b & 1 \\ 4 & -c & 1 \end{vmatrix} = 0$$

$$2(-b + c) + a(3 - 4) + 1(-3c + 4b) = 0$$

$$-2b + 2c + 3a - 4a - 3c + 4b = 0$$

$$\therefore \quad 2b = a + c \quad \therefore \quad a, b, c \text{ are in A.P}$$

***Corollary*: The equation of any line passing through the point of intersection of two lines $L_1 = 0$, $L_2 = 0$ is of the form $L_1 + \lambda L_2 = 0$, where λ is parameter.**

Ex : Find the equation of line passing through the point of intersection of the lines $x + y + 1 = 0$, $2x - y + 5 = 0$ and the point (5, –2).

Sol. Equation of any line passing through point of intersection of two lines is of the form $L_1 + \lambda L_2 = 0$.

i.e., $(x + y + 1) + \lambda(2x - y + 5) = 0$

If it is passing through the point (5, –2) then $(5 - 2 + 1) + \lambda(10 + 2 + 5) = 0$

$$4 + \lambda(17) = 0 \quad \lambda = \frac{-4}{17}$$

$$\therefore \quad (x + y + 1) \frac{-4}{17} (2x - y + 5) = 0$$

$$17x + 17y + 17 - 4(2x - y + 5) = 0$$

$$9x + 11y - 3 = 0$$

$$3x + 7y - 1 = 0$$

Alternative Method

Find the point of intersection of two lines. Let it be A and the given point is say B. Find the equation of $\overleftrightarrow{AB}$. It is the required equation line.

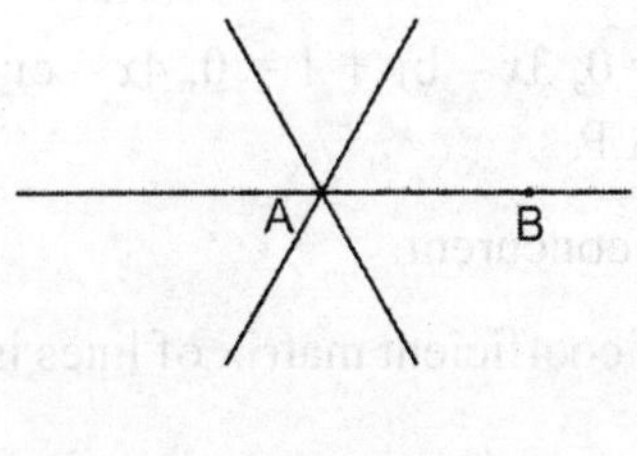

14.5 Angle between Two Lines

If θ is anlge between the two lines $a_1x + b_1y + c_1 = 0$, $a_2x + b_2y + c_2 = 0$ then

$$\cos\theta = \frac{a_1a_2 + b_1b_2}{\sqrt{a_1^2 + b_1^2}\sqrt{a_2^2 + b_2^2}}$$

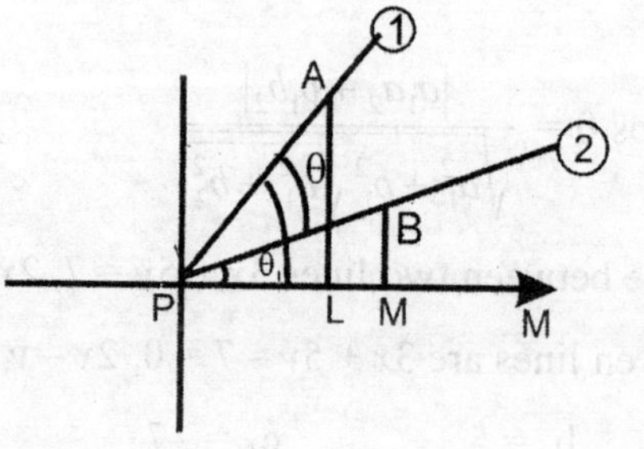

Suppose the lines $a_1x + b_1y + c_1 = 0$, $a_2x + b_2y + c_2 = 0$. Intersect at P. Draw a line $\overline{PM}$ through P and parallel to x-axis.

Let A, B two points on $a_1x + b_1y + c_1$ and $a_2x + b_2y + c_2 = 0$ respectively. Draw two perpendiculars AL, BM from A, B to $\overrightarrow{PM}$.

Let θ_1, θ_2 be inclination of lines respectively.

$$\therefore \quad \tan\theta_1 = \frac{-a_1}{b_1}, \qquad \tan\theta_2 = \frac{-a_2}{b_2}$$

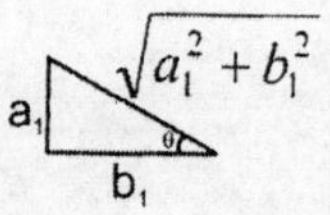

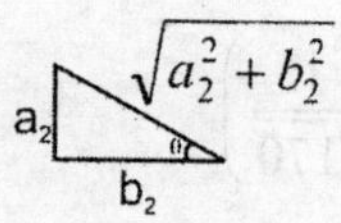

$$\cos\theta_1 = \frac{b_1}{\sqrt{a_1^2 + b_1^2}} \qquad \cos\theta_2 = \frac{b_2}{\sqrt{a_2^2 + b_2^2}}$$

$$\sin\theta_1 = \frac{a_1}{\sqrt{a_1^2 + b_2^2}} \qquad \sin\theta_2 = \frac{a_2}{\sqrt{a_1^2 + b_2^2}}$$

$\therefore$ from fig $\theta = \theta_2 - \theta_1$

$$\cos\theta = \cos(\theta_2 - \theta_1)$$

$$\cos\theta_2 \cos\theta_1 + \sin\theta_2 \sin\theta_1$$

$$= \frac{b_2}{\sqrt{b_2^2 + a_2^2}} \cdot \frac{b_1}{\sqrt{a_1^2 + b_1^2}} + \frac{a_1}{\sqrt{a_1^2 + b_1^2}} \cdot \frac{a_2}{\sqrt{a_2^2 + b_2^2}}$$

$$\therefore \quad \cos\theta = \frac{a_1 a_2 + b_1 b_2}{\sqrt{a_1^2 + b_1^2} \cdot \sqrt{a_1^2 + b_2^2}}$$

If θ is acute then $\cos\theta = \frac{|a_1 a_2 + b_1 b_2|}{\sqrt{a_1^2 + b_1^2}\sqrt{a_1^2 + b_2^2}}$

Ex : Find the acute angle between two lines $3x + 5y = 7$, $2x - y + 4 = 0$.

Sol. The equation of given lines are $3x + 5y - 7 = 0$, $2x - y + 4 = 0$

$a_1 = 3$, $b_1 = 5$, $c_1 = -7$

$a_2 = 2$ $b_2 = -1$ $c_2 = 4$

Let θ be acute angle between the two lines

$$\therefore \quad \cos\theta = \frac{|a_1 a_2 + b_1 b_2|}{\sqrt{a_1^2 + b_1^2} \cdot \sqrt{a_2^2 + b_2^2}}$$

$$= \left| \frac{(3)(2) + (5)(-1)}{\sqrt{(3)^2 + (5)^2} \cdot \sqrt{(2)^2 + (-1)^2}} \right| = \frac{(6-5)}{\sqrt{34} \cdot \sqrt{5}} = \frac{1}{\sqrt{34} \cdot \sqrt{5}} = \frac{1}{\sqrt{170}}$$

$$\therefore \quad \theta = \cos^{-1}\left(\frac{1}{\sqrt{170}}\right)$$

14.6 Foot of the Perpendicular from given Point to a Line

If p(h, k) be foot of perpendicular drawn from A(x_1, y_1) to the line $ax + by + c = 0$ then P is obtained by $\frac{h - x_1}{a} = \frac{k - y_1}{b} = \frac{-(ax_1 + by_1 + c)}{a^2 + b^2}$

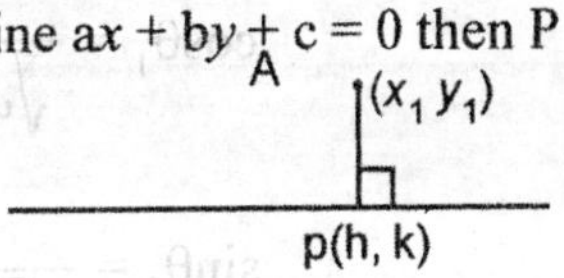

14.7 Image of Point with Respect to Line

If Q(h, k) is image of the given point P(x_1, y_1) w.r.t line $ax + by + c = 0$ then Q is obtained by $\frac{h - x_1}{a} = \frac{k - y_1}{b} = \frac{-2(ax_1 + by_1 + c)}{a^2 + b^2}$

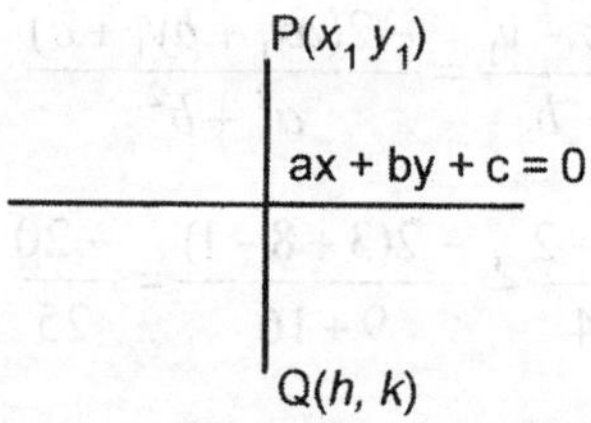

Ex 1. Find the foot of perpendicular from (4, 1) to the line $3x - 4y + 12 = 0$.

Sol. Let $(x_1\ y_1) = (4, 1)$; the line is $3x - 4y + 12 = 0$

$\therefore$ a = 3, b = –4, c = 12

Let (h, k) be foot of perpendicular of (x_1, y_1) w.r.t $3x - 4y + 1 = 0$

$$\therefore \quad \frac{h - x_1}{a} = \frac{k - y_1}{b} = \frac{-(ax_1 + by_1 + c)}{a^2 + b^2}$$

$$\frac{h-4}{3} = \frac{k-1}{-4} = \frac{-(12 + (-4) + 12)}{9+16}$$

$$\Rightarrow \frac{h-4}{3} = \frac{k-1}{-4} = \frac{-(20)}{25}$$

$$= \frac{-4}{5}$$

$$\therefore \quad \frac{h-4}{3} = \frac{-4}{5} \quad \Rightarrow \quad h - 4 = \frac{-12}{5} \Rightarrow h = 4 - \frac{-12}{5} = \frac{8}{5}$$

$$\frac{k-1}{-4} = \frac{-4}{5} \quad \Rightarrow \quad k - 1 = \frac{16}{5} \Rightarrow k = = \frac{5+16}{5} = \frac{21}{5}$$

$$\therefore \quad (h, k) = \left(\frac{8}{5}, \frac{21}{5}\right)$$

2. Find the image of the point (1, 2) w.r.t the line $3x + 4y - 1 = 0$.

Sol. Let P = (x_1, y_1) (1, 2) and equation of line is $3x + 4y - 1 = 0$

$\therefore$ a = 3, b = 4, c = –1

Let Q(h, k) be image of the line, then θ is obtained by,

$$\therefore \quad \frac{h-x_1}{a} = \frac{k-y_1}{b} = \frac{-2(ax_1+by_1+c)}{a^2+b^2}$$

$$\frac{h-1}{3} = \frac{k-2}{4} = \frac{-2(3+8-1)}{9+16} = \frac{-20}{25} = \frac{-4}{5}$$

$$\therefore \quad \frac{h-1}{3} = \frac{-4}{5}, \quad \frac{k-2}{4} = \frac{-4}{5}$$

$$h-1 = \frac{-12}{5} \quad \Rightarrow \quad h = 1\frac{-12}{5} = \frac{7}{5}, \quad \frac{k-2}{4} = \frac{-4}{5} \quad \Rightarrow$$

$$k-2 = \frac{-16}{5} \quad \Rightarrow \quad k = \frac{-16}{5} + 2 = \frac{-6}{5}$$

$$\therefore (h, k) = \left(\frac{-7}{5}, \frac{-6}{5}\right)$$

14.8 Angular Bisector of Lines

The equations of angular bisectors of lines $l_1x + m_1y + n_1 = 0$ and $l_2x + m_2y + n_2 = 0$ are

$$\frac{l_1x+m_1y+n_1}{\sqrt{l_1^2+m_1^2}} = \pm\frac{l_2x+m_2y+n_2}{\sqrt{l_2^2+m_2^2}}$$

Ex : Find the equation of angular bisectors of the angles between the lines $3x + 4y = 5$, $12x - 5y = 41$.

Sol. The equation of bisectors of angle made by the lines $3x + 4y - 5 = 0$, $12x - 5y - 41 = 0$ are

$$\left(\frac{3x+4y-5}{\sqrt{9+16}}\right) = \pm\left(\frac{12x-5y-41}{\sqrt{144+25}}\right)$$

$$\frac{3x+4y-5}{5} = \pm\frac{(12x-5y-41)}{13}$$

i.e., $\quad 39x + 52y - 65 = \pm(60x - 25y - 205)$

$\therefore \quad 11x + 3y = 30, \quad 3x - 11y = 20$

Solved Examples

1. Find the point of intersection of lines $\frac{x}{a}+\frac{y}{b}=1, \frac{x}{b}+\frac{y}{a}=1$ $(a \neq \pm b)$

Sol. Given equation of lines are

$$\frac{x}{a}+\frac{y}{b}=1 \quad \Rightarrow \quad bx + ay - ab = 0$$

$$\frac{x}{b}+\frac{y}{a}=1 \quad \Rightarrow \quad ax + by - ab = 0$$

Let (x_1, y_1) be point of intersection of lines

$$bx_1 + ay_1 - ab = 0$$

$$ax_1 + by_1 - ab = 0$$

$$\therefore \quad \begin{matrix} & x_1 & & y_1 & & 1 & \\ a & \times & -ab & \times & b & \times & a \\ b & & -ab & & a & & b \end{matrix}$$

$$\therefore \quad \frac{x_1}{-a^2b+ab^2}=\frac{y_1}{-a^2b+ab^2}=\frac{1}{b^2-a^2}$$

$$\therefore \quad \frac{x_1}{ab(b-a)}=\frac{y_1}{ab(b-a)}=\frac{1}{(b+a)(b-a)}$$

$$\therefore \quad x_1=\frac{ab(b-a)}{(b+a)(b-a)}=\frac{ab}{b+a}=\frac{ab}{a+b}$$

$$y_1=\frac{ab(b-a)}{(b+a)(b-a)}=\frac{ab}{a+b}$$

$\therefore$ Point of intersection

$$=\left(\frac{ab}{a+b}, \frac{ab}{a+b}\right)$$

2. Find the value of λ if the lines $2x-3y+\lambda=0$, $3x-4y-13=0$, $8x-11y-33=0$ are concurent.

Sol. First we find the point of intersection of lines $3x-4y-13=0$, $8x-11y-33=0$. Let it be (x_1, y_1)

$$\therefore \quad \begin{matrix} & x_1 & & y_1 & & 1 & \\ -4 & \times & -13 & \times & 3 & \times & -4 \\ -11 & & -33 & & 8 & & -11 \end{matrix}$$

$$\Rightarrow \quad \frac{x_1}{132-143}=\frac{y_1}{-104+99}=\frac{1}{-33+32}$$

$$\therefore \quad x_1 = \frac{-11}{-1}, y_1 = \frac{-5}{-1}$$

$$\Rightarrow \quad x_1 = 11, y_1 = 5$$

$(x_1 \, y_1) = (11, 5)$ lies on $2x - 3y + \lambda = 0$ ($\because$ the three lines are concurent)

$$2(+11) - 3(+5) + \lambda = 0$$

$$22 - 15 + \lambda = 0$$

$$\lambda = -7$$

3. Find the equation of straight line passing through point of intersection of lines $x - 2y - 3 = 0$, $x + 3y - 6 = 0$ and parallel to $3x + 4y = 7$.

Sol. Let $(x_1 . y_1)$ be the point of intersection of lines $x - 2y - 3 = 0$, $x + 3y - 6 = 0$

$$\begin{array}{ccccccc} & x_1 & & y_1 & & 1 & \\ \therefore \quad -2 & \times & -3 & \times & 1 & \times & -2 \\ 3 & & -6 & & 1 & & 3 \end{array}$$

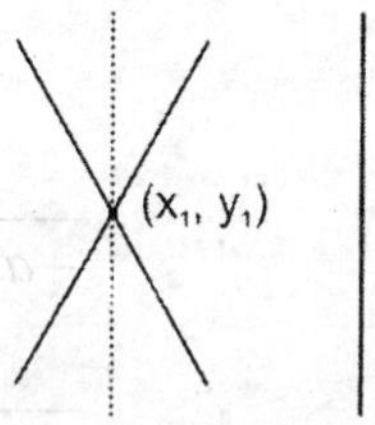

$$\frac{x_1}{12+9} = \frac{y_1}{-3+6} = \frac{1}{3+2}$$

$$\therefore \quad x_1 = \frac{21}{5}, \quad y_1 = \frac{3}{5}$$

$$\therefore \quad (x_1 \, y_1) = \left(\frac{21}{5} \; \frac{3}{5}\right)$$

the slope of line parallel to the line $3x + 4y = 7$ is $\frac{-3}{4}$.

$\therefore$ Equation of required line is

$$y - \frac{3}{5} = \frac{-3}{4}\left(x - \frac{21}{5}\right) \qquad (\because \text{ parallel lines have equal slope})$$

$$\therefore \quad \frac{5y-3}{5} = \frac{-3}{4}\left(\frac{5x-21}{5}\right)$$

$$20y - 12 = -15x + 63$$

$$\therefore \quad 15x + 20y - 75 = 0$$

$$\therefore \quad 3x + 4y - 15 = 0$$

Alternative Method

Equation of any line passing through point of intersection of two lines

$x - 2y - 3 = 0$ and $x + 3y - 6 = 0$ is of the form

$$x - 2y - 3 + \lambda (x + 3y - 6) = 0 \quad \text{.... (1)}$$

i.e., $(1 + \lambda)x + (-2 + 3\lambda)y + (-3 - 6\lambda) = 0$

If it is parallel to given line $3x + 4y = 7$ then

$$\frac{-(1+\lambda)}{(-2+3\lambda)} = \frac{-3}{4} \qquad (\because \text{ Slope of Parallel lines are equal})$$

$$\frac{1+\lambda}{-2+3\lambda} = \frac{3}{4}$$

$\Rightarrow \quad 4 + 4\lambda = -6 + 9\lambda$

$5\lambda = 10 \qquad \lambda = 2$

$\therefore$ substitute n in (1) we get,

$(x - 2y - 3) + 2(x + 3y - 6) = 0$

$3x + 4y - 15 = 0$

4. Find the equation of line passing through point of intersection of $x + 3y - 1 = 0$, $x - 2y + 4 = 0$ and perpendicular $2x + 3y = 0$.

Sol. Let (x_1, y_1) be point of intersection of two lines

$x + 3y - 1 = 0, \quad x - 2y + 4 = 0,$

$$\begin{array}{cccccc} & x_1 & & y_1 & & 1 \\ 3 & & -1 & & 1 & & 3 \\ -2 & & 4 & & 1 & & -2 \end{array}$$

$$\Rightarrow \frac{x_1}{12-2} = \frac{y_1}{-1-4} = \frac{1}{-2-3}$$

$$\Rightarrow \frac{x_1}{10} = \frac{y_1}{-5} = \frac{1}{-5} \quad \Rightarrow x_1 = \frac{10}{-5} = -2,\ y_1 = \frac{-5}{-5} = 1$$

$\therefore \quad (x_1, y_1) = (-2, 1)$

slope of line $2x + 3y = 0$ is $m = \dfrac{-2}{3}$

$\therefore$ Slope of any line perpendicular to $2x + 3y = 0$ is $\dfrac{-1}{m} = \dfrac{-1}{\left(\dfrac{-2}{3}\right)} = \dfrac{3}{2}$

$\therefore$ equation of line passing through (x_1, y_1) and slope $\dfrac{3}{2}$ is

$$y - 1 = \frac{3}{2}(x + 2)$$

$$\therefore\ 2y - 2 = 3x + 6 \Rightarrow \quad 3x - 2y + 8 = 0$$

5. Find the perpendicular distance of the straight line $7x + 24y - 15 = 0$ from the point of intersection of lines $3x + 2y + 4 = 0$, $2x + 5y - 1 = 0$.

Sol. Let $P(x_1, y_1)$ be the point of intersection of straight lines $3x + 2y + 4 = 0$, $2x + 5y - 1 = 0$

$$\begin{array}{ccccccc} & x_1 & & y_1 & & 1 & \\ \therefore\ 2 & \times & 4 & \times & 3 & \times & 2 \\ 5 & & -1 & & 2 & & 5 \end{array}$$

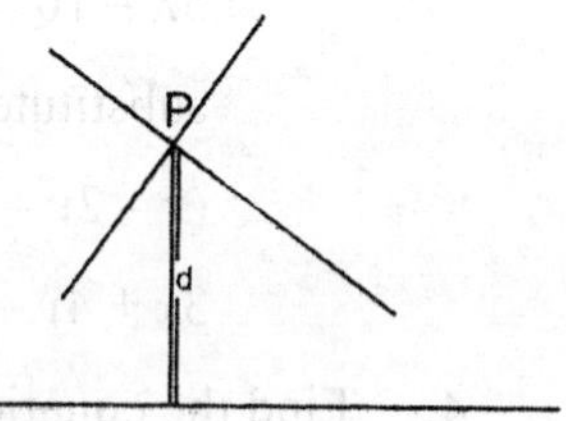

$$\therefore\ \frac{x_1}{-2-20} = \frac{y_1}{8+3} = \frac{1}{15-4} = \frac{1}{11}$$

$$\therefore\ \frac{x_1}{-22} = \frac{y_1}{11} = \frac{1}{11}$$

$$\therefore\ x_1 = \frac{-22}{11} = -2, \quad y_1 = \frac{11}{11} = 1$$

$(x_1\ y_1) = (-2, 1)$

the perpendicular distance from $(-2, 1)$ to line $7x + 24\,y - 15 = 0$

$$\left|\frac{ax_1 + by_1 + c}{\sqrt{a^2 + b^2}}\right| = \left|\frac{7(-2) + 24(1) - 15}{\sqrt{49 + 576}}\right| = \left|\frac{-14 + 24 - 15}{25}\right| = \frac{5}{25} = \frac{1}{5} \text{ square units}$$

6. (i) Transform the equation $(2 + 5k)\,x - 3\,(1 + 2k)\,y + 2 - k = 0$ into $L_1 + KL_2 = 0$ and find the point of concurence of the family of the straight lines.

(ii) Find the condition that the lines $ax + hy + y = 0$, $hx + by + f = 0$, $gx + fy + c = 0$ to be concurent.

Sol. (i) Given equation is $(2 + 5k)\,x - 3(1+2k)y + (2 - k) = 0$

i.e., $2x + 5kx - 3y - 6ky + 2 - k = 0$

$(2x - 3y + 2) + (5kx - 6ky - k = 0$

$(2x - 3y + 2) + k\ (5x - 6y - 1) = 0$

it is of the form $L_1 + kL_2 = 0$

all these lines are concurent at the point of intersection of $L_1 = L_2$,

i.e., $2x - 3y + 2 = 0,\ 5x - 6y - 1 = 0.$

$$\begin{array}{cccc} & x_1 & y_1 & 1 \\ -3 & 2 & 2 & -3 \\ -6 & -1 & 5 & -6 \end{array}$$

$$\frac{x_1}{3+12} = \frac{y_1}{10+2} = \frac{1}{-12+15}$$

$$\Rightarrow \quad \frac{x_1}{15} = \frac{y_1}{12} = \frac{1}{3}$$

$$\therefore \quad x_1 = \frac{15}{3}, \quad y_1 = \frac{12}{3}$$

$$\therefore \quad (x_1, y_1) = \left(\frac{15}{3}, \frac{12}{3}\right) = (5, 4)$$

(ii) Since the lines $ax + hy + g = 0$, $hx + by + f = 0$, $gx + fy + c = 0$ are concurent

$$\therefore \quad \begin{vmatrix} a & h & g \\ h & b & f \\ g & f & c \end{vmatrix} = 0$$

$\therefore\ a(bc - f^2) - h(hc - gf) + g(hf - bg) = 0$

$\therefore\ abc - af^2 - ch^2 + gfh + ghf - bg^2 = 0$

$\therefore\ abc + 2fgh - af^2 - bg^2 - ch^2 = 0$

7. Find the circum centre of triangle formed by the points (1, 3), (0, –2), (–3, 1).

Sol. Let $S(x_1, y_1)$ be circum centre of traingle formed by the points A(1, 3), B(0, –2) C = (–3, 1)

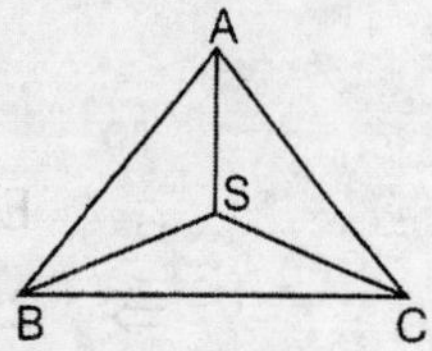

$\therefore \quad SA = SB = SC$

$\therefore \quad SA = SB$

$\Rightarrow \quad (SA)^2 = (SB)^2$

$\Rightarrow \quad (x_1 - 1)^2 + (y_1 - 3)^2 = (x_1 - 0)^2 + (y_1 + 2)^2$

$\Rightarrow \quad x_1^2 + y_1^2 - 2x_1 - 6y_1 + 10 = x_1^2 + y_1^2 + 4y_1 + 4$

$\Rightarrow \quad -2x_1 - 6y_1 + 10 = 4y_1 + 4$

$\Rightarrow \quad 2x_1 + 10y_1 - 6 = 0$

$\Rightarrow \quad x_1 + 5y_1 - 3 = 0 \quad$ ...(1)

also SB = SC $\Rightarrow (SB)^2 = (SC)^2$

$\therefore \quad (x_1 - 0)^2 + (y_1 + 2)^2 = (x_1 + 3)^2 + (y_1 - 1)^2$

$\because \quad x_1^2 + y_1^2 + 4y_1 + 4 = x_1^2 + 9 + 6x_1 + y_1^2 + 1 - 2y_1$

$\Rightarrow \quad 6x_1 - 6y_1 + 6 = 0$

$x_1 - y_1 + 1 = 0 \quad$ ....(2)

Solving (1) and (2)

$$\begin{array}{cccccc} & x_1 & & y_1 & & 1 \\ 5 & & -3 & & 1 & & 5 \\ -1 & & 1 & & 1 & & -1 \end{array}$$

$$\frac{x_1}{5-3} = \frac{y_1}{-3-1} = \frac{1}{-1-5}$$

$$\Rightarrow \quad x_1 = \frac{2}{-6},\ y_1 = \frac{-4}{-6}$$

$$(x_1\ y_1) = \left(\frac{-1}{3}, \frac{2}{3}\right)$$

8. Find the ortho centre of triangle formed by the points (–5, –7) (13, 2) (–5, 6).

Sol. Let A = (–5, –7), B = (13, 2) C = (–5, 6) and Let 'O' be the orthocentre of traingle.

$\overrightarrow{AD}, \overrightarrow{BE}, \overrightarrow{CF}$ are altitude of triangle through A, B, C respectively.

Now slope of $\overline{AB} = \dfrac{2-(-7)}{13-(-5)} = \dfrac{9}{18} = \dfrac{1}{2}$

$\therefore \quad$ Slope of $\overline{CF} = \dfrac{-1}{\frac{1}{2}} = -2 \quad (\because \overline{CF} \perp \overline{AB})$

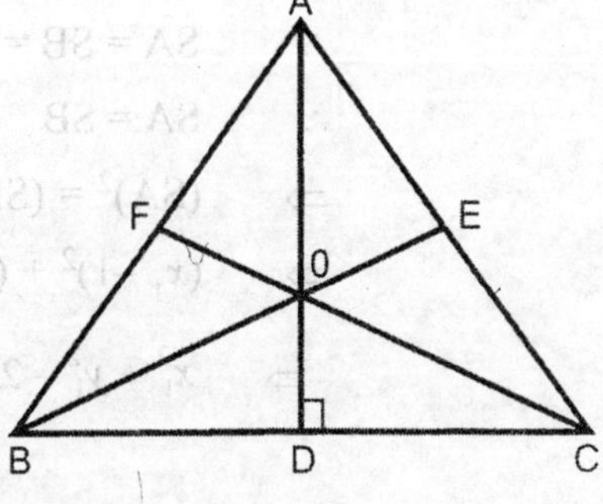

$\therefore \quad$ Equation of $\overline{CF}$ is $y - 6 = -2(x + 5)$

$\Rightarrow \quad 2x + y + 4 = 0$ (altitude) .....(1)

Slope of $\overline{BC}$ is $\dfrac{6-2}{-5-13} = \dfrac{4}{-18} = \dfrac{-2}{9}$

$\therefore \quad$ slope of $\overline{AD} = \dfrac{9}{2}$

Equation of $\overline{AD}$ is $y-(-7)=\dfrac{9}{2}\,(x-(-5))$

$\Rightarrow \quad y+7=\dfrac{9}{2}\,(x+5)$

$\Rightarrow \quad 2y+14=9x+45$

$\Rightarrow \quad 9x-2y+31=0 \quad$ (altitude) .....(2)

solving (1) and (2) we get orthocentre

($\because$ point of concurence of altitudes is orthocentre)

$$\begin{array}{cccccc} & x & & y & & 1 \\ 1 & & 4 & & 2 & & 1 \\ -2 & & 31 & & 9 & & -2 \end{array}$$

$$\frac{x}{31+8}=\frac{1}{36-62}=\frac{1}{-4-9}$$

$$x=\frac{39}{-13}=-3, \qquad y=\frac{-26}{-13}=2$$

$(x, y)=(-3, 2) \quad O=(-3, 2)$

Note : Suppose equations of sides of triangle are given, find the vertices by solving the equations of sides and hence find the ortho centre as above

9. Find the acute angle between the lines $y=4-2x$; $y=3x+7$

Sol. Given equations of lines are $2x+y-4=0$, $3x-y+7=0$

$a_1=2, \quad b_1=1, \quad c_1=-4, \quad a_2=3, \quad b_2=-1 \quad c_2=7$

If θ is acute angle between the lines then

$$\cos\theta=\frac{|a_1a_2+b_1b_2|}{\sqrt{a_1^2+b_1^2}\,.\sqrt{a_2^2+b_2^2}}=\frac{|(2)(3)+(1)(-1)|}{\sqrt{2^2+1^2}\,\sqrt{3^2+(-1)^2}}$$

$$=\left|\frac{6-1}{\sqrt{5}.\sqrt{10}}\right|=\frac{5}{\sqrt{50}}=\frac{5}{5\sqrt{2}}=\frac{1}{\sqrt{2}}$$

$$\therefore \quad \cos\theta=\frac{1}{\sqrt{2}} \quad \Rightarrow \quad \theta=\frac{\pi}{4}$$

(or) $m_1 = -2$, $m_2 = 3$ (slope of lines)

$$\therefore \quad \tan\theta = \left|\frac{m_1 - m_2}{1 + m_1 m_2}\right| = \left|\frac{-2-3}{1+(-2)(3)}\right| = \left|\frac{-5}{1-6}\right| = 1$$

$$\therefore \quad \theta = \frac{\pi}{4}$$

10. If the acute angle between the lines $4x - y + 7 = 0$, $kx - 5y - 9 = 0$ is 45° then find the value of k.

Sol. Given equation of lines are

$$4x - y + 7 = 0 \quad \text{... (1)}$$

$$kx - 5y - 9 = 0 \quad \text{... (2)}$$

$a_1 = 4$ $\quad b_1 = -1,$ $\quad c_1 = 7$

$a_2 = k$ $\quad b_2 = -5$ $\quad c_2 = -9$

If the angle between two lines is 45° then

$$\cos\theta = \cos 45^o = \left|\frac{a_1 a_2 + b_1 b_2}{\sqrt{a_1^2 + b_1^2}\sqrt{a_2^2 + b_2^2}}\right|$$

$$\therefore \quad \frac{1}{2} = \left|\frac{(4)(k) + (-1)(-5)}{\sqrt{4^2 + 1^2}\sqrt{k^2 + 25}}\right|$$

$$\Rightarrow \quad \frac{1}{2} = \left|\frac{(4k+5)^2}{17(k^2+25)}\right|$$

$$\therefore \quad 17k^2 + 17 \times 25 = 2(16k^2 + 25 + 40k)$$

$$\therefore \quad 17k^2 + 425 = 32k^2 + 50 + 80k$$

$$\Rightarrow \quad 15k^2 + 80k - 375 = 0$$

$$\Rightarrow \quad 3k^2 + 16k - 75 = 0$$

$$3k(k-3) + 25(k-3) = 0$$

$$k = -\frac{25}{3} \text{ or } k = 3$$

11. Show that the lines $x - 7y - 22 = 0$, $3x + 4y + 9 = 0$, $7x + y - 54 = 0$ form a right angled isosceles triangle.

Sol. Given equations of lines are

$$x - 7y - 22 = 0 \quad .....(1)$$

$$3x + 4y + 9 = 0 \quad .....(2)$$

$$7x + y - 54 = 0 \quad ....(3)$$

Slope of (1) is $\frac{1}{7}$, slope of (2) is $\frac{-3}{4}$, slope of (3) is -7

$\therefore$ slope of (1) $\times$ slope of (3) $= -1$

(1) and (3) are (perpendicular)

Let θ_1 be angle between (1), (2)

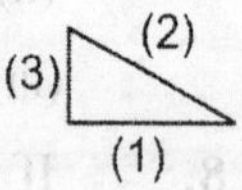

$$\therefore \cos\theta_1 = \left|\frac{3-28}{\sqrt{1+49}.\sqrt{9+16}}\right| = \left|\frac{-25}{\sqrt{50}.5}\right| = \frac{1}{\sqrt{2}}$$

$$\Rightarrow \theta_1 = \frac{\pi}{4}$$

Let θ_2 be angle between (2) & (3)

$$\cos\theta_2 = \left|\frac{21+4}{\sqrt{9+16}.\sqrt{49+1}}\right|$$

$$= \left|\frac{25}{5\sqrt{50}}\right| = \frac{1}{\sqrt{2}}$$

and (1) and (3) are $\perp$er

$\therefore$ The triangle is right angled isosceles triangle

Exercise - 14.4

1. Find the point of intersection of lines.

   (i) $3x + y + 4 = 0, 2x + 3y - 2 = 0$

   (ii) $x + y - 3 = 0, 2x - 3y + 8 = 0$

2. (i) Show that the lines $2x + y - 3 = 0$, $3x + y - 2 = 0$, $2x - 3y + 17 = 0$ are concurent

   (ii) Find the value of λ if the three lines $3x + 4y = 5$, $2x + 3y = 4$ and $\lambda x + 4y = 6$ are concurent.

   (iii) Find the condition that the lines $ax + by + c = 0$, $bx + cy + a = 0$,

   $cx + ay + b = 0$ to be concurent.

3. Find the equations of line passing through point of intersection of lines $2x + 3y = 1$, $3x + 4y = 6$ and

   (i) parallel to

   (ii) perpendicular to the line $5x - 2y = 7$

4. (i) If 3a + 2b + 4c = 0 then show that ax + by + c = 0, represents a set of concurent lines then find the point of concurence.

(ii) Transform the equation $(k + 1)x + (k + 2)y + 5 = 0$ into $l_1 + kl_2 = 0$ and find the point of concurence of family lines .

5. Find the circum centre of triangle formed by the points (1, 3), (–3, 5), (5, –1).

6. Find the ortho centre of triangle formed by the points (–2, –1), (6, –1), (2, 5).

7. (i) Find the angle between the lines $x + y + 1 = 0$, $x - 5 = 0$.

(ii) If the lines $2x + 3y + 5 = 0$, $kx + 6y + 7 = 0$ are parallel find k.

(iii) If $2x + 3y + 5 = 0$, $kx + 6y + 7 = 0$ are perpendicular. find k.

8. If the acute angle between the lines

(i) $3x - y + 1 = 0$, $2x + ky + 5 = 0$ is 45^0 then find the value of k

(ii) $2x + 3y - 5 = 0$, $5x + ky - 6 = 0$ is 45^0 then find the value of k.

9. Find the area of parallelogram formed by the lines $3x + 4y + 5 = 0$, $3x + 4y - 2 = 0$, $2x + 3y + 1 = 0$, $2x + 3y - 7 = 0$.

Answers

1. (i) (–2, 2) (ii) $\left(\frac{1}{5}, \frac{14}{5}\right)$

2. (ii) $\lambda = 2$ (iii) $a^3 + b^3 + c^3 = 3abc$

3. (i) $5x - 2y = 88$ (ii) $2x + 5y = -17$

4. (i) $\left(\frac{3}{4}, \frac{1}{2}\right)$ (ii) (5, –5)

5. (–8, –10)

6. $\left(2, \frac{5}{3}\right)$

7. (i) 45^0 or 135^0 (ii) 4 (iii) –9

8. (i) 1, –4 (ii) +1, –25

9. 56 square units

Hint : Area formed by $a_1x + by_1 + c_1 = 0$, $a_2x + b_2y + c_2 = 0$ and $a_1x + b_1y + d_1 = 0$, $a_2x + b_2y + d_2 = 0$

$$\frac{(c_1 - d_1)(c_2 - d_2)}{a_1b_2 - a_2b_1} = \frac{(7)(8)}{9-8} = \frac{56}{1} = 56 \text{ square units}$$

15

Circles

15.1 Equation of Circle, Standard Form, Centre and Radius

A circle is the set of points in a plane such that they are equidistant from a fixed point lying in the plane.

(or) The locus of a point which moves in a plane such that its distance from fixed point is equal to given distance called a circle.

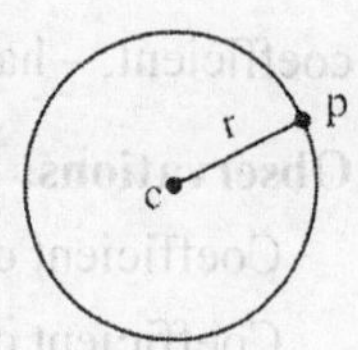

Here fixed point is called centre of the cirlce and the given distance is called the radius of the circle.

So the distance from any point on circle to its centre is radius of the circle.

Theorem: The equation of circle with centre at (x_1, y_1) and radius r is

$$(x - x_1)^2 + (y - y_1)^2 = r^2.$$

Proof: Let p(h, k) be any point on circle with centre at $c(x_1, y_1)$ and radius r.

$\therefore$ by definition CP = r

$\Rightarrow$ $(CP)^2 = r^2$

$\Rightarrow$ $(h - x_1)^2 + (k - y_1)^2 = r^2$

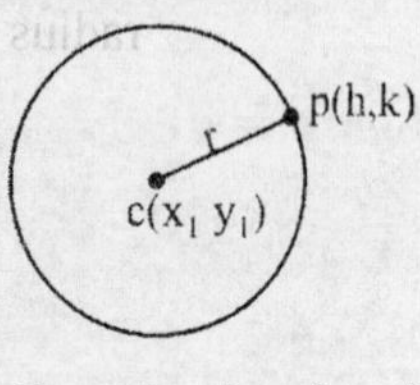

locus of (h, k) is $(x - x_1)^2 + (y - y_1)^2 = r^2$

Note: The equation of circle with centre at (0, 0) and radius r is $x^2 + y^2 = r^2$

EX: 1. The equation of circle with centre (2, 3) and radius 1 is $(x - 2)^2 + (y - 3)^2 = 1^2$

i.e., $(x^2 - 4x + 4) + (y^2 - 6y + 9) = 1$

$\Rightarrow$ $x^2 + y^2 - 4x - 6y + 12 = 0$

2. The equation of circle with centre at (4, –1) and radius 3 is

$$(x-4)^2 + (y+1)^2 = 1^2$$

i.e., $$(x^2 - 8x + 16) + (y^2 + 2y + 1) = 1$$

$\Rightarrow$ $$x^2 + y^2 - 8x + 2y + 16 = 0$$

Standard form of Circle

We have the equation of circle with centre at (x_1, y_1) and radius r is $(x - x_1)^2 + (y - y_1)^2 = r^2$

i.e., $$x^2 + y^2 - 2x_1x - 2y_1y + (x_1^2 + y_1^2 - r^2) = 0$$

put $-x_1 = g, -y_1 = f$ and $x_1^2 + y_1^2 - r^2 = c$

$\Rightarrow$ $g^2 + f^2 - r^2 = c$

$\Rightarrow$ $(x_1, y_1) = (-g, -f)$ $r^2 = g^2 + f^2 - c$

so, $r = \sqrt{g^2 + f^2 - c}$

$\therefore$ above equation becomes

$$x^2 + y^2 + 2gx + 2fy + c = 0 \quad \text{.....} (1)$$

It is called the equation circle in the standard form with centre at $(-g, -f)$ = (– half of x coefficient, – half of y coefficient) and radius $r = \sqrt{g^2 + f^2 - c}$

Observations: in the equation (1)

Coefficient of x^2 = coefficient of y^2 =1

Coefficient of xy = 0

EX: 1. $x^2 + y^2 - 2x + 4y - 1 = 0$ compare with $x^2 + y^2 + 2gx + 2fy + c = 0$

$2g = -2, 2f = 4, c = -1$

$\Rightarrow$ $g = -1, f = 2, c = -1$

$\therefore$ centre $c = (-g, -f) = (1, -2)$

radius $= \sqrt{g^2 + f^2 - c}$

$= \sqrt{(-1)^2 + (2)^2 - (-1)} = \sqrt{1 + 4 + 1}$

$= \sqrt{6}$

2. $x^2 + y^2 - ax - by = 0$

here $2g = -a, 2f = -b, c = 0$

$g = -a/2, f = -b/2$

$\therefore$ centre $c = (-g, -f) = (a/2, b/2)$

radius $r = \sqrt{g^2 + f^2 - c} = \sqrt{\frac{a^2}{4} + \frac{b^2}{4} - 0}$

$= \frac{\sqrt{a^2 + b^2}}{2}$

Note:

1. **Any general second degree equation $ax^2 + 2hxy + by^2 + 2gx + 2fg + c = 0$ represents a circle iff (i) $a = b \neq 0$; (ii) $h = 0$; (iii) $g^2 + f^2 - ac \geq 0$**

   So the equation becames

   $$ax^2 + ay^2 + 2gx + 2fy + c = 0$$

   $$\therefore \quad x^2 + y^2 + \frac{2g}{a}x + \frac{2f}{a}y + y_a = 0 \qquad (\because a \neq 0)$$

   its centre $c = \left(\frac{-g}{a}, \frac{-f}{a}\right)$

   radius $r = \sqrt{\frac{g^2}{a^2} + \frac{f^2}{a^2} - c/a} = \frac{\sqrt{g^2 + f^2 - ac}}{|a|}$

2. **If the circle $x^2 + y^2 + 2gx + 2fy + c = 0$ passing through (0, 0) then $c = 0$**

   $\therefore$ **$x^2 + y^2 + 2gx + 2fy = 0$ represents a circle passing through origin.**

3. **If the centre of circle $x^2 + y^2 + 2gx + 2fy + c = 0$ lies on x-axis then $f = 0$**

   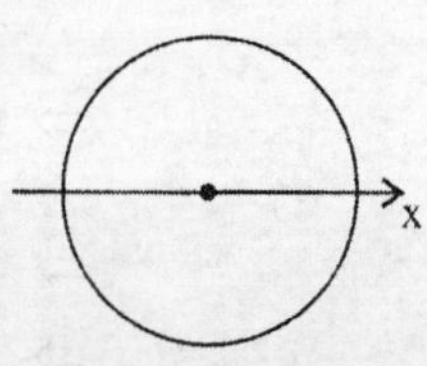

   $\therefore$ the equation of circle whose centre lies on x-axis is of the form

   $$x^2 + y^2 + 2gx + c = 0$$

4. **If the centre of circle $x^2 + y^2 + 2gx + 2fy + c = 0$ lies on y-axis then $g = 0$,**

   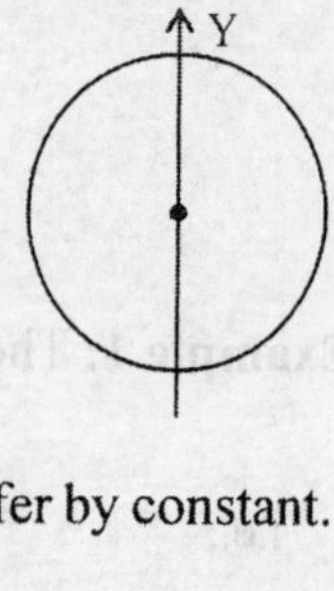

   $\therefore$ the equation of circle whose centre lies on y-axis is of the form

   $$x^2 + y^2 + 2fg + c = 0.$$

5. **If two or more circles have same centre then they are said to be concentric circles and the equations of concentric circles are only differ by constant.**

6. **A circle of radius 1 is called unit circle.**

15.2 Chord - Diameter - Lengths of Intercepts

Chord: If A and B are any two points on circle then the line segment joining of A, B is called chord of a circle.

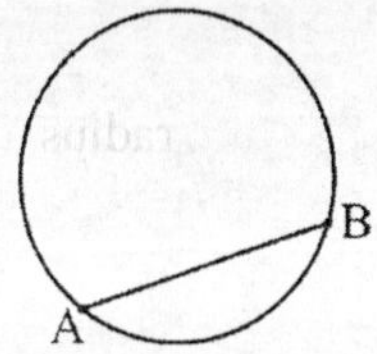

Diameter: The largest chord (of joining of two points on circle) is called diameter of circle.

Note:

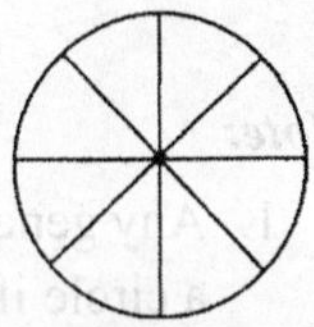

1. There exists infinite number of diameters to a circle.
2. Every diameter passing through centre of the circle.
3. Every circle is symmetric about every diameter of circle.
4. Length of diameter of circle is equal to twice the radius of circle.
5. The point of intersection as of any two diameters is centre of the circle.
6. Angle in a semi circle is 90^0
7. Two mid point of extremities of a diameter is centre of the circle.

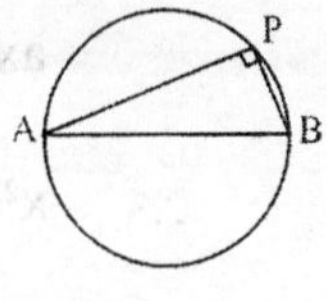

Theorem: The equation of circle whose ends of a diameter are $A(x_1, y_1)$ $B(x_2, y_2)$ is

$$(x - x_1)(x - x_2) + (y - y_1)(y - y_2) = 0$$

Proof: Let P(h, k) be any point on circlé whose ends of a diameter are $A(x_1, y_1)$ $B(x_2, y_2)$.

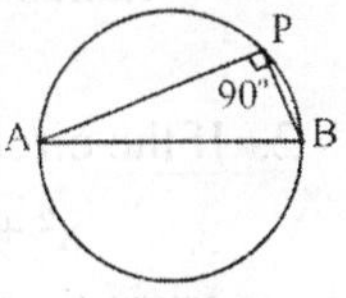

Since angle in semi circle is 90^0

$\therefore$ $\angle APB = 90^0$

$\therefore$ slope of PA × slope of PB = – 1

$$\Rightarrow \frac{k-y_1}{h-x_1} \times \frac{k-y_2}{h-x_2} = -1$$

$$\Rightarrow (k - y_1)(k - y_2) = -(h - x_1)(h - x_2)$$

$$\Rightarrow (h - x_1)(h - x_2) + (k - y_1)(k - y_2) = 0$$

$\therefore$ locus of (h, k) is

$$(x - x_1)(x - x_2) + (y - y_1)(y - y_2) = 0$$

it is the equation of circle whose ends of diameter are $A(x_1, y_1)$ $B(x_2, y_2)$.

Example 1: The equation of circle whose ends of a diameter are (1, 2) (3, 4) is

$$(x - 1)(x - 3) + (y - 2)(y - 4) = 0$$

i.e., $$(x^2 - 3x - x + 3) + (y^2 - 4y - 2y + 8) = 0$$

or $$x^2 + y^2 - 4x - 6y + 11 = 0$$

Example 2: The equation of circle whose ends of a diameter are (3, – 1) (– 4, 5) is

$$(x-3)(x-(-4))+(y-(-1))(y-5)=0$$

i.e.,
$$(x-3)(x+4)+(y+1)(y-5)=0$$

$$(x^2+4x-3x-12)+(y^2-5y+y-5)=0$$

$$\Rightarrow \quad x^2+y^2+x-4y-17=0$$

Length of x, and y–intercepts made by a Circle.

Suppose a circle intersects x-axis at A, B then distance AB is called length of x-intercept made the circle. Similarly if a circle intersect y-axis and C, D then distance CD is called length of y-intercept made by the circle.

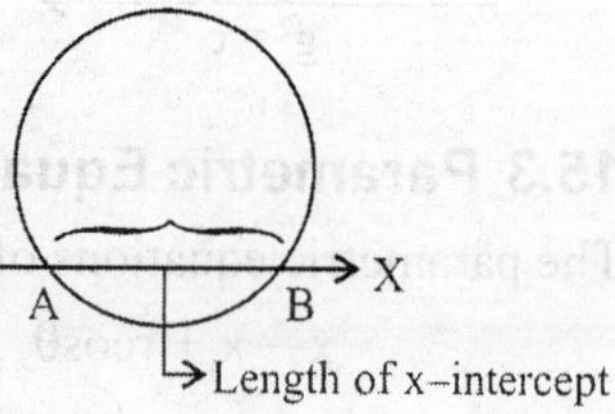

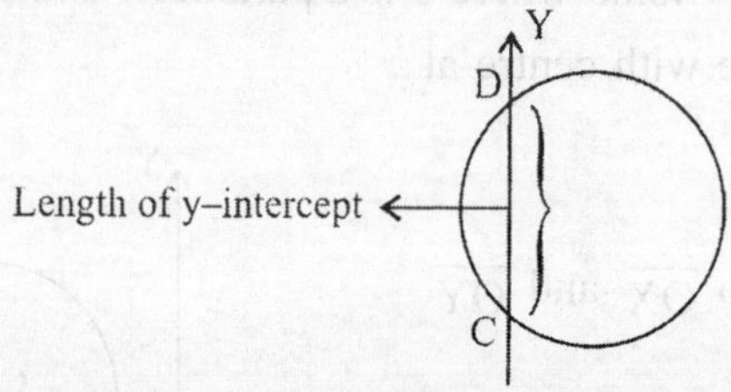

Theorem: The length of x-intercept and y-intercept made by the circle $x^2+y^2+2gx+2fy+c=0$ are $2\sqrt{g^2-c}$ and $2\sqrt{f^2-c}$ respectively.

Proof: Suppose $x^2+y^2+2gx+2fy+c=0$ .....(1)

intersets x-axis (y = 0) at A, B.

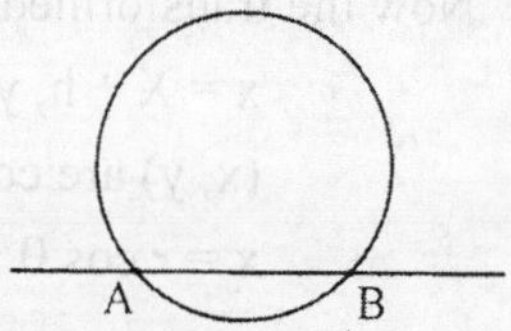

∴ the length AB is x-intercept.

put y = 0 in eq. (1) we get

$$x^2+2gx+c=0$$

it is a quadratic equation in 'x' its roots are x-coordinates of points of intersections made by x-axis and the circle. Let them be x_1, x_2 say

$$\therefore \quad x_1+x_2=-2g \quad \text{(sum of roots)}$$

$$x_1 x_2 = c \qquad \text{(product of roots)}$$

Now A = $(x_1, 0)$, B = $(x_2, 0)$

$$\therefore \quad AB=|x_1-x_2|=\sqrt{(x_1+x_2)^2-4x_1x_2}$$

$$=\sqrt{4g^2-4.c}=2\sqrt{g^2-c}$$

Similarly we can prove length of y-intercept

$$=2\sqrt{f^2-c}$$

Note: If a circle $x^2 + y^2 + 2gx + 2fy + c = 0$ touches x-axis of $g^2 = c$, and touches y-axis if $f^2 = c$ and touches both the x- and y-axis if $g^2 = f^2 = c$.

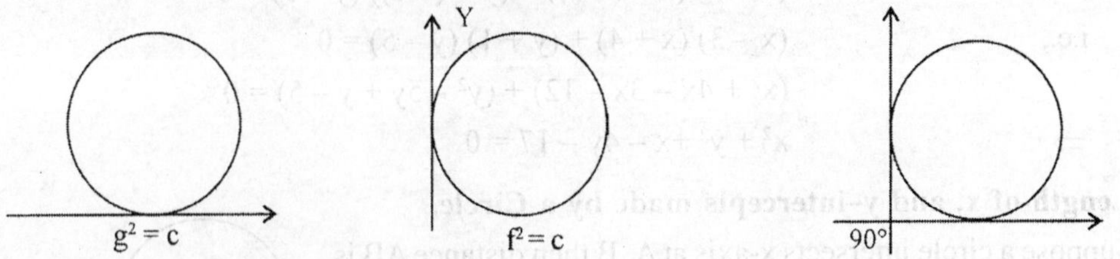

15.3 Parametric Equations of Circle

The parametric equations of circle with centre at (x_1, y_1) and radius r are

$$x = x_1 + r\cos\theta,\ y = y_1 + r\sin\theta \text{ where } \theta \text{ is a parameter and } 0 \le \theta < 2\pi.$$

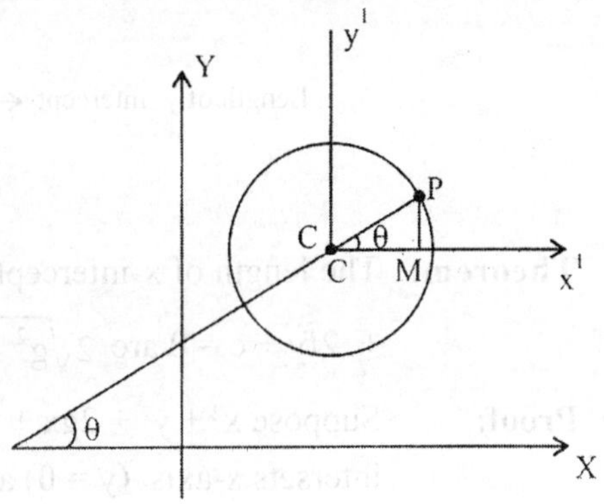

Let P(x, y) be any point of circle with centre at $c(x_1\ y_1)$ and radius r.

$\therefore \quad CP = r$

Draw cx' and CY^1 parallel to $\overline{OX}$ and $\overline{OY}$ respectively.

Let $\angle Pcx^1 = \theta$.

Now shifting the origin to the point $c(x_1\ y_1)$ with out changing the direction of axes.

Now the transformed equations are

$$x = X + h,\ y = Y + k$$

(x, y) are coordinates of P w.r.t new coordinates

$$\Rightarrow \quad x = r\cos\theta + x_1 \qquad y = r\sin\theta + y_1$$

$$\left(\because \cos\theta = \frac{x}{r}, \sin\theta = \frac{y}{r}\right)$$

$$\therefore \quad x = x_1 + r\cos\theta,\ y = y_1 + r\sin\theta \text{ where } \theta \text{ is parameter and } 0 \le \theta < 2\pi$$

Solved Problems

1. Find the equation circle with centre at (4, 1) and radius 5.

Sol. Given centre = C = $(x_1\ y_1)$ = (4, 1) radius r = 5

$\therefore$ the equation of circle with centre at $(x_1\ y_1)$ and radius r is

$$(x - x_1)^2 + (y - y_1)^2 = r^2$$

i.e., $(x - 4)^2\ (y - 1)^2 = 5^2$

$\Rightarrow \quad x^2 + y^2 - 8x - 2y + 16 + 1 - 25 = 0$

i.e., $x^2 + y^2 - 8x - 2y - 8 = 0$

2. Find the equation of circle whose centre is at (1, 1) and passing through the point (6, 5)

Sol. Given centre c = (1, 1) and p = (6, 5) is a point on circle.

$\therefore$ radius $r = cp = \sqrt{(6-1)^2+(5-1)^2} = \sqrt{25+16} = \sqrt{41}$

so centre $c = (1, 1)$, radius $r = \sqrt{41}$

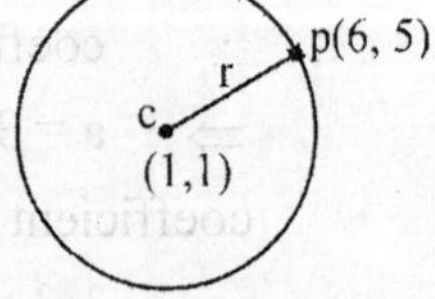

$\therefore$ equation of circle is

$$(x-1)^2+(y-1)^2 = (\sqrt{41})^2$$

$\Rightarrow \quad (x^2-2x+1)+(y^2-2y+1) = 41$

$\Rightarrow \quad x^2+y^2-2x-2y-39 = 0$

3. Find the centre and radius of the circle $x^2+y^2-2x+4y-4 = 0$

Sol. Here $2g = -2, 2f = 4, c = -4$

$\Rightarrow \quad g = -1, f = 2, c = -4$

centre $= (-g,-f) = (1, -2)$

radius $r = \sqrt{g^2+f^2-c} = \sqrt{1+4+4} = 3$

4. Find the centre and radius of circle $2x^2+2y^2-4x+6y-1 = 0$

Sol. $2x^2+2y^2-4x+6y-1 = 0$

i.e., $x^2+y^2-2x+3y-1/2 = 0$

here $2g = -2, 2f = 3, c = -1/2$

$g = -1, f = 3/2, c = -1/2$

centre $= (-g, -f) = (1, -3/2)$

radius $r = \sqrt{g^2+f^2-c}$

$= \sqrt{1+9/4+1/2}$

$= \sqrt{\dfrac{4+9+2}{4}} = \sqrt{\dfrac{15}{4}}$

$= \dfrac{\sqrt{15}}{2}$

5. Find the equation of circle passing through (2, 1) and concentric with the circle $x^2+y^2+6x+4y-1 = 0$

Sol. The equation of any circle concentric with the given circle is of the form

$$x^2+y^2+6x+4y+k = 0$$

if it is passing through (2, 1) then $4 + 1 + 12 + 4 + k = 0$

$21 + k = 0 \Rightarrow k = -21$

$\therefore \quad x^2 + y^2 + 6x + 4y - 21 = 0$

6. Find the values of a, b if $ax^2 + bxy + 3y^2 + 5x - 2y - 3 = 0$ represents a circle also find the centre and radius.

Sol. $ax^2 + bxy + 3y^2 + 5x - 2y - 3 = 0$ represents a circle

$\therefore$ coefficient of x^2 = coefficient of y^2

$\Rightarrow \quad a = 3$

coefficient of xy = 0 $\Rightarrow b = 0$

$\therefore \quad 3x^2 + 3y^2 + 5x - 2y - 3 = 0$

$$\therefore \quad x^2 + y^2 + \frac{5}{3}x - \frac{2}{3}y - 1 = 0$$

$\therefore$ centre c = (–5/6, 1/3)

$$\text{radius } r = \sqrt{\frac{25}{36} + \frac{1}{9} + 1}$$

$$= \sqrt{\frac{25 + 4 + 36}{36}} = \frac{\sqrt{65}}{6}$$

7. If the circle $x^2 + y^2 - 4x + 6y + a = 0$ has radius 3, then find a.

Sol. Given equation of circle is $x^2 + y^2 - 4x + 6y + a = 0$

$\therefore$ centre c = (2, –3)

$$\text{radius} = \sqrt{4 + 9 - a} = 3$$

$$= \sqrt{13 - a} = 3$$

$\Rightarrow \quad 13 - a = 9 \quad \Rightarrow \quad a = 13 - 9 = 4$

$\therefore \quad a = 4$

8. Find the equation of circle whose ends of a diameter are (1, 2) and (4, 5).

Sol. The equation of circle whose ends of a diameter are $(x_1\ y_1)\ (x_2\ y_2)$ is

$$(x - x_1)(x - x_2) + (y - y_1)(y - y_2) = 0$$

here $(x_1 y_1) = (1, 2), (x_2 y_2) = (4, 5) \Rightarrow x_1 = 1, y_1 = 2, x_2 = 4, y_2 = 5$

$\therefore \quad (x - 1)(x - 4) + (y - 2)(y - 5) = 0$

$\Rightarrow \quad (x^2 - 5x + 4) + (y^2 - 7y + 10) = 0$

i.e., $\quad x^2 + y^2 - 5x - 7y + 14 = 0$

9. Find the other end of diameter of the circle $x^2+y^2-8x-8y+27=0$. If one end of it is (2, 3).

Sol. Let B (x_1, y_1) be other end of diameter of $x^2+y^2-8x-8y+27=0$ whose one ends is A(2, 3).

Now centre C = (4, 4)

$\therefore$ C is mid point of AB.

$$\therefore \quad (4,4)=\left(\frac{x_1+2}{3},\frac{y_1+3}{2}\right) \Rightarrow \frac{x_1+2}{3}=4,\quad \frac{y_1+3}{2}=4$$

$\therefore \quad x_1+2=12$

$x_1=10$

$y_1+3=8$

and $y_1=5$

$\therefore \quad (x_1, y_1)=(10, 5)$

10. Find the centre and radius of circle passing through the points (0, 0) (1, 0) (0, 1)

Sol. Let O = (0, 0) A = (1, 0) B = (0, 1)

$\therefore$ OA =- 1, OB = 1

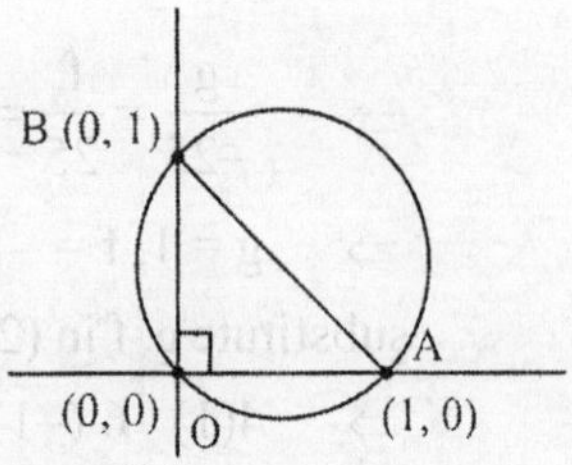

Clearly $\angle AOB = 90^\circ$

$\therefore$ AB is a diameter of circle.

$\therefore \quad (x-1)(x-0)+(y-0)(y-1)=0$

$x^2+y^2-x-y=0$

11. Obtain the parametric equations of circle $(x-3)^2+(y+4)^2=32$

Sol. Given $(x-3)^2+(y+4)^2=6^2$

here centre $C=(3,-4)=(x_1, y_1)$; radius = 6 = r

$\therefore$ the parametric equations of circle with centre at (x_1, y_1) and radius r are

$x=x_1+r\cos\theta,\ y=y_1+r\sin\theta$

$\therefore \quad x=3+6\cos\theta,\ y=-4+6\sin\theta$

where θ is a parameter and $0\le\theta<2\pi$

12. Find the equation of circle passing through (2, –3) and (–4, 5) and having centre on $4x+3y+1=0$.

Sol. Let A = (2, –3), B = (–4, 5) and $4x+3y+1=0$ ..... (1)

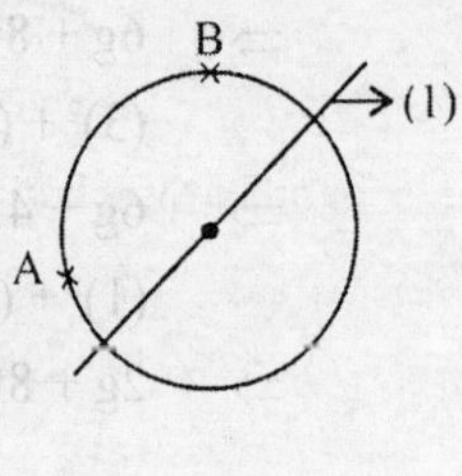

Let $S=x^2+y^2+2gx+2fy+c=0$ be required equation of circle

$\therefore$ A, B lies on it

$\Rightarrow \quad (2)^2+(-3)^2+2g(2)+2f(-3)+c=0$

$\Rightarrow \quad 4g - 6f + c = -13$ ..... (2)

and $\quad (-4)^2 + (5)^2 + 2g(-4) + 2f(5) + c = 0$

$\Rightarrow \quad -8g + 10f + c = -41$ ..... (3)

$(2)-(3) \Rightarrow$

$$12g - 16f = 28$$

i.e., $\quad 3g - 4f - 7 = 0$ ..... (4)

also centre $(-g, -f)$ lies on $4x + 3y + 1 = 0$

$\Rightarrow \quad -4g - 3f + 1 = 0$ ..... (5)

Solving (4) and (5)

$$\begin{matrix} & g & & f & & c & \\ -4 & & -7 & & 3 & & -4 \\ -3 & & 1 & & -4 & & -3 \end{matrix}$$

$$\Rightarrow \quad \frac{g}{-4-21} = \frac{f}{28-3} = \frac{1}{-9-16}$$

$$\Rightarrow \quad \frac{g}{-25} = \frac{f}{25} = \frac{1}{-25}$$

$\Rightarrow \quad g = 1, f = -1$

substitute g, f in (2)

$\Rightarrow \quad 4(1) - 6(-1) + c = -13$

$c = -13 - 10 = -23$

substitute g, f, c in S = 0

$\therefore \quad x^2 + y^2 + 2x - 2y - 23 = 0$

13. Find the equation of circle passing through three points (3, 4) (3, 2) (1, 4)

Sol. Suppose the required equation of circle is

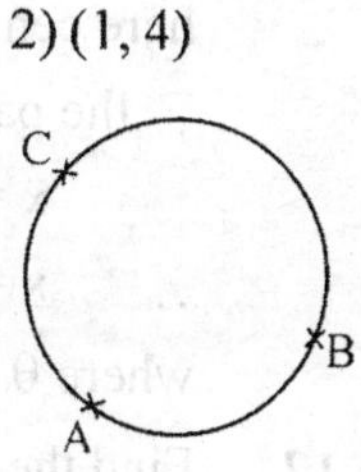

$S = x^2 + y^2 + 2gx + 2fy + c = 0$

$\therefore$ it is passing through the given points

A = (3, 4), B = (3, 2), C = (1, 4)

we get $\quad (3)^2 + (4)^2 + 2(3)g + 2(4)f + c = 0$

$\Rightarrow \quad 6g + 8f + c = -25$ ..... (1)

$(3)^2 + (2)^2 + 2(3)g + 2(2)f + c = 0$

$\Rightarrow \quad 6g + 4f + c = -13$ ..... (2)

$(1)^2 + (4)^2 + 2(1)g + 2(4)f + c = 0$

$\Rightarrow \quad 2g + 8f + c = -17$ ..... (3)

$(1) - (2) \Rightarrow 4f = -12 \Rightarrow f = -3$

$(2) - (3) \Rightarrow 4g - 4f = 4$

$\Rightarrow \quad g - f = 1 \Rightarrow g + 3 = 1$

$\Rightarrow \quad g = -2$

substitute g, f in (1)

$6(-2) + 8(-3) - c = -25$

$\Rightarrow \quad -12 - 24 + c = -25$

$\Rightarrow \quad -36 + c = -25$

$\Rightarrow \quad c = 36 - 25 = 11$

$\therefore \quad x^2 + y^2 - 4x - 6y + 11 = 0$

14. Find the equation of circle passing through (0, 0) and making intercepts 4, 3 on x-axis and y-axis respectively.

Sol. Suppose the required equation of circle is

$S = x^2 + y^2 + 2gx + 2y + c = 0$

it is passing through (0, 0)

$\Rightarrow \quad c = 0$

length of x intercept $= 2\sqrt{g^2 - c} = 4$

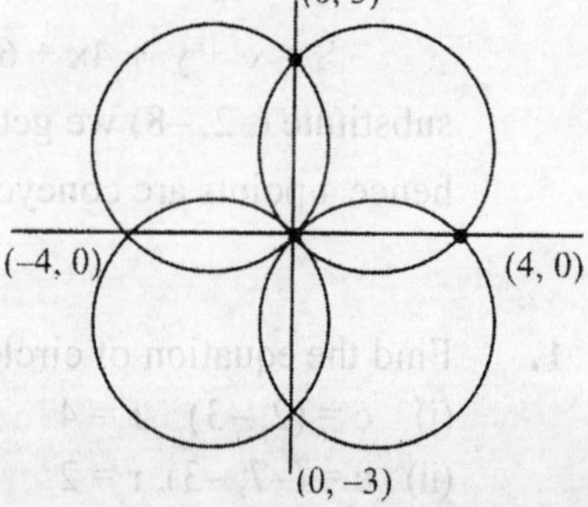

$\Rightarrow \quad 2\left(\sqrt{g^2}\right) = 4 \quad (\because c = 0)$

$\Rightarrow \quad 2|g| = 4$

$\Rightarrow \quad |g| = 2$

$\Rightarrow \quad g = \pm 2$

and length of y-intercept = 3

$\Rightarrow \quad 2\sqrt{f^2 - c} = 3$

$\Rightarrow \quad 2\sqrt{f^2} = 3 \qquad (\because c = 0)$

$\Rightarrow \quad 2|f| = 3$

$\therefore \quad |f| = 3/2$

$\Rightarrow \quad f = \pm 3/2$

so we have $g = \pm 2$, $f = \pm 3/2$, $c = 0$

substitute in $S = 0$

we get $x^2 + y^2 \pm 4x \pm 3y = 0$ it is the required equation.

15. Show that the points (1, 1), (–6, 0), (–2, 2) and (–2, –8) are concyclic.

Sol. We have to show that the given four points lies on a circle. For this first we find the equation of circle passing through three points. (1, 1), (–6, 0), (–2, 2)

Suppose the equation is $S = x^2 + y^2 + 2gx + 2fy + c = 0$

$\therefore$ substitute (1, 1), (–6, 0), (–2, 2). we get

$$2g + 2f + c = -2 \quad \text{..... (1)}$$

$$-12g + c = -36 \quad \text{..... (2)}$$

$$-4g + 4f + c = -8 \quad \text{..... (3)}$$

$(1) - (2) \Rightarrow 14g + 2f = 34 \Rightarrow 7g + f = 17$ ..... (4)

$(2) - (3) \Rightarrow -8g - 4f = 28 \Rightarrow -2g - f = -7$ ..... (5)

$(4) + (5) \Rightarrow 5g = 10 \Rightarrow g = 2$

substitute $g = 2$ in (4)

$$14 + f = 17 \Rightarrow f = 3$$

substitute g, f in (1) $\Rightarrow 4 + 6 + c = -2$

$$c = -12$$

$\therefore \quad S = x^2 + y^2 + 4x + 6y - 12 = 0$

substitute (–2, –8) we get $4 + 64 - 8 - 48 - 12 = 68 - 68 = 0$

hence 4 points are concyclic.

Exercise 15.1

1. Find the equation of circle with centre at c and radius r where
   (i) $c = (2, -3)$, $r = 4$
   (ii) $c = (-7, -3)$, $r = 2$
2. Find the equation of circle passing through origin and having centre at (–2, –4)
3. Find the value of a if $4x^2 + ay^2 - 3x + 2y - 1 = 0$ represents a circle and find its radius also.
4. If $x^2 + y^2 - 4x + 6y + c = 0$ represents a circle of radius 6 then find c.
5. Find the centre and radius of circle
   (i) $x^2 + y^2 + 8x + 6y - 96 = 0$
   (ii) $2x^2 + 2y^2 + 2x - 3y - 1 = 0$
6. Find the equation of circle whose ends of diameter are
   (i) (4, 1) (2, 5)
   (ii) (3, 2) (1, 7)

7. Obtain the parametric equations of circle
   (i) $x^2 + y^2 = 16$
   (ii) $x^2 + y^2 - 6x - 4y - 12 = 0$
8. If (3, –1) is one end of diameter of circle $x^2 + y^2 - 2x + 4y = 0$ then find the other end of diameter through the point.
9. Find the equation of circle passes through (4, 1), (6, 5) and having centre on $4x + 3y - 24 = 0$.
10. Find the equation of circle passing through the points (1, 2), (3, –4) (5, –6).
11. Find the equation of circle passing through (0, 0) and having intercepts 4 units on x-axis and 6 units on y-axis.
12. Show that the four points (1, 2) (3, –4) (5, –6) (19, 8) are concyclic.
13. If (2, 0) (0, 1) (4, 5) and (0, c) are concyclic, find c.

Answers

1. (i) $x^2 + y^2 - 4x + 6y - 3 = 0$
   (ii) $x^2 + y^2 + 14x + 6y + 54 = 0$
2. $x^2 + y^2 + 4x + 8y = 0$
3. $a = 4,\ r = (\sqrt{17})/4$
4. –23
5. (i) $c = (-4, -3),\ r = 11$
   (ii) $c = \left(-1/2, 3/4\right)\quad r = \sqrt{\frac{1}{4} + \frac{9}{16} - \frac{1}{2}} = \sqrt{\frac{4+9-8}{16}} = \frac{\sqrt{5}}{4}$
6. (i) $x^2 + y^2 - 6x - 6y + 13 = 0$
   (ii) $x^2 + y^2 - 4x - 9y + 17 = 0$
7. (i) $x = 4\cos\theta,\ y = 4\sin\theta$
   (ii) $x = 3 + 5\cos\theta,\ y = 2 + 5\sin\theta$
8. (–1, –3)
9. $x^2 + y^2 - 6x - 8y + 15 = 0$
10. $x^2 + y^2 - 22x - 4y + 25 = 0$
11. $x^2 + y^2 \pm 4x \pm 6y = 0$
12. 14/3

16

Parabola

Parabola is one of conic section. Conic section is a section of double napped right circular cone with a plane. In view of the analytical approach we set the following basic definitions.

16.1 Basic Definitions

A Conic is the locus of a point moving on a plane such that its distance from fixed point and fixed line are in the constant ratio. Here the fixed point is called 'focus', fixed line is called 'directrix' and the constant ratio is called eccentricity of conic. Focus is denoted by S. directrix is denoted by L and eccentricity is denoted by 'e'.

$$\therefore \quad \frac{SP}{PM} = e$$

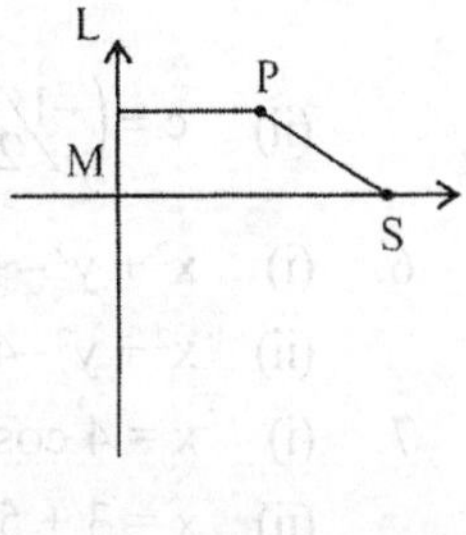

where PM is perpendicular distance from point (point on locus) P to directrix.

If e = 1 then the conic is called a parabola.

If e < 1 then the conic is called an ellipse.

If e > 1 then the conic is called an hyperbola.

Axis: The line passing through focus and perpendicular to directrix is called axis.

Vertex: The point where the axis meet the conic is called vertex.

Chord: The line segment joining of any two points on conic is called chord.

Focal Chord: A chord passing through focus is called a focal chord.

Double Ordinate: Any chord perpendicular to axis is called double ordinate.

Latus rectum: The focal chord perpendicular to axis is called latus rectum.

Focal Distance: Let P be any point on conic with focus S, then the distance SP is called the focal distance of point P with respect to conic.

16.2 Standard Equation of Parabola

Statement: The standard equation of parabola is $y^2 = 4ax$ $(a > 0)$

Proof: Let S be the focus and line L be the directrix. Draw a line SZ perpendicular from focus S to L as shown in the figure.

Let A be the mid point of SZ such that SA = AZ = a.

Choose A as origin and $\overrightarrow{AS}$ as x-axis then the line passing through A and perpendiular to $\overrightarrow{AS}$ is y-axis.

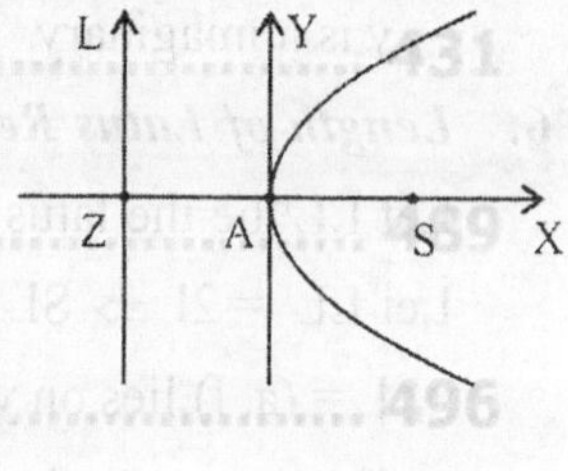

$\therefore$ now S = (a, 0); Z = (–a, 0)

directrix is perpendicular to x-axis, it is of the form

$x + k = 0$ it is passing through (–a, 0)

$\therefore$ $-a + k = 0, \Rightarrow k = a$

$\therefore$ $x + a = 0$

so we have focus S = (a, 0); directrix is x + a = 0.

Let $P(x_1, y_1)$ be any point on parabola

$\therefore$ by definition $\frac{SP}{PM} = 1$

$\therefore$ $SP = PM$

$\Rightarrow$ $(SP)^2 = (PM)^2$

$\Rightarrow$ $(x_1 - a)^2 + y_1^2 = \left(\frac{x_1 + a}{\sqrt{1}}\right)^2$

$\Rightarrow$ $(x_1 + a)^2 - (x_1 - a)^2 = y_1^2$

$\therefore$ $y_1^2 = 4ax_1$

$\therefore$ Locus of (x_1, y_1) is $y^2 = 4ax$

It is the required equation of parabola.

16.3 Nature of the Curve $y^2 = 4ax$

1. If (x, y) lies on parabola then (–x, y) lies on it. The curve is symmetric about x-axis. x-axis is also the line passing through focus (a, 0) and perpendicular to directrix $x + a = 0$

   $\therefore$ axis is x-axis i.e., y = 0

2. The point of intersection of axis ($y = 0$) and curve ($y^2 = 4ax$) is $(0, 0)$.

$\therefore$ Vertex is $(0, 0)$

3. Put $x = 0$ in $y^2 = 4ax$; we get $y^2 = 0$ is $y = 0, 0$ both point of intersections of $x = 0$, $y^2 = 4ax$ coinsides with $(0, 0)$.

$\therefore$ $x = 0$ is tangent at vertex $(0, 0)$ of $y^2 = 4ax$.

4. $y^2 = 4ax \Rightarrow y = \pm 2\sqrt{ax}$ as x increases from 0 to ∞ both the values of y increases from 0 to ∞ numerically.

5. There is no curve left side of y-axis. Since if $x < 0$ then $y^2 = 4ax < 0$ i.e., $y^2 < 0$.

$\therefore$ y is immaginary.

6. ***Length of Latus Rectun:***

Let LL^1 be the latus rectum of parabola $y^2 = 4ax$ whose focus is S.

Let $LL^1 = 2l \Rightarrow SL = SL^1 = l$ and $AS = a$

$\therefore$ $L = (a, l)$ lies on $y^2 = 4ax$

$\therefore$ $l^2 = 4a \Rightarrow l = 2a, \Rightarrow 2l = 4a$

$\therefore$ $L = (a, 2a)$; $L^1 = (a, -2a)$

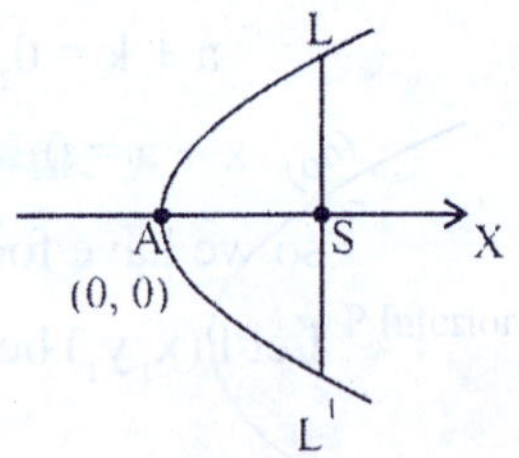

So length of latus rectun is 4a and ends of latus rectun are (a, 2a) (a, –2a)

7. **Focal distance of a point $p(x_1, y_1)$**

$$\text{Focal distance } SP = PM = \left|\frac{x_1 + a}{\sqrt{1}}\right| = |x_1 + a|$$

here PM is for distance from p to directrix.

16.4 Different forms of Parabola

$y^2 = 4ax$

Vertex: (0, 0) Focus (a, 0)

Directrix $x + a = 0$ LLR = 4a

axis x-axis ($y = 0$)

Tangent at vertex y-axis ($x = 0$)

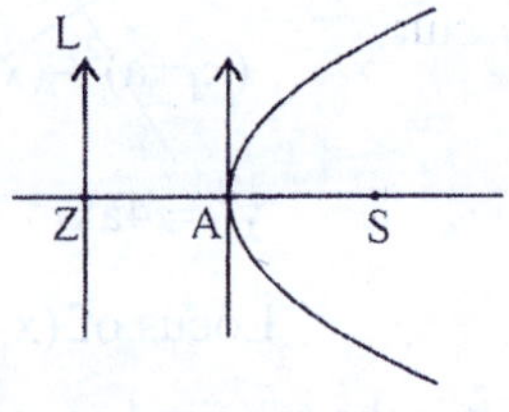

$y^2 = -4ax$

Vertex (0, 0) Focus (–a, 0)

directrix $x - a = 0$ LLR 4a

axis x-axis ($y = 0$)

Tangent at vertex y-axis ($x = 0$)

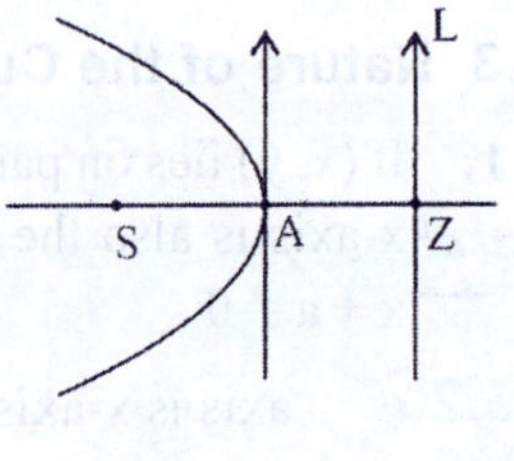

$x^2 = 4ay$

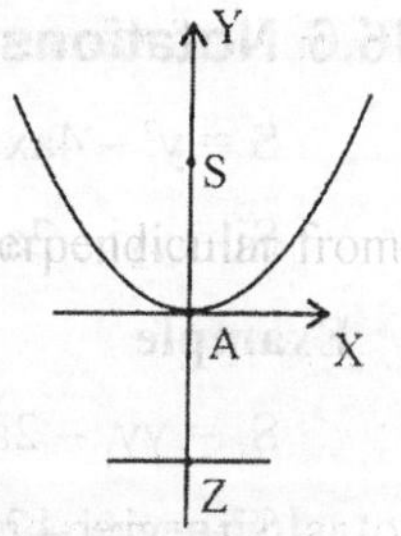

Vertex (0, 0) Focus (0, a)

directrix $y + a = 0$ LLR = 4a (length of latus rectun)

axis y-axis $(x = 0)$

Tangent at vertex x-axis $(y = 0)$

$x^2 = -4ay$

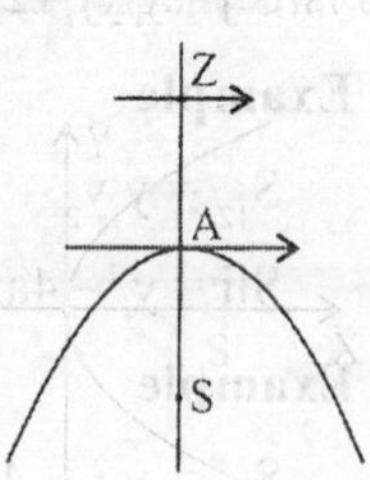

Vertex (0, 0) Focus (0, –a)

directrix $x + a = 0$ LLR = 4a

axis y-axis $(x = 0)$

Tangent at vertex x-axis $(y = 0)$

The equation of parabola whose axis parallel x-axis with vertex at (h,k) is

$(y - k)^2 = \pm 4a(x - h)$

+ for rightwards

– for leftwards

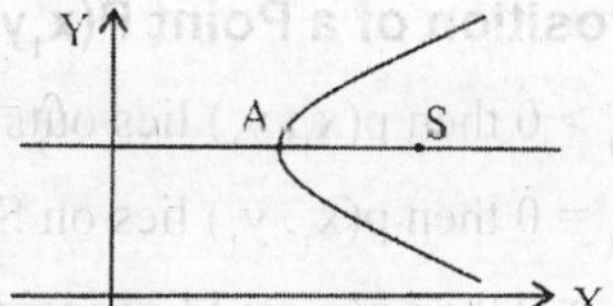

(or) $x = ly^2 + my + n$

The equation of parabola whose axis is parallel to y-axis with vertex at (h, k) is

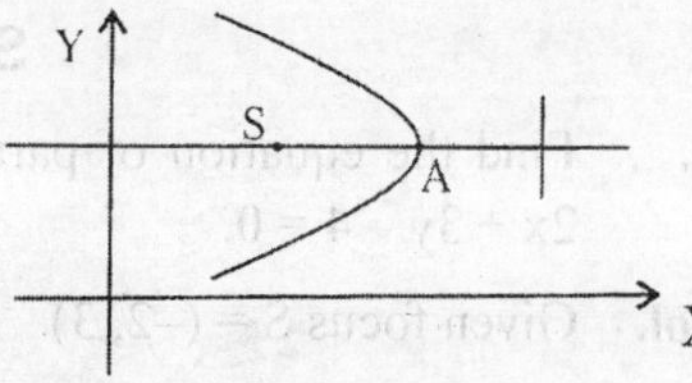

$(x - h)^2 = \pm 4a(y - k)$

'+' for upwards

'–' for downwards

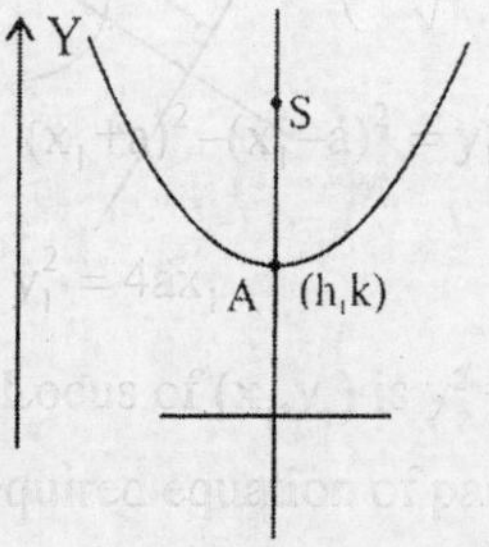

or

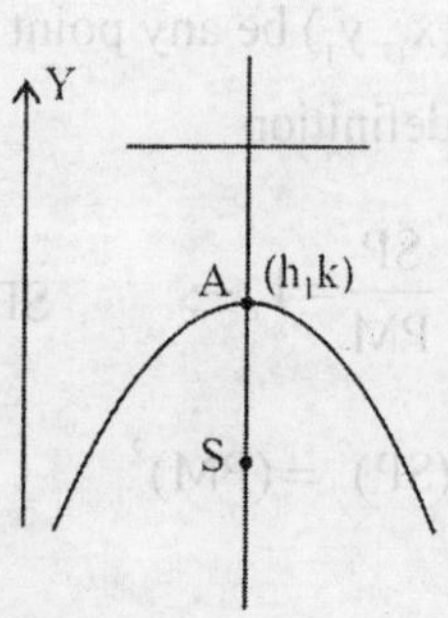

16.5 Parametric Equation of Parabola $y^2 = 4ax$

The point $(at^2, 2at)$ lies on parabola $y^2 = 4ax$ for all real values of t.

So we take $x = at^2$, $y = 2at$ are the parametric equations of parabola.

16.6 Notations

$S = y^2 - 4ax$

$S_i = yy_i - 2a\,(x+x_i)\ i \in N$

Example

$S_1 = yy_1 - 2a\,(x + x_1)$

$S_{ij} = y_iy_j - 2a\,(x_i + x_j)\ i, j \in N$

Example

$S_{12} = y_1y_2 - 2a\,(x_1+x_2)$

$S_{ii} = y_i^2 - 4ax_i\ i \in N$

Example

$S_{11} = y_1^2 - 4ax_1$

16.7 Position of a Point $P(x_1y_1)$ with Respect to $S = y^2 = 4ax$

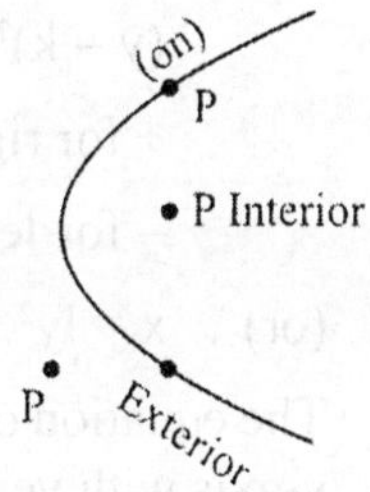

If $S_{11} > 0$ then $p(x_1, y_1)$ lies outside of $S = 0$

If $S_{11} = 0$ then $p(x_1, y_1)$ lies on $S = 0$

If $S_{11} < 0$ then $p(x_1, y_1)$ lies inside of $S = 0$

Solved Problems

1. Find the equation of parabola whose focus is (–2, 3) and directrix is the line $2x + 3y - 4 = 0$.

Sol. Given focus $S = (-2, 3)$

directrix is $L = 2x + 3y - 4 = 0$

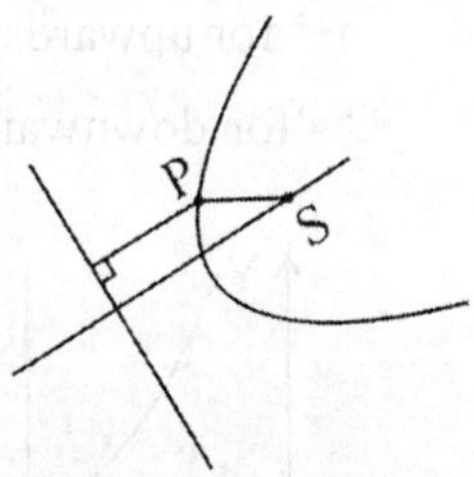

Let $P(x_1, y_1)$ be any point on parabola.

$\therefore$ by definition

$$\frac{SP}{PM} = 1 \Rightarrow \qquad SP = PM$$

$$\therefore \quad (SP)^2 = (PM)^2$$

$$\Rightarrow \quad (x_1 + 2)^2 + (y_1 - 3)^2 = \left(\frac{2x_1 + 3y_1 - 4}{\sqrt{4+9}}\right)^2$$

$$\Rightarrow \quad 13\{(x_1 + 2)^2 + (y_1 - 3)^2\} = (2x_1 + 3y_1 - 4)^2$$

$$\Rightarrow \quad 13\{x_1^2+4+4x_1+y_1^2+9-6y_1\} = 4x_1^2+9y_1^2+16+12x_1y_1-16x_1-24y_1$$

$$\Rightarrow \quad 13x_1^2+13y_1^2+52x_1-78y_1+169$$

$$= 4x_1^2+9y_1^2+12x_1y_1-16x_1-24y_1+16$$

$$\Rightarrow \quad 9x_1^2+4y_1^2-12x_1y_1+68x_1+54y_1+153=0$$

$\therefore$ locus of $(x_1 y_1)$ is

$$9x^2+4y^2-12xy+68x+54y+153=0$$

2. Find the coordinates of vertex, focus, equation of directrix and axis of the following parabolas.

(i) $y^2 = 16x$ (ii) $x^2 = -4y$

Sol. (i) $y^2 = 16x$

Compare with $y^2 = 4ax$

So we have $4a = 16 \Rightarrow a = 4$

Vertex = (0, 0) Focus = (a, 0) = (4, 0)

directrix $x + a = 0$ i.e., $x + 4 = 0$

axis $y = 0$

(ii) $x^2 = -4y$

Compare with $x^2 = 4ay$

$4a = -4 \Rightarrow a = -1$

Vertex = (0, 0)

Focus = (0, a) = (0, –1)

directrix $y + a = 0$, $y + (-1) = 0$, $y - 1 = 0$

axis $x = 0$

3. Find the coordinates of the vertex and focus, the equation of directrix and axis of the following parabolas.

(i) $y^2 + 4x + 4y - 3 = 0$

(ii) $x^2 - 2x + 4y - 3 = 0$

Sol. Consider $y^2 + 4x + 4y - 3 = 0$

$y^2 + 4y = -4x - 3$

$$y^2 + 4y + 4 = -4x - 3 + 4$$

$$(y + 2)^2 = -4x + 1 = -4(x - 1/4)$$

$$\therefore \quad (y + 2)^2 = -4(x - 1/4)$$

Let it be $y^2 = 4ax$

$$Y = y + 2,\ X = x - 1/4,\ 4a = -4,\ a = -1$$

Vertex = (0, 0)

$$\therefore \quad X = 0 \qquad Y = 0$$

$$x - 1/4 = 0 \quad \Rightarrow \quad x = 1/4$$

$$y + 2 = 0 \quad \Rightarrow \quad y = -2$$

$\therefore$ Vertex = (1/4, –2)

Focus S = (a, 0)

$$X = a,$$

$$x - 1/4 = -1 \quad \Rightarrow \quad x = -1 + \tfrac{1}{4} = \frac{-4+1}{4} = \frac{-3}{4}$$

$$y + 2 = 0 \quad \Rightarrow \quad y = 2$$

$\therefore$ focus = (–3/4, –2)

directrix is $x + a = 0$

$$x - 1/4 - 1 = 0$$

$$4x - 5 = 0$$

axis $Y = 0 \quad y + 2 = 0$

(ii) $x^2 - 2x + 4y - 3 = 0$

$$x^2 - 2x = -4y + 3$$

$$x^2 - 2x + 1 = -4y + 3 + 1$$

$$\Rightarrow \quad (x - 1)^2 = -4y + 4$$

$$(x - 1)^2 = -4(y - 1)$$

Let it be $X^2 = 4ay$

$\therefore \quad X = x - 1,\ Y = y - 1,\ 4a = -4 \Rightarrow a = -1$

Vertex = (0, 0) Focus = (0, a)

$X = 0 \quad Y = 0$ $\qquad X = 0, \quad Y = 0$

$\Rightarrow x - 1 = 0 \Rightarrow x = 1$ $\qquad x - 1 = 0 \quad x = 1$

$y - 1 = 0 \Rightarrow y = 1$ $\qquad y - 1 = -1 \quad y = 0$

$\therefore$ Vertex = (1, 1) $\therefore$ Focus = (1, 0)

directrix $y + a = 0$

$y - 1 - 1 = 0$

$y = 2$

axis $x = 0$

$x - 1 = 0$

4. Find the equation of parabola whose focus is S (1, –7) and Vertex A (1, –2)

Sol. Given Focus S = (1, –7) Vertex A = (1, –2)

Slope of axis = slope of $AS = \infty$.

$\therefore$ axis is parallel to y-axis and focus is downwards to vertex and

$4a = 4AS = (4)(5) = 20$

Vertex $(h, k) = (1, -2)$

equation of parabola is

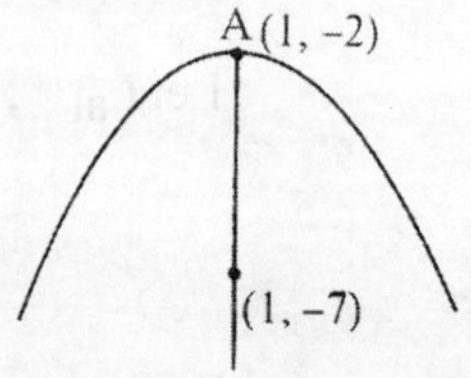

$$(x - h)^2 = -4a\,(y - k)$$

$$(x - 1)^2 = -20\,(y + 2)$$

5. Find the coordinates of points on parabola $y^2 = 8x$ whose focal distance is 10.

Sol. Given equation of parabola is $y^2 = 8x$.

Let $P(x_1, y_1)$ be point on parabola whose focal distance is 10.

$\therefore$ SP = 10

$\Rightarrow |x_1 + a| = 10$, $4a = 8 \Rightarrow a = 2$

$\therefore |x_1 + 2| = 10$

$x_1 + 2 = \pm 10$

$x_1 = \pm 10 - 2$

$x_1 = 8,\ x_1 = -12$

$\Rightarrow x_1 = 8 \quad (\because x_1 > 0)$

(x_1, y_1) lies on $y^2 = 8x$

$\Rightarrow y_1^2 = 8x_1$

$\Rightarrow \quad y_1^2 = 8.8 = 64$

$\Rightarrow \quad y_1 = \pm 8$

$\therefore \quad (x_1, y_1) = (8, \pm 8)$

6. If (1/2, 2) is are extremity of a focal chord of parabole $y^2 = 8x$, find the coordinates of other extremity.

Sol. Given equation of parabola is $y^2 = 8x$

$\therefore \quad 4a = 8 \Rightarrow a = 2$

Let $\quad (at^2, 2at) = (1/2, 2)$

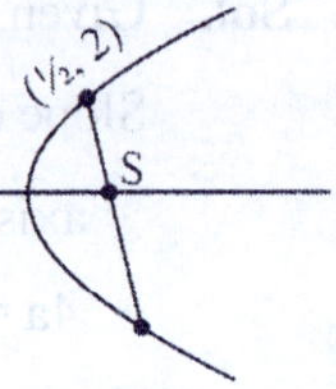

$\Rightarrow \quad (2t^2, 4t) = (1/2, 2) \Rightarrow 4t = 2 \quad \Rightarrow \quad t = 1/2$

Let $(at'^2, 2at')$ be other extremity then

$$tt' = -1 \quad \Rightarrow \quad t' = \frac{-1}{t} = \frac{-1}{(1/2)} = -2$$

$\therefore \quad (at'^2, 2at') = (2.(-2)^2, 2.(2)(-2))$

$= (8, -8)$

7. Find the equation of parabola whose axis is parallel to y-axis and passing through the points (4, 5), (–2, 11), (–4, 21)

Sol. The required equation of parabola is of the form

$y = lx^2 + mx + n$

It is passing through (4, 5) (–2, 11) (–4, 21)

$\therefore$ Substitute the poins in $y = lx^2 + mx + n$

$5 = l(6) + m(4) + n \qquad 16l + 4m + n = 5 \qquad \ldots (1)$

$11 = l(4) + m(-2) + n \qquad 4l - 2m + n = 11 \qquad \ldots (2)$

$21 = l(16) + m(-4) + n \qquad 16l - 4m + n = 21 \qquad \ldots (3)$

$(1) - (2) \Rightarrow 12l + 6m = -6 \Rightarrow 2l + m = -1$

$(1) - (3) \Rightarrow 8m = -16 \Rightarrow m = -2$

$\therefore 2l - 2 = -1 \Rightarrow l = 1/2$, substitute l, m in 2 we get

$4(1/2) - 2(-2) + n = 11$

$2 + 4 + n = 11 \Rightarrow n = 5$

$\therefore\ y = lx^2 + mx + n$

$y = 1/2\ x^2 - 2x + 5$

$x^2 - 4x - 2y + 10 = 0$

8. Find the locus of the point of trisection of double ordinate of parabola $y^2 = 4ax\ (a > 0)$

Sol. Let $P = (at^2, 2at)$ be one end of double ordinate of PQ then $Q = (at^2, -2at)$

Let $R\ (x_1, y_1)$ be trisection of PQ

$\therefore$ R divides PQ in the ratio 2 : 1

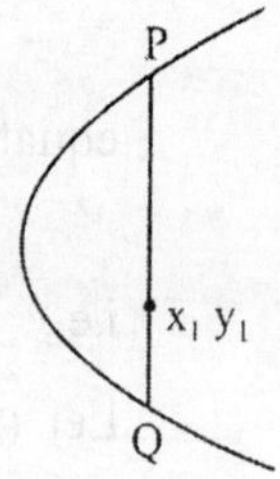

$$(x_1, y_1) = \left(\frac{2at^2 + at^2}{3}, \frac{-4at + 2at}{3}\right)$$

$$(x_1, y_1) = \left(at^2, \frac{-2at}{3}\right)$$

$$x_1 = at^2,\ y_1 = -\frac{2at}{3} \Rightarrow t = \frac{-3y_1}{2a}$$

$$\Rightarrow\ x_1 = a\left(\frac{9y_1^2}{4a^2}\right) \quad \Rightarrow \quad 9y_1^2 = 9ax_1$$

locus of (x_1, y_1) is $9y^2 = 4ax$

9. If the coordinates of ends of a focal chord of parabola $y^2 = 4ax$ are (x_1, y_1), (x_2, y_2) then prove that $x_1x_2 = a^2$; $y_1y_2 = -4a^2$.

Sol. Let $(x_1, y_1) = (at_1^2, 2at_1)$

$(x_2, y_2) = (at_2^2, 2at_2)$

$$x_1x_2 = (at_1^2)(at_1^2) = a^2(t_1t_2)^2 = a^2(-1)^2 = a^2 \qquad (\because t_1t_2 = -1)$$

$$y_1y_2 = (2at_1)(2at_2) = 4a^2(t_1t_2)$$

$$= 4a^2(-1) = -4a^2 \qquad (\because t_1t_2 = -1)$$

10. If L and L^1 are ends of latus rectun of parabola $x^2 = 6y$, find the equations of OL and OL^1 where where O is origin, also find the angle between them.

Sol. $x^2 = 6y \quad \Rightarrow \quad 4a = 6 \quad \Rightarrow \quad a = 3/2$

$\therefore\ L = (2a, a) = (3, 3/2)$

$L^1 = (-2a, a) = (-3, 3/2)$

$$\text{slope of OL} = m_1 = \frac{3/2-0}{3-0} = 1/2$$

$$\text{slope of OL}^1 = m_2 = \frac{3/2-0}{-3-0} = -1/2$$

$\therefore$ equation of OL is $y - 0 = 1/2\ (x - 0)$

$$2y = x \text{ i.e., } x - 2y = 0$$

equation of OL^1 is $y - 0 = -1/2\ (x - 0)$

$$2y = -x$$

i.e., $x + 2y = 0$

Let θ be angle between the OL, OL$'$

$$\therefore \quad \tan\theta = \left|\frac{m_1 - m_2}{1 + m_1 m_2}\right|$$

$$= \frac{1/2-(-1/2)}{1+(1/2)(-1/2)}$$

$$= \frac{1}{(1-1/4)} = \frac{1}{3/4} = \frac{4}{3}$$

$$\therefore \quad \theta = \tan^{-1}(4/3)$$

Excercise 16.1

1. Find the vertex, focus, directrix and axis of
   (i) $y^2 - x + 4y + 5 = 0$
   (ii) $3x^2 - 9x + 5y - 2 = 0$
2. Find the equation of parabola whose vertex is (3, –2) and focus (3, 1).
3. Find the equation of parabola whose axis is parallel to x-axis and which passes through the points (–2, 1) (1, 2) (–1, 3).
4. Find the equation of parabola whose vertex and focus are on positive x-axis at a distances a and b from origin respectively.
5. Find the coordinates of point on the parabola $y^2 = 2x$ whose focal distance is 5/2.
6. A commet is in a parabolic orbit with sun as focus when the comet is 2×10^{12} km from the sun to it makes an angle $\frac{\pi}{2}$ of the orbit. Find how near the commet comes to the sun.

7. Find the position of the following points with respect to the parabola $y^2 = 6x$.
(i) (6, –6) (ii) (0, 1) (iii) (2, 3)

8. For a focal chord PQ of parabola $y^2 = 4ax$ of SP = l, SQ = l^1 then prove that

$$\frac{1}{l}+\frac{1}{l^1}=\frac{1}{a}$$

9. A double ordinate of the curve $y^2 = 4ax$ is of length 8a. Prove that the lines from the vertex to its ends are at right angles.

10. If Q is the foot of the perpendicular from point P on the parabola $y^2 = 8(x-3)$ to its directrix, S is the fous of parabola and if SPQ is an equilateral triangle then find the length of side of triangle.

Answers

1. (i) Vertex (1, –2) Focus (5/4, –2)
directrix $4x - 3 = 0$ axis $y+2 = 0$
(ii) Vertex (3/2, 7/4) Focus (3/2, 4/3)
directrix $6x - 13 = 0$ axis $2x - 3 = 0$

2. $(x-3)^2 = 12(y+2)$

3. $5y^2 + 2x - 21y + 20 = 0$

4. $y^2 = 4(b-a)(x-a)$

5. (2, ±2)

6. 10^{12}

7. (i) on (ii) Outside (iii) Inside

10. 8

Unit - III

Exercise Questions

12. Coordinate System

1. Find the coordinates of points which divide the join of points (–1, –7) and (1, 2) internally and externally in the ratio 2 : 1.
2. If (–2, 1) (1, 0) and (4, 3) are three successive vertices of a parallelogram, find the fourth vertex.
3. Find the coordinates of point which divides the join of points A(–1, –7) and B(1, 2) internally and externally in the ratio 2 : 1.
4. Show that the points A(–5, 1), B(5, 5) and C = (10, 7) are collinear.
5. Find the coordinates of the point which divides the joining points (8, 9) and (–7, 4).

   (i) internally in the ratio 2 : 3

   (ii) externally in the ratio 4 : 3
6. If P(6, –1), Q(1, 3), R(x, 8) are points such that PQ = QR Find x.
7. Find the area of triangle having vertices

   (i) (1, –4), (3, –2) and (–3, 16)

   (ii) (3, 1), (–2, 5) (–4, –5)
8. Show that the triangle formed by (1, 4) (3, 2) (2, 5) is a right angled triangle.
9. Show that the points (–1, 1), (0, –3), (5, –2) and (4, 6) are the vertices of parallelogram and find its area.
10. Find the area of Δle formed by (1, –2), (2, 3), (–3, 4).
11. Find the perimeter of Δle whose vertices are (1, –2), (2, 3), and (–3, 4).

13. Locus

1. Find the locus of a point which moves so that its distance from the origin is thrice its distance from the y-axis.
2. Find the equation of path of the point P which moves such that PA = PB where A is (1, 2) and B is (3, 4).

14. Straight Lines

1. Find the equation of line which makes positive intercepts 5 and 6 on axes of coordinates

2. The three straight lines $px + qy + r = 0$, $qx + ry + p = 0$ and $rx + py + q = 0$ are concurent if $p = q = r$ or $p + q + r = 0$.

3. Find the equation of line which passes through the point of intersection of lines $5x - 6y = 1$ and $3x + 2y + 5 = 0$ and is perpendicular to $3x - 5y + 11 = 0$.

4. Derive the formula for finding the angle between the straight lines $y = mx + c$ and $y = m'x + c'$.

5. Find the equation of line having intercepts a, b on axis such that $a + b = 5$, $ab = 6$.

6. Find the parametric equations of line l which has equation $x - \sqrt{3}y = 1 + \sqrt{3}$.

7. If the acute angle between lines $2x + 3y - 5 = 0$ and $5x + ky - 6 = 0$ is $\frac{\pi}{4}$ then find the value of k.

8. Find the equation of line passing through (1, 1) and making an angle 45^0 with the line $2x - y + 7 = 0$.

9. Find the equation of straight line whose slope is $\frac{1}{3}$ and which divides the line segment joining the points A(3, 2), B(5, –3) in the ratio 4 : 7.

10. Find the distance of the point P(–2, 3) from the line AB which is $x - y = 5$.

11. Find the equation of line passing through (5, –2) and intersecting the point of $2x - y + 5 = 0$ and $x + y + 1 = 0$.

12. Find the point of intersection of lines $2x + 3y = 8$, $7x - 3y = 1$.

13. Find the equation of straight line passing through (2, 6) and parallel to the line joining (1, 2) and (–2, –4).

14. Find the equation of straight line passing through (0, 1) and parallel to line joining of (0, 0) and (1, 2).

15. Find the point of intersection of straight lines $2x + 3y = 8$, $7x - 3y = 1$ and also find the acute angle between the lines.

16. Find the angle between the lines $y = \sqrt{3}x + 7$, $y = \sqrt{3}x + 5$.

17. Find the ratio in which the line joining (3, –1) and (6, –4) is divided by (4, –2).

18. Find the point of intersection and angle between the lines $5x - 2y + 12 = 0$ and $4x - 7y = 15$.

19. Find the equation of line passing through the point (3, –2) and make an angle 45° with the line $3x - y + 4 = 0$.

Unit - III

Answers to Exercise Questions

12. Coordinate System

1. $\left(\frac{1}{3}, -1\right)$ (3, 11) **2.** (1,4)

3. $\left(\frac{1}{3}, -1\right)(3, 11)$ **5.** (2, 7) (–52, –11)

6. 5 **7.** (i) 24 (ii) 29

9. 33 square units **10.** 13 square units

11. $\sqrt{26}\left(2+\sqrt{2}\right)$

13. Locus

1. $8x^2 - y^2 = 0$ **2.** $x + y = 5$

14. Straight lines

1. $\frac{x}{5} + \frac{y}{6} = 1$ **3.** $5x + 3y + 8 = 0$

4. $\tan\theta = \left|\frac{m_1 - m_2}{1 + m_1 m_2}\right|$ **5.** $2x + 3y = 6,\ 3x + 2y = 6$

6. $x = x_1 + r\cos\frac{\pi}{6},\ y = y_1 + r\sin\frac{\pi}{6}$ **7.** k = 1, k = –25

8. $3x + y - 4 = 0,\ x - 3y + 2 = 0$ **9.** $11x - 33y = 35$

10. $5\sqrt{2}$ **11.** $3x + 7y = 1$

12. (1, 2) **13.** $2x - y - 10 = 0$

14. $2x - y + 1 = 0$ **15.** P.I = (+1, +2), $\theta = \cos^{-1}\left(\frac{5}{\sqrt{754}}\right)$

16. 60° **17.** –1 : 2 i.e., 1 : 2 externally

18. $\left(\frac{-114}{27}, \frac{123}{27}\right)$ **19.** $x - 2y - 7 = 0$; $2x + y + 8 = 0$

Unit - III

Self Test Questions

Geometry

1. Find the distance between the pair of points $(\sqrt{3},-1),(\sqrt{2},\sqrt{2})$?

2. Show that the points (2, –1), (3, 4) (–2, 3) and (–3, –2) from a rhombus.

3. Find the equation of the line whose y-intercept is –2 and slope is $\frac{3}{2}$?

4. Find the point of intersection of lines 3x + 4y + 1 = 0, 2x – y – 3 = 0?

5. Find the point of intersection of lines 4x + 8y – 1 = 0, 2x – y + 1 = 0.

6. Find the point of intersection of lines 3x + 4y + 1 = 0, 2x – y – 3 = 0?

7. Find the equation of the straight line perpendicular to the line 5x – 2y = 7 and passing through the point of intersection of lines 2x + 3y = 1, 3x + 4y = 6.

8. Find the value of P, if the straight lines x + p = 0, y + 2 = 0 and 3x + 2y + 5 = 0 are concurrent.

9. The angle between the lines is 45° and the slope of one of the lines is 1/2. Find the slope of another line.

10. Find the angle between the lines OB and CD, where O = (0, 0), B = (2,3), C = (2, –2), D = (3, 5)?

11. If the acute angle between the lines 4x – y + 7 = 0 and kx – 5y – 9 = 0 is 46°, find k.

12. If the area of triangle whose vertices are (x, y), (1, 2), (2, 1) is 6. Show that x + y = 15.

13. Find the distance between the parallel straight lines 3x + 4y – 3 = 0, 6x + 8y – 1 = 0.

UNIT - IV
DIFFERENTIAL CALCULUS

UNIT - IV

DIFFERENTIAL CALCULUS

17

Limits

17.1 Limit of a Function

Let $f(x)$ be a function and 'a' be a real number when we give values for x which are nearer and nearer to a if $f(x)$ takes values nearer and nearer to a real number l, then we say that $f(x)$ approaches l as x approaches a, or limit of $f(x)$ as x tends to a is l.

This is symbolically denoted by $\underset{x \to a}{Lt} f(x) = l$

Ex : (i) Let $f(x) = x + 5$. Here as x approaches 4 it is clear that $f(x)$ approaches 9.

This can be seen from the following two tables.

x	3	3.5	3.9	3.99	approaches 4
$f(x)$	8	8.5	8.9	8.99	approaches 9

x	5	4.5	4.1	4.01	approaches 4
$f(x)$	10	9.5	9.1	9.01	approaches 9

(ii) Let us take $f(x) = \dfrac{x^2 - 25}{x - 5}$ $(x \neq 5)$

Here also we see that $f(x)$ is same as above

$$\left(\because f(x) = \frac{(x-5)(x+5)}{x-5} = x + 5 \right)$$

Here $\underset{x \to 5}{Lt} f(x) = \underset{x \to 5}{Lt} (x+5) = 5+5 = 10$

in Example (i) x approaches a from leftside (we are taking the values for x which are nearer and nearer to 4 and they are less than 4). in this case we write

$$\underset{x \to 4-}{Lt} f(x) = \underset{x \to 4-}{Lt} (x+5) = 9$$

Similarly from 2nd table x approaches 4 from right side

i.e., $\underset{x \to 4+}{Lt} f(x) = \underset{x \to 4+}{Lt} x+5 = 9$

$\therefore$ the limit function is exists if $\underset{x \to a-}{Lt} f(x) = \underset{x \to a+}{Lt} (fx)$

i.e., left hand limit = right hand limit.

17.2 Basic Properties of Limits

1. If $\underset{x \to a}{Lt} f(x) = l$, $\underset{x \to a}{Lt} g(x) = m$ then $\underset{x \to a}{Lt} (f \pm g)(x) = l \pm m$

2. If $\underset{x \to a}{Lt} f(x) = l$, $C \in R$ then $\underset{x \to a}{Lt} (cf)(x) = cl$

3. If $\underset{x \to a}{Lt} f(x) = l$, $\underset{x \to a}{Lt} g(x) = m$ then $\underset{x \to a}{Lt} (fg)(x) = lm$.

4. If $f(x) = g(x)$ then $\underset{x \to a}{Lt} (fx) = \underset{x \to a}{Lt} (gx)$

5. If $\underset{x \to a}{Lt} (fx) = 0$ and $g(x)$ is bounded then $\underset{x \to a}{Lt} (fx)g(x) = 0$

6. If $\underset{x \to a}{Lt} f(x) = \pm\infty \Rightarrow \underset{x \to a}{Lt} \frac{1}{f(x)} = 0$.

7. If $\underset{x \to a}{Lt} f(x) = 0$ then $\underset{x \to a}{Lt} \frac{1}{f(x)} = \infty$ (f is +ve)

   $= -\infty$ (f is –ve)

8. If $f(x)$ is a polynomial function then $\underset{x \to a}{Lt} f(x) = f(a)$

Ex : (i) $\underset{x \to 2}{Lt} \left(6x^2 + 4x + 3\right) = 6(2)^2 + 4(2) + 3$

$= 24 + 8 + 3 = 35$

(ii) $\underset{x \to 1}{Lt} \dfrac{x^2 + 4}{x - 1} = \infty$

since $f(x) = \dfrac{x - 1}{x^2 + 4}$

Clearly $\underset{x \to 1}{Lt} f(x) = \dfrac{1 - 1}{1^2 + 4} = 0$

$\therefore \underset{x \to 1}{Lt} \dfrac{1}{f(x)} = \infty$

17.3 Indeterminate Forms

In the process of finding the values of limits, same time we obtain the following forms like, $\frac{0}{0}, \frac{\infty}{\infty}, 0 \times \infty, \infty - \infty, 0^0, 1^\infty, \infty^0$ which are not determined. These forms are known as indeterminate forms.

Ex : (i) Consider $\underset{x \to 2}{Lt} \dfrac{x^2 - 4}{x - 2} = (\frac{0}{0} \textit{ form})$

$= \underset{x \to 2}{Lt} \dfrac{(x+2)(x-2)}{x-2} = \underset{x \to 2}{Lt} x + 2 = 4$

Ex : (ii) Consider $\underset{x \to 1}{Lt} \dfrac{x^2 - 2x + 1}{x^2 - 3x + 2} = (\frac{0}{0} \textit{ form})$

$= \underset{x \to 1}{Lt} \dfrac{(x-1)^2}{(x-1)(x-2)} = \underset{x \to 1}{Lt} \dfrac{x-1}{x-2}$

$= \dfrac{0}{-1} = 0$

17.4 Standard Limits

- If n is a real number then $\underset{x \to a}{Lt} \dfrac{x^n - a^n}{x - a} = n.a^{n-1}$

- If m, n are two real numbers then $\underset{x \to a}{Lt} \frac{x^m - a^m}{x^n - a^n} = \frac{m}{n}.a^{m-n}$
- $\underset{x \to 0}{Lt} \frac{\sin x}{x} = 1$
- $\underset{x \to 0}{Lt} \frac{\tan x}{x} = 1$
- $\underset{x \to 0}{Lt} \frac{e^x - 1}{x} = 1$
- $\underset{x \to 0}{Lt} \frac{a^x - 1}{x} = \log_e^a$
- $\underset{x \to \infty}{Lt} \left(1 + \frac{1}{x}\right)^x = e$
- $\underset{x \to 0}{Lt} (1 + x)^{\frac{1}{x}} = e$

Solved Examples

1. Evaluate

(i) $\underset{x \to 1}{Lt} (x+1)(x+2)$

(ii) $\underset{x \to 2}{Lt} \frac{1}{x+5}$

(iii) $\underset{x \to 2}{Lt} \frac{x+5}{3x^2 - 4x + 3}$

(iv) $\underset{x \to 2}{Lt} \frac{x+1}{x^2 - 9}$

(v) $\underset{x \to 1}{Lt} \left(\frac{1}{x+4} + \frac{2}{x}\right)$

Sol. (i) $\underset{x \to 1}{Lt} (x+1)(x+2) = (1+1)(1+2) = 6$

(ii) $\underset{x \to 2}{Lt} \frac{1}{x+5} = \frac{1}{2+5} = \frac{1}{7}$

(iii) $\underset{x \to 2}{Lt} \frac{x+5}{3x^2 - 4x + 3} = \frac{2+5}{12 - 8 + 3} = \frac{7}{7} = 1$

(iv) $\underset{x \to 2}{Lt} \dfrac{x+1}{x^2-9} = \dfrac{2+1}{4-9} = \dfrac{3}{-5} = \dfrac{-3}{5}$

(v) $\underset{x \to 1}{Lt} \left(\dfrac{1}{x+4} + \dfrac{2}{x}\right) = \dfrac{1}{1+4} + \dfrac{2}{1} = \dfrac{1}{5} + 2 = \dfrac{11}{5}$

2. Evaluate

(i) $\underset{x \to 2}{Lt} \dfrac{x^2-4}{x-2}$ (ii) $\underset{x \to 3}{Lt} \dfrac{x^3-27}{x-3}$

(iii) $\underset{x \to 2}{Lt} \dfrac{x^4-16}{x^2-4}$ (iv) $\underset{x \to 1}{Lt} \dfrac{x^{\frac{1}{2}}-1}{x-1}$

Sol. (i) We have $\underset{x \to a}{Lt} \dfrac{x^n-a^n}{x-a} = n.a^{n-1}$

$\therefore \underset{x \to 2}{Lt} \dfrac{x^2-4}{x-2} = \underset{x \to 2}{Lt} \dfrac{x^2-2^2}{x-2} = (2).(2)^{2-1}$

$= 2.2 = 4$ $(\because n = 2, a = 2)$

(ii) $\underset{x \to 3}{Lt} \dfrac{x^3-27}{x-3} = \underset{x \to 3}{Lt} \dfrac{x^3-3^3}{x-3} = (3).(3)^{3-1} = 27$

(iii) $\underset{x \to 2}{Lt} \dfrac{x^4-16}{x^2-4} = \underset{x \to 2}{Lt} \dfrac{x^4-2^4}{x^2-2^2}$

we have $\underset{x \to a}{Lt} \dfrac{x^n-a^n}{x^m-a^m} = \left(\dfrac{n}{m}\right).a^{n-m}$

$= \dfrac{4}{2}.(2)^{4-2}$

$= 2 \times 2^2 = 8$

(iv) $\underset{x \to 1}{Lt} \dfrac{x^{\frac{1}{2}}-1^{\frac{1}{2}}}{x-1} = \left(\dfrac{1}{2}\right).(1)^{\frac{1}{2}-1} = \dfrac{1}{2}.(1)^{\frac{-1}{2}} = \dfrac{1}{2}$

(here $n = \dfrac{1}{2}$, a = 1)

3. Show that

(i) $\underset{x \to 1}{Lt} \dfrac{(2x-1)(\sqrt{x}-1)}{(2x^2+x-3)} = \dfrac{1}{10}$ (ii) $\underset{x \to 0}{Lt} \dfrac{\sqrt{x+1}-1}{x} = \dfrac{1}{2}$

(iii) $\underset{x \to 0}{Lt} \dfrac{(1+x)^{\frac{3}{2}}-1}{x} = \dfrac{3}{2}$ (iv) $\underset{x \to 0}{Lt} \dfrac{(1+x)^{\frac{1}{8}}-(1-x)^{\frac{1}{8}}}{x} = \dfrac{1}{4}$

Sol. (i) $\underset{x \to 1}{Lt} \dfrac{(2x-1)(\sqrt{x}-1)}{2x^2+x-3} = \dfrac{0}{0}$ *form*

$$= \underset{x \to 1}{Lt} \frac{(2x-1)(\sqrt{x}-1)}{2x^2+3x-2x-3}$$

$$= \underset{x \to 1}{Lt} \frac{(2x-1)(\sqrt{x}-1)}{2x(x-1)+3(x-1)}$$

$$= \underset{x \to 1}{Lt} \frac{(2x-1)(\sqrt{x}-1)}{(2x+3)(x-1)} = \underset{x \to 1}{Lt} \frac{(2x-1)}{(2x+3)(\sqrt{x}+1)}$$

$$= \frac{2-1}{(2+3)(1+1)} = \frac{1}{10}$$

(ii) $\underset{x \to 0}{Lt} \dfrac{\sqrt{(1+x)}-1}{x} = \underset{x \to 0}{Lt} \dfrac{(1+x)^{\frac{1}{2}}-1}{x} = \underset{x \to 0}{Lt} \dfrac{(1+x)^{\frac{1}{2}}-1}{(1+x)-1}$

$$= \underset{x \to 0}{Lt} \frac{(1+x)^{\frac{1}{2}}-1^{\frac{1}{2}}}{(1+x)-1} = \underset{1+x \to 1}{Lt} \frac{(1+x)^{\frac{1}{2}}-1^{\frac{1}{2}}}{(1+x)-1}$$

$$= \left(\frac{1}{2}\right).(1)^{\frac{1}{2}-1} = \frac{1}{2}$$

Alternative method :

$$\underset{x \to 0}{Lt} \frac{\sqrt{1+x}-1}{x} = \underset{x \to 0}{Lt} \frac{\left(\sqrt{1+x}-1\right)\left(\sqrt{1+x}+1\right)}{x\left(\sqrt{1+x}+1\right)}$$

$$= \underset{x \to 0}{Lt.} \frac{(1+x)-1}{(\sqrt{1+x}+1)} = \underset{x \to 0}{Lt} \frac{x}{x(\sqrt{1+x}+1)} = \underset{x \to 0}{Lt} \frac{1}{\sqrt{1+x}+1} = \frac{1}{\sqrt{1}+1} = \frac{1}{2}$$

(iii) $\underset{x \to 0}{Lt} \dfrac{(1+x)^{\frac{3}{2}} - 1}{x} = \underset{x \to 0}{Lt} \dfrac{(1+x)^{\frac{3}{2}} - 1^{\frac{3}{2}}}{(1+x)-1}$

$$= \underset{x+1 \to 1}{Lt} \frac{(1+x)^{\frac{3}{2}} - 1^{\frac{3}{2}}}{(1+x)-1}$$

$$= \frac{3}{2}(1)^{\frac{3}{2}-1} = \frac{3}{2} \qquad \left(\because \underset{x \to a}{Lt} \frac{x^n - a^n}{n-a} = n.a^{n-1}\right)$$

(iv) $\underset{x \to 0}{Lt} \dfrac{(1+x)^{\frac{1}{8}} - (1-x)^{\frac{1}{8}}}{x}$

$$\underset{x \to 0}{Lt} \frac{\left((1+x)^{\frac{1}{8}} - 1\right) - \left((1-x)^{\frac{1}{8}} - 1\right)}{x}$$

$$= \underset{x \to 0}{Lt} \frac{\left((1+x)^{\frac{1}{8}} - 1\right)}{x} - \underset{x \to 0}{Lt} \frac{(1-x)^{\frac{1}{8}} - 1}{x}$$

$$= \underset{x \to 0}{Lt} \frac{(1+x)^{\frac{1}{8}} - 1}{1+x-1} + \underset{x \to 0}{Lt} \frac{(1-x)^{\frac{1}{8}} - 1}{(1-x)-1}$$

$$= \underset{1+x \to 1}{Lt} \frac{(1+x)^{\frac{1}{8}} - 1^{\frac{1}{8}}}{(1+x)-1} + \underset{(1-x) \to 1}{Lt} \frac{(1-x)^{\frac{1}{8}} - 1}{(1-x)-1}$$

$$= \frac{1}{8}.(1)^{\frac{1}{8}-1} + \frac{1}{8}.(1)^{\frac{1}{8}-1} = \frac{1}{8} + \frac{1}{8} = \frac{2}{8} = \frac{1}{4}$$

4. Show that

(i) $\underset{x \to 2}{Lt} \left(\dfrac{1}{x-2} - \dfrac{4}{x^2-4}\right) = \dfrac{1}{4}$ (ii) $\underset{x \to 4}{Lt} \left(\dfrac{2x^2 - 4x - 24}{x^2 - 16} - \dfrac{1}{4-x}\right) = \dfrac{13}{8}$

Sol. (i) $\underset{x \to 2}{Lt} \left(\dfrac{1}{x-2} - \dfrac{4}{x^2-4}\right) = \underset{x \to 2}{Lt} \left(\dfrac{(x+2)-4}{(x^2-4)}\right)$

$$= \underset{x \to 2}{Lt} \frac{x-2}{x^2-4}$$

$$= \underset{x \to 2}{Lt} \frac{x-2}{(x+2)(x-2)} = \underset{x \to 2}{\text{Lt}} \frac{1}{x+2} = \frac{1}{2+2} = \frac{1}{4}$$

(ii) $\underset{x \to 4}{Lt} \left(\frac{2x^2-4x-24}{x^2-16} - \frac{1}{4-x} \right)$

$$\underset{x \to 4}{Lt} \frac{2x^2-4x-24}{x^2-16} + \frac{1}{x-4}$$

$$\underset{x \to 4}{Lt} \frac{2x^2-4x-24+x+4}{(x^2-16)}$$

$$\underset{x \to 4}{Lt} \frac{2x^2-3x-20}{(x+4)(x-4)} = \underset{x \to 4}{Lt} \frac{2x^2-8x+5x-20}{(x+4)(x-4)}$$

$$= \underset{x \to 4}{Lt} \frac{2x(x-4)+5(x-4)}{(x+4)(x-4)}$$

$$= \underset{x \to 4}{Lt} \frac{(2x+5)(x-4)}{(x+4)(x-4)}$$

$$= \underset{x \to 4}{Lt} \frac{(2x+5)}{x+4}$$

$$= \frac{8+5}{4+4} = \frac{13}{8}$$

5. Evaluate

(i) $\underset{x \to 0}{Lt} \frac{\sin bx}{x \cos x}$ (ii) $\underset{x \to 2}{Lt} \frac{\sin(x-2)}{x^2-4}$

(iii) $\underset{x \to 3}{Lt} \frac{\tan(x-3)}{x^2-9}$ (iv) $\underset{x \to \frac{\pi}{2}}{Lt} \frac{\cos x}{x - \frac{\pi}{2}}$

(v) $\underset{x \to a}{Lt} \frac{\sin(x-a).\tan^2(x-a)}{(x^2-a^2)^2}$

(i) $\underset{x \to 0}{Lt} \dfrac{\sin bx}{x \cos x}$

$$= \underset{x \to 0}{Lt} \frac{\sin bx}{bx} . \frac{b}{\cos x}$$

$$= \underset{bx \to 0}{Lt} \frac{\sin bx}{bx} . \underset{x \to 0}{Lt} \frac{b}{\cos x}$$

$$= 1 . \frac{b}{1} = b$$

(ii) $\underset{x \to 2}{Lt} \dfrac{\sin(x-2)}{x^2 - 4}$

$$= \underset{(x-2) \to 0}{Lt} \frac{\sin(x-2)}{(x+2).(x-2)}$$

$$= \underset{(x-2) \to 0}{Lt} \frac{\sin(x-2)}{(x-2)} . \underset{x \to 2}{Lt} \frac{1}{x+2}$$

$$= 1 . \frac{1}{4} = \frac{1}{4}$$

(iii) $\underset{x \to 3}{Lt} \dfrac{\tan(x-3)}{x^2 - 9} = \underset{x \to 3}{Lt} \dfrac{\tan(x-3)}{(x+3).(x-3)}$

$$= \underset{x \to 3}{Lt} \frac{1}{x+3} . \underset{x \to 3}{Lt} \frac{\tan(x-3)}{(x-3)}$$

$$= \frac{1}{6} . (1) = \frac{1}{6}$$

(iv) $\underset{x \to a}{Lt} \dfrac{\sin(x-a).\tan^2(x-a)}{(x^2 - a^2)^2}$

$$= \underset{x \to a}{Lt} \frac{\sin(x-a).\tan^2(x-a)}{(x-a)^2.(x+a)^2}$$

$$= \underset{x \to a}{Lt} \frac{\tan^2(x-a)}{(x-a)^2} . \underset{x \to a}{Lt} . \frac{\sin(x-a)}{(x+a)^2}$$

$$= 1 \times \frac{0}{a^2} = 0$$

6. Show that

(i) $\underset{x \to a}{Lt} \dfrac{x \sin a - a \sin x}{x - a} = \sin a - a \cos a$

(ii) $\underset{x \to a}{Lt} \dfrac{\tan(x) - \tan a}{x - a} = \sec^2 a$

(iii) $\underset{x \to 0}{Lt} \dfrac{1 - \cos 2mx}{\sin^2 nx} = \dfrac{2m^2}{n^2}$

(iv) $\underset{x \to 0}{Lt} \dfrac{\cos px - \cos qx}{x^2} = \dfrac{q^2 - p^2}{2}$

(v) $\underset{x \to 0}{Lt} \dfrac{\sin(a + bx) - \sin(a - bx)}{x} = 2b \cos a$

(vi) $\underset{x \to 0}{Lt} \dfrac{\operatorname{cosec} x - \cot x}{x} = \dfrac{1}{2}$

(vii) $\underset{x \to 0}{Lt} \dfrac{\tan x - \sin x}{x^3} = \dfrac{1}{2}$

(viii) $\underset{x \to \frac{\pi}{2}}{Lt} \dfrac{1 - \sin^3 x}{\cos^2 x} = \dfrac{3}{2}$

(ix) $\underset{x \to \frac{\pi}{2}}{Lt} \dfrac{\cos x}{x - \frac{\pi}{2}} = -1$

(i) $\underset{x \to a}{Lt} \dfrac{x.\sin a - a \sin x}{x - a}$

$$= \underset{x \to a}{Lt} \frac{x.\sin a - a \sin a + a \sin a - a \sin x}{x - a}$$

$$= \underset{x \to a}{Lt} \frac{\sin a(x - a) + a(\sin a - \sin x)}{x - a}$$

$$= \underset{x \to a}{Lt} \frac{\sin a(x - a)}{x - a} + a. \underset{x \to a}{Lt} \frac{\sin a - \sin x}{x - a}$$

$$= \sin a - a.\ \underset{x \to a}{Lt} \left(\frac{\sin x - \sin a)}{x - a} \right)$$

$$= \sin a - a\ .\ \underset{x \to a}{Lt} \frac{2\cos(\frac{x+a}{2}).\sin(\frac{x-a}{2})}{(x-a)}$$

$$= \sin a - a.\ \underset{x \to a}{Lt} \cos\left(\frac{x+\text{a}}{2}\right).\ \underset{x \to a}{Lt} \frac{\sin\left(\frac{x-a}{2}\right)}{\left(\frac{x-a}{2}\right)}$$

$$= \sin a - a\ .\ \cos a\ \underset{\frac{x-a}{2} \to 0}{Lt} \frac{\sin\left(\frac{x-a}{2}\right)}{\left(\frac{x-a}{2}\right)}$$

$= \sin a - a\cos a.1 = \sin a - a \cos a$

(ii) $\underset{x \to a}{Lt} \dfrac{\tan x - \tan a}{x - a}$

$$= \underset{x \to a}{Lt} \frac{\frac{\sin x}{\cos x} - \frac{\sin a}{\cos a}}{x - a}$$

$$= \underset{x \to a}{Lt} \frac{\sin x \cos a - \cos x \sin a}{(x-a)\cos x.\cos a}$$

$$= \underset{x \to a}{Lt} \frac{\sin(x-a)}{(x-a)\cos x.\cos a}$$

$$= \underset{x \to a}{Lt} \frac{\sin(x-a)}{x-a}.\ \underset{x \to a}{Lt} \frac{1}{\cos x.\cos a}$$

$$= 1 \times \frac{1}{\cos a.\cos a} = \frac{1}{\cos^2 a} = \sec^2 a$$

(iii) $\underset{x \to 0}{Lt} \dfrac{1-\cos 2mx}{\sin^2 nx}$

$$= \underset{x \to 0}{Lt} \frac{2\sin^2 mx}{\sin^2 nx} \qquad (\because 1 - \cos 2\theta = 2\sin^2\theta)$$

$$= 2 \underset{x \to 0}{Lt} \frac{\dfrac{\sin^2 mx}{m^2 x^2}.x^2 m^2}{\dfrac{\sin^2 nx}{x^2}.x^2.n^2}$$

$$= \frac{2m^2}{n^2} \underset{x \to 0}{Lt} \left(\frac{\dfrac{\sin^2 mx}{m^2 x^2}}{\dfrac{\sin^2 nx}{x^2}} \right)$$

$$= \frac{2m^2}{n^2} \times \frac{1}{1} = \frac{2m^2}{n^2}$$

(iv) $\underset{x \to 0}{Lt} \dfrac{\cos px - \cos qx}{x^2}$

$$= \underset{x \to 0}{Lt} \frac{2\sin\left(\dfrac{px+qx}{2}\right)\sin\left(\dfrac{qx-px}{2}\right)}{x^2}$$

$$= \underset{x \to 0}{Lt} \frac{2\sin\left(\dfrac{(p+q)}{2}x\right)}{x} \frac{\sin\left(\dfrac{(q-p)x}{2}\right)}{x}$$

$$= \underset{x \to 0}{Lt} \frac{2\sin\left(\dfrac{(p+q)}{2}x\right)}{\left(\dfrac{p+q}{2}\right)x}.\left(\frac{p+q}{2}\right).\frac{\sin\left(\dfrac{(q-p)x}{2}\right)}{\left(\dfrac{q-p}{2}\right).x}\left(\frac{q-p}{2}\right)$$

$$= 2.\left(\frac{p+q}{2}\right)\left(\frac{q-p}{2}\right). \underset{x \to 0}{Lt} \frac{\sin\left(\dfrac{p+q}{2}\right)x}{\left(\dfrac{p+q}{2}\right)x}. \underset{x \to 0}{Lt} \frac{\sin\left(\dfrac{q-p}{2}\right)x}{\left(\dfrac{q-p}{2}\right)x}$$

$$= 2.\frac{(p+q)(q-p)}{2 \times 2}.(1).(1) = \frac{q^2 - p^2}{2}$$

(v) $\underset{x \to 0}{Lt} \dfrac{\sin(a+bx)-\sin(a-bx)}{x}$

$$= \underset{x \to 0}{Lt} \frac{\dfrac{2\cos(a+bx+a-bx)}{2}.\sin\dfrac{(a+bx-a+bx)}{2}}{x}$$

$$= \underset{x \to 0}{Lt} \frac{2\cos a.\sin bx}{x} \quad \left(\because \sin C - \sin D = 2\cos\left(\frac{C+D}{2}\right)\sin\left(\frac{C-D}{2}\right)\right)$$

$$= 2\cos a. \underset{x \to 0}{Lt} \frac{\sin bx}{x} = 2(\cos a).b$$

(vi) $\underset{x \to 0}{Lt} \dfrac{\operatorname{cosec} x - \cot x}{x}$

$$= \underset{x \to 0}{Lt} \frac{\dfrac{1}{\sin x} - \dfrac{\cos x}{\sin x}}{x}$$

$$= \underset{x \to 0}{Lt} \frac{1-\cos x}{\sin x.x}$$

$$= \underset{x \to 0}{Lt} \frac{2\sin^2 \dfrac{x}{2}}{\sin x.x}$$

$$= \underset{x \to 0}{Lt} \frac{2}{\sin x}.\frac{\left(\sin\dfrac{x}{2}\right)^2}{\left(\dfrac{x}{2}\right)^2}.\frac{\left(\dfrac{x}{2}\right)^2}{x}$$

$$= \underset{x \to 0}{Lt} \frac{2}{\sin x}.\frac{x^2}{4.x} \quad \left(\because \underset{x \to 0}{Lt} \frac{\left(\sin\dfrac{x}{2}\right)^2}{\left(\dfrac{x}{2}\right)^2} = 1\right)$$

$$= \underset{x \to 0}{Lt} \frac{2x}{4\sin x} = \frac{1}{2} \cdot \underset{x \to 0}{Lt} \frac{x}{\sin x}$$

$$= \frac{1}{2} \cdot \underset{x \to 0}{Lt} \frac{1}{\left(\frac{\sin x}{x}\right)} = \frac{1}{2}$$

(vii) $\underset{x \to 0}{Lt} \dfrac{\tan x - \sin x}{x^3}$

$$= \underset{x \to 0}{Lt} \frac{\frac{\sin x}{\cos x} - \sin x}{x^3}$$

$$= \underset{x \to 0}{Lt} \frac{\sin x\left[\frac{1}{\cos x} - 1\right]}{x^3}$$

$$= \underset{x \to 0}{Lt} \frac{\sin x}{x^3}\left(\frac{1 - \cos x}{\cos x}\right)$$

$$= \underset{x \to 0}{Lt} \frac{\sin x . 2\sin^2 \frac{x}{2}}{x . x^2} \frac{1}{\cos x}$$

$$= \underset{x \to 0}{Lt} \frac{\sin x}{x} \cdot \underset{x \to 0}{Lt} \frac{2\sin^2 \frac{x}{2}}{\frac{x^2}{4} 4} \cdot \frac{1}{\cos x} = 1 \times \frac{2}{4} \times 1 = \frac{1}{2}$$

(viii) $\underset{x \to \frac{\pi}{2}}{Lt} \dfrac{1 - \sin^3 x}{\cos^2 x}$

$$= \underset{x \to \frac{\pi}{2}}{Lt} \frac{(1 - \sin x)(1 + \sin^2 x + \sin x)}{(1 - \sin^2 x)}$$

$$= \underset{x \to \frac{\pi}{2}}{Lt} \frac{(1-\sin x)(1+\sin^2 x+\sin x)}{(1+\sin x)(1-\sin x)}$$

$$= \underset{x \to \frac{\pi}{2}}{Lt} \frac{1+\sin^2 x+\sin x}{1+\sin x} = \frac{1+1+1}{1+1} = \frac{3}{2}$$

(ix) $\underset{x \to \frac{\pi}{2}}{Lt} \frac{\cos x}{x-\frac{\pi}{2}}$

$$= \underset{x \to \frac{\pi}{2}}{Lt} \frac{\sin\left(\frac{\pi}{2}-x\right)}{x-\frac{\pi}{2}}$$

$$= \underset{(x-\frac{\pi}{2}) \to 0}{Lt} \frac{\sin\left(\frac{\pi}{2}-x\right)}{-\left(\frac{\pi}{2}-x\right)} = \underset{\left(x-\frac{\pi}{2}\right) \to 0}{Lt} \frac{-\sin\left(\frac{\pi}{2}-x\right)}{\left(\frac{\pi}{2}-x\right)} = -1$$

7. Evaluate

(i) $\underset{x \to \infty}{Lt} \frac{x^2+5x+2}{2x^2-5x+1}$ (ii) $\underset{x \to \infty}{Lt} \frac{6x^2-x+7}{(x+3)}$

(iii) $\underset{X \to \infty}{\text{Lt}} \frac{3X^2+4X+5}{2X^3+3X-7}$ (iv) $\underset{x \to \infty}{Lt} \frac{1^2+2^2+3^2+.......+x^2}{x^3} = \frac{1}{3}$

Sol. (i) $\underset{x \to \infty}{Lt} \frac{x^2+5x+2}{2x^2-5x+1}$

$$= \underset{x \to \infty}{Lt} \frac{x^2\left[1+\frac{5}{x}+\frac{2}{x^2}\right]}{x^2\left[2-\frac{5}{x}+\frac{1}{x^2}\right]}$$

$$= \frac{1+0+0}{2-0+0} = \frac{1}{2} \qquad \left(\because as\ x \to \infty\ \frac{1}{x} \to 0\right)$$

(ii) $$\underset{x\to\infty}{Lt}\frac{x^2\left[6-\frac{1}{x}+\frac{7}{x^2}\right]}{x\left[1+\frac{3}{x}\right]}$$

$$=\underset{x\to\infty}{Lt}\frac{x\left[6-\frac{1}{x}+\frac{7}{x^2}\right]}{\left[1+\frac{3}{x}\right]}$$

$$=\frac{\infty(6-0+0)}{1+0}=\infty$$

(iii) $$\underset{x\to\infty}{Lt}\frac{3x^2+4x+5}{2x^3+3x-7}$$

$$=\underset{x\to\infty}{Lt}\frac{x^2\left[3+\frac{4}{x}+\frac{5}{x^2}\right]}{x^3\left[2+\frac{3}{x^2}-\frac{7}{x^3}\right]}$$

$$=0 \qquad \left(\because as\ x\to\infty,\frac{1}{x}\to 0\right)$$

(iv) $$\underset{x\to\infty}{Lt}\frac{1^2+2^2+3^2+\ldots..+x^2}{x^3}$$

$$=\underset{x\to\infty}{Lt}\frac{x(x+1)(2x+1)}{6}\frac{1}{x^3}$$

$$=\underset{x\to\infty}{Lt}\frac{x^3\left[1+\frac{1}{x}\right]\left[2+\frac{1}{x}\right]}{x^3 6}$$

$$=\frac{(1).(2)}{6}=\frac{1}{3}$$

8. Show that

(i) $\underset{x\to 0}{Lt}\dfrac{e^x-1}{\sqrt{1+x}-1}=2$ (ii) $\underset{x\to 0}{Lt}\dfrac{3^x-1}{\sqrt{1+x}-1}=2\log 3$

(iii) $\underset{x \to 0}{Lt} \frac{a^x - 1}{b^x - 1} = \frac{\log a}{\log b}$

Sol. (i) $\underset{x \to 0}{Lt} \frac{(e^x - 1).(\sqrt{1+x}+1)}{(\sqrt{1+x}-1)(\sqrt{1+x}+1)}$

$= \underset{x \to 0}{Lt} \frac{(e^x - 1).(\sqrt{1+x}+1)}{(1+x-1)}$

$= \underset{x \to 0}{Lt} \frac{(e^x - 1)}{x}(\sqrt{1+x}+1)$

$= 1(\sqrt{1+0}+1) = 2$

(ii) $\underset{x \to 0}{Lt} \frac{3^x - 1}{\sqrt{1+x}-1}$

$= \underset{x \to 0}{Lt} \frac{(3^x - 1)(\sqrt{1+x}+1)}{(\sqrt{1+x}-1)(\sqrt{1+x}+1)}$

$= \underset{x \to 0}{Lt} \frac{(3^x - 1)(\sqrt{1+x}+1)}{x}$

$= (\log 3).(1 + 1)$

$= 2 \log 3$

(iii) $\underset{x \to 0}{Lt} \frac{a^x - 1}{b^x - 1}$

$= \underset{x \to 0}{Lt} \frac{\left(\frac{a^x - 1}{x}\right)}{\left(\frac{b^x - 1}{x}\right)} = \frac{\log a}{\log b}$

9. **Find the right and left limits of the function $f(x) = \left\{\frac{x}{2}(x < 2), \frac{x^2}{3}(x \geq 2)\right\}$ at the point $x = 2$.**

Sol. $\underset{x \to 2-}{Lt} f(x) = \underset{x \to 2}{Lt} \frac{x}{2} = \frac{2}{2} = 1$

$\underset{x \to 2+}{Lt} f(x) = \underset{x \to 2}{Lt} \frac{x^2}{3} = \frac{4}{3}$

10. Show that

(i) $\underset{x \to 2-}{Lt} \frac{|x-2|}{x-2} = -1$ (ii) $\underset{x \to 0+}{Lt} \left(\frac{2|x|}{x} + x + 1 \right) = 3$

Sol. (i) when $x < 2 \Rightarrow |x-2| = -(x-2)$

$$\therefore \underset{x \to 2-}{Lt} \frac{|x-2|}{x-2} = \underset{x \to 2}{Lt} \frac{-(x-2)}{(x-2)} = -1$$

(ii) when $x > 0$, $\underset{x \to 0+}{Lt} \left(\frac{2|x|}{x} + x + 1 \right) = \underset{x \to 0}{Lt} \frac{2x}{x} + x + 1$

$\Rightarrow |x| = x$ $= 2 + 0 + 1 = 3$

Exercise - 17.1

1. Evaluate

(i) $\underset{x \to 2}{Lt} \frac{x+1}{x+3}$ (ii) $\underset{x \to 1}{Lt} \left(\frac{1}{x+5} - \frac{1}{x+2} \right)$

(iii) $\underset{x \to 3}{Lt} (x+1)(x+2)$ (iv) $\underset{x \to 0}{Lt} (x+1)(x+2)(x+3)$

(v) $\underset{x \to 0}{Lt} \frac{x^2+3x+5}{x^2-2x+1}$

2. (i) $\underset{x \to 4}{Lt} \frac{x^2-16}{x-4}$ (ii) $\underset{x \to 1}{Lt} \frac{x^2-4x+3}{(x-1)}$

(iii) $\underset{x \to 3}{Lt} \frac{x-3}{x^3-27}$ (iv) $\underset{x \to 0}{Lt} \frac{x^3+x^2}{x^4+x^2}$

(v) $\underset{x \to 2}{Lt} \frac{x^2-4}{x^2-5x+6}$

3. (i) $\underset{x \to 3}{Lt} \frac{x^{\frac{5}{2}}-3^{\frac{5}{2}}}{x-3}$ (ii) $\underset{x \to 2}{Lt} \frac{x^{-5}-2^{-5}}{x-2}$

(iii) $\underset{x \to 4}{Lt} \frac{x^{100}-4^{100}}{x-4}$ (iv) $\underset{x \to 2}{Lt} \frac{x^5\sqrt{x}-32\sqrt{2}}{x^3\sqrt{x}-8\sqrt{2}}$

(v) $\underset{x\to 3}{Lt} \dfrac{x^4\sqrt{x}-81\sqrt{3}}{x^2\sqrt{x}-9\sqrt{3}}$

4. (i) $\underset{x\to 0}{Lt} \dfrac{x}{\sqrt{x+9}-3}$ (ii) $\underset{x\to 0}{Lt} \dfrac{x}{\sqrt{x+16}-4}$

(iii) $\underset{x\to 0}{Lt} \dfrac{x^2}{\sqrt{x^2+25}-5}$ (iv) $\underset{x\to 0}{Lt} \dfrac{\sqrt{x+81}-9}{x}$

(v) $\underset{x\to 0}{Lt} \dfrac{\sqrt{x^2+100}-10}{x^2}$ (vi) $\underset{x\to 4}{Lt} \dfrac{3-\sqrt{5+x}}{x-4}$

5. (i) $\underset{x\to 0}{Lt} \dfrac{(1+x)^{\frac{5}{2}}-1}{x}$ (ii) $\underset{x\to 0}{Lt} \dfrac{(1+x)^{\frac{7}{2}}-1}{x}$

(iii) $\underset{x\to 0}{Lt} \dfrac{\sqrt[3]{2+x}-\sqrt[3]{2-x}}{x}$ (iv) $\underset{x\to 0}{Lt} \dfrac{(1+x)^{\frac{1}{5}}-(1-x)^{\frac{1}{5}}}{x}$

(v) $\underset{x\to 0}{Lt} \dfrac{(1+x)^{\frac{3}{5}}-(1-x)^{\frac{3}{5}}}{x}$

6. (i) $\underset{x\to 1}{Lt} \left(\dfrac{1}{x-1}-\dfrac{2}{x^2-1}\right)$ (ii) $\underset{x\to 2}{Lt} \left(\dfrac{1}{x-2}-\dfrac{4}{x^2-4}\right)$

7. (i) $\underset{x\to 0}{Lt} \dfrac{\sin 2x}{x}$ (ii) $\underset{x\to 0}{Lt} \dfrac{\tan 3x}{x}$

(iii) $\underset{x\to 0}{Lt} \dfrac{\sin 2x}{\sin 3x}$ (iv) $\underset{x\to 0}{Lt} \dfrac{\tan 3x}{\tan 4x}$

(v) $\underset{x\to 0}{Lt} \dfrac{\sin px}{x\cos x}$ (vi) $\underset{x\to 0}{Lt} \dfrac{\tan 5x}{x.\sec x}$

(vii) $\underset{x\to 2}{Lt} \dfrac{\sin(x-2)}{x^2-4}$ (viii) $\underset{x\to 4}{Lt} \dfrac{\tan(x-4)}{x^2-16}$

(ix) $\underset{x\to 3}{Lt} \dfrac{\sin(x-3)\tan^2(x-3)}{(x^2-9)^2}$ (x) $\underset{x\to 3}{Lt} \dfrac{\sin^2(x-3)\tan(x-3)}{(x^2-9)^2}$

8. (i) $\underset{x \to 0}{Lt} \dfrac{1-\cos 2x}{x^2}$ (ii) $\underset{x \to 0}{Lt} \dfrac{1-\cos 2x}{\sin^2 x}$

(iii) $\underset{x \to 0}{Lt} \dfrac{1-\cos 2px}{\sin^2 qx}$ (iv) $\underset{x \to 0}{Lt} \dfrac{\cos ax - \cos bx}{x^2}$

(v) $\underset{x \to 0}{Lt} \dfrac{\sin(p+qx)-\sin(p-qx)}{x}$ (vi) $\underset{x \to \frac{\pi}{2}}{Lt} \dfrac{1-\sin^4 x}{\cos^2 x}$

(vii) $\underset{x \to 0}{Lt} \dfrac{\cos x}{\frac{\pi}{2}-x}$ (viii) $\underset{x \to 0}{Lt} \dfrac{\cot x}{x-\frac{\pi}{2}}$

(ix) $\underset{x \to \frac{\pi}{2}}{Lt} \dfrac{\cot x}{\frac{\pi}{2}-x}$ (x) $\underset{x \to 0}{Lt} \dfrac{3\sin x^0 - \sin 3x^0}{x^3}$

9. (i) $\underset{x \to \infty}{Lt} \dfrac{x^2+3x+2}{x^2+7x+4}$ (ii) $\underset{x \to \infty}{Lt} \dfrac{x^3+3x^2+1}{x+2}$

(iii) $\underset{x \to \infty}{Lt} \dfrac{x+1}{x^2+7x+4}$ (iv) $\underset{x \to \infty}{Lt} \dfrac{1^3+2^3+3^3+\ldots\ldots+x^3}{x^4}$

(v) $\underset{x \to \infty}{Lt} \dfrac{1+2+3+\ldots\ldots+x}{x^2}$ (vi) $\underset{x \to \infty}{Lt} \dfrac{1+2+3+\ldots\ldots+x}{3x^2+5}$

10. (i) $\underset{x \to 0}{Lt} \dfrac{e^{2x}-1}{x}$ (ii) $\underset{x \to 0}{Lt} \dfrac{e^{4x}-1}{e^{5x}-1}$

(iii) $\underset{x \to 0}{Lt} \dfrac{e^x-1}{\sqrt{4+x}-2}$ (iv) $\underset{x \to 0}{Lt} \dfrac{5^x-1}{\sqrt{x+1}-1}$

(v) $\underset{x \to 0}{Lt} \dfrac{3^x-1}{4^x-1}$ (vi) $\underset{x \to 0}{Lt} \dfrac{e^x-1}{\sin x}$

11. (i) $\underset{x \to 0-}{Lt} \dfrac{|x|}{x}$ (ii) $\underset{x \to 0+}{Lt} \dfrac{|x|}{x}$

(iii) $\underset{x \to 0}{Lt} \frac{|x|}{x}$ (iv) $\underset{x \to 2-}{Lt} \frac{|x-2|}{x-2}$

(v) $\underset{x \to 2+}{Lt} \frac{|x-2|}{x-2}$ (vi) $\underset{x \to 2}{Lt} \frac{|x-2|}{x-2}$

12. Find the right and left limits of the function

$$f(x) = \frac{x}{3} \quad \text{if} \quad x < 2$$

$$= \frac{x^2}{6} \quad \text{if} \quad x \geq 2$$

at the point $x = 2$

Answers

1. (i) $\frac{3}{5}$ (ii) $\frac{-1}{6}$ (iii) 20 (iv) 6 (v) 5

2. (i) 8 (ii) -2 (iii) $\frac{1}{27}$ (iv) 1 (v) -4

3. (i) $\frac{5}{2}(3)^{\frac{3}{2}}$ (ii) $\frac{-5}{64}$ (iii) 100.4^{99} (iv) $\frac{44}{7}$ (v) $\frac{81}{5}$

4. (i) 6 (ii) 8 (iii) 10 (iv) $\frac{1}{18}$ (v) $\frac{1}{20}$

(vi) $\frac{-1}{6}$

5. (i) $\frac{5}{2}$ (ii) $\frac{7}{2}$ (iii) $\frac{2^{\frac{1}{3}}}{3}$ (iv) $\frac{2}{5}$ (v) $\frac{6}{5}$

6. (i) $\frac{1}{2}$ (ii) $\frac{1}{4}$

7. (i) 2 (ii) 3 (iii) $\frac{2}{3}$ (iv) $\frac{3}{4}$ (v) p

(vi) 5 (vii) $\frac{1}{4}$ (viii) $\frac{1}{8}$ (ix) 0 (x) 0

8. (i) 2 (ii) 2 (iii) $\frac{2p^2}{q^2}$ (iv) $\frac{b^2 - a^2}{2}$ (v) 2q cosp

(vi) 2 (vii) +1 (viii) −1 (ix) +1 (x) $4\left(\frac{\pi}{180}\right)^3$

9. (i) 1 (ii) ∞ (iii) 0 (iv) $\frac{1}{4}$ (v) $\frac{1}{2}$

(vi) $\frac{1}{6}$

10. (i) 2 (ii) $\frac{4}{5}$ (iii) 4 (iv) 2log5 (v) $\frac{\log 3}{\log 4}$

(vi) 1

11. (i) −1

(ii) 1

(iii) does not exists

(iv) −1

(v) 1

(vi) does not exist

12. (i) $\frac{2}{3}$ (ii) $\frac{2}{3}$

18

Continuity

18.1 Continuity of a Function at a Point

A function f is said to be continuous at a if

$$\underset{x \to a}{Lt} f(x) = f(a)$$

Ex : (i) $f(x) = x^3$ is continuous at $x = 1$ since

$$\underset{x \to 1}{Lt} f(x) = \underset{x \to 1}{Lt} x^3 = 1 \text{ also}$$

$$f(1) = 1^3 = 1$$

$$\therefore \quad \underset{x \to 1}{Lt} f(x) = f(1)$$

(ii) $f(x) = \dfrac{x^2 - 1}{x - 1}$ is not continuous at $x = 1$

$$\text{since} \quad \underset{x \to 1}{Lt} \frac{x^2 - 1}{x - 1} = \underset{x \to 1}{Lt} (x + 1) = 2$$

$$\text{but } f(1) = \frac{x^2 - 1}{x - 1} = \frac{0}{0} \text{ not defined}$$

$$\therefore f(x) = \frac{x^2 - 1}{x - 1} \text{ is not continuous at } x = 1$$

A function f is said to be left continuous at a if

$$\underset{x\to a-}{Lt} f(x)=f(a) \text{ or } \underset{x\to 0}{Lt} f(a-x)=f(a)$$

Ex : (i) $f(x) = |x-2|$ is left continuous at $x = 2$ since

$$\underset{x\to 2-}{Lt} f(x)=\underset{x\to 2-}{Lt} |x-2|=\underset{x\to 0-}{Lt} |2-x-2|$$

$$=\underset{x\to 0}{Lt} |-x|=\underset{x\to 0-}{Lt} x=0$$

and $f(2) = |2-2|=0$

$$\therefore \underset{x\to 2-}{Lt} f(x)=f(2)$$

Ex : (ii) $f(x) = x - 2 \qquad x \geq 2$

$= 1 \qquad x < 2$ is not left continuous at $x = 2$

since $\underset{x\to 2-}{Lt} f(x)=\underset{x\to 2}{Lt} (1)=1$

also $f(2) = x - 2 = 2 - 2 = 0$

A function f is said to be right continuous at a if

$$\underset{x\to a+}{Lt} f(x)=f(a) \text{ (or) } \underset{x\to 0}{Lt} f(a+x)=f(a).$$

Ex : (i) $f(x) = |x-2| = \underset{x\to 0}{Lt} |2+x-2|=\underset{x\to 0}{Lt} |x|=0$

and $f(2) = |2-2|=0$.

(ii) $f(x) = x^2 - 2 \quad$ if $\quad x > 2$

$= 1 \quad$ if $\quad x \leq 2$

is not right continuous at $x = 2$

since $\underset{x \to 2+}{Lt} f(x) = \underset{x \to 2}{Lt} (x^2 - 2) = 4 - 2 = 2$

and $f(2) = 1$ (by given function)

$\therefore \underset{x \to 2+}{Lt} f(x) \neq f(2)$

Note that it is left continuous at $x = 2$ $\quad \because \underset{x \to 2-}{Lt} f(x) = \underset{x \to 2}{Lt} 1 = 1$

Note: A function f is said to be discontinuous at a

if f is not continuous at a

if f is discontinuous at a, then

either $\underset{x \to a}{Lt} f(x)$ exists and not equal to $f(a)$

or $\underset{x \to a}{Lt} f(x)$ does not exists.

Solved Examples

1. Check the continuity of f given by

$$f(x) = \frac{x^2 - 4}{x - 2} \quad \text{if} \quad x \neq 2$$

$$= 4 \quad \text{if} \quad x = 2 \quad \text{at the point 2}$$

Sol. $\underset{x \to 2}{Lt} f(x) = \underset{x \to 2}{Lt} \frac{x^2 - 4}{x - 2} = \underset{x \to 2}{Lt} (x + 2) = 2 + 2 = 4$ also given $f(2) = 4$.

$\therefore \underset{x \to 2}{Lt} f(x) = f(2)$

hence f is continuous at $x = 2$

2. Check the continuity of f given by

$$f(x) = \frac{x^2 - 4}{2} \quad \text{if} \quad 0 < x < 2$$

$= 0$ if $x = 2$

$= 2 - 8\,.x^{-3}$ if $n > 2$

at the point 2

Sol. $\underset{x \to 2-}{Lt} f(x) = \underset{x \to 2}{Lt} \dfrac{x^2 - 4}{2} = 0$

$\underset{x \to 2+}{Lt} f(x) = \underset{x \to 2}{Lt} 2 - 8.x^{-3} = 0$

also given $f(2) = 0$

$\therefore \underset{x \to 2-}{Lt} f(x) = \underset{x \to 2+}{Lt} f(x) = f(2)$ i.e., $\underset{x \to 2}{Lt} f(x) = f(2)$

hence f is continuous at $x = 2$.

3. Check the continuity of f given by

$f(x) = 4 - x^2$ if $x \leq 0$

$= x - 5$ if $0 < x \leq 1$

$= 4x^2 - 9$ $1 < x < 2$

$= 3x + 4$ $x \geq 2$

at the point 0, 1, 2

Sol. $\underset{x \to 0-}{Lt} f(x) = \underset{x \to 0}{Lt} 4 - x^2 = 4$, $\underset{x \to 0+}{Lt} f(x) = \underset{x \to 0}{Lt} x - 5 = -5$

$\therefore \underset{n \to 0-}{Lt} f(x) = \underset{x \to 0+}{Lt} f(x)$

So $\underset{x \to 0}{Lt} f(x)$ not exists

$\therefore f$ is not continuous at $x = 0$

again, $\underset{x \to 1-}{Lt} f(x) = \underset{x \to 1}{Lt} f(x - 5) = 1 - 5 = -4$

$\underset{x \to 1+}{Lt} f(x) = \underset{x \to 1}{Lt} (4x^2 - 9) = 4 - 9 = -5$

$f(1) = 1 - 4 = -4$

$$\therefore \lim_{x \to 1-} f(x) \neq \lim_{x \to 1+} f(x)$$

$\therefore f$ is not continuous at $x = 1$

also $\displaystyle\lim_{x \to 2-} f(x) = \lim_{x \to 2} 4x^2 - 9 = 7$; $\displaystyle\lim_{x \to 2+} f(x) = \lim_{x \to 2} 3x + 4 = 10$

$$\therefore \lim_{x \to 2-} f(x) \neq \lim_{x \to 2+} f(x)$$

$\therefore f$ is not continuous at $x = 2$

Hence, f is not continuous at $x = 0, 1, 2$

4. If f is defined by $f(x) = \begin{cases} \dfrac{\sin 2x}{x} & \text{if } x \neq 0 \\ 2 & \text{if } x = 0 \end{cases}$

then show that f is continuous at $x = 0$

Sol. $\displaystyle\lim_{x \to 0} f(x) = \lim_{x \to 0} \frac{\sin 2x}{x} = \lim_{x \to 0} \frac{\sin 2x}{2x}.2 = 1 \times 2 = 2$

also $f(0) = 2$

$\therefore \displaystyle\lim_{x \to 0} f(x) = f(0)$ hence f is continuous at $x = 0$

5. Show that

$$f(x) = \begin{cases} \dfrac{\cos ax - \cos bx}{x^2} & \text{if } x \neq 0 \\ \dfrac{1}{2}(b^2 - a^2) & \text{if } x = 0 \end{cases}$$

where a and b are real constants, continuous at $x = 0$.

Sol. $\displaystyle\lim_{x \to 0} f(x) = \lim_{x \to 0} \frac{\cos ax - \cos bx}{x^2}$

$$= \lim_{x \to 0} \frac{2\sin\left(\dfrac{ax + bx}{2}\right)\sin\left(\dfrac{bx - ax}{2}\right)}{x^2}$$

$$= \underset{x \to 0}{Lt} \frac{2\sin\left(\frac{ax+bx}{2}\right)\sin\left(\frac{bx-ax}{2}\right)}{\left(\frac{a+b}{2}\right)x.\left(\frac{b-a}{2}\right)x}\left(\frac{b^2-a^2}{4}\right)$$

$$= 2\left(\frac{b^2-a^2}{4}\right)\underset{x \to 0}{Lt} \frac{\sin\left(\frac{(a+b)x}{2}\right)}{\left(\frac{a+b}{2}\right)x}\underset{x \to 0}{Lt} \frac{\sin\left(\frac{b-a}{2}x\right)}{\left(\frac{b-a}{2}\right)x}$$

$$= \frac{b^2-a^2}{2} \times 1 \times 1 = \frac{b^2-a^2}{2}$$

also $f(0) = \frac{b^2-a^2}{2}$

$\therefore \underset{x \to 0}{Lt} f(x) = f(0)$

$\therefore f$ is continuous a $x = 0$

6. Show that the function $f(x) = \frac{3x + 4\tan x}{x}$ for $x \neq 0$,

$f(0) = 7$

is continuous at $x = 0$

Sol. $\underset{x \to 0}{Lt} f(x) = \underset{x \to 0}{Lt} \frac{3x + 4\tan x}{x} = \underset{x \to 0}{Lt}\left(3 + \frac{4\tan x}{x}\right) = 3 + 4 = 7$

also $f(0) = 7$

$\therefore \underset{x \to 0}{Lt} f(x) = f(0)$

$\therefore$ f is continuous at $x = 0$

7. Find real constants a, b so that the function f given by

$$f(x) = \begin{cases} \sin x & \text{if } x \leq 0 \\ x^2 + a & \text{if } 0 < x < 1 \\ bx + 3 & \text{if } 1 \leq x \leq 3 \\ -3 & \text{if } x > 3 \end{cases}$$

is continuous on R

Sol. f is continuous at $x = 0$ $\quad \therefore \displaystyle \underset{x \to 0}{Lt} f(x) = f(0)$

$$\therefore \underset{x \to 0-}{Lt} f(x) = \underset{x \to 0}{Lt} \sin x = 0$$

$$\underset{x \to 0+}{Lt} f(x) = \underset{x \to 0}{Lt} x^2 + a = 0 + a = a$$

$$f(0) = \sin 0 = 0$$

$$\underset{x \to 0-}{Lt} f(x) = \underset{x \to 0+}{Lt} f(x) = f(0) \Rightarrow a + 0 = 0$$

$\therefore$ a = 0

f is continuous at $x = 1$

$$\therefore \underset{x \to 1-}{Lt} f(x) = \underset{x \to 1+}{Lt} f(x) = f(1)$$

$$\underset{x \to 1-}{Lt} f(x) = \underset{x \to 1}{Lt} (x^2 + a) = 1 + a$$

$$\underset{x \to 1+}{Lt} f(x) = \underset{x \to 1}{Lt} bx + 3 = b + 3$$

$$\therefore \underset{x \to 1-}{Lt} f(x) = \underset{x \to 1+}{Lt} f(x) \Rightarrow \quad 1 + a = b + 3$$

$$1 + 0 = b + 3 \quad (\because a = 0)$$

$$\therefore \quad b = -2$$

$\therefore$ a = 0, b = – 2

8. If $f(x) = \begin{cases} \dfrac{x.2^x - x}{1 - \cos x} & \text{for } x \neq 0 \\ \log 4 & \text{for } x = 0 \end{cases}$

then show that f is continuous at $x = 0$.

Sol. $$\underset{x \to 0}{Lt} \frac{x\,2^x - x}{1 - \cos x} = \underset{x \to 0}{Lt} \frac{x(2^x - 1)}{1 - \cos x} = \underset{x \to 0}{Lt} \frac{(2^x - 1)}{\left(\dfrac{1 - \cos x}{x}\right)}$$

$$= \underset{x \to 0}{Lt} \frac{\left(\frac{(2^x - 1)}{x}\right)}{\left(\frac{1 - \cos x}{x^2}\right)} = \frac{\log 2}{\left(\frac{1}{2}\right)} = 2 \log 2 = \log 2^2 = \log 4$$

$$(\because \underset{x \to 0}{Lt} \frac{1 - \cos x}{x^2} = \frac{1}{2} \text{ is proved in limits chapter})$$

$$\therefore \underset{x \to 0}{Lt} \frac{x\,2^x - x}{1 - \cos x} = \log 4$$

9. If $f(x) = \begin{cases} \frac{2}{x} \log(1+x) & \text{when } x \neq 0 \\ 2 & \text{when } x = 0 \end{cases}$

then show that f is continuous at $x = 0$

Sol. $\underset{x \to 0}{Lt} \frac{2}{x}.\log(1+x) = \underset{x \to 0}{Lt} \log(1+x)^{\frac{2}{x}}$

$$= ln \underset{x \to 0}{Lt} \left[(1+x)^{\frac{1}{x}}\right]^2 = ln \left[\underset{x \to 0}{Lt} (1+x)^{\frac{1}{x}}\right]^2$$

$$\text{In. } (e^2) = 2 \log e = 2$$

given $f(0) = 2$

$$\therefore \underset{x \to 0}{Lt} \frac{2}{x}.\log(1+x) = 2$$

10. If $f(x) = \dfrac{e^{\frac{1}{x}} - 1}{e^{\frac{1}{x}} + 1}$ for $x \neq 0$,

$f(0) = 0$ then show that $f(x)$ is discontinuous at $x = 0$.

Sol. $\underset{x \to 0-}{Lt} f(x) = \underset{x \to 0-}{Lt} \dfrac{e^{\frac{1}{x}} - 1}{e^{\frac{1}{x}} + 1} = \underset{h \to 0-}{Lt} \dfrac{e^{\frac{1}{0-h}} - 1}{e^{\frac{1}{0-h}} + 1}$

$$= \underset{h\to 0}{Lt}\frac{e^{\frac{1}{-h}}-1}{e^{\frac{1}{h}}+1} = \underset{h\to 0}{Lt}\frac{e^{h}-1}{e^{\frac{1}{0h}}+1} = \frac{1-1}{1+1} = 0$$

$$\underset{x\to 0+}{Lt} f(x) = \underset{h\to 0+}{Lt}\frac{e^{\frac{1}{x}}-1}{e^{\frac{1}{x}}+1} = \underset{h\to 0}{Lt}\frac{e^{\frac{1}{0+h}}-1}{e^{\frac{1}{0+h}}+1} = \underset{h\to 0}{Lt}\frac{e^{\frac{1}{h}}-1}{e^{\frac{1}{h}}+1}$$

$$= \underset{h\to 0}{Lt}\frac{e^{\frac{1}{h}}\left[1-e^{\frac{-1}{h}}\right]}{e^{\frac{1}{h}}\left[1+e^{\frac{-1}{h}}\right]} = \underset{x\to 0}{Lt}\frac{1-e^{\frac{-1}{h}}}{1+e^{\frac{-1}{h}}} = \frac{1-0}{1+1} = 1$$

$$\therefore \underset{x\to 0-}{Lt} f(x) \neq \underset{x\to 0+}{Lt} f(x)$$

$$\left[\because h\to 0,\ \frac{1}{h}\to\infty,\ e^{\frac{-1}{h}}\to+\infty,\ \frac{1}{e^{\frac{1}{h}}}\to 0,\ e^{\frac{-1}{h}}\to 0\right]$$

$\therefore$ f is not continuous at $x = 0$

Exercise - 18.1

Show that the function

1. (i) $f(x) = \begin{cases} \dfrac{x^2-9}{x-3} & \text{if } x \neq 3 \\ 6 & \text{if } x = 3 \end{cases}$

   is continuous at $x = 3$

   (ii) $f(x) = \begin{cases} \dfrac{x^3-8}{x-2} & \text{if } x \neq 2 \\ 12 & \text{if } x = 2 \end{cases}$

   is continuous at $x = 2$

(iii)
$$f(x) = \begin{cases} \dfrac{x^3+8}{x^5+32} & \text{for} \quad x \neq -2 \\[2ex] \dfrac{3}{20} & \text{for} \quad x = -2 \end{cases}$$

is continuous at $x = -2$

(iv)
$$f(x) = \begin{cases} \dfrac{x - \sin x}{x} & \text{for} \quad x \neq 0 \\[2ex] 0 & \text{for} \quad x = 0 \end{cases}$$

is continuous at $x = 0$

(v)
$$f(x) = \begin{cases} \dfrac{\cos 3x - \cos 4x}{x \sin 2x} & \text{for} \quad x \neq 0 \\[2ex] \dfrac{7}{4} & \text{for} \quad x = 0 \end{cases}$$

is continuous at $x = 0$

(vi)
$$f(x) = \begin{cases} \dfrac{\sin 2x \sin 3x}{x^2} & \text{for} \quad x \neq 0 \\[2ex] 6 & \text{for} \quad x = 0 \end{cases}$$

is continuous at $x = 0$

(vii) $f(x) = \sin x$ continuous on R

(viii) $f(x) = \dfrac{x^2 - 9}{x^2 - 2x - 3}$ for $x \neq 3$

$= 1.5$ for $x = 3$

is continuous at $x = 3$

(ix)
$$f(x) = \begin{cases} \dfrac{\sqrt{x^2+3} - 2}{x - 1} & \text{for} \quad x \neq 1 \\[2ex] = \dfrac{1}{2} & \text{for} \quad x = 1 \end{cases}$$

is continuous at $x = 1$

2. Show that the function

$$f(x) = \begin{cases} x+2 & \text{if} \quad x \le 1, \\ 3x & \text{if} \quad 1 < x < 2, \\ 1+x^2 & \text{if} \quad x \ge 2. \end{cases}$$

is continuous at $x = 1$, discontinuous at $x = 2$

3. Show that the functions

(i) $$f(x) = \begin{cases} \dfrac{x\tan 2x}{\sin 3x.\sin 5x} & \text{for} \quad x \ne 0 \\ \dfrac{2}{17} & \text{for} \quad x = 0 \end{cases}$$ is discontinuous at $x = 0$

(ii) $$f(x) = \begin{cases} \dfrac{1-\cos x}{x} & \text{for} \quad x \ne 0 \\ 1 & \text{for} \quad x = 0 \end{cases}$$ is discontinuous at $x = 0$

(iii) $$f(x) = \begin{cases} \dfrac{1-\cos ax}{1-\cos bx} & \text{for} \quad x \ne 0 \end{cases}$$
$$= \dfrac{a}{b} \quad \text{for} \quad x = 0$$ is discontinuous at $x = 0$

(iv) $$f(x) = \begin{cases} \dfrac{7|x|+5x}{7|x|-5x} & \text{for} \quad x \ne 0 \\ 6 & \text{for} \quad x = 0 \end{cases}$$ is discontinuous at $x = 0$

(v) $$f(x) = \begin{cases} \dfrac{x}{1+e^{\frac{1}{x}}} & \text{for} \quad x \ne 0 \\ 0 & \quad x = 0 \end{cases}$$ is continuous at $x = 0$

4. (i) If $f(x) = \begin{cases} ax^2 + 9x - 5 & \text{if} \quad x < 1 \\ b & \text{if} \quad x = 1 \\ (x+3)(2x-a) & \text{if} \quad x > 1 \end{cases}$ is continuous on R

then show that $a = \frac{4}{5}$, $b = \frac{24}{5}$

(ii) If $f(x) = \begin{cases} ax + 3 & \text{if} \quad x < 3 \\ 3 - x + 2x^2 & \text{if} \quad x \geq 3 \end{cases}$

is continuous on R, then show that a = 5

19

Differentiation

19.1 Derivative of a Function

Let $y = f(x)$ be a function of real variable x, defined over an interval $A \subset R$. Suppose the variable x be changed from x to δx. Then the corresponding change in y from $y + \delta y$ say, that is $y + \delta y$, is the value of the function at $x + \delta x$.

$$\therefore y + \delta y = f(x + \delta x) \qquad ..... (1)$$

$$\text{we have } y = f(x) \qquad ..... (2)$$

$$(1) - (2) \Rightarrow \quad (y + \delta y) - (y) = f(x + \delta x) - f(x)$$

$$\therefore \delta y = f(x + \delta x) - f(x)$$

$$\Rightarrow \quad \frac{\delta y}{\delta x} = \frac{f(x+\delta x) - f(x)}{\delta x}$$

This is the ratio gives to average rate of change of y w.r.t x per unit.

If the change in x i.e, δx is very very small i.e., $\delta x \to 0$ then

$$\underset{\delta x \to 0}{Lt} \frac{\delta y}{\delta x} = \underset{\delta x \to 0}{Lt} \frac{f(x+\delta x) - f(x)}{dx}$$

If this limit exists and finite, then we say the function $y = f(x)$ is differentiable at x and the limit is called 'derivative' or differential coefficient or rate of change of y w.r.t x. This is denoted by $\frac{dy}{dx}, \frac{d}{dx}[f(x)]$ or $f'(x)$ *or* y'.

$$\therefore f'(x) = \frac{dy}{dx} = \underset{\delta x \to 0}{Lt} \frac{\delta y}{\delta x} = \underset{\delta x \to 0}{Lt} \frac{f(x+\delta x) - f(x)}{\delta x}$$

If δx = h, the above formula becomes

$$f'(x) \underset{h\to 0}{Lt} \frac{f(x+h)-f(x)}{h}$$

suppose we take x = a then we get

$$f'(x)=f'(a)=\underset{h\to 0}{Lt} \frac{f(a+h)-f(a)}{h} \qquad \text{.... (i)}$$

This is the derivative of the function f(x) at x = a, it is denoted by $\left(\frac{dy}{dx}\right)_{x=a}$ or y'_a

Now let us take a + h = x in (i)

then $h \to 0$ changes to $x \to$ a and we have

$$f'(a)=\underset{x\to a}{Lt} \frac{f(x)-f(a)}{x-a} \qquad (\because h = x - a)$$

It is another form of expressing derivative of $f(x)$ at x = a.

So $y = f(x)$ is said to be differentiable at x = a if $\underset{x\to a}{Lt} \frac{f(x)-f(a)}{x-a}$ is exists and finite

i.e, $\underset{x\to a-}{Lt} \frac{f(x)-f(a)}{x-a}, \underset{x\to a+}{Lt} \frac{f(x)-f(a)}{x-a}$ are exist and equal.

(i.e., left hand limit = right hand limit)

Now $\underset{x\to a-}{Lt} \frac{f(x)-f(a)}{x-a}$ if exists and finite then it is called left hand derivative of $f(x)$ at x = a and is denoted by $Lf'(a)$.

$\underset{x\to a+}{Lt} \frac{f(x)-f(a)}{x-a}$ if exists and finite then it is called right hand derivative of $f(x)$ at x = a and is denoted by $Rf'(a)$.

So a function of $f(x)$ is said to be differentiable at x = a if $L(f'(a)), R(f'(a))$ exists and equal. If they are exist and not equal we say the function is not 'differentiable' at x = a.

19.2 Relation between Differentiability and Continuity

Theorem : Every differentiable function is continuous but every continuous function is need not be differentiable in the given interval.

Proof : Let a be any point in the interval A where the function $f(x)$ is defined and that $f(x)$ is differentiable at $x = a$.

by definition $f'(a) = \underset{x \to a}{Lt} \dfrac{f(x) - f(a)}{x - a}$ is exists and finite.

Consider $f(x) - f(a) = \dfrac{[f(x) - f(a)]}{(x - a)}(x - a)$

taking $\underset{x \to a}{Lt}$ on both sides we get

$$\underset{x \to a}{Lt} f(x) - f(a) = \underset{x \to a}{Lt} \frac{f(x) - f(a)}{(x - a)}(x - a)$$

$$\underset{x \to a}{Lt} (f(x) - f(a)) = f'(a)\ 0$$

$$\underset{x \to a}{Lt} (f(x) - f(a)) = 0$$

$$\therefore \quad \underset{x \to a}{Lt} \{f(x)\} - \underset{x \to a}{Lt} f(a) = 0$$

$$\underset{x \to a}{Lt} f(x) - f(a) = 0$$

$$\underset{x \to a}{Lt} f(x) = f(a)$$

hence $f(x)$ is continuous at $x = a$

Note : The converse of the above theorem is need not be true., i.e., every continuous function is need not be differentiable.

for example take the function $f(x) = |x|$ on R.

clearly $f(x)$ is continuous at $x = 0$

since $\underset{x \to 0-}{Lt} f(x) = \underset{x \to 0}{Lt} -x = 0$

$$\underset{x\to 0+}{Lt} f(x) = \underset{x\to 0}{Lt} x = 0$$

$$f(0) = 0$$

now consider $L(f'(0)) = \underset{x\to 0-}{Lt} \dfrac{f(x)-f(0)}{x-0}$

$$= \underset{x\to 0}{Lt} \frac{-x-0}{x-0} \qquad (\because |x| = -x \text{ if } x < 0)$$

$$= \underset{x\to 0}{Lt} \frac{-x}{x} = \underset{x\to 0}{Lt} -1 = -1$$

$$R(f'(0)) = \underset{x\to 0+}{Lt} \frac{f(x)-f(0)}{x-0} = \underset{x\to 0}{Lt} \frac{x-0}{x-0} \ (\because |x| = x \text{ if } x > 0)$$

$$= \underset{x\to 0}{Lt} \frac{x}{x} = \underset{x\to 0}{Lt} x = 1$$

$$\therefore L(f'(0)) \neq R(f'(0))$$

$\therefore f$ is not differentiable at $x = 0$

From the above theorem we can conclude that :

(i) a function is differentiable then it is continuous,

(ii) a function is continuous, it may or may not differentiable,

(iii) a function is not continuous then it is not differentiable.

19.3 Differentiation of Functions from the First Principle

The process of finding the derivatives of a function is called differentiation or by obtaining the derivative of a function using definition is called differentiation from the first principle.

1. To find the derivative of constant function from the first principle

Let $y = f(x) = k\ \forall\ x \in$ R and k is constant be a constant function, we get $f(x + a) = k$

by definition $\qquad f'(x) = \dfrac{dy}{dx} \underset{h\to 0}{Lt} \dfrac{f(x+h)-f(x)}{h}$

$$= \underset{h\to 0}{Lt} \frac{k-k}{h} = \underset{x\to 0}{Lt} 0 = 0$$

Thus the derivative of constant function is zero.

Ex : (i) $\frac{d}{dx}(7) = 0$ (ii) $\frac{d}{dx}(\log 5) = 0$

2. To find the derivative of x^n from first principle

Let $y = f(x) = x^n$

by definition we have

$$f'(x) = \frac{dy}{dx} = \underset{h \to 0}{Lt} \frac{f(x+h) - f(x)}{h} = \underset{h \to 0}{Lt} \frac{(x+h)^n - x^n}{h}$$

$$= \underset{x+h \to x}{Lt} \frac{(x+h)^n - x^n}{(x+h) - n}$$

$$= n.(x)^{n-1} \qquad \left(\because \underset{x \to a}{Lt} \frac{x^n - a^n}{x - a} = n.a^{n-1}\right)$$

$$\therefore \frac{dy}{dx} = n.x^{n-1}$$

Ex : (i) if $y = x^{10}$ then $\frac{dy}{dx} = 10.x^{10-1} = 10x^9$

(ii) if $y = x^{-5}$ then $\frac{dy}{dx} = (-5) \cdot x^{-5-1} = -5.x^{-6}$.

(iii) If $y = \frac{1}{x}$ then $\frac{dy}{dx} = (-1)\, x^{-1-1} = -x^{-2}$ $\left(\because \frac{1}{x} = x^{-1}\right)$

(iv) If $y = x^{\frac{3}{2}}$ then $\frac{dy}{dx} = \frac{3}{2}.(x)^{\frac{3}{2}-1} = \frac{3}{2}.(x)^{\frac{1}{2}}$

3. To find the derivative of sinx w.r.t x.

Let $y = f(x) = \sin x$ $\quad x \in R$ (angle measured in radians)

by definition $\frac{dy}{dx} = \underset{h \to 0}{Lt} \frac{f(x+h) - f(x)}{n}$

$$= \underset{h \to 0}{Lt} \frac{\sin(x+h) - \sin x}{h}$$

$$= \underset{h \to 0}{Lt} \frac{2\cos\left(\frac{x+h+x}{2}\right).\sin\left(\frac{x+h-x}{2}\right)}{h}$$

($\because$ by using $\sin C - \sin D = 2\cos\left(\frac{C+D}{2}\right)\sin\left(\frac{C-D}{2}\right)$)

$$= \underset{h \to 0}{Lt} \frac{2\cos\left(x+\frac{h}{2}\right)\sin\left(\frac{h}{2}\right)}{h}$$

$$= \underset{h \to 0}{Lt} \frac{\cos\left(x+\frac{h}{2}\right).\sin\left(\frac{h}{2}\right)}{\left(\frac{h}{2}\right)}$$

$$= \underset{h \to 0}{Lt} \cos\left(x+\frac{h}{2}\right)\frac{\sin\left(\frac{h}{2}\right)}{\left(\frac{h}{2}\right)}$$

$= \cos x\,(1)$ $\qquad [\because \underset{x \to 0}{Lt} \frac{\sin x}{x} = 1]$

$\therefore \frac{dy}{dx} = \cos x$

$\therefore$ The derivative of sin$x$ w.r.t x is cos$x$

i.e $y = \sin x \quad \Rightarrow \quad \frac{dy}{dx} = \cos x$

4. To find the derivative of cosx w.r.t x

Let $y = f(x) = \cos x$, $\qquad x \in R$ (x is measured in radians)

by definition $\frac{dy}{dx} = \underset{h \to 0}{Lt} \frac{f(x+h) - f(x)}{h}$

$$= \underset{h \to 0}{Lt} \frac{\cos(x+h) - \cos x}{h}$$

$$= \underset{h \to 0}{Lt} \frac{2\sin\left(\frac{x+h+x}{2}\right)\sin\left(\frac{x-(x+h)}{2}\right)}{h}$$

$$[\because \text{ by using } \cos C - \cos D = 2\sin\left(\frac{C+D}{2}\right)\sin\left(\frac{D-C}{2}\right)]$$

$$= \underset{h\to 0}{Lt} \frac{(\sin(x+\frac{h}{2}).\sin(-\frac{h}{2})}{\left(\frac{h}{2}\right)}$$

$$= \underset{h\to 0}{Lt} \sin(x+\frac{h}{2}) \frac{\sin\left(\frac{h}{2}\right)}{\left(\frac{h}{2}\right)} \qquad [\because \sin(-x) = -\sin x]$$

$$= - \underset{h\to 0}{Lt} \sin(x+\frac{h}{2}) \underset{\frac{h}{2}\to 0}{Lt} \frac{\sin\left(\frac{h}{2}\right)}{\frac{h}{2}}$$

$$= -\sin x \times 1 \qquad \left[\because \underset{x\to 0}{Lt} \frac{\sin x}{x} = 1\right]$$

$$= -\sin x$$

$$\therefore \frac{dy}{dx} = -\sin x$$

hence if $y = \cos x \Rightarrow \frac{dy}{dx} = -\sin x$

5. To find the derivative of tanx w.r.t 'x' by using first principle

Let $y = f(x) = \tan x$, x is taken in radians

by definition, $\frac{dy}{dx} = \underset{h\to 0}{Lt} \frac{\tan(x+h) - \tan x}{h}$

$$= \underset{h\to 0}{Lt} \frac{\frac{\sin(x+h)}{\cos(x+h)} - \frac{\sin x}{\cos x}}{h}$$

$$= \underset{h\to 0}{Lt} \frac{\sin(x+h)\cos x - \cos(x+h)\sin x}{h\cos(x+h)\cos x}$$

($\because$ by taking LCM)

$$= \underset{h \to 0}{Lt} \frac{\sin[(x+h-x)]}{h\cos(x+h)\cos x}$$

[(∵ by using sin A cosB – cos A sin B = sin (A – B)]

$$= \underset{x \to 0}{Lt} \frac{\sinh}{h.\cos(x+h)\cos x}$$

$$= \underset{x \to 0}{Lt} \frac{\sinh}{h} \underset{h \to 0}{Lt} \frac{1}{\cos(x+h)\cos x}$$

$$= 1 \times \frac{1}{\cos x.\cos x} = \frac{1}{\cos^2 x} = \sec^2 x$$

$\therefore$ if $y = \tan x$ $\Rightarrow$ $\frac{dy}{dx} = \sec^2 x$

6. To find the derivative of cotx w.r.t x by using first principle

Let $y = f(x) = \cot x$ x is taken in radians

by definition, $\frac{dy}{dx} = \underset{h \to 0}{Lt} \frac{f(x+h) - f(x)}{h}$

$$= \underset{h \to 0}{Lt} \frac{\cot(x+h) - \cot x}{h}$$

$$= \underset{h \to 0}{Lt} \frac{\frac{\cos(x+h)}{\sin(x+h)} - \frac{\cos x}{\sin x}}{h}$$

$$= \underset{h \to 0}{Lt} \frac{\cos(x+h)\sin x - \sin(x+h)\cos x}{\sin(x+h).\sin x.h}$$

$$= \underset{h \to 0}{Lt} \frac{\sin[x-(x+h)]}{h.\sin(x+h)\sin x}$$

[∵ by using sinA cosB – cosA sinB = sin(A – B)]

$$= \underset{h \to 0}{Lt} \frac{\sin(-h)}{h.\sin(x+h)\sin x}$$

$$= - \underset{h \to 0}{Lt} \frac{\sinh}{h} \underset{h \to 0}{Lt} \frac{1}{\sin(x+h).\sin x}$$

$$= -(1).\frac{1}{\sin^2 x}$$

$$= \frac{-1}{\sin^2 x} = -\operatorname{cosec}^2 x$$

$\therefore$ if $y = \cot x \Rightarrow \frac{dy}{dx} = -\operatorname{cosec}^2 x$

7. **To find the derivative of 'secx' w.r.t x by using first principle**

Let $y = f(x) = \sec x$, x is taken in radians

by definition, $\frac{dy}{dx} = f'(x) = \underset{h \to 0}{Lt} \frac{f(x+h) - f(x)}{h}$

$$= \underset{h \to 0}{Lt} \frac{\sec(x+h) - \sec x}{h}$$

$$= \underset{h \to 0}{Lt} \frac{\frac{1}{\cos(x+h)} - \frac{1}{\cos x}}{h}$$

$$= \underset{h \to 0}{Lt} \frac{\cos x - \cos(x+h)}{h.\cos(x+h).\cos x}$$

$$= \underset{h \to 0}{Lt} \frac{2\sin\left(\frac{x+x+h}{2}\right)\sin\left(\frac{x+h-x}{2}\right)}{h.\cos(x+h).\cos x}$$

[$\because$ by using $\cos C - \cos D = 2\sin\left(\frac{C+D}{2}\right)\sin\left(\frac{D-C}{2}\right)$

$$= \underset{h \to 0}{Lt} \frac{2\sin\left(\frac{2x+h}{2}\right)\sin\left(\frac{h}{2}\right)}{h.\cos(x+h).\cos x}$$

$$= \underset{h \to 0}{Lt} \frac{2\sin\left(x+\frac{h}{2}\right)\sin\left(\frac{h}{2}\right)}{\cos(x+h)\cos x.\left(\frac{h}{2}\right).2}$$

$$= \underset{h\to 0}{Lt} \sin\left(x+\frac{h}{2}\right) \cdot \underset{\frac{h}{2}\to 0}{Lt} \frac{\sin\left(\frac{h}{2}\right)}{\frac{h}{2}} \cdot \underset{h\to 0}{Lt} \frac{1}{\cos(x+h)\cos x}$$

$$= (\sin x)(1) \cdot \frac{1}{(\cos x)(\cos x)}$$

$$= \frac{\sin x}{\cos^2 x} = \frac{\sin x}{\cos x.\cos x} = \frac{\sin n}{\cos x} \cdot \frac{1}{\cos x} = \tan n.\sec x$$

$\therefore$ if $y = \sec x$, then $\frac{dy}{dx} = \sec x \tan x$

8. To find the derivative of cosec x w.r.t x by using first principle

Let $y = f(x) = \operatorname{cosec} x$ $\quad x$ is taken in radians

by definition, $\frac{dy}{dx} = \underset{h\to 0}{Lt} \frac{\operatorname{cosec}(x+h) - \operatorname{cosec} x}{h}$

$$= \underset{h\to 0}{Lt} \frac{\frac{1}{\sin(x+h)} - \frac{1}{\sin x}}{h}$$

$$= \underset{h\to 0}{Lt} \frac{\sin x - \sin(x+h)}{\sin(x+h).(\sin x)(h)}$$

$$= \underset{h\to 0}{Lt} \frac{2\cos\left(\frac{x+x+h}{2}\right)\sin\left(\frac{x-(x+h)}{2}\right)}{\sin(x+h)\sin(x)\,h}$$

$$= \underset{h\to 0}{Lt} \frac{2\cos\left(\frac{2x+h}{2}\right)\sin\left(\frac{-h}{2}\right)}{\sin(x+h)\sin(x).(\frac{h}{2}).2}$$

$$= -\underset{h\to 0}{Lt} \frac{\cos\left(\frac{2x+h}{2}\right)}{\sin(x+h).\sin(x)} \underset{\frac{h}{2}\to 0}{Lt} \frac{\sin\left(\frac{h}{2}\right)}{\left(\frac{h}{2}\right)}$$

$$= \frac{-\cos(x)}{\sin x.\sin x} \times 1 = \frac{-\cos x}{\sin x}.\frac{1}{\sec x}$$

$$= -\cot x \,.\, \text{cosec}\, x$$

$$= -\text{cosec}\, x \,.\, \cot x$$

$\therefore$ if $y = \text{cosec}\, x$ then $\frac{dy}{dx} = -\text{cosec} x \,.\, \cot x$

9. To find the derivative of e^x w.r.t x by using first principle.

Let $y = f(x) = e^x$

by definition, $\frac{dy}{dx} = \underset{h \to 0}{Lt} \frac{f(x+h) - f(x)}{h}$

$$= \underset{h \to 0}{Lt} \frac{e^{x+h} - e^x}{h}$$

$$= \underset{h \to 0}{Lt} \frac{e^x.e^h - e^x}{h} \qquad [\because \text{by } a^{m+n} = a^m \,.\, a^n]$$

$$= \underset{h \to 0}{Lt} e^x \frac{[e^h - 1]}{h}$$

$$= e^x \underset{h \to 0}{Lt} \frac{e^h - 1}{h} = e^x \qquad [\because \underset{x \to 0}{Lt} \frac{e^x - 1}{x} = 1]$$

$\therefore$ if $y = e^x$ then $\frac{dy}{dx} = e^x$

10. To find the derivative of a^x w.r.t x and by using first principle.

Let $y = f(x) = a^x$ and by definition,

$$\frac{dy}{dx} = \underset{h \to 0}{Lt} \frac{f(x+h) - f(x)}{h}$$

$$= \underset{h \to 0}{Lt} \frac{a^{x+h} - a^x}{h}$$

$$= \underset{h \to 0}{Lt} \frac{a^x.a^h - a^x}{h}$$

$$= \lim_{h \to 0} \frac{a^x(a^h - 1)}{h}$$

$$= a^x \lim_{h \to 0} \frac{a^h - 1}{h} = a^x.\log a \qquad \left[\because \lim_{x \to 0} \frac{a^x - 1}{x} = \log a\right]$$

$\therefore$ If $y = a^x$ then $\frac{dy}{dx} = a^x \log a$

11. To find the derivative of $\log x$ w.r.t x ($x > 0$).

Let $y = f(x) = \log x$.

by definition $\frac{dy}{dx} = \lim_{h \to 0} \frac{f(x+h) - f(x)}{h}$

$$= \lim_{h \to 0} \frac{\log(x+h) - \log x}{h}$$

$$= \lim_{h \to 0} \frac{\log\left(\frac{x+h}{x}\right)}{h} \qquad \left[\because \log m - \log n = \log\left(\frac{m}{n}\right)\right]$$

$$= \lim_{h \to 0} \frac{\log\left(1 + \frac{h}{x}\right)}{h}$$

$$= \lim_{h \to 0} \log\left(1 + \frac{h}{x}\right)^{\frac{1}{h}}$$

$$= \lim_{h \to 0} \log\left(1 + \frac{h}{x}\right)^{\frac{x}{h}\cdot\frac{1}{x}}$$

$$= \lim_{h \to 0} \frac{1}{x}.\log\left(1 + \frac{h}{x}\right)^{\frac{1}{\left(\frac{h}{x}\right)}}$$

$$= \frac{1}{x} \lim_{\frac{h}{x} \to 0} \log\left(1 + \frac{h}{x}\right)^{\frac{1}{\left(\frac{h}{x}\right)}} = \frac{1}{x}.(1) = \frac{1}{x}$$

$\therefore$ If $y = \log x$ then $\frac{dy}{dx} = \frac{1}{x}$

19.4 Algebraic Properties of Differentiable Functions

1. If f is a differentiable function at x and $K \in R$ then kf is differentiable and

$$\frac{d}{dx}(kf) = k \cdot \frac{df}{dx}$$

Let $y = kf$, i.e., $(kf)(x) = k.f(x)$

since f is differentiable, at x, $f'(x)$ exists.

$$\therefore f'(x) = \underset{h \to 0}{Lt} \frac{f(x+h) - f(x)}{h}$$

$$\therefore kf'x = \underset{h \to 0}{Lt} \frac{(kf)(x+h) - kf(x)}{h}$$

$$= \underset{h \to 0}{Lt} \frac{k.f(x+h) - kf(x)}{h}$$

$$= \underset{h \to 0}{Lt} \frac{k[f(x+h) - f(x)]}{h}$$

$$= k. \underset{h \to 0}{Lt} \left(\frac{f(x+h) - f(x)}{h} \right) = k.f'(x)$$

$$\therefore (kf)'x = k.f'(x)$$

$$\text{i.e } \frac{d}{dx}(kf) = k.\frac{d}{dx}(f) = k.\frac{df}{dx}$$

$\therefore$ kf is differentiable and $\frac{d}{dx}(kf) = k.\frac{df}{dx}$

Ex : (i) $\frac{d}{dx}(3x) = 3.\frac{d}{dx}(x) = 3(1)x^{1-1} = 3(1) = 3$

(ii) $\frac{d}{dx}(4\tan x) = 4.\frac{d}{dx}(\tan x) = 4\sec^2 x$

2. If f and g are two differentiable functions at x then $f + g$ is differentiable at x and

$$\frac{d}{dx}((f+g)x) = \frac{d}{dx}(f(x)) + \frac{d}{dx}(g(x))$$

i.e., $(f+g)'(x) = f'(x) + g'(x)$.

Since f and g are differentiable at x

$\therefore\ f'(x), g'(x)$ exists

$$\therefore\ f'(x) \lim_{h\to 0} \frac{f(x+h)-f(x)}{h} \text{ and } g'(x) \lim_{h\to 0} \frac{g(x+h)-g(x)}{h}$$

Now $(f+g)'x = \frac{d}{dx}(f+g)^{(x)} = \lim_{h\to 0} \frac{(f+g)(x+h)-(f+g)(x)}{h}$

$$= \lim_{h\to 0} \frac{f(x+h)+g(x+h)-f(x)-g(h)}{h}$$

$$= \lim_{h\to 0} \left\{\left(\frac{(f(x+h)-f(x)}{h}\right)+\left(\frac{g(x+h)-g(x)}{h}\right)\right\}$$

$$= \lim_{h\to 0} \frac{f(x+h)-f(x)}{h} + \lim_{h\to 0} \frac{f(x+h)-g(x)}{h}$$

$$\therefore (f+g)'x = f'(x)+g'(x)$$

$$\frac{d}{dx}((f+g)x) = \frac{d}{dx}(f'(x))+\frac{d}{dx}(g(x))$$

$\therefore\ (f+g)(x)$ is differentiable and $\frac{d}{dx}((f+g)x) = \frac{d}{dx}f(x)+\frac{d}{dx}g(x)$

Ex : $\frac{d}{dx}(\sin x + \cos x) = \frac{d}{dx}(\sin x) + \frac{d}{dx}(\cos x) = \cos x - \sin x$

Note : If f, g are two differentiable functions at x, y and $k_1\ k_2 \in R$ then

$$\frac{d}{dx}(k_1 f + k_2 g)(x) = k_1 \frac{d}{dx}(f(x)) + k_2 \frac{d}{dx}(g(x))$$

Ex : $\frac{d}{dx}(5x^2 + 6\sin x)$

$= 5.\frac{d}{dx}(x^2) + 6.\frac{d}{dx}(\sin x)$

$= 5.(2x) + 6(\cos x)$

$= 10x + 6\cos x$

3. If f and g are two differentiable functions at x then fg is differentiable at x and

$$(fg)'(x) = f(x)g^1(x) + g(x)f'(x).$$

Since f and g are two differentiable functions

$\therefore f'(x),\ g'(x)$ are exists

$$\therefore f'(x) = \underset{h\to 0}{Lt} \frac{f(x+h)-f(x)}{h}, \quad g'(x) = \underset{h\to 0}{Lt} \frac{g(x+h)-g(x)}{h}$$

$$\text{now } (f'g)x = \underset{h\to 0}{Lt} \frac{(fg)(x+h)-(fg)(x)}{h}$$

$$= \underset{h\to 0}{Lt} \frac{f(x+h)g(x+h)-f(x)g(x)}{h}$$

$$= \underset{h\to 0}{Lt} \frac{f(x+h)g(x+h)-f(x+h)g(x)+f(x+b)g(x)-f(x)g(x)}{h}$$

$$= \underset{h\to 0}{Lt} \frac{f(x+h)[g(x+h)-g(x)[+g(x)[f(x+h)-f(x)]}{h}$$

$$= \underset{h\to 0}{Lt} f(x+h) \underset{h\to 0}{Lt} \frac{g(x+h)-g(x)}{h} + \underset{h\to 0}{Lt} g(x). \underset{h\to 0}{Lt} \frac{f(x+h)-f(x)}{h}$$

$$= f(x).g'(x)+g(x).f'(x)$$

$$\therefore (fg)'(x) = f(x).g'(x)+g(x).f'(x)$$

Corollary : *u* and *v* are two differentiable functions at *x*, then *u v* is also differentiable at *x*

and $\frac{d}{dx}(u\,v) = u\,.\frac{dv}{dx} + v.\frac{du}{dx}$ (it is called *u v* rule)

Ex : (i) $\frac{d}{dx}(x\sin x) = x\,.\frac{d}{dx}(\sin x) + \sin x\,.\frac{d}{dx}(x)$

$= x\,.\cos x + \sin x\,.1$

(ii) $\frac{d}{dx}(e^x \sin x) = e^x\,.\frac{d}{dx}(\sin x) + \sin x.\frac{d}{dx}(e^x)$

$= e^x\,.\cos x + \sin x\,.\,e^x$

(iii) $\frac{d}{dx}(x^n\,.\tan x) = x^n\,.\frac{d}{dx}(\tan x) + \tan x\,.\frac{d}{dx}(x^n)$

$= x^n\,.\sec^2 x + \tan x\,.\,(n\,x^{n-1})$

$= x^n \sec^2 x + n.\tan x\,.\,x^{n-1}$

Corollary

$$\frac{d}{dx}(u\,v\,w) = u\,v\,\frac{dw}{dx} + vw\frac{du}{dx} + uw\frac{dv}{dx}$$

4. If f and g are two differentiable functions at x and $g(x) \neq 0$ then $\frac{f}{g}$ is differentiable at x and $\left(\frac{f}{g}\right)'(x) = \frac{g(x).f'(x) - f(x).g'(x)}{[g(x)]^2}$.

Since f and g are differentiable at x

$\therefore$ $f'(x)$, $g'(x)$ are exists\

and $f'(x) = \underset{h\to 0}{Lt}\frac{f(x+h)-f(x)}{h}$, $\quad g'(x) = \underset{h\to 0}{Lt}\frac{g(x+h)-g(x)}{h}$

now $\left(\frac{f'}{g}\right)(x) = \underset{h\to 0}{Lt}\frac{\left(\frac{f}{g}\right)(x+h) - \left(\frac{f}{g}\right)(x)}{h}$

$$= \underset{h\to 0}{Lt}\frac{\frac{f(x+h)}{g(x+h)} - \left(\frac{f(x)}{g(x)}\right)}{h}$$

$$= \underset{h\to 0}{Lt}\frac{f(x+h)g(x) - f(x)f(x+h)}{h.\ g(x+h)\ g(x)}$$

$$= \underset{h\to 0}{Lt}\frac{f(x+h)g(x) - f(x)g(x) + f(x)g(x) - f(x)g(x+h)}{h.\ g(x+h)\ g(x)}$$

$$= \underset{h\to 0}{Lt}\frac{g(x)[f(x+h)-f(x)] - f(x)[g(x+h)-g(x)]}{h.\ g(x+h).g(x)}$$

$$= \underset{h\to 0}{Lt}\frac{1}{g(x+h)\ g(x)}\left\{g(x)\underset{h\to 0}{Lt}\frac{f(x+h)-f(x)}{h} - f(x)\right\}\underset{h\to 0}{Lt}\frac{[g(x+h)-g(x)]}{h}$$

$$= \frac{1}{\{g(x)\}^2}\{g(x)f'(x) - f(x).g'(x)\}$$

$$= \frac{g(x)f'(x) - f(x)g'(x)}{\{g(x)\}^2}$$

Note : If u and v are two differentiable functions in x then

$$\frac{d}{dx}\left\{\frac{u}{v}\right\}=\frac{v.\frac{du}{dx}-u.\frac{dv}{dx}}{v^2}$$

(it is known as quotient rule of u/v formula)

Ex : (i) $$\frac{d}{dx}\left(\frac{x^n}{e^x}\right)=\frac{e^x.\frac{d}{dx}(x^n)-x^n.\frac{d}{dx}(e^x)}{(e^x)^2}$$

$$=\frac{e^x.n.x^{n-1}-x^n.e^n}{e^{2x}}$$

$$=\frac{e^x.x^{n-1}[n-x]}{e^{2x}}$$

$$=\frac{x^{n-1}[n-x]}{e^x}$$

(ii) $$\frac{d}{dx}\left(\frac{\sin x}{ax+b}\right)=\frac{(ax+b).\frac{d}{dx}(\sin x)-\sin x\frac{d}{dx}(ax+b)}{(ax+b)^2}$$

$$=\frac{(ax+b)\cos x-(\sin x)(a)}{(ax+b)^2}$$

Solved Examples

1. Find the derivative of the following functions by first principle (by definition)

(i) x^2 (ii) $\frac{i}{x^2+1}$ (iii) $\sin^2 x$

Sol. Let $y=x^2$

by definition, $$\frac{dy}{dx}=f'(x)=\underset{h\to 0}{Lt}\frac{f(x+h)-f(x)}{h}$$

$$=\underset{h\to 0}{Lt}\frac{(x+h)^2-x^2}{h}$$

$$= \underset{h \to 0}{Lt} \frac{(x+h+x)(x+h-x)}{h}$$

$$= \underset{h \to 0}{Lt} \frac{(2x+h)(h)}{h} = \underset{h \to 0}{Lt}(2x+h) = 2x+0 = 2x$$

$\therefore$ if $y = x^2$ then $\frac{dy}{dx} = 2x$

(ii) Let $y = \frac{1}{x^2+1}$

by definition, $\frac{dy}{dx} = \underset{h \to 0}{Lt} \frac{f(x+h) - f(x)}{h}$

$$= \underset{h \to 0}{Lt} \frac{\frac{1}{(x+h)^2+1} - \frac{1}{x^2+1}}{h}$$

$$= \underset{h \to 0}{Lt} \frac{\{(x^2+1)\} - \{(x+h)^2+1\}}{((x+h)^2+1)(x^2+1).h}$$

$$= \underset{h \to 0}{Lt} \frac{x^2-(x+h)^2}{((x+h)^2+1)(x^2+1).h}$$

$$= \underset{h \to 0}{Lt} \frac{(x+x+h)(x-x-h)}{((x+h)^2+1)(x^2+1).h}$$

$$= -\underset{h \to 0}{Lt} \frac{(2x+h)}{((x+h)^2+1)(x^2+1)} = \frac{-2x}{(x^2+1)(x^2+1)} = \frac{-2x}{(x^2+1)^2}$$

(iii) $y = \sin^2 x$

by definition $\frac{dy}{dx} = \underset{h \to 0}{Lt} \frac{\sin^2(x+h) - \sin^2(x)}{h}$

$$= \underset{h \to 0}{Lt} \frac{\sin^2(x+h+x)\sin(x+h-x)}{h}$$

($\because$ by using $\sin^2 A - \sin^2 B = \sin(A+B)\sin(A-B)$)

$$= \underset{h \to 0}{Lt} \frac{\sin(2x+h)\sin h}{h}$$

$$= \sin(2x) \,.\, 1 = \sin 2x$$

$$\therefore y = \sin^2 x \quad \Rightarrow \quad \frac{dy}{dx} = \sin 2x$$

2. Show that the function

$$f(x) = x \quad \text{for} \quad 0 \le x < 2$$

$$= 2 \quad \text{for} \quad x \ge 2 \qquad \text{is not differentiable at } x = 2$$

Sol. $$L(f'(a)) = \underset{x \to a}{Lt} \frac{f(x) - f(a)}{x - a}$$

$$\therefore L(f'(2)) = \underset{x \to 2}{Lt} \frac{x-2}{x-2} = 1 \qquad (\because f(x) = x \text{ for } x \ge 2)$$

$$R(f'(2)) = \underset{x \to 2}{Lt} \frac{2-2}{x-2} = 0 \qquad (\because f(x) = 2 \text{ for } x > 2)$$

$$\therefore L(f'(x)) \neq R(f'(x))$$

Hence f is not differentiable at $x = 2$

3. Find the derivative of the following functions w.r.t x.

(i) $3e^x + 5 \sin x$ (ii) $e^x + x^n + 5 \log x$

(iii) $\log_{10} x$ (iv) $\dfrac{x^{10} + 3x^5 + 15x - 1}{x^2}$

(v) $\sqrt{2} \sin x + 5x^7 - \dfrac{8}{x^3}$ (vi) $\sqrt{x} + 3x^{\frac{3}{4}} + 2x^{\frac{5}{6}}$

Sol. (i) Let $y = 3e^x + 5\sin x$

$$\frac{dy}{dx} = \frac{d}{dx}(3e^x + 5\sin x)$$

$$= 3.\frac{d}{dx}(e^x) + 5.\frac{d}{dx}(\sin x)$$

$$\frac{dy}{dx} = 3.e^x + 5.\cos x$$

(ii) Let $y = e^x + x^n + 5\log x$

$$\frac{dy}{dx} = \frac{d}{dx}\{e^x + x^n + 5\log x\}$$

$$= \frac{d}{dx}(e^x) + \frac{d}{dx}(x^n) + \frac{d}{dx}(5\log x)$$

$$= e^x + n \,.\, x^{n-1} + 5 \,.\, \frac{d}{dx}(\log x)$$

$$= e^x + n.\, x^{n-1} + 5.\, \frac{1}{x}$$

(iii) $\log_{10} x = \dfrac{\log_e x}{\log_e 10}$

$$\therefore \frac{d}{dx}(\log_{10} x) = \frac{d}{dx}\left\{\frac{\log_e x}{\log_e 10}\right\} = \frac{1}{\log_e 10}\,\frac{d}{dx}\{\log_e x\}$$

$$= \frac{1}{\log_e 10} \cdot \frac{1}{x}$$

(iv) Let $y = \dfrac{x^{10} + 3x^5 + 15x - 1}{x^2}$

$$\frac{dy}{dx} = \frac{d}{dx}\left\{\frac{x^{10} + 3x^5 + 15x - 1}{x^2}\right\}$$

$$= \frac{d}{dx}\left\{x^8 + 3.x^3 + \frac{15}{x} - \frac{1}{x^2}\right\}$$

$$= \frac{d}{dx}\{x^8\} + 3.\frac{d}{dx}(x^3) + 15\frac{d}{dx}\left(\frac{1}{x}\right) - \frac{d}{dx}\left\{\frac{+1}{x^2}\right\}$$

$$= 8.x^7 + 3.\,(3x^2) + 15\,(-1)\,(x^2) - \frac{d}{dx}\,(x^{-2}) - (-2)\,x^{-2-1}$$

$$= 8x^7 + 9x^2 - 15\,(x^{-2}) + 2x^{-3}$$

(v) Let $y = \sqrt{2}\ \sin x + 5x^7 - \dfrac{8}{x^3}$

$$\frac{dy}{dx} = \frac{d}{dx}\left\{\sqrt{2}\sin x + 5x^7 - 8x^{-3}\right\}$$

$$= \sqrt{2}.\frac{d}{dx}(\sin x) + 5.\frac{d}{dx}(x^7) - 8.\frac{d}{dx}(x^{-3})$$

$$= \sqrt{2}\ .\ \cos x + 5.\,(7\,.\,x^6) - 8.\,(-3)\,x^{-3-1}$$

$$= \sqrt{2}\ \cos x + 35\,x^6 + 24\,.\,x^{-4}$$

(vi) $\frac{d}{dx}\left\{\sqrt{x}+3.x^{\frac{3}{4}}+2x^{\frac{5}{6}}\right\}=\frac{1}{2}x^{\frac{-1}{2}}+\frac{9}{4}.x^{\frac{-1}{4}}+2.\frac{5}{6}.x^{\frac{-1}{6}}$

4. Find the derivative of following functions w.r.t x.

(i) $e^x(x^4)$ (ii) $e^x . (x^5 + 3)$ (iii) $e^x \sin^x$

(iv) $(\log x)(x^n)$ (v) $x^2 . e^x \sin x$ (vi) $(x^2 - 3)(4x^3 + 1)$

Sol (i) by $u\,v$ rule we have

$$\frac{d}{dx}(u\,v) = u.\frac{d}{dx}(v) + v.\frac{d}{dx}(u)$$

$$\therefore \frac{d}{dx}(e^x x^4) = e^x.\frac{d}{dx}(x^4) + x^4.\frac{d}{dx}(e^x)$$

$$= e^x.(4x^3) + x^4.e^x$$

$$= x^3e^x(4 + x)$$

(ii) $\frac{d}{dx}(e^x.(x^5 + 3)$

$$= e^x.\frac{d}{dx}(x^5 + 3) + (x^5 + 3).\frac{d}{dx}(e^x)$$

$$= e^x.\left\{\frac{d}{dx}(x^5) + \frac{d}{dx}(3)\right\} + (x^5 + 3).(e^x)$$

$$= e^x.\{5x^4 + 0\} + e^x.(x^5 + 3)$$

$$= 5\,e^x x^4 + e^x x^5 + 3\,e^x$$

$$= e^x[5x^4 + x^5 + 3]$$

(iii) $\frac{d}{dx}(e^x.\sin x)$

$$= e^x.\frac{d}{dx}(\sin x) + (\sin x).\frac{d}{dx}(e^x)$$

$$= e^x(\cos x) + \sin^x.e^x$$

(iv) $\frac{d}{dx}(\log x.x^n) = \log x.\frac{d}{dx}(x^n) + x^n.\frac{d}{dx}(\log x)$

$$= (\log x)(n.x^{n-1}) + x^n.\frac{1}{x}$$

$$= n.x^{n-1} \cdot \log x + x^{n-1}$$
$$= x^{n-1} \{ n \log x + 1\}$$

(v) $$\frac{d}{dx}(x^2 \cdot e^x \cdot \sin x) = x^2 e^x \cdot \frac{d}{dx}(\sin x) + e^x \sin x \frac{d}{dx}(x^2)$$
$$+ \sin x \cdot x^2 \cdot \frac{d}{dx}(e^x)$$
$$= x^2 e^x \cdot \cos x + e^x \sin x \cdot (2x) + x^2 \cdot \sin x \cdot e^x$$

(vi) $$\frac{d}{dx}\{(x^2 - 3)(4x^3 + 1)\}$$
$$= (x^2 - 3) \cdot \frac{d}{dx}(4x^3 + 1) + (4x^3 + 1) \cdot \frac{d}{dx}(x^2 - 3)$$
$$= (x^2 - 3).\left\{4.\frac{d}{dx}(x^3) + \frac{d}{dx}(1)\right\} + (4x^3 + 1)\left\{\frac{d}{dx}(x^2) - \frac{d}{dx}(3)\right\}$$
$$= (x^2 - 3) \cdot \{ 4(3x^2) + 0 \} + (4x^3 + 1)(2x - 0\}$$
$$= 12x^2 (x^2 - 3) + 2x (4x^3 + 1)$$
$$= 12x^4 - 36x^2 + 8x^4 + 2x$$
$$= 20x^4 - 36x^2 + 2x$$

5. Find the derivative of the following functions w.r.t x.

(i) $\frac{\sin x}{x}$ (ii) $\frac{x}{\tan x}$ (iii) $\frac{e^x}{x^n}$

(iv) $\frac{x^3 + 5}{2x + 3}$ (v) $\frac{\sin x}{\sin x + \cos x}$

Sol. (i) by $\frac{u}{v}$ rule

$$\frac{d}{dx}\left(\frac{u}{v}\right) = \frac{v.\frac{du}{dx} - u\frac{dv}{dx}}{v^2}$$

$$\therefore \frac{d}{dx}\left(\frac{\sin x}{x}\right) = \frac{x.\frac{d}{dx}(\sin x) - \sin x.\frac{d}{dx}(x)}{(x)^2}$$

$$= \frac{x.\cos x - \sin x.(1)}{x^2}$$

(ii) $$\frac{d}{dx}\left(\frac{x}{\tan x}\right)=\frac{\tan x.\frac{d}{dx}(x)-x.\frac{d}{dx}(\tan x)}{(\tan x)^2}$$

$$=\frac{\tan x(1)-x.\sec^2 x}{(\tan x)^2}$$

(iii) $$\frac{d}{dx}\left(\frac{e^x}{x^n}\right)=\frac{x^n.\frac{d}{dx}(e^x)-e^x.\frac{d}{dx}(x^n)}{(x^n)^2}$$

$$=\frac{x^n.e^x-e^x.n.x^{n-1}}{(x^n)^2}$$

$$=\frac{x^{n-1}e^x[x-n]}{x^{2n}}=\frac{e^x(x-n)}{x^{n+1}}$$

(iv) $\dfrac{x^3+5}{2x+3}$

$$\frac{d}{dx}\left(\frac{x^3+5}{2x+3}\right)=\frac{(2x+3).\frac{d}{dx}(x^3+5)-(x^3+5)\frac{d}{dx}(2x+3)}{(2x+3)^2}$$

$$=\frac{(2x+3)(3x^2+0)-(x^3+5).(2+0)}{(2x+3)^2}$$

$$=\frac{3x^2(2x+3)-(x^3+5)2}{(2x+3)^2}$$

$$=\frac{6x^3+9x^2-10-2x^3}{(2x+3)^2}\Rightarrow\frac{4x^3+9x^2-10}{(2x+3)^2}$$

(v) $\dfrac{\sin x}{\sin x+\cos x}$

$$\frac{d}{dx}\left\{\frac{\sin x}{\sin x+\cos x}\right\}$$

$$=\frac{(\sin x+\cos x)\frac{d}{dx}(\sin x)-\sin x.\frac{d}{dx}(\sin x+\cos x)}{(\sin x+\cos x)^2}$$

$$= \frac{\sin x \cos x + \cos^2 x - \sin x \cos x + \sin^2 x}{(\sin x + \cos x)^2}$$

$$= \frac{1}{(\sin x + \cos x)^2}$$

6. Find the derivative of the following functions w.r.t x.

(i) $\dfrac{\log x}{2 + \log x}$ (ii) $\dfrac{x + \tan x}{x^2 + \sin x}$ (iii) $\dfrac{\log x}{1 + e^x}$

(iv) $\dfrac{a^x + b^x}{\cos ec\, x}$ (v) $\dfrac{e^x + 1}{e^x - 1}$ (vi) $\dfrac{\left(\sqrt{x} + \dfrac{1}{\sqrt{x}}\right)^2}{\sin x}$

(vii) $\dfrac{\sqrt{x}}{3x + 4}$

Sol. (i) Let $y = \dfrac{\log x}{2 + \log x}$

$$\frac{dy}{dx} = \frac{(2 + \log x)\dfrac{d}{dn}(\log x) - (\log x).\dfrac{d}{dn}(2 + \log x)}{(2 + \log x)^2}$$

$$= \frac{(2 + \log x).\left(\dfrac{1}{x}\right) - (\log x).\left(\dfrac{1}{x}\right)}{(2 + \log x)^2} = \frac{\dfrac{2}{x}}{(2 + \log x)^2} = \frac{2}{x(2 + \log x)^2}$$

(ii) $y = \dfrac{x + \tan x}{x^2 + \sin x}$

$$\frac{dy}{dx} = \frac{(x^2 + \sin x)\dfrac{d}{dx}(x + \tan x) - (x + \tan x)\dfrac{d}{dx}(x^2 + \sin x)}{(x^2 + \sin x)^2}$$

$$= \frac{(x^2 + \sin x)(1 + \sec^2 x) - (x + \tan x)(2x + \cos x)}{(x^2 + \sin x)^2}$$

$$= \frac{x^2 + x^2 \sec^2 x + \sin x + \sin x.\sec^2 x - 2x^2 - x\cos x - 2x\tan x - \tan x.\cos x}{(x^2 + \sin x)^2}$$

$$= \frac{x^2 \sec^2 x + \sin x + \sin x.\sec^2 x - x^2 - x\cos x - 2x\tan x - \sin x}{(x^2 + \sin x)^2}$$

$$= \frac{(\sec^2 x)(x^2 + \sin x) - x^2 - x\cos x - 2x\tan x}{(x^2 + \sin x)^2}$$

(iii) Let $y = \frac{\log x}{1+e^x}$

$$\frac{dy}{dx} = \frac{(1+e^x)\frac{d}{dx}(\log x) - \log x.\frac{d}{dx}\left(1+e^x\right)}{(1+e^x)^2}$$

$$= \frac{(1+e^x)\frac{1}{x} - (\log x).e^x}{(1+e^x)^2}$$

(iv) Let $y = \frac{a^x + b^x}{\operatorname{cosec} x}$

$$\frac{dy}{dx} = \frac{(\operatorname{cosec} x)(a^x \log a + b^x \log b) - (a^x + b^x)(-\operatorname{cosec} x \cot x)}{\operatorname{cosec}^2 x}$$

$$= \frac{(a^x \log a + b^x \log b) + (a^x + b^x)\cot x}{\operatorname{cosec} x}$$

$= \sin x(a^x \log a + b^x \log b) + (a^x + b^x)\cos x$

$= a^x(\sin x . \log a + \cos x) + b^x(\sin x \log b + \cos x)$

(v) Let $y = \frac{e^x + 1}{e^x - 1}$

$$\frac{dy}{dx} = \frac{(e^x - 1).\frac{d}{dx}(e^x + 1) - (e^x + 1).\frac{d}{dx}(e^x - 1)}{(e^x - 1)^2}$$

$$= \frac{(e^x - 1).e^x - (e^x - 1).e^x}{(e^x - 1)^2}$$

$$= \frac{e^x\left[e^x - 1 - e^x - 1\right]}{\left[e^x - 1\right]^2}$$

$$= \frac{e^x[-2]}{\left[e^x - 1\right]^2} = \frac{-2e^x}{(e^x - 1)^2}$$

(vi) Let $y = \dfrac{\left(\sqrt{x} + \dfrac{1}{\sqrt{x}}\right)^2}{\sin x} = \dfrac{x + \dfrac{1}{x} + 2}{\sin x}$

$$\frac{dy}{dx} = \frac{(\sin x).\frac{d}{dx}(x + \frac{1}{x} + 2) - (x + \frac{1}{x} + 2).\frac{d}{dx}(\sin x)}{(\sin x)^2}$$

$$= \frac{(\sin x)(1 - \frac{1}{x^2}) - (x + \frac{1}{x} + 2).\cos x}{\sin^2 x}$$

(vii) $\dfrac{dy}{dx} = \left[\dfrac{(3x+4).\dfrac{1}{2\sqrt{x}} + \sqrt{x}.3}{(3x+4)^2}\right]$

Exercise - 19.1

1. Find the derivative of the following functions by using first principle.

   (i) x^4 (ii) e^{2x} (iii) $\sin 3x$

   (iv) $\sec^2 x$ (v) $\operatorname{cosec} 3x$ (vi) $\sqrt{x+3}$

   (vii) $\dfrac{1}{x+1}$ (viii) $ax^2 + bx + c$

2. Show that the function $f(x) = 3 + x$ for $x > 0$

   $= 3 - x$ for $x < 0$, is not differentiable at $x = 0$

3. Find the derivative of the following functions w.r.t to x.

   (i) x^{25} (ii) $e^x + x^n$ (iii) $\sin x + \tan x$

   (iv) $a^x + e^x + x^n$ (v) $\dfrac{x^4 + 4x^3 + 3x + 1}{x^3}$ (vi) $5^x + \log x + \sec x$

(vii) $\sec x - \tan x$ (viii) $x^3 + \frac{1}{x} + \log x$ (ix) $\cot x + \tan x$

(x) $\sqrt{x} + 2x^{\frac{3}{4}} + 3x^{\frac{5}{6}}$

4. Find the derivative of the following functions by using first principle.

(i) $e^x(x^2 + 2)$ (ii) $a^x + \sin x \cos x$ (iii) $10^x + \log x + x^4 e^x$

(iv) $(x^3 + 3)(4x^2 + 7)$ (v) $\left(\sqrt{x} - 1\right)(x^2 + 4x + 3)$ (vi) $5\cos x + a^x \log x$

(vii) $x \cdot e^x \cdot \cos x$ (viii) $x^3 e^x \sin x$ (ix) $x\, 3^x \tan x$

(x) $a^x \cdot \log x \cdot e^x$

5. Find the derivative of the following functions.

(i) $\frac{x}{\cot x}$ (ii) $\frac{ax+b}{cx+d}$ (iii) $\frac{x^n}{e^x}$

(iv) $\frac{\cos x}{\cos x - \sin x}$ (v) $\frac{x^2 - x + 1}{x^2 + x + 1}$ (vi) $\frac{a - b\cos x}{a + b\cos x}$

(vii) $\frac{xe^x}{1 + \tan x}$ (viii) $\frac{x(x+3)}{2x-5}$ (ix) $\frac{x^3 + 2}{x^2 - x - 2}$

(x) $(\cos x)(1 - \sin x)$ (xi) $\frac{\sin x + \cos x}{\sqrt{1 + \sin 2x}}$

6. Find the derivative of the following functions w.r.t x.

(i) $\frac{\log x}{1 - \log x}$ (ii) $\frac{x + \cos x}{x + \sin x}$ (iii) $\frac{\log x}{x + \sqrt{x}}$

(iv) $\frac{5^x + 3^x}{\sin x}$ (v) $\frac{\sec x + 1}{\sec x - 1}$ (vi) $\frac{\cos x - \sin x}{\cos x + \sin x}$

(vii) $\frac{e^x + \sin x}{e^x - \cos x}$ (viii) $\frac{e^x + \sin x}{1 + \cos x}$

7. Find the derivative of the following functions.

(i) $\sqrt[3]{x^5} . e^x . \log x$ (ii) $x\sqrt{x} - 2^x \sin x$

(iii) $(2x - 1)(3x^2 + 2)(4x^2 - 7)$ (iv) $\left(\frac{1}{3}\right)^x (\sin x + \log x)$

8. Find the derivative of the following w.r.t x.

(i) $\dfrac{x\sin x}{\sin x+\cos x}$ (ii) $\dfrac{e^x(x+1)}{\sin x}$

(iii) $\dfrac{3^x\tan x}{\sqrt[3]{x}}$ (iv) $\dfrac{(\sqrt{x}+1)(2^x+1)}{\sin x}$

Answers

1. (i) $4x^3$ (ii) $2e^{2x}$ (iii) $3\cos 3x$

(iv) $2\sec^2 x\,.\tan x$ (v) $-3\operatorname{cosec} x\cot x$ (vi) $\frac{1}{2}(x+3)^{\frac{-1}{2}}$

(vii) $\dfrac{-1}{(x+1)^2}$ (viii) $2ax + b$

3. (i) $25x^{24}$ (ii) $e^x + nx^{n-1}$ (iii) $\cos x + \sec^2 x$

(iv) $a^x \log a + e^x + nx^{n-1}$ (v) $1-\dfrac{3}{x^2}-\dfrac{3}{x^4}$ (vi) $5^x\log 5+\dfrac{1}{x}+\sec x\,.\tan x$

(vii) $\sec x\tan x - \sec^2 x$ (viii) $3x^2-\dfrac{1}{x^2}+\dfrac{1}{x}$ (ix) $-\operatorname{cosec}^2 x + \sec^2 x$

(x) $\dfrac{1}{2\sqrt{x}}+\dfrac{3}{2}x^{\frac{-1}{4}}+\dfrac{5}{2}.x^{\frac{-1}{6}}$

4. (i) $e^x(x^2 + 2x + 2)$ (ii) $a^x \log a + \dfrac{1}{2}\,.\,2\cos 2x$

(iii) $10^x\log 10+\dfrac{1}{x}+e^x(x^4+4x^3)$

(iv) (Hint : $(x^3 + 3)(8x) + (4x^2 + 7)(3x^2) = (20x^4 + 21x^2 + 24x)$)

(v) (Hint : $\left[(\sqrt{x}-1)(2x+4)+(x^2+4x+3)\dfrac{1}{2\sqrt{x}}\right]$

$$= 2x\sqrt{x}+4\sqrt{x}-2x-4+\frac{1}{2}x\sqrt{x}+4\sqrt{x}+\frac{3}{2}\frac{1}{\sqrt{x}})$$

$$= \frac{5}{2}x\sqrt{x}+8\sqrt{x}-2x-\frac{3}{2\sqrt{x}}-4$$

(vi) $-5\sin x + \frac{a^x}{x} + \log x.a^x.\log a$

(vii) $e^x[x(\cos x - \sin x) + \cos x]$

(viii) $e^x[x^3(\sin x + \cos x) + 3x^2 \sin x]$

(ix) $3^x[2\sec^2 x + (\log x)(\log 3) + (\tan x)(\log 3)\} + 2\tan x]$

(x) $\frac{(ae)^x}{x} + (\log x)(ae)^x.(1 + \log a)$

5. (i) $\frac{\cot x + x\operatorname{cosec}^2 x}{\cot^2 x} = \tan x + x.\sec^2 x$ (ii) $\frac{ad - bc}{(cx+d)^2}$

(iii) $\frac{x^{n-1}[x+n]}{e^x}$ (iv) $\frac{1}{(\cos x - \sin x)^2}$

(v) $\frac{2x^3 + 2x^2 - 2}{(x^2 + x + 1)^2}$ (vi) $\frac{2ab\sin x}{(a + b\cos x)^2}$

(vii) $e^x \frac{[(1+\tan x)(x+1) - x\sec^2 x]}{(1+\tan x)^2}$ (viii) $\frac{2x^2 - 10x - 15}{(2x-5)^2}$

(ix) $\frac{x^4 - 2x^3 - 6x^2 - 4x + 2}{(x^2 - x - 2)^2}$ (x) $-\sin x - \cos 2x$

(xi) 0

6. (i) $\frac{1}{(1 - \log x)^2}$

(ii) $\frac{\sin x - \cos x - x(\sin x + \cos x) - 1}{(x + \sin x)^2}$ (iii) $\frac{(x - \log x) + \left(\frac{2 - \log x}{2\sqrt{x}}\right)}{(x + \sqrt{x})^2}$

(iv) $\frac{\sin x(5^x \log 5 + 3^x \log 3) - (5^x + 3^x)\cos x}{\sin^2 x}$

(v) $-\cot\left(\frac{x}{2}\right).\operatorname{cosec}^2\left(\frac{x}{2}\right)$ (vi) $-\sec^2\left(\frac{\pi}{4} - x\right)$

(vii) $\frac{2.e^x.\sin x - 1}{(e^x - \cos x)^2}$ (viii) $\frac{(1+\cos x) + e^x(1 + \sin x + \cos x)}{(1+\cos x)^2}$

7. (i) $e^x\left(x^{\frac{5}{3}}\log x+\frac{5}{3}x^{\frac{2}{3}}\log x+x^{\frac{2}{3}}\right)$ (ii) $\frac{3}{2}\sqrt{x}-\left(2^x\cos x+\sin x.2^x\log 2\right)$

(iii) $120x^4 - 48x^3 - 78x^2 + 26x - 28$

(iv) $3^{-x}\left[\ (\cos x + \frac{1}{x}) - (\log 3)\ (\sin x + (\log x))\ \right]$

8. (i) $\dfrac{x+\sin x(\sin x+\cos x)}{(\sin x+\cos x)^2}$ (ii) $e^x\left\{\dfrac{(x+2)\sin x-(x+1)\cos x}{\sin^2 x}\right\}$

(iii) $\dfrac{x^{\frac{3}{2}}\,3^x\left(\sec^2 x-(\tan x)(\log 3)\right)-3^x\tan x.\frac{3}{2}\sqrt{x}}{x^3}$

(iv) $\dfrac{(\sin x)\left\{\frac{1}{2\sqrt{x}}(2^x+1)-(\sqrt{x}+1)(2^x\log 2)\right\}-(\sqrt{x}+1)(2^x+1)\cos x}{\sin^2 x}$

19.5 Differentiation of Composite Functions (Chain Rule)

Theorem : (Chain rule)

If f is a differentiable function at x and g is differentiable function at $f(x)$ then gof is differentiable at x and $(gof)'(x) = g'(f(x)).f'(x)$.

Proof : Since f is differentiable at x and g is differentiable at $f(x)$, it follows that $f'(x)$, $g'(f(x))$ exists.

$$\underset{h\to 0}{Lt}\ \frac{(gof)(x+h)-(gof)x}{h}$$

$$=\underset{h\to 0}{Lt}\ \frac{g(f(x+h))-g(f(x))}{h}$$

$$=\underset{h\to 0}{Lt}\ \frac{g(f(x+h)-g(f(x))}{f(x+h)-f(x)}\times\frac{f(x+h)-f(x)}{h}$$

$$=g'f(x+h).f'(x)$$

$\therefore$ gof is differentiable at x and

$$(gof)'(x)=g'(f(x))f'(x)$$

Note : (i) If u is a function in x and y is a function in u then $\frac{dy}{dx}=\frac{dy}{du}\cdot\frac{du}{dx}$, it is known as chain rule.

(ii) If $y = f(u),\ u = g(v),\ v = h(x)$

then $\frac{dy}{dx}=\frac{dy}{du}\cdot\frac{du}{dv}\cdot\frac{dv}{dx}$

Ex : (i) If $y = (3x + 2)^n$ then $\frac{dy}{dx} = n(3x + 2)^{n-1} \cdot \frac{d}{dx}(3x + 2)$

$= n(3x + 2)^{n-1} \cdot (3)$

(ii) If $y = \sin(4x + 7)$ then $\frac{dy}{dx} = \cos(4x + 7)\frac{d}{dx}(4x + 7)$

$= \cos(4x + 7) \cdot (4)$

Solved Examples

1. Find the derivative of following w.r.t x.

(i) $(2x + 3)^{10}$ (ii) $\cos^4 x$ (iii) $\sin(e^x)$

(iv) $\log(\tan x)$ (v) $e^{\operatorname{cosec} x}$ (vi) $\sqrt{\tan x}$

Sol. (i) Let $y = (2x + 3)^{10}$

$$\therefore \frac{dy}{dx}=\frac{d}{dx}(2x+3)^{10}$$

$$= 10 \cdot (2x + 3)^9 \cdot \frac{d}{dn}(2x + 3)$$

$$= 10 \cdot (2x + 3)^9 \cdot (2) = 20(2x + 3)^9$$

(ii) Let $y = \cos^4 x = (\cos x)^4$

$$\frac{dy}{dx} = 4.(\cos x)^{4-1} \cdot \frac{d}{dx}(\cos x)$$

$$= 4(\cos x)^3 \cdot (-\sin x) = -4 \sin x \cdot \cos^3 x$$

(iii) Let $y = \sin(e^x)$

$$\frac{dy}{dx}=\frac{d}{dx}(\sin(e^x))$$

$$= \cos(e^x) \cdot \frac{d}{dx}(e^x) = (\cos(e^x))(e^x)$$

(iv) Let $y = \log(\tan x)$

$$\frac{dy}{dx} = \frac{d}{dx}\{\log(\tan x)\}$$

$$= \frac{1}{\tan x}.\frac{d}{dx}(\tan x)$$

$$= \frac{1}{\tan x}.\sec^2 x$$

$$= \frac{\cos x}{\sin x} \times \frac{1}{\cos^2 x} = \frac{1}{\sin x \cos x} = \frac{2}{\sin 2x} = 2 \text{ cosec } 2x$$

(v) Let $y = e^{\text{cosec } x}$

$$\frac{dy}{dx} = \frac{d}{dx}(e^{cosecx}) = e^{cosecx}.\frac{d}{dx}(cosecx)$$

$$= e^{cosecx}.(-\text{cosec } x \cot x)$$

$$= -\text{cosec } x \cot x \,.\, e^{cosecx}$$

(vi) Let $y = \sqrt{\tan x}$

$$\frac{dy}{dx} = \frac{d}{dx}\left(\sqrt{\tan x}\right)$$

$$= \frac{1}{2\sqrt{\tan x}}.\frac{d}{dx}(\tan x) = \frac{1}{2\sqrt{\tan x}} \times \sec^2 x$$

2. Find the derivative of following function w.r.t x.

(i) $\sin\left(e^{\sqrt{x}}\right)$ (ii) $\log(\sin(x^3))$

(iii) $e^{\tan(x^3)}$ (v) $e^{\tan}(2^x)$

Sol. (i) Let $y = \sin\left(e^{\sqrt{x}}\right)$

$$\frac{dy}{dx} = \frac{d}{dx}(\sin(e^{\sqrt{x}}))$$

$$= \cos(e^{\sqrt{x}}).\frac{d}{dx}\left(e^{\sqrt{x}}\right)$$

$$= \cos(e^{\sqrt{x}}).e^{\sqrt{x}}.\frac{d}{dx}\left(\sqrt{x}\right)$$

$$= \cos(e^{\sqrt{x}}).e^{\sqrt{x}}.\frac{1}{2\sqrt{x}}$$

(ii) Let $y = \log(\sin(x^3))$

$$\frac{dy}{dx} = \frac{d}{dx}(\log(\sin(x^3))$$

$$= \frac{1}{\sin(x^3)} \cdot \frac{d}{dx}(\sin(x^3))$$

$$= \frac{1}{\sin(x^3)} .\cos(x^3) \frac{d}{dx}(x^3)$$

$$= \cot(x^3) \,.\, (3x^2)$$

$$= 3x^2 \cot\,(x^3)$$

(iii) Let $y = e^{\tan(x^3)}$

$$\frac{dy}{dx} = \frac{d}{dx}\left(e^{\tan(x^3)}\right)$$

$$\frac{dy}{dx} = e^{\tan(x^3)} . \frac{d}{dx}[\tan(x^3)]$$

$$= e^{\tan(x^3)} \,.\, \sec^2(x^3) \,.\, \frac{d}{dx}(x^3)$$

$$= e^{\tan(x^3)} \,.\, \sec^2(x^3) \,.\, (3x^2)$$

$$= 3x^2\, e^{\tan(x^3)} \,.\, \sec^2\,(x^3)$$

(iv) Let $y = e^{\tan(2^x)}$

$$\frac{dy}{dx} = \frac{d}{dx}\left(e^{\tan(2^x)}\right)$$

$$= e^{\tan(2^x)} . \frac{dy}{dx}\,(\tan\,(2^x))$$

$$= e^{\tan(2^x)} \,.\, \sec^2\,(2^x) \,.\, \frac{d}{dx}(2^x)$$

$$= e^{\tan(2^x)} \,.\, \sec^2(2^x) \,.\, (2^x) \log 2$$

3. Find the drivative of the following functions w.r.t x.

(i) $\log(\tan\sqrt{x}\,)$ (ii) $\log\sqrt{\tan x}$ (iii) $\sqrt{\tan(\log x)}$

(iv) $\sqrt{\cos\sqrt{x}}$ (v) $\sin\,(\log(\tan x))$ (vi) $\sec(\log\sqrt{2x+3})$

(vii) $\sin^4(\log(\tan x))$ (viii) $\log(\sqrt{3x^2-8x+1})$ (ix) $\frac{1}{3x+7}$

(x) $\left(\sqrt{x}+\frac{1}{\sqrt{x}}\right)^{10}$

Sol. (i) Let $y = \log(\tan\sqrt{x})$

$$\therefore \frac{dy}{dx} = \frac{d}{dx}\{\log(\tan\sqrt{x}\}$$

$$= \frac{1}{\tan\sqrt{x}}.\frac{d}{dx}(\tan\sqrt{x})$$

$$= \frac{1}{\tan\sqrt{x}}.\sec^2(\sqrt{x}).\frac{d}{dx}(\sqrt{x})$$

$$= \frac{1}{\tan\sqrt{x}}.\sec^2(\sqrt{x}).\frac{1}{2\sqrt{x}}$$

$$= \frac{\cos\sqrt{x}}{\sin\sqrt{x}}.\frac{1}{\cos^2\sqrt{x}}\frac{1}{2\sqrt{x}}$$

$$= \frac{1}{2\sin\sqrt{x}.\cos.\sqrt{x}.\sqrt{x}} = \frac{1}{\sqrt{x}.\sin 2\sqrt{x}}$$

(ii) Let $y = \log\sqrt{\tan x}$

$$\frac{dy}{dx} = \frac{d}{dx}\{\log(\sqrt{\tan x})\}$$

$$\frac{dy}{dx} = \frac{1}{\sqrt{\tan x}}.\frac{d}{dx}(\sqrt{\tan x})$$

$$= \frac{1}{\sqrt{\tan x}}.\frac{1}{2\sqrt{\tan x}}.\frac{d}{dx}.(\tan x)$$

$$= \frac{1}{\sqrt{\tan x}}.\frac{1}{2\sqrt{\tan x}}.\sec^2 x$$

$$= \frac{\sec^2 x}{2\tan x}$$

$$= \frac{1}{\cos^2 x} \cdot \frac{\cos x}{2\sin x}$$

$$= \frac{1}{2\sin x \cos x}$$

$$= \frac{1}{\sin 2x} = \operatorname{cosec} 2x$$

(iii) Let $y = \sqrt{\tan(\log x)}$

$$\frac{dy}{dx} = \frac{d}{dx}(\sqrt{\tan(\log x)})$$

$$= \frac{1}{2\sqrt{\tan(\log x)}} \times \frac{d}{dx}(\tan \log x)$$

$$= \frac{1}{2\sqrt{\tan(\log x)}} . \sec^2(\log x) . \frac{d}{dx}(\log x)$$

$$= \frac{1}{2\sqrt{\tan(\log x)}} \sec^2(\log x) . \frac{1}{x}$$

(iv) Let $y = \sqrt{\cos\sqrt{x}}$

$$\frac{dy}{dx} = \frac{d}{dx}(\sqrt{\cos\sqrt{x}})$$

$$= \frac{1}{2\sqrt{\cos\sqrt{x}}} . \frac{d}{dx}(\cos\sqrt{x})$$

$$= \frac{1}{2\sqrt{\cos\sqrt{x}}} . (-\sin\sqrt{x}) . \frac{d}{dx}(\sqrt{x})$$

$$= \frac{-\sin\sqrt{x}}{2\sqrt{\cos\sqrt{x}}} . \frac{1}{2\sqrt{x}} = \frac{-\sin\sqrt{x}}{4\sqrt{x}.\sqrt{\cos\sqrt{x}}}$$

(v) Let $y = \sin(\log(\tan x))$

$$\frac{dy}{dx} = \cos(\log(\tan x)) \frac{d}{dx}(\log(\tan x))$$

$$= \cos(\log(\tan x)) \cdot \frac{1}{\tan x} \cdot \frac{dy}{dx}(\tan x)$$

$$= \cos(\log(\tan x)) \cdot \frac{1}{\tan x} \cdot \sec^2 x$$

$$= \frac{2\cos(\log(\tan x))}{\sin 2x}$$

(vi) Let $y = \sec(\log(\sqrt{2x+3}))$

$$\frac{dy}{dx} = \sec(\log\sqrt{2x+3})\tan(\log\sqrt{2x+3}).\frac{d}{dx}(\log\sqrt{2x+3})$$

$$= \sec(\log\sqrt{2x+3})\tan(\log\sqrt{2x+3}).\frac{1}{\sqrt{2x+3}} \times \frac{d}{dx}(\sqrt{2x+3})$$

$$= \sec(\log\sqrt{2x+3})\tan(\log\sqrt{2x+3}).\frac{1}{\sqrt{2x+3}}.\frac{1}{2\sqrt{2x+3}}.2$$

$$= \sec(\log\sqrt{2x+3})\tan(\log\sqrt{2x+3}).\frac{1}{2x+3}$$

(vii) Let $y = \sin^4(\log(\tan x) = [\sin(\log\tan x)]^4$

$$\frac{dy}{dx} = 4.(\sin(\log(\tan x)))^3 \quad \frac{d}{dx}(\sin(\log\tan x)) \qquad \left[\frac{d}{dx}(x^n) = n.x^{n-1}\right]$$

$$= 4.(\sin(\log(\tan x)))^3 . \cos(\log(\tan x)) . \frac{d}{dx}(\log\tan x)$$

$$= 4.\sin(\log(\tan x))^3 . \cos(\log(\tan x)) . \frac{1}{\tan x}\frac{d}{dx}(\tan x)$$

$$= 4.\sin(\log(\tan x))^3 . \cos(\log(\tan x)) . \frac{1}{\tan x}.\sec^2 x$$

(viii) Let $y = \log\left(\sqrt{3x^2 - 8x + 1}\right)$

$$\frac{dy}{dx} = \frac{1}{\sqrt{3x^2 - 8x + 1}} \times \frac{d}{dx}\left(\sqrt{3x^2 - 8x + 1}\right)$$

$$= \frac{1}{\sqrt{3x^2 - 8x + 1}}.\frac{1}{2\sqrt{3x^2 - 8x + 1}} \times \frac{d}{dx}(3x^2 - 8x + 1)$$

$$= \frac{1}{2(3x^2 - 8x + 1)}(6x - 8)$$

$$= \frac{6x - 8}{2(3x^2 - 8x + 1)} = \frac{3x - 4}{3x^2 - 8x + 1}$$

(ix) Let $y = \frac{1}{3x + 7}$

$$\frac{dy}{dx} = \frac{d}{dx}\left(\frac{1}{3x+7}\right) = \frac{d}{dx}\left((3x+7)^{-1}\right)$$

$$= -(3x+7)^{-2}\frac{d}{dx}(3x+7)$$

$$= \frac{-1}{(3x+7)^2}.(3)$$

$$= \frac{-3}{(3x+7)^2}$$

(x) Let $y = \left(\sqrt{x} + \frac{1}{\sqrt{x}}\right)^{10}$

$$\frac{dy}{dx} = 10.\left(\sqrt{x} + \frac{1}{\sqrt{x}}\right)^{10-1}.\frac{d}{dx}\left(\sqrt{x} + \frac{1}{\sqrt{x}}\right)$$

$$= 10.\left(\sqrt{x} + \frac{1}{\sqrt{x}}\right)^{9}.\left(\frac{1}{2\sqrt{x}} + \left(\frac{-1}{2}x^{\frac{-1}{2}-1}\right)\right)$$

$$= 10.\left(\sqrt{x} + \frac{1}{\sqrt{x}}\right)^{9}.\left(\frac{1}{2\sqrt{x}} - \frac{1}{2}.\frac{1}{x^{\frac{3}{2}}}\right)$$

4. Find the drivative of the following functions w.r.t x.

(i) $\log\left(x + \sqrt{1 + x^2}\right)$ (ii) $\tan\left(x^2 - \frac{1}{x^2}\right)$ (iii) $e^{\sqrt{\sin x}}$

(iv) $\sin(3^{\log x})$ (v) $\log(\sin x + 2^x - 3\tan x)$

Sol. (i) Let $y = \log\left(x+\sqrt{1+x^2}\right)$

$$\frac{dy}{dx} = \frac{1}{x+\sqrt{1+x^2}} \times \frac{d}{dx}\left(x+\sqrt{1+x^2}\right)$$

$$= \frac{1}{x+\sqrt{1+x^2}} \cdot \left[\frac{d}{dx}(x) + \frac{d}{dx}(\sqrt{1+x^2})\right]$$

$$= \frac{1}{x+\sqrt{1+x^2}} \cdot \left[1 + \frac{1}{2\sqrt{1+x^2}} \cdot \frac{d}{dx}(1+x^2)\right]$$

$$= \frac{1}{x+\sqrt{1+x^2}} \cdot \left[1 + \frac{1}{2\sqrt{1+x^2}} .(2x)\right]$$

$$= \frac{1}{x+\sqrt{1+x^2}} \cdot \left[\frac{\sqrt{1+x^2}+x}{\sqrt{1+x^2}}\right]$$

$$= \frac{1}{\sqrt{1+x^2}}$$

(ii) Let $y = \tan\left(x^2 - \frac{1}{x^2}\right)$

$$\frac{dy}{dx} = \sec^2\left(x^2 - \frac{1}{x^2}\right) \cdot \frac{d}{dx}\left(x^2 - \frac{1}{x^2}\right)$$

$$= \sec^2\left(x^2 - \frac{1}{x^2}\right)\left[\frac{d}{dx}(x^2) - \frac{d}{dx}\left(\frac{1}{x^2}\right)\right]$$

$$= \sec^2\left(x^2 - \frac{1}{x^2}\right)\left[2x - \frac{d}{dx}\left(x^{-2}\right)\right]$$

$$= \sec^2\left(x^2 - \frac{1}{x^2}\right)\left[2x - \left(-2.x^{-3}\right)\right]$$

(iii) Let $y = e^{\sqrt{\sin x}}$

$$\frac{dy}{dx} = e^{\sqrt{\sin x}} \frac{d}{dx}(\sqrt{\sin x})$$

$$= e^{\sqrt{\sin x}} \frac{1}{2\sqrt{\sin x}} \cdot \frac{d}{dx}(\sin x)$$

$$= e^{\sqrt{\sin x}} \frac{1}{2\sqrt{\sin x}} . \cos x$$

(iv) Let $y = \sin(3^{\log x})$

$$\frac{dy}{dx} = \cos(3^{\log x}) . \frac{d}{dx}(3^{\log x})$$

$$= \cos (3^{\log x}) . 3^{\log x} . (\log 3) . \frac{d}{dx} (\log x)$$

$$= \cos (3^{\log x}) . 3^{\log x} . (\log 3) . \frac{1}{x}$$

(v) Let $y = \log (\sin x + 2^x - 3 \tan x)$

$$\frac{dy}{dx} = \frac{1}{\sin x + 2^x - 3\tan x} \frac{d}{dx} \{\sin x + 2^x - 3\tan x\}$$

$$= \frac{1}{\sin x + 2^x - 3\tan x} \{\cos x + 2^x \log 2 - 3\sec^2 x\}$$

5. Find the drivative of the following functions w.r.t x.

(i) $x^2 \tan x^3$ (ii) $e^{\tan x} \cos (2^x)$ (iii) $\tan(x^2 e^x)$

(iv) $\sin^4 x . \cos^3 x$

Sol. (i) Let $y = x^2 . \tan(x^3)$

$$\frac{dy}{dx} = \frac{d}{dx}\{x^2 . \tan(x^3)\}$$

$$= x^2 . \frac{d}{dx} (\tan (x^3)) + \tan (x^3) . \frac{d}{dx} (x^2) \quad \text{(by u - v formula)}$$

$$= x^2 . \sec^2 (x^3) . \frac{d}{dx} (x^3) + \tan (x^3) . (2x)$$

$$= x^2 . \sec^2 (x^3) (3x^2) + 2x . \tan(x^3)$$

(ii) Let $y = e^{\tan x} . \cos (2^x)$

$$\frac{dy}{dx} = \frac{d}{dx} \{e^{\tan x} \cos(2^x)\}$$

$$= e^{\tan x} \cdot \frac{d}{dx}\{\cos(2^x)\} + \cos(2^x)\frac{d}{dx}\{e^{\tan x}\}$$

$$= e^{\tan x} - \sin 2x \frac{d}{dx}(2^x) + \cos 2^x \cdot e^{\tan x}\frac{d}{dx}(\tan x)$$

$$= e^{\tan x} - \sin(2^x)\cdot(2^x)\log 2 + \cos 2^x \cdot e^{\tan x}\cdot \sec^2 x$$

$$= e^{\tan x}(\cos 2^x \cdot \sec^2 x - \sin 2^x \cdot 2^x \cdot \log^2)$$

(iii) Let $y = \tan(x^2 e^x)$

$$\frac{dy}{dx} = \sec^2(x^2 e^x)\frac{d}{dx}\{x^2 e^x\}$$

$$= \sec^2(x^2 e^x)\left[x^2 \cdot \frac{d}{dx}e^x + e^x \frac{d}{dx}(x^2)\right\} \quad \text{(by } u\text{ - }v \text{ rule)}$$

$$= \sec^2(x^2 e^x)[x^2 e^x + e^x \cdot 2x]$$

$$= \sec^2(x^2 e^x)(e^x)(x^2 + 2x)$$

$$= x(x+2)\cdot e^x \cdot \sec^2(x^2 e^x)$$

(iv) Let $y = \sin^4 x \cdot \cos^3 x$

$$y = (\sin x)^4 \cdot (\cos x)^3$$

$$\therefore \frac{dy}{dx} = (\sin x)^4 \cdot \frac{d}{dx}(\cos x)^3 + (\cos x)^3 \cdot \frac{d}{dx}(\sin x)^4$$

$$= (\sin x)^4 \cdot 3(\cos x)^2 \cdot \frac{d}{dx}(\cos x) + (\cos x)^3 \cdot 4(\sin x)^3 \cdot \frac{d}{dx}(\sin x)$$

$$= 3(\sin x)^4(\cos x)^2(-\sin x) + 4(\cos x)^3 \cdot (\sin x)^3 \cdot (\cos x)$$

$$= (\sin^3 x)(\cos^2 x)[-3\sin^2 x + 4.\cos^2 x]$$

6. Find the drivative of the following functions.

(i) $\dfrac{\log(\log x)}{\log(\cos x)}$ (ii) $\sqrt{\dfrac{1+x}{1-x}}$ (iii) $\sqrt{\dfrac{1+\cos x}{1-\cos x}}$

(iv) $\sqrt{\dfrac{1-e^x}{1+e^x}}$ (v) $\log\left(\dfrac{1-\sin x}{1+\sin x}\right)$ (vi) $\log\left(x^3 + \dfrac{1}{x^3}\right)$

(vii) $\dfrac{\sqrt{2x+1}}{x}$

Sol. (i) Let $y = \dfrac{\log(\log x)}{\log(\cos x)}$

$$\frac{dy}{dx} = \frac{\log(\cos x).\frac{d}{dx}(\log(\log x)) - \log(\log x)\frac{d}{dx}\log(\cos x)}{(\log(\cos x))^2}$$

$$= \frac{\log(\cos x).\frac{1}{\log x}.\frac{d}{dx}(\log x) - \log(\log x).\frac{1}{\cos x}\frac{d}{dx}(\cos x)}{(\log(\cos x))^2}$$

$$= \frac{\log(\cos x).\frac{1}{\log x}.\frac{1}{x} - \log(\log x).\frac{-\sin x}{\cos x}}{(\log(\cos x))^2}$$

$$= \frac{\frac{1}{x\log x}.\log(\cos x) + \frac{\sin x\log(\log x)}{\cos x}}{[\log(\cos x)]^2}$$

(ii) Let $y = \sqrt{\dfrac{1+x}{1-x}}$

$$\frac{dy}{dx} = \frac{1}{2\sqrt{\frac{1+x}{1-x}}}.\frac{d}{dx}\left\{\frac{1+x}{1-x}\right\}$$

$$= \frac{1}{2}\sqrt{\frac{1-x}{1+x}}\left(\frac{(1-x)\frac{d}{dx}(1+x) - (1+x)\frac{d}{dx}(1-x)}{(1-x)^2}\right)$$

$$= \frac{1}{2}\sqrt{\frac{1-x}{1+x}}\left(\frac{(1-x)(1) - (1+x)(-1)}{(1-x)^2}\right)$$

$$= \frac{1}{2}\sqrt{\frac{1-x}{1+x}}\left(\frac{1-x+1+x)}{(1-x)^2}\right)$$

$$= \frac{\sqrt{1-x}}{\sqrt{1+x}}.\frac{1}{(1-x)^2}$$

(iii) Let $y = \sqrt{\dfrac{1+\cos x}{1-\cos x}}$

$$\frac{dy}{dx} = \frac{1}{2\sqrt{\dfrac{1+\cos x}{1-\cos x}}} \cdot \frac{d}{dx}\left(\frac{1+\cos x}{1-\cos x}\right)$$

$$= \frac{1}{2\sqrt{\dfrac{1+\cos x}{1-\cos x}}}\left[\frac{(1-\cos x)(-\sin x)-(1+\cos x)(\sin x)}{(1-\cos x)^2}\right]$$

$$= \frac{1}{2}\,\frac{\sqrt{1-\cos x}}{\sqrt{1+\cos x}}\,\frac{-\sin x+\sin x\cos x-\sin x-\sin x\cos x}{(1-\cos x)^2}$$

$$= -\frac{\sqrt{1-\cos x}}{\sqrt{1+\cos x}} \cdot \frac{(\sin x)}{(1-\cos x)^2}$$

(iv) Let $y = \sqrt{\dfrac{1-e^x}{1+e^x}}$

$$\frac{dy}{dx} = \frac{1}{2\sqrt{\dfrac{1-e^x}{1+e^x}}} \cdot \frac{d}{dx}\left(\frac{1-e^x}{1+e^x}\right)$$

$$= \frac{1}{2} \cdot \sqrt{\frac{1+e^x}{1-e^x}}\left(\frac{(1+e^x)(-e^x)-(1-e^x)(e^x)}{(1+e^x)^2}\right)$$

$$= \sqrt{\frac{1-e^x}{1+e^x}}\,\frac{(-e^x)}{(1+e^x)^2}$$

(v) Let $y = \log\left(\dfrac{1-\sin x}{1+\sin x}\right)$

$$\frac{dy}{dx} = \frac{1}{\left(\dfrac{1-\sin x}{1+\sin x}\right)} \cdot \frac{d}{dx}\left(\frac{1-\sin x}{1+\sin x}\right)$$

$$= \frac{1+\sin x}{1-\sin x}\left[\frac{(1+\sin x)(-\cos x)-(1-\sin x)(\cos x)}{(1+\sin x)^2}\right]$$

$$= \left(\frac{1+\sin x}{1-\sin x}\right)\left[\frac{-\cos x-\sin x\cos x-\cos x+\sin x\cos x}{(1+\sin x)^2}\right]$$

$$= \left(\frac{1+\sin x}{1-\sin x}\right)\left[\frac{-2\cos x}{(1+\sin x)^2}\right]$$

$$= \frac{-2\cos x}{(1-\sin^2 x)} = \frac{-2\cos x}{\cos^2 x} = \frac{-2}{\cos x} = -2\sec x$$

(vi) Let $y = \log\left(x^3 + \frac{1}{x^3}\right)$

$$\frac{dy}{dx} = \frac{1}{(x^3+\frac{1}{x^3})}\cdot\frac{d}{dx}\left(x^3+\frac{1}{x^3}\right)$$

$$= \frac{x^3}{(x^3)^2+1}\cdot(3x^2+(-3)\cdot x^{-2})$$

$$= \frac{x^3}{x^6+1}\ (3x^2 - \frac{3}{x^2})$$

$$= \frac{x^3}{x^6+1}\ (\frac{3x^4-3}{x^2}) = \frac{3x(x^4-1)}{(x^6+1)}$$

(vii) Let $y = \frac{\sqrt{2x+1}}{x}$

$$\frac{dy}{dx} = \frac{x.\frac{d}{dx}\sqrt{2x+1} - \sqrt{2x+1}.\frac{d}{dx}(x)}{x^2}$$

$$= \frac{x.\frac{1}{2\sqrt{2x+1}}.2 - \sqrt{2x+1}(1)}{x^2}$$

$$= \frac{1-(2x+1)}{x^2\left(\sqrt{2x+1}\right)} = \frac{-2}{x\sqrt{2x+1}}$$

Excercise - 19.2

1. Find the drivative of the following functions w.r.t x.

(i) $\sin 3x$ (ii) $\cos 4x$ (iii) $\tan(5x)$

(iv) $\cot 6x$ (v) $\sec\left(x+\dfrac{1}{x}\right)$ (vi) $\operatorname{cosec} 8x$

(vii) $\sin (x^4)$ (viii) $\cos(\sqrt{x})$ (ix) $\tan(e^x)$

(x) $\cot^4 x$ (xi) $e^{\sin x}$ (xii) e^{x^3}

(xiii) $(5x + 7)^{100}$ (xiv) $\dfrac{1}{\sqrt{x^3+2}}$ (xv) $\sqrt{\tan x^2}$

(xvi) $\sqrt{\sec x - \tan x}$ (xvii) $\sqrt{10x^3 + 3\log x}$ (xviii) $3^{\sin x}$

(xix) $5^{\cos\sqrt{x}}$ (xx) $7^{\log(\sin x)}$ (xxi) $\log (\sec x + \tan x)$

(xxii) $\log\left(\sqrt{\log(\sin x)}\right)$ (xxiii) $\log (\sin^4 x)$ (xxiv) $\log\left(\sqrt{\sin x}\right)$

(xxv) $\tan\left(2^{(x^3)}\right)$

2. Find the derivatives of the following functions w.r.t x.

(i) $\sin 3x \cos 4x$ (ii) $e^{2x} . \log x$ (iii) $e^x \log (x^3)$

(iv) $e^{3x} . \sin 4x$ (v) $e^{4x} . \cos 3x$ (vi) $(2x + 5) \sqrt{3x-7}$

(vii) $x^3 . \sin^4 x$ (viii) $\log\left(e^{5x}.\sqrt{x}\right)$ (ix) $e^{\cos x} . \sin\sqrt{x}$

(x) $2^{x^3}.\log (2x)$

3. Differentiate the following functions w.r.t x.

(i) $\sqrt{\dfrac{x}{\sin x}}$ (ii) $\dfrac{e^{\cos x}}{\sqrt{\log x}}$ (iii) $\dfrac{\cos^5 x}{e^x+2}$

(iv) $\sqrt{\dfrac{3+e^x}{3-e^x}}$ (v) $\sqrt{\dfrac{1-\cos x}{1+\cos x}}$ (vi) $\log\left(\dfrac{1+\cos x}{1-\cos x}\right)$

(vii) $\dfrac{e^x \sin x+\cos x}{\log x+x}$ (viii) $\dfrac{e^x \tan x+\cos x}{2^x+e^x}$ (ix) $\dfrac{1-\cos 2x}{1+\cos 2x}$

(x) $\dfrac{x\cos x}{\sqrt{1+x^2}}$ (xi) $\sqrt{\dfrac{1+x^2}{1-x^2}}$

Answers

1. (i) $3\cos 3x$ (ii) $-4\sin 4x$

(iii) $5\sec^2 5x$ (iv) $-6\text{cosec}^2 x$

(v) $\sec\left(x+\frac{1}{x}\right)\tan\left(x+\frac{1}{x}\right)\left(1-\frac{1}{x^2}\right)$ (vi) $-8\text{cosec}\,8x\cot 8x$

(vii) $1\cos(x^4)\,(4x^3)$ (viii) $-\sin\left(\sqrt{x}\right).\left(\frac{1}{2\sqrt{x}}\right)$

(ix) $\sec^2(e^x)\,.\,(e^x)$ (x) $-4\cot^3 x\,.\,(\text{cosec}^2 x)$

(xi) $e^{\sin x}\cos x$ (xii) $e^{x^3}\,.\,(3x^2)$

(xiii) $(500)\,(5x+7)^{99}$ (xiv) $\frac{-3}{2}x^2.\left(x^3+2\right)^{\frac{-3}{2}}$

(xv) $\frac{1}{\sqrt{\tan x^2}}.\sec^2(x^2).x$ (xvi) $-\frac{1}{2}\sec x\left(\sqrt{\sec x-\tan x}\right)$

(xvii) $\frac{1}{2\sqrt{10x^3+3\ln x}}\left(30x^2+\frac{3}{x}\right)$ (xviii) $3^{\sin x}\,.\,(\log 3)\,.\,(\cos x)$

(xix) $5^{\cos\sqrt{x}}\,.\,(\log 5)\left(-\sin\sqrt{x}\right)\left(\frac{1}{2\sqrt{x}}\right)$

(xx) $(\log 7)\,(\cot x)\,7^{\log(\sin x)}$

(xxi) $\sec x$ (xxii) $\frac{1}{2\sqrt{\log(\sin x)}}.\cot x$

(xxiii) $\frac{1}{\sin^4 x}\,.\,4\,.\,\sin^3 x\,.\,\cos x$ (or) $4\,.\,\cot x$

(xxiv) $\frac{1}{2}\cot x$ (xxv) $3(\log 2).x^2.2^{(x^3)}.\sec^2(2^{(x^3)})$

2. (i) $\frac{1}{2}[7\cos 7x-\cos x]$

(ii) $e^{2x}\,.\,\frac{1}{x}+\log x\,.\,e^{2x}\,(2)$ (or) $e^{2x}\left[\frac{1}{x}+2\log x\right]$

(iii) $3.e^x\left[\log x+\frac{1}{x}\right]$ (iv) $e^{3x}\,[\sin 4x+12\cos 4x]$

(v) e^{4x} [cos $3x$ – 12 sin $3x$]

(vi) $\frac{2x+5}{2\left(\sqrt{3x-7}\right)}.3+\left(\sqrt{3x-7}\right)(2)$

(vii) $3x^2 . \sin^4 x + 4x^3 \sin^3 x \cos x$

(viii) $5+\frac{1}{2x}$

(ix) $e^{\cos x}\left[\frac{\cos\sqrt{x}}{2\sqrt{x}}-(\sin x)\sin\sqrt{x}\right]$

(x) $\frac{2^{(x^3)}}{x}+3.(\log 2)(x^2)\,2^{(x^3)}\,(\log(2x))$

3. (i) $\frac{1}{2\sqrt{x}}\left\{\frac{\sin x - x\cos x}{(\sin x)^{\frac{3}{2}}}\right\}$

(ii) $\frac{e^{\cos x}\left[\frac{1}{2x\sqrt{\log x}}+\frac{\sin x}{\sqrt{\log x}}\right]}{(\log x)}$

(iii) $\frac{(e^x+2)\{-5\sin x\cos^4 x\}-e^x.\cos^5 x}{(e^x+2)^2}$

(iv) $\frac{-4(e^x)^2}{(\sqrt{3+e^x})(3-e^x)^{\frac{3}{2}}}$

(v) $\frac{1}{2}\sec^2\left(\frac{x}{2}\right)$

(vi) –2cosec x + c

(vii) $\frac{(\log x + x)\{e^x(\sin x+\cos x)-\sin x\}-(e^x\sin x+\cos x)(\frac{1}{x}+1)}{(\log x + x)^2}$

(viii) $\frac{(2^x+e^x)\{e^x(\tan x+\sec^2 x)-\cos x\}-(e^x\tan x+\cos x)(2^x\log 2+e^x)}{(2^x+e^x)^2}$

(ix) 2 tan x . $\sec^2 x$

(x) $\frac{(1+x^2)(\cos x - x\sin x)-x^2\cos x}{(1+x^2)^{\frac{3}{2}}}$

(xi) $\frac{2x}{\sqrt{1+x^2}.\left(1-x^2\right)^{\frac{3}{2}}}$

19.6 Logarithmic Differentiation

Suppose the given function is of the form $y = f(x)^{g(x)}$ when $f(x)$, $g(x)$ are functions in x then we use logarithms (taking 'log' on both sides) to find $\frac{dy}{dx}$. This method of finding $\frac{dy}{dx}$ is known as logarithmic differentiation.

While differentiating, after taking logarithms we apply chain rule to differentiate $\log y$.

i.e., $\frac{d}{dx}(\log y) = \frac{1}{y}.\frac{dy}{dx}$

This method is also useful in finding the derivatives of a function which is the product of number of functions.

Solved Examples

1. Find the derivative of the following functions w.r.t x.

(i) x^x (ii) $x^{\sin x}$ (iii) $(\tan x)^x$

(iv) $(\sin x)^{\tan x}$ (v) $(\log x)^{\sin x}$ (vi) x^{x^x}

(vii) $(x^x)^x$

Sol. (i) Let $y = x^x$

taking 'log' on both sides we get

$$\log y = \log x^x = x \log x \qquad (\because \log n^m = m \log n)$$

$$\therefore \quad \log y = x \log x$$

Differentiate w.r.t 'x' on both sides we get

$$\frac{d}{dx}(\log y) = \frac{d}{dx}(x \log x)$$

$$\Rightarrow \quad \frac{1}{y}.\frac{d}{dx}(y) = x.\frac{d}{dx}(\log x) + (\log x).\frac{d}{dx}(x) \qquad \text{(by } u\,v \text{ rule)}$$

$$\Rightarrow \quad \frac{1}{y}.\frac{dy}{dx} = x.\frac{1}{x} + (\log x)(1)$$

$$= 1 + \log x$$

$$\therefore \quad \frac{dy}{dx} = y(1 + \log x) = x^x(1 + \log x) \qquad (\because y = x^x)$$

(ii) Let $y = x^{\sin x}$

taking 'log' on both sides we get

$$\log y = \log (x^{\sin x}) \Rightarrow \log y = (\sin x) \log x$$

Differentiate w.r.t 'x' on both sides we get

$$\frac{1}{y}.\frac{dy}{dx} = (\sin x).\frac{d}{dx}(\log x) + (\log x).\frac{d}{dx}(\sin x)$$

$$\Rightarrow \quad \frac{1}{y}.\frac{dy}{dx} = \sin x.\frac{1}{x} + \log x.(\cos x)$$

$$\therefore \quad \frac{dy}{dx} = y\left[\frac{\sin x}{x} + (\log x).(\cos x)\right]$$

$$\therefore \quad \frac{dy}{dx} = x^{\sin x}\left[\frac{\sin x}{x} + (\log x).(\cos x)\right]$$

(iii) Let $y = (\tan x)^x \Rightarrow \quad \log y = \log(\tan x)^x) = x \log (\tan x)$

$$\Rightarrow \quad \frac{1}{y}\frac{dy}{dx} = x\left(\frac{1}{\tan x}.(\sec^2)\right) + (\log(\tan x)) \quad (1)$$

$$\therefore \quad \frac{dy}{dx} = y\left[\frac{x\sec^2 x}{\tan x} + \log(\tan x)\right]$$

$$= (\tan x)^x\left[\frac{x\sec^2 x}{\tan x} + \log(\tan x)\right]$$

(iv) Let $y = (\sin x)^{\tan x}$

$$\Rightarrow \quad \log y = \log((\sin x)^{\tan x}) \quad \Rightarrow \quad \log y = (\tan x) . \log (\sin x)$$

$$\Rightarrow \quad \frac{1}{y}\frac{dy}{dx} = (\tan x).\left(\frac{1}{\sin x}.\cos x\right) + \log(\sin x).\sec^2 x$$

$$\Rightarrow \quad \frac{1}{y}\frac{dy}{dx} = (\tan x).(\cot x) + (\sec^2 x).\log(\sin x)$$

$$\Rightarrow \quad \frac{1}{y}\frac{dy}{dx} = 1 + (\sec^2 x)(\log(\sin x))$$

$$\Rightarrow \quad \frac{dy}{dx} = y[1 + (\sec^2 x).\log(\sin x)]$$

$$= (\sin x)^{\tan x} \, [\, 1 + (\sec^2 x) \log (\sin x) \,]$$

(v) Let $y = (\log x)^{\sin x}$

$\Rightarrow \quad \log y = \log((\log x)^{\sin x}) = (\sin x)(\log(\log x))$

$\therefore \quad \log y = (\sin x)(\log(\log(x))$

$$\Rightarrow \quad \frac{1}{y}.\frac{dy}{dx} = (\sin x).\left(\frac{1}{\log x}.\frac{1}{x}\right) + \log(\log x).\cos x$$

$$\Rightarrow \quad \frac{dy}{dx} = y\left\{(\sin x)\left[\frac{1}{x\log x}\right] + (\log(\log x)).(\cos x)\right\}$$

$$= (\log x)^{\sin x}\left\{\frac{(\sin x)}{x\log x} + (\cos x).\log(\log x)\right\}$$

(vi) Let $y = x^{x^x}$

$$\Rightarrow \quad \log y = \log\left(x^{x^x}\right) = (x^x)(\log x)$$

$$\Rightarrow \quad \frac{1}{y}.\frac{dy}{dx} = \left(x^x\right)\left[\frac{1}{x}\right] + (\log x)\left(x^x(1+\log x)\right)$$

$$= x^{x-1} + x^x.(\log x)(1+\log x)$$

$$\therefore \quad \frac{dy}{dx} = y\left[x^{x-1} + x^x(\log x)(1+\log x)\right]$$

(vii) Let $y = \left(x^x\right)^x$

$$\Rightarrow \quad \log y = \log((x^x)^x) = \log\left(x^{x^2}\right) = x^2 \log x$$

$$\Rightarrow \quad \frac{1}{y}.\frac{dy}{dx} = x^2.\left(\frac{1}{x}\right) + (\log x).(2x)$$

$$\Rightarrow \quad \frac{1}{y}.\frac{dy}{dx} = x + (2x)(\log x)$$

$$\Rightarrow \quad \frac{dy}{dx} = y[x + (2x)(\log x)]$$

$$\therefore \quad \frac{dy}{dx} = \left(x^x\right)^x\left[x + 2x(\log x)\right]$$

2. Find derivative of the following functions w.r.t x.

(i) $(\sin x)^{\log x} + x^{\sin x}$ (ii) $x^{\tan x} + (\sin x)^{\cos x}$

Sol. (i) Let $y = (\sin x)^{\log x} + x^{\sin x}$

and $u = (\sin x)^{\log x}$; $v = (x)^{\sin x}$

$\therefore\ y = u + v$

$$\Rightarrow \quad \frac{dy}{dx} = \frac{du}{dx} + \frac{dv}{dx} \qquad \text{..... (i)}$$

we have $u = (\sin x)^{\log x}$

taking 'log' on both sides we get

$\log u = \log((\sin x)^{\log x})$

$\log u = (\log x) . \log (\sin x)$

Differentiate w.r.t x on both sides we get

$$\frac{1}{u}.\frac{du}{dx} = (\log x)\left(\frac{1}{\sin x}.\cos x\right) + \log(\sin x).\frac{1}{x}$$

$$\therefore \frac{du}{dx} = u\left[(\log x).(\cot x) + \frac{\log(\sin x)}{x}\right]$$

$$= (\sin x)^{\log x}\left[(\log x).(\cot x) + \frac{\log(\sin x)}{x}\right]$$

similarly we have, $v = x^{\sin x}$

$\Rightarrow \quad \log v = \log(x^{\sin x}) = (\sin x)(\log x)$

$$\therefore \frac{1}{v}.\frac{du}{dx} = (\sin x).\left(\frac{1}{x}\right) + (\log x).(\cos x)$$

$$\therefore \frac{dv}{dx} = v\left[\frac{\sin x}{x} + (\log x).(\cos x)\right]$$

$$= x^{\sin x}\left[\frac{\sin x}{x} + (\log x).(\cos x)\right]$$

$\therefore$ Substitute $\frac{du}{dx}, \frac{dv}{dx}$ in *(i)* we get

$$\frac{dy}{dx} = (\sin x)^{\log x}\left[(\log x)(\cos x) + \frac{\log(\sin x)}{x}\right] + x^{\sin x}\left[\frac{\sin x}{x} + (\log x)(\cos x)\right]$$

(ii) Let $y = x^{\tan x} + (\sin x)^{\cos x}$ and

$u = x^{\tan x}$, $v = (\sin x)^{\cos x}$

we have $u = x^{\tan x}$

$$\Rightarrow \quad \log u = \log (x^{\tan x}) = (\tan x) . (\log x)$$

$$\Rightarrow \quad \frac{1}{u}.\frac{du}{dx} = (\tan x)\left(\frac{1}{x}\right) + (\log x)(\sec^2 x)$$

$$\Rightarrow \quad \frac{du}{dx} = u\left[\frac{\tan x}{x} + (\log x).\sec^2 x\right]$$

$$= x^{\tan x}\left[\frac{\tan x}{x} + (\log x)\sec^2 x\right]$$

again $v = (\sin x)^{\cos x}$

$$\log v = \log ((\sin x)^{\cos x}) = (\cos x) \log (\sin x)$$

$$\frac{1}{v}.\frac{dv}{dx} = (\cos x)\left[\left(\frac{1}{\sin x}\right)\cos x\right] + \log (\sin x) . (-\sin x)$$

$$= \frac{\cos^2 x}{\sin x} - \sin x \log (\sin x)$$

$$\therefore \quad \frac{dv}{dx} = v\left[\frac{\cos^2 x}{\sin x} - \sin(\log(\sin x))\right]$$

$$= (\sin x)^{\cos x}\left[\frac{\cos^2 x}{\sin x} - \sin(\log(\sin x))\right]$$

$$\therefore \quad \frac{dy}{dx} = \frac{du}{dx} + \frac{dv}{dx}$$

i.e., $$\frac{dy}{dx} = x^{\tan x}\left[\frac{\tan x}{x} + (\log x)\sec^2 x\right] + (\sin x)^{\cos x}\left[\frac{\cos^2 x}{\sin x} - \sin(\log(\sin x))\right]$$

3. Find the derivative of $\dfrac{x^3\sqrt{2+3x}}{(2+x)(1-x)}$

Sol. Let $y = \dfrac{x^3\sqrt{2+3x}}{(2+x)\,(1-x)}$

taking 'log' on both sides we get

$$\log y = \log\left\{\frac{x^3\sqrt{2+3x}}{(2+x)(1-x)}\right\}$$

$$= \log\left(x^3\sqrt{2+3x}\right) - \log(2+x)(1-x)$$

$$\left[\because \log\left(\frac{m}{n}\right) = \log m - \log n\right]$$

$$= \left(\log x^3 + \log\sqrt{2+3x}\right) - \log(2+x) - \log(1-x)$$

$$(\because \log mn = \log m + \log n)$$

$$\log y = \left(3\log x + \frac{1}{2}\log(2+3x)\right) - \log(2+x) - \log(1-x)$$

$$\therefore \quad \frac{1}{y}\cdot\frac{dy}{dx} = \frac{3}{x} + \frac{1}{2}\cdot\frac{1}{2+3x}.3 - \frac{1}{2+x} - \frac{1}{1-x}.(-1)$$

$$\therefore \quad \frac{dy}{dx} = y\left[\frac{3}{x} + \frac{3}{2}\left(\frac{1}{2+3x}\right) - \frac{1}{2+x} + \frac{1}{1-x}\right]$$

Exercise 19.3

1. Find the derivative of the following functions w.r.t x.

(i) $(\log x)^{\tan x}$ (ii) $(\tan x)^{\sin x}$

2. Find the derivative of the following functions w.r.t x.

(i) $x^x + (\cot x)^x$ (ii) $(\sin x)^x + x^{\sin x}$

3. Find the derivative of the following functions w.r.t x.

(i) $\dfrac{(1-2x)^{\frac{2}{3}}(1+3x)^{\frac{-3}{4}}}{(1-6x)^{\frac{5}{6}}.(1+7x)^{\frac{-6}{7}}}$ (ii) $\dfrac{x^4\sqrt[3]{x^2+4}}{\sqrt{4x^2-7}}$

(iii) $\dfrac{(a-x)^2(b-x)^3}{(c-2x)^3}$

Answers

1. (i) $(\log x)^{\tan x}\left[\dfrac{\tan x}{x\log x}+\sec^2 x\log(\log x)\right]$

(ii) $(\tan x)^{\sin x}$ [cos x. log (tan x) + sec x]

2. (i) $x^x(1+\log x)+(\cot x)^x\left[\log(\cot x)-\dfrac{2x}{\sin 2x}\right]$

(ii) $(\sin x)^x[\log(\sin x)+x\cot x]+x^{\sin x}\left[\cos x\log x+\dfrac{\sin x}{x}\right]$

3. (i) $y\left[\dfrac{5}{1-6x}+\dfrac{6}{1+7x}-\dfrac{4}{3(1-2x)}-\dfrac{9}{4(1+3x)}\right]$ when y is given function.

(ii) $\dfrac{x^4\sqrt[3]{x^2+4}}{\sqrt{4x^2-7}}\left(\dfrac{4}{x}+\dfrac{2x}{3(x^2+4)}-\dfrac{4x}{4x^2-7}\right)$

(iii) $\dfrac{(a-x)^2(b-x)^3}{(c-2x)^3}\left[\dfrac{6}{c-2x}-\dfrac{3}{b-x}-\dfrac{2}{a-x}\right]$

19.7 Differentiation of the Function in the Parametric Form

Let $x = g(t)$, $y = h(t)$ are two differentiable functions at t such that g^{-1} exists, then

$$\frac{dy}{dx}=\frac{\left(\frac{dy}{dt}\right)}{\left(\frac{dx}{dt}\right)}$$

Ex : (i) If $x = at^2$, $y = 2at$ then find $\dfrac{dy}{dx}$

Sol. $\dfrac{dx}{dt}=2at,\ \dfrac{dy}{dt}=2a$

$$\frac{dy}{dx}=\frac{\left(\frac{dy}{dt}\right)}{\left(\frac{dx}{dt}\right)}=\frac{2a}{2at}=\frac{1}{t}$$

(ii) If $x = ct$, $y = \frac{c}{t}$ then find $\frac{dy}{dx}$

Sol. $\frac{dx}{dt} = c, \quad \frac{dy}{dt} = \frac{-c}{t^2}$

$$\therefore \quad \frac{dy}{dx} = \frac{\left(\frac{dy}{dt}\right)}{\left(\frac{dx}{dt}\right)} = \frac{\frac{-c}{t^2}}{c} = \frac{-1}{t^2}$$

19.8 Differentiation of Functions which are in Implicit Form

The method of finding $\frac{dy}{dx}$ of an implicit functions given by the relation $f(x, y) = 0$ is known as implicit function.

To find $\frac{dy}{dx}$, taking differentiation w.r.t x on both sides of $f(x, y) = 0$ and then find $\frac{dy}{dx}$.

Ex : (i) If $x + xy + y = 0$ then find $\frac{dy}{dx}$

Sol. we have $x + xy + y = 0$

$$\Rightarrow \quad \frac{d}{dx}(x + xy + y) = \frac{d}{dx}(0) = 0$$

$$\therefore \quad 1 + \left(x.\frac{dy}{dx} + y(1)\right) + \frac{dy}{dx} = 0$$

$$\therefore \quad (x + 1)\frac{dy}{dx} + (y + 1) = 0$$

$$\therefore \quad \frac{dy}{dx} = \frac{-(y+1)}{(x+1)}$$

(ii) If $x^2 + y^2 + 3xy = 7$ then find $\frac{dy}{dx}$

Sol. given, $x^2 + y^2 + 3xy = 7$

$$\therefore \quad \frac{d}{dx}\{x^2 + y^2 + 3xy\} = \frac{d}{dx}(7) = 0$$

$$\therefore\ 2x + 2y\,.\,\frac{dy}{dx} + 3\left(x.\frac{dy}{dx} + y(1)\right) = 0$$

$$\therefore\ (2x + 3y) + \frac{dy}{dx}(2y + 3x) = 0$$

$$\therefore\ \frac{dy}{dx} = -\left(\frac{2x+3y}{3x+2y}\right)$$

(iii) If $x^y = e^{x-y}$ then show that $\frac{dy}{dx} = \frac{\log x}{(1+\log x)^2}$

Sol. given, $x^y = e^{x-y}$

taking 'log' on both sides we get

$y \ln x = (x - y) \ln e$

$\Rightarrow\quad y \log x = (x - y)$

Differentiate w.r.t x we get

$$y.\frac{1}{x} + (\log x)\frac{dy}{dx} = \left(1 - \frac{dy}{dx}\right)$$

$$\therefore\quad \frac{y}{x} + (\log x + 1)\frac{dy}{dx} = 1$$

$$\therefore\quad (1+\log x)\frac{dy}{dx} = 1 - \frac{y}{x} = \frac{x-y}{x}$$

$$= \frac{y\log x}{x} \qquad (\because x - y = y \log x)$$

$$\therefore\quad \frac{dy}{dx} = \frac{y\log x}{x(1+\log x)}$$

$$= \frac{\log x}{(1+\log x)(1+\log x)} \qquad (\because y \log x = x - y = y\,(1+ \log x) = x$$

$$\therefore \frac{y}{x} = \frac{1}{1+\log x})$$

(iv) If $y = x^y$ then show that $\dfrac{dy}{dx} = \dfrac{y^2}{x(1 - y\log y)}$

Sol. given, $y = x^y$

taking 'log' on both sides we get

$$\log y = y \log x$$

Differentiate w.r.t x on both sides we get

$$\frac{1}{y}\frac{dy}{dx} = y.\frac{1}{x} + (\log x)\left(\frac{dy}{dx}\right)$$

$$\therefore \left(\frac{1}{y} - \log x\right)\frac{dy}{dx} = \frac{y}{x}$$

$$\therefore \left(\frac{1 - y\log y}{y}\right)\frac{dy}{dx} = \frac{y}{x}$$

$$\therefore \frac{dy}{dx} = \left(\frac{y}{x}\right)\left(\frac{y}{1 - y\log x}\right) = \frac{y^2}{x(1 - y\log x)}$$

19.9 Derivative of a Function with Respect to Another Function

Let $f(x)$, and $g(x)$ are functions. Now we have to find the derivative of $f(x)$ w.r.t $g(x)$. For this

Let $U = f(x)$, $V = g(x)$

$$\frac{dU}{dx} = f'(x), \quad \frac{dV}{dx} = g^1(x)$$

$$\therefore \frac{dU}{dV} = \frac{\left(\dfrac{dU}{dx}\right)}{\left(\dfrac{dV}{dx}\right)} = \frac{f'(x)}{g'(x)}$$

Ex : (i) Find the derivative of e^x w.r.t $\sin x$

Let $u = e^x$, $v = \sin x$

$$\frac{du}{dx} = e^x \quad \frac{dv}{dx} = \cos x,$$

$$\therefore \quad \frac{du}{dv} = \frac{\left(\frac{du}{dx}\right)}{\left(\frac{dv}{dx}\right)} = \frac{e^x}{\cos x}$$

(ii) Find the derivative of $e^{\tan x}$ w.r.t $\tan x$.

Let $u = e^{\tan x}$, $v = \tan x$

$$\frac{du}{dx} = e^{\tan x}.\sec^2 x, \quad \frac{dv}{dx} = \sec^2 x$$

$$\therefore \quad \frac{du}{dv} = \frac{\left(\frac{du}{dx}\right)}{\left(\frac{dv}{dx}\right)} = \frac{e^{\tan x}.\sec^2 x}{\sec^2 x} = e^{\tan x}$$

Exercise - 19.3

1. Find $\frac{dy}{dx}$ if

(i) $x = a\cos^3 t$, $y = a\sin^3 t$

(ii) $x = a(\cos t + t\sin t)$, $y = a(\sin t - t\cos t)$

(iii) $x = \log t + \sin t$, $y = e^t + \cos t$

(iv) $x = a\left(\frac{1-t^2}{1+t^2}\right)$, $y = \frac{2bt}{1+t^2}$

2. Find $\frac{dy}{dx}$ if

(i) $x^3 + y^3 = 3axy$ (ii) $e^{x+y} = xy$ (iii) $x^4 + y^4 - a^2xy = 0$

3. If $\sin y = x\sin(a + y)$ then show that $\frac{dy}{dx} = \frac{\sin^2(a+y)}{\sin a}$

4. If $x^{\log y} = \log x$ then show that $\frac{dy}{dx} = \frac{y}{x}\left[\frac{1-\log x \log y}{(\log x)^2}\right]$

5. If $x^y + y^x = a^b$ then show that $\frac{dy}{dx} = -\left[\frac{y.x^{y-1} + y^x \log x}{x^y \log x + xy^{x-1}}\right]$

6. Find the derivative of

(i) $\sqrt{x}$ w.r.t e^x (ii) tan $2x$ w.r.t x^5 (iii) $\sin^2 x$ w.r.t log (cos x)

Answers

1. (i) –tan t (ii) tan t (iii) $\frac{t(e^t - \sin t)}{1 + t\cos t}$ (iv) $\frac{b(t^2-1)}{2at}$

2. (i) $\frac{x^2 - ay}{ax - y^2}$ (ii) $\frac{y - e^{x+y}}{e^{x+y} - x}$ (iii) $\frac{a^2 y - 4x^3}{4y^3 - a^2 x}$

6. (i) $\frac{1}{2\sqrt{x}\, e^x}$ (ii) $\frac{2\sec^2 2x}{5x^4}$ (iii) $2\cos^2 x$

20

Successive Differentiation

When $y = f(x)$ is a differentiable function of x, its differential coefficient $\frac{dy}{dx} = f'(x)$ is also a function in x. If f' is also differentiable then the derivative of $f'(x)$ with respect to x is called second derivative of y wrt to x. This second derivative of y is denoted by $f''(x)$ or

$$f^{(2)}(x) \text{ or } \frac{d^2y}{dx^2} \text{ or } y_2.$$

For a positive integer n, if f is differentiable n times with respect to x we define

$$f^{(n)}(x) \text{ or } \frac{d^nx}{dx^n} \text{ or } y_n = \underset{h\to 0}{\text{Lt}} \frac{f^{(n-1)}(x+h) - f^{(n-1)}(x)}{h}$$

If f and g are two differentiable functions of n times then

(i) $(f \pm g)^{(n)}(x) = f^{(n)}(x) + g^{(n)}(x)$

(ii) $(cf)^{(n)}(x) = c.f^{(n)}(x)$ where 'c' is constant

n^{th} Derivative of Some Standard Functions

S.No.	Function	n^{th} derivative
1.	$(ax+b)^m$, $m \in Z^+$	$\begin{cases} m!a^m & \text{if } n = m \\ 0 & \text{if } n > m \end{cases}$
2.	$(ax+b)^m$ $m \in R$	$m(m-1)(m-2)...(m-n+1)\times(ax+b)^{m-n}.\ a^n$

Table *contd....*

S.No.	Function	n^{th} Derivative
3.	$\frac{1}{ax+b}$	$\frac{(-1)^n\, n!\, a^n}{(ax+b)^{n+1}}$
4.	$\log\|ax+b\|$	$\frac{(-1)^{n-1}(n-1)!\, a^n}{(ax+b)^n}$
5.	sin (ax+b)	$a^n \sin\left(ax+b+\frac{n\pi}{2}\right)$
6.	cos (ax+b)	$a^n \cos\left(ax+b+\frac{n\pi}{2}\right)$
7.	e^{ax+b}	$a^n.e^{ax+b}$
8.	a^{cx+d}	$c^n.(\log a)^n\, a^{cx+d}$
9.	$e^{ax}\sin(bx+c)$	$(\sqrt{a^2+b^2})^n e^{ax}\sin(bx+c+n\tan^{-1}(b/a))$
10.	$e^{ax}\cos(bx+c)$	$(\sqrt{a^2+b^2})^n e^{ax}\cos(bx+c+n\tan^{-1}(b/a))$

Lenbnitz's Theorem

For any two functions f and g of x each is derivable n times and positive integer n,

$$(fg)^n(x) = f^{(n)}(x)g^{(0)}(x) + n_{c1}.f^{(n-1)}(x)g(x) + ...n_{cr}f^{(n-r)}(x)g^r(x) + ... + f^0(x)g^n(x)$$

$$= \sum_{r=0}^{n} n_{cr}.f^{(n-r)}(x)\, g^{(r)}(x)$$

Solved Problems

1. If $y = \frac{6+5x}{2+3x}$ find $\frac{d^2y}{dx^2}$

Sol. $y = \frac{6+5x}{2+3x}$

$$\frac{dy}{dx} = \frac{(2+3x)(5)-(6+5x)(3)}{(2+3x)^2}$$

$$= \frac{10+15x-18-15x}{(2+3x)^2} = \frac{-8}{(2+3x)^2}$$

$$\therefore \quad \frac{dy}{dx} = -8(2+3x)^{-2}$$

$$\therefore \quad \frac{d^2y}{dx^2} = -8.(-2)(2+3x)^{-3}$$

$$= \frac{16}{(2+3x)^3}$$

2. If $y = \sqrt{\sec 2x}$ then show that $y_2 = 3y^5 - y$

Sol. $y^2 = \sec 2x$

$2yy_1 = 2\sec 2x.\tan 2x$

$2yy_1 = 2.y^2 \tan 2x$

$y_1 = y \tan 2x$

$$\Rightarrow \quad y_2 = \sec^2 2x(2.y) + \tan 2x.y_1$$

$$y_2 = 2(y^4)y + y(\sec^2 2x - 1)$$

$$= 2y^5 + y(y^4 - 1)$$

$$= 3y^5 - y$$

3. If $x = t^2$ $y = f^3$ then find y^2

Sol. $x = t^2$ $\qquad y = f^3$

$$\Rightarrow \quad \frac{dx}{dt} = 2t \quad \Rightarrow \quad \frac{dy}{dt} = 3f^2$$

$$\therefore \quad \frac{dy}{dx} = \frac{(dy/dt)}{\left(\frac{dx}{dt}\right)} = \frac{3t^2}{2t} = 3/2\,t$$

$$\therefore \quad \frac{d^2y}{dx^2} = 3/2\,(1).\frac{dt}{dx} = 3/2 \times \frac{1}{2t} = \frac{3}{4t}$$

4. If y = cos (log x) show that

$x^2 y_2 + xy^1 + y = 0$

Sol. $y = \cos(\log x)$

Differentiate wrt x we get

$$y_1 = -\sin(\log x).\left(\frac{1}{x}\right)$$

$$xy_1 = -\sin(\log x)$$

again differentiate wrt 'x' we get

$$\therefore \quad xy_2 + y_1 = -\cos(\log x).\frac{1}{x}$$

$$\Rightarrow x^2y_2 + xy_1 = -\cos(\log x)$$

$$\Rightarrow x^2y_2 + xy_1 = -y$$

or $x^2y_2 + xy_1 + y = 0$

5. If $y = e^x \cos x \cos 2x$ then find y_n

Sol. $y = e^x \cos x \ \cos 2x$

$$\text{i.e., } y = \frac{e^x}{2}[2\cos x.\cos 2x]$$

$$= \frac{e^x}{2}[\cos(3x) + \cos(-x)]$$

$$y = \frac{e^x}{2}[\cos 3x + \cos x]$$

$$y = \frac{1}{2}\left[e^x \cos 3x + e^x \cos x\right]$$

$$\therefore \quad y_n = \frac{1}{2}\left[\frac{d^n}{dx^n}(e^x \cos 3x) + \frac{d^n}{dx^n}(e^x \cos x)\right]$$

$$= \frac{1}{2}\left[(\sqrt{1+9})^n \cos(3x + n\tan^{-1}(3) + (\sqrt{1+1})^n \cos(x + n\tan^{-1}(1))\right]$$

$$= \frac{1}{2}\left[(\sqrt{10})^n \cos(3x + n\tan^{-1}3) + (\sqrt{2})^n \cos(x + \frac{n\pi}{4})\right]$$

6. If $y = \cos^4 x$ then find y_n

$$y = \cos^4 x$$

$$= (\cos^2 x)^2$$

$$= \left(\frac{1+\cos 2x}{2}\right)^2$$

$$= \frac{1}{4}\left[1+\cos^2 2x + 2\cos 2x\right]$$

$$y = \frac{1}{4}\left[1+\left(\frac{1+\cos 4x}{2}\right)+2\cos 2x\right]$$

$$= \frac{1}{4}+\frac{1}{8}(1+\cos 4x)+\frac{1}{2}\cos 2x$$

$$y_n = 0+\frac{1}{8}\left[0+4^n\cos(4x+\frac{n\pi}{2})+\frac{1}{2}.2^n\cos(2x+\frac{n\pi}{2})\right]$$

$$= 2^{2n-3}\cos(4x+\frac{n\pi}{2})+2^{n-1}\cos(2x+\frac{n\pi}{2})$$

7. If $y = \sin(3\sin^{-1}x)$ then find $\frac{d^3y}{dx^3}$

Sol. Given $y = \sin\ (3\sin^{-1}x)$

Let $\sin^{-1}x = \theta \Rightarrow x = \sin\theta$

$\therefore\ y = \sin\ (3\ \sin^{-1}n)$

$= \sin\ (3\theta)$

$= 3\ \sin\theta - 4\ \sin^3\theta$

$y = 3x - 4x^3$

$\Rightarrow\ y_1 = 3 - 12x^2$

$y_2 = -24x$

$y_3 = -24$

8. Find the nth derivative of $y = \log\ (4x^2 - 9)$

Sol. Given $y = \log\ (4x^2 - 9)$

$$= \log\left[(2x+3)(2x-3)\right]$$

$$y = \log[2x+3] + \log[2x-3]$$

$$\therefore \quad y_n = \frac{d^n}{dx^n}[\log(2x+3)] + \frac{d^n}{dx^n}[\log(2x-3)]$$

$$= \frac{(-1)^{n-1}.2^n(n-1)!}{(2x+3)^n} + \frac{(-1)^n.2^n(n-1)!}{(2x-3)^n}$$

$$= (-1)^{n-1}(n-1)!\ 2^n\left[\frac{1}{(2x+3)^n} + \frac{1}{(2x-3)^n}\right]$$

$$\left[\because D^n(\log(ax+b) = \frac{(-1)^{n-1}.a^n.(n-1)!}{(ax+b)^n}\right]$$

Excercise 20.1

1. If $y = \sin^{-1}x$ then show that $(1 - x^2)\, y_2 - xy_1 = 0$
2. If $y = \sin^2 x$ then find y_n

   Ans: $-2^{n-1}\cos(2x + \frac{n\pi}{2})$

3. If $xy = ac^x + bc^{-x}$ then show that $xy_2 + 2y_1 = xy$.
4. If $y = x^3 e^x$ then find y_n

   Ans: $e^x(x^3 + 3nx^2 + 3(n^2 - n)x + n(n-1)(n-2))$

5. If $y = e^{2x}\sin 3x$ then find y_n

   Ans: $13^{n/2} e^{2x}\sin(3x + n\tan^{-1}(3/2))$

6. Find the nth derivative of $y = \frac{2x+1}{x^2-4}$

   Ans: $\frac{(-1)^n n!}{4}\left[\frac{5}{(x-2)^{n+1}} + \frac{3}{(x+2)^{n+1}}\right]$

7. If $x = \sin^{-1}t$, $y = \sqrt{1-t^2}$ then find y_2 at $t = 1/2$

   Ans: $-\frac{\sqrt{3}}{2}$

8. If $y = \sqrt{ax} + \frac{a^2}{\sqrt{ax}}$ then find y_2 at $x = a$

Ans: 1/2a

9. If $y = e^{m\cos^{-1}(x)}$ then show that $(1 - x^2)y_{n+2} - (2n + 1)xy_{n+1} - (n^2 - m^2)y_n = 0$

10. If $y = (x^2 - 1)^n$ then prove that $(x^2 - 1)y_{n+2} + 2xy_{n+1} = n(n + 1)y_n$

21

Partial Differentiation

21.1 Partial Derivatives of First Order

Let $u = f(x, y)$ be a function of two variables defined in the given interval, then the partial derivative of u with reference to x is denoted by $\frac{\partial u}{\partial x}$ or u_x and is obtained by differentiating u w.r.t x by keeping y as constant. As well as the partial derivative of u w.r.t y is denoted $\frac{\partial u}{\partial y}$ or u_y and is obtained by differentiate u w.r.t y by keeping x as constant.

for example $u = f(x, y) = x^2 + y^2$ then

$\frac{\partial u}{\partial x}$ is obtained by differentiating u w.r.t x by keeping y as constant.

$$\therefore \quad \frac{\partial u}{\partial x} = \frac{\partial}{\partial x}(x^2 + y^2) = 2x + 0 \qquad (\because y \text{ is treated constant } \frac{\partial}{\partial x}(y^2) = 0)$$

Similarly, let us consider $u = f(x,y) = x^2y$

$$\frac{\partial u}{\partial x} = \frac{\partial}{\partial x}(x^2 y) = y.\frac{\partial}{\partial x}(x^2) = y.(2x) = 2xy$$

$$\frac{\partial u}{\partial y} = \frac{\partial}{\partial y}(x^2 y) = x^2\frac{\partial}{\partial y}(y) = x^2(1) = x^2$$

Let us see some more examples

Ex : (i) If $u = x^3y^2 - y \sin x$ then find $\frac{\partial u}{\partial x}$, $\frac{\partial u}{\partial y}$

Sol. $$\frac{\partial u}{\partial x} = \frac{\partial}{\partial x}\{x^3 y^2 - y \sin x\}$$

$$= y^2 . \frac{\partial}{\partial x}(x^3) - y\frac{\partial}{\partial x}(\sin x)$$

$$= y^2 . (3x^2) - y \cos x$$

$$\frac{\partial u}{\partial y} = \frac{\partial}{\partial y}\{x^3y^2 - y \sin x\} = x^3 . \frac{\partial}{\partial y}(y^2) - (\sin x)\frac{\partial}{\partial y}(y)$$

$$= 2yx^3 - \sin x - (\sin x)(1)$$

(ii) If u = $\frac{\cos x}{\sin y}$ then find $\frac{\partial u}{\partial x}, \frac{\partial u}{\partial y}$

Sol. $$\frac{\partial u}{\partial x} = \frac{\partial}{\partial x}\left(\frac{\cos x}{\sin y}\right) = \frac{1}{\sin y}\frac{\partial}{\partial x}(\cos x)$$

$$= \frac{1}{\sin y}(-\sin x)$$

$$\frac{\partial u}{\partial y} = \frac{\partial}{\partial y}\left(\frac{\cos x}{\sin y}\right) = \cos x . \frac{\partial}{\partial y}\left(\frac{1}{\sin y}\right) = \cos x \frac{\partial}{\partial y}(\operatorname{cosec} y)$$

$$= \cos x\,(-\operatorname{cosec} y \cot y)$$

$$= -\operatorname{cosec} y . \cot y . \cos x$$

(iii) If $u = x . e^y + y.e^x$ then find u_x, u_y

$$u_x = \frac{\partial}{\partial x}\{xe^y + y.e^x\} = e^y . \frac{\partial}{\partial x}(x) + y . \frac{\partial}{\partial x}(e^x)$$

$$= e^y(1) + y . e^x$$

$$= e^y + y. e^x$$

$$u_y = \frac{\partial}{\partial y}[x.e^y + ye^x] = x\frac{\partial}{\partial y}(e^y) + e^x\frac{\partial}{\partial y}(y)$$

$$= x.e^y + e^x.1$$

***Corollary* :** If v = $g(u)$ and $u = f(x, y)$

then

$$\frac{\partial v}{\partial x} = \frac{\partial v}{\partial u}\cdot\frac{\partial u}{\partial x} \text{ and}$$

$$\frac{\partial v}{\partial y} = \frac{dv}{du}\cdot\frac{\partial u}{\partial y}$$

Examples

1. If v = $\sin(x + y)$ find $\frac{\partial v}{\partial x}$

Sol. Let u = $x + y$ $\Rightarrow$ $\frac{\partial u}{\partial x} = \frac{\partial}{\partial x}(x + y) = 1 + 0 = 1$

$\therefore$ $v = \sin u$

$\therefore$ $\frac{\partial v}{\partial x} = \frac{\partial}{\partial u}(\sin u)\frac{\partial u}{\partial x}$

$$= \cos u\frac{\partial u}{\partial x} = \cos u\,.\,(1)$$

$$= \cos u = \cos(x + y)$$

2. If v = $e^{x^2y^3}$ then find $\frac{\partial v}{\partial x}, \frac{\partial v}{\partial y}$

Sol. Given v = $e^{x^2y^3}$

Put x^2y^3 = u $\Rightarrow$ $\frac{\partial u}{\partial x} = \frac{\partial}{\partial x}(x^2y^3) = y^3.(2x)$

$$\frac{\partial u}{\partial y} = \frac{\partial}{\partial y}(x^2y^3) = x^2.3y^2 = 3x^2y^2$$

now v = e^u

$$\frac{\partial v}{\partial x} = \frac{d}{du}(e^u)\frac{\partial u}{\partial x} \qquad = e^u.\frac{\partial v}{\partial x} = e^u.(2x\,y^3)$$

$$= e^{x^2y^3}.(2xy^3)$$

and $\dfrac{\partial v}{\partial y}=\dfrac{d}{du}\left(e^{u}\right)\dfrac{\partial u}{\partial y}$ $= e^{u} . 3x^2 y^2$

$$= e^{x^2y^3}.3x^2y^2$$

$$= 3e^{x^2y^3}.x^2y^2$$

3. If $z = 3x . e^{y^2} + 4y$ then find $\dfrac{\partial z}{\partial x}, \dfrac{\partial z}{\partial y}$

Sol. Given $z = 3x . e^{y^2} + 4y$

$$\frac{\partial z}{\partial x}=\frac{\partial}{\partial x}\left\{3x\,e^{y^2}+4y\right\}$$

$$=\frac{\partial}{\partial x}\left(3xe^{y^2}\right)+\frac{\partial}{\partial x}(4y)$$

$$= e^{y^2} . (3) + 0 = 3\,e^{y^2}$$

again $\dfrac{\partial z}{\partial y}=\dfrac{\partial}{\partial y}\,[\,3x . e^{y^2} + 4y\,]$

$$=\frac{\partial}{\partial y}\left(3x.e^{y^2}\right)+\frac{\partial}{\partial y}(4y)$$

$$= (3x)\,(e^{y^2} . (2y)) + 4(1)$$

$$= 6xy . e^{y^2} + 4$$

4. Find the partial derivatives of the following functions

(i) $\log(\tan x + \tan y)$ (ii) $\log(x^2 + y^2)$

Sol. Let $z = \log(\tan x + \tan y)$

and Let $u = \tan x + \tan y$

$\therefore$ $z = \log u$

$$\frac{\partial z}{\partial x}=\frac{d}{du}(z).\frac{\partial u}{\partial x}$$

$$= \frac{d}{du}(\log u) . \frac{\partial}{dx}(\tan x + \tan y)$$

$$= \frac{1}{u} . \sec^2 u$$

$$\frac{\partial z}{\partial x} = \frac{dz}{du} . \frac{\partial u}{\partial x}$$

$$= \frac{1}{\tan x + \tan y} \sec^2 x = \frac{\sec^2 x}{\tan x + \tan y}$$

Similarly $\dfrac{\partial z}{\partial y} = \dfrac{dz}{du} . \dfrac{\partial u}{\partial y}$

$$= \frac{1}{u} . \sec^2 y = \frac{1}{\tan x + \tan y} . \sec^2 y = \frac{\sec^2 y}{\tan x + \tan y}$$

(ii) Let $z = \log(x^2 + y^2)$

$$\frac{\partial z}{\partial x} = \frac{1}{x^2 + y^2} . \frac{\partial}{\partial x}(x^2 + y^2) = \frac{1}{x^2 + y^2} . 2x$$

$$\frac{\partial z}{\partial y} = \frac{1}{x^2 + y^2} \frac{\partial}{\partial x}(x^2 + y^2) = \frac{1}{x^2 + y^2} . 2y$$

5. If $z = f(x^2 + y^2)$ then prove that $x \dfrac{\partial z}{\partial y} - y . \dfrac{\partial z}{\partial x} = 0$

Sol. Given $z = f(x^2 + y^2)$

$$\frac{\partial z}{\partial x} = \frac{\partial}{\partial x}\left(f(x^2 + y^2)\right)$$

$$= f'(x^2 + y^2) . \frac{\partial}{\partial x}(x^2 + y^2)$$

$$= f'(x^2 + y^2)\, 2x$$

$$\frac{\partial z}{\partial y}=\frac{\partial}{\partial y}\left(f(x^2+y^2)\right)=f'\left(x^2+y^2\right)\frac{\partial}{\partial y}\left(x^2+y^2\right)$$

$$=f'\left(x^2+y^2\right)(2y)$$

$$\therefore\quad x.\frac{\partial z}{\partial y}-y.\frac{\partial z}{\partial x}$$

$$= x(\ f'(x^2+y^2)\ .\ 2y)-y(\ f'(x^2+y^2)\ .\ 2x)$$

$$= 2xy\ f'(x^2+y^2)-2xy\ .\ f'(x^2+y^2)=0$$

$$\therefore\quad x.\frac{\partial z}{\partial y}-y.\frac{\partial z}{\partial x}=0$$

6. If $V = \pi r^2 h$ then show that $r.v_r + 2h\ v_h = 4v$

Sol. Given $V = \pi r^2 h$

$$V_r = \pi h (2r) = 2\pi r h$$

$$rv_r = 2\pi r^2 h \qquad ....(1)$$

again $V_h = \pi r^2 \qquad .... (1)$

$$2hv_h = (2h)(\pi r^2) = 2\pi r^2 h \qquad ..... (2)$$

$$\therefore\quad (1)+(2) \quad\Rightarrow\quad rv_r + 2hv_h = 2\pi r^2 h + 2\pi r^2 h$$

$$= 4\pi r^2 h$$

$$= 4v$$

7. If $au + b = a^2x + y$ then show that $u_x + u_y = 1$.

Sol. Given $au + b = a^2x + y$

$$\frac{\partial}{\partial x}[au+b]=\frac{\partial}{\partial x}[a^2x+y] = a^2 \quad\Rightarrow\quad au_x = a^2 \quad\Rightarrow u_x = \frac{a^2}{a} = a$$

$$\frac{\partial}{\partial y}[au+b] = \frac{\partial}{\partial y}[a^2x+y] \Rightarrow\quad au_y = 1 \quad\Rightarrow u_y = \frac{1}{a}$$

$$\Rightarrow u_x\ .\ u_y = a.\ \frac{1}{a} = 1$$

Exercise - 21.1

1. Find $\frac{\partial z}{\partial x}, \frac{\partial z}{\partial y}$ if

(i) $z = x^2 - y^2$ (ii) $e^x \sin y$ (iii) $3x\, e^{y^2} + 4y$

(iv) $\frac{1}{\sqrt{1+x+y^2}}$ (v) $e^x \cos y$ (vi) $\frac{y}{x^2+y^2}$

(vii) $e^{2xy} \cos (y^2 - x^2)$ (viii) $z = e^{2x} . \cos 3y$

2. If $u = e^{ax + by} f(ax - by)$ then show that $bu_x + au_y = 2abu$.

3. If $u = \frac{x+y}{x-y}$ then find the value of $\frac{\partial u}{\partial x} + \frac{\partial u}{\partial y}$

4. If $u = \log(x^3 + y^3 + z^3 - 3xyz)$ then find the value of $\frac{\partial u}{\partial x} + \frac{\partial u}{\partial y} + \frac{\partial u}{\partial z}$

5. If $u = e^{-x^2+y^2}$ then show that $y\, u_x = x\, u_y$.

6. If $u = (x^2 + y^2 + z^2)^{3/2}$ then show that $\left(\frac{\partial u}{\partial x}\right)^2 + \left(\frac{\partial u}{\partial y}\right)^2 + \left(\frac{\partial u}{\partial z}\right)^2 = 9u^{\frac{4}{3}}$

7. If $u = \log(\sec x + \sec y + \sec z)$ then show that $\sum \cot x . \frac{\partial u}{\partial x} = 1$

8. If $x^x y^y z^z = c$ then show that $\frac{\partial_z}{\partial_x} = \frac{-(1+\log x)}{1+\log z}$

9. If $(2z - ay^2 - 2b)^2 = 16ax$ then show that $z_y = xy . (z_x)^2$.

10. If $x = r\cos \theta$, $y = r \sin \theta$ then prove that $\left(\frac{\partial r}{\partial x}\right)^2 + \left(\frac{\partial r}{\partial y}\right)^2 = 1$

Answers

1. (i) $2x, -2y$

(ii) $e^x \sin y$, $e^x \cos y$

(iii) $3\, e^{y^2}$, $6xy\, e^{y^2} + 4$

(iv) $\frac{-1}{2}(1+x+y^2)^{\frac{-3}{2}}, \frac{-1}{2}(1+x+y^2)^{\frac{-3}{2}} 2y$

(v) $e^x \cos y, - e^x \sin y$

(vi) $\frac{-2xy}{(x^2+y^2)} \frac{x^2-y^2}{(x^2+y^2)^2}$

(vii) $2e^{2xy}$ [$x \sin (y^2 - x^2) + y \cos (y^2 - x^2)$], $2\, e^{2xy}$ [$x \cos (y^2 - x^2) - y \sin (y^2 - x^2)$]

(viii) $2e^{2x} \cos 3y$; $-3e^{2x} \sin 3y$

3. $\frac{2}{x-y}$ **4.** $\frac{3}{x+y+z}$

21.2 Partial Derivatives of Second Order

Let $u = f(x, y)$ is a function of two variables and $\frac{\partial u}{\partial x}, \frac{\partial u}{\partial y}$ are partial derivatives of f and are exists. If the partial derivatives of $\frac{\partial u}{\partial x}, \frac{\partial u}{\partial y}$ are exists then they are called second order partial derivatives of $u = f(x, y)$ and these are denoted by

$$\frac{\partial^2 u}{\partial x^2} = f_{xx}, \frac{\partial^2 u}{\partial y^2} = f_{yy}, \frac{\partial^2 u}{\partial x \partial y} = f_{xy}, \frac{\partial^2 u}{\partial y \partial x} = f_{yx} \text{ and these are obtained by}$$

$$\frac{\partial^2 u}{\partial x^2} = \frac{\partial}{\partial x}\left(\frac{\partial u}{\partial x}\right), \frac{\partial^2 u}{\partial y^2} = \frac{\partial}{\partial y}\left[\frac{\partial u}{\partial y}\right], \frac{\partial^2 u}{\partial x \partial y} = \frac{\partial}{\partial x}\left[\frac{\partial u}{\partial y}\right]$$

$$\frac{\partial^2 u}{\partial y . \partial x} = \frac{\partial}{\partial y}\left[\frac{\partial u}{\partial x}\right]$$

Ex 1. Find the second order partial derivatives of the following functions

(i) $e^x \sin y$ (ii) $\log (x^2 + y^2)$

Sol. (i) Let $z = e^x \sin y$

$$\frac{\partial z}{\partial x} = \frac{\partial}{\partial x}\left[e^x \sin y\right] = e^x \sin y$$

$$\frac{\partial^2 z}{\partial x^2} = \frac{\partial}{\partial x}\left[e^x \sin y\right] = e^x \sin y$$

again $z = e^x \sin y$

$$\frac{\partial z}{\partial y} = \frac{\partial}{\partial y}\left[e^x \sin y\right]$$

$$= e^x \cdot \frac{\partial}{\partial y}[\sin y] = e^x \cos y$$

$$\frac{\partial^2 z}{\partial y^2} = \frac{\partial}{\partial y}\left[\frac{\partial z}{\partial y}\right] = \frac{\partial}{\partial y}\left[e^x \cos y\right]$$

$$= e^x \cdot \frac{\partial}{\partial y}[\cos y]$$

$$= e^x(-\sin y) = -e^x \cdot \sin y$$

$$\therefore \quad \frac{\partial^2 z}{\partial y^2} = -e^x \cdot \sin y$$

also $\dfrac{\partial^2 z}{\partial x \partial y} = \dfrac{\partial}{\partial x}[e^x \cos y] = e^x \cos y$; $\dfrac{\partial^2 z}{\partial y \partial x} = \dfrac{\partial}{\partial y}\left[\dfrac{\partial z}{\partial x}\right] = \dfrac{\partial}{\partial y}\left[e^x \sin y\right] = e^x \cdot \cos y$

(ii) Let $z = \log(x^2 + y^2)$

$$\frac{\partial z}{\partial x} = \frac{\partial}{\partial x}[\log(x^2 + y^2)] = \left(\frac{1}{x^2 + y^2}\right) \cdot \frac{\partial}{\partial x}(x^2 + y^2)$$

$$= \left(\frac{1}{x^2 + y^2}\right) \cdot (2x)$$

again, $\dfrac{\partial^2 z}{\partial x^2} = \dfrac{\partial}{\partial x}\left[\dfrac{\partial z}{\partial x}\right] = \dfrac{\partial}{\partial x}\left[\dfrac{2x}{x^2 + y^2}\right]$

$$= \frac{(x^2 + y^2) \cdot (2) - (2x)(2x)}{(x^2 + y^2)^2}$$

$$= \frac{2y^2 - 2x^2}{(x^2 + y^2)^2} = \frac{2(y^2 - x^2)}{(x^2 + y^2)^2}$$

$$\therefore \quad \frac{\partial^2 z}{\partial y^2} = \frac{2(y^2 - x^2)}{(x^2 + y^2)^2}$$

consider,

$$\frac{\partial z}{\partial y} = \frac{1}{x^2 + y^2} \cdot \frac{\partial}{\partial y}(x^2 + y^2) = \frac{1}{x^2 + y^2}(2y) \quad \Rightarrow \quad \frac{\partial z}{\partial y} = \frac{2y}{x^2 + y^2}$$

$$\frac{\partial^2 z}{\partial y^2} = \frac{\partial}{\partial y}\left[\frac{2y}{x^2 + y^2}\right] = \frac{(x^2 + y^2)\frac{\partial}{\partial y}(2y) - (2y)\frac{\partial}{\partial y}(x^2 + y^2)}{(x^2 + y^2)^2}$$

$$= \frac{(x^2 + y^2)(2) - (2y)(2y)}{(x^2 + y^2)^2}$$

$$= \frac{2x^2 - 2y^2}{(x^2 + y^2)^2} = \frac{2(x^2 - y^2)}{(x^2 + y^2)^2}$$

$$\therefore \quad \frac{\partial^2 z}{\partial y^2} = \frac{2(x^2 - y^2)}{(x^2 + y^2)^2}$$

again consider, $\frac{\partial z}{\partial y} = \frac{2y}{x^2 + y^2}$

$$\frac{\partial^2 z}{\partial x . \partial y} = \frac{\partial}{\partial x}\left[\frac{\partial z}{\partial y}\right] = \frac{\partial}{\partial x}\left[\frac{2y}{x^2 + y^2}\right] = 2y . \frac{\partial}{\partial x}\left(\frac{1}{x^2 + y^2}\right)$$

$$= 2y . \frac{-1}{(x^2 + y^2)^2} . \frac{\partial}{\partial x}(x^2 + y^2)$$

$$= \frac{-2y}{(x^2 + y^2)^2} . (2x) = \frac{-4xy}{(x^2 + y^2)^2}$$

$$\therefore \quad \frac{\partial^2 z}{\partial x \partial y} = \frac{-4xy}{(x^2 + y^2)^2}$$

we have $\frac{\partial z}{\partial x} = \frac{2x}{x^2 + y^2}$

$$\frac{\partial^2 z}{\partial y \partial x} = \frac{\partial}{\partial y}\left[\frac{\partial z}{\partial x}\right] = \frac{\partial}{\partial y}\left[\frac{2x}{x^2+y^2}\right] = 2x.\frac{\partial}{\partial y}\left[\frac{1}{x^2+y^2}\right]$$

$$= 2x \,.\, \frac{-1}{\left(x^2+y^2\right)^2} \,.2y = \frac{-4xy}{\left(x^2+y^2\right)^2}$$

2. If $z = \dfrac{y}{x^2+y^2}$ then find $\dfrac{\partial^2 z}{\partial x^2}, \dfrac{\partial^2 z}{\partial y^2}$

To find $\dfrac{\partial z}{\partial x} = \dfrac{\partial}{\partial x}\left[\dfrac{y}{x^2+y^2}\right] = y.\dfrac{\partial}{\partial x}\left[\dfrac{1}{\left(x^2+y^2\right)}\right]$

$$= y \,.\, \frac{-1}{\left(x^2+y^2\right)^2} \,.\, \frac{\partial}{\partial x}(x^2+y^2)$$

$$= \frac{-y}{(x^2+y^2)} .(2x) = \frac{-2xy}{(x^2+y^2)^2}$$

To find $\dfrac{\partial^2 z}{\partial x^2}$

$$\frac{\partial^2 z}{\partial x^2} = \frac{\partial}{\partial x}\left[\frac{\partial z}{\partial x}\right] = \frac{\partial}{\partial x}\left[\frac{-2xy}{(x^2+y^2)}\right]$$

$$= -2y\, \frac{\partial}{\partial x}\left[\frac{x}{(x^2+y^2)^2}\right]$$

$$= (-2y)\left[\frac{(x^2+y^2)^2(1) - x.2(x^2+y^2).(2x)}{(x^2+y^2)^4}\right]$$

$$= (-2y)\left[\frac{(x^2+y^2)[x^2+y^2-4x^2]}{(x^2+y^2)^4}\right]$$

To find $\dfrac{\partial z}{\partial y}$

$$z = \frac{y}{x^2+y^2}$$

$$\frac{\partial z}{\partial y}=\frac{\partial}{\partial y}\left[\frac{y}{x^2+y^2}\right]=\frac{(x^2+y^2).(1)-y(2y)}{(x^2+y^2)^2}=\frac{x^2-y^2}{(x^2+y^2)^2}$$

To find $\frac{\partial^2 z}{\partial y^2}$

$$\frac{\partial^2 z}{\partial y^2}=\frac{\partial}{\partial y}\left[\frac{\partial z}{\partial y}\right]=\frac{\partial}{\partial y}\left[\frac{x^2-y^2}{(x^2+y^2)^2}\right]$$

$$=\frac{(x^2+y^2)^2(2x)-(x^2-y^2)(2(x^2+y^2)(2x)}{(x^2+y^2)^4}$$

$$=\frac{2x(x^2+y^2)[(x^2+y^2)-(x^2-y^2)2]}{(x^2+y^2)^2}$$

$$=\frac{2x(3y^2-x^2)}{(x^2+y^2)^3}$$

3. **If z = sin(x – y) + log (x + y) then prove that $z_{xx} = z_{yy}$.**

Sol. Given z = sin (x – y) + log (x + y)

$$z_x=\cos(x-y).(1)+\frac{1}{x+y}(1)=\cos(x-y)+\frac{1}{x+y}$$

$$z_{xx}=-\sin(x-y)(1)+\frac{-1}{(x+y)^2}(1)$$

$$=-\sin(x-y)-\frac{1}{(x+y)^2}$$

also $z_y=\cos(x-y)(-1)+\frac{1}{x+y}.(1)$

$$=-\cos(x-y)+\frac{1}{x+y}$$

$$z_{yy}=-[-\sin(x-y)(-1)]+\frac{-1}{(x+y)^2}(1)$$

$$=-\sin(x-y)-\frac{1}{(x+y)^2}$$

$\therefore\ z_{xx}=z_{yy}$

4. If $z = e^{x+y} + f(x) + g(y)$ prove that $z_{xy} = e^{x+y}$

Sol. $z_y = \dfrac{\partial}{\partial y}\{e^{x+y} + f(x) + g(y)\}$

$$= e^{x+y}(1) + 0 + \frac{\partial}{\partial y}(g(y))$$

$$z_{xy} = e^{x+y}(1) + 0 + 0 = e^{x+y}$$

Exercise - 21.2

1. Find the second order derivatives of following functions.

(i) $\sin xy$ (ii) e^{x-2y} (iii) $\sin(ax + by)$

2. Show that the following functions z, $z_{xx} + z_{yy} = 0$

(i) $x^2 - y^2$ (ii) $e^x(x \cos y - y \sin x)$ (iii) $e^{2xy}(\cos(y^2 - x^2)$

3. If $u = 3xy - y^3 + (y^2 - 2x)^{3/2}$ then show that $u_{xx}\, u_{yy} - (u_{xy})^2 = 0$.

4. If $z = \tan(y + ax) + (y - ax)^{\frac{1}{2}}$ then show that $z_{xx} - a^2 z_{yy} = 0$.

5. If $u = e^{xy}$ show that $u(u_{xx} + u_{yy}) = u_{x^2} + u_{y^2}$.

6. If $u^2 = \dfrac{1}{x^2 + y^2 + z^2}$ then show that $\dfrac{\partial^2 u}{\partial x^2} + \dfrac{\partial^2 u}{\partial y^2} + \dfrac{\partial^2 u}{\partial z^2} = 0$

[*Hint :* $u^{-2} = x^2 + y^2 + z^2$, then partial differentiation w.r.t x]

7. If $u = \log r$, $r^2 = x^2 + y^2 + z^2$ then show that $\dfrac{\partial^2 u}{\partial x^2} + \dfrac{\partial^2 u}{\partial y^2} + \dfrac{\partial^2 u}{\partial z^2} = \dfrac{1}{r^2}$.

8. If $z = \sec(y - ax) + \tan(y + ax)$ then show that $\dfrac{\partial^2 z}{\partial x^2} - a^2.\dfrac{\partial^2 z}{\partial y^2} = 0$

9. If $z = \log \dfrac{(x^2 + y^2)}{xy}$ then show that $\dfrac{\partial^2 z}{\partial x.\partial y} - \dfrac{\partial^2 z}{\partial y \partial x} = 0$

10. If $u = x^2 \sin y + y^2 \sin x$ then show that $\dfrac{\partial^2 u}{\partial x.\partial y} = \dfrac{\partial^2 u}{\partial y \partial x}$

Answers

1. $f_{xx} = -y^2 \sin xy$, $f_{yy} = -x^2 \sin xy$, $f_{xy} = f_{yx} = -xy \sin xy + \cos xy$
2. $f_{xx} = e^{x-2y}$, $f_{yy} = 4e^{x-2y}$, $f_{xy} = f_{yx} = -2 \cdot e^{x-2y}$.

21.3 Euler's Theorem on Homogeneous Functions

Homogenious functions : A function $f(x, y)$ is said to be Homogenious functions of degree n in x, y if $f(kx, ky) = k^n (f(x, y))$.

Ex : (i) $f(x, y) = x^3 + 3x^2y + y^3$ is a Homogenious function of deg 3

Since $f(kx, ky) = (kx)^3 + 3(kx)^2 (ky) + (ky)^3$

$= k^3 \{ x^3 + 3x^2y + y^3 \} = k^3 f(x, y)$

$\therefore$ $f(kx, ky) = k^3 \{f(x, y)\}$

$\therefore$ f is Homogeneous function of degree 3

(ii) $f(x, y) = \dfrac{x^2y - xy^2}{x^3 - y^3}$

$f(kx, ky) = \dfrac{k^3}{k^3} (f(x, y)) = k^o f(x, y)$

$\therefore$ f is Homogeneous function of degree '0'.

Euler's Theorem : If $u = f(x, y)$ is a Homogeneous function of degree n in x, y then

$$x.\frac{\partial u}{\partial x} + y.\frac{\partial u}{\partial y} = nu$$

If $u = f(x, y)$ is a homogeneous function of degree n in x, y then

Result

(i) $x.\dfrac{\partial^2 u}{\partial x^2} + y\dfrac{\partial^2 u}{\partial x.\partial y} = (n-1)\dfrac{\partial u}{\partial x}$

(ii) $x.\dfrac{\partial^2 u}{\partial y \partial x} + y.\dfrac{\partial^2 u}{\partial y^2} = (n-1)\dfrac{\partial u}{\partial y}$

(iii) $x^2\dfrac{\partial^2 u}{\partial x^2} + 2xy\dfrac{\partial^2 u}{\partial x \partial y} + y^2\dfrac{\partial^2 u}{\partial y^2} = n(n-1)u$

Solved Examples

1. If $u = (x^2 + y^2 + z^2)^{-1/2}$ then find the value of $x.\frac{\partial u}{\partial x} + y\frac{\partial u}{\partial y} + z\frac{\partial u}{\partial z}$

Sol. Let $u(x, y, z) = (x^2 + y^2 + z^2)^{-1/2}$

now $u(kx, ky, kz) = (k^2x^2 + k^2y^2 + k^2z^2)^{\frac{1}{2}} = (k^2)^{\frac{-1}{2}}(x^2 + y^2 + z^2)^{\frac{-1}{2}}$

$$= k^{-1}(x^2 + y^2 + z^2)^{\frac{1}{2}} = k^{-1}.u(x, y, z)$$

$\therefore$ $u(kx, ky, kz) = k^{-1}\, u(x, y, z)$

$\therefore$ u is Homogeneous function of degree -1

$\therefore$ by Euler's theorem $x.\frac{\partial u}{\partial x} + y.\frac{\partial u}{\partial y} + z.\frac{\partial u}{\partial z} = nu = (-1)u$

$$= -u$$

$$\therefore\ x.\frac{\partial u}{\partial x} + y.\frac{\partial u}{\partial y} + z.\frac{\partial u}{\partial z} = -u = -(x^2 + y^2 + z^2)^{\frac{-1}{2}}$$

2. If $u = \frac{x^2(x^2 - y^2)^3}{(x^2 + y^2)^2}$ then show that $x.\frac{\partial u}{\partial x} + y.\frac{\partial u}{\partial y} = 4u$

Sol. Given $u(x, y) = \frac{x^2(x^2 - y^2)^3}{(x^2 + y^2)^2}$

now $u(kx, ky) = \frac{k^2(k^2x^2 - k^2y^2)^3}{(k^2x^2 + k^2y^2)^2} = \frac{k^2(x^2 - y^2)(k^2)^3}{(k^2)^2(x^2 + y^2)^2}$

$$= \frac{k^8(x^2 - y^2)}{k^4(x^2 + y^2)^2} = k^4.u(x, y)$$

$\therefore$ $u(kx, ky) = k^4\, u(x, y)$

$\therefore$ u is Homogenous function of degree 4

$\therefore$ By Euler's theorem $x.\frac{\partial u}{\partial x} + y.\frac{\partial u}{\partial y} = nu = 4u$

3. If $u = \frac{1}{x^2} + \frac{1}{y^2} + \frac{\log x - \log y}{x^2 + y^2}$ then show that $x\frac{\partial u}{\partial x} + y.\frac{\partial u}{\partial y} = -2u$

Sol. Given $u(x, y) = \frac{1}{x^2} + \frac{1}{y^2} + \frac{\log x - \log y}{x^2 + y^2}$

$$\therefore\ u(kx, ky) = \frac{1}{k^2x^2} + \frac{1}{k^2y^2} + \frac{\log kx - \log ky}{k^2x^2 + k^2y^2}$$

$$= \frac{1}{k^2x^2} + \frac{1}{k^2y^2} + \frac{\log k + \log x - \log k - \log y}{k^2(x^2 + y^2)}$$

[$\therefore$ log mn = log m + log n]

$$= \frac{1}{k^2}\left[\frac{1}{x^2} + \frac{1}{y^2} + \frac{\log x - \log y}{(x^2 + y^2)}\right]$$

$\therefore$ $u(kx, ky) = k^{-2}\, u\,(x, y)$

$\therefore$ u is Homogeneous function of degree –2

$\therefore$ by Euler's theorem

$$x.\frac{\partial u}{\partial x} + y.\frac{\partial u}{\partial y} = nu = -2.u$$

$$\therefore \quad x.\frac{\partial u}{\partial x} + y.\frac{\partial u}{\partial y} = -2u$$

4. If $z = \frac{x^{\frac{1}{25}} - y^{\frac{1}{25}}}{x^{\frac{1}{20}} + y^{\frac{1}{20}}}$ then find the value of $x\frac{\partial z}{\partial x} + y\frac{\partial z}{\partial y}$

Sol. Given $z(x, y) = \frac{x^{\frac{1}{25}} - y^{\frac{1}{25}}}{x^{\frac{1}{20}} + y^{\frac{1}{20}}}$

$$\text{now } z(kx, ky) = \frac{(kx)^{\frac{1}{25}} - (ky)^{\frac{1}{25}}}{(kx)^{\frac{1}{20}} + (ky)^{\frac{1}{20}}} = \frac{k^{\frac{1}{25}}\left[x^{\frac{1}{25}} - y^{\frac{1}{25}}\right]}{k^{\frac{1}{20}}\left[x^{\frac{1}{20}} + y^{\frac{1}{20}}\right]}$$

$$= k^{\frac{1}{25} - \frac{1}{20}}\left[\frac{x^{\frac{1}{25}} - y^{\frac{1}{25}}}{x^{\frac{1}{20}} + y^{\frac{1}{20}}}\right]$$

$$= k^{\frac{4-5}{100}}\left[\frac{x^{\frac{1}{25}} - y^{\frac{1}{25}}}{x^{\frac{1}{20}} + y^{\frac{1}{20}}}\right]$$

$$= k^{\frac{-1}{100}} z(x, y)$$

$\therefore$ $z(kx, ky) = k^{\frac{-1}{100}} z(x, y)$

$\therefore$ Z is Homogeneous function of degree $\frac{-1}{100}$

$\therefore$ By Euler's theorem $x.\frac{\partial z}{\partial x} + y\frac{\partial z}{\partial y} = nz = \frac{-1}{100} z = \frac{-z}{100}$

5. If $u = \cos^{-1}\left(\frac{x+y}{\sqrt{x}+\sqrt{y}}\right)$ then show that $x.\frac{\partial u}{\partial x} + y.\frac{\partial u}{\partial y} = \frac{-1}{2}\cot u$

Sol. Given $u = \cos^{-1}\left(\frac{x+y}{\sqrt{x}+\sqrt{y}}\right)$

$\Rightarrow$ $\cos u = \frac{x+y}{\sqrt{x}+\sqrt{y}}$, Let z = cos u

$\therefore$ $z = \frac{x+y}{\sqrt{x}+\sqrt{y}}$ i.e., $z(x, y) = \frac{x+y}{\sqrt{x}+\sqrt{y}}$

$\therefore$ $z(kx, ky) = \frac{kx+ky}{\sqrt{kx}+\sqrt{ky}} = \frac{k}{\sqrt{k}}\left(\frac{x+y}{\sqrt{x}+\sqrt{y}}\right) = k^{\frac{1}{2}}\left(\frac{x+y}{\sqrt{x}+\sqrt{y}}\right)$

$\therefore$ $z(kx, ky) = k^{\frac{1}{2}} z(x, y)$

$\therefore$ z is Homogeneous function of degree $\frac{1}{2}$, hence by Euler's theorem

$\therefore$ $x.\frac{\partial z}{\partial x} + y.\frac{\partial z}{\partial y} = nz = \frac{1}{2} z$

$$\therefore \quad x.\frac{\partial}{\partial x}(\cos u) + y.\frac{\partial}{\partial y}(\cos u) = \frac{1}{2}\cos u \qquad (\because z = \cos u)$$

$$\therefore \quad x.(-\sin u)\frac{\partial u}{\partial x} + y(-\sin u)\frac{\partial u}{\partial y} = \frac{1}{2}\cos u$$

$$\therefore \quad x.\frac{\partial u}{\partial x} + y\frac{\partial u}{\partial y} = \frac{-1}{2}\frac{\cos u}{\sin u} = \frac{-1}{2}\cot u$$

$$\therefore \quad x.\frac{\partial u}{\partial x} + y.\frac{\partial u}{\partial y} = \frac{-1}{2}\cot u$$

6. If $u = \log(x^3 + y^3 + z^3 - 3xyz)$ then show that $x.\frac{\partial u}{\partial x} + y.\frac{\partial u}{\partial y} + z\frac{\partial u}{\partial z} = 3$

Sol. Given $u = \log(x^3 + y^3 + z^3 - 3xyz)$

$\Rightarrow \quad e^u = (x^3 + y^3 + z^3 - 3xyz)$

Let $f = e^u \quad \Rightarrow \quad f = x^3 + y^3 + z^3 - 3xyz$

$\therefore$ f is Homogeneous function of degree 3

$(\because 2(kx, ky) = k^3 (f(x, y))$

Hence by Euler's theorem,

$$x.\frac{\partial f}{\partial x} + y.\frac{\partial f}{\partial y} + 2.\frac{\partial f}{\partial z} = nf = 3f$$

but $f = e^u \quad \Rightarrow \quad x\frac{\partial}{\partial x}(e^u) + y.\frac{\partial}{\partial y}(e^u) + z.\frac{\partial}{\partial z}(e^u) = 3e^u$

$$\Rightarrow \quad x.e^u\frac{\partial u}{\partial x} + y.e^u\frac{\partial u}{\partial y} + z.e^u\frac{\partial u}{\partial z} = 3e^u$$

$$\Rightarrow \quad x.\frac{\partial u}{\partial x} + y.\frac{\partial u}{\partial y} + z\frac{\partial u}{\partial z} = \frac{3e^u}{e^u} = 3$$

7. If $u = x^2 - xy + y^2$ then find the value of $x.\frac{\partial^2 u}{\partial x^2} + y.\frac{\partial^2 u}{\partial x \partial y}$

Sol. Given $u(x, y) = x^2 - xy + y^2$

$\Rightarrow$ $u(kx, ky) = k^2 [x^2 - xy + y^2] = k^2 u(x, y)$

$\therefore$ u is a Homogeneous function of degree 2

$\therefore$ by Euler's theorem

$$x.\frac{\partial u}{\partial x} + y.\frac{\partial u}{\partial y} = nu = 2u$$

$$\therefore \quad x.\frac{\partial u}{\partial x} + y.\frac{\partial u}{\partial y} = 2u \quad \text{..... (1)}$$

Now Partial differentiation of (1) w.r.t x on both sides we get

$$\frac{\partial}{\partial x}\left[x.\frac{\partial u}{\partial x} + y\frac{\partial u}{\partial y}\right] = \frac{\partial}{\partial x}[2u]$$

$$\frac{\partial}{\partial x}\left(x.\frac{\partial u}{\partial x}\right) + \frac{\partial}{\partial x}\left[y.\frac{\partial u}{\partial y}\right] = 2.\frac{\partial u}{\partial x}$$

$$\Rightarrow \quad x.\frac{\partial^2 u}{\partial x^2} + \frac{\partial u}{\partial x}(1) + y.\frac{\partial^2 u}{\partial x \partial y} + \frac{\partial u}{\partial y}.\frac{\partial}{\partial x}(y) = 2.\frac{\partial u}{\partial x}$$

$$\Rightarrow \quad x.\frac{\partial^2 u}{\partial x^2} + \frac{\partial u}{\partial x} + y\frac{\partial^2 u}{\partial x \partial y} = 2\frac{\partial u}{\partial x} \qquad \left[\because \frac{\partial}{\partial x}(y) = 0\right]$$

$$\Rightarrow \quad x.\frac{\partial^2 u}{\partial x^2} + y.\frac{\partial^2 u}{\partial x \partial y} = \frac{\partial u}{\partial x}$$

8. If $u = x^3 + y^3 - x^2y + xy^2$ then find the value of $x^2\frac{\partial^2 u}{\partial x^2} + 2xy\frac{\partial^2 u}{\partial x \partial y} + y^2\frac{\partial^2 u}{\partial y^2}$

Sol. Given $u(x, y) = x^3 + y^3 - x^2y + xy^2$

$u(kx, ky) = k^3 [u(x, y)]$

$\therefore$ u is Homogeneous function of degree 3

$$\therefore \quad x.\frac{\partial u}{\partial x} + y.\frac{\partial u}{\partial y} = nu = 3u \quad \text{.... (1)}$$

Partial Differentiation of (1) w.r.t to x we get

$$x\frac{\partial^2 u}{\partial x^2}+\frac{\partial u}{\partial x}+y.\frac{\partial^2 u}{\partial x\partial y}+0=3\frac{\partial u}{\partial x}$$

$$\therefore \quad x\frac{\partial^2 u}{\partial x^2}+y.\frac{\partial^2 u}{\partial x\partial y}= 3\frac{\partial u}{\partial x}-\frac{\partial u}{\partial x}=2\frac{\partial u}{\partial x} \quad .... (2)$$

$$\Rightarrow \quad x^2\frac{\partial^2 u}{\partial x^2}+xy.\frac{\partial^2 u}{\partial x\partial y}=2x\frac{\partial u}{\partial x}$$ (∵ by multiplying on both sides by x)

..... (3)

again partial differentiation of (1) with reference to y we get

$$x\,.\,\frac{\partial^2 u+0}{\partial x.\partial y}+y.\frac{\partial^2 u}{\partial y^2}+\frac{\partial u}{\partial y}=3\frac{\partial u}{\partial y}$$

$$\therefore \quad x.\frac{\partial^2 u}{\partial x\partial y}+y.\frac{\partial^2 u}{\partial y^2}=2\frac{\partial u}{\partial y} \quad ..... (4)$$

$$\Rightarrow \quad xy\frac{\partial^2 u}{\partial x\partial y}+y^2\frac{\partial^2 u}{\partial y^2}=2y\frac{\partial u}{\partial y}$$ (∵ by multiplying on both sides by y)

..... (5)

(3) + (4)

$$x^2\frac{\partial^2 u}{\partial x^2}+2xy\frac{\partial^2 u}{\partial x\partial y}+y^2\frac{\partial^2 u}{\partial y^2}=2\left[x.\frac{\partial u}{\partial x}+y.\frac{\partial x}{\partial y}\right]$$

$$= 2.(3u) \quad \because \text{by (1)}$$

$$\therefore \quad x^2\frac{\partial^2 u}{\partial x^2}+2xy\frac{\partial^2 u}{\partial x\partial y}+y^2\frac{\partial^2 u}{\partial y^2}=6u$$

Exercise - 21.3

1. If $u=x^2+y^2-xy$ then show that $x\frac{\partial u}{\partial x}+y\frac{\partial u}{\partial y}=2u$

2. If $u=x^3+y^3+z^3-xyz$ then show that $x\frac{\partial u}{\partial x}+y\frac{\partial u}{\partial y}+z.\frac{\partial u}{\partial z}=3u$

3. If u = $\frac{x}{y} + \frac{y}{z} + \frac{z}{x}$ then show that $x.\frac{\partial u}{\partial x} + y\frac{\partial u}{\partial y} + z\frac{\partial u}{\partial z} = 0$

4. If z = $xy\ f\left(\frac{x}{y}\right)$ then show that $x.\frac{\partial z}{\partial x} + y\frac{\partial z}{\partial y} = 2z$

5. If $z^2 = \frac{x^{\frac{1}{2}} + y^{\frac{1}{2}}}{x^{\frac{1}{3}} + y^{\frac{1}{3}}}$ then show that $x.\frac{\partial z}{\partial x} + y\frac{\partial z}{\partial y} = \frac{z}{12}$

6. If u = $xy^2 \tan^{-1}\left(\frac{y}{x}\right)$ then show that $x.\frac{\partial u}{\partial x} + y.\frac{\partial u}{\partial y} = 3u$

7. If u = $\tan^{-1}(x + y)$ then show that $x.\frac{\partial u}{\partial x} + y.\frac{\partial u}{\partial y} = \frac{1}{2}\sin 2u$

8. If u = tán–1 $\left(\frac{x^3 + y^3}{x - y}\right)$ then show that $x.\frac{\partial u}{\partial x} + y.\frac{\partial u}{\partial y} = \sin 2u$

9. If u = $\log\left(\frac{x^2 + y^2}{\sqrt{x} + \sqrt{y}}\right)$ then show that $x.\frac{\partial u}{\partial x} + y.\frac{\partial u}{\partial y} = \frac{3}{2}$

11. If $u = \frac{x^5 + y^5}{x^2 - y^2}$ then show that $x.\frac{\partial^2 u}{\partial y \partial x} + y.\frac{\partial^2 u}{\partial y^2} = 2\frac{\partial u}{\partial y}$

12. If $u = y\sin^{-1}\left(\frac{x}{y}\right)$ then show that $x^2.\frac{\partial^2 u}{\partial x^2} + 2xy\frac{\partial^2 u}{\partial x.\partial y} + y^2.\frac{\partial^2 u}{\partial y^2} = 0$

22

Maxima - Minima

Let $y = f(x) = x + 1$ is a function defined on [0, 3].

x	0	1	2	3
f(x)	1	2	3	4

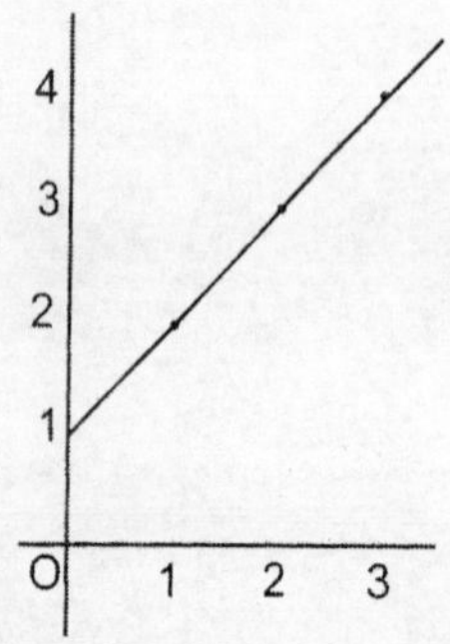

$\therefore$ Clearly we can observe that the function is increases (i.e., as x increases from 0 to 3 then $f(x)$ increases from 1 to 4), so at $x = 0$ the function has minimum value 1, and at $x = 3$ the function has maximum value 4. So we conclude that the function $f(x)$ has maxima value at $x = 3$ and minimum value at $x = 0$, in the given interval.

Here 1, 4 are called minimum, maximum values of $f(x)$ in the interval [0, 3]

Note

If $y = f(x)$ is a function defined in [a, b] then the values f(a), f(b) may or may not be the minimum or maximum values of $f(x)$.

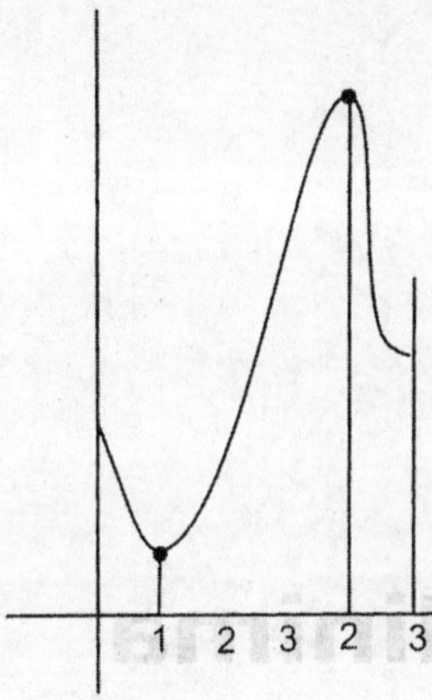

From the diagram, a function is defined in the interval [0, 3] and at $x = 1$ the function has minimum value, and at $x = 2$ the function has maximum value.

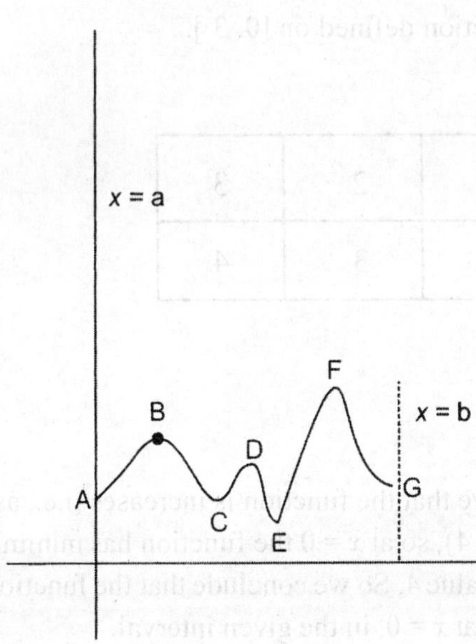

Now observe the another function from its graph here the function is defined in the interval [a, b]

We can conclude that the function has minimum values at A, C, E, G and maximum values at B, D, E .

Now A, C, E, G are called relative minimum values of the function, B, D, E are called relative maximum values of the function.

The minimum of relative minimum values of f on [a, b] is called absolute minimum value of f on [a, b], and

The maximum of relative maximum values of *f* on [a, b] is called absolute maximum value of f on [a, b].

Absolute maximum of *f* on [a, b] = max { *f*(a), *f*(b), max *f* in [a, b] }and the absolute mimimum of f on [a, b] = min { f(a), f(b), min f(b) }

Definition

Let f be a function defined on [a, b]. The relative maximum and the relative minimum values of *f* are called extreme values of *f*.

Algorithm to finding relative maximum or relative minimum of a given function $y = f(x)$ defined in the given interval (a, b).

(i) Find α such that $f'(\alpha) = 0$

(ii) If $f''(\alpha) < 0$ then $f(x)$ has maximum value at α that is equal to $f(\alpha)$.

If $f''(\alpha) > 0$, then $f(x)$ has minimum value at α that is equal to $f(\alpha)$.

Note

(α, f(α)) is called stationary point.

Ex : (i) Consider the function $f(x) = 4x^2 - 4x + 11$ for any $x \in R$.

$\Rightarrow \quad f'(x) = 8x - 4$

equate $f'(x)$ to zero, we get $8x - 4 = 0$

$\therefore\ 8x = 4 \qquad x = \frac{4}{8} = \frac{1}{2}$

at $\alpha = \frac{1}{2} \qquad f'(\alpha) = 0$

$f''(x) = 8$

Now $\quad f''(\alpha) = 8 > 0$

$\therefore$ at $\alpha = \frac{1}{2}$ the function has minimum value that is equal to $f(\alpha) = f\left(\frac{1}{2}\right)$

$$= 4\left(\frac{1}{2}\right)^2 - 4\left(\frac{1}{2}\right) + 11$$

$$= 1 - 2 + 11$$

$$= 10$$

Solved Examples

1. Find (local) maxima and (local) minima of function $x^3 - 6x^2 + 12x - 8$.

Sol. Let $y = f(x) = x^3 - 6x^2 + 9x + 15$

$$f'(x) = 3x^2 - 12x + 9 = 3(x^2 - 4x + 3)$$

take $f'(x) = 0 \quad \Rightarrow \quad x^2 - 4x + 3 = 0$

$$\Rightarrow \quad x^2 - 3x - x + 3 = 0$$

$$\Rightarrow \quad x(x-3) - 1(x-3) = 0$$

$$x = 1, x = 3$$

$\therefore \quad f'(x) = 0$ at $x = 1, 3$

$$f''(x) = 6x - 12$$

$$f''(x) = f''(1) = 6(1) - 12 = -6 < 0$$

$$f''(3) = 18 - 12 > 0 = 6 > 0$$

$\therefore \quad f(x)$ has minimum value at $x = 2$, and is equal to

$$f(3) = 27 - 54 + 27 + 15 = 15$$

and $f(x)$ has maximum value at $x = 1$ and is equal to

$$f(1) = 1 - 6 + 9 + 15 = 9$$

2. Find all the points of (local) maxima and (local) minima of the function $(x-1)(x+2)^2$

Sol. Let $y = f(x) = (x-1)(x+2)^2$

$$f'(x) = (x-1)(2(x+2)) + (x+2)^2(1)$$

take $f'(x) = 0$

$$\Rightarrow \quad 2(x-1)(x+2) + (x+2)^2 = 0 \Rightarrow (x+2)[2(x-1) + x + 2] = 0$$

$\Rightarrow \quad x+2=0, \quad 3x=0$

$\therefore \quad x=-2, \quad x=0$

$\therefore \quad f'(\alpha)=0$ at $\alpha = 0, -2$

Now $f''(x) = 2\{(x-1)[1]+(x+2)(1)\}+2(x+2)(1)$

$= 2(x-1+x+2)+2x+4$

$= 2(2x+1)+2x+4 = 6x+6$

$f''(\alpha)$ at $\alpha = 0$ is $6(0)+6 = 6 > 0$

$\therefore$ $f(x)$ has minimum at $x = 0$

the minimum value is $f(0) = (0-1)(0+2)^2$

$= -1(2)^2 = -4$

also $f''(\alpha)$ at $\alpha = -2$ is $6(-2)+6 = -6 < 0$

$\therefore$ $f(x)$ has maximum value at $x = -2$

the minimum value is $f(0) = (0-1)(0+2)^2 = -1(2)^2 = -4$

$\therefore$ $f(x)$ has maximum value at $x = -2$ and the value is $f(-2) = (-2-1)(-2+2)^2 = 0$

$\therefore$ the function has maximum $= 0$ at $x = -2$ and minimum $= -4$ at $x = 0$

3. Find all the points of (local) maxima and (local) minima of the function

$$\frac{x}{2}+\frac{2}{x} \quad (x > 0).$$

Sol. Let $y = f(x) = \frac{x}{2}+\frac{2}{x}$

$$f'(x) = \frac{1}{2}-\frac{2}{x^2}$$

take $f'(x) = 0 \quad \Rightarrow \quad \frac{1}{2}-\frac{2}{x^2} = 0 \Rightarrow \frac{1}{2} = \frac{2}{x^2} \Rightarrow x^2 = 4 \quad \Rightarrow \quad x = \pm 2$

$\therefore \quad f'(\alpha) = 0$ at $\alpha = -2, 2$

we take only $\alpha = 2$ $(\because x > 0)$

now $f''(x) = 0 - 2(-2) \,.\, x^{-3}$ $\left(\because \frac{d}{dx}\left(\frac{1}{x}\right) = \frac{d}{dx}x^{-2} = -2x^{-3}\right)$

$= 4x^{-3} = \frac{4}{x^3}$

$$(f''(x))_{x=2} = \frac{4}{(+2)^3} = \frac{4}{8} = \frac{1}{2} > 0$$

$\therefore$ $f(x)$ has minimum value at $x = 2$ and is equal to $f(2) = \frac{2}{2} + \frac{2}{2} = 1 + 1 = 2$

$\therefore$ the function has minimum at $x = 2$ and is equal to 2 its maximum value is ∞.

4. Show that the function $f(x) = \frac{x}{\log x}$ has a minimum value at $x = e$.

Sol. Let $f(x) = \frac{x}{\log x}$ $\Rightarrow$ $f'(x) = \frac{\log x(1) - x.\frac{1}{x}}{(\log x)^2} = \frac{\log x - 1}{(\log x)^2}$

also $f''(x) = \frac{(\log x)^2 \frac{1}{x} - (\log x - 1) 2 \log x \,.\, \frac{1}{x}}{(\log x)^4}$

now $f'(x) = 0$ $\Rightarrow$ $\log x - 1 = 0 \Rightarrow \log x = 1$ $\Rightarrow$ $x = e$

$$f''(e) = \frac{\frac{1}{e} - 0}{1} = \frac{1}{e} > 0$$

$\therefore$ $x = e$, $f(x)$ has minimum value and is equal to $f(e) = \frac{e}{\log e} = e$

5. Show that xe^{-x} has minimum value at $x = 1$.

Sol. Let $y = f(x) = xe^{-x}$

$\therefore \quad f'(x) = x.(e^{-x}(-1)) + e^{-x}(1)$

$= e^{-x}(1-x)$

$f''(x) = e^{-x}(-1) + (1-x)e^{-x}(-1)$

$= e^{-x}(-1+1-x) = -x.e^{-x}$

take $f'(x) = 0 \Rightarrow \quad e^{-x}(1-x) = 0 \quad \Rightarrow \quad x = 1$

$f''(1) = -1.e^{-1} = \frac{-1}{e} < 0$

$\therefore \quad f(x)$ has maximum at $x = 1$ and its value is $f(e) = 1.e^{-1} = \frac{1}{e}$

6. Show that $f(x) = \sin x(1 + \cos x)$ has maximum value at $x = \frac{\pi}{3}$.

Sol. Given $f(x) = \sin x(1 + \cos x)$

$f'(x) = \sin x(-\sin x) + (1 + \cos x)\cos x$

$= -\sin^2 x + \cos x + \cos^2 x$

$= \cos^2 x - \sin^2 x + \cos x = \cos 2x + \cos x$

$f''(x) = -2\sin 2x - \sin x$

take $f'(x) = 0 \Rightarrow \quad \cos x + \cos 2x = 0$

$\Rightarrow \quad 2\cos\frac{3x}{2}.\cos\left(\frac{x}{2}\right) = 0$

$\Rightarrow \quad \frac{\cos 3x}{2} = 0 \quad \Rightarrow \quad \frac{3x}{2} = \frac{\pi}{2} \qquad \cos\left(\frac{-x}{2}\right) = 0$

$x = \frac{\pi}{3}, \qquad \cos x = \frac{\pi}{2} = 0$

$\frac{\pi}{2} = \pi$

$\Rightarrow \quad x = \pi$

at $x = \frac{\pi}{3}$ $\quad f''(x) = -2 \sin\left(\frac{2\pi}{3}\right) - \sin\frac{\pi}{3} = -2 \cdot \frac{\sqrt{3}}{2} - \frac{\sqrt{3}}{2}$

$$= \frac{-3\sqrt{3}}{2} < 0$$

$\therefore$ $f(x)$ has maximum at $x = \frac{\pi}{3}$ and is equal to

$$f\left(\frac{\pi}{3}\right) = \sin\frac{\pi}{3}(1 + \cos\frac{\pi}{3}) = \frac{\sqrt{3}}{2}\left(1 + \frac{1}{2}\right) = \frac{\sqrt{3}}{2}\left(\frac{3}{2}\right)$$

$$= \frac{3\sqrt{3}}{2}$$

7. Find the greatest and least values of 2 sin$x$ + sin 2x over $[0, 2\pi]$

Sol. Let $f(x) = 2 \sin x + \sin 2x$

$$f'(x) = 2 \cos x + 2 \cos 2x$$

$$f'(x) = 0 \quad \Rightarrow \quad \cos x + \cos 2x = 0$$

$$\Rightarrow \quad \cos x + 2 \cos^2 x - 1 = 0$$

$$2 \cos^2 x + \cos x - 1 = 0$$

$$\Rightarrow \quad (2 \cos x - 1)(\cos x + 1) = 0$$

The solution of $\cos x = \frac{1}{2}$ in $[0, 2\pi]$ are $x = \frac{\pi}{2}, \frac{5\pi}{3}$

The solutions of $\cos x = -1$ is $x = \pi$ in $[0, 2\pi]$

Now it is enough to find the values of f at π, $\frac{\pi}{3}, \frac{5\pi}{3}$ at the extremities of the interval $[0, 2\pi]$ $f(0) = 0$, $f\left(\frac{\pi}{3}\right) = \frac{3\sqrt{3}}{2}$, $f(\pi) = 0$, $f\left(\frac{5\pi}{3}\right) = \frac{3\sqrt{3}}{2}$, $f(2\pi) = 0$

$\therefore$ f has greatest value $\frac{3\sqrt{3}}{2}$ at $\frac{\pi}{3}$

f has least value $\frac{-3\sqrt{3}}{2}$ at $\frac{5\pi}{3}$

8. Find the maximum (absolute) and the minimum (absolute) values of the following functions in the given interval.

(i) $(x-1)^2+3$ in $[-3, 1]$ (ii) $x^{40}-x^{20}$ in $[0, 1]$

(iii) $x+\sin 2x$ in $[0, 2\pi]$

Sol. (i) Let $f(x) = (x-1)^2+3$

$$f'(x) = 2(x-1)+0 = 2x-2$$

$$f'(x)=0 \quad \Rightarrow \quad 2x-2=0 \quad \Rightarrow \quad x=1$$

at $x = (-3)$ $f(-3) = (-3-1)^2+3 = 16+3 = 19$

at $x = 1$ $f(1) = (1-1)^2+3 = 3$

$\therefore$ absolute maximum $= \text{Max}\{f(-3), (1)\}$

$= \text{Max}\{19, 3\} = 19$

absolute minimum $= \min\{f(1), f(-3)\}$

$= \{3, 19\} = 3$

$\therefore$ Max = 19, Min = 3

(ii) $x^{40}-x^{20}$ in $[0, 1]$

Let $y = f(x) = x^{40}-x^{20}$

$$f'(x) = 40\,x^{39}-20x^{19} \quad \Rightarrow \quad 20\,x^{19}[2x^{20}-1]$$

$$f'(x)=0 \quad \Rightarrow \quad x^{19}=0,\ 2x^{20}-1=0 \Rightarrow \quad x=0,\ x=\left(\frac{1}{2}\right)^{\frac{1}{20}}$$

$$f(x) = 0^{40}-0^{40} = 0,\ f(1) = 1^{40}-1^{20} = 0$$

$$f\left(\frac{1}{2}^{20}\right) = \left(\frac{1}{2^{\frac{1}{20}}}\right)^{40} - \left(\frac{1}{2^{\frac{1}{20}}}\right)^{20} \quad \frac{1}{2} = \frac{1}{4} - \frac{1}{2} = \frac{-1}{4}$$

$$\text{Max}f(x) = \left\{0, 0, -\frac{1}{4}\right\} = 0$$

$$\min(f(x)) = \{0, 0, -\frac{1}{4}\} = \frac{-1}{4}$$

$\therefore$ $f(x)$ has maximum value 0 at $x = 0$

$f(x)$ has minimum value $\frac{-1}{4}$ at $x = \left(\frac{1}{2}\right)^{\frac{1}{20}}$

(iii) Let $f(x) = x + \sin 2x$

$$f'(x) = 1 + 2\cos 2x$$

take $f'(x) = 0 \quad \Rightarrow \quad 1 + 2\cos 2x = 0$

$$\cos 2x = -\frac{1}{2}$$

$$\Rightarrow x = \frac{\pi}{3}, \frac{2\pi}{3}, \frac{4\pi}{3}$$

$\Rightarrow \quad x = x = \frac{\pi}{3}, \frac{2\pi}{3}, \frac{4\pi}{3}$ in the given interval $[0, 2\pi]$

$$f\left(\frac{\pi}{3}\right) = \frac{\pi}{3} + \sin\frac{2\pi}{3} = \frac{\pi}{3} + \frac{\sqrt{3}}{2}$$

$$f\left(\frac{2\pi}{3}\right) = \frac{2\pi}{3} + \sin\frac{4\pi}{3} = \frac{2\pi}{3} - \frac{\sqrt{3}}{2}$$

$$f\left(\frac{4\pi}{3}\right) = \frac{4\pi}{3} + \sin\left(\frac{8\pi}{3}\right) = \frac{4\pi}{3} + \frac{\sqrt{3}}{2}$$

$$f(2\pi) = 2\pi, \quad f(0) = 0$$

$$\text{Max } f_{(x)} = \left\{\frac{\pi}{3} + \frac{\sqrt{3}}{2}, \frac{2\pi}{3} - \frac{\sqrt{3}}{2}, \frac{4\pi}{3} + \frac{\sqrt{3}}{2}, 2\pi, 0\right\}$$

$$= 2\pi$$

9. If the sum of two numbers is 12. Find the numbers so that sum of squares is minimum.

Sol. Let the two numbers be x, y

$\therefore\ x + y = 12$

we have to find x, y such that $x^2 + y^2$ is minimum

$\therefore\ x^2 + y^2$

$= x^2 + (x - 12)^2$ $\qquad (\because\ x + y = 12)$

$= f(x)$ (say)

$\therefore\ f'(x) = 2x + 2(x - 12)$

$f''(x) = 2 + 2 = 4 > 0$

$f'(x) = 0 \quad \Rightarrow \quad 4x - 24 = 0 \Rightarrow \quad x = 6$

at $x = 6$ $\ f''(x) > 0$

$\therefore\ f(x)$ has minimum value at $x = 6$

$\therefore\ x = 6, x + y = 12$

$\Rightarrow \quad y = 12 - x = 12 - 6 = 6$

$\therefore\ x = 6, y = 6$

10. Find the positive numbers x and y such that $x + y = 60$ and xy^3 is maximum.

Sol. Given $x + y = 60 \quad \Rightarrow \quad y = 60 - x$

$\therefore \quad xy^3 = x(60 - x)^3$

Let $f(x) = x(60 - x)^3$

we find x such that $f(x)$ is maximum

$\therefore \quad f'(x) = (x)\ 3(60 - x)^2\ (-1) + (1)\ (60 - x)^3$

$f'(x) = 0 \quad \Rightarrow \quad (60 - x)^2\ [-3x + (60 - x)\ ] = 0$

$\Rightarrow \quad 60 - 4x = 0 \Rightarrow \quad 4x = 60$ and

$60 - x - 3x = 0$

$4x = 60 \quad \Rightarrow \quad x = 15$

$$f''(x) = 6(60 - x)(1) + 3(60 - x)^2(-1)$$

$$= 6(60 - x) - 3(60 - x)^2$$

$$f''(60) = 0,\ f''(15) = 6(60 - 15) - 3(60 - 15)^2 < 0$$

$\therefore$ $f(x)$, has maximum at $x = 15$

$$x = 15 \quad \Rightarrow \quad y = 60 - x = 60 - 15 = 45$$

$\therefore$ $x = 15, y = 45$

11. Show that the area of a rectangle inscribed in a circle is maximum when it is square.

Sol. Let $2x$, $2y$ be lengths of side of rectantle ABCD inscribed in a circle of radius R.

$\therefore$ OD = y AD = x

from Δle AOD, $R^2 = x^2 + y^2$ ....(1)

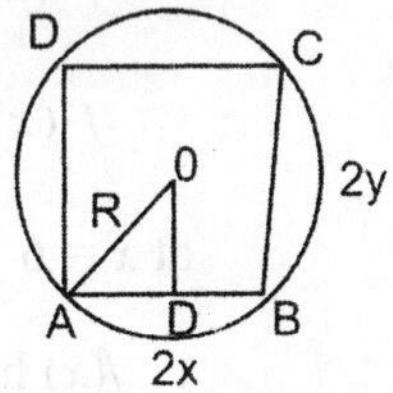

we have to maximise the area of rectangle

$\therefore$ area of rectangle = xy is maximum

$$\Delta = x\left(\sqrt{R^2 - x^2}\right) \qquad (\because y = \sqrt{R^2 - x^2})$$

$$\frac{d}{dx}(\Delta) = x.\frac{1}{2\sqrt{R^2 - x^2}}.(2x)(-1) + \sqrt{R^2 - x^2} \quad .....(1)$$

$$= \frac{-x^2}{\sqrt{R^2 - x^2}} + \sqrt{R^2 - x^2}$$

$$= -x^2 + (R^2 - x^2);\ \text{also}\ \frac{d^2}{dx^2}(\Delta) = -4x < 0$$

$$\frac{d}{dx}(\Delta) = 0 \Rightarrow -2x^2 + R^2 = 0 \Rightarrow R^2 = 2x^2 \Rightarrow R = \sqrt{2}\,x$$

from (1) $\Rightarrow$ $2x^2 = x^2 + y^2$

$\Rightarrow$ $x^2 = y^2$

$\Rightarrow$ $x = y$

$\therefore$ sides of rectangle are equal

$\therefore$ the rectangle is square, when the area of rectangle if maximum which is inscribed in a circle.

12. A line segment of length 10 cm is divided in to two parts and a rectangle is formed with these as adjacent sides. Find the dimensions of the rectangle in order that its area is maximum.

Sol. Let two line segment of length 10 cm be divided in to two parts x and $10 - x$ then we have to maximise $A = x(10 - x)$

$$\frac{dA}{dx} = 10 - 2x$$

$$\frac{dA}{dx} = 0 \Rightarrow 10 - 2x = 0 \Rightarrow x = 5$$

$\therefore\ y = 10 - x = 10 - 5 = 5$

$\therefore$ dimensions of rectangle are 5, 5

Exercise 22.1

1. Find all the points of (local) maxima and (local) minima of the functions.

(i) $x^3 - 12x$ (ii) $(1 - x)^3 (x + 1)^2$

(iii) $\dfrac{1}{x^2 + 2}$ (iv) $5x - x^2 - 6$

2. Find the absolute maximum value and the absolute minimum value of the following functions in the given intervals.

(i) $4x^3 - 8x^2 + 1$ in $[-1, 1]$ (ii) $\sin x + \cos x$ in $[0, \pi]$

3. For what value of $x > 0$ the ratio of $ln\, x$ to x is greater.

4. Show that $f(x) = \sin^m x \cos^n x$ has maximum values at $x = \tan^{-1} \sqrt{\dfrac{m}{n}}$.

5. Find two positive numbers whose sum is 24 and whose product is as large as possible.

6. If $x > 0$ then find the minimum value of $x + \dfrac{1}{x}$

7. Find the minimum value of $x^2 + \dfrac{250}{x}$

8. Find the minimum value of the following functions.

(i) x^x

(ii) $\dfrac{a^2}{x} + \dfrac{b^2}{1-x}$ in (0,1)

(iii) $a \cot x + b \tan x$

(iv) $a^2 \sec^2 x + b^2 \operatorname{cosec}^2 x$

(v) $4 \sec^2 x + 9 \operatorname{cosec}^2 x$

(vi) $64 \sec \theta + 27 \operatorname{cosec} \theta$ where θ lies in $(0, \frac{\pi}{2})$

(vii) $x + y$ subject to $xy = 1, x > 0$.

(viii) $x^2 + y^2$ subject to $x + y = 12$

9. Find the maximum values of the following functions.

(i) x^{-x}

(ii) $\sin^3 x + \cos^3 x$

(iii) $(x-1)(x-2)(x-3)$

(iv) xy subject to $x + y = 7$

(v) $l + m$ subject to $l^2 + m^2 = 1$

10. The sum of the two positive numbers is 8, then find the two numbers, so that the sum of their cubes is minimum.

11. The sum of the two number is 20. If the product of the square of one number and cube of the other is maximum, then find the numbers.

12. Find the point on the curve $y^2 = 4x$ which is nearest to (2, 1).

13. Show that when curved surface of a cylinder inscribes in sphere of radius R is maximum, then height of the cylinder is $\sqrt{2}$ R.

14. Find the rectangle of maximum perimeter that can be inscribed in a circle.

15. Show that semivertical angle of the cone of volume and of given slant height is $\tan^{-1}\sqrt{2}$

Answers

1. (i) Maximum = 16 at $x = -2$, minimum = -16 at $x = 2$.

   (ii) Maximum = $\frac{3456}{3125}$ at $x = \frac{1}{5}$ and minimum = 0 at $x = -1$

   (iii) Maximum = $\frac{1}{2}$ at $x = 0$.

   (iv) Maximum = $\frac{1}{4}$ at $x = \frac{5}{2}$

2. (i) Minimum = -11, maximum = 1

   (ii) Maximum $\sqrt{2}$ at $x = \frac{\pi}{4}$ and minimum = -1 at $x = \pi$.

3. $x = e$

5. 12, 12

6. 2

7. 75

8. (i) $e^{\frac{-1}{e}}$ (ii) $(a + b)^2$ (iii) $2\sqrt{ab}$

   (iv) $(a + b)^2$ (v) 25 (vi) 125

   (vii) 2 (viii) 72

9. (i) $e^{\frac{1}{e}}$ (ii) 1 (iii) $\frac{2}{3\sqrt{3}}$

   (iv) $\frac{49}{4}$ (v) $\sqrt{2}$

10. 4, 4,

11. 12, 8

12. (9, 6)

14. Square

Unit - IV

Exercise Questions

17. Limits and 18. Continuity

1. Evaluate

(i) $\underset{x \to 1}{Lt}\left(\frac{8}{x^2-1}-\frac{4}{x-1}\right)$ (ii) $\underset{x \to 2}{Lt}\left(\frac{x^2-3x+2}{x^2-5x+6}\right)$

2. Evaluate $\underset{x \to 0}{Lt}\ \frac{1-\cos mx}{1-\cos nx}$

3. Define continuity of a function at a point. Show that the function $f(x) = \cot x$ is continuous on $(0, \pi)$

4. Evaluate $\underset{x \to 0}{Lt}\left(\frac{1}{\sin x}-\frac{1}{\tan x}\right)$

5. Find $\underset{x \to 0}{Lt}\ \frac{1-\cos x}{x^2}$

6. Show that the function $f(x) = \frac{\cos 3x - \cos 4x}{x \sin 2x}$ $x \neq 0$.

$= \frac{7}{4}$ $x = 0$ is continuous at $x = 0$.

7. Find $\underset{x \to a}{Lt}\ \frac{\tan x - \tan a}{x-a}$

8. Find $\underset{x \to \pi/2}{Lt}\left(\frac{\cot x}{\frac{\pi}{2}-x}\right)$

9. Show that sin*x* is continuous on R.

10. (i) $\underset{x \to 0}{Lt}\ \frac{x^2-3x+2}{x^2-5x+6}$ (ii) $\underset{x \to 1}{Lt}\left(\frac{8}{x^2-1}-\frac{4}{x-1}\right)$

11. $\underset{n \to \infty}{\text{Lt}} \dfrac{(1+2+3+....+n)}{n^2}$

12. $\underset{n \to \infty}{\text{Lt}} \dfrac{n(1^2+2^2+....+n^2)}{(1+2+3+.....n)^2}$

13. Find $\underset{x \to 1}{Lt} \dfrac{\cot\left(\dfrac{\pi x}{2}\right)}{x-1}$

19. Differentiation

1. Find the left hand and right hand derivatives of $f(x) = 1 + x, x < 2$; $f(x) = 5 - x$ $x > 2$ at $x = 2$.

2. Find $\dfrac{dy}{dx}$ if $y + \sqrt{xy} = x^2$

3. Find $\dfrac{dy}{dx}$ if $x = a(\theta - \sin\theta), y = a(1 - \cos\theta)$

4. Find left and right hand derivatives of $f(x) = x^2 - 1$ $[x \geq 1]$

   $f(x) = 1 - x$ $x < 1$, at $x = 1$.

5. Find left and right hand derivative of $f(x) = |x - 1|$ at $x = 1$.

6. Find the derivative of

   (i) $\dfrac{x^2-3}{x^2+5}$ (ii) $3x^4 + (2x - 1)^2$

7. Find the derivative of x^{2x} w.r.t x.

8. Find the derivative of $\log_{10}x + \log_x 10 + \log_e x^3$.

9. If $y = \log\left[\dfrac{\sqrt{x+a^2}+x}{\sqrt{x^2+a^2}-x}\right]$; find $\dfrac{dy}{dx}$

10. Find the derivative of $\dfrac{x^2 - 3(\cos x)(e^x)}{5x^2 + \operatorname{cosec} x}$

11. Find the derivative of $y = \dfrac{x^{\frac{1}{2}}(5-2x)^{\frac{2}{3}}}{(4-3x)^{\frac{3}{4}}(7-4x)^{\frac{4}{5}}}$

12. If $x = at^2$, $y = 2at$ then find $\frac{dy}{dx}$

13. Find $\frac{d}{dx}\left(\cos\left(\frac{1-x^2}{1+x^2}\right)\right)$

14. Find $\frac{d}{dx}\left[x^2(2x-3)^4\tan^{-1}x\right]$

15. If $y = \tan^{-1}\left(\frac{\sqrt{1+x^2}-1}{x}\right)$, find $\frac{dy}{dx}$

16. Find $\frac{dy}{dx}$ where $y = 3\sqrt{x^2} - \frac{4}{\sqrt{x}}$

17. If $y = e^{3x} . \cot x$ find $\frac{dy}{dx}$

18. Differentiate w.r.t x, (i) $x.e^{2x}$ (ii) $x^a + a^x$

19. Find $\frac{dy}{dx}$ if $y = (\tan x)^{\cot x} + (\cot x)^{\tan x}$

20. If $x = a(\cos t + t \sin t)$, $y = a(\sin t - t \cos t)$ then find $\frac{dy}{dx}$

21. Find the differential coefficient of $e^{ax}\cos(b\tan^{-1}x)$

22. Find the differential coefficient of $x^2 \log(\tan^{-1}x)$

23. Differentiate $x^{\sin x}$

24. Differentiate from first principles $y = \frac{\cos 2x}{x}$

21. Partial Differentiation

1. If $u = \tan^{-1}\left(\frac{x^3+y^3}{x=y}\right)$ show that $xu_x + yu_y = \frac{1}{2}\sin 2u$.

2. Using Eulers theorem show that $xu_x + yu_y = \frac{1}{2}\tan x$ for the function

$$u = \sin^{-1}\left(\frac{x+y}{\sqrt{x}+\sqrt{y}}\right)$$

3. If u = (y – z) (z – x) (x – y) find the value of $\frac{\partial u}{\partial x}+\frac{\partial u}{\partial y}+\frac{\partial u}{\partial z}$

4. If $z = x^2y - x\sin xy$ then find $\frac{\partial z}{\partial x},\frac{\partial z}{\partial y}$

5. If $u = x^4 + y^4 + 3x^2y^2$ prove that $x.\frac{\partial u}{\partial x}+y\frac{\partial u}{\partial y}=4u$

6. If $f = \log(x^2 + y^2)$ show that $\frac{\partial^2 f}{\partial x^2}+\frac{\partial^2 f}{\partial y^2}=0$

7. If $e^{x^3+y^3}=u$ then prove that $x.\frac{\partial u}{\partial x}+y.\frac{\partial u}{\partial y}=3u\log u$

8. If $u=\frac{x+y}{x-y}$ prove that $x.\frac{\partial u}{\partial x}+y.\frac{\partial u}{\partial y}=0$

9. If $z = \tan^{-1}\left(\frac{y}{x}\right)$ show that $\frac{\partial^2 z}{\partial x^2}+\frac{\partial^2 z}{\partial y^2}=0$

10. If $u=\frac{y}{z}+\frac{z}{x}$ then show that $x.\frac{\partial u}{\partial x}+y.\frac{\partial u}{\partial y}+z.\frac{\partial u}{\partial z}=0$

22. Maxima-Minima

1. Show that $\sin x(1 + \cos x)$ is maximum, when $x = \frac{\pi}{3}$.
2. Find the maximum and minimum values of $f(x) = 3x^5 - 5x^3 + 2$.
3. Find the maximum and minimum of the function $f(x) = x^3 - 12x$.
4. Find the maximum and minimum values of $(x - 3)^5 . (x + 1)^4$.
5. Investigate the Maximum and minimum of $2x^3 - 15x^2 + 36x + 10$.
6. Determine Maxima and minima of $(x^4 - 8x^2 + 10)$
7. Find two numbers whose product is 100 and whose sum is minimum
8. Show that the maximum value of $\left(\frac{1}{x}\right)^x$ is $e^{\frac{1}{e}}$, x being positive.
9. Examine for maximum and minimum values of the function $f(x) = (x - 2)^2 (x - 3)$
10. Find the maximum value of $x^2 y^2 z^2$ subject to $\frac{x^2}{a^2}+\frac{y^2}{b^2}+\frac{z^2}{c^2}=1$.

Unit - IV
Answers to Exercise Questions

17. Limits and 18. Continuity

1. -2

2. $\frac{m^2}{n^2}$

4. 0

5. $\frac{1}{2}$

7. 1

8. 1

10. -1

19. Differentiation

2. $\frac{dy}{dx} = \frac{4x\sqrt{xy} - 1}{2\sqrt{xy} + 1}$

3. $\cot\frac{\theta}{2}$

4. -1

5. 0

6. (i) $\frac{16x}{(x^2+5)^2}$ (ii) $12x^3 + 8x - 4$

7. $\frac{dy}{dx} = 2.x^{2x}(1 + lnx)$

8. $\frac{1}{x}\left(\frac{1}{\log_{10}^{e}}\right)$

9. $\frac{2}{\sqrt{x^2 + a^2}}$

10. $\frac{(5x^2 + \text{cosec } x)(2x - 3e^x(\cos x - \sin x) - (x^2 - 3\cos x\, e^x)(10x - \text{cosec } x \cos x)}{(5x^2 + \text{cosec } x)^2}$

11. $y\left[\dfrac{1}{2x}-\dfrac{4}{5-2x}+\dfrac{9}{4(4-3x)}+\dfrac{16}{5}\dfrac{1}{(7-4x)}\right]$

12. $\dfrac{1}{t}$

13. $\sin\left(\dfrac{1-x^2}{1+x^2}\right)\left(\dfrac{4x}{(1+x^2)^2}\right)$

14. $\dfrac{x^2(2x-3)^4}{1+x^2}+8x^2\tan^{-1}x(2x-3)^3+2(2x-3)^4 x.\tan^{-1}x$

15. $\dfrac{1}{2(1+x^2)}$

16. $\dfrac{2}{3}x^{\frac{-1}{3}}+2.x^{\frac{-3}{2}}$

17. $-\operatorname{cosec}^2 x + 3\cot x\, e^{3x}$

18. (i) $2x\, e^{2x} + e^{2x}$ (ii) $ax^{a-1} + a^x \ln a$

19. $(\tan x)^{\cot x} (\operatorname{cosec}^2 x\,(1 - \ln(\tan x)) + (\cot x)^{\tan x}((\sec^2 x)(\ln(\cot x) - 1)$

20. $\tan t$

21. $a \,.\, e^{ax}\cos(b\tan^{-1}x) - \dfrac{e^{ax}}{1+x^2}\sin(b\tan^{-1}x)$

22. $2x\log(\tan^{-1}x) - \dfrac{x^2}{1+x^2\tan^{-1}x}$

23. $x^{\sin x}\left(\dfrac{\sin x}{x}+\cos x\log x\right)$

24. $\dfrac{-2x\sin 2x-\cos 2x}{x^2}$

21. Partial Differentiation

3. 0

4. $2xy - (x \cos xy\,(y)\,x^2 - x^2 \cos xy + \sin xy$

22. Maxima - Minima

2. Maximum = 4, Minimum = 0

3. Maximum = 16, Minimum = –16

4. $\text{Min} = \dfrac{-(20)^5\,(16)^4}{9^9}$

5. Maximum value = 48, minimum value = 37

6. Maximum value = 10, Minimum value = –6

7. 10, 10

9. Minimum value = $^{-4}/_{27}$

Unit - IV

Self Test Questions

17. Limits and 18. Continuity

1. Evaluate $\underset{x\to\infty}{\text{Lt}} \dfrac{3x^2-5x-1}{x^2-2x+6}$

2. Evaluate $\underset{x\to 1}{\text{Lt}} \dfrac{\sqrt{x^2-1}+\sqrt{x-1}}{\sqrt{x^2-1}}$

3. Compute $\underset{x\to\infty}{\text{Lt}} \dfrac{x^2-\sin x}{x^2-2}$

4. Compute $\underset{x\to 0}{\text{Lt}} \dfrac{a^x-1}{b^x-1}$ $(a>0,\ b>0,\ b\neq 1)$

5. Show that $\underset{x\to 2}{\text{Lt}} \dfrac{x-1}{2x^2-7x+5} = -\dfrac{1}{3}$

6. Evaluate $\underset{x\to\infty}{\text{Lt}} \dfrac{3^{x+1}+4}{3^{x+2}+4}$

19. Differentiation

1. (i) If y = f(x) is differentiable at x = a then f is continuous at x = a
   (ii) Find the derivative of $\log_e^x$
   (iii) Show that the derivative of tanx is $\sec^2 x$ and the derivative of sinx is cosx.
2. Differentiate the following wrt to x
   (i) 3tanx + logx + 7 (ii) Secxtanx
3. Differentiate $\tan^{-1}\left(\dfrac{x-\sqrt{x}}{1+x^{3/2}}\right)$
4. Find the derivative of sin2x and $\tan^2 5x$

5. Find the derivative of $y = \sqrt{\tan x}$

6. Find $\frac{dy}{dx}$ when $x = a\cos^3 t$, $y = a\sin^3 t$

7. (i) Find the derivative of $y = \sin(x^x)$

(ii) Find the derivative of $y = \sin^2(\cos 3x)$

8. (i) Differentiate x^x w.r.t x.

(ii) If $y = (\tan x)^{\sin x}$ find $\frac{dy}{dx}$

9. If $x^y = e^{x-y}$ show that $\frac{dy}{dx} = \frac{\tan x}{(1+\log x)^2}$

10. Find the derivative of $x = \log\left(1+\sqrt{y}\right)$

21. Partial Differention

1. If $z = e^{x-2y}$ find $\frac{\partial z}{\partial x}, \frac{\partial z}{\partial y}$

2. Evaluate $\frac{\partial z}{\partial x}$ and $\frac{\partial z}{\partial y}$ of

(i) $z = x^2 y - x\sin xy$ (ii) $z = x^3 + y^3 - 3axy$

3. If $u = \log(x^2 + y^2)$ find $\frac{\partial u}{\partial x}, \frac{\partial u}{\partial y}$

22. Maxima-Minima

1. Find maxima and minima of the function

$f(x) = 3x^3 - 9x^2 - 27x + 30$

2. Show that x^x is minimum at $x = 1/e$

3. Discuss the maxima and minima of $u = x^4 + y^4 - 2x^2 + 4xy - 2y^2 = 0$

4. Find the maximum of the $3\cos x + \sqrt{3}\sin x$ $0 < x < \pi$

UNIT - V

INTEGRAL CALCULUS

UNIT - V

INTEGRAL CALCULUS

23

Indefinite Integrals

23.1 Indefinite Integral

Anti derivative : If $f(x)$, $g(x)$ are two functions such that $f'(x) = g(x)$ then $f(x)$ is called anti derivative of $g(x)$ with respect to x.

Ex: 1. $\frac{d}{dx}\{x^4 + 5\} = 4x^3 \Rightarrow x^4 + 5$ is anti derivative of $4x^3$.

2. $\frac{d}{dx}\{\tan x\} = \sec^2 x \Rightarrow \tan x$ is anti derivative of $\sec^2 x$

Note: If $f(x)$ is anti derivative of $g(x)$ then $f(x) + c$ is also anti derivative of $g(x)$.

for example $\frac{d}{dx}\{x\} = 1$; $\frac{d}{dx}\{x + 5\} = 1$

Antiderivative of x, $x + 5$ is same as 1.

Indefinite Integral: If $g(x)$ is antiderivative of $f(x)$ then $g(x) + C$, $C \in R$ is called indefinite integral of $f(x)$ with respect to x. It is denoted by $\int (f(x))\,dx$. The real number C is called constant of Integration.

23.2 Standard Integrals

1. $\int x^n dx = \frac{x^{n+1}}{n+1} + c$ *for* $n \neq -1$ $\left(\because \frac{d}{dx}\left(\frac{x^{n+1}}{n+1} = x^n\right)\right)$

Ex : (i) $\int x^5 dx = \frac{x^{5+1}}{5+1} + c = \frac{x^6}{6} + c$

(ii) $\int 1\,dx = \int x^0\,dx = \frac{x^{0+1}}{0+1} + c = x + c$

2. $\int \frac{1}{x}\,dx = \log|x| + c \quad \left(\because \frac{d}{dx}(ln\,x) = \frac{1}{x}\right)$

3. $\int e^x dx = e^x + c$

4. If $a > 0$. $a \neq 1$ then $\int a^x dx = \frac{a^x}{\log a} + c$

5. $\int \cos x\,dx = \sin x + c$

6. $\int \sin x\,dx = -\cos x + c$

7. $\int \sec^2 x\,dx = \tan x + c$

8. $\int \operatorname{cosec}^2 x\,dx = -\cot x + c$

9. $\int \sec x \tan x\,dx = \sec x + c$

10. $\int \operatorname{cosec} x \cot x\,dx = -\operatorname{cosec} x + c$

11. $\int \frac{1}{\sqrt{1-x^2}}\,dx = \sin^{-1}x + c = -\cos^{-1}x + c$

12. $\int \frac{1}{1+x^2}\,dx = \tan^{-1}x + c = -\cot^{-1}x + c$

13. $\int \frac{1}{|x|\sqrt{x^2-1}}\,dx = \sec^{-1}x + c = -\operatorname{cosec}^{-1}x + c$

14. $\int \sinh x\,dx = -\cosh x + c$

15. $\int \cosh x\,dx = \sin hx + c$

16. $\int \sec h^2 x\,dx = \tan hx + c$

17. $\int \operatorname{cosech}^2 x\, dx = -\coth x + c$

18. $\int \operatorname{sech} x \tanh x\, dx = \operatorname{sech} x + c$

19. $\int \operatorname{cosech} x \coth x\, dx = -\operatorname{cosech} x + c$

20. $\int \frac{1}{\sqrt{1+x^2}}\, dx = \sinh^{-1} x + c$

21. $\int \frac{1}{\sqrt{x^2-1}}\, dx = \cosh^{-1} x + c$

23.3 Fundamental Rules of Integration

1. If $f(x)$ is an integrable function and K is a real number then $\int Kf(x)dx = K\int f(x)dx$

Ex : $\int (5x)dx = 5\int x\, dx = 5\frac{x^2}{2} + c$

2. *If $f(x)$, $g(x)$ are two integrable functions then* $\int (f+g)x\, dx = \int f(x)\, dx + \int g(x)dx$.

Ex : $\int (x^2 + \sin x)dn = \int x^2 dx + \int \sin x dx = \frac{x^3}{3} - \cos x + c$

3. If $f(x)$, $g(x)$ are two integrable functions, k_1, k_2 are two real numbers then $\int [k_1 f(x) + k_2 g(x)]dx = K_1 \int f(x)dx + k_2 \int g(x)dx$

Ex : $\int (5x^2 + 6e^x)dx = 5\int x^2 dx + 6\int e^x dx = \frac{5.x^3}{3} + 6.e^x + c$

Solved Examples

1. Evaluate $\int \sqrt[3]{x}\, dx$

Sol. $\int \sqrt[3]{x} dx = \int x^{\frac{1}{3}} dx = \frac{x^{\frac{1}{3}+1}}{\frac{1}{3}+1} = \frac{x^{\frac{4}{3}}}{\frac{4}{3}} = \frac{3}{4}.\, x^{\frac{4}{3}} + c$ $\left[\because \int x^n dx = \frac{x^{n+1}}{n+1} + c\right]$

2. Evaluate $\int\left(\frac{ax^3+bx^2+cx+d}{x}\right)dx$

Sol. $\int\frac{ax^3+bx^2+cx+d}{x}dx = \int\left(\frac{ax^3}{x}+\frac{bx^2}{x}+\frac{cx}{x}+\frac{d}{x}\right)dx$

$$= a\int x^2dx + b\int xdx + c\int 1dx + d\int\frac{1}{x}dx$$

$$= \frac{ax^3}{3}+\frac{bx^2}{2}+cx+d\ln(x)+c$$

3. Evaluate (i) $\int\frac{1}{x\sqrt{x}}dx$ (ii) $\int\frac{1}{\sqrt[4]{x}}dx$

Sol. (i) $\int\frac{1}{x\sqrt{x}}dx = \int\frac{1}{x^{\frac{3}{2}}}dx = \int x^{\frac{-3}{2}}dx = \frac{x^{\frac{-3}{2}+1}}{-\frac{3}{2}+1}+c = \frac{x^{\frac{-1}{2}}}{-\frac{1}{2}}+c = -2x^{\frac{-1}{2}}+c$

(ii) $\int\frac{1}{\sqrt[4]{x^7}}dx = \int\frac{1}{x^{\frac{7}{4}}}dx = \int x^{-\frac{7}{4}}dx = \frac{x^{\frac{-7}{4}+1}}{-\frac{7}{4}+1}+c = \frac{x^{\frac{-3}{4}}}{-\frac{3}{4}}+c = -\frac{4}{3}.x^{-\frac{3}{4}}+c$

4. Evaluate

(i) $\int e^{2\log x}dx$ (ii) $\int e^{2ln\sec x}dx$ (iii) $\int 7^x dx$

Sol. (i) $\int e^{lnx^2}dx = \int x^2dx = \frac{x^3}{3}+c$ $\left[\because e^{\log f(x)} = f(x)\right]$

(ii) $\int e^{2\ln(\sec x)}dx = \int e^{ln(\sec^2 x)}dx = \int\sec^2 x\,dx = \tan x + c$

(iii) $\int 7^x dx = \frac{7^x}{\log 7}+c$ $\left[\because \int a^x dx = \frac{a^x}{\log a}+c\right]$

5. Evaluate

(i) $\int\tan^2 xdx$ (ii) $\int\sec^2 x\,cosec^2 xdx$

(iii) $\int\frac{1-\cos 2x}{1+\cos 2x}dx$ (iv) $\int\frac{\sin x}{1+\cos 2x}dx$

Sol. (i) $\int \tan^2 x dx = \int (\sec^2 x - 1)dx = \int \sec^2 x dx - \int 1\, dx = \tan x - x + c$

(ii) $\int (\sec^2 x . \operatorname{cosec}^2 x)dx = \int \frac{1}{\sin^2 x . \cos^2 x} dx$

$$= \int \frac{\sin^2 x + \cos^2 x}{\sin^2 x \cos^2 x} dx \qquad (\because \sin^2 x + \cos^2 x = 1)$$

$$= \int \frac{\sin^2 x}{\sin^2 x \cos^2 x} + \int \frac{\cos^2 x}{\sin^2 x \cos^2 x}$$

$$= \int (\sec^2 x + \operatorname{cosec}^2 x)\, dx = \tan x - \cot x + c$$

(iii) $\int \frac{1 - \cos 2x}{1 + \cos 2x} dn = \int \frac{2\sin^2 x}{2\cos^2 x} dx = \int \tan^2 x dx = \int (\sec^2 x - 1)dx = \tan x - x + c$

(iv) $\int \frac{\sin x}{1 + \cos 2x} dx$

$$= \int \frac{\sin x}{2\cos^2 x} dx$$

$$= \frac{1}{2} \int \tan x . \sec x\, dx$$

$$= \frac{1}{2} \sec x + c$$

6. Evaluate $\int \frac{\sin^2 x}{1 + \cos x} dx$

Sol. $\int \frac{\sin^2 x}{1 + \cos x} dx = \int \frac{1 - \cos^2 x}{1 + \cos x} dx = \int \frac{(1 + \cos x)(1 - \cos x)}{(1 + \cos x)} dx$

$$= \int (1 - \cos x)dx = x - \sin x + c$$

7. Evaluate $\int\sqrt{1+\sin 2x}\,dx\,x$

Sol. $\int\sqrt{1+\sin 2x}\,dx = \int\sqrt{(\sin^2 x+\cos^2 x)+2\sin x\cos x}$

$\int\sqrt{(\sin x+\cos x)^2} = \int \sin x+\cos x\,dx$

$= (-\cos x + \sin x) + c$

8. Evaluate $\int\frac{1}{1+\cos x}dx$

$$= \int\frac{1-\cos x}{(1+\cos x)(1-\cos x)}dx = \int\frac{1-\cos x}{(1-\cos^2 x)}dx$$

$$= \int\frac{1-\cos x}{\sin^2 x}dx$$

$$= \int\left(\frac{1}{\sin^2 x}-\frac{\cos x}{\sin^2 x}\right)dx$$

$$= \int(\operatorname{cosec}^2 x-\operatorname{cosec} x.\cot x)\,dx$$

$$= -\cot x + \operatorname{cosec} x + c$$

9. Evaluate $\int\frac{\cos x+\sin x}{\sqrt{1+\sin 2x}}dx \qquad x\in(\frac{\pi}{2},\frac{3\pi}{4})$

Sol. $\int\frac{\cos x+\sin x}{\sqrt{\sin^2 x+\cos^2 x+2\sin x\cos x}}dx$

$\int\frac{\cos x+\sin x}{\sqrt{(\cos x+\sin x)^2}}dx$

$= \int\frac{\cos x+\sin x}{\cos x+\sin x}dx = \int 1\,dx = x+c$

10. Evaluate $\int\frac{(a^x+b^x)^2}{a^x.b^x}dx$

Sol. $\int\frac{(a^x+b^x)^2}{a^x.b^x} = \int\frac{(a^x)^2+(b^x)^2+2a^x.b^x}{a^x.b^x}dx$

$$= \int\left(\frac{a^x}{b^x}+\frac{b^x}{a^x}+2\right)dx = \int\left(\left(\frac{a}{b}\right)^x+\left(\frac{b}{a}\right)^x+2\right)dx$$

$$= \frac{\left(\frac{a}{b}\right)^x}{ln\left(\frac{a}{b}\right)}+\frac{\left(\frac{b}{a}\right)^x}{ln\left(\frac{b}{a}\right)}+2x+c \qquad (\because \int a^x = \frac{a^x}{\log a})$$

11. Evaluate $\int\frac{a\cos^3 x+b\sin^3 x}{\cos^2 x\sin^2 x}dx$

Sol. $\int\frac{a\cos^3 x+b\sin^3 x}{\cos^2 x\sin^2 x}dx = a\int\frac{\cos^3 x}{\cos^2 x\sin^2 x}dx+b\int\frac{\sin^3 x}{\cos^2 x\sin^2 x}dx$

$$= a\int\frac{\cos x}{\sin^2 x}dx+b\int\frac{\sin x}{\cos^2 x}dx$$

$$= a\int\cot x.\operatorname{cosec} x dx+b\int\tan x.\sec x dx$$

$$= -\text{a cosec } x + \text{b sec } x + \text{c}$$

12. Evaluate (i) $\int\frac{x^4}{x^2+1}dx$, (ii) $\int\frac{x^2+5}{x^2+1}dx$

(iii) $\int\frac{x^4+x^2+1}{x^2+1}dx$

(i) $\int\frac{x^4}{x^2+1}dx = \int\frac{x^4-1+1}{x^2+1}dx = \int\left(\frac{x^4-1}{x^2+1}+\frac{1}{x^2+1}\right)dx$

$$= \int\frac{(x^2-1)(x^2+1)}{x^2+1}dx+\int\frac{1}{x^2+1}dx$$

$$= \int(x^2-1)dx+\int\frac{1}{x^2+1}dx$$

$$= \frac{x^3}{3}-x+\tan^{-1}x+c$$

(ii) $$\int \frac{x^2+5}{x^2+1}dn = \int \frac{x^2+1+4}{x^2+1}dx = \int\left(\frac{x^2+1}{x^2+1}+\frac{4}{x^2+1}\right)dx$$

$$= \int\left(1+\frac{4}{1+x^2}\right)dx = \int 1\,dx + 4\int\frac{1}{1+x^2}dx$$

$$= x + 4.\tan^{-1} x + c$$

(iii) $$\int\left(\frac{x^4+x^2+1}{x^2+1}\right)dx = \int\frac{(x^2+1)+x^4}{x^2+1}dx$$

$$= \int\frac{x^2+1}{x^2+1}dn + \int\frac{x^4}{x^2+1}dx$$

$$= x + \frac{x^3}{3} - x + \tan^{-1} x + c$$

$$= \frac{x^3}{3} + \tan^{-1} x + c$$

$$\left(\because \text{ by (i), (ii) } \int\frac{x^4}{x^2+1} = \frac{x^3}{3} - x + \tan^{-1} x\right)$$

13. Evaluate $\displaystyle\int\frac{x^2}{\sqrt{1+x^2}\left(1+\sqrt{1+x^2}\right)}dx$

Sol. $$\int\frac{x^2\left(1-\sqrt{1+x^2}\right)}{\sqrt{1+x^2}\left(1-\sqrt{1-x^2}\right)\left(1+\sqrt{1+x^2}\right)}dx = \int\frac{x^2\left(1-\sqrt{1+x^2}\right)}{\sqrt{1+x^2}\left(1-1-x^2\right)}dx$$

$$= \int\frac{x^2\left(1-\sqrt{1+x^2}\right)}{\sqrt{1+x^2}\left(1-1-x^2\right)}dx$$

$$= \int\frac{x^2\left(1-\sqrt{1+x^2}\right)}{\sqrt{1+x^2}\,(-x^2)}dx = \int\left(\frac{-1+\sqrt{1+x^2}}{\sqrt{1+x^2}}\right)dx = \int\left(\frac{-1}{\sqrt{1+x^2}}+1\right)dx$$

$$= -\sinh^{-1} x + x + c$$

$$= x - \sin h^{-1} x + c$$

14. Evaluate $\int \frac{1-\sqrt{x}}{1+\sqrt[4]{x}}\,dx$

Sol. $\int \frac{1-\sqrt{x}}{1+\sqrt[4]{x}}\,dx = \int \frac{\left(1-\sqrt[4]{x}\right)\left(1+\sqrt[4]{x}\right)}{\left(1+\sqrt[4]{x}\right)}\,dx$

$\left(\because 1-\sqrt{x} = (1-\sqrt[4]{x})(1+\sqrt[4]{x})\right)$

$= \int (1-\sqrt[4]{x})\,dx$

$= x - \frac{x^{\frac{1}{4}+1}}{\frac{1}{4}+1} + c$

$= x - \frac{4}{5}.x^{\frac{5}{4}} + c$

15. Evaluate $\int \left(\frac{1}{x} - \frac{2}{x\sqrt{x^2-1}} + \sec x \tan x\right) dx$

Sol. $\int \frac{1}{x}\,dx - 2\int \frac{1}{x\sqrt{x^2-1}}\,dx + \int \sec x \tan x\,dx$

$= \ln x - 2\sec^{-1}x + \sec x + c$

Exercise - 23.1

Integrate the following with respect x.

1. (i) x^{17} (ii) x^{-9}

(iii) $\frac{7}{x^6} - \frac{5}{x^4} + \frac{3}{x^2} - 70x$ (iv) $\frac{x^3 - 3x^2 + 2}{x}$

(v) $(2-3x)(5-4x)(1+x)$ (vi) $\frac{1}{\sqrt[4]{x^9}}$

(vii) $e^{3\log x}$ (viii) $\cot^2 x$

(ix) $\frac{1}{1-\cos 2x}$ (x) $(a\tan x - b\cot x)^2$

(xi) $\frac{1}{\sqrt{1-x^2}} + 2^x + e^x$

2. (i) $2^{2x} . 3^{2x} . 5^{x}$ (ii) $\frac{(a^x - b^x)^2}{a^x . b^x}$

3. (i) $\frac{\cos^2 x}{1+\sin x}$ (ii) $\frac{\sin^2 x}{1-\cos x}$

(iii) $\frac{2+3\sin x}{\cos^2 x}$ (iv) $\frac{\cos^3 x}{\sin^2 x \cos^2 x}$

4. (i) $\frac{1+\cos^2 x}{1+\cos 2x}$ (ii) $\frac{1+\sin^2 x}{1-\cos 2x}$

5. (i) $\sqrt{1+\sin 2x}\, dx$ (ii) $\sqrt{1+\cos 2x}\, dx$

(iii) $\sqrt{1-\sin 2x}\, dx$ (iv) $\sqrt{1-\cos 2x}\, dx$

6. (i) $\frac{1}{1+\cos x}$ (ii) $\frac{1}{1-\cos x}$

(iii) $\frac{1}{1+\sin x}$

To get the integral of given functions we use the following methods.

(i) Integration by substitution

(ii) Integration of rational functions using partial fractions

(iii) Integration biparts

(iv) Integration by succesive reduction

Answers

1. (i) $\frac{x^{18}}{18}+c$ (ii) $\frac{x^{-8}}{-8}+c$

(iii) $\frac{7.x^{-5}}{-5}-\frac{5x^{-3}}{-3}-\frac{3}{x}-\frac{70x^2}{2}+c$ (iv) $\frac{x^3}{3}-\frac{3x^2}{2}+2lnx+c$

(v) $10x - \frac{13}{2}x^2 - \frac{11}{3}x^3 + 3x^4 + c$ (vi) $-\frac{4}{5}x^{\frac{-5}{4}} + c$

(vii) $\frac{x^4}{4}+c$ (viii) $-\cot x - x + c$

(ix) $-\frac{1}{2}\cot x + c$ (x) $a^2 \tan x - b^2 \cot x - (a+b)^2 x + c$

(xi) $\sin^{-1}x + \frac{2^x}{\log 2} + e^x + c$

2. (i) $\frac{(180)^x}{\ln 180} + c$ (ii) $\frac{\left(\frac{a}{b}\right)^x - \left(\frac{b}{a}\right)^x}{\ln a - \ln b} - 2x + c$

3. (i) $x + \cos x + c$ (ii) $x + \sin x + c$

(iii) $2\tan x + 3\sec x + c$ (iv) $-\operatorname{cosec} x + c$

4. (i) $\frac{1}{2}\tan x + \frac{1}{2}x + c$ (ii) $\frac{1}{2}x - \frac{1}{2}\cot x + c$

5. (i) $\pm(\cos x - \sin x) + c$ (ii) $\pm\sqrt{2}\,.\sin x + c$

(iii) $\pm(\cos x + \sin x) + c$ (iv) $\pm\sqrt{2}\,.\cos x + c$

6. (i) $-\cot x + \operatorname{cosec} x + c$ (ii) $-\cot x - \operatorname{cosec} x + c$

(iii) $\tan x - \sec x + c$

23.4 Integration by Substitution

Theorem : If $\int f(x)dx = g(x)$ then $\int f(ax+b)dx = \frac{1}{a}g(ax+b)+c$

Proof : given $\int f(x)dx = g(x)$

consider $\int f(ax+b)dx$

Let $ax + b = t$, differentiate with *respect to x* on both sides

$\Rightarrow a\,dx = dt$

$\Rightarrow dx = \frac{dt}{a}$

$$\therefore \int f(ax+b)dx = \int f(t).\frac{dt}{a} = \frac{1}{a}\int f(t)dt$$

$$= \frac{1}{a} g(t)$$

$$= \frac{1}{a} g(ax+b)$$

Ex : (i) $\int e^{2x}dx = \frac{e^{2x}}{2} + c$ (ii) $\int \cos 4x\, dx = \frac{\sin 4x}{4} + c$

Theorem : $\int (f(x))^n . f^1(x).dx = \frac{f(x)^{n+1}}{n+1} + c$ where $f^1(x)$ *is* derivative of $f(x)$.

Proof : Consider $\int (f(x))^n . f^1(x)dx$

Let $f(x) = t$; differentiate with respect to 'x' we get

$$f'(x) . dx = dt$$

$$\therefore \int (f(x)^n . f^1(x)dx = \int t^n .dt = \frac{t^{n+1}}{n+1} + c$$

$$= \frac{(f(x))^{n+1}}{n+1} + c$$

Ex : (i) $\int \sin^4 x.\cos x dx = \frac{\sin^5 x}{5} + c$

($\because$ here $f(x) = \sin x \Rightarrow f'(x) = \cos x$ dx)

(ii) $\int (e^x)^3 .e^x .dx = \frac{(e^x)^4}{4} + c$

($\because$ here $f(x) = e^x \Rightarrow f'(x) = e^x$. dx)

Theorem : If $f(x)$ is differentiable then

$$\int \frac{f^1(x)}{f(x)} dx = \ln|f(x)| + c$$

Proof : Consider $\int \frac{f^1(x)}{f(x)} dx$

Let $f(x) = t \quad \Rightarrow f^1(x)dx = dt$

$$\therefore \int \frac{f^1(x)}{f(x)} dx = \int \frac{dt}{t} = ln|t| + c$$

$$= ln|\,f(x)\,| + c$$

Ex : (i) $\int \cot x\, dx = \int \frac{\cos x}{\sin x} dx = \int \frac{d(\sin x)}{\sin x} dx = \ln|\sin x| + c$

(ii) $\int \frac{1}{xlnx} dx = \int \frac{1/x}{lnx} dx = \int \frac{d(lnx)}{lnx} dx = ln(lnx) + c$

Theorem If $f(x)$ is differentiable then

$$\int \frac{f^1(x)}{\sqrt{f(x)}} dx = 2\sqrt{f(x)} + c$$

Proof: Consider $\int \frac{f^1(x)}{\sqrt{f(x)}} dx$

Let $f(x) = t \quad \Rightarrow \quad f^1(x)\, dx = dt$

$$\therefore \int \frac{f^1(x)}{\sqrt{f(x)}} dx = \int \frac{dt}{\sqrt{t}} = \int t^{-1/2} dt = \frac{t^{-1/2+1}}{-1/2+1} = 2\sqrt{t}$$

$$= 2\sqrt{f(x)} + c$$

Ex : (i) $\int \frac{\sec^2 x}{\sqrt{\tan x}} dx$

$$\int \frac{\frac{d}{dx}(\tan x)}{\sqrt{\tan x}} dx = 2\sqrt{\tan x} + c$$

(ii) $\int \frac{1}{\sqrt{x}} dx = \int \frac{\frac{d}{dx}(x)}{\sqrt{x}} dx = 2\sqrt{x} + c$

Solved Examples

1. Evaluate $\int (2x+3)^{10}\, dx$

Sol. $\int (2x+3)^{10}\, dx = \frac{1}{2}.\frac{2x+3)^{10+1}}{11} + c = \frac{(2x+3)^{11}}{22} + c$

$$\left(\because \int (ax+b)^n\, dx \frac{1}{a}\frac{(ax+b)^{n+1}}{n+1} + c \right)$$

2. Evaluate $\int \frac{1}{7x+4} dx$

Sol. $\int \frac{1}{7x+4} dx = \frac{1}{7}.\ln |7x+4| + c$

3. Evaluate $\int \frac{1}{\sqrt{ax+b}} dx$

Sol. $\int \frac{1}{\sqrt{ax+b}} dx = \frac{1}{a} 2\sqrt{ax+b} = \frac{2}{a}\sqrt{ax+b} + c$

4. Evaluate $\int e^{4x+7}\, dx$

Sol. $\int e^{4x+7} dx = \frac{1}{4}.e^{4x+7} + c$

5. Evaluate $\int 5^{4x-3} dx$

Sol. $\int 5^{4x-3} dx = \frac{1}{4}\frac{5^{4x-3}}{ln\, 5} + c$

6. Evaluate $\int \sin 4x\, dx$

Sol. $\int \sin 4x\, dx = \frac{1}{4}.(-\cos 4x) + c = \frac{-1}{4}\cos 4x + c$

7. Evaluate $\int \sin 3x \cos 4x dx$

Sol. $\int \sin 3x \cos 4x dx = \frac{1}{2}\int 2\sin 3x \cos 4x dx$

$$= \frac{1}{2}\int \sin 7x + \sin(-x)dx$$

$[\because \sin(A+B) + \sin(A-B) = 2\sin A \cos B]$

$$= \frac{1}{2}\int \sin 7x - \sin x\, dx$$

$$= \frac{1}{2}\left(\frac{1}{7}(-\cos 7x)\right) - \frac{1}{2}(-\cos x) + c$$

$$= -\frac{1}{14}\cos 7x + \frac{1}{2}\cos x + c$$

8. Evaluate $\int \sin^2 x\, dx$

Sol. $\int \sin^2 x\, dx = \int\left(\frac{1-\cos 2x}{2}\right)dx = \int \frac{1}{2}dx - \frac{1}{2}\int \cos 2x\, dx$

$$= \frac{1}{2}x - \frac{1}{2}\frac{\sin 2x}{2} + c$$

$$= \frac{1}{2}x - \frac{1}{4}.\sin 2x + c$$

9. Evaluate $\int \cos^3 x\, dx$

Sol. We know that $\cos 3x = 4\cos^3 x - 3\cos x$

$$4\cos^3 x = \cos 3x + 3\cos x$$

$$\Rightarrow \cos^3 x = \frac{1}{4}[\cos 3x + 3\cos x]$$

$$\therefore \int \cos^3 x\, dx = \frac{1}{4}\int(\cos 3x + 3\cos x)dx$$

$$= \frac{1}{4}.\frac{1}{3}.(\sin 3x) + \frac{3}{4}.\sin x + c$$

$$= \frac{1}{12}\sin 3x + \frac{3}{4}\sin x + c$$

10. Evaluate $\int \cos^4 x dx$

Sol. $\int \cos^4 x dx = \int (\cos^2 x)^2 dx = \int \left(\frac{1+\cos 2x}{2}\right)^2 dx$

$$\left[\because \cos 2x = 2\cos^2 x - 1 \Rightarrow \cos^2 x = \frac{1+\cos 2x}{2} \right]$$

$$= \int \frac{(1+\cos^2 2x + 2\cos 2x)}{4} dx$$

$$= \frac{1}{4}\left[\int 1 dx + \int \cos^2 2x dx + 2\int \cos 2x dx\right]$$

$$= \frac{1}{4}\left[x + \int \left(\frac{1+\cos 4x}{2}\right) dx + \frac{2}{2}\sin 2x\right] + c \qquad \left(\because \cos^2 2x = \frac{1+\cos 4x}{2}\right)$$

$$= \frac{1}{4}\left[x + \frac{1}{2}x + \frac{1}{2}.\frac{1}{4}\sin 4x + \sin 2x\right] + c$$

$$= \frac{1}{4}\left[x + \frac{1}{2}x + \frac{1}{2}.\frac{1}{4}\sin 4x + \sin 2x\right] + c$$

$$= \frac{3}{8}x + \frac{1}{32}\sin 4x + \frac{1}{4}\sin 2x + c$$

11. Evaluate $\int \frac{\cos x}{2+3\sin x} dx$

Sol. Let 2 + 3 sin$x$ = t, differentiate w.r.t x on both sides we get

0 + 3 cos x dx = dt

$\Rightarrow$ cos$x$. dx = $\frac{dt}{3}$

$$\therefore \int \frac{\cos x}{2+3\sin x} dn = \int \frac{\frac{dt}{3}}{t} = \frac{1}{3}\int \frac{dt}{t} = \frac{1}{3} ln\,(t)$$

$$= \frac{1}{3}\ln|2+3\sin x| + c$$

$$= \frac{1}{3}\ln|2+3\sin x| + c$$

12. Evaluate $\int \frac{1}{1+e^{-x}} dx$

Sol. $\int \frac{1}{1+e^{-x}} dn = \int \frac{1}{1+\frac{1}{e^x}} dx = \int \frac{e^x}{e^x+1} dx = \int \frac{\frac{d}{dx}(e^x+1)}{e^x+1} = ln\ (e^x + 1) + c$

13. Evaluate $\int \frac{3\cos 3x - 2\sin 2x}{\cos 2x + \sin 3x} dx$

Sol. $\int \frac{3\cos 3x - 2\sin 2x}{\cos 2x + \sin 3x} dx$

Let $\cos 2x + \sin 3x = t$

$\Rightarrow (-2\sin 2x + 3\cos 3x)\, dx = dt$

$\therefore \int \frac{3\cos 3x - 2\sin 2x}{\cos 2x + \sin 3x} = \int \frac{dt}{t} = ln(t) + c$

$= ln(\cos 2x + \sin 3x) + c$

14. Evaluate $\int \frac{1-\tan x}{1+\tan x} dx$

Sol. $\int \frac{1-\frac{\sin x}{\cos x}}{1+\frac{\sin x}{\cos x}} dx = \int \frac{\cos x - \sin x}{\cos x + \sin x} dx$

Put, $\cos x + \sin x = t$

$= (-\sin x + \cos x)\, dx = dt$

$\therefore \int \frac{1-\tan x}{1+\tan x} = \int \frac{dt}{t} = \ln |t| + c$

$= \ln | \cos x + \sin x | + c$

15. Evaluate $\int \frac{1}{xlnx.(ln(lnx)} dx$

Sol. Consider $I = \int \frac{1}{x.lnx.(ln(lnx)} dx$

Put *ln*(*lnx*) = t $\Rightarrow \frac{1}{\ln x}.\frac{1}{x}.dx = dt$

$\therefore$ I = $\int \frac{1}{t} dt$ = *ln* | t | +c = *ln* (*ln* (*ln x*)) + c

16. Evaluate $\int \frac{1}{x(2+3lnx)} dx$

Sol: Let 2 +3 *ln x* = t

$$\therefore \Rightarrow \frac{3}{x} dx = dt \Rightarrow \frac{dx}{x} = \frac{dt}{3}$$

$$\therefore \int \frac{1}{x(2+3lnx)} dx = \int \frac{dt/3}{t} = \frac{1}{3} ln|t| + c$$

$$= \frac{1}{3}.ln|2+3lnx| + c$$

17. Evaluate (i) $\int \frac{1}{1+e^x} dx$ (ii) $\int e^x.\sin(e^x)dx$

Sol. $\int \frac{1}{1+e^x} dx = \int \frac{1}{e^x\left[\frac{1}{e^x}+1\right]} dx = \int \frac{e^{-x}}{e^{-x}+1} dx$

Put $e^{-x} + 1 = t \Rightarrow -e^{-x}.\ dx = dt \Rightarrow e^{-x}\ dx = -dt$

$$\therefore \int \frac{e^{-x}}{e^{-x}+1} dx = \int \frac{-dt}{t} = -\ln|t| + c$$

$$= -ln\ (1 + e^{-x}) + c$$

(or) $\int \frac{1}{1+e^x} dx = \int \frac{1+e^x-e^x}{1+e^x} dx$

$$= \int \left(1 - \frac{e^x}{1+e^x}\right) dx$$

$$= x - \int \frac{e^x}{1+e^x} dx$$

$$= x - ln\ |1+e^x| + c$$

(ii) Put $e^x = t \Rightarrow e^x\,dx = dt \Rightarrow \int e^x \sin(e^x)dx = \int \sin t\,dt$

$= -\cos t + c = -\cos(e^x) + c$

18. Evaluate $\int \frac{1}{e^x + e^{-x}}dx$

Sol. $\int \frac{1}{e^x + e^{-x}}dx = \int \frac{1}{e^x + \frac{1}{e^x}}dx = \int \frac{e^x}{(e^x)^2 + 1}dx$

Put $e^x = t \Rightarrow e^x\,dx = dt$

$\therefore \int \frac{e^x}{(e^x)^2 + 1} - \int \frac{dt}{t^2 + 1} = \tan^{-1}(t) + c = \tan^{-1}(e^x) + c$

19. Evaluate $\int \frac{2}{x(1 + (lnx))^2}dx$

Sol. Put $lnx = t \Rightarrow \frac{1}{x}\,dx = dt$

$\therefore \int \frac{2}{x\left((1 + (lnx)^2\right)}dx = \int \frac{2}{1 + t^2}dt$

$= 2.\tan^{-1}(t) + c$

$= 2\tan^{-1}(lnx) + c$

20. Evaluate $\int x^3.\sin(x^4)dx$

Sol. Let $x^4 = t \Rightarrow 4.x^3\,dx = dt$

$\therefore x^3\,dx = \frac{1}{4}dt$

$\int x^3.\sin(x^4)dx = \int \sin(x^4).x^3dx = \int (\sin t)(\frac{1}{4}dt)$

$= \frac{1}{4}\int \sin t\,dt = \frac{1}{4}.(-\cos t) + c$

$= -\frac{1}{4}.\cos(x^4) + c$

21. Evaluate (i) $x^3 . \sec^2 (x^4)$ dx (ii) $\cos^3 x. \sin x$ dx

Sol. (i) Put $x^4 = t$

$$\Rightarrow 4x^3 \, dx = dt \qquad \therefore x^3 \, dx = \frac{dt}{4}$$

$$\therefore \int x^3 . \sec^2(x^4) dx = \int \sec^2(t) . \left(\frac{dt}{4}\right) = \frac{1}{4} \int \sec^2 dt$$

$$= \frac{1}{4} . \tan t + c$$

$$= \frac{1}{4} . \tan(x^4) + c$$

(ii) $\int \cos^3 x . \sin x \, dx$

Put $\cos x = t$

$\Rightarrow -\sin x \, dx = dt \Rightarrow \sin x \, dx = -dt$

$\int t^3(-dt) = -\int t^3 dt$

$$= -\frac{t^4}{4} + c = \frac{-(\cos x)^4}{4} + c$$

22. Evaluate (i) $\int \sqrt{\sin x} \cos x \, dx$ (ii) $\int \left(1 - \frac{1}{x^2}\right) e^{x + 1/x} dx$

Sol. (i) $\int \sqrt{\sin x} \cos x \, dx$

Put $\sin x = t \Rightarrow \cos x \, dx = dt$

$$\therefore \int \sqrt{t} \, dt = \frac{t^{\frac{1}{2}+1}}{1/2 + 1} + c = \frac{2}{3} (\sin x)^{3/2} + c$$

(ii) $\int \left(1 - \frac{1}{x^2}\right) e^{x + 1/x} dx$

Put $x + 1/x = t \Rightarrow \left(1 - \frac{1}{x^2}\right) dx = dt$

$$\therefore \int \left(1 - \frac{1}{x^2}\right) . e^{(x + \frac{1}{x})} dx = \int e^{(x + \frac{1}{x}) . (1 - \frac{1}{x^2})} dx = \int e^t dt$$

$$= e^t + c$$

$$= e^{x + \frac{1}{x}} + c$$

23. Integrate the following

(i) $\frac{x^3}{\sqrt{1-x^8}}$ (ii) $\frac{x}{1+x^4}$ (iii) $\frac{x^8}{x^6+1}$

(iv) $\frac{2x^3}{1+x^8}$ (v) $\frac{x^5}{1+x^{12}}$

Sol. (i) $\int\frac{x^3}{\sqrt{1-x^8}}dx = \int\frac{x^3}{\sqrt{1-(x^4)^2}}dx$

Put $x^4 = t \Rightarrow 4x^3dx = dt \Rightarrow x^3dx = \frac{1}{4}dt$

$$\int\frac{x^3}{\sqrt{1-(x^4)^2}} = \frac{1}{4}\int\frac{dt}{\sqrt{1-t^2}} = \frac{1}{4}.\sin^{-1}(t) = \frac{1}{4}\sin^{-1}(x^4)$$

(ii) $\int\frac{x}{1+x^4}dx$

Put $x^2 = t \quad \Rightarrow \quad 2x\,dx = dt$

$\Rightarrow \quad x.dx = \frac{1}{2}dt$

$$\therefore \quad \int\frac{xdx}{1+x^4} = \int\frac{\frac{1}{2}dt}{1+t^2} = \frac{1}{2}\int\frac{dt}{1+t^2}$$

$$= \frac{1}{2}\tan^{-1}(t) + c$$

$$= \frac{1}{2}\tan^{-1}(x^2) + c$$

(iii) $\int\frac{x^8}{x^6+1}dx$

$$\int\frac{x^8}{x^6+1}dx = \int\frac{x^6.x^2}{1+x^6}dx = \int\frac{(x^3)^2x^2}{1+(x^3)^2}dx$$

Put $x^3 = t \Rightarrow \quad 3x^2\,dx = dt$

$$\therefore \quad \int\frac{(x^3)^2x^2dx}{1+(x^3)^2} = \frac{1}{3}\int\frac{t^2.dt}{1+t^2} = \frac{1}{3}\int\frac{t^2+1-1}{t^2+1}dt$$

$$= \frac{1}{3}\int\left(1-\frac{1}{t^2+1}\right)dt = \frac{1}{3}\left[t-\tan^{-1}t\right]+c$$

$$= \frac{1}{3}\left[x^3 - \tan^{-1}(x^3)\right] + c$$

(iv) $\int \frac{2x^3}{1+x^8} dx$

$$\int \frac{2x^3}{1+x^8} dx = \int \frac{2x^3}{1+(x^4)^2} dx$$

Put $x^4 = t$ $\Rightarrow 4x^3\ dx = dt$ $\Rightarrow 2x^3\ dx = \frac{dt}{2}$

$$\therefore \int \frac{2x^3 dx}{1+(x^4)^2} = \int \frac{\left(\frac{dt}{2}\right)}{1+t^2} = \frac{1}{2}\int \frac{dt}{1+t^2} = \frac{1}{2}\tan^{-1} t + c$$

$$= \frac{1}{2}\tan^{-1} x^4 + c$$

(v) $\int \frac{x^5}{1+x^{12}} dx$

$\int \frac{x^5}{1+(x^6)2} dx$ Put $x^6 = t$

$\Rightarrow 6x^5\ dx = dt$

$\Rightarrow x^5\ dx = \frac{dt}{6}$

$$\therefore \int \frac{\left(\frac{dt}{6}\right)}{1+t^2} = \frac{1}{6}\int \frac{dt}{1+t^2} = \frac{1}{6}\tan^{-1}(t)$$

$$= \frac{1}{6}\tan^{-1}(x^6) + c$$

24. Evaluate $\int \sec x\, dx$

Sol. $\int \frac{\sec x.(\sec x + \tan x)}{\sec x + \tan x} dx = \int \frac{\sec^2 x + \sec x \tan x}{\sec x + \tan x} dx$

$$= \int \frac{\frac{d}{dx}(\sec x + \tan x)}{(\sec x + \tan x)} dx = ln|\sec x + \tan x| + c$$

25. Evaluate $\int \frac{\cos\sqrt{x}}{\sqrt{x}}dx$

Sol. Put $\sqrt{x}$ = t $\Rightarrow \frac{1}{2\sqrt{x}}$ dx = dt $\Rightarrow \frac{dx}{\sqrt{x}}$ = 2dt

$$\therefore \int \frac{\cos\sqrt{x}}{\sqrt{x}}dx = \int \cos t.(2)dt = 2\int \cos t dt = 2\sin t + c$$

$$= 2\sin\sqrt{x} + c$$

26. Evaluate $\int \frac{e^x(1+x)}{\cos^2(xe^x)}dx$

Sol. Put $x.e^x$ = t $\Rightarrow$ ($x.e^x + e^x$) dx = dt

$\Rightarrow$ (1+x) e^x dx = dt

$$\therefore \int \frac{dt}{\cos^2 t} = \int \sec^2 t\, dt = \tan t + c = \tan(xe^x) + c$$

27. Evaluate $\int \frac{e^{\tan^{-1}x}}{1+x^2}dx$

Sol. Put $\tan^{-1}x$ = t $\Rightarrow \frac{1}{1+x^2}dx = dt$

$$\therefore \int \frac{e^{\tan^{-1}x}}{1+t^2} = \int e^t.dt = e^t + c$$

$$= e^{\tan^{-1}x} + c$$

28. Evaluate $\int \frac{x^2}{\sqrt{x+5}}dx$

Sol. Put x + 5 = t^2 $\Rightarrow$ dx = 2t dt ; also x = t^2 –5

$$\therefore \int \frac{x^2}{\sqrt{x+5}}dx = \int \frac{(t^2-5)^2 2tdt}{t} = 2\int (t^4 + 25 - 10t^2)dt$$

$$= 2\left(\frac{t5}{5} + 25t - \frac{10t^3}{3}\right) + c$$

when t = $\sqrt{x+5}$

29. Evaluate $\int \frac{x}{\sqrt{1-x}}dx$

Sol. Put $1-x = t^2 \Rightarrow 0 - dx = 2tdt$

$\Rightarrow dx = -2tdt$

also $x = 1-t^2$

$$\therefore \int \frac{xdx}{\sqrt{1-x}} = \int \frac{(1-t^2)(-2tdt)}{t} = -2\int(1-t^2)dt$$

$$= -2\left(t - \frac{t^3}{3}\right) + c = 2\left(\frac{t^3}{3} - t\right) + c \quad \text{where } t = \sqrt{1-x}$$

30. Evaluate $\int \frac{dx}{(x+5)\sqrt{x+4}}$

Sol. Put $x + 4 = t^2$

$\Rightarrow dx = 2tdt$; $x + 5 = x + 4 + 1 = t^2 + 1$

$$\therefore \int \frac{dx}{(x+5)\sqrt{x+4}} = \int \frac{2t\,dt}{(t^2+1)t} = 2\int \frac{dt}{1+t^2}$$

$$= 2\tan^{-1}t + c$$

$$= 2\tan^{-1}\sqrt{x+4} + c$$

31. Evaluate $\int \frac{\cos(x-a)}{\sin x}dx$

Sol. $\int \frac{\cos(x-a)}{\sin x}dx = \int \frac{\cos x.\cos a + \sin x \sin a}{\sin x}dx$

$$= \int(\cos a.\cot x + \sin a)dx$$

$= \cos a \,.\, ln\,|\sin x| + (\sin a).\, x + c$

32. $\int \frac{\sec x}{(\sec x + \tan x)^n}dx$

Sol. Put $\sec x + \tan x = t$

$\therefore (\sec x \tan x + \sec^2 x)\, dx = dt$

$\sec x(\tan x + \sec x)\, dx = dt$

$$\Rightarrow \sec x.dx = \frac{dt}{t}$$

$$\therefore \int \frac{\left(\frac{dt}{t}\right)}{t^n} = \int \frac{dt}{t^{n+1}} = \int t^{-(n+1)} dt$$

$$= \frac{t^{-(n+1)+1}}{-(n+1)+1} = \frac{t^{-n}}{n} + c$$

$$= -\frac{1}{n}\frac{1}{(\sec x + \tan x)^n} + c$$

33. Evaluate

(i) $\int x^2 . e^{x^3} \cos(e^{x^3}) dx$

(ii) $\int \frac{x^3 \sin(\tan^{-1} x^4)}{1+x^8} dx$

(iii) $\int \frac{e^{2x}+1}{e^{2x}-1} dx$

(iv) $\int \frac{1}{x^2} \cos\left(\frac{1}{x}\right) dx$

Sol. (i) $\int x^2 e^{x^3} \cos(e^{x^3}) dx$

Put $e^{x^3} = t \Rightarrow e^{x^3} . 3x^2 dx = dt$

$$\therefore e^{x^3} x^2 . dx = \frac{dt}{3}$$

$\therefore$ Our Integral becomes

$$\int \cos(t) . \frac{dt}{3} = \frac{1}{3}(\sin t) + c$$

$$= \frac{1}{3} \sin(e^{x^3}) + c$$

(ii) $\int \frac{x^3 \sin(\tan^{-1}(x^4))}{1+x^8} dx$

Put $\tan^{-1}(x^4) = t$

$$\Rightarrow \qquad \frac{1}{1+(x^4)^2}.(4x^3)dx = dt$$

$$\therefore \qquad \frac{x^3 dx}{1+x^8} = \frac{dt}{4}$$

$\therefore$ our integral becomes

$$\frac{1}{4}\int \sin t dt = -\frac{1}{4}\cos t + c$$

$$= -\frac{1}{4}\cos(\tan^{-1}(x^4)) + c$$

(iii) $\int \frac{e^{2x}+1}{e^{2x}-1} dx$

$$= \int \frac{e^x + e^{-x}}{e^x - e^{-x}} dx$$

($\therefore$ by taking e^x common from both numarator and denominator)

$$= \int \frac{\frac{d}{dx}(e^x - e^{-x})}{(e^x - e^{-x})} dx$$

$= ln\ (e^x - e^{-x}) + c$

(iv) $\int \frac{1}{x^2}\cos\left(\frac{1}{x}\right)dx$

Put $\frac{1}{x} = t \quad \Rightarrow \frac{-1}{x^2}\ dx = dt$

$$\therefore \quad \int \frac{1}{x^2}\cos\left(\frac{1}{x}\right)dx = -\int \cos t\, dt$$

$$= -\sin t + c$$

$$= -\sin\left(\frac{1}{x}\right) + c$$

34. Evaluate

(i) $\int \frac{\sin x \cos x}{4\cos^2 x + 8\sin^2 x} dx$ (ii) $\frac{\sin 2x}{1+\sin^4 x} dx$

(iii) $\int \frac{\tan x.\sec^2 x}{\sec^2 x + \tan^2 x} dx$ (iv) $\int \sqrt{1 + 2\tan x(\tan x + \sec x)} dx$

Sol. (i) $\int \frac{\sin x \cos x dx}{4(1-\sin^2 x) + 8\sin^2 x} = \int \frac{\sin x.\cos x dx}{4 + 4\sin^2 x} = \frac{1}{4}\int \frac{\sin x \cos x}{1+\sin^2 x} dx$

Put $\sin x = t \Rightarrow \cos x\, dx = dt$

$$= \frac{1}{4}\int \frac{tdt}{1+t^2} = \frac{1}{4}.\frac{1}{2}.\int \frac{2tdt}{1+t^2} = \frac{1}{8} ln(l + t^2) + c$$

$$= \frac{1}{8} ln(1 + \sin^2 x) + c$$

(ii) $\int \frac{\sin 2x}{1+\sin^4 x} dx$

$$= \int \frac{\sin 2x}{1 + (\sin^2 x)^2} dx$$

Put $\sin^2 x = t \Rightarrow 2 \sin x \cos x\, dx = dt \quad \Rightarrow \sin 2x\, dx = dt$

$$\Rightarrow \int \frac{\sin 2x}{1+(\sin^2 x)^2} \Rightarrow \int \frac{dt}{1+t^2}$$

$$= \tan^{-1}(t) + c = \tan^{-1}(\sin^2 x) + c$$

(iii) $\int \frac{\tan x.\sec^2 x}{\sec^2 x + \tan^2 x} dx = \int \frac{\tan x.\sec^2 x}{(1+\tan^2 x) + \tan^2 x} dx$

$$= \int \frac{\tan x \sec^2 x\, dx}{1 + 2\tan^2 x}$$

Put $\tan x = t \Rightarrow \sec^2 x\, dx = dt$

Integral becomes $\int \frac{t.dt}{1+2t^2} = \frac{1}{4}\int \frac{4tdt}{1+2t^2} = \frac{1}{4} ln(1 + 2t^2)$

$$= \frac{1}{4} ln(1 + 2\tan^2 x) + c$$

(iv) $\int \sqrt{\sec^2 x - \tan^2 x + 2\tan^2 x + 2\tan \sec}\, dx$

$$= \int \sqrt{\sec^2 x + \tan^2 x + 2\tan x \sec x}\, dx = \int (\sec x + \tan x) dx$$

$$ln\ |\sec x + \tan x\ | + ln\ |\ \sec x\ | + c$$

Integration of some Standard functions

1. $$\int \frac{dx}{x^2 + a^2} = \frac{1}{a}\tan^{-1}\left(\frac{x}{a}\right) + c$$

Proof : Let $x = a \tan \theta$

$\Rightarrow \quad dx = a \sec^2 \theta\, d\theta$

$$\therefore \quad \int \frac{dx}{x^2 + a^2} = \int \frac{a \sec^2 \theta\, d\theta}{a^2 \tan^2 \theta + a^2}$$

$$= \int \frac{a \sec^2 \theta\, d\theta}{a^2 \sec^2 \theta}$$

$$= \frac{1}{a}\int d\theta = \frac{1}{a}\theta$$

$$= \frac{1}{a}\tan^{-1}\left(\frac{x}{a}\right)$$

2. $$\int \frac{dx}{\sqrt{a^2 - x^2}} dx = \sin^{-1}\left(\frac{x}{a}\right) + c$$

Proof : Put $x = a \sin \theta \Rightarrow dx = a \cos \theta\, d\theta$

$$\therefore \quad \int \frac{1}{\sqrt{a - x^2}} dx = \int \frac{a \cos \theta d\theta}{\sqrt{a^2 - a^2 \sin^2 \theta}} = \int \frac{a \cos \theta d\theta}{a \cos \theta}$$

$$\int d\theta = \theta = \sin^{-1}\left(\frac{x}{a}\right) + c$$

$$\therefore \quad \int \frac{1}{\sqrt{a - x^2}} dx = \sin^{-1}\left(\frac{x}{a}\right) + c$$

Ex : 1. $\int \frac{dx}{x^2+9} = \int \frac{dx}{3^2+x^2} = \frac{1}{3}\tan^{-1}\left(\frac{x}{3}\right) + c$

2. $\int \frac{dn}{3x^2+7} = \int \frac{dn}{(\sqrt{3}x)^2+\left(\sqrt{7}\right)^2} = \frac{\frac{1}{\sqrt{7}}\tan^{-1}\left(\frac{\sqrt{3}x}{\sqrt{7}}\right)}{\sqrt{3}}$

$$= \frac{1}{\sqrt{21}}\tan^{-1}\left(\frac{\sqrt{3}x}{\sqrt{7}}\right) + c$$

3. $\int \frac{dn}{3+4x^2} = \int \frac{dn}{(\sqrt{3})^2+(2x)^2} = \frac{1}{\sqrt{3}}.\frac{\tan^{-1}\left(\frac{2x}{\sqrt{3}}\right)}{2}$

$$= \frac{1}{2\sqrt{3}}.\tan^{-1}\left(\frac{2x}{\sqrt{3}}\right) + c$$

4. $\int \frac{1}{\sqrt{25-x^2}}dx$

$$= \int \frac{1}{\sqrt{5^2-x^2}}dx = \sin^{-1}\left(\frac{x}{5}\right) + c$$

3. $\int \frac{1}{a^2-x^2}dx = \frac{1}{2a}\log\left|\frac{a+x}{a-x}\right| + c$

Proof : $\int \frac{1}{a^2-x^2}dx = \int \frac{1}{(\mathrm{a}+\mathrm{x})(\mathrm{a}-\mathrm{x})}dx = \frac{1}{2a}\int\left(\frac{1}{a+x}+\frac{1}{a-x}\right)dx$

$$= \frac{1}{2a}\left[\int \frac{1}{a+x}dx + \int \frac{1}{a-x}dx\right]$$

$$= \frac{1}{2a}\left[ln(a+x) - ln(a-x)\right]$$

$$= \frac{1}{2a}ln\left(\frac{\mathrm{a}+x}{\mathrm{a}-x}\right) + c$$

Ex : 1. $\int \frac{1}{25-x^2}dx = \int \frac{1}{(5)^2-x^2}dx = \frac{1}{2.5}\, ln\left|\frac{5+x}{5-x}\right| + c$

2. $\int \frac{1}{1-25x^2} = \int \frac{1}{1-(5x)^2}dx = \frac{1}{2.1}\frac{ln\left|\frac{1+5x}{1-5x}\right|}{5}$

$\frac{1}{10}\, ln\left|\frac{1+5x}{1-5x}\right| + c$

4. $\int \frac{1}{x^2-a^2}dx = \frac{1}{2a}\ln\left|\frac{x-a}{x+a}\right| + c$

Proof : $\int \frac{1}{x^2-a^2}dx = \int \frac{1}{(x-a)(x+a)} = \frac{1}{2a}\int \frac{1}{x-a} - \frac{1}{x+a}$

$$= \frac{1}{2a}\left[\int \frac{1}{x-a}dx - \int \frac{1}{x+a}dx\right] = \frac{1}{2a}\, ln\left|\frac{x-a}{x+a}\right| + c$$

Ex : 1. $\int \frac{1}{x^2-9}dx = \int \frac{1}{x^2-(3)^2} = \frac{1}{2.3}\, ln\left|\frac{x-3}{x+3}\right| + c$

2. $\int \frac{1}{4x^2-25}dx = \int \frac{1}{(2x)^2-(5)^2} = \frac{1}{2}.\frac{1}{2.5}\, ln\left|\frac{2x-5}{2x+5}\right|$

$$= \frac{1}{20}\ln\left|\frac{2x-5}{2x+5}\right| + c$$

5. $\int \frac{1}{\sqrt{a^2+x^2}}dx = \sinh^{-1}\left(\frac{x}{a}\right) + c$

Proof : $x = a\, sinh\theta \Rightarrow \mathrm{dx} = \mathrm{a \cos h\, \theta\, d\theta}$

$$= \int \frac{a\cosh\theta d\theta}{\sqrt{a^2+a^2\sinh^2\theta}} = \int \frac{a\cosh\theta}{a\cosh\theta}d\theta = \int 1 d\theta = \theta \ = \sinh^{-1}\left(\frac{x}{a}\right) + c$$

Ex : 1. $\int \frac{1}{\sqrt{9+x^2}}dx = \sinh^{-1}\left(x/3\right) + c$

2. $\int \frac{1}{\sqrt{16+2x^2}} = \int \frac{1}{\sqrt{4^2+\left(\sqrt{2x}\right)^2}} = \frac{1}{\sqrt{2}}.\sinh^{-1}\left(\frac{\sqrt{2x}}{4}\right) + c$

6. $\int \frac{1}{\sqrt{x^2-a^2}}\,dx = \cosh^{-1}\left(\frac{x}{a}\right)+c$

Put $x = a\cosh\theta \Rightarrow dx = a\sinh\theta\, d\theta$

$$\therefore \int \frac{1}{\sqrt{x^2-a^2}}\,dx = \int \frac{a\sinh\theta\, d\theta}{\sqrt{a^2\cosh^2\theta - a^2}} = \int \frac{\sinh\theta}{\sinh\theta}\,d\theta$$

$$= \int 1 d\theta$$

$$= \theta = \cosh^{-1}\left(\frac{x}{a}\right)+c$$

Ex : 1. $\int \frac{1}{\sqrt{x^2-9}}\,dx = \cosh^{-1}\left(\frac{x}{3}\right)+c$

2. $\int \frac{1}{\sqrt{3x^2-4}}\,dx = \int \frac{1}{\sqrt{\left(\sqrt{3}x\right)^2-2^2}} = \frac{1}{\sqrt{3}}.\cosh^{-1}\left(\frac{\sqrt{3}x}{2}\right)+c$

7. $\int \sqrt{a^2-x^2}\,dx = \frac{x}{2}\sqrt{a^2-x^2}+\frac{a^2}{2}\sin^{-1}\left(\frac{x}{a}\right)+c$

8. $\int \sqrt{a^2+x^2}\,dx = \frac{x}{2}\sqrt{a^2-x^2}+\frac{a^2}{2}\sinh^{-1}\left(\frac{x}{a}\right)+c$

9. $\int \sqrt{x^2-a^2}\,dx = \frac{x}{2}\sqrt{x^2-a^2}-\frac{a^2}{2}\cosh^{-1}\left(\frac{x}{a}\right)+c$

Exercise 23.2

(Problems on Integration by Substitution)

Evaluate the following integrals.

1. (i) $\int (2x+3)^{11}\,dx$ (ii) $\frac{1}{\sqrt{7x+1}}$

(iii) $\frac{1}{x+5}$ (iv) $\sqrt{3x+4}$

2. (i) $\int e^{5x-4}$ (ii) $\int e^{\frac{x}{3}}$ (iii) $\int 7^{2x+3}$

3. $\int \frac{1}{\sqrt{x+3}+\sqrt{x+4}}$

4. (i) $\int \frac{3x^2}{1+x^3}dn$ (ii) $\int \frac{2x+6}{x^2+6x+11}dn$ (iii) $\int \frac{1+\cos x}{x+\sin x}dn$

5. (i) $\int \frac{5x^{n-1}}{12x^n+c}$ (ii) $\int \frac{x+5}{x^2+1}dn$

6. (i) $\int \frac{3x+7}{3x^2+14x-5}dn$ (ii) $\int \sec x \operatorname{cosec} x\, dn$ (iii) $\int \operatorname{cosec} x\, dn$

7. (i) $\int x.\sin(x^2)dx$ (ii) $\int x^2.\cos(x^3)\, dx$

(iii) $\int x^3.\tan(x^4)\, dx$ (iv) $\int x^4.\sec^2(x^5)dx$

8. $\int \frac{1}{\sqrt{x}}.\sec^2(\sqrt{x})\, dx$

9. $\int \frac{e^x}{\sqrt{e^x+1}}dx$

10. (i) $\int \sqrt[4]{\sin x}\cos x\, dx$ (ii) $\frac{\cos(lnx)}{x}dx$

11. $\int \tan^4 x.\sec^2 x\, dx$

12. $\int \frac{1}{\sqrt{\sin^{-1}x}.\sqrt{1-x^2}}dx$

13. $\int \frac{e^{\sin^{-1}x}}{\sqrt{1-x^2}}dx$

14. (i) $\int \frac{1-\tan^2 x}{1+\tan^2 x}dx$ (ii) $\int \frac{\sin(x+a)}{\sin x}dx$

15. $\int \frac{1}{a\sin x+b\cos x}dx$

16. (i) $\int \sin^3 x\, dx$ (ii) $\int \sin^4 x\, dx$

17. (i) $\int \frac{4x^3}{1+x^8} dx$ (ii) $\int \frac{3.x^8}{1+x^{18}} dx$ (iii) $\int \frac{4.x^5}{1+x^{12}} dx$

(iv) $\int \frac{x^2}{\sqrt{x+3}} dx$ (v) $\int \frac{x^3}{\sqrt{x+3}} dx$

18. $\int \frac{1}{(1+e^{-x})(1+e^{+x})} dx$

19. $\int \frac{1+\cos x}{(x+\sin x)^3} dx$

20. (i) $\int \frac{4x+3}{\sqrt{2x^2+3x+7}} dx$ (ii) $\int \frac{\operatorname{cosec}^2 x}{\sqrt{\cot x}} dx$

21. (i) $\int \frac{x^2+\tan^{-1}(x^3)}{1+x^6} dx$ (ii) $\int \frac{\cos(\tan^{-1} x)}{1+x^2} dx$

22. $\int \frac{(1+x)e^x}{\cos^2(xe^x)} dx$

23. $\int \tan^4 x dx$

24. $\int \frac{\sin 2x}{3\cos^2 x + 4\sin^2 x} dx$

25. $\int \frac{\sec \mathrm{x}}{(\sec \mathrm{x} + \tan x)^{10}} dx$

Answers

1. (i) $\frac{1}{2}.\frac{(2x+3)^{12}}{12}+c$ (ii) $\frac{2}{7}\sqrt{7x+1}+c$

(iii) log|x+5| +c (iv) $\frac{2}{9}(3x+4)^{\frac{3}{2}}+c$

2. (i) $\frac{e^{5x-4}}{5}+c$ (ii) $3e^{\frac{x}{3}}+c$ (iii) $\frac{1}{2}\frac{7^{2x+3}}{\log 7}+c$

3. $\frac{2}{3}(x+4)^{\frac{3}{2}} - \frac{2}{3}(x+3)^{\frac{3}{2}} + c$

4. (i) $\log|1+x^3| + c$ (ii) $\log(x^2 + 6x + 11) + c$ (iii) $\log(x + \sin x) + c$

5. (i) $\frac{5}{12n} \ln(12x^n + c) + k$ (ii) $\frac{1}{2} \log(x^2+1) + 5\tan^{-1}x + c$

6. (i) $\frac{1}{2} \ln(3x^2 + 14x - 5)$ (ii) $\log(\tan x) + c$ (iii) $\log|\tan x/2| + c$

7. (i) $-\frac{1}{2}\cos^2 x + c$ (ii) $\frac{1}{3}\sin(x^3) + c$

(iii) $\frac{1}{4} \ln|\sec x^4| + c$ (iv) $\frac{1}{5}\tan(x^5) + c$

8. $2\tan\sqrt{x} + c$

9. $2\sqrt{e^x + 1} + c$

10. (i) $\frac{4}{5}(\sin x)^{\frac{5}{4}} + c$ (ii) $\sin(\log x) + c$

11. $\frac{\tan^5 x}{5} + c$

12. $2\sqrt{\sin^{-1} x} + c$

13. $e^{\sin^{-1}x} + c$

14. (i) $\frac{\sin 2x}{2} + c$ (ii) $x\cos a + \log(\sin x)\sin a + c$

15. $\left[\frac{1}{\sqrt{a^2+b^2}} \log\left|\sec(x-\alpha) + \tan(x-\alpha)\right|\right]$ where $\alpha = \tan^{-1}\frac{a}{b}$

16. (i) $\frac{1}{4}\left[-3\cos x + \frac{\cos 3x}{3}\right]$ (ii) $\frac{3x}{8} + \frac{\sin 4x}{32} - \frac{\sin 2x}{4} + c$

17. (i) $\tan^{-1} x^4 + c$ (ii) $\frac{1}{3}\tan^{-1} x^9 + c$

(iii) $\frac{2}{3}\tan^{-1}(x^6) + c$

(iv) $2\left[\frac{\left(\sqrt{x+1}\right)^5}{5}+9\sqrt{x+3}-2\left(\sqrt{x+3}\right)^3+c\right]$

(v) $2\left[\frac{t^7}{7}-27t-\frac{9t^5}{5}+9t^3\right]+c$ where t = $\sqrt{x+1}$

18. $\frac{-1}{1+e^x}+c$

19. $-\frac{1}{2}\frac{1}{(x+\sin x)^2}+c$

20. (i) $2\sqrt{2x^2+3x+7}$ (ii) $2\sqrt{\cot x}+c$

21. (i) $\frac{1}{3}\frac{\left(\tan^{-1}x^3\right)^2}{2}+c$ (ii) $\sin(\tan^{-1}x)+c$

22. $\tan(x.e^x)+c$

23. $\frac{\tan^3 x}{3}-\tan x+x+c$

24. $\log\left|3+\sin^2 x\right|+c$

25. $\frac{1}{-12[\sec x+\tan x]^{12}}+c$

23.5 Evaluation of Integrals of Some Special type of Functions

Type 1 : Evaluation of integrals of the form

$$\int\frac{1}{ax^2+6x+c}dx$$

Working rule

(i) Reduce ax^2+bx+c into

$a\left[(x+\alpha)^2\pm\beta^2\right]$ get the form

$$\int\left[\frac{1}{(x+\alpha)^2\pm\beta^2}\right]dx$$

(iii) take $x+\alpha=t$

(iv) Convert into $\frac{1}{a}\int\frac{1}{t^2\pm\beta^2}dt$

Ex : 1. Evaluate $\int \frac{dx}{x^2+4x+5}$

Sol. $\int \frac{dx}{(x^2+4x+4)+1} = \int \frac{dx}{(x+2)^2+1^2}$

Put $x + 2 = t \Rightarrow dx = dt$

$$\therefore \int \frac{dx}{(x+2)^2+1^2} = \int \frac{dt}{t^2+1} = \frac{1}{1}.\tan^{-1}(t)$$

$$= \tan^{-1}(x+2) + c$$

2. Evaluate $\int \frac{1}{3x^2+x+1} dx$

Sol. $\int \frac{1}{3x^2+x+1} dx = \int \frac{1}{3\left[x^2+\frac{x}{3}+\frac{1}{3}\right]} dx$

$$= \frac{1}{3}\int \frac{1}{x^2+2.\frac{1}{6}.x+\frac{1}{36}+\frac{1}{3}-\frac{1}{36}} dx$$

$$= \frac{1}{3}\int \frac{1}{(x+\frac{1}{6})^2+\frac{11}{36}} dx = \frac{1}{3}\int \frac{1}{(x+\frac{1}{6})^2+(\frac{\sqrt{11}}{6})^2}$$

$$= \frac{1}{3}.\frac{1}{(\frac{\sqrt{11}}{6})}.\tan^{-1}\left(\frac{x+\frac{1}{6}}{\frac{\sqrt{11}}{6}}\right)$$

$$= \frac{2}{\sqrt{11}}\tan^{-1}\left(\frac{6x+1}{\sqrt{11}}\right)+c$$

Type 2

Evaluation of integrals of the form

(i) $\int \frac{dx}{\sqrt{ax^2+bx+c}}$ (ii) $\int \sqrt{ax^2+bx+c}$

Working rule :

Convert $ax^2 + bx + c$ into

$a[(x+\alpha)^2 \pm \beta^2]$ [if (a > 0)] or $(-a)\,[\beta^2 - (x+\alpha)^2]$ [if a < 0) and

then integrate

Ex. 1. Evaluate $\int \frac{dx}{\sqrt{x^2+2x+17}}$

$x^2 + 2x + 17 = (x^2 + 2x + 1) + 16 = (x + 1)^2 + 4^2$

$$\therefore \int \frac{dx}{\sqrt{x^2+2x+17}} = \int \frac{dx}{\sqrt{(x+1)^2+4^2}} = \frac{1}{4}.\ \sinh^{-1}\left(\frac{x+1}{4}\right)+c$$

2. Evaluate $\int \frac{dx}{\sqrt{1+x-x^2}}$

Sol. $$\int \frac{dx}{\sqrt{1+x-x^2}} - \int \frac{dx}{\sqrt{-(x^2-x+1)}}$$

$$= \int \frac{dx}{\sqrt{-[x^2 - 2.\frac{1}{2}x + \frac{1}{4} - \frac{1}{4} - 1}}$$

$$= \int \frac{dx}{\sqrt{-[(x-\frac{1}{2})^2 - \frac{5}{4}]}}$$

$$= \int \frac{dx}{\sqrt{\left(\frac{5}{2}\right)^2 - (x-\frac{1}{2})^2}}$$

$$= \sin^{-1}\left(\frac{x-\frac{1}{2}}{\sqrt{\frac{5}{2}}}\right)+c$$

$$= \sin^{-1}\left(\frac{2x-1}{\sqrt{5}}\right)+c \qquad \left[\because \int \frac{1}{\sqrt{a^2-x^2}} = \sin^{-1}(\frac{x}{a})+c\right]$$

2. Evaluate $\int \sqrt{1+3x-x^2}\,dx$

Sol. $\int \sqrt{1+3x-x^2}\,dx$

$$= \int \sqrt{-(x^2-3x-1)}\,dx = \int \sqrt{-\left(x^2-2.\frac{3}{2}x+\frac{9}{4}-\frac{9}{4}-1\right)}\,dx$$

$$= \int \sqrt{\left[-(x-\frac{3}{2})^2-(\frac{\sqrt{13}}{2})^2\right]}\,dx = \int \sqrt{(\frac{\sqrt{13}}{2})^2-(x-\frac{3}{2})^2}\,dx$$

$$\therefore \int \sqrt{(\frac{\sqrt{13}}{2})^2-\left(x-\frac{3}{2}\right)^2}\,dx$$

$$= \frac{x-\frac{3}{2}}{2}\sqrt{(\frac{\sqrt{13}}{2})^2-(x-\frac{3}{2})^2}+\frac{(\frac{13}{4})}{2}.\sin^{-1}\left(\frac{x-\frac{3}{2}}{\frac{\sqrt{13}}{2}}\right)+c$$

$$= \frac{2x-3}{4}\sqrt{(\frac{\sqrt{13}}{2})^2-(x-\frac{3}{2})^2}+\frac{13}{8}\sin^{-1}\left(\frac{2x-3}{\sqrt{13}}\right)+c$$

$$\left[\because \sqrt{a^2-x^2}\,dn = \frac{x}{2}\sqrt{a^2-x^2}+\frac{a^2}{2}\sin^{-1}\left(\frac{x}{a}\right)+c\right]$$

Type 3

To evaluate the integrals of the form

(i) $\int \frac{px+q}{ax^2+bx+c}\,dx$

(ii) $\int (px+q)\sqrt{ax^2+bx+c}\,dx$

(iii) $\int \frac{px+q}{\sqrt{ax^2+bx+c}}$

Working rule

(i) Convert $px + q$ into the form of

$$A\frac{d}{dx}(ax^2 + bx + c) + B \qquad \text{i.e., take}$$

$$px + q = A\frac{d}{dx}(ax^2 + bx + c) + B$$

(ii) find A, B by comparing like coefficients

(iii) convert the above integral into Type (1) or Type (2)

Ex : Evaluate $\int \frac{2x+5}{x^2-2x+10}dx$

Sol. $\int \frac{2x+5}{x^2-2x+10}dx$

take $2x + 5 = A\left(\frac{d}{dx}(x^2-2x+10)\right) + B$

$\therefore 2x + 5 = A(2x - 2) + B$

$\therefore 2 = 2A$ (bycomparing x coefficient)

$\Rightarrow A = 1$

also $5 = -2A + B$ (by comparing constant term)

$\therefore 5 = -2 + B$

$\therefore B = 7$

$$\therefore \int \frac{2x+5}{x^2-2x+10}dx = \int \frac{1(2x-2)+7}{x^2-2x=10}dx$$

$$= \int \frac{2x-2}{x^2-2x+10}dx + \int \frac{7}{x^2-2x+10}dx \qquad \left(\because \int \frac{f'(x)}{f(x)} = ln\, f(x)\right)$$

$$= \ln(x^2-2x+10) + 7\int \frac{1}{(x-1)^2+9}dx$$

$$= ln\,(x^2 - 2x + 10) + 7.\,\frac{1}{3}\,.\,\tan^{-1}\left(\frac{x-1}{3}\right) + c$$

2. Evaluate $\int \frac{2x+5}{\sqrt{x^2-2x+10}}\,dx$

$$= \int \frac{(2x-2)+7}{\sqrt{x^2-2x+10}}\,dx$$

$$= \int \frac{2x-2}{\sqrt{x^2-2x+10}} + 7\int \frac{1}{\sqrt{x^2-2x+10}}\,dx$$

$$= 2\sqrt{x^2-2x+10} + 7\int \frac{1}{\sqrt{(x-1)^2+9}} + c$$

$$\left(\because \int \frac{f'(x)}{\sqrt{f(x)}}\,dx = 2\sqrt{f(x)} + c\right)$$

$$= 2\sqrt{x^2-2x+10} + 7\sin x^{-1}\left(\frac{x-1}{9}\right) + c$$

3. Evaluate $\int (2x+5)\sqrt{x^2-2x+10}\,dx$

Sol. $\int (2x+5)\sqrt{x^2-2x+10}$

$$= \int (2x-2+7)\sqrt{x^2-2x+10}$$

$$= \int (2x-2)\sqrt{x^2-2x+10} + 7\int \sqrt{x^2-2x+10}\,dx$$

$$= \frac{(x^2-2x+10)^{\frac{3}{2}}}{\frac{3}{2}} + 7\int \sqrt{(x-1)^2+9}$$

$$\left(\because \int \sqrt{f(x)}.f'(x)dx = \frac{f(x)^{\frac{3}{2}}}{\frac{3}{2}} + c\right)$$

$$= \frac{2}{3}(x^2-2x+10)^{\frac{3}{2}} + 7\left[\frac{x-1}{2}\sqrt{(x-1)^2+9} + \frac{9}{2}\sinh^{-1}\left(\frac{x-1}{3}\right)\right] + c$$

$$\left(\because \int\sqrt{a^2+x^2} = \frac{x}{2}\sqrt{a^2+x^2}+\frac{a^2}{2}\sin^{-1}h\frac{x}{a}\right)$$

$$=\frac{2}{3}(x^2-2x+10)^{\frac{3}{2}}+7\left[\frac{x-1}{2}\sqrt{x^2-2x+10}+\frac{9}{2}\sinh^{-1}\left(\frac{x-1}{3}\right)\right]+c$$

Type 4

To evaluate integral of the form

$$\int\frac{dx}{(px+q)\sqrt{ax+b}},\quad \int\frac{px+q}{\sqrt{ax+b}}\,dx \quad \text{and}$$

$$\int(px+q)\sqrt{ax+b}$$

Working rule : Take $ax + b = t^2$

Ex: $\displaystyle\int\frac{dx}{(x+5)\sqrt{x+4}}$

Sol. Put $x+4=t^2 \Rightarrow x+5=t^2+1$

$dx = 2t\,dt$

$$\int\frac{2t\,dt}{(t^2+1).t} = 2\int\frac{dt}{t^2+1}$$

$$=2\tan^{-1}t = 2\tan^{-1}(\sqrt{x+4})+c$$

Type 5

To evaluate integral of the form

(i) $\displaystyle\int\frac{1}{a+b\sin x}dx$ (ii) $\displaystyle\int\frac{1}{a\cos x+b}dx$

(iii) $\displaystyle\int\frac{1}{a+b\sin x+c\cos x}dx$

Working rule : (i) Take $\tan\frac{x}{2}=t$

(ii) convert

$$\sin x = \frac{2t}{1+t^2}$$

$$\cos x = \frac{1-t^2}{1+t^2}$$

$$dx = \frac{2dt}{1+t^2}$$

and find the integration.

Ex : Evaluate $\int \frac{dx}{3\cos x + 4\sin x + 6}$

Sol. Put tan $x/2$ = t $\Rightarrow$ $\sin x = \frac{2t}{1+t^2}$, $\cos x = \frac{1-t^2}{1+t^2}$

$$dx = \frac{2dt}{1+t^2}$$

$$\therefore \int \frac{dx}{3\cos x + 4\sin x + 6} = \int \frac{\frac{2}{1+t^2}dt}{3\left(\frac{1-t^2}{1+t}\right)+4\left(\frac{2t}{1+t^2}\right)+6}$$

$$= \int \frac{2}{3(1-t^2)+4(2t)+6(1+t^2)}dt$$

$$= \int \frac{2}{3-3t^2+8t+6+6t^2} = \int \frac{2}{9+8t+3t^2}$$

$$= 2\int \frac{dt}{3t^2+8t+9} = \frac{2}{3}\int \frac{dt}{t^2+\frac{8}{3}.t+\frac{9}{3}}$$

$$= \frac{2}{3}\int \frac{dt}{t^2+2.\frac{4}{3}.t+\frac{16}{9}+\frac{9}{3}-\frac{16}{9}}$$

$$= \frac{2}{3}\int \frac{dt}{(t+\frac{4}{3})^2+\frac{11}{9}}$$

$$=\frac{2}{3}\int\frac{dt}{\left(t+\frac{4}{3}\right)^2+\left(\frac{\sqrt{11}}{3}\right)^2}$$

$$=\frac{2}{3}\cdot\frac{1}{\left(\frac{\sqrt{11}}{3}\right)}.\tan^{-1}\left(\frac{t+\frac{4}{3}}{\frac{\sqrt{11}}{3}}\right)+c$$

$$=\frac{2}{\sqrt{11}}\tan^{-1}\left(\frac{3t+4}{\sqrt{11}}\right)+c$$

$$=\frac{2}{\sqrt{11}}\tan^{-1}\left(\frac{3\tan\frac{x}{2}+4}{\sqrt{11}}\right)+c$$

Type 6

Evaluation of integrals of type

$$\int\frac{a\cos x+b\sin x}{c\cos x+d\sin x}\,dx$$

Working rule

take Nr = A $\frac{d}{dx}$ (Dr) + B(Dr)

where Nr → Numerator of above function and

Dr → Denominator of above function i.e., of $\left(\frac{a\cos x+b\sin x}{c\cos x+d\sin x}\right)$

Ex. Evaluate $\int\frac{\cos x+2\sin x}{2\cos x+3\sin x}\,dx$

Sol. Take Nr = A $\frac{d}{dx}$ (Dr) + B. (Dr)

$\therefore$ cos x + 2sin x = A(–2sin x + 3cos x) + B(2cos x + 3sin x)

Comparing the coffecients of cos x and sin x we get

1 = 3A + 2B

2 = –2A + 3B solving we get

$$A = -\frac{1}{13}, \quad B = \frac{8}{13}$$

$$\therefore \int \frac{\cos x + 2\sin x}{2\cos x + 3\sin x} dx = \int \frac{\frac{-1}{13} . \frac{d}{dx}(Dr)}{Dr} + \int \frac{8}{13} . \frac{(Dr)}{Dr} dx$$

$$= -\frac{1}{13} . ln\,(Dr) + \frac{8}{13} . x + c$$

$$= -\frac{1}{13} . ln\,(2\cos x + 3\sin x) + \frac{8}{13} . x + c$$

Exercise - 23.3

1. Evaluate $\int \frac{dx}{x^2 + x + 1}$

2. Evaluate $\int \frac{dx}{x^2 + 6x + 10}$

3. Evaluate $\int \frac{dx}{5 - 2x^2 + 4x}$

4. Evaluate $\int \frac{dn}{\sqrt{5x - 6 - x^2}}$

5. Evaluate $\int \frac{1}{\sqrt{x^2 + 2x + 10}} dx$

6. Evaluate $\int \frac{1}{\sqrt{1 + x - x^2}} dx$

7. Evaluate $\int \frac{2x-2}{2x^2+3x-4}\,dx$

8. Evaluate $\int \frac{x+4}{6x-7-x^2}\,dx$

9. Evaluate $\int \frac{x+1}{\sqrt{x^2-x+1}}\,dx$

10. Evaluate $\int \frac{2x-1}{\sqrt{1-5x-6x^2}}\,dx$

11. Evaluate $\int \sqrt{\frac{5-x}{3+x}}\,dx$

12. Evaluate $\int (3x-2)\sqrt{2x^2-x+1}\,dx$

13. Evaluate $\int \frac{1}{(x+1)\sqrt{3+2x-x^2}}\,dx$

14. Evaluate (i) $\int \frac{2x+3}{\sqrt{4x+3}}$ (ii) $\int (2x+3)\sqrt{2-3x}\,dx$

(iii) $\int \frac{1}{(x+2)\sqrt{x+1}}\,dx$

15. Evaluate $\int \frac{1}{5+4\cos x}\,dx$

16. Evaluate $\int \frac{1}{\cos x+\sin x}\,dx$

17. Evaluate $\int \frac{1}{1+\sin x+\cos x}\,dx$

18. Evaluate $\int \frac{1}{4\cos x+3\sin x}\,dx$

19. Evaluate $\int \frac{3\cos x+2\sin x}{4\cos x+3\sin x}\,dx$

20. Evaluate $\int \frac{2\cos x + 3\sin x}{4\cos x + 5\sin x} dx$

21. Evaluate $\int \frac{1}{1+\tan x} dx$

22. Evaluate $\int \frac{1}{4\sin^2 x + 9\cos^2 x} dx$

Answers

1. $\frac{2}{\sqrt{3}} \tan^{-1}\left(\frac{2x+1}{\sqrt{3}}\right) + c$

2. $\tan^{-1}(x+3) + c$

3. $\frac{1}{2\sqrt{7}} \log\left|\frac{\sqrt{7}+\sqrt{2x}-\sqrt{2}}{\sqrt{7}-\sqrt{2x}+\sqrt{2}}\right| + c$

4. $\sin^{-1}(2x-5) + c$

5. $\sinh^{-1}\left(\frac{x+1}{3}\right) + c$

6. $\sin^{-1}\left(\frac{2x-1}{\sqrt{5}}\right) + c$

7. $\frac{5}{4} \log\left|2x^2+3x-4\right| - \frac{23}{2\sqrt{41}} \log\left|\frac{4x+3-\sqrt{41}}{4x+3+\sqrt{41}}\right| + c$

8. $-\frac{1}{2}\log\left|6x-7-x^2\right| - \frac{7}{2\sqrt{2}} \log\left|\frac{x-3-\sqrt{2}}{x-3+\sqrt{2}}\right| + c$

9. $\sqrt{x^2-x+1} + \frac{3}{2}\sinh^{-1}\frac{2x-1}{\sqrt{3}} + c$

10. $\frac{-1}{3}\sqrt{1-5x-6x^2} \frac{-11}{6\sqrt{6}} \sin^{-1}\left(\frac{12x+5}{7}\right) + c$

11. $\sqrt{15+2x-x^2} + 4\sin^{-1}\left(\frac{x-1}{4}\right) + c$

[**Hint:** Rationalize numerator}

12. $\frac{1}{2}(2x^2-3x+1)^{\frac{3}{2}}$

$$-\frac{5\sqrt{2}}{4}\left[\frac{x-\frac{1}{4}}{2}\sqrt{(x-\frac{1}{4})^2+\frac{7}{16}}+\frac{7}{32}\log\left(x-\frac{1}{4}\right)+\left[\sqrt{(x-\frac{1}{4})^2+\frac{7}{16}}\right]\right]$$

13. $\frac{-1}{2}\sqrt{\frac{3-x}{1+x}}+c$

(Hint : take $x+1=\frac{1}{t}$)

14. (i) $\frac{1}{12}(4x+3)^{\frac{3}{2}}+\frac{3}{4}\sqrt{4x+3}+c$

(ii) $\frac{-1}{135}(2-3x)^{\frac{3}{2}}\ (36x+106)+c$

(iii) $2\tan^{-1}(\sqrt{x+1})+c$

15. $\frac{2}{3}\tan^{-1}\left(\frac{1}{3}\tan\frac{x}{2}\right)+c$

16. $\frac{1}{\sqrt{2}}\log\left|\frac{\sqrt{2}+\tan\frac{x}{2}-1}{\sqrt{2}-\tan\frac{x}{2}+1}\right|+c$

17. $\log\left|1+\tan\frac{x}{2}\right|+c$

18. $\frac{1}{5}\log\left|\frac{1+2\tan\frac{x}{2}}{4-2\tan\frac{x}{2}}\right|+c$

19. $\frac{1}{25}\log|4\cos x+3\sin x|+\frac{18}{25}x+c$

20. $\frac{-2}{41}\log|4\cos x+5\sin x|+\frac{23}{41}x+c$

21. $\frac{1}{2}\log|\cos x+\sin x|+\frac{1}{2}x+c$

[Hint : $\int\frac{1}{1+\frac{\sin x}{\cos x}}dx=\int\frac{\cos x}{\cos x+\sin x}dx$]

22. $\frac{1}{6}\tan^{-1}(\frac{2}{3}\tan x)+c$

[Hint : Multiply Nr and Dr by $\sec^2 x$]

23.6 Integration of Rational Functions using Partial Fractions

Working rule : Resolve the given rational function in to partial fractions. (using the methods in partial fraction chapter) and integrate the function.

Solved Examples

1. Evaluate $\int\frac{1}{(2x-3)(3x-2)}dx$

Sol. Consider $\frac{1}{(2x-3)(3x-2)}=\frac{A}{(2x-3)}+\frac{B}{(3x-2)}$

$$\frac{1}{(2x-3)(3x-2)}=\frac{A(3x-2)+B(2x-3)}{(2x+3)(3x-2)}$$

$\therefore$ $1 = A(3x-2) + B(2x-3)$

Put $x=\frac{2}{3}$ $\Rightarrow 1=B\left(\frac{4}{3}-3\right)=B(-\frac{5}{3})\Rightarrow B=-\frac{3}{5}$

Put $x=\frac{3}{2}$ $\Rightarrow 1=A\left(\frac{9}{2}-2\right)=A\frac{5}{2}\Rightarrow A=\frac{2}{5}$

$$\therefore \int\frac{1}{(2x+3)(3x-2)}dx=\int\frac{\frac{2}{5}}{2x+3}dx+\int\frac{-\frac{3}{5}}{3x-2}dx$$

$$= \frac{1}{5} ln|2x+3| - \frac{1}{5} ln|3x-2| + c$$

$$= \frac{1}{5} ln\left|\frac{2x+3}{3x-2}\right| + c$$

2. Evaluate $\int \frac{1}{(x-a)(x-b)(x-c)} dx$

Consider $\frac{1}{(x-a)(x-b)(x-c)} = \frac{A}{x-a} + \frac{B}{x-b} + \frac{C}{x-c}$

$\therefore$ 1 = A(x – b) (x – c) + B(x – a) (x – c) + c(x – a) (x – b)

Put x = a $\Rightarrow$ 1 = A(a – b) (a – c) $\Rightarrow$ A = $\frac{1}{(a-b)(a-c)}$

Similarly B = $\frac{1}{(b-a)(b-c)}$ C = $\frac{1}{(c-a)(c-b)}$

$$\therefore \int \frac{1}{(x-a)(x-b)(x-c)} dx$$

$$= \int \frac{1}{(a-b)(b-c)} \cdot \frac{1}{x-a} + \int \frac{1}{(b-c)(b-a)} \frac{1}{x-b} + \int \frac{1}{(c-a)(c-b)} \frac{1}{x-c} dx$$

$$= \frac{1}{(a-b)(b-c)} ln|x-a| + \frac{1}{(b-c)(c-a)} ln|x-b| + \frac{1}{(c-a)(c-b)} ln|x-c| + c$$

3. Evaluate $\int \frac{7x-4}{(x-1)^2(x+2)} dx$

Sol. Consider $\frac{7x-4}{(x-1)^2(x+2)} = \frac{A}{(x-1)} + \frac{B}{(x-1)^2} + \frac{C}{x+2}$

$\therefore$ 7x – 4 = A(x – 1) (x + 2) + B (x + 2) + c(x – 1)^2 ..... (1)

Put x = 1 in (1) we get

3 = 3B $\Rightarrow$ B = 1

Put x = –2 in (1) $\Rightarrow$ –18 = 9c $\Rightarrow$ c = –2

Comparing consistant terms of (1) on both sides we get

$$-4 = -2A + 2B + c$$

$$\therefore -4 = -2A + 2(1) + -2 \Rightarrow 2A = 4 \Rightarrow A = 2$$

$$\therefore \int \frac{7x-4}{(x-1)^2(x+2)} = \int \left(\frac{2}{x-1} + \frac{1}{(x-1)^2} + \frac{-2}{x+2} \right) dx$$

$$= 2ln|x-1| - \frac{1}{x-1} - 2\ln|x+2| + c$$

$$= 2ln\left(\frac{x-1}{x+2}\right) - \frac{1}{x-1} + c$$

4. Evaluate $\int \frac{x}{(1+x)(1+x^2)} dx$

Sol. Consider $\frac{x}{(1+x)(1+x^2)} = \frac{A}{1+x} + \frac{Bx+c}{1+x^2}$

$\Rightarrow \quad x = A(1 + x^2) + (Bx + C)(1 + x)$ ..... (1)

Put $x = -1$ in (1) we get

$$-1 = A(1 + 1) + (-B + C)(1 - 1)$$

$$\Rightarrow \quad -1 = 2A \Rightarrow A = -1/2$$

Comparing x^2 cofficients on both sides $O = A + B$

$$\Rightarrow \quad B = -A = -\left(\frac{-1}{2}\right) = \frac{1}{2}$$

Comparing constant terms on both sides we get

$$O = A + C \Rightarrow C = -A = +1/2$$

$$\therefore \int \frac{x}{(1+x)(1+x^2)} dx = \int \frac{-\frac{1}{2}}{1+x} dx + \int \frac{+\frac{1}{2}x + \frac{1}{2}}{1+x^2} dx$$

$$= \frac{-1}{2} ln|1+x| + \frac{1}{2} \int \frac{x+1}{x^2+1} dx$$

$$= \frac{-1}{2} \ln|x+1| + \frac{1}{2}\left[\frac{1}{2}\int \frac{2x}{x^2+1}dx + \int \frac{1}{1+x^2}dx\right]$$

$$= \frac{-1}{2} \ln|x+1| + \frac{1}{4}.\ln(x^2+1) + \frac{1}{2}\tan^{-1}(x) + c$$

5. Evaluate $\int \frac{1}{1+x^3}dx$

Ans. Consider $\int \frac{1}{1+x^3}dx = \int \frac{1}{(1+x)(x^2-x+1)}dx$

$$\frac{1}{(x+1)(x^2-x+1)} = \frac{A}{x+1} + \frac{Bx+c}{x^2-x+1}$$

$$\therefore\ 1 = A(x^2 - x + 1) + (Bx + c)(x + 1) \qquad \text{..... (1)}$$

Put $x = -1$ in (1) $\Rightarrow 1 = A(1+1+1) = A = \frac{1}{3}$

Comparing the coefficient of x^2 we get $o = A + B \Rightarrow B = -A = -\frac{1}{3}$

Comparing constant terms in (1) we get $1 = A + C \Rightarrow C = 1 - A = 1 - \frac{1}{3} = \frac{2}{3}$

$$\therefore \frac{1}{1+x^3} = \frac{\frac{1}{3}}{1+x} + \frac{\frac{-1}{3}x + \frac{2}{3}}{x^2-x+1}$$

$$\therefore \int \frac{1}{1+x^3}dx = \frac{1}{3}\int \frac{1}{x+1}dx - \frac{1}{3}\int \frac{x-2}{x^2-x+1}dx$$

$$= \frac{1}{3}\log|x+1| - \frac{1}{3}\int \frac{x-2}{x^2-x+1}dx$$

Consider $I_1 = \int \frac{x-2}{x^2-x+1}dx$

$$\therefore\ x - 2 = P\left(\frac{d}{dx}(x^2-x+1)\right) + q$$

$$x - 2 = P(2x - 1) + q$$

$$2p = 1 \Rightarrow p = \frac{1}{2}$$

$$-p + x = -2 \Rightarrow q = P - 2 = \frac{1}{2} - 2 = \frac{-3}{2}$$

$$\therefore I_1 = \int \left(\frac{\frac{1}{2}(2x-1)}{x^2 - x + 1} + \frac{\frac{-3}{2}}{x^2 - x + 1} \right) dx$$

$$= \frac{1}{2} \ln\left|x^2 - x + 1\right| - \frac{3}{2} \int \frac{1}{x^2 - x + 1} dx$$

$$= \frac{1}{2} \ln\left|x^2 - x + 1\right| - \frac{3}{2} \int \frac{1}{(x - \frac{1}{2})^2 + \left(\frac{\sqrt{3}}{2}\right)^2} dx$$

$$= \frac{1}{2} ln\left|x^2 - x + 1\right| - \frac{3}{2} \frac{1}{\left(\frac{\sqrt{3}}{2}\right)} . \tan^{-1}\left(\frac{2x-1}{\sqrt{3}}\right) + c$$

Substitute I_1 in $\int \frac{1}{1+x^3} dx = \frac{1}{3} \int \frac{1}{x+1} dx - \frac{1}{3} \int \frac{x-2}{x^2 - x + 1} dx$

$$\therefore \int \frac{1}{1+x^3} dx = \frac{1}{3} ln|x+1| - \frac{1}{3}\left\{ \frac{1}{2} ln\left((x^2 - x + 1) - \sqrt{3} \tan^{-1}\left(\frac{2x+1}{\sqrt{3}}\right) \right) \right\}$$

$$= \frac{1}{3} ln|x+1| - \frac{1}{6} ln\left|x^2 - x + 1\right| + \frac{1}{\sqrt{3}} \tan^{-1}\left(\frac{2x+1}{\sqrt{3}}\right) + C$$

Exercise - 23.4

Evaluate the following integrals.

1. $\int \frac{1}{x(x+1)(x+2)} dx$

2. $\int \frac{3x-2}{(x-1)(x+2)(x-3)} dx$

3. $\int \frac{x^2}{(x+1)(x+2)^2} dx$

4. $\int\frac{2x^2+x+1}{(x+3)(x-2)^2}dx$

5. $\int\frac{2x+3}{(x+2)(x^2+4)}dx$

6. $\int\frac{1}{(1-x)(4+x^2)}dx$

7. $\int\frac{1}{(x^2+a^2)(x^2+b^2)}dx$

8. $\int\frac{x^3-2x+3}{x^2+x-2}dx$

Answers

1. $\frac{1}{2}\ln|x|-\ln|x+1|+\frac{1}{2}\ln|x+2|+c$

2. $\frac{-1}{6}\,ln|x-1|\frac{-8}{15}\,ln|x+2|+\frac{7}{10}\ln|x-3|+c$

3. $ln|x+1|+\frac{4}{x+2}+C$

4. $\frac{16}{25}\,ln|x+3|+\frac{34}{25}\,ln|x-2|\frac{-11}{5(x-2)}+c$

5. $\frac{-1}{8}ln|x+2|+\frac{1}{16}ln|x^2+4|+\frac{7}{8}\tan^{-1}(\frac{x}{2})+c$

6. $\frac{-1}{5}ln|1-x|+\frac{1}{10}ln|x^2+4|+\frac{1}{10}\tan^{-1}(\frac{x}{2})+c$

7. $\frac{1}{b^2-a^2}\left[\frac{1}{a}\tan^{-1}\left(\frac{x}{a}\right)-\frac{1}{b}\tan^{-1}\left(\frac{x}{b}\right)\right]$

[Hint : $\frac{1}{(x^2+a^2)(x^2+b^2)}=\frac{1}{b^2-a^2}\left[\frac{1}{x^2+a^2}-\frac{1}{x^2+b^2}\right]$ **]**

8. $\dfrac{(x-1)^2}{2}+\dfrac{1}{3}ln|x+2|+\dfrac{2}{3}ln|x-1|+c$

[**Hint :** $\dfrac{x^3-2x+3}{x^2+x-2}=(x-1)+\dfrac{x+1}{x^2+x-2}=(x-1)+\dfrac{x+1}{(x-1)(x+2)}$]

23.7 Integration by Parts

If f(x), g(x) are two integrable functions then $\int f(x)g(x)dx$

$$= f(x)\int g(x)dx - \int f'(x)\left(\int g(x)dx\right)dx$$

In the integration by parts, the first function will be taken as follows

I, L, A, T E

I $\rightarrow$ Inverse functions Ex : $\sin^{-1}$, $\cos^{-1}$ ....

L $\rightarrow$ Logarithmic functions Ex : log ....

A $\rightarrow$ Algebric functions Ex : x, x^2 ....

T $\rightarrow$ Trigonometric functions Ex : sin, cos x ....

E $\rightarrow$ Exponential functions Ex : e^x, e^{2n}........

To remember the formulae, we write

$$\text{i.e., } f(x)\ \underbrace{\int g(x)dx} - \int f'(x)(\ \nearrow\ )dx - \int f'(x).\left(\int g(x)dx\right)dx$$

Solved Examples

1. Evaluate $\int x^2 \log x\, dx$

Sol. Here given functions are x^2, log x..
take first function f(x) = log x, second function g(x) = x^2 from ILATE rule

$$\therefore \int f(x)\, g(x)\, dx = f(x)\int g(x)dx - \int f'(x)\left(\int g(x)\, dx\right)dx$$

$$= \log x\int x^2 dx - \int\left(\frac{1}{x}\right).\left(\int x^2 dx\right)dx$$

$$= \log x.\frac{x^3}{3} - \int \left(\frac{1}{x}\right).\frac{x^3}{3}\,dx$$

$$= \frac{x^3}{3}\log x - \frac{1}{3}\int x^2 dx$$

$$= \frac{x^3}{3}\log x - \frac{1}{3}.\frac{x^3}{3} + c$$

$$= \frac{x^3}{3}.\log x - \frac{1}{9}x^3 + c$$

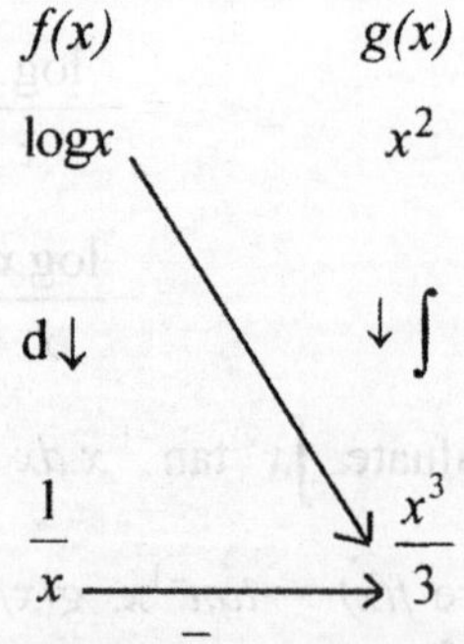

2. Evaluate $\int x \log(1+x)\,dx$

here $f(x) = \log(1 + x)$ $g(x) = x$

by using integral biparts

$$\int f(x)g(x)dx = \log(1+x)\ \int (xdx) - \int \left(\frac{1}{1+x}.\left(\int x\,dx\right)\right)dx$$

$$= \frac{x^2}{2}\log(1+x) - \int \frac{x^2}{2(1+x)}dx$$

$$= \frac{x^2}{2}\log(1+x) - \frac{1}{2}\int \frac{x^2-1+1}{(x+1)}dx$$

$$= \frac{x^2}{2}\log(1+x) - \frac{1}{2}\int (x-1) + \frac{1}{(x+1)}dx$$

$$= \frac{x^2}{2}\log(1+x) - \frac{1}{2}\int \left(\frac{x^2}{2} - x\right) + \frac{-1}{2}ln\,(x+1) + c$$

$$= \left(\frac{x^2-1}{2}\right)\log(1+x) - \frac{1}{2}\left(\frac{x^2}{2} - x\right) + c$$

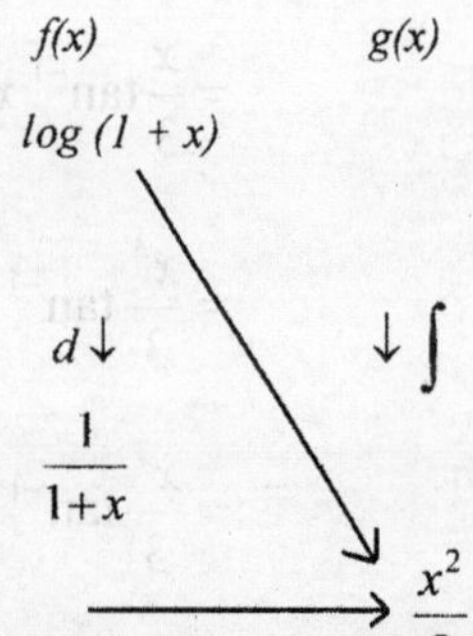

3. Evaluate $\int \frac{\log x}{x^2}dx$

Here $f(x) = \log x$ $\quad g(x) = \frac{1}{x^2}$

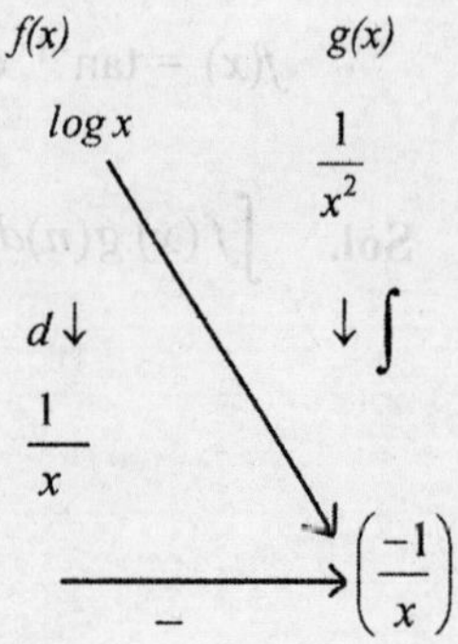

$$\therefore \int f(x)g(x)dx = (\log x)\left(-\frac{1}{x}\right) - \int \frac{1}{x}.\left(\frac{-1}{x}\right)dx$$

$$= -\frac{\log x}{x} + \int \frac{1}{x^2}dx$$

$$= -\frac{\log x}{x} - \frac{1}{x} + c \quad = -\frac{1}{x}(\log x + 1) + c$$

4. Evaluate $\int x^2 \tan^{-1} x.dx$

Sol. Here $f(x) = tan^{-1}x,\ g(x) = x^2$

$$\therefore \int f(x)g(x)dx = f(x) \int g(x)dx - \int f'(x)\left(\int g(x)dx\right)dx$$

$$(\tan^{-1} x)\frac{x^3}{3} - \int \frac{1}{1+x^2}.\frac{x^3}{3}dx$$

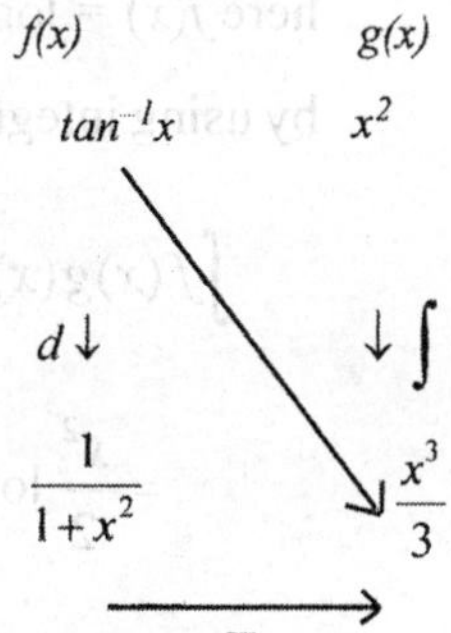

$$= \frac{x^3}{3}.\tan^{-1} x - \frac{1}{3}\int \frac{x^3}{x^2+1}dx$$

$$= \frac{x}{3}\tan^{-1} x - \frac{1}{3}\int\left(x - \frac{x}{x^2+1}\right)dx$$

$$= \frac{x^3}{3}\tan^{-1} x - \frac{1}{3}\frac{x^2}{2} + \frac{1}{6}\int \frac{2x}{x^2+1}dx$$

$$= \frac{x^3}{3}\tan^{-1} x - \frac{x^2}{6} + \frac{1}{6}\, ln\,(1+x^2) + c$$

5. Evaluate $\int \frac{\tan^{-1} x}{x^2}dx$

$f(x) = \tan^{-1} x \qquad g(x) = \dfrac{1}{x^2}$

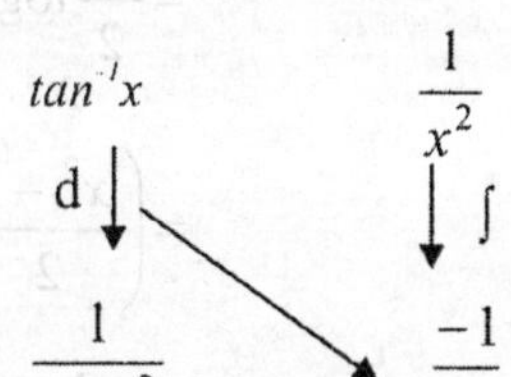

Sol. $\int f(x).g(n)dx = \tan^{-1} x.\left(\frac{-1}{x}\right) - \int\left(\frac{1}{1+x^2}\right)\left(\frac{-1}{x}\right)dx$

$$= \frac{-1}{x}.\tan^{-1} x + \int \frac{1}{x(1+x^2)}dx$$

$$= \frac{-1}{x}.\tan^{-1} x + \int\left(\frac{1}{x} - \frac{x}{1+x^2}\right)dx$$

$$= \frac{-1}{x}.\tan^{-1} x + ln|x| - \frac{1}{2}\, ln\left|1+x^2\right| + c$$

6. Evaluate $\int x^2 \sin x dx$

Sol. Here $f(x) = x^2$, $g(x) = \sin x$

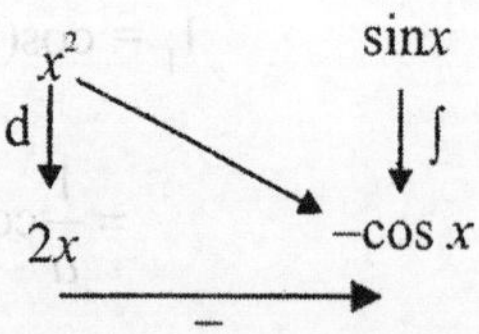

$\int f(x)g(x)dx$

$= x^2 (-\cos x) - \int (2x)(-\cos x)dx$

$= -x^2 \cos x + 2\int x\cos x\, dx$

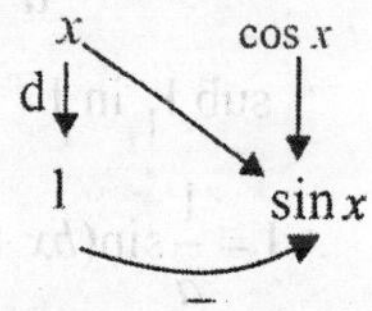

$= -x^2\cos x + 2\left[x.\sin x - \int (1).\sin x\right] + c$

$= -x^2 \cos x + 2x \sin x + 2 \cos x + c$

7. Evaluate $\int e^x . x^2 dx$

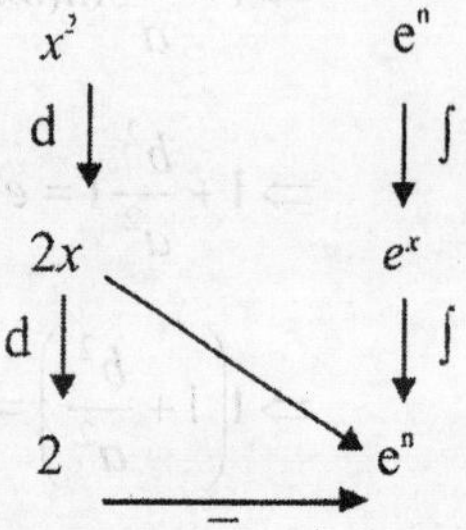

$f(x) = x^2$, $g(x) = e^x$

$\therefore \int f(x).g(x)\, dx = x^2.e^x - \int 2x\, e^x dx$

$= x^2e^x - 2\int xe^x dx$

$= x^2 e^x - 2\left[x.e^x - \int 1.e^x dx\right]$

$= x^2 e^x - 2x e^x + 2e^x + c$

$= (x^2 - 2x + 2) e^x + c$

8. Evaluate $\int e^{ax}.\sin(bx + c)\, dx$

Sol. $f(x) = \sin(bx + c)$, $g(x) = e^{ax}$

Let $I = \int f(x).g(n)dx = \sin(bx+c).\frac{e^{ax}}{a} - \int \cos(bx+c).\frac{b.e^{ax}}{a}dx$

$$= \frac{1}{a}.\sin(bx+c)e^{ax} - \frac{b}{a}\int \cos(bx+c)e^{ax}dx$$

$$= \frac{1}{a}.\sin(bx+c)e^{an} - \frac{b}{a} I_1$$

where $I_1 = \int e^{ax}.\cos(bx+c).dx$

again apply by parts we get

$$I_1 = \cos(bx+c) \cdot \frac{e^{ax}}{a} - \int -b\sin(bx+c).\frac{e^{ax}}{a}\, dx$$

$$= \frac{1}{a}\cos(bx+c)\, e^{ax} + \frac{b}{a}\int \sin(bx+c)e^{an}\, dx$$

$$= \frac{1}{a}\cos(bx+c)\, e^{ax} + \frac{b}{a}\, I$$

$\therefore$ sub I_1 in I

$$\therefore I = \frac{1}{a}\sin(bx+c)\, e^{ax} - \frac{b}{a}\left[\frac{1}{a}\cos(bx+c)e^{ax} + {}^{b}\!/_{a}\, I\right]$$

$$\Rightarrow I = \frac{1}{a}\sin(bx+c)\, e^{ax} - \frac{b}{a^2}\cos(bx+c)e^{ax} + {}^{b^2}\!/_{a^2}\, I$$

$$\Rightarrow I + \frac{b^2}{a^2} I = e^{ax}\left[\frac{1}{a}\frac{\sin(bx+c)}{a} - \frac{b}{a^2}\cos(bx+c)\right]$$

$$\Rightarrow I\left(1 + \frac{b^2}{a^2}\right) = e^{ax}\left[\frac{1}{a}\sin(bx+c) - \frac{b}{a^2}\cos(bx+c)\right]$$

$$\therefore I\left(\frac{a^2+b^2}{a^2}\right) = e^{ax}\left[\frac{a\sin(bx+c) - b\cos(bx+c)}{a^2}\right]$$

$$\therefore I\,(a^2+b^2) = e^{ax}\,(a\sin(bx+c) - b\cos(bx+c))$$

$$I = \frac{e^{ax}}{a^2+b^2}\,(a\sin(bx+c) - b\cos(bx+c) + c$$

$$\therefore \int e^{ax}.\sin(bx+c) = \frac{e^{ax}}{a^2+b^2}[a\sin(bx+c) - b\cos(bx+c) + c$$

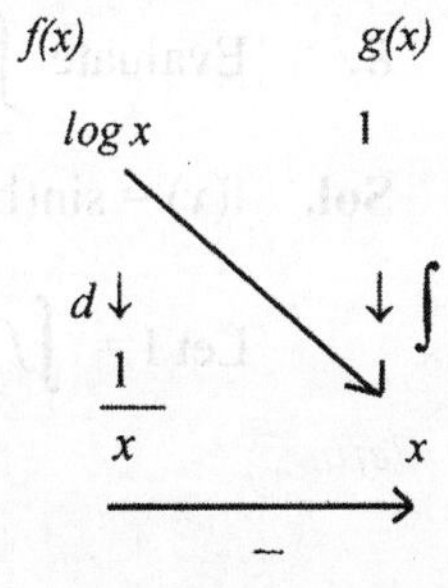

9. Evaluate $\int \log x.1dx$

Sol. $\int \log x.1\, dx$

$$\log x \, . \, x - \int \frac{1}{x} . x.dx$$

$$x(\log x) - x + c$$

10. Evaluate $e^x \cos^2 x$ dx

Sol. $\int e^x \left(\frac{1 + \cos 2x}{2} \right) dx$

$$\int \left(e^x . \frac{1}{2} + e^x . \frac{\cos 2x}{2} \right) dx$$

$$\int e^x . \frac{1}{2} + e^x . \frac{\cos 2x}{2}) \, dx$$

$$= \frac{1}{2} \int e^x + \frac{1}{2} \int e^x \cos 2x \, dx$$

$$= \frac{1}{2} . e^x + \frac{1}{2} \left[\frac{e^x}{1^2 + 2^2} (1 \cos 2x + 2 \sin 2x) \right] + c$$

$$\left(\because \int e^{ax} \cos(bx + c^{dx} = \frac{e^{ax}}{a^2 + b^2} a \cos(bx + c) + \sin(bx + c) \right)$$

$$= \frac{e^x}{2} + \frac{e^x}{10} (\cos 2x + 2 \sin 2x) + c$$

Theorem : $\int e^x (f(x) + f'(x) = e^x . f(x) + c$

Proof : $\int e^x (f(x) + f'(x) dx$

$$= \int e^x f(x) dx + \int e^x . f'(x) dx$$

$$= f(x) e^x - \int f'(x) . e^x dx + \int e^x . f'(x) dx \quad [\because \text{by using by parts}]$$

$$= f(x) \, . \, e^x = e^x \, . \, f(x)$$

$$\therefore \int e^x [f(x) + f'(x)] dx = e^x . f(x) + c$$

11. Evaluate $\int e^x (\sin x + \cos x) dx$

Sol. If $f(x) = \sin x$ then $f'(x) = \cos x$

$$\therefore \int e^x(\sin x+\cos x)\,dx = \int e^x(f(x)+f'(x)\,dx$$

$$= e^n . f(x) + c$$

$$= e^x . \sin x + c$$

12. Evaluate $\int e^x\left(\tan^{-1}x+\frac{1}{1+x^2}\right)dx$

Sol. $f(x) = \tan^{-1} x, \quad \Rightarrow \quad f'(x)=\frac{1}{1+x^2}$

$$\therefore \int e^x.(f(x)+f'(x)_{dx} = e^x . f(x)$$

$$= e^x . \tan^{-1} x + c$$

Exercise - 23.5

Evaluate the following integrals

1. $\int x\cos x\,dx$

2. $\int x\cos^{-1}x\,dx$

3. $\int x\sin^{-1}x\,dx$

4. $\int e^{2x}.\cos 3x\cos x\,dx$

5. $\int e^x\cos^3 x dx$

6. $\int \frac{x.e^x}{(x+1)^2}dx$

7. $(\sin(\log x) + \cos(\log x)\,dx$

8. (i) $\int \sin^{-1}x\,dx$ (ii) $\int \cot^{-1}x\,dx$

9. $\int x^2.\sin^2 x dx$

10. $\int \cos(\log\ x)dx$

Answers

1. $x \sin x + \cos x + c$

2. $\dfrac{x^2 \cos^{-1} x}{2} - \dfrac{\cos^{-1} x}{4} - \dfrac{x\sqrt{1-x^2}}{4} + c$

3. $\dfrac{1}{2}\left[\left(x^2 - \dfrac{1}{2}\right)\sin^{-1} x + \dfrac{x}{2}\sqrt{1-x^2}\right] + c$

4. $\dfrac{e^{2x}}{8}\left[\dfrac{2}{5}\cos 4x + \dfrac{4}{5}\sin 4x + \cos 2x + \sin 2x\right] + c$

5. $\dfrac{1}{4}e^x\left[\left(\dfrac{3}{2}(\cos x + \sin x)\right) + \dfrac{1}{10}(\cos 3x + 3\sin 3x)\right] + c$

6. $\dfrac{1}{x+1}e^x + c$

7. $x \sin(\log x) + c$

8. (i) $x \sin^{-1} x + \sqrt{1-x^2} + c$ (ii) $x \cot^{-1} x + \dfrac{1}{2}\log(1 + x^2) + c$

9. $\dfrac{1}{2}\left[\dfrac{x^3}{3} - \dfrac{x^2}{4}\sin 2x - \dfrac{x}{4}\cos 2x + \dfrac{1}{8}\sin 2x\right] + c$

10. $\dfrac{x}{2}\,[\,\cos(\log x) + \sin(\log x)\,] + c$

24

Definite Integrals

24.1 Definite Integrals

Suppose $f(x)$ be a function defined on [a, b]. If $\int f(x)dx = F(x)$ then F(b) – F(a) is called definite integral of $f(x)$ over [a, b]. It is denoted by $\int_a^b f(x)dx$. Here a is called lower limit and b is called upper limit.

$$\therefore \int_a^b f(x)dx = F(b) - F(a)$$

Note that if $\int f(x)dx = F(x) + c \Rightarrow \int_a^b f(x)dx = F(b) - F(a)$

Ex : (i) $\int_1^2 x\,dx = \left[\frac{x^2}{2}\right]_1^2 = \frac{(2)^2}{2} - \frac{(1)^2}{2} = \frac{4}{2} - \frac{1}{2} = \frac{3}{2}$

(ii) $\int_0^{\frac{\pi}{4}} \sin x\,dx = [-\cos x]_0^{\frac{\pi}{4}} = -\cos\left(\frac{\pi}{4}\right) - (-\cos 0) = \frac{-1}{\sqrt{2}} + 1 = \frac{\sqrt{2}-1}{\sqrt{2}}$

Theorem 1: $\int_a^b f(x)dx = \int_a^b f(t)\,dt$

Proof : Let $\int f(x)dx = F(x) \Rightarrow \int f(t)dt = F(t)$

$$\therefore \int_a^b f(x)\,dx = [f(x)]_a^b = \text{F(b)} - \text{F(a)},$$

$$\int_a^b f(t)dt = [F(t)]_a^b = F(b) - F(a)$$

$$\therefore \int_a^b f(x)dx = \int_a^b f(t)\,dt$$

Theorem 2 : If $f(x)$ is an integrable function on [a, b] and $g(x)$ is derivable on [a, b]

then $\displaystyle\int_a^b (fog)(x)g'(x)\,dx = \int_{g(a)}^{g'(b)} f(x)\,dx$

Proof : $\displaystyle\int_a^b (fog)(x)g(x)dx = \int_a^b f(g(x).g'(x).\,dx$

Let $g(x) = t$

$\Rightarrow g'(x)dx = dt$

when $x = a$	then	t = g(a)
$x = b$	then	t = g(b)

$\therefore$ given integration becomes $\displaystyle\int_{g(a)}^{g(b)} f(t).\,dt = \int_{g(a)}^{g(b)} f(x)dx$

Solved Examples

1. Evaluate $\displaystyle\int_0^1 (2x^2 + 3x + 1)dx$

Sol. $\displaystyle\int_0^1 (2x^2 + 3x + 1)dx = 2\int_0^1 x^2dx + 3\int_0^1 xdx + \int_0^1 dx$

$$= 2\left(\frac{x^3}{3}\right)_0^1 + 3\left(\frac{x^2}{2}\right)_0^1 + (x)_0^1$$

$$= 2\left(\frac{1}{3} - 0\right) + 3\left(\frac{1}{2} - 0\right) + (1 - 0) = \frac{2}{3} + \frac{3}{2} + 1$$

$$= \frac{4 + 9 + 6}{6} = \frac{19}{6}$$

2. Evaluate $\int_0^{\frac{1}{2}} \frac{1+x}{1-x} dx$

Sol. $\int_0^{\frac{1}{2}} \left(-1+\frac{2}{1-x}\right) dx = \left[-x-2ln(1-x)\right]_0^{\frac{1}{2}}$

$$= \left(\frac{-1}{2} - 2\ln\left(1-\frac{1}{2}\right)\right) - [-0-2ln\,1]$$

$$= \frac{-1}{2} - 2\ln\frac{1}{2}^2 = \frac{-1}{2} + 2\log 2$$

3. Evaluate $\int_0^1 \frac{dx}{\sqrt{x+1}+\sqrt{x}}$

Sol. $\int_0^1 \frac{dx}{\sqrt{x+1}+\sqrt{x}} = \int_0^1 \frac{\sqrt{x+1}-\sqrt{x}}{\left(\sqrt{x+1}+\sqrt{x}\right)\left(\sqrt{x+1}-\sqrt{x}\right)} dx$

(by rationalising the denominator)

$$= \int_0^1 \frac{\sqrt{x+1}-\sqrt{x}}{(x+1)-(x)} dx$$

$$= \int_0^1 \left(\sqrt{x+1}-\sqrt{x}\right) dx$$

$$= \left(\frac{(x+1)^{\frac{3}{2}}}{\frac{3}{2}} - \frac{x^{\frac{3}{2}}}{\frac{3}{2}}\right)_0^1$$

$$= \frac{2}{3}\left[\left(2^{\frac{3}{2}}-1\right)-1\right]$$

$$= \frac{2}{3}\left(2\sqrt{2}-2\right) = \frac{4}{3}(\sqrt{2}-1)$$

4. Evaluate $\int_0^{\frac{\pi}{4}} \sec^2 x dx$ (ii) $\int_{\frac{\pi}{6}}^{\frac{\pi}{3}} \cot^2 x dx$

Sol. (i) $\int_0^{\frac{\pi}{4}} \sec^2 x dx = (\tan x)_0^{\frac{\pi}{4}} = 1 - 0 = 1$

(ii) $\int_{\frac{\pi}{6}}^{\frac{\pi}{3}} \cot^2 x\, dx = \int_{\frac{\pi}{6}}^{\frac{\pi}{3}} (\cos ec^2 x - 1) = (-\cot x - x)_{\frac{\pi}{6}}^{\frac{\pi}{3}}$

$$= \left(\frac{-1}{\sqrt{3}} - \frac{\pi}{3}\right) - \left(\sqrt{3} - \frac{\pi}{6}\right)$$

$$= -\frac{\pi}{6} + \sqrt{3} - \frac{1}{\sqrt{3}}$$

$$= -\frac{\pi}{6} + \frac{2}{\sqrt{3}} = \frac{2}{\sqrt{3}} - \frac{\pi}{6}$$

5. Evaluate $\int_0^{\frac{\pi}{4}} \frac{1 + \sin 2x}{\cos x + \sin x} dx$

Sol. $\int_0^{\frac{\pi}{4}} \frac{(\sin x + \cos x)^2}{\sin x + \cos x} dx = \int_0^{\frac{\pi}{4}} (\sin x + \cos x) dx$

$$= (-\cos x + \sin x)_0^{\frac{\pi}{4}}$$

$$= \left(\frac{-1}{\sqrt{2}} + \frac{1}{\sqrt{2}}\right) - (-1 + 0) = 1$$

6. (i) $\int_0^{\frac{\pi}{2}} \frac{\cos x}{1+\sin^2 x} dx$ (ii) $\int_0^{\frac{\pi}{3}} \frac{\cos x}{3+4\sin x} dx$

Sol. (i) $\int_0^{\frac{\pi}{2}} \frac{\cos x}{1+\sin^2 x} dx$

Put $\sin x = t$ when $x = 0 \Rightarrow t = \sin 0 = 0$

$\Rightarrow \cos x \, dx = dt$ $x = \frac{\pi}{2} \Rightarrow t = \sin\frac{\pi}{2} = 1$

$$\therefore \int_0^{\frac{\pi}{2}} \frac{\cos x \, dx}{1+\sin^2 x} = \int_0^1 \frac{dt}{1+t^2} = (\tan^{-1}(t))_0^1 = \tan^{-1}(1) - 0$$

$$= \frac{\pi}{4} - 0$$

$$= \frac{\pi}{4}$$

(ii) $\int_0^{\frac{\pi}{3}} \frac{\cos x}{3+4\sin x} dx$

Put $3 + 4\sin x = t$ $\Rightarrow 0 + 4\cos x \, dx = dt$

$\therefore \cos x \, dx = \frac{dt}{4}$; also when

$x = 0 \Rightarrow t = 3 + 4 \sin x$

$= 3 + 4 \sin 0 = 3$

$x = \frac{\pi}{3} \Rightarrow t = 3 + 4 . \sin \frac{\pi}{3}$

$= 3 + 4 . \frac{\sqrt{3}}{2}$

$= 3 + 2\sqrt{3}$

$$\therefore \int_0^{\frac{\pi}{3}} \frac{\cos x}{3+4\sin x}\,dx = \int_3^{3+2\sqrt{3}} \frac{\left(\frac{dt}{4}\right)}{t} = \frac{1}{4}(\ln t)_3^{3+2\sqrt{3}}$$

$$= \frac{1}{4}\left[ln(3+2\sqrt{3}) - ln3\right]$$

$$= \frac{1}{4} ln\left[\frac{3+2\sqrt{3}}{3}\right]$$

7. Evaluate

(i) $\int_0^a \frac{a}{\sqrt{a^2-x^2}}\,dx$ (ii) $\int_0^1 \frac{x^2}{1+x^2}\,dx$

(iii) $\int_1^2 \frac{1}{x\sqrt{x^2-1}}\,dx$ (iv) $\int_0^3 \frac{xdx}{\sqrt{x^2+16}}$

Sol. (i) $\int_0^a \frac{a}{\sqrt{a^2-x^2}}\,dx = \text{a}\,.\int_0^a \frac{1}{\sqrt{a^2-x^2}}\,dx$

$$= a.\left[\sin^{-1}\left(\frac{x}{a}\right)\right]_0^a = a.(\sin^{-1}{}_{(1)} - \sin^{-1}{}_{(0)})$$

$$= a.\left(\frac{\pi}{2} - 0\right)$$

$$= a\frac{\pi}{2} = \frac{\pi}{2}a$$

(ii) $\int_0^1 \frac{x^2}{1+x^2}\,dx = \int_0^1 \frac{x^2+1-1}{x^2+1}\,dx = \int_0^1 \left(1 - \frac{1}{x^2+1}\right)dx$

$$= (x - \tan^{-1} x)_0^1$$

$$= (1 - \tan^{-1}{}_{(1)}) - (0 - 0)$$

$$= 1 - \frac{\pi}{4} = \frac{4-\pi}{4}$$

(iii) $\int_1^2 \frac{1}{x\sqrt{x^2-1}}dx$

$$\int_1^2 \frac{1}{x\sqrt{x^2-1}}dx = \left[\sec^{-1}(x)\right]_1^2 = \sec^{-1}(2) - \sec^{-1}(1)$$

$$= \frac{\pi}{3} - 0 = \frac{\pi}{3}$$

(iv) $\int_0^3 \frac{x}{\sqrt{x^2+16}}dx$

$$\int_0^3 \frac{x}{\sqrt{x^2+16}}dx = \frac{1}{2}\int_0^3 \frac{2x}{\sqrt{x^2+16}}dx = \frac{1}{2}\left[2.\sqrt{x^2+16}\right]_0^3$$

$$\left(\because \int \frac{f'(x)}{f(x)} = 2\sqrt{f(x)}\right)$$

$$= \frac{1}{2}\left[2(\sqrt{25}-\sqrt{16})\right]$$

$$= 5 - 4 = 1$$

8. (i) $\int_0^1 \frac{dx}{\sqrt{3-2x}}$ (ii) $\int_0^1 (2x+3)\sqrt{3-2x}\,dx$

Sol. (i) $\int_0^1 \frac{dx}{\sqrt{3-2x}}$

$$= -\frac{1}{2}\int_0^1 \frac{-2}{\sqrt{3-2x}}dx$$

$$= -\frac{1}{2}\left(2\sqrt{3-2x}\right)_0^1 \qquad \left[\because \int \frac{f'(x)}{\sqrt{f(x)}}dx = 2\sqrt{f(x)}\right]$$

$$= -(\sqrt{3}-2-\sqrt{3}) = -\left(1-\sqrt{3}\right) = \sqrt{3}-1$$

(ii) $\int_0^1 (2x+3)\sqrt{3-2x}\,dx$

Put $3 - 2x = t^2$

$$\therefore \quad x = \frac{3-t^2}{2}$$

$\Rightarrow -2dx = 2t\ dt$ when $x = 0 \Rightarrow t^2 = 3 \quad \Rightarrow t = \sqrt{3}$

$dx = -t\ dt$

where $x = 1 \Rightarrow t^2 = 1 \Rightarrow t = 1$

$\therefore$ The Integration becomes $\int_{\sqrt{3}}^{1}\left(3 - t^2 + 3\right)t(-t)dt$

$$\int_{\sqrt{3}}^{1}\left(-3t^2 + t^4 - 3t^2\right)dt = \left(-2t^3 + \frac{t^5}{5}\right)_{\sqrt{3}}^{1} = \frac{(-9+21\sqrt{3})}{5}$$

(iii) $$\int_0^{\frac{\pi}{4}} \sec^4\theta d\theta = \int_0^{\frac{\pi}{4}} (\sec^2\theta).\sec^2\theta\, d\theta$$

$$= \int_0^{\frac{\pi}{4}} (1+\tan^2\theta)\sec^2\theta\, d\theta$$

$$= \int_0^{\frac{\pi}{4}} (\sec^2\theta + \tan^2\theta.\sec^2\theta)d\theta$$

$$= \left[\tan\theta + \frac{\tan^3\theta}{3}\right]_0^{\frac{\pi}{4}}$$

$$= \left(1+\frac{1}{3}\right) - (0+0) = \frac{4}{3}$$

9. Evaluate

(i) $\int_0^{16}\left(\frac{x^{\frac{1}{4}}}{1+x^{\frac{1}{2}}}\right)dx$ (ii) $\int_0^{1}\frac{x}{1+\sqrt{x}}\,dx$

Sol. (i) $\int_0^{16} \frac{x^{\frac{1}{4}}}{1+x^{\frac{1}{2}}} dx$

Put $x = t^4 \Rightarrow dx = 4t^3\, dt$

when $x = 0 \Rightarrow t = 0$ $(\because x = t^4)$

when $x = 16 \Rightarrow t^4 = 16 \Rightarrow t = 2$

$$\therefore \int_0^{16} \frac{x^{\frac{1}{4}}}{1+x^{\frac{1}{2}}} dx = \int_0^2 \frac{t.4t^3 dt}{1+t^2} = 4\int_0^2 \frac{t^4}{1+t^2} dt$$

$$= 4\int_0^2 \frac{t^4-1+1}{t^2+1} dt = 4\int_0^2 (t^2-1) + \frac{1}{(t^2+1)} dt$$

$$= 4\left[\frac{t^3}{3} - t + \tan^{-1} t\right]_0^2$$

$$= 4\left[\frac{8}{3} - 2 + \tan^{-1}(2)\right]$$

$$= 4\left(\frac{2}{3} + \tan^{-1}(2)\right)$$

(ii) $\int_0^1 \frac{x}{1+\sqrt{x}} dx$

Put $x = t^2 \Rightarrow dx = 2t\, dt$

when $x = 0 \Rightarrow t = 0$ $(\because x = t^2)$

$x = 1 \Rightarrow t = 1$

$$\therefore \int_0^1 \frac{x}{1+\sqrt{x}} dx = \int_0^1 \frac{t^2.2tdt}{1+t} = 2\int_0^1 \frac{t^3}{t+1} dt$$ $(\because$ By division$)$

$$= 2\int_0^1 (t^2 - t + 1) + \frac{(-1)}{(t+1)} dt$$

$$= 2\left[\frac{t^3}{3} - \frac{t^2}{2} + t - \ln(t+1)\right]_0^1$$

$$= 2\left[\frac{1}{3} - \frac{1}{2} + 1 - ln\,2\right]$$

$$= 2\left[\frac{2-3+6}{6} - ln\,2\right]$$

$$= 2\left[\frac{5}{6} - ln\,2\right]$$

10. Evaluate $\int_0^{\frac{\pi}{2}} \frac{1}{2+3\sin x}dx$

Sol. Put $\tan\frac{x}{2} = \text{t} \quad \Rightarrow \quad dx = \frac{2}{1+t^2}$

$$\sin x = \frac{2t}{1+t^2}$$

when $x = 0 \quad \Rightarrow \quad \text{t} = 0$

$x = \frac{\pi}{2} \quad \Rightarrow \quad \text{t} = 1$

$$\therefore \int_0^{\frac{\pi}{2}} \frac{1}{2+3\sin x}dx = \int_0^1 \frac{\frac{2}{1+t^2}}{2+3\left(\frac{2t}{1+t^2}\right)}dt$$

$$= \int_0^1 \frac{2}{2(1+t^2)+6t}dt = \int_0^1 \frac{1}{1+t^2+3t}dt = \int_0^1 \frac{dt}{\left(t+\frac{3}{2}\right)^2 - \frac{9}{4} + 1}$$

$$= \int_0^1 \frac{dt}{(t+\frac{3}{2})^2 - (\frac{\sqrt{5}}{2})^2} = \left[\frac{1}{2.\frac{\sqrt{5}}{2}}.\log\left|\frac{t+\frac{3}{2}-\frac{\sqrt{5}}{2}}{t+\frac{3}{2}+\frac{\sqrt{5}}{2}}\right|\right]_0^1$$

$$= \frac{1}{\sqrt{5}} \log \left| \frac{2t+3-\sqrt{5}}{2t+3+\sqrt{5}} \right|_0^1$$

$$= \frac{1}{\sqrt{5}} \log \left| \frac{5-\sqrt{5}}{5+\sqrt{5}} \right| - \frac{1}{\sqrt{5}} \ln \left| \frac{3-\sqrt{5}}{3+\sqrt{5}} \right|$$

11. Evaluate $\int_0^{\frac{\pi}{2}} \frac{1}{4\cos^2 x + 9\sin^2 x} dx$

Sol. $\int_0^{\frac{\pi}{2}} \frac{1}{4\cos^2 x + 9\sin^2 x} dx = \int_0^{\frac{\pi}{2}} \frac{\sec^2 x dx}{4 + 9\tan^2 x}$

($\because$ by multiplying Nr and Dr by $\sec^2 x$)

Put $\tan x = t$ $\Rightarrow$ $\sec^2 x \, dx = dt$

also when $x = 0$ $\Rightarrow$ $t = 0$

$x = \frac{\pi}{2}$ $\Rightarrow t = \infty$,

$$\therefore \int_0^{\frac{\pi}{2}} \frac{\sec^2 x}{4 + 9\tan^2 x} dx = \int_0^{\infty} \frac{dt}{4 + 9t^2} = \int_0^{\infty} \frac{dt}{4 + (3t)^2}$$

$$= \left[\frac{1}{2} \cdot \frac{\tan^{-1}\left(\frac{3t}{2}\right)}{3} \right]_0^{\infty}$$

$$= \frac{1}{2}\left[\frac{\pi}{6} - 0\right] = \frac{\pi}{12}$$

12. Evaluate

(i) $\int_0^{\frac{\pi}{2}} x^2 \sin x dx$ (ii) $\int_1^2 \frac{\log x}{x^2} dx$

(iii) $\int_0^1 \frac{xe^x}{(1+x)^2}\,dx$ (iv) $\int_0^1 (x\sin^{-1}x)\,dx$

(v) $\int_0^1 x\tan^{-1}x\,dx$

Sol. (i) $\int_0^{\frac{\pi}{2}} x^2 \sin x\,dx$

by using by parts, $\int f(x)g(x)dx = f(x)\int g(x)dx - \int f'(x).(\int g(x)dx)dx$

$$\int_0^{\frac{\pi}{2}} x^2 \sin x dx = \left[x^2(-\cos x)\right]_0^{\frac{\pi}{2}} - \int_0^{\frac{\pi}{2}} 2x(-\cos x)\,dx$$

$$= \left(\frac{\pi^2}{4}(-0) - 0\right) + 2\int_0^{\frac{\pi}{2}} x\cos x\,dx$$

$$= 0 + 2\left[x.(\sin x)\right]_0^{\frac{\pi}{2}} - \int_0^{\frac{\pi}{2}} (1).\sin x\,dx$$

$$= 2\left[\left(\frac{\pi}{2}\right)(1) - (-\cos x)_0^{\frac{\pi}{2}}\right]$$

$$= \left[\left(\frac{\pi}{2}\right) - (-0+1)\right]$$

$$= 2\left[\frac{\pi}{2} - 1\right] = 2\left[\frac{\pi - 2}{2}\right] = \pi - 2$$

(ii) $\int_1^2 \frac{\log x}{x^2}\,dx$

$$= \int_1^2 (\log x)\left(\frac{1}{x^2}\right)dx = (\log x)\int_1^2 \frac{1}{x^2}\,dx - \int_1^2 \frac{d}{dx}(\log x)\int \frac{1}{x^2}\,dx$$

$$= \log x.\left(\frac{-1}{x}\right) - \int_1^2 \frac{1}{x}.\left(\frac{-1}{x}\right)dx$$

$$= \left(\frac{-\log x}{x}\right)_1^2 + \int_1^2 \frac{1}{x^2}dx$$

$$= \left(\frac{-\log x}{x}\right)_1^2 - \left(\frac{1}{x}\right)_1^2$$

$$= \left(\frac{-\log 2}{2} + 0\right) - \left(\frac{1}{2} - 1\right)$$

$$= \frac{-ln2}{2} + \frac{1}{2}$$

$$= \frac{1 - \log 2}{2}$$

(iii) $\int_0^1 \frac{xe^x}{(1+x)^2}dx$

$$= \int_0^1 \frac{(x+1-1)e^x}{(1+x)^2}dx$$

$$= \int_0^1 \left(\frac{x+1}{(x+1)^2} - \frac{1}{(x+1)^2}\right)e^x dx$$

$$= \int_0^1 \left(\frac{1}{x+1} - \frac{-1}{(x+1)^2}\right)e^x dx$$

$$= \left[\frac{e^x}{x+1}\right]_0^1 \qquad \left[\because \int (f(x) + f'(x))e^x dx = e^x . f(x)\right]$$

$$= \frac{e^1}{0+1} - \frac{e^0}{0+1} = \frac{e}{2} - 1 = \frac{e-2}{2}$$

(iv) $\int_0^1 x \sin^{-1} x \, dx$

using byparts

$$\int_0^1 (.\sin^{-1} x)(x)dx = \left(\sin^{-1} x \int (x)dx\right)_0^1 - \int_0^1 \left(\frac{1}{\sqrt{1-x^2}}\left(\int x dx\right)\right)dx$$

$$= \left(\sin^{-1} x\left(\frac{x^2}{2}\right)\right)_0^1 - \int_0^1 \frac{x^2}{2\sqrt{1-x^2}}dx$$

Put $x = \sin\theta \Rightarrow dx = \cos\theta \, d\theta$

$$= \left((\frac{\pi}{2})\frac{1}{2} - 0\right) - \int_0^{\frac{\pi}{2}} \frac{\sin^2\theta.\cos\theta}{2.\cos\theta}d\theta$$

$$= \frac{\pi}{4} - \frac{1}{2}\int_0^{\frac{\pi}{2}} \sin^2\theta d\theta$$

$$= \frac{\pi}{4} - \frac{1}{2}.\frac{1}{2}.\frac{\pi}{2} = \frac{\pi}{4} - \frac{\pi}{8} = \frac{\pi}{8}$$

(v) $$\int_0^1 x.\tan^{-1} x dx = \left[\tan^{-1} x.\int (x)dx\right]_0^1 - \int_0^1 \frac{1}{1+x^2}\left(\int x dx\right)dx$$

$$\left[\frac{(\tan^{-1} x)x^2}{2}\right]_0^1 - \int_0^1 \frac{x^2}{2(x^2+1)}dx$$

$$\left(\frac{\frac{\pi}{4}.(1)}{2}\right) - \frac{1}{2}\int_0^1 \frac{x^2}{x^2+1}dx$$

$$= \frac{\pi}{8} - \frac{1}{2}\int_0^1 \left(\frac{x^2+1-1}{x^2+1}\right)dx$$

$$= \frac{\pi}{8} - \frac{1}{2}\int_0^1 \left(1 - \frac{1}{x^2+1}\right)dx$$

$$= \frac{\pi}{8} - \frac{1}{2}\left[x - \tan^{-1} x\right]_0^1$$

$$= \frac{\pi}{8} - \frac{1}{2}\left[\left(1 - \frac{\pi}{4}\right) - 0\right]$$

$$= \frac{\pi}{8} - \frac{1}{2} + \frac{\pi}{8} = \frac{\pi}{4} - \frac{1}{2} = \frac{\pi - 2}{4}$$

13. Evaluate (i) $\int_0^1 \sqrt{\frac{1-x}{1+x}}\, dx$ (ii) $\int_0^1 \sin^{-1}\sqrt{x}\, dx$

Sol. (i) $\int_0^1 \sqrt{\frac{1-x}{1+x}}\, dx = \int_0^1 \frac{1-x}{\sqrt{1-x^2}}\, dx$

$$= \int_0^1 \frac{1}{\sqrt{1-x^2}} - \int_0^1 \frac{x}{\sqrt{1-x^2}}\, dx$$

$$= \left(\sin^{-1} x\right)_0^1 - \frac{1}{2}\int_0^1 \frac{2x}{\sqrt{1-x^2}}\, dx$$

$$= \left(\frac{\pi}{2} - 0\right) + \frac{1}{2}.\left(2\sqrt{1-x^2}\right)_0^1 = \frac{\pi}{2} + (0-1)$$

$$= \frac{\pi}{2} - 1 = \frac{\pi - 2}{2}$$

(ii) $\int_0^1 \sin^{-1}(\sqrt{x})\, dx$

Let $x = t^2$ $\Rightarrow$ $dx = 2t\, dt$ also when $x = 0 \Rightarrow t = 0$

$x = 1 \Rightarrow t = 1$

$(\because x = t^2)$

$$\therefore \int_0^1 \sin^{-1}(\sqrt{x})\, dx = \int_0^1 \sin^{-1}(t).2t\, dt$$

$$= 2\int_0^1 \sin^{-1}(t)\, t\, dt$$

($\because$ solving this by using Integration By parts)

$$= 2\left(\sin^{-1} t.\left(\frac{t^2}{2}\right) - \int_0^1 \frac{1}{\sqrt{1-t^2}}.\frac{t^2}{2}dt \right)_0^1$$

(∵ by problem 12 (iv)

$$= 2.\frac{\pi}{8} = \frac{\pi}{4}$$

14. Evaluate (i) $\int_0^1 \frac{1}{e^x + e^{-x}} dx$ (ii) $\int_0^{\frac{\pi}{2}} \sqrt{\cos x}.\sin^5 x\, dn$

(iii) $\int_0^4 \frac{1}{1+\sqrt{x}} dx$

Sol. (i) $\int_0^1 \frac{1}{e^x + e^{-x}} = \int_0^1 \frac{1}{e^x + \frac{1}{e^x}} dx = \int_0^1 \frac{e^x}{(e^x)^2 + 1} dx$

Put $e^x = t \Rightarrow e\ dx = dt$

when $x = 0 \Rightarrow t = e^0 = 1$

$x = 1 \Rightarrow t = e^1 = e$

$$\therefore \int_0^1 \frac{e^x}{(e^x)^2+1} dx = \int_1^e \frac{dt}{t^2+1} = \left[\tan^{-1}(t)\right]_1^e = \tan^{-1}(e) - \tan^{-1} (1)$$

$$= \tan^{-1}(e) - \frac{\pi}{4}$$

(ii) $\int_0^{\frac{\pi}{2}} \sqrt{\cos x}\ \sin^5 x\ dx$

Put $\cos x = t \Rightarrow -\sin x\ dx = dt$

when $x = 0 \Rightarrow t = \cos 0 = 1$

$x = \frac{\pi}{2} \Rightarrow t = \cos\frac{\pi}{2} = 1$

$$\therefore \int_0^{\frac{\pi}{2}} \sqrt{\cos x}\ .\ \sin^5 x\ dx = \therefore \int_0^{\frac{\pi}{2}} \sqrt{\cos x}.(1-\cos^2 x)^2.\sin x\, dx$$

$$= -\int_1^0 \sqrt{t}(1-t^2)^2\,dt$$

$$= -\int_1^0 \sqrt{t}(1+t^4-2t^2)dt$$

$$= -\int_1^0 (t^{\frac{1}{2}}+t^{\frac{9}{2}}-2.t^{\frac{5}{2}})dt$$

$$= -\left[\frac{t^{\frac{3}{2}}}{\frac{3}{2}}+\frac{t^{\frac{11}{2}}}{\frac{11}{2}}-2\frac{t^{\frac{7}{2}}}{\frac{7}{2}}\right]_1^0$$

$$= -\left\{(0)-\left(\frac{2}{3}+\frac{2}{11}-\frac{4}{7}\right)\right\}$$

$$= \frac{64}{231}$$

(iii) $\displaystyle\int_0^4 \frac{1}{1+\sqrt{x}}dx$

Put $x = t^2$; $dx = 2t\,dt$

when $x = 0 \Rightarrow t^2 = 0 \Rightarrow t = 0$

$x = 4 \Rightarrow t^2 = 4 \Rightarrow t = 2$

$$\int_0^2 \frac{1}{1+t} \times 2t\,dt$$

$$= 2\int_0^2 \frac{t}{1+t}dt$$

$$= 2\int_0^2 \left(\frac{1+t-1}{1+t}\right)dt$$

$$= 2\int_0^2 \left(1-\frac{1}{1+t}\right)dt$$

$$= 2[t-\ln(1+t)]_0^2 = 2 \;\; = 2[\,2 - ln\,3] = 4 - 2\,ln\,3$$

15. Evaluate

(i) $\int_0^{\frac{\pi}{2}} \cos 5x \cos 3x \, dx$ (ii) $\int_0^{\frac{\pi}{2}} \cos^4 x \sin x \, dx$

(iii) $\int_0^{\frac{\pi}{4}} \tan^6 x \, . \sec^2 x \, dx$ (iv) $\int_0^1 \frac{\cos^{-1} x}{\sqrt{1-x^2}} dx$

Sol. (i) $\int_0^{\frac{\pi}{2}} \cos 5x \cos 3x \, dx$

$$= \frac{1}{2}\int_0^{\frac{\pi}{2}} 2\cos 5x . \cos 3x \, dx$$

$$= \frac{1}{2}\int_0^{\frac{\pi}{2}} (\cos 8x + \cos 2x) dx$$

[∵ cos (A + B) + cos(A – B) = 2cos A cos B]

$$= \frac{1}{2}\int_0^{\frac{\pi}{2}} \cos 8x . \, dx + \frac{1}{2}\int_0^{\frac{\pi}{2}} \cos 2x \, dx$$

$$= \frac{1}{2}\left[\frac{\sin 8x}{8}\right]_0^{\frac{\pi}{2}} + \frac{1}{2}\left[\frac{\sin 2x}{2}\right]_0^{\frac{\pi}{2}}$$

$$= \frac{1}{16}[\sin 4\pi - \sin 0] + \frac{1}{4}[\sin \pi - \sin 0]$$

$$= 0 + 0 = 0$$

(ii) $\int_0^{\frac{\pi}{2}} \cos^4 x . \sin x dx$

put $\cos x = t \Rightarrow -\sin x \, dx = dt$

when $x = 0 \quad \Rightarrow \quad t = \cos o = 1$ (∵ $t = \cos x$)

when $x = \frac{\pi}{2} \quad \Rightarrow \quad t = \cos\frac{\pi}{2} = 0$

$$\therefore \int_0^{\frac{\pi}{2}} \cos^4 x.\sin x dx = \int_1^0 t^4.(-dt)$$

$$= -\left(\frac{t^5}{5}\right)_1^0 = -\left(0 - \frac{1}{5}\right) = \frac{1}{5}$$

(iii) $\int_0^{\frac{\pi}{4}} \tan^6 x.\sec^2 x dx$

Put $\tan x = t \quad \Rightarrow \quad \sec^2 x\, dx = dt$

when $x = 0 \quad \Rightarrow \quad t = \tan 0 = 0$

$x = \frac{\pi}{4} \quad \Rightarrow \quad t = \tan\frac{\pi}{4} = 1$

$$\therefore \int_0^{\frac{\pi}{4}} \tan^6 x.\sec^2 x dx = \int_0^1 t^6.dt = \left[\frac{t^7}{7}\right]_0^1 = \frac{1}{7} - \frac{0}{7} = \frac{1}{7}$$

(iv) $\int_0^1 \frac{\cos^{-1} x}{\sqrt{1-x^2}} dx$

put $\cos^{-1}x = t \quad \Rightarrow \quad \frac{-1}{\sqrt{1-x^2}} dx = dt$

when $x = 0 \quad \Rightarrow \quad t = \cos^{-1} 0 = \frac{\pi}{2}$

$x = 1 \quad \Rightarrow \quad t = \cos^{-1} = 0$

$$\therefore \int_0^1 \frac{\cos^{-1} x}{\sqrt{1-x^2}} dn = \int_{\frac{\pi}{2}}^0 t(-dt) = \int [\frac{-t^2}{2}]_{\frac{\pi}{2}}^0 = 0 + \left(\frac{\pi^2}{8}\right) = \frac{\pi^2}{8}$$

16. Evaluate (i) $\int_0^{\frac{\pi}{2}} \frac{\sin x \cos x}{1+\sin^4 x} dx$ (ii) $\int_0^{\frac{\pi}{2}} \frac{\sin x \cos x}{\cos^2 x + 3\cos x + 2} dx$

Sol. (i) $\int_0^{\frac{\pi}{2}} \frac{\sin x \cos x}{1+\sin^4 x} dx$ (ii) *Hint:* Take $\cos x = t$

Put $\sin x = t \Rightarrow \cos x\, dx = dt$

when $x = 0 \Rightarrow t = \sin 0 = 0$

$x = \frac{\pi}{2} \Rightarrow t = \sin \frac{\pi}{2} = 1$

$$\therefore \int_0^{\frac{\pi}{2}} \frac{\sin x.\cos x}{1+\sin^4 x} dx = \int_0^1 \frac{t.dt}{1+t^4} = \frac{1}{2}\int_0^1 \frac{2tdt}{1+(t^2)^2}$$

$$= \frac{1}{2}.\left[\tan^{-1}(t^2)\right]_0^1 = \frac{1}{2}\left[\tan^{-1}(1) - \tan^{-1}(0)\right] = \frac{1}{2}\left(\frac{\pi}{4} - 0\right) = \frac{\pi}{8}$$

17. (i) $\int_1^3 \frac{dx}{(x+1)(x+3)}$ (ii) $\int_0^{\frac{\pi}{2}} \frac{\cos x}{(2+\sin x)(3+\sin x)} dx$

Sol: (i) $\int_1^3 \frac{dx}{(x+1)(x+3)} = \frac{1}{2}\int_1^3 \left[\frac{1}{(x+1)} - \frac{1}{(x+3)}\right] dx$ ($\because$ by partial fractions)

$$= \frac{1}{2}\left[ln(x+1) - ln(x+3)\right]_1^3$$

$$= \frac{1}{2}\left[(ln4 - ln6) - (ln2 - ln4)\right]$$

$$= \frac{1}{2}\left[2ln4 - ln6 - ln2\right]$$

$$= \frac{1}{2}\left[ln16 - ln12\right]$$

$$= \frac{1}{2} ln\left[\frac{16}{12}\right] = \frac{1}{2} ln\frac{4}{3} = ln\left(\frac{2}{\sqrt{3}}\right)$$

(ii) $\int_0^{\frac{\pi}{2}} \frac{\cos x}{(2+\sin x)(3+\sin x)} dx$

Put $\sin x = t \quad \Rightarrow \quad \cos x\, dx = dt$

when $x = 0 \quad \Rightarrow \quad t = \sin 0 = 0$

$x = \frac{\pi}{2} \quad \Rightarrow \quad t = \sin \frac{\pi}{2} = 1$

Integral becomes $\therefore \int_0^1 \frac{dt}{(2+t)(3+t)} = \int_0^1 \left[\frac{1}{(t+2)} - \frac{1}{(t+3)}\right] dt$

$= \left(\ln(t+2) - \ln(t+3)\right)_0^1$

$= \ln\left(\frac{t+2}{t+3}\right)\Bigg|_0^1 = ln\left(\frac{3}{4}\right) - ln\left(\frac{2}{3}\right)$

Exercise - 24.1

Find the values of the following integrals

1. (i) $\int_0^1 x^2 dx$ (ii) $\int_1^2 c^x dx$

(iii) $\int_0^{\frac{\pi}{2}} \sin x\, dx$ (iv) $\int_0^{\frac{\pi}{3}} \sec^2 x\, dx$

(v) $\int_{\frac{\pi}{6}}^{\frac{\pi}{3}} \tan^2 x\, dx$

2. (i) $\int_0^a (a^2 x - x^3) dx$ (ii) $\int_0^a (\sqrt{a} - \sqrt{x})^2 dx$

(iii) $\int_0^1 \frac{dx}{\sqrt{x+1+\sqrt{x}}}$ (iv) $\int_1^2 \frac{(x+1)^2}{\sqrt{x}} dx$

3. (i) $\int_2^3 \frac{1}{x} dx$ (ii) $\int_0^1 \frac{1}{1+x} dx$

(iii) $\int_1^2 \frac{2x}{1+x^2} dx$ (iv) $\int_0^1 \frac{1-x}{1+x} dx$

4. (i) $\int_{\frac{1}{\sqrt{2}}}^1 \frac{1}{\sqrt{1-x^2}} dx$ (ii) $\int_0^a \frac{1}{\sqrt{a^2-x^2}} dx$

(iii) $\int_{-1}^1 \frac{1}{1+x^2} dx$ (iv) $\int_0^1 \frac{1}{a^2+x^2} dx$

(v) $\int_1^4 x\sqrt{x^2-1}\, dx$

5. (i) $\int_0^1 \frac{4x^3}{\sqrt{1-x^8}} dx$ (ii) $\int_1^5 \frac{dx}{\sqrt{2x-1}}$

(iii) $\int_0^1 x.e^{-x^2} dx$

6. (i) $\int_1^2 \log x\, dx$ (ii) $\int_1^{\sqrt{e}} x \log x\, dx$

(iii) $\int_0^1 \sin^{-1} x\, dn$ (iv) $\int_1^2 x^2 \log x\, dx$

(v) $\int_0^1 (1+x).\log(1+x) dx$

7. (i) $\int_2^3 \frac{1}{x(\log x)^2} dx$ (ii) $\int_1^3 \frac{\sin(\log x)}{x} dx$

(iii) $\int_0^2 \frac{5x+1}{x^2+4} dx$ (iv) $\int_0^1 \frac{\cos(\tan^{-1} x)}{1+x^2} dx$

(v) $\int_0^{\frac{\pi}{2}} \frac{\sin\theta}{\sqrt{1+\cos\theta}} d\theta$

Answers

1. (i) $\frac{1}{3}$ (ii) $e^2 - e$ (iii) 1

(iv) $\sqrt{3}$ (v) $\frac{2}{\sqrt{3}} - \frac{\pi}{6}$

2. (i) $\frac{a^4}{4}$ (ii) $\frac{a^2}{6}$ (iii) $\frac{4}{3}(\sqrt{2}-1)$

(iv) $\frac{94\sqrt{2}-56}{15}$

3. (i) $ln\left(\frac{3}{2}\right)$ (ii) $\log 2$ (iii) $\log\frac{5}{2}$

(iv) $2\log 2 - 1$

4. (i) $\frac{\pi}{4}$ (ii) $\frac{\pi}{2}$ (iii) $\frac{\pi}{2}$

(iv) $\frac{\pi}{4a}$ (v) $5\sqrt{15}$

5. (i) $\frac{\pi}{2}$ (ii) 2 (iii) $\frac{1}{2}\left(1-\frac{1}{e}\right)$

6. (i) $2\log 2 - 1$ (ii) $\frac{1}{4}$ (iii) $\frac{\pi-2}{2}$

(iv) $\frac{8}{3}\log 3 - \frac{7}{9}$ (v) $2 \ln 2 - \frac{3}{4}$

7. (i) $\dfrac{\log\left(\dfrac{3}{2}\right)}{\log 2.\log 3}$ (ii) $1 - \cos(\log 3)$ (iii) $\dfrac{5}{2}(\log 2) + \dfrac{\pi}{8}$

(iv) $\dfrac{1}{\sqrt{2}}$ (v) $2\sqrt{2} - 2$

24.2 Properties of Definite Integrals

Property

1. $$\int_a^b f(x)dx = -\int_b^a f(x)dx$$

Proof : Let $\int_a^b f(x)dx = F(x)$

then $\int_a^b f(x)dx = [F(x)]_a^b$ = F(b) – F(a)

and $\int_b^a f(x)dx = [F(x)]_b^a$ = F(a) – F(b)

= –(F(b) – F(a))

$= -\int_a^b f(x)dx$

$$\therefore \int_b^a f(x)dx = -\int_a^b f(x)dx$$

$$\therefore \int_a^b f(x)dx = -\int_b^a f(x)dx$$

2. $$\int_0^a f(x)dx = \int_0^a f(a-x)dx$$

Proof : Put a – x = t ⇒ –dx = dt ⇒ dx = (–dt)

also, when x = 0 ⇒ t = a – 0 = a

when $x = a \Rightarrow t = a - a = 0$

$$\text{R.H.S} = \int_0^a f(a-x)dx = -\int_a^0 f(t)(-dt)$$

$$= -\int_a^0 f(t)dt = -\left(-\int_0^a f(t)dt\right) \quad (\because \text{ by property (1)})$$

$$= \int_0^a f(t)dt$$

$$= \int_0^a f(x)dx = \text{L.H.S}$$

$$\therefore \int_0^a f(x)dx = \int_0^a f(a-x)dx$$

3. If $a < 0 < b$ then $= \int_a^b f(x)dx = \int_a^c f(x)dx + \int_c^b f(x)dx$

Proof: Let $\int f(x)dx = F(x)$

$\therefore$ R.H.S = (F(c) – F(a)) + F(b) – F(c)
= F(b) – F(a) = L.H.S

4. $\int_{-a}^a f(x)dx = 2\int_0^a f(x)dx$ if $f(x)$ is an even function if

$f(x)$ is an odd function = 0

Proof: A function $f(x)$ is said to be even if $f(x) = f(-x)$

A function $f(x)$ is said to be odd if $f(x) = -f(x)$

$$\int_{-a}^a f(x)dx = \int_{-a}^0 f(x)dx + \int_0^a f(x)dx \quad (\because -a < 0 < a) \text{ and by property 3)}$$

$$= I_1 + \int_0^a f(x)dx$$

Consider $I_1 = \int_{-a}^0 f(x)dx$

Let $x = -t \Rightarrow dx = -dt$

and when $x = -a \qquad -a = -t \Rightarrow t = a$

$x = 0 \Rightarrow 0 = -t \Rightarrow t = 0$

$$\therefore \int_{-a}^{0} f(x)dx = \int_{-a}^{0} f(-t)(-dt)$$

$$= \int_{0}^{a} f(-t)dt \qquad (\because \text{ by property (1)})$$

$$= \int_{0}^{a} f(-x)dx$$

Case (i) if $f(x)$ is even then $f(-x) = f(x)$

$$\therefore \int_{-a}^{0} f(x)dx = \int_{0}^{a} f(-x)dx = \int_{0}^{a} f(x)dx = I_1$$

$$\therefore \int_{-a}^{a} f(x)dx = I_1 + \int_{0}^{a} f(x)dx = \int_{0}^{a} f(x)dx + \int_{0}^{a} f(x)dx$$

$$= 2\int_{0}^{a} f(x)dx$$

Case (ii) if $f(x)$ is odd then $f(-x) = -f(x)$

$$\therefore \int_{-a}^{0} f(x)dx = \int_{0}^{a} f(-x)dn = -\int_{0}^{a} f(x)dx$$

$$\therefore \int_{-a}^{a} f(x)dx = I_1 + \int_{0}^{a} f(x)dx = -\int_{0}^{a} f(x)dx + \int_{0}^{a} f(x)dx = 0$$

Solved Examples

1. Find the values of the following integrals.

(i) $\displaystyle\int_{0}^{\frac{\pi}{2}} \frac{\sin x}{\sin x + \cos x} dx$ (ii) $\displaystyle\int_{0}^{\frac{\pi}{2}} \frac{\cos x}{\sin x + \cos x} dx$

(iii) $\displaystyle\int_{0}^{\frac{\pi}{2}} \frac{\tan x}{\tan x + \sec x} dx$ (iv) $\displaystyle\int_{0}^{\frac{\pi}{2}} \frac{\sqrt{\sin x}}{\sqrt{\sin x} + \sqrt{\cos x}} dn$

(v) $\int_0^{\frac{\pi}{2}} \frac{\cos^{\frac{5}{7}} x}{\sin^{\frac{5}{7}} x + \cos^{\frac{5}{7}} x} dx$ (vi) $\int_0^{\frac{\pi}{2}} \frac{2\sin x + 3\cos x}{\sin x + \cos x} dx$

Sol. (i) Let $I = \int_0^{\frac{\pi}{2}} \frac{\sin x}{\sin x + \cos x} dx$ .....(1)

$$= \int_0^{\frac{\pi}{2}} \frac{\sin\left(\frac{\pi}{2} - x\right)}{\sin\left(\frac{\pi}{2} - x\right) + \cos\left(\frac{\pi}{2} - x\right)} dx \qquad \left(\because \int_0^a f(x)dx = \int_0^a f(a-x)dx\right)$$

$$I = \int_0^{\frac{\pi}{2}} \frac{\cos x}{\cos x + \sin x} dx \qquad .....(2)$$

$$(1) + (2) \Rightarrow \quad I + I = \int_0^{\frac{\pi}{2}} \frac{\sin x}{\sin x + \cos x} dx + \int_0^{\frac{\pi}{2}} \frac{\cos x}{\sin x + \cos x} dx$$

$$2I = \int_0^{\frac{\pi}{2}} \left(\frac{\sin x}{\sin x + \cos x} + \frac{\cos x}{\sin x + \cos x}\right) dx$$

$$= \int_0^{\frac{\pi}{2}} \left(\frac{\sin x + \cos x}{\sin x + \cos x}\right) dx$$

$$= \int_0^{\frac{\pi}{2}} 1 dx = [x]_0^{\frac{\pi}{2}} = \frac{\pi}{2}$$

$$\therefore 2I = \frac{\pi}{2} \quad \Rightarrow \quad I = \frac{\pi}{4}$$

(ii) Let $I = \int_0^{\frac{\pi}{2}} \frac{\cos x}{\sin x + \cos x} dx$

$$= \int_0^{\frac{\pi}{2}} \frac{\cos(\frac{\pi}{2} - x)}{\sin(\frac{\pi}{2} - x) + \cos(\frac{\pi}{2} - x)} dx$$

$$I = \int_0^{\frac{\pi}{2}} \frac{\sin x}{\sin x + \cos x} dx$$

$$2I = \int_0^{\frac{\pi}{2}} \frac{\sin x + \cos x}{\sin x + \cos x} dx = \int_0^{\frac{\pi}{2}} 1 dx = [x]_0^{\frac{\pi}{2}} = \frac{\pi}{2}$$

$$\therefore I = \frac{\pi}{4}$$

(iii) Let $I = \int_0^{\frac{\pi}{2}} \frac{\tan x}{\tan x + \cot x} dx$

$$= \int_0^{\frac{\pi}{2}} \frac{\tan\left(\frac{\pi}{2} - x\right)}{\tan(\frac{\pi}{2} - x) + \cot\left(\frac{\pi}{2} - x\right)} dx$$

$$= \int_0^{\frac{\pi}{2}} \frac{\cot x}{\cot x + \tan x} dx$$

$$\therefore 2I = \int_0^{\frac{\pi}{2}} \frac{\tan x + \cot x}{\tan x + \cot x} dx$$

$$= \int_0^{\frac{\pi}{2}} 1 dx = (x)_0^{\frac{\pi}{2}} = \frac{\pi}{2}$$

$$\therefore I = \frac{\pi}{4}$$

(iv) Let $= \int_0^{\frac{\pi}{2}} \frac{\sqrt{\sin x}}{\sqrt{\sin x}+\sqrt{\cos x}}dx$

$$= \int_0^{\frac{\pi}{2}} \frac{\sqrt{\sin\left(\frac{\pi}{2}-x\right)}}{\sqrt{\sin(\frac{\pi}{2}-x)}+\sqrt{\cos\left(\frac{\pi}{2}-x\right)}}dx$$

$$I = \int_0^{\frac{\pi}{2}} \frac{\sqrt{\cos x}}{\sqrt{\cos x}+\sqrt{\sin x}}dx$$

$$2I = \int_0^{\frac{\pi}{2}} \left(\frac{\sqrt{\sin x}}{\sqrt{\sin x}+\sqrt{\cos x}}+\frac{\sqrt{\cos x}}{\sqrt{\sin x}+\sqrt{\cos x}}\right)dx$$

$$= \int_0^{\frac{\pi}{2}} 1dx = \frac{\pi}{2}$$

$$I = \frac{\pi}{4}$$

(v) Same as above

(vi) Let $I = \int_0^{\frac{\pi}{2}} \frac{2\sin x+3\cos x}{\sin x+\cos x}dx$

$$= \int_0^{\frac{\pi}{2}} \frac{2\sin(\frac{\pi}{2}-x)+3\cos(\frac{\pi}{2}-x)}{\sin\left(\frac{\pi}{2}-x\right)+\cos\left(\frac{\pi}{2}-x\right)}$$

$$I = \int_0^{\frac{\pi}{2}} \frac{2\cos x+3\sin x}{\cos x+\sin x}dx$$

$$\therefore\ I + I = 2I = \int_0^{\frac{\pi}{2}} \left[\left(\frac{2\sin x + 3\cos x}{\sin x + \cos x}\right) + \left(\frac{2\cos x + 3\sin x}{\cos x + \sin x}\right)\right] dx$$

$$= \int_0^{\frac{\pi}{2}} \left(\frac{5\sin x + 5\cos x}{\sin x + \cos x}\right) dx$$

$$= 5\int_0^{\frac{\pi}{2}} 1dx = 5(x)_0^{\frac{\pi}{2}} = \frac{5\pi}{2}$$

$$\therefore 2I = \frac{5\pi}{2} \quad \Rightarrow \quad I = \frac{5\pi}{4}$$

Note $\int_0^{\frac{\pi}{2}} \frac{a\sin x + b\cos x}{\sin x + \cos x} dx = \frac{(a+b)}{4}\pi$

2. (i) $\int_0^{\frac{\pi}{2}} \log(\tan x)dx$ (ii) $\int_0^{\frac{\pi}{2}} \log(\cot x)dx$

(iii) $\int_0^{\frac{\pi}{2}} \frac{\cos x - \sin x}{1 + \cos x \sin x} dx$ (iv) $\int_0^{\frac{\pi}{2}} \frac{\cos^2 x - \sin^2 x}{\sin^3 x + \cos^3 x} dx$

Sol. (i) Let $I = \int_0^{\frac{\pi}{2}} \log(\tan x)dx$

$$= \int_0^{\frac{\pi}{2}} \log(\tan(\frac{\pi}{2} - x)dx \qquad \left(\because \int_0^a f(x)dx = \int_0^a f(a-x)dx\right)$$

$$I = \int_0^{\frac{\pi}{2}} \log(\cot n)dx$$

$$\therefore \quad I + I = \int_0^{\frac{\pi}{2}} \log(\tan x)dx + \int_0^{\frac{\pi}{2}} \log(\cot x)dx$$

$$= \int_0^{\frac{\pi}{2}} [\log(\tan x) + \ln(\cot x)]dx$$

$$= \int_0^{\frac{\pi}{2}} \log(\tan x.\cot x)dx \qquad (\because \log m + \log n = \log mn)$$

$$2I = 0 \Rightarrow I = 0$$

(ii) Let $I = \int_0^{\frac{\pi}{2}} \log(\cot x)dx$

$$= \int_0^{\frac{\pi}{2}} \log(\cot(\frac{\pi}{2} - x))dx$$

$$I = \int_0^{\frac{\pi}{2}} \log(\tan x))dx$$

$$\therefore I + I = \int_0^{\pi} [\log(\cot x) + (\log(\tan x))]dx$$

$$= \int_0^{\frac{\pi}{2}} \log(\cot x.\tan x)\, dx$$

$$= \int_0^{\frac{\pi}{2}} \log 1\, dx = 0 \qquad (\because \log 1 = 0 \therefore \int_a^b dx = 0)$$

$$\therefore 2I = 0 \qquad \Rightarrow I = 0$$

(iii) Let $I = \int_0^{\frac{\pi}{2}} \frac{\cos x - \sin x}{1 + \cos x \sin x} dx$

$$= \int_0^{\frac{\pi}{2}} \frac{\cos(\frac{\pi}{2} - x) - \sin(\frac{\pi}{2} - x)}{1 + \cos(\frac{\pi}{2} - x)\sin(\frac{\pi}{2} - x)} dx$$

$$I = \int_0^{\frac{\pi}{2}} \frac{\sin x - \cos x}{1 + \sin x \cos x} dx$$

$$I + I = 2I = \int_0^{\frac{\pi}{2}} \left(\frac{\cos x - \sin x + \sin x - \cos x}{1 + \sin x \cos x} \right) dx$$

$$= \int_0^{\frac{\pi}{2}} 0 \, dx = 0$$

$\therefore 2I = 0 \Rightarrow I = 0$

(iv) Let $I = \int_0^{\frac{\pi}{2}} \frac{\cos^2 x - \sin^2 x}{\sin^3 x + \cos^3 x} dx$

$$= \int_0^{\frac{\pi}{2}} \frac{\cos^2(\frac{\pi}{2} - x) - \sin^2\left(\frac{\pi}{2} - x\right)}{\sin^3(\frac{\pi}{2} - x) + \cos^3(\frac{\pi}{2} - x)} dx$$

$$I = \int_0^{\frac{\pi}{2}} \frac{\sin^2 x - \cos^2 x}{\cos^3 x + \sin x} dx$$

$$I + I = \int_0^{\pi/2} \frac{\cos^2 x - \sin^2 x + \sin^2 x - \cos^2 x}{\sin^3 x + \cos^3 x} dx$$

$$= \int_0^{\pi/2} 0\,dx = 0$$

$\therefore\ I = 0$

3. Show that $\int_0^5 x(5-x)^{10}\,dx = \frac{(5)^{12}}{132}$

Sol. $\int_0^5 x(5-x)^{10}\,dx = \int_0^5 (5-x)[5-(5-x)]^{10}\,dx = \int_0^5 (5-x)(x)^{10}$

$$\left(\because \int_0^a f(x)dx = \int_0^a f(a-x)\right)$$

$$= \int_0^5 (5-x)x^{10}\,dx$$

$$= \int_0^5 \left(5x^{10} - x^{11}\right)dx$$

$$= \left[\frac{5.x^{11}}{11} - \frac{x^{12}}{12}\right]_0^5 = \frac{5}{11}(5)^{11} - \frac{(5)^{12}}{12}$$

$$= \frac{5^{12}}{11} - \frac{5^{12}}{12}$$

$$= 5^{12}\left(\frac{1}{11} - \frac{1}{12}\right)$$

$$= 5^{12}\left(\frac{1}{132}\right)$$

4. Prove that $\int_{-2}^{2} \left(x^{11}\cos x + \sin x\right) = 0$

Sol. $\int_{-2}^{2} x^{11}\cos x + \int_{-2}^{2} \sin x\,dx$

$= 0 + 0 = 0$ ($\because$ $x^{11}\cos x$, $\sin x$ are odd functions)

5. Evaluate $\int_0^4 |2-x|\,dx$

Sol. $$\int_0^4 |2-x| = \int_0^2 |2-x|\,dx + \int_2^4 |2-x|\,dx$$

$$= \int_0^2 (2-x)\,dx + \int_2^4 (x-2)\,dx$$

$$= \left(2x - \frac{x^2}{2}\right)_0^2 + \left(\frac{x^2}{2} - 2x\right)_2^4 = \left(4 - \frac{4}{2}\right) + \left((8-8)-(2-4)\right) = 4$$

6. (i) $\int_0^{\pi/2} \frac{1}{1+\tan x}\,dx$ (ii) $\int_0^{\pi/2} \frac{e^{\sin x}}{e^{\sin x} + e^{\cos x}}\,dx$

Sol. (i) $\int_0^{\pi/2} \frac{1}{1+\tan x} dn$

$$= \int_0^{\pi/2} \frac{1}{1+\frac{\sin x}{\cos x}}\,dn = \int_0^{\pi/2} \frac{\cos x}{\cos x + \sin x}\,dn = \pi/4 \qquad \text{(by example 1)}$$

(ii) Let $$I = \int_0^{\pi/2} \frac{e^{\sin x}}{e^{\sin x} + e^{\cos x}} dx = \int_0^{\pi/2} \frac{e^{\sin\left(\frac{\pi}{2}-x\right)}}{e^{\sin\left(\frac{\pi}{2}-x\right)} + e^{\cos\left(\frac{\pi}{2}-x\right)}}\,dx$$

$$\therefore\ I = \int_0^{\pi/2} \frac{e^{\cos x}}{e^{\cos x} + e^{\sin x}}\,dx$$

$$\therefore\ 2I = \int_0^{\pi/2} \left(\frac{e^{\sin x}}{e^{\sin x} + e^{\cos x}} + \frac{e^{\cos x}}{e^{\cos x} + e^{\sin x}}\right) dx$$

$$= \int_0^{\pi/2} \left(\frac{e^{\sin x} + e^{\cos x}}{e^{\sin x} + e^{\cos x}}\right) dx = \int_0^{\pi/2} 1\,dx = (x)_0^{\pi/2}$$

$$\therefore\ I = \frac{\pi}{4}$$

7. Evaluate

(i) $\int_0^{\pi/4} \log(1+\tan x)\,dx$ (ii) $\int_0^1 \frac{\log(1+x)}{1+x^2}\,dn$

Sol. (i) Let $I = \int_0^{\pi/4} \log(1+\tan x)\,dx$

$$= \int_0^{\pi/4} \log\left(1+\tan\left(\frac{\pi}{4}-x\right)\right)dx$$

$$= \int_0^{\pi/4} \log\left(1+\left(\frac{1-\tan x}{1+\tan x}\right)\right)dx$$

$$= \int_0^{\pi/4} \log\left(\frac{1+\tan x+1-\tan x}{1+\tan x}\right)dx$$

$$= \int_0^{\pi/4} \log\left(\frac{2}{1+\tan x}\right)\cdot dx$$

$$I = \int_0^{\pi/4} \log 2\,dx - \int_0^{\pi/4} \log(1+\tan x)\,dx$$

$$= \log 2 \int_0^{\pi/4} 1\,dx - I$$

$$\therefore \quad 2I = \log 2 \int_0^{\pi/4} 1\,dx = (\log 2).(x)_0^{\pi/4} = (\log 2).(\pi/4)$$

$$\therefore \quad 2I = \frac{\pi}{4}\log 2 \Rightarrow \quad I = \frac{\pi}{8}\log 2$$

(ii) $\int_0^1 \frac{\log(1+x)}{1+x^2}\,dx$

Sol. Put $x = \tan\theta \Rightarrow d\theta = \sec^2\theta\,d\theta$

when $x = 0 \Rightarrow \tan\theta = 0 \Rightarrow \theta = 0$

$x = 1 \Rightarrow \tan\theta = 1 \Rightarrow \theta = \pi/4$

$$\therefore \quad \int_0^1 \frac{\log(1+x)}{1+x^2}\,dx = \int_0^{\pi/4} \frac{\log(1+\tan\theta)}{1+\tan^2\theta}\sec^2\theta\, d\theta$$

$$= \int_0^{\pi/4} \log(1+\tan\theta)\, d\theta$$

$$= \pi/8 \log 2 \qquad \text{(by (i))}$$

Exercise - 24.2

1. Evaluate the following integrals

(i) $\displaystyle\int_0^{\pi/2} \frac{\sin^3 x}{\sin^3 x + \cos^3 x}\,dx$ (ii) $\displaystyle\int_0^{\pi/2} \frac{\sin^{5/2} x}{\sin^{5/2} x + \cos^{5/2} x}\,dx$

(iii) $\displaystyle\int_0^{\pi/2} \frac{\sqrt{\tan x}}{\sqrt{\tan x} + \sqrt{\cot x}}\,dx$ (iv) $\displaystyle\int_0^{\pi/2} \frac{1}{1+\cot x}\,dx$

2. Evaluate the following integrals

(i) $\displaystyle\int_0^{\pi/2} \frac{3\sin x + 4\cos x}{\sin x + \cos x}\,dx$ (ii) $\displaystyle\int_0^{\pi/2} \frac{4\tan x + 5\cot x}{\tan x + \cot x}\,dx$

(iii) $\displaystyle\int_0^{\pi/2} \frac{5\tan x - 3\cot x}{\tan x + \cot x}\,dx$

3. Evaluate the following integrals

(i) $\displaystyle\int_0^{\pi/2} \log(\cot x)\,dx$ (ii) $\displaystyle\int_0^{\pi/2} \log(\tan x)\,dx$

(iii) $\displaystyle\int_0^{\pi/2} \frac{\sin x - \cos x}{1+\sin^2 x.\cos^2 x}\,dn$ (iv) $\displaystyle\int_0^{\pi/2} \frac{\sec x - \operatorname{cosec} x}{1+\sec x.\operatorname{cosec} x}\,dx$

(v) $\displaystyle\int_{-1}^{1} \log\left(\frac{3+x}{3-x}\right)dx$

4. Evaluate the following integrals

(i) $\int_{-1}^{1} |x|\, dx$ (ii) $\int_{0}^{2} |x-1|\, dx$

(iii) $\int_{-2}^{2} |1-x^2|\, dx$

5. Evaluate the following integrals

(i) $\int_{0}^{\pi} \frac{x \tan x}{\sec x + \tan x}\, dx$ (ii) $\int_{0}^{\pi/2} \frac{x}{\sin x + \cos x}\, dx$

Answers

1.	(i) $\pi/4$	(ii) $\pi/4$	(iii) $\pi/4$	(iv) $\pi/4$
2.	(i) $7\pi/4$	(ii) $9\pi/4$	(iii) $\pi/2$	
3.	(i) 0 (v) 0	(ii) 0	(iii) 0	(iv) 0
4.	(i) 1	(ii) 1	(iii) 4	
5.	(i) $\pi^2/2 - \pi$	(ii) $\frac{\pi}{4\sqrt{2}} \log\left|\frac{\sqrt{2}+1}{\sqrt{2}-1}\right|$		

25

Areas

25.1 Some Standard Curves

1. $x^2 + y^2 = a^2$ (Circle)

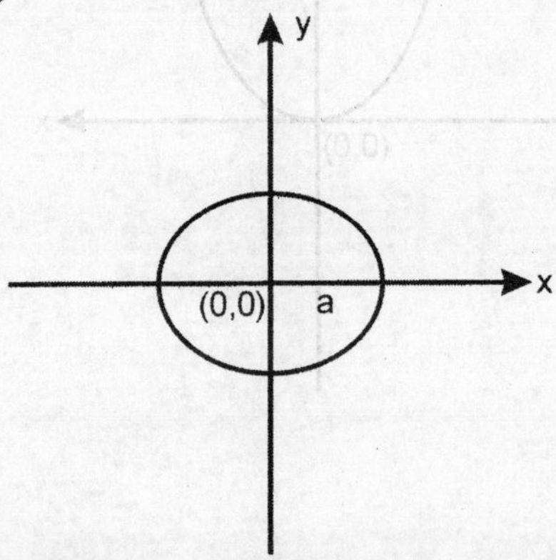

2. $y^2 = 4ax$ (Parabola)

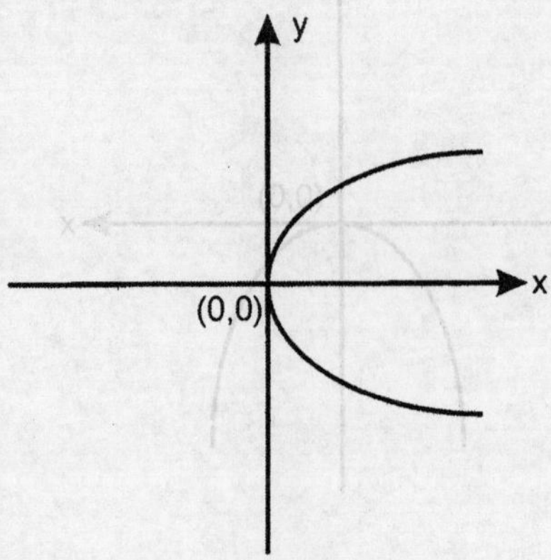

3. $y^2 = -4ax$ (Parobola)

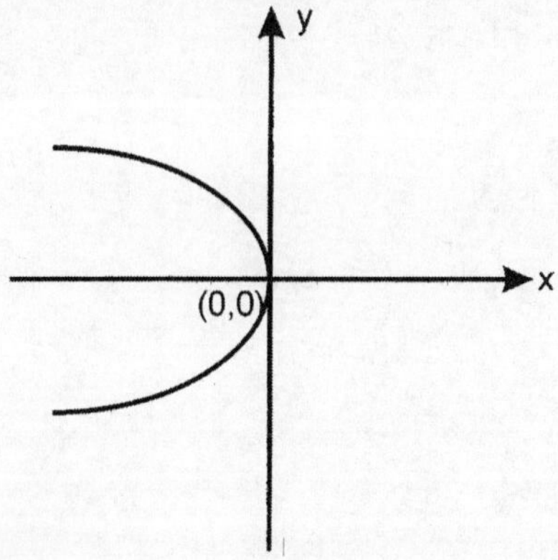

4. $x^2 = +4ay$ (Parabola)

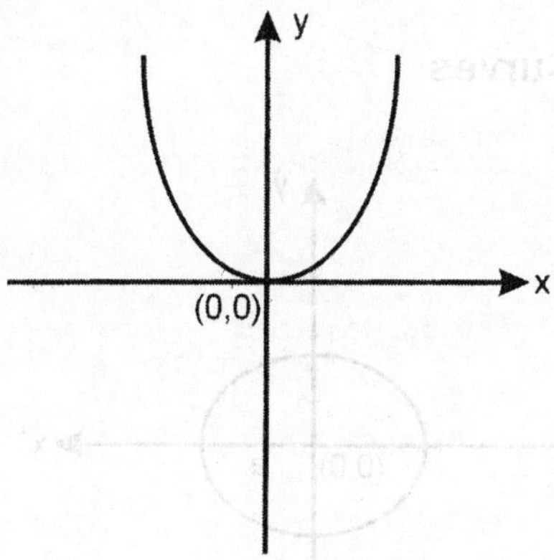

5. $x^2 = -4ay$

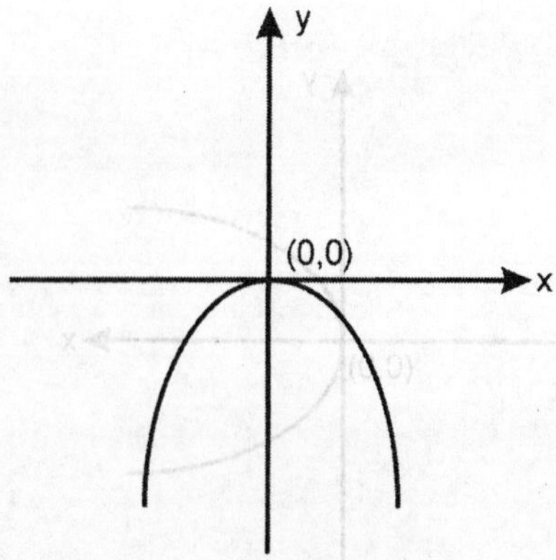

6. $\dfrac{x^2}{a^2}+\dfrac{y^2}{b^2}=1$ (Ellipse)

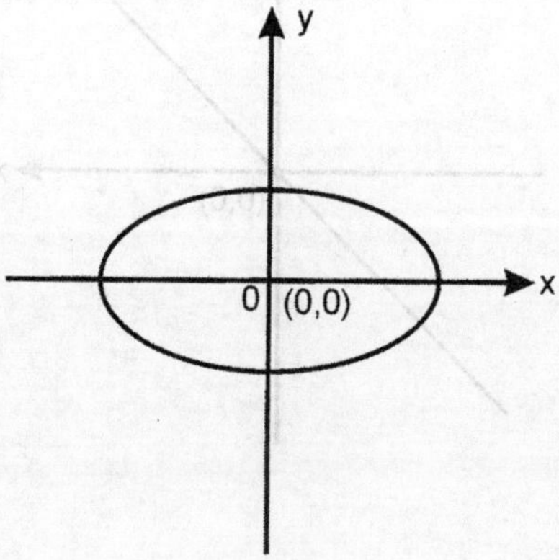

7. $y=\sqrt{x} \quad x>0$

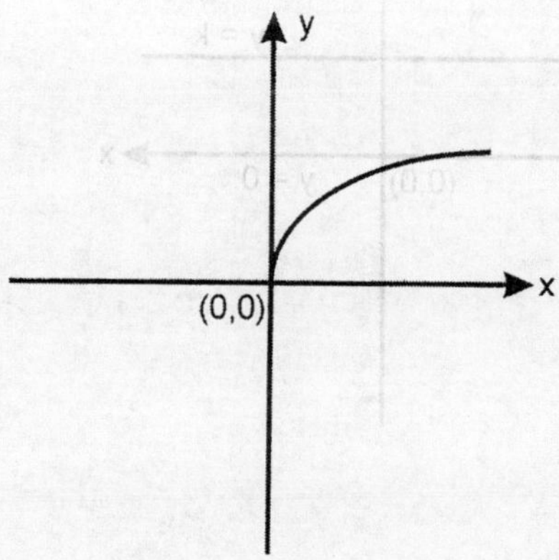

8. $y=x^3$

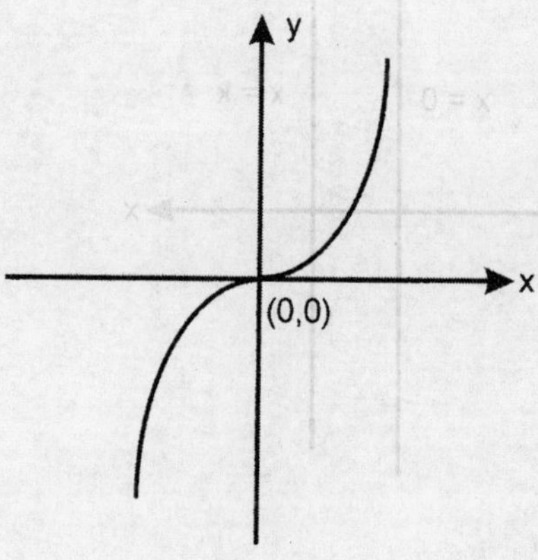

9. $y = x$

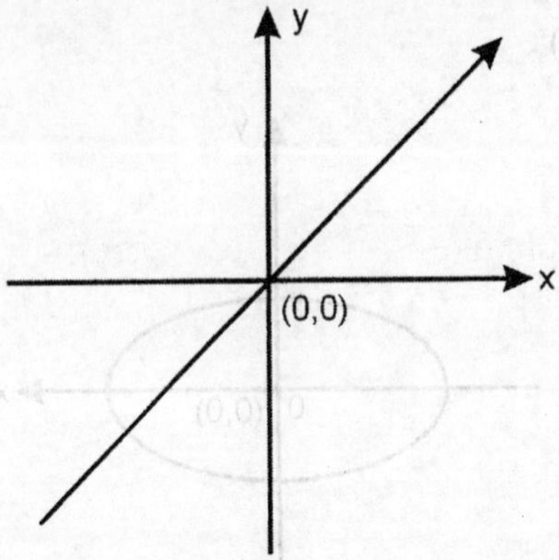

10. $y = k$

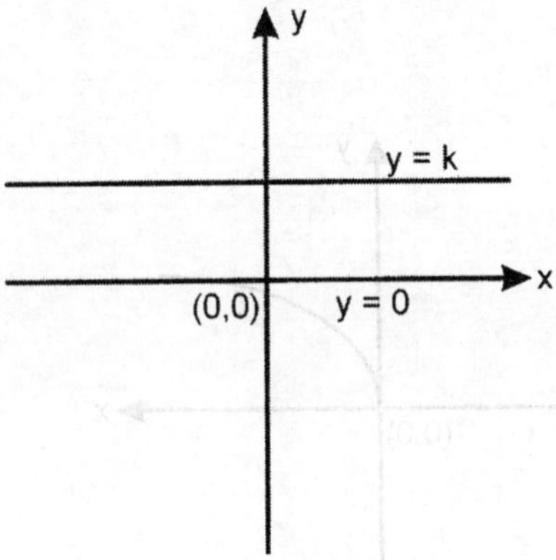

11. $x = k$

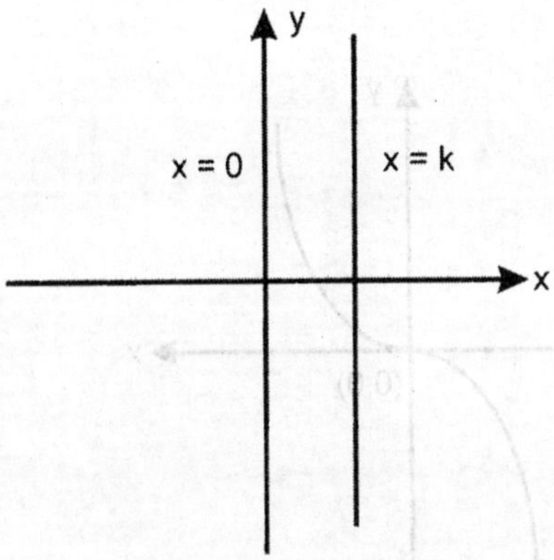

12. $y = \sin x$

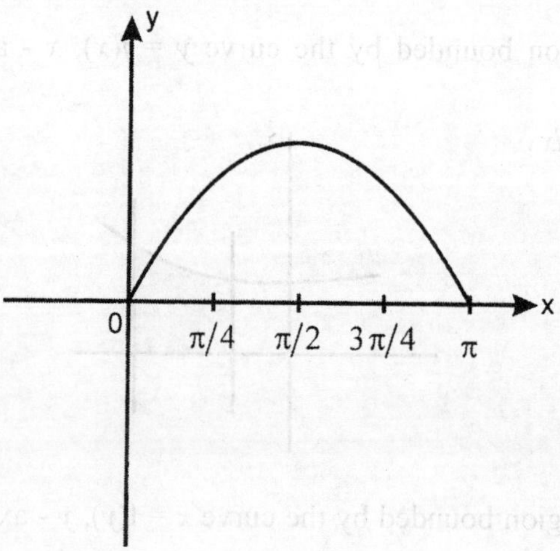

13. $y = \cos x$

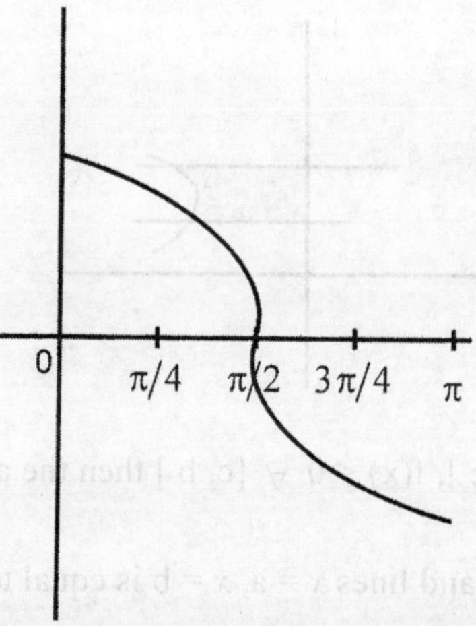

- A curve $y = f(x)$ is said to be symmetric about x-axis if (x, y) lies on the curve then $(x, -y)$ lies on it. Ex : $y^2 = 4ax$.
- A curve i.e., $y = f(x)$ is said to be symmetric about y-axis if (x, y) lies on the curve then $(-x, y)$ lies on it. Ex : $x^2 = 4ay$.
- A curve $y = f(x)$ is said to be symmetric about both x and y axis if (x, y) lies on the curve then $(-x, y)$ $(+x, -y)$, $(-x, -y)$ lies on it.

Ex : (i) $x^2 + y^2 = a^2$ (ii) $\frac{x^2}{a^2} + \frac{y^2}{b^2} = 1$

25.2 Area of Regions Bounded by Curves with Axes

- The area of the region bounded by the curve $y = f(x)$, x - axis and the ordinates $x = a, x = b$ is $\int_a^b y dx$.

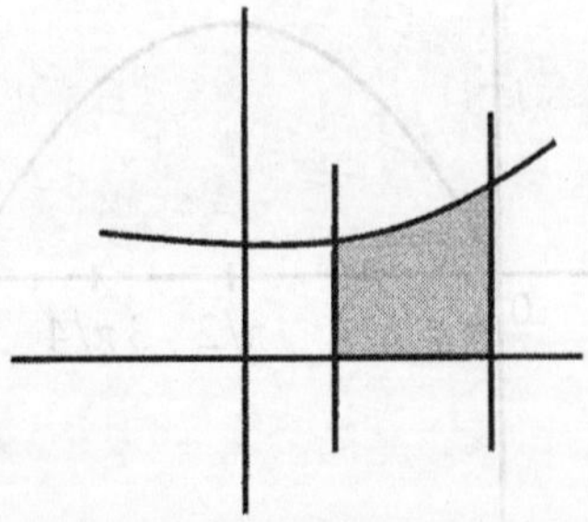

- The area of the region bounded by the curve $x = f(y)$, y - axis and the lines $y = a$, $y = b$ is $\int_a^b x dy$

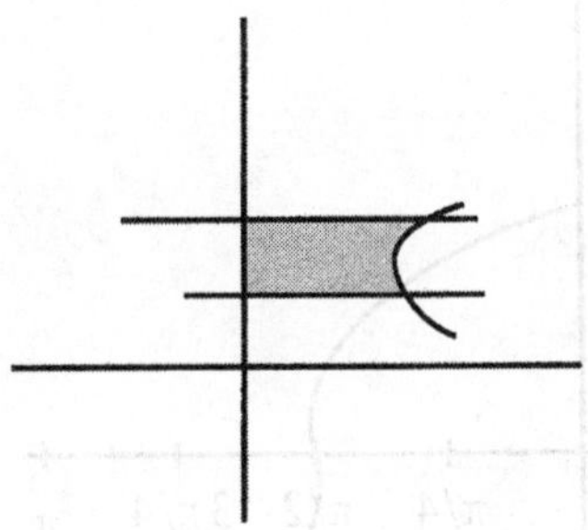

- If $f(x) > 0 \ \forall \ x \in [a, c]$, $f(x) < 0 \ \forall \ [c, b]$ then the area of region bounded by the curve $y = f(x)$, x - axis and lines $x = a$, $x = b$ is equal to $\int_a^c f(x)dx - \int_c^b f(x)dx$.

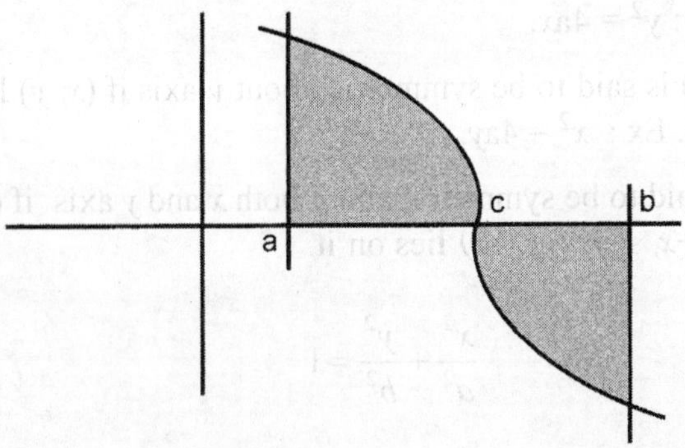

- Let $y = f(x)$, $y = g(x)$ be two curves such that $f(x) > g(x)\ \forall\ x \in [a, b]$ then the area bounded by curves $y = f(x)$, $y = g(x)$ and the lines $x = a$, $x = b$ is $\int_a^b f(x)dx - \int_a^b g(x)dx$

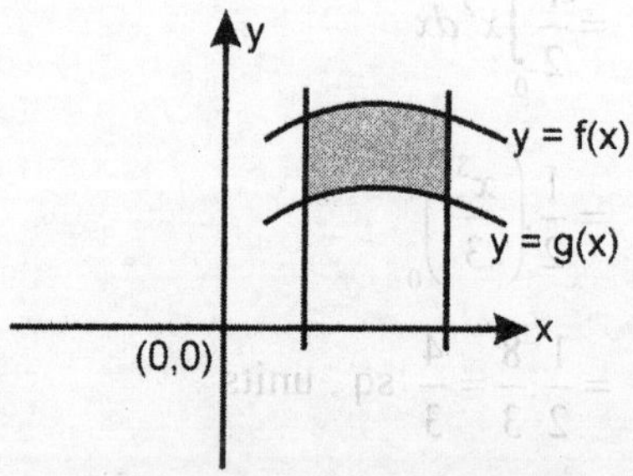

Solved Examples

1. Find the area bounded by the curve $y = x^3$, x - axis and the ordinates $x = 1, x = 4$.

Sol.

x	1	2	3	4	
$y=x^3$	1	8	27	64	

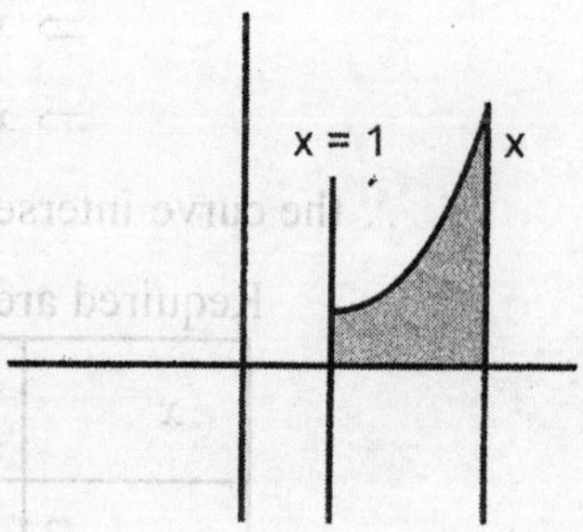

Required area is

$$\int_a^b ydx = \int_1^4 x^3 dx = \left[\frac{x^4}{4}\right]_1^4$$

$$= \frac{1}{4}\left[4^4 - 1\right] = \frac{255}{4} \text{ sq. units}$$

2. Find the area bounded by the curve $y = \frac{x^2}{2}$, bounded by $x = 0$, $x = 2$, and $y = 0$.

x	0	1	2
$y=\frac{x^2}{2}$	0	$\frac{1}{2}$	2

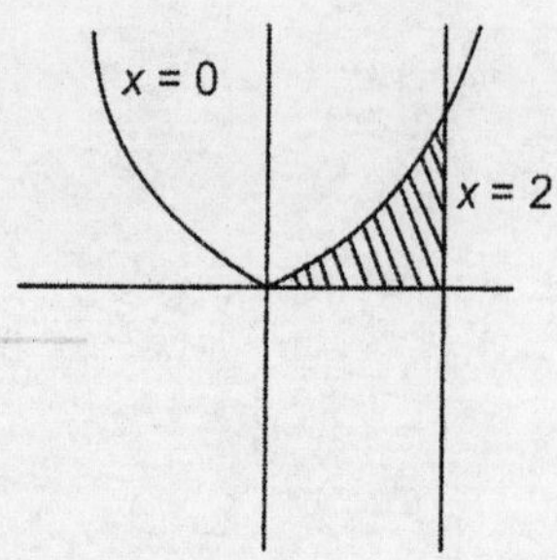

$\therefore$ Required area is

$$\int_0^2 y\,dx = \int_0^2 \frac{x^2}{2}\,dx$$

$$= \frac{1}{2}\int_0^2 x^2\,dx$$

$$= \frac{1}{2}\cdot\left(\frac{x^3}{3}\right)_0^2$$

$$= \frac{1}{2}\cdot\frac{8}{3} = \frac{4}{3} \text{ sq . units}$$

3. Find the area bounded by the curve $y = 4x - x^2$ with x - axis.

Sol. given curve is $y = 4x - x^2$

Put y = 0 we get $0 = 4x - x^2$

$$\Rightarrow x(4 - x) = 0$$

$$\Rightarrow x = 0, x = 4$$

$\therefore$ the curve intersect x - axis at 0, 4

$\therefore$ Required area is

x	0	1	2	3	4	
$y=4x-x^2$	0	3	4	3	0	

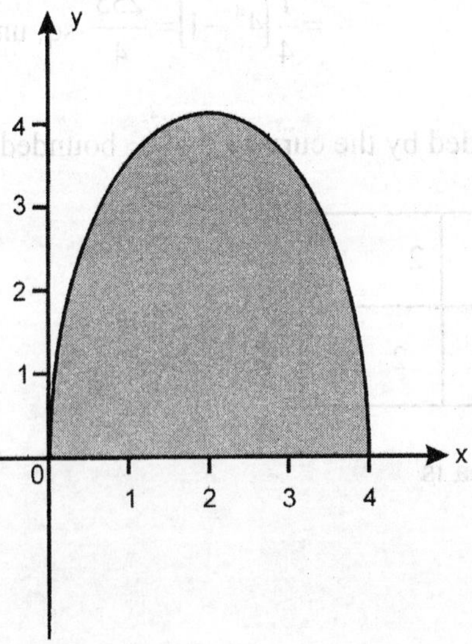

$$\int_0^4 y\,dx = \int_0^4 4x - x^2 dx$$

$$= \left(\frac{4.x^2}{2} - \frac{x^3}{3}\right)_0^4$$

$$= 2.(16) - \frac{1}{3}.64 = 32 - \frac{64}{3} = 32\left(1 - \frac{2}{3}\right) = \frac{32}{3} \text{ sq. units}$$

4. **Find the area cut off between $y = o$, $y = 1 - x - 6x^2$**

Sol: Put $y = 0$ in $y = 1 - x - 6x^2$

$$1 - x - 6x^2 = 0$$

$$\Rightarrow \quad 6x^2 + x - 1 = 0$$

$$6x^2 + 3x - 2x - 1 = 0$$

$$3x(2x + 1) - 1(2x + 1) = 0$$

$$x = \frac{-1}{2},\ x = \frac{1}{3}$$

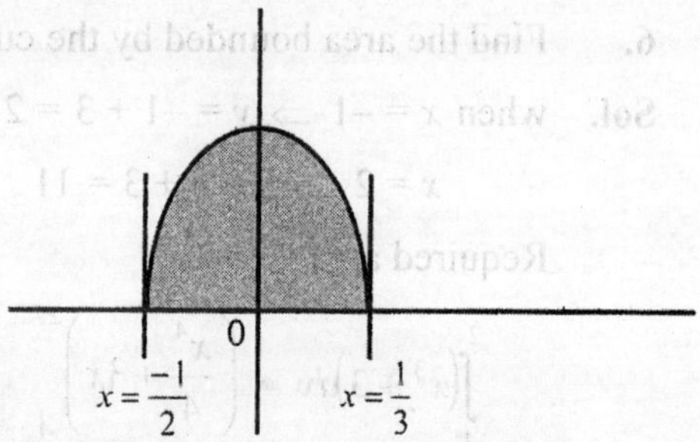

x	$\frac{-1}{2}$	0	$\frac{1}{3}$	
y	0	1	0	

$\therefore$ Required area is $\int_{\frac{-1}{2}}^{\frac{1}{3}} (1 - x - 6x^2)dx$

$$= \left(x - \frac{x^2}{2} - \frac{6x^3}{3}\right)_{-\frac{1}{2}}^{\frac{1}{3}}$$

$$= \frac{125}{216} \text{ square units}$$

5. Find the area bounded by the curve $y = x^2 + 2$; x–axis; $x = 1, x = 2$

Sol. Required area is

$$\int_1^2 y\,dx = \int_1^2 (x^2 + 2)\,dx$$

$$= \left(\frac{x^3}{3} + 2x\right)_1^2$$

$$= \left(\frac{8}{3} + 4\right) - \left(\frac{1}{3} + 2\right) = \frac{20}{3} - \frac{7}{3} = \frac{13}{3} \text{ square units}$$

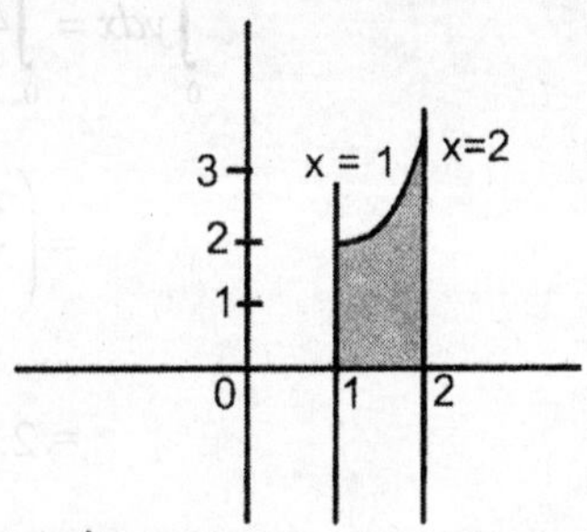

6. Find the area bounded by the curves $y = x^3 + 3, y = 0, x = -1, x = 2$

Sol. when $x = -1 \Rightarrow y = -1 + 3 = 2$

$x = 2 \Rightarrow y = 8 + 3 = 11$

Required area is

$$\int_{-1}^{2} (x^3 + 3)\,dx = \left(\frac{x^4}{4} + 3x\right)_{-1}^{2}$$

$$= (4 + 6) - \left(\frac{1}{4} - 3\right) = 10 - \left(\frac{-11}{4}\right) = \frac{51}{4} \text{ square units}$$

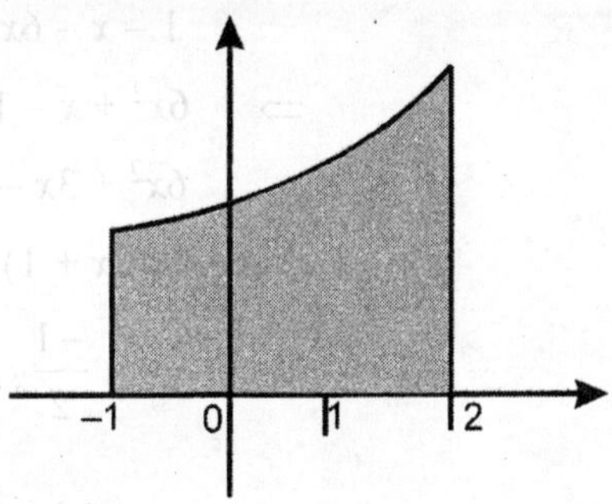

7. Find the area bounded by $y^2 = 4x$ and lines $x = 1, x = 9$

Sol. when $x = 1 \Rightarrow y^2 = 4 \Rightarrow y = \pm 2$

$x = 9 \Rightarrow y^2 = 36 \Rightarrow y = \pm 6$

$y^2 = 4x$

x	1	4	9
y	± 2	± 4	± 6

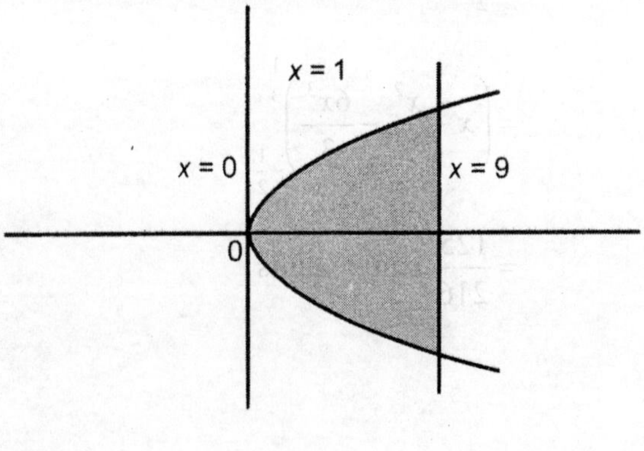

Required area is $2\int_1^9 \sqrt{4x}dx$

$$= 2\int_1^9 2\sqrt{x}dx = 4.\left.\frac{x^{3/2}}{\frac{3}{2}}\right|_1^9 = \frac{8}{3}\left(9\sqrt{9}-1\right) = \frac{208}{3} \text{ square units}$$

8. Find the area bounded by $y^2 = 4ax$ and its latus rectum

Sol. Required area is

$$2\int_0^a ydx = 2\int_0^a 2\sqrt{ax}dx \quad (\because \text{The equation of latus rectum is } x = a)$$

$$= 4\int_0^a \sqrt{ax}dx = 4\sqrt{a}\int_0^a \sqrt{x}\,dx$$

$$= 4\sqrt{a}.\left[\frac{x^{\frac{3}{2}}}{\frac{3}{2}}\right]_0^a$$

$$= 4\sqrt{a}.\frac{2}{3}.a\sqrt{a}$$

$$= \frac{8a^2}{3} \text{ Square Units}$$

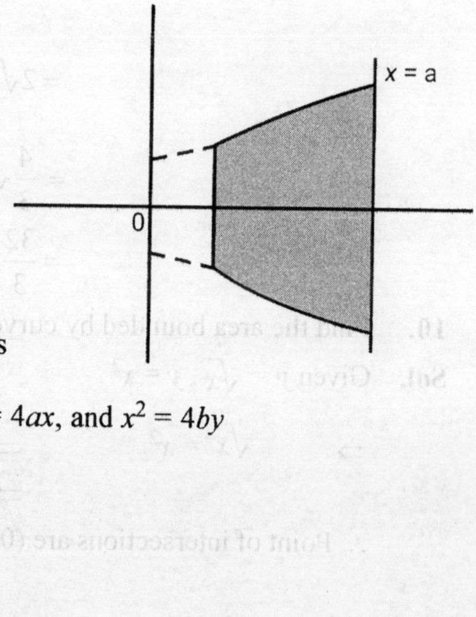

9. Find the area bounded by the curves $y^2 = 4ax$, and $x^2 = 4by$

Sol. Given curves are

$y^2 = 4ax, \rightarrow (1) \qquad x^2 = 4by \rightarrow (2)$

$(1) \Rightarrow y = \dfrac{x^2}{4b}$ sub in (2) we get

$$\left(\frac{x^2}{4b}\right)^2 = 4ax \Rightarrow \frac{x^4}{16b^2} = 4ax$$

$$\Rightarrow \quad x = 0,\ x^3 = 64ab^2$$

$$x = 4a^{1/3}b^{2/3}$$

$$y = \frac{x^2}{4b} = \frac{16a^{2/3}b^{4/3}}{4b} = 4a^{\frac{2}{3}}\,b^{\frac{1}{3}}$$

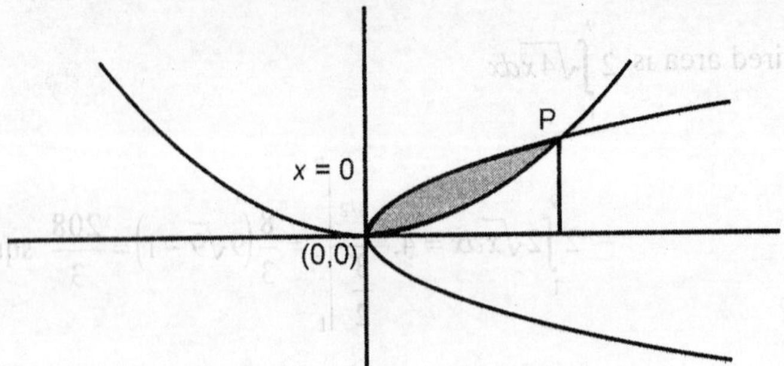

$\therefore$ Point of intersection of curves

$$P = \left(4a^{1/3}b^{2/3}, 4a^{2/3}b^{1/3}\right)$$

Required area is $\displaystyle\int_0^{4a^{\frac{1}{3}}b^{\frac{2}{3}}} \left[\sqrt{4ax} - \frac{x^2}{4b}\right] dy$

$$= 2\sqrt{a}\,\frac{2}{3}\left(x^{\frac{3}{2}}\right)^{4a^{\frac{1}{3}}b^{\frac{2}{3}}} - \left(\frac{x^3}{12b}\right)^{4a^{\frac{1}{3}}b^{\frac{2}{3}}}$$

$$= \frac{4}{3}\sqrt{a}.8.\sqrt{a}\,.b - \frac{1}{12b}.64\,.a\,.b^2$$

$$= \frac{32}{3}ab - \frac{16}{3}ab = \frac{16ab}{3} \text{ square units}$$

10. Find the area bounded by curves $y = \sqrt{x}$, $y = x^2$

Sol. Given $y = \sqrt{x}$, $y = x^2$

$\Rightarrow \quad \sqrt{x} = x^2 \quad \Rightarrow \quad x = 0, x = 1$

$\Rightarrow \quad y = 0, y = 1$

$\therefore$ Point of intersections are (0, 0) (1, 1)

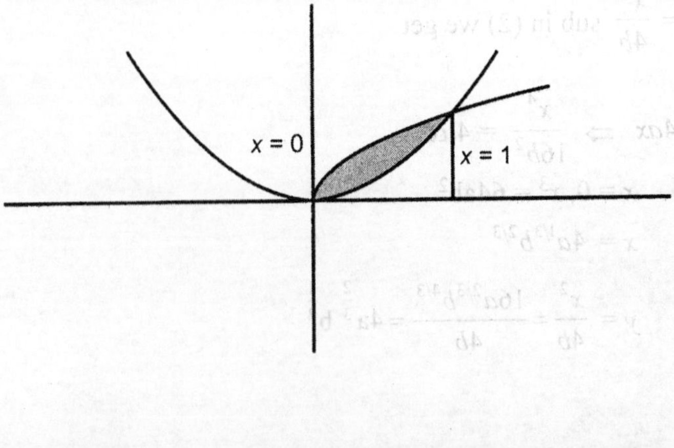

$\therefore$ Required area is

$$\int_0^1 \left(\sqrt{x} - x^2\right) dx$$

$$= \left(\frac{x^{3/2}}{3/2} - \frac{x^3}{3}\right)_0^1 = \frac{2}{3} - \frac{1}{3} = \frac{1}{3} \text{ Square Units}$$

11. Find the area bounded by $y = x^2, y = 2x$

Sol. Given $y = x^2, y = 2x$

$\Rightarrow \quad x^2 = 2x$

$\Rightarrow \quad x = 0, x = 2$

$y = 0, y = 4$

$\therefore$ (0,0), (2,4)

$\therefore$ curves intersect at (0,0), (2,4)

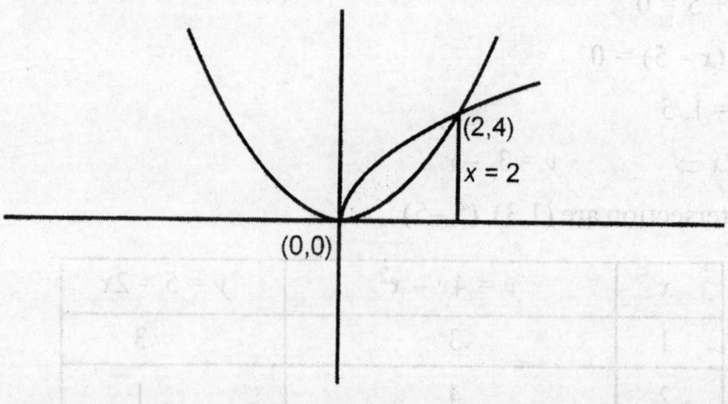

$\therefore$ Required area is $\int_0^2 \left(2x - x^2\right) dn$

$$= \left(\frac{2x^2}{2} - \frac{x^3}{3}\right)_0^2$$

$$= \left(4 - \frac{8}{3}\right) - (0) = \frac{4}{3} \text{ Square Units}$$

12. Find the area bounded by $y = x^3, y = x$

Sol. Given curves are $y = x^3, y = x$

$\Rightarrow \quad x^3 = x$

$x(x^2 - 1) = 0$

$x = 0, x = \pm 1$

$\Rightarrow \quad y = 0, y = +1$

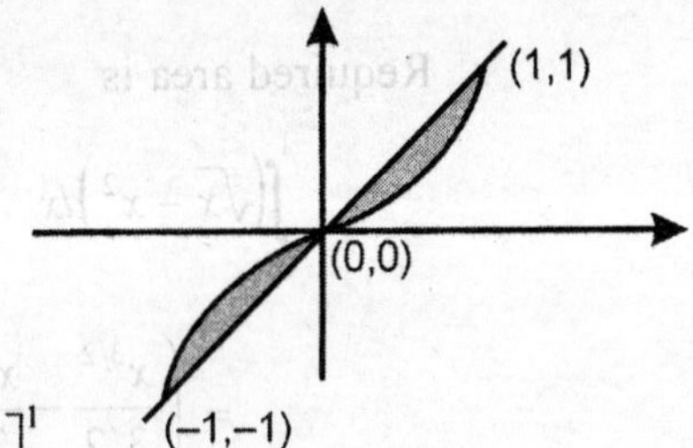

$\therefore$ the curve intersect at (–1,–1), (0,0), (1,1)

$\therefore$ Required area is $2\int_0^1 (x - x^3)\,dx = 2\left[\frac{x^2}{2} - \frac{x^4}{4}\right]_0^1$

$= 2\left(\frac{1}{2} - \frac{1}{4}\right) = 2\left(\frac{1}{4}\right) = \frac{1}{2}$ square units

13. Find the area bounded by the curves $y = 4x - x^2$, $y = 5 - 2x$

Sol. The curves are $y = 4x - x^2$, $y = 5 - 2x$

$\therefore\ 4x - x^2 = 5 - 2x$

$\therefore\ x^2 - 6x + 5 = 0$

$x^2 - 5x - x + 5 = 0$

$x(x - 5) - 1(x - 5) = 0$

$x = 1, 5$

$\therefore\ y = 5 - 2x \Rightarrow \quad y = 3, -5$

Points of intersection are (1,3), (5,–5)

x	$y = 4x - x^2$	$y = 5 - 2x$
1	3	3
2	4	1
3	3	–1
4	0	–3
5	–5	–5

Required area is

$$\int_1^5 (4x - x^2) - (5 - 2x)\,dx$$

$$= \int_1^5 (6x - x^2 - 5)\,dx$$

$$\left(\frac{6x^2}{2} - \frac{x^3}{3} - 5x\right)_1^5$$

$$= \left(75 - \frac{125}{3} - 25\right) - \left(3 - \frac{1}{3} - 5\right)$$

$$= \left(\frac{150 - 125}{3}\right) - \left(\frac{-7}{3}\right) = \frac{25 + 7}{3} = \frac{32}{3} \text{ square units}$$

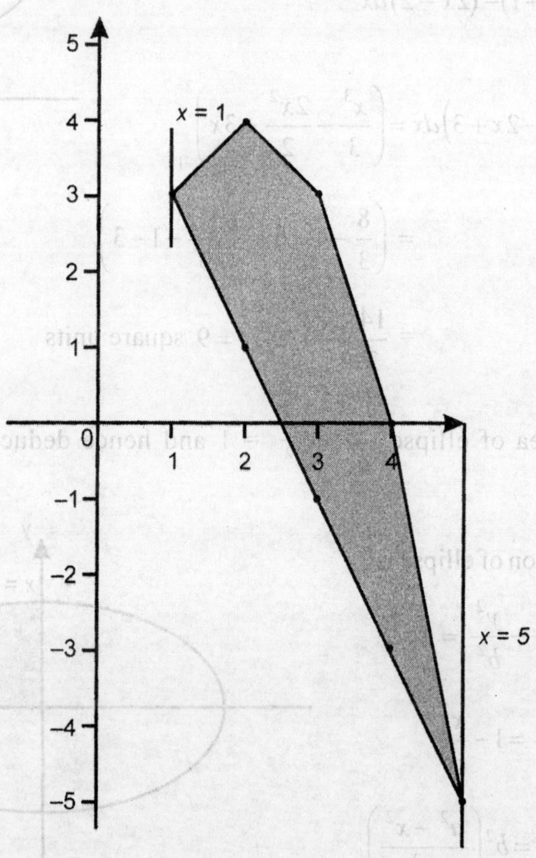

14. Find the area enclosed between the curve $y = x^2 + 1$ $y = 2x - 2$, $x = -1$, $x = 2$

Sol. Given $y = x^2 + 1$ $y = 2x - 2$

x	$y = x^2 + 1$	$y = 2x - 2$
–1	2	–4
0	1	–2
1	2	0
2	5	2

Required area is

$$\int_{-1}^{2} (x^2+1)-(2x-2)\,dx$$

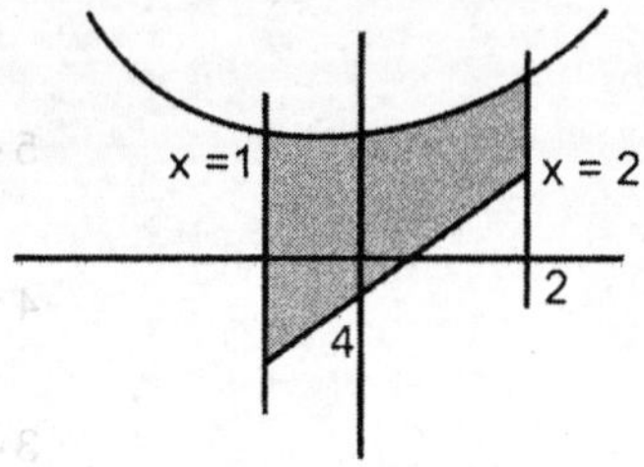

$$\int_{-1}^{2} (x^2-2x+3)\,dx = \left(\frac{x^3}{3}-\frac{2x^2}{2}+3x\right)_{-1}^{2}$$

$$= \left(\frac{8}{3}-4+6\right)-\left(\frac{-1}{3}-1-3\right)$$

$$= \frac{14}{3}+\frac{13}{3} = \frac{27}{3} = 9 \text{ square units}$$

15. Find the area of ellipse $\frac{x^2}{a^2}+\frac{y^2}{b^2} = 1$ and hence deduce the area of circle $x^2 + y^2 = a^2$

Sol. Given equation of ellipse is

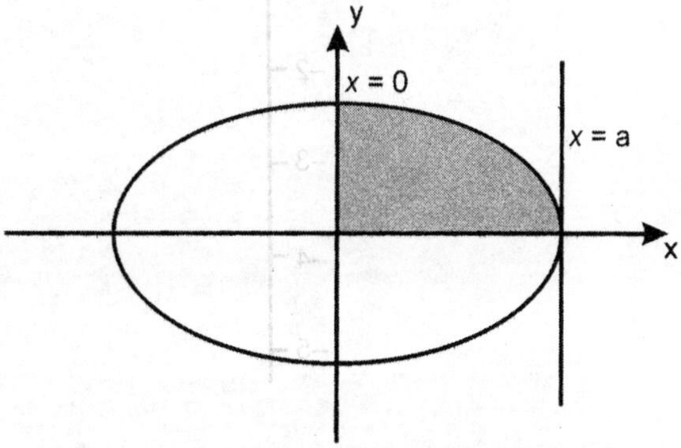

$$\frac{x^2}{a^2}+\frac{y^2}{b^2} = 1$$

$$\Rightarrow \quad \frac{y^2}{b^2} = 1-\frac{x^2}{a^2}$$

$$\Rightarrow \quad y^2 = b^2\left(\frac{a^2-x^2}{a^2}\right)$$

$$\therefore \quad y = \frac{b}{a}\sqrt{a^2-x^2} \qquad y = 0 \quad \Rightarrow \quad x = +a$$

Clearly the curve is symmetric about both x and y–axis

∴ The requested area is obtained by

$$4\int_0^a y\,dx = 4\int_0^a \frac{b}{a}\sqrt{a^2-x^2}\,dx$$

$$= \frac{4b}{a}.\left[\int_0^a \sqrt{a^2-x^2}\,dx\right]$$

$$= \frac{4b}{a}.\left[\frac{x}{2}\sqrt{a^2-x^2}+\frac{a^2}{2}\sin^{-1}\left(\frac{x}{a}\right)\right]_0^a$$

$$= \frac{4b}{a}\left[0+\frac{a^2}{2}.\sin^{-1}(1)-(0)\right]$$

$$= \frac{4b}{a}.\frac{a^2}{2}.\frac{\pi}{2} = \frac{4a}{a}.\frac{a^2\pi}{4} = \pi ab \text{ square units}$$

Put a = b we obtain area of circle

∴ area of circle = π.a.a = πa^2

16. Find the area bounded by $|x| + |y| = 1$

Sol. $x + y = 1$ if $x > 0, y > 0$

$y = 1 - x$

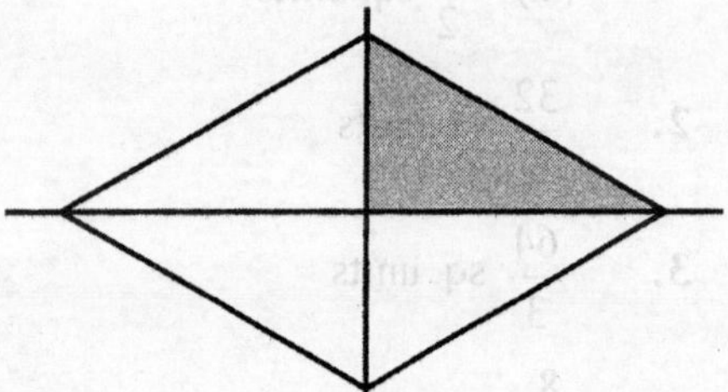

required area = $4\int_0^1 (1-x)\,dx$

$$= 4.\left(x-\frac{x^2}{2}\right)_0^1$$

$$= 4\left(1-\frac{1}{2}\right) = 2 \text{ square units}$$

Exercise - 25.1

1. Find the area cut off between

   (i) $y = 0$ and $y = x^2 - 4x + 3$ (ii) $y = x^2 - 5x + 6, y = 0$

   (iii) $y = 5x - x^2 - 4, y = 0$

2. Find the area bounded by curve $x = y^2 + 4y$ with y axis

3. Find the area bounded by the curves $y^2 = 8x$ and $x^2 = 8y$

4. Find the area enclosed between $y = 2 - x^2, y = x^2$
5. Find the area bounded by $y = x^2$ and $y = 2x$
6. Find the area enclosed between $y = 3x$, and $y = 6x - x^2$
7. Find the area enclosed between $y = x^2 - 5x$, and $y = 4 - 2x$
8. Find the area enclosed between $y = mx$, and $y^2 = 4ax$
9. Find the area enclosed between curve $y = x^2$, and $y = x^3$
10. Find the area of region bounded by curve $y = \sin x$ and x - axis in $[0, 2\pi]$
11. Find the area enclosed between $y^2 = 4x$, and $y^2 = 4(4 - x)$
12. Find the area bounded by $x^2 = 4ay$ and line $y = 2a$
13. Find the area bounded by the curve $y^2 = 4x$ and the line $y = 2x - 4$
14. Find the area bounded by the circle $x^2 + y^2 = a^2$ by the method of integration
15. Find the area bounded by $xy = 16, x = 4, x = 8, y = 0$

Answers

1. (i) $\frac{4}{3}$ sq. units (ii) $\frac{1}{6}$ sq. units

   (iii) $\frac{9}{2}$ sq. units

2. $\frac{32}{3}$ sq. units

3. $\frac{64}{3}$ sq. units

4. $\frac{8}{3}$ sq. units

5. $\frac{4}{3}$ sq. units

6. $\frac{9}{2}$ sq. units

7. $\frac{125}{6}$ sq. units

8. $\frac{8a^2}{3m^3}$ sq. units

9. $\frac{1}{12}$ sq. units

10. 4 sq. units

11. $\frac{32\sqrt{2}}{3}$

12. $\frac{16\sqrt{2}a^2}{3}$ sq. units

13. 9 sq. units

14. πa^2

15. 16 *ln* 2

Unit - V

Exercise Questions

23. Indefinite Integrals

1. Find $\int \frac{x^2}{\sqrt{x+5}} dx$

2. Evaluate $\int x \sin^{-1} dx$

3. Evaluate $\int x^2 \log x \, dx$

4. Integrate $\int \frac{x^2 . dx}{\sqrt{2x+3}}$

5. Integrate $\int \frac{e^{\tan^{-1} x}}{1+x^2} dx$

6. Evaluate $\int \frac{x^2+5x+41}{(x-1)(x+3)(2x-1)}$

7. Evaluate $\int \sin^4 x dx$

8. Evaluate $\int \frac{1}{(x+1)\sqrt{x+4}} dx$

9. Evaluate $\int x \ln x \, dx$

10. (i) $\int \frac{4x^3-2x}{3x} dx$ (ii) $\int \left(6x^2 - \frac{4}{x^2}\right) dx$

    (iii) $\int \left(t+\frac{1}{t}\right)^2 dt$ (iv) $\int (x+1)(2x+3) \, dx$

11. Find $\int \frac{xe^x}{(1+x)^2} dx$

12. Find $\int \sqrt{4-9x^2} dx$

13. Find $\int \frac{dx}{(x^2+4)}$

14. Find $\int \sqrt{1+\sin 2x}\, dx$

15. Find $\int \frac{\log x}{x}\, dx$

16. Find $\int (\tan x + \sec^2 x) e^x\, dx$

17. Find $\int \tan^{-1} x\, dx$

18. Find $\int \frac{dx}{5+4\cos x}$

19. Find $\int \frac{2x+3}{x^2+x-30}$

20. Find $\int \frac{x^3 dx}{\sqrt{1+x^8}}$

21. $\int \sqrt{\sin x}\cos x\, dx$

24. Definite Integrals

1. Evaluate $\int_0^{\frac{\pi}{2}} \frac{\sin^5 x}{\sin^5 x + \cos^5 x}\, dx$

2. Evaluate $\int_1^4 (3x^4 + 4x^2 + x + 1)\, dx$

3. Evaluate $\int_0^{\pi} \sin^5 x\, dx$

4. Evaluate $\int_{-3}^{1} \left(\frac{1}{x^2} - \frac{1}{x^3}\right) dx$

5. Evaluate $\int_{-1}^{2} \frac{dx}{x^2 - 9}$

6. $\int_{0}^{\frac{\pi}{2}} \frac{dx}{4 + 5\cos x}$

25. Areas

1. Find the area of ellipse $\frac{x^2}{a^2} + \frac{y^2}{b^2} = 1$

2. Find the area bounded by the curve $y = 3x - x^2$ x-axis and the lines $x = 0$, $x = 3$.

3. Show that the area between a Parabola $y^2 = 4ax$ and double ordinate (h, k) on it is $\frac{4hk}{3}$.

4. Find the area enclosed by the curve $y = x^2$, $y = x^3$.

5. Find the area of circle $x^2 + y^2 = a^2$

6. Find the area enclosed by $y^2 = (x + 1)$ between $x = 1$ and $x = 2$.

7. Find the area enclosed by $y^2 = 4x$ and $x = 2$.

8. Find the area bounded by the parabola $y = 4 - x^2$, $y = 0$ and $y = 3$.

9. Find the area between the x-axis and the curve $y = \sin x$ from $x = 0$ to $x = \pi$.

Unit - V

Answers to Exercise Questions

23. Indefinite Integrals

1. $2\left(\frac{t^5}{5}+25t-\frac{10t^3}{3}\right)+c$ where $t=\sqrt{x+5}$

2. $\left(\frac{2x^2-1}{4}\right)\sin^{-1}x-\frac{x}{4}\sqrt{1-x^2}+c$

3. $\frac{x^3}{3}\log x-\frac{x^3}{9}+c$

4. $\frac{1}{4}\left[\frac{t^5}{5}+9t-2t^3\right]$ where $t=\sqrt{2x+3}$

5. $e^{\tan^{-1}x}+c$

6. $\frac{47}{4}\log(x-1)+\frac{35}{28}\ln|x+3|-\frac{357}{14}\ln|2x-1|$

7. $\frac{3}{8}x+\frac{1}{32}\sin 4x-\frac{1}{4}\sin 2x+c$

8. $\frac{1}{\sqrt{3}}ln\left|\frac{\sqrt{x+4}-\sqrt{3}}{\sqrt{x+4}+\sqrt{3}}\right|$

9. $\frac{x^2}{2}\ln x-\frac{x^2}{4}+c$

10. (i) $\frac{4}{9}x^3-\frac{2}{3}x+c$ (ii) $2x^3+\frac{4}{x}+c$

(iii) $\frac{t^3}{3}-\frac{1}{t}+2t+c$ (iv) $\frac{2x^3}{3}+\frac{5x^2}{2}+3x+c$

11. $\frac{e^x}{(1+x)}+c$

12. $3\left[\frac{x}{2}\sqrt{\frac{4}{9}-x^2}+\frac{2}{9}\sin^{-1}\left(\frac{3x}{2}\right)+c\right]$

13. $\frac{1}{2}\tan^{-1}\left(\frac{x}{2}\right)+c$

14. $\sin x - \cos x + c$

15. $\frac{(\log x)^2}{2}+c$

16. $e^x(\tan x)+c$

17. $(\tan^{-1}x)(x)-\frac{1}{2}\ ln\,|1+x^2|+c$

18. $\frac{2}{3}\tan^{-1}\left(\frac{\tan\frac{x}{2}}{3}\right)+c$

19. $ln\left|x^2+x-30\right|\frac{-2}{11}\ln\frac{x+6}{x-5}$

20. $\frac{1}{4}\sin h^{-1}(x^4)+c$

21. $\frac{2}{3}(\sin x)^{\frac{3}{2}}+c$

24. Definite Integrals

1. $\frac{\pi}{4}$

2. $\frac{7083}{10}$

3. $\frac{16}{15}$

4. $\frac{-8}{9}$

5. $\frac{-1}{6}\log_e 10$

6. $\frac{1}{3}ln2$

25. Areas

1. π ab

2. $\frac{9}{2}$ square units

5. πa^2 square units

6. $\frac{2}{3}(3\sqrt{3}-2\sqrt{2})$ square units

7. $\frac{16}{3}\sqrt{2}$ square units

8. $\frac{28}{3}$ square units

9. 2 square units

Unit - V

Self Test Questions

23. Indefinite Integrals

1. (i) Find $\int 2x^7 \, dx$ on R (ii) Find $\int (\sin x + x^3) dx$

2. $\int \frac{e^{\sin^{-1} x}}{\sqrt{1-x^2}} dx$

3. $\int \frac{\sin 2x}{a^2 \sin^2 x + b^2 \cos^2 x}$

4. $\int \frac{\tan \sqrt{x} \sec^2 \sqrt{x}}{\sqrt{x}} dx$

5. $\int \sin 4x \cos 2x \, dx$

6. $\int \frac{x^4 + 1}{x^2 + 1} dx$

7. Evaluate (i) $\int \operatorname{cosec} x \, dx$ (ii) $\int \cot x \, dx$ (iii) $\int \sec x \, dx$

8. Evaluate (i) $\int x \sin x \, dx$ (ii) $\int x \cos x \, dx$

9. Evaluate $\int \frac{dx}{1 + \cot x}$

24. Definite Integrals

1. $\int_0^{\pi/2} \tan^2 x \, dx$

2. $\int_0^{\pi/4} \frac{\sqrt{\sin x}}{\sqrt{\sin x} + \sqrt{\cos x}} dx$

3. $\int_0^1 \frac{xe^x}{(x+1)^2}$

25. Areas

1. Find the area bounded by the curve $y = x^2 - 7x + 10$ and x-axis.
2. Find the area between the curves $y^2 = 2x - 2$ and $y = x - 5$
3. Find the area of circle $x^2 + y^2 = a^2$ by method of integration.
4. Find the area enclosed between the curves $y^2 = 4x$ and the line $y = 2x - 4$
5. Find the area bounded by the curve $x^2 = 4y$ and $x = 4y - 2$

UNIT - VI

DIFFERENTIAL EQUATIONS

UNIT - VI

DIFFERENTIAL EQUATIONS

26

Differential Equations

26.1 Differential Equation

Definition : Differential equation is an equation involving one dependent variable and its derivatives with respect to one or more independent variables is called a differential equation.

If a differential equation contains an independent variable then it is called an ordinary differential equation otherwise it is called Partial Differential Equation.

Ex : (i) $\frac{dy}{dx} + \sin x = 5x$ [x is an independent variable, y is a dependent variable]

(ii) $\frac{d^2y}{dx^2} + \left(\frac{dy}{dx}\right)^3 + e^x = 0$

(iii) $\frac{\delta^2 u}{\delta x^2} + \frac{\delta^2 u}{\delta y^2} + \frac{\delta^2 u}{\delta z^2} = 0$ (x, y, z are independent variables, u is dependent variable)

So, ex (i), ex (ii) are ordinary differential equations and ex (iii) is partial differential equation.

26.2 Order and Degree of Differential Equation

Order : The order of differential equation is the order of the heighest derivative occur in it.

Ex : (i) Order of $\frac{d^2y}{dx^2} + \frac{dy}{dn} + x = e^x$ is 2 since its order of highest order derivative is 2

(i.e., $\frac{d^2y}{dx^2}$ is occur in the equation)

$\therefore$ order of the Differential equation is 2

(ii) order of $\frac{d^3y}{dx^3}+3\left(\frac{dy}{dn}\right)^{10}+\sin x=0$ is 3

(iii) order of $1+\left(\frac{d^2y}{dx^2}\right)^2=\left[2+\left(\frac{dy}{dx}\right)^2\right]^{\frac{3}{2}}$ is 2

(iv) order of $\left[\left(\frac{dy}{dx}\right)^2+\left(\frac{d^2y}{dx^2}\right)\right]^{\frac{5}{3}}=\frac{d^3y}{dx^3}$ is 3

(v) order of $x=\sin\left(\frac{dy}{dx}\right)$ is 1

Degree : Degree of a differential equation is the degree (lowest positive integer) of highest order derivative occuring it after the equation has been expressed a form free from radicals and fractions so far as the derivatives are concerned (i.e., can be expressed as a polynomial equation in the derivatives occuring in it).

Ex : (i) The degree of the differential euqation

$$\frac{d^2y}{dx^2}=\left[1+\left(\frac{dy}{dx}\right)^3\right]^{\frac{4}{3}}$$ is 3

[Since the above equation can be written as (by cubing on both sides)

$\left(\frac{d^2y}{dx^2}\right)^3=\left[1+\left(\frac{dy}{dx}\right)^3\right]^4$ after expanding it, the equation has been expressed as a form free from radicals and fractions so far as the derivatives $\left(\frac{d^2y}{dx^2},\left(\frac{dy}{dx}\right)^3\right)$

In this case degree of highest derivative is 3.

$\therefore$ degree = 3]

(ii) The degree of the differential equation

$$\left(1+\left(\frac{d^2y}{dx^2}\right)\right)=\left(2+\left(\frac{dy}{dx}\right)^{10}\right)^{\frac{3}{7}} \quad \text{is 7}$$

(iii) The degree of the differential equation

$$2+\left(\frac{d^2y}{dx^2}\right)^3=\left(5+\frac{d^3y}{dx^3}\right)^{\frac{5}{2}} \quad \text{is 5}$$

$$\left[\because\left(2+\left(\frac{d^2y^3}{dx^2}\right)\right)^2=\left(5+\frac{d^3y}{dx^3}\right)\right]^5$$

order of highest order is 3. Its power is 5

(iv) The degree of $x^{\frac{1}{2}}\left(\frac{d^2y}{dx^2}\right)^{\frac{1}{3}}+x\frac{dy}{dx}+y=0$ is 1

(v) Degree of $\left(\frac{dy}{dx}\right)^{\frac{5}{2}}=x$ is 1

[$\because \left(\frac{dy}{dx}\right)^{\frac{5}{2}}=x \Rightarrow \left(\frac{dy}{dx}\right)=x^{\frac{2}{5}}$

its derivatives are free from radicals or fractions.

so, here order of highest derivative = 1 and its power is 1

$\therefore$ degree is 1]

(vi) Degree of $\left(\frac{dy}{dx}\right)^{\frac{2}{3}}=\left(\frac{d^2y}{dx^2}\right)^{\frac{3}{2}}$ is 9

$$[\because \quad \left(\frac{dy}{dx}\right)^{\frac{2}{3}}=\left(\frac{d^2y}{dx^2}\right)^{\frac{3}{2}}$$

$$\Rightarrow \quad \left[\left(\frac{dy}{dx}\right)^{\frac{2}{3}}\right]^6 = \left[\left(\frac{d^2y}{dx^2}\right)^{\frac{3}{2}}\right]^6$$

(L.C.M of 3, 2 = 6, and taking power of 6 on both sides)

$$\Rightarrow \quad \left(\frac{dy}{dx}\right)^4 = \left(\frac{d^2y}{dx^2}\right)^9$$

$\therefore$ order highest ordery derivative = 2, its power is 9

$\therefore$ degree = 9]

(vii) degree of $x = \sin\left(\frac{dy}{dx}\right)$ is not defined

(viii) degree of $\frac{d^2y}{dx^2} + 3\frac{dy}{dx} + y = \log\left(\frac{dy}{dx}\right)$ is not defined.

The general form of an ordinary differential equation of nth order is

$$F\left(x, y, \frac{dy}{dx}, \frac{d^2y}{dx^2}, \ldots \frac{d^ny}{dx^n}\right) = 0$$

(may not all involve except $\frac{d^ny}{dx^n}$) or

$F(x, y, y, y_1\, y_2 \ldots\ldots\, y_n) = 0$

26.3 Solution of Differential Equation

It is a relation between the dependent and independent variables which satisfies the Differential Equation.

Consider $\frac{dy}{dx} = \cos x$, its solution is $y = \sin x$ or $y = \sin x + k_1$,

or $y = \sin x + k_2$ (k_1, k_2 ... are constants)

$\because \quad \frac{d}{dx}(\sin x + k) = \cos x + 0 = \cos x$

$\therefore \quad y = \sin x$ satisfies $\frac{dy}{dx} = \cos x$

So, $y = \sin x$ is a solution of the differential equation.

General Solution of Differential equation : The general solution of a differential equation is the solution which contains the number of arbitrary constants equal to the order of the differential equation.

If $F(x, y, y^1 \dots y^{(n)}) = 0$ is a differential equation then its general solution is of the form $\phi(x, y\, c_1\, c_2 \dots\dots c_n)$.

where $c_1, c_2 \dots\dots\dots c_n$ are n arbitrary constants.

Ex : $y = mx$ (m is a arbitrary constants) is general solution of the Differential equation

$$x\frac{dy}{dx} = y$$

$y = \sin x + k$ (k is a parameter or arbitrary constant) is general solution of

Differential equation $\frac{dy}{dx} = \cos x$.

Particular Solution : Particular solution is a solution of the differential equation obtained from the general solution by giving particular values to the arbitrary constants.

Ex : $y = 2x$ is particular solution of $x\frac{dy}{dx} = y$

which is obtained from $y = mx$ by giving $m = 2$.

26.4 Formation of the Differential Equation of given Equation of Family Curves

Suppose $y = \phi(x, c_1, c_2 \dots\dots\dots c_n)$ is an equation of family of curves where $c_1, c_2 \dots\dots\dots c_n$ are n arbitrary constant. For this we obtain the Differential Equation as follows.

Step (i) : Differentiate the function $y = \phi(x, c_1 \dots\dots c_n)$ n times (the number of arbitrary constants).

we obtain $\frac{d\phi}{dx} = 0, \quad \frac{d^2\phi}{dx^2} = 0 \quad \dots\dots\dots \quad \frac{d^n\phi}{dx^n} = 0$

Step (ii) eliminate $C_1, C_2 \dots\dots\dots C_n$ by using above differential equations.

Ex : (i) Form the differential equation of family of curves $y = A\cos 3x + B\sin 3x$ where A and B are parameters.

Sol. Given equation is $y = A\cos 3x + B\sin 3x$ ...... (1)

here the number of parameters is 2 (A , B). so we differentiate (1) w.r.t x two times.

Differentiate (1) w.r.t to x we get

$$\frac{dy}{dx} = A((-\sin 3x)(3)) + B((\cos 3x)(3))$$

$$\frac{dy}{dx} = -3A\sin 3x + 3B\cos 3x \quad \text{..... (2)}$$

Again differentiating (2) w.r.t x, we get

$$\frac{d^2y}{dx^2} = -3A(\cos 3x\,(3)) + 3B\,((-\sin 3x)\,(3))$$

$$= -9A\cos 3x - 9B\sin 3x$$

$$\frac{d^2y}{dx^2} = -9\,[\,A\cos 3x + B\sin 3x\,]$$

$$\frac{d^2y}{dx^2} = -9\,y \qquad (\because \text{ by } (1))$$

so the required differential equation is

$$\frac{d^2y}{dx^2} = -9y$$

(ii) Form the differential equation of $xy = ae^x + be^{-x}$ where a, b are arbitrary constants.

Sol. The given equation is $xy = ae^x + be^{-x}$ ...(1)

the number of arbitrary constants is 2

So, Differentiate (1) w.r.t x, we get

$$x\,\frac{dy}{dx} + y(1) = ae^x + b.e^{-x}\,(-1)$$

$$\therefore \quad x.\,\frac{dy}{dx} + y = ae^x - be^{-x} \quad \text{..... (2)}$$

Again Diffenting (2) w.r.t x, we get

$$x.\frac{d^2y}{dx^2} + \left(\frac{dy}{dx}\right)(1) + \frac{dy}{dx} = a.e^x - b\,e^{-x}\,(-1)$$

$$\therefore \quad x.\frac{d^2y}{dx^2} + \frac{dy}{dx} + \frac{dy}{dx} = a.e^x + be^{-x}$$

$$\therefore \quad x.\frac{d^2y}{dx^2} + 2\frac{dy}{dx} = xy \qquad (\because \text{ by } (1))$$

This is the required differential equation

Solved Examples

1. Form the differential equation of the following family of curves where arbitrary constants (parameters) are given in brackets.

(i) $y = ax^2 + bx$ (a, b) (ii) $xy = ax^2 + \frac{b}{x}$

Sol. (i) $y = ax^2 + bx$ ..... (1)

Differentiating (1) w.r.t x we get

$$\frac{dy}{dx} = 2ax + b \quad ..... (2)$$

Differentiation (2) w.r.t x we get

$$\frac{d^2y}{dx^2} = 2a(1) + 0 = 2a \Rightarrow \left(a = \frac{1}{2}\frac{d^2y}{dx^2}\right) \quad ..... (3)$$

Substitute (3) in (2) we get

$$\frac{dy}{dx} = \left(\frac{d^2y}{dx^2}\right)x + b \Rightarrow b = \frac{dy}{dx} - x\left(\frac{d^2y}{dx^2}\right)$$

substitute b, a in (1) we get

$$y = \frac{1}{2}\frac{d^2y}{dx^2}x^2 + \left(\frac{dy}{dx} - x\left(\frac{d^2y}{dx^2}\right)\right)x$$

$$\therefore \quad 2y = \frac{d^2y}{dx^2}.x^2 + 2\frac{dy}{dx}.x - 2x^2\frac{d^2y}{dx^2}$$

$$\Rightarrow \quad -x^2\frac{d^2y}{dx^2} + 2x.\frac{dy}{dx} = 2y$$

$$\therefore \quad x^2.\frac{d^2y}{dx^2} - 2x.\frac{dy}{dx} + 2y = 0$$

(ii) Given equation is $xy = ax^2 + \frac{b}{x}$

$$\therefore \quad x^2y = ax^3 + b \quad ..... (1)$$

Differentiating (1) w.r.t 'x' we get

$$(2x)y + \frac{dy}{dx}.(x^2) = 3ax^2$$

$$\Rightarrow \qquad 2y + x\,.\frac{dy}{dx} = 3ax \qquad \text{......(2)}$$

Again differentiating (2) w.r.t x we get

$$2.\frac{dy}{dx} + \left(x.\frac{d^2y}{dx^2} + \frac{dy}{dx}.1\right) = 3a$$

substitute '3a' in (2) we get,

$$2y + x.\frac{dy}{dx} = \left(2\frac{dy}{dx} + x.\frac{d^2y}{dx^2} + \frac{dy}{dx}\right)x$$

$$2y + x\,.\frac{dy}{dx} = 3x\,.\frac{dy}{dx} + x^2\,.\frac{d^2y}{dx^2}$$

$$\Rightarrow \qquad x^2.\frac{d^2y}{dx^2} + 2x.\frac{dy}{dx} - 2y = 0$$

2. Form the differential equation of

(i) $ax^2 + by^2 = 1$ (ii) $y = ae^{-x} + b$

where a, b are arbitrary constants

Sol. (i) $ax^2 + by^2 = 1$ ......(1)

Differentiating (1) w.r.t x, we get

$$2ax + 2by\,.\frac{dy}{dx} = 0 \qquad \text{..... (2)}$$

again differentiatin (2) w.r.t x, we get

$$2a + 2b\,.\left[y.\frac{d^2y}{dx^2} + \left(\frac{dy}{dx}\right)^2\right] = 0$$

$$\therefore \qquad 2a = -2b\left[y.\frac{d^2y}{dx^2} + \left(\frac{dy}{dx}\right)^2\right] \qquad \text{..... (3)}$$

substitute '2a' in (2) we get

$$-2b\left[y.\frac{d^2y}{dx^2} + \left(\frac{dy}{dx}\right)^2\right]x + 2b.y\,\frac{dy}{dx} = 0$$

$$\therefore \quad 2b\left[-\left(y.\frac{d^2y}{dx^2}+\left(\frac{dy}{dx}\right)^2\right)x+y.\frac{dy}{dx}\right]=0$$

$$\therefore \quad -\left(y.\frac{d^2y}{dx^2}+\left(\frac{dy}{dx}\right)^2\right)x+y.\frac{dy}{dx}=0$$

$$\therefore \quad -xy\frac{d^2y}{dx^2}-x\left(\frac{dy}{dx}\right)^2+y\frac{dy}{dx}=0$$

$$\therefore \quad xy\frac{d^2y}{dx^2}+x\left(\frac{dy}{dx}\right)^2-y\frac{dy}{dx}=0$$

(ii) we have $y = ae^{-x} + b$

Differentiate w.r.t x on both sides we get

$$\frac{dy}{dx} = a\,e^{-x}\,.\,(-1)+0=-ae^{-x} \quad \Rightarrow \quad \frac{dy}{dx}=-ae^{-x} \qquad \text{..... (1)}$$

again Differentiate w.r.t x on both sides we get

$$\frac{d^2y}{dx^2}=-ae^{-x}\,.\,(-1)=ae^{-x}=\frac{-dy}{dx} \qquad (\because \text{ by (1)})$$

$$\therefore \quad \frac{d^2y}{dx^2}+\frac{dy}{dx}=0$$

3. Form the differential equation of

(i) $y = a\cos(nx + b)$ (ii) $y = (a + bx)\,e^{kx}$

where a, b are arbitrary constants

Sol. (i) Given equation is $y = a\cos(nx + b)$ ..... (1)

Differentiating (1) w.r.t x, on both sides we get

$$\frac{dy}{dx} = a\,(-\sin(nx+b))\,(n)$$

$$\frac{dy}{dx} = -\,an\,.\,\sin(nx+b) \qquad \text{.....(2)}$$

Again differentiating (2) w.r.t x we get

$$\frac{d^2y}{dx^2} = -\text{an}.(\cos(\text{n}x + \text{b}))\,\text{n}$$

$$\frac{d^2y}{dx^2} = -\text{an}^2(\cos(\text{n}x + \text{b}))$$

$$\therefore \quad \frac{d^2y}{dx^2} = -\text{n}^2(\text{a}\cos(\text{n}x + \text{b})) = -\text{n}^2y \qquad (\because \text{by (1)})$$

$$\therefore \quad \frac{d^2y}{dx^2} = -\text{n}^2y \quad \text{(or)} \quad \frac{d^2y}{dx^2} + \text{n}^2y = 0$$

(ii) Given equation is $y = (\text{a} + \text{b}x)\,\text{e}^{kx}$ ..... (1)

Differentiating (1) w.r.t x, we get

$$\frac{dy}{dx} = (\text{a} + \text{b}x)(\text{e}^{kx}.\text{k}) + \text{e}^{kx}(0 + \text{b})$$

$$= \text{k}.(\text{a} + \text{b}x)\,\text{e}^{kx} + \text{e}^{kx}.\text{b}$$

$$\frac{dy}{dx} = \text{k}.y + \text{be}^{kx} \qquad \text{..... (2)}$$

Again differentiating (2) w.r.t x we get

$$\frac{d^2y}{dx^2} = k.\frac{dy}{dx} + b.e^{kx}.k \qquad \text{.....(3)}$$

from (2) we have $\text{be}^{kx} = \left(\frac{dy}{dx} - ky\right)$

substitute in 3

$$\frac{d^2y}{dx^2} = k.\frac{dy}{dx} + \left(\frac{dy}{dx} - ky\right)k + \frac{dy}{dx}$$

$$\therefore \quad \frac{d^2y}{dx^2} - 2k.\frac{dy}{dx} + k^2y = 0$$

Which is required Differential equation

4. Form the differential equation of

(i) $y = cx - 2c^2$ (ii) $y = c(x - c)^2$

(iii) $y = mx + a/m$ (iv) $y = m(x + m)$

where m is a parameter

Sol. (i) Given equation is

$$y = cx - 2c^2 \quad ..... (1)$$

Differentiating (1) w.r.t x, we get

$$\frac{dy}{dx} = c(1) - 0 \quad \Rightarrow \quad \frac{dy}{dx} = c$$

Substitute the value of 'c' in (1) we get

$$y = \frac{dy}{dx}\, x - 2\left(\frac{dy}{dx}\right)^2$$

It is the required differential equation

(ii) Given equation is

$$y = c\,(x - c)^2 \quad ..... (1)$$

Differentiating (1) w.r.t x, we get

$$\frac{dy}{dx} = c\,.\,2(x - c)\,\frac{d}{dx}\,(x - c)$$

$$\frac{dy}{dx} = c\,.\,2(x - c)\,(1) = 2c(x - c) \quad ..... (2)$$

$$\frac{(2)}{(1)} \quad \Rightarrow \quad \frac{\frac{dy}{dx}}{y} = \frac{2c(x-c)}{c(x-c)^2} = \frac{2}{(x-c)}$$

$$x - c = \frac{2y}{\left(\frac{dy}{dx}\right)} \quad \Rightarrow \quad c = x - \frac{2y}{\left(\frac{dy}{dx}\right)}$$

substitute $x - c$, c in (1) we get

$$\therefore \quad y = \left(x - \frac{2y}{\left(\frac{dy}{dx}\right)}\right)\left(\frac{2y}{\left(\frac{dy}{dx}\right)}\right)^2$$

$$\left(\frac{dy}{dx}\right)^2 y = \left(\frac{x.\frac{dy}{dx} - 2y}{\frac{dy}{dx}}\right).4y^2 \Rightarrow \left(\frac{dy}{dx}\right)^3 = 4xy\frac{dy}{dx} - 8y^2$$

$$\Rightarrow \quad \left(\frac{dy}{dx}\right)^3 - 4xy + 8y^2 = 0$$

(iii) Given $y = mx + \frac{a}{m}$ ..... (1)

Differentiating (1) w.r.t x, we get

$$\frac{dy}{dx} = m(1) + 0 \quad \Rightarrow \quad m = \frac{dy}{dx}$$

Substitute m in (1) we get

$$y = \left(\frac{dy}{dx}\right)x + \frac{a}{\left(\frac{dy}{dx}\right)}$$

$$\Rightarrow \quad y.\frac{dy}{dx} = \left(\frac{dy}{dx}\right)^2 x + a$$

$$\therefore \quad x.\left(\frac{dy}{dx}\right)^2 - y.\frac{dy}{dx} + a = 0$$

is the required differential equation

(iv) $y = m(x + m) \quad \Rightarrow \quad y = mx + m^2$ .....(1)

Differentiating (1) w.r.t x, we get

$$\frac{dy}{dx} = m(1) + 0 \quad \Rightarrow \quad m = \frac{dy}{dx}$$

Substitute m in (1) we get

$$y = \frac{dy}{dx}x + \left(\frac{dy}{dx}\right)^2 = \frac{dy}{dx}\left(x + \frac{dy}{dx}\right)$$

$$\therefore \quad y = \frac{dy}{dx}\left(x + \frac{dy}{dx}\right)$$

is the required differential equation

Equation of some curves

1. Equation of circle with centre at (x_1, y_1) and radius a is

$$(x - x_1)^2 + (y - y_1)^2 = r^2.$$

2. Equation of circle which touches x - axis at origin is (or centre lies on y-axis and passing through (0, 0)

$$x^2 + y^2 + 2fy = 0.$$

3. Equation of circle which touches y - axis at origin is (or centre lies on x-axis and passing through (0, 0)

$$x^2 + y^2 + 2gx = 0$$

4. Equation of parabola with vertex at (h, k) and length of latus rectum 4a and its axis parallel to x - axis is

$$(y - k)^2 = 4a(x - h).$$

5. Form the differential equation of family of circles of radius r given by $(x - a)^2 + (y - b)^2 = r^2$ where a, b are parameters.

Sol. Given equation is $(x - a)^2 + (y - b)^2 = r^2$ ..... (1)

Differentiating (1) w r t x, we get

$$2(x - a) + 2(y - b) \cdot \frac{dy}{dx} = 0 \Rightarrow (x - a) + (y - b)\frac{dy}{dx} = 0 \quad .....(2)$$

Again differentiating (2) w.r. t x, we get

$$1 + (y - b) \cdot \frac{d^2y}{dx^2} + \left(\frac{dy}{dx}\right) \cdot \left(\frac{dy}{dx}\right) = 0$$

$$\therefore \quad 1 + (y - b) \cdot \frac{d^2y}{dx^2} + \left(\frac{dy}{dx}\right)^2 = 0$$

$$\therefore \quad (y - b) \cdot \frac{d^2y}{dx^2} = -\left(1 + \left(\frac{dy}{dx}\right)^2\right)$$

$$\therefore \quad y - b = -\left(\frac{1 + \left(\frac{dy}{dx}\right)^2}{\left(\frac{d^2y}{dx^2}\right)}\right)$$

Substitute in (2) we get

$$(x-a)+\frac{-\left(1+\left(\frac{dy}{dx}\right)^2\right)}{\left(\frac{d^2y}{dx^2}\right)}\left(\frac{dy}{dx}\right)=0$$

$$\therefore \qquad (x-a)=\frac{1+\left(\frac{dy}{dx}\right)^2}{\left(\frac{d^2y}{dx^2}\right)}\left(\frac{dy}{dx}\right)$$

Now substitute $(x-a)$, $(y-b)$ in (1) we get

$$\therefore \frac{\left[1+\left(\frac{dy}{dx}\right)^2\right]^2}{\left(\frac{d^2y}{dx^2}\right)^2}\left(\frac{dy}{dx}\right)^2+\left(\frac{1+\left(\frac{dy}{dx}\right)^2}{\left(\frac{d^2y}{dx^2}\right)}\right)^2=r^2$$

$$\Rightarrow r^2\left(\frac{d^2y}{dx^2}\right)^2=\left(1+\left(\frac{dy}{dx}\right)^2\right)^2\left(\left(\frac{dy}{dx}\right)^2+1\right)$$

$$\Rightarrow r^2\left(\frac{d^2y}{dx^2}\right)^2=\left(1+\left(\frac{dy}{dx}\right)^2\right)^3$$

6. Form the differential equation of family of circles which touches x - axis at (0, 0).

Sol. The equation of family of circles is

$$x^2+y^2+2fy=0 \qquad \text{..... (1)}$$

where f is parameter, now differentiating (1) w.r.t 'x' we get

$$2x+2y\,.\,\frac{dy}{dx}+2f\,.\,\frac{dy}{dx}=0$$

$$\therefore \quad 2f = \frac{-\left(2x+2y\dfrac{dy}{dx}\right)}{\left(\dfrac{dy}{dx}\right)}$$

Substitute '2*f*' in (1) we get [to eliminate f]

$$x^2 + y^2 - \frac{\left(2x+2y\dfrac{dy}{dx}\right)}{\left(\dfrac{dy}{dx}\right)} y = 0$$

$$(x^2 + y^2) \cdot \frac{dy}{dx} - (2x + 2y) \cdot \frac{dy}{dx})\, y = 0$$

$$\therefore \quad x^2 \cdot \frac{dy}{dx} + y^2 \cdot \frac{dy}{dx} - 2x \cdot y - 2y^2 \cdot \frac{dy}{dx} = 0$$

$$(x^2 - y^2) \cdot \frac{dy}{dx} - 2xy = 0$$

7. Form the differential equation of $y = a.e^{2x} + be^{3x}$

Sol. Given $y = ae^{2x} + be^{3x}$ ..... (1)

Differentiating (1) w. r. t x we get

$y_1 = 2a\, e^{2x} + 3be^{2x}$ ..... (2)

again differentiating w.r.t x we get

$y_2 = 4a\, e^{2x} + 9\, be^{3x}$ ..... (3)

from (1), (2), (3)

$$\begin{vmatrix} e^{2x} & e^{3x} & -y \\ 2e^{2x} & 3e^{3x} & -y_1 \\ 4e^{2x} & 9e^{3x} & y_2 \end{vmatrix} = 0$$

$$\therefore -e^{2x} \cdot e^{3x} \cdot \begin{vmatrix} 1 & 1 & y \\ 2 & 3 & y_1 \\ 4 & 9 & y_2 \end{vmatrix} = 0$$

$$\therefore \begin{vmatrix} 1 & 1 & y \\ 2 & 3 & y_1 \\ 4 & 9 & y_2 \end{vmatrix} = 0 \quad \Rightarrow \quad 1(3y_2 - 9y_1) - 1\,(2y_2 - 4y_1) + y(18 - 12) = 0$$

$$\Rightarrow \quad 3y_2 - 9y_1 - 2y_2 + 4y_1 + 6y = 0$$

$$\Rightarrow \quad y_2 - 5y_1 + 6y = 0$$

$$\therefore \quad \frac{d^2y}{dx^2} - 5.\frac{dy}{dx} + 6.y = 0$$

Excercise - 26.1

1. Find the order and degree of following differential equations

(i) $1 + \left(\frac{d^2y}{dx^2}\right)^2 = \left[2 + \left(\frac{dy}{dx}\right)^2\right]^{\frac{3}{2}}$ (ii) $\dfrac{\left[1 + \left(\frac{dy}{dx}\right)^2\right]^{\frac{3}{2}}}{\left(\frac{d^2y}{dx^2}\right)} = \alpha$

2. Form the differential equations whose solution if

(i) $y = \text{a} \cos x + \text{b} \sin x$

(ii) $y = \text{a} \cos\left(\frac{n}{x} + b\right)$ where a and b are constants

3. Form the differential equation of $y = \text{a}e^x + \text{b}e^{-x}$ where a, b are arbitrary constants.

4. Form the differential equation of $y = e^x(\text{A}\cos x - \text{B} \sin x)$, where A, B are arbitrary constants.

5. Form the differential equation of $y = \text{a}x^3 + \text{b}x^2$ where a and b are arbitrary constants.

6. Form the differential equation of $y^2 = 4\text{a}\,(x + \text{a})$ where a is parameter.

7. Form the differential equation $y = \text{a}x^2 + \text{b}x + \text{c}$ as solution, where a, b, c are arbitrary constants.

8. Form the differential equations of circles of radius 6 with centres on y-axis.

Answers

1. (i) order degree

	order	degree
(i)	2	4
(ii)	2	2

2. (i) $\frac{d^2y}{dx^2} + y = 0$

(ii) $x^4 \frac{d^2y}{dx^2} + 2x^3 . \frac{dy}{dx} + n^2 y = 0$

3. $\frac{d^2y}{dx^2} - y = 0$

4. $\frac{d^2y}{dx^2} - 2\frac{dy}{dx} + 2y = 0$

5. $x^2 \frac{d^2y}{dx^2} - 4x\frac{dy}{dx} + 6y = 0$

6. $y\left(\frac{dy}{dx}\right)^2 + 2x\left(\frac{dy}{dx}\right) - y = 0$

7. $\frac{d^3y}{dx^3} = 0$

8. $\left(1+\left(\frac{dy}{dx}\right)^2\right)x^2 = 36\left(\frac{dy}{dx}\right)^2$

26.5 Solutions of the First Order, First Degree Differential Equations

Variables separable method

The first order first degree differential equation is of the form $\frac{dy}{dx} = f(x, y)$.

If it is possible to separate like variables in the equation we can solve the equation by this method.

To solve the differential equation by seperable method

Step I : separate the like variables in the equation

Step II : Taking integration on both sides

Ex: Solve $x\,dy = y\,dx$

Sol : The given equation is $x\,dy = y\,dx$

separate the like variables, we get

$$\frac{dy}{y} = \frac{dx}{x}$$

Integrating on both sides we get

$$\int \frac{dy}{y} = \int \frac{dx}{x}$$

$\Rightarrow \quad ln\, y = lnx + lnc$

$\Rightarrow \quad ln\, y = ln\, cx \quad \Rightarrow \quad y = cx$ is required solution

Solved Examples

1. Solve $\frac{dy}{dx} = e^{y-x}$

Sol. Given, $\frac{dy}{dx} = e^{y-x} \quad = e^{y} \,.\, e^{-x} \quad = \frac{e^y}{e^x}$

$\therefore \quad \frac{dy}{dx} = \frac{e^y}{e^x} \quad \Rightarrow \quad e^{-y} \,.\, dy = e^{-x} \,.\, dx$

taking integration of both sides we get

$$\int e^{-y} dy = \int e^{-x} dx$$

$$\Rightarrow \frac{e^{-y}}{-1} = \frac{e^{-x}}{-1} + c$$

$\therefore \quad e^{-x} - e^{-y} = c$

2. Solve $\frac{dy}{dx} = e^{x-y} + x^2 \,.\, e^{-y}$

$$\frac{dy}{dx} = e^x \,.\, e^{-y} + x^2 \,.\, e^{-y} = (e^x + x^2)\, e^{-y}$$

$$\therefore \quad \frac{dy}{dx} = e^{-y}(e^x + x^2) \Rightarrow e^y \frac{dy}{dx} = e^x + x^2 \Rightarrow e^y . dy = (e^x + x^2)dx$$

taking integration on both sides $\int e^y dy = \int (e^x + x^2)dx$

$$\Rightarrow e^y = e^x + \frac{x^3}{3} + c$$

3. Solve

(i) $\sqrt{1+x^2}\,dx + \sqrt{1+y^2}\,dy = 0$, (ii) $\tan y\, dx + \tan x\, dy = 0$

Sol. (i) $\sqrt{1+x^2}\,dx = -\sqrt{1+y^2}\,dy$

$\therefore$ taking integration on both sides

$$\int \sqrt{1+x^2}\,dx = -\sqrt{1+y^2}\,dy$$

$$\Rightarrow \quad \frac{x}{2}\sqrt{1+x^2} + \frac{1}{2}\sinh^{-1} x = -\left(\frac{y}{2}\sqrt{1+y^2} + \frac{1}{2}\sinh^{-1}(y)\right) + c$$

$$\left[\because \int \sqrt{a^2+x^2} = \frac{x}{2}\sqrt{a^2+x^2} + \frac{a^2}{2}\sinh^{-1}\left(\frac{x}{a}\right)\right]$$

(ii) $\tan y\, dx + \tan x\, dy = 0$

$$\Rightarrow \quad \frac{dx}{\tan x} = -\frac{dy}{\tan y}$$

$\therefore$ taking integration on both sides we get

$$\int \frac{dx}{\tan x} = -\int \frac{dy}{\tan y} \quad \Rightarrow \quad \int \frac{\cos x}{\sin x} dx = -\int \frac{\cos y}{\sin y} dy$$

$$\Rightarrow \quad ln\,|\sin x| = -ln\,|\sin y| + ln\,|c|$$

$$\therefore \quad \log|\sin x| = ln\left|\frac{c}{\sin y}\right|$$

$$\Rightarrow \quad \sin x = \frac{c}{\sin y} \quad \Rightarrow \quad \sin x . \sin y = c$$

4. Solve

(i) $\dfrac{dy}{dx} = \dfrac{xy+y}{xy+x}$ (ii) $(xy^2 + x)\, dx + (yx^2 + y)\, dy = 0$

Sol. (i) Given $\dfrac{dy}{dx}=\dfrac{xy+y}{xy+x}$

$$\Rightarrow \quad \frac{dy}{dx}=\frac{y(x+1)}{x(y+1)} \quad \Rightarrow \quad \frac{dy}{dx}=\frac{(x+1)}{(x)}\left(\frac{y}{y+1}\right)$$

$$\Rightarrow \quad \frac{(y+1)}{y}\frac{dy}{dx}=\frac{(x+1)}{x} \quad \Rightarrow \quad \frac{(y+1)}{y}dy=\frac{(x+1)}{x}.dx$$

Integrating on both sides we get

$$\int\frac{(y+1)}{y}.dy=\int\frac{x+1}{x}dx$$

$$\Rightarrow \quad \int\left(1+\frac{1}{y}\right)dy=\int\left(1+\frac{1}{x}\right)dx \quad \Rightarrow \quad y+ln\,y=x+ln\,x+c$$

(ii) Given equation is $(xy^2+x)\,dx+(yx^2+y)\,dy=0$

$$\therefore \quad x\,(y^2+1)\,dx+y(x^2+1)\,dy=0$$

$$\therefore \quad x(y^2+1)\,dx+y(x^2+1)\,dy=0$$

$$\therefore \quad x(y^2+1)\,dx=-\,y(x^2+1)\,dy$$

$$\therefore \quad \frac{x.dx}{(x^2+1)}=-\int\frac{ydy}{y^2+1}$$

taking integration on both sides we get

$$\int\frac{x.dx}{(x^2+1)}=-\int\frac{ydy}{y^2+1}$$

$$\Rightarrow \quad \frac{1}{2}\,ln\,(x^2+1)=\frac{-1}{2}\,ln\,(y^2+1)+ln\,c$$

$$\left(\because \int\frac{f'(x)}{f(x)}dx=ln|f(x)|+c\right)$$

$$\Rightarrow \quad \frac{1}{2}\,ln\,(x^2+1)\,(y^2+1)=ln\,c$$

$$\Rightarrow \quad (x^2+1)\,(y^2+1)=c^2$$

5. Solve $\frac{dy}{dx} = 2xy - 3y + 2x - 3$

Sol. $\frac{dy}{dx} = y(2x-3) + 1(2x-3)$

$$\frac{dy}{dx} = (y+1)(2x-3)$$

$$\Rightarrow \quad \frac{dy}{y+1} = (2x-3)\,dx$$

taking integration on both sides we get

$$\int \frac{dy}{y+1} = \int (2x-3)\,dx$$

$$\Rightarrow \quad ln\,(y+1) = 2.\frac{x^2}{2} - 3x + c$$

$$\therefore \quad ln(y+1) = x^2 - 3x + c$$

6. Solve $\frac{dy}{dx} + \frac{x(1+y^3)}{y^2(1+x^2)} = 0$

Sol. $\frac{dy}{dx} = -\frac{x(1+y^3)}{y^2(1+x^2)} = -\left(\frac{x}{1+x^2}\right)\left(\frac{1+y^3}{y^2}\right)$

$$\therefore \quad \left(\frac{y^2}{1+y^3}\right)dy = \frac{-x}{1+x^2}dx$$

$$\int \frac{y^2}{1+y^3}dy = -\int \frac{x}{1+x^2}dx$$

$$\Rightarrow \quad \frac{1}{3}\int \frac{3y^2}{1+y^3} = -\frac{1}{2}\int \frac{2x}{1+x^2}dx$$

$$\Rightarrow \quad \frac{1}{3}ln(1+y^3) = \frac{-1}{2}ln(1+x^2) + c$$

7. Solve $(1-x^2)\dfrac{dy}{dx} + xy = 5x$

Sol. $(1-x^2)\dfrac{dy}{dx} = 5x - xy = (5-y)\,x$

$$\Rightarrow \quad \frac{dy}{5-y} = \frac{xdx}{1-x^2}$$

$$\therefore \quad \int\frac{dy}{5-y} = \int\frac{xdx}{1-x^2}$$

$$-\int\frac{-dy}{5-y} = \frac{-1}{2}\int\frac{-2x}{1-x^2}$$

$$-\ln(5-y) = -\frac{1}{2}\ln(1-x^2) + k$$

$$\therefore \quad -\ln(5-y) = -\frac{1}{2}\ln(1-x^2) + c$$

where c = –k

8. Solve $\sqrt{1+x^2+y^2+x^2y^2} + xy.\dfrac{dy}{dx} = 0$

Sol. $\sqrt{(1+x^2)+y^2(1+x^2)} = -xy.\dfrac{dy}{dx}$

$$\therefore \quad \sqrt{(1+x^2)(1+y^2)} = -xy\,\frac{dy}{dx}$$

$$\therefore \quad \frac{\sqrt{1+x^2}}{x}dx = \frac{-y}{\sqrt{1+y^2}}dy$$

$$\therefore \quad \int\frac{\sqrt{1+x^2}}{x}dx = \frac{-1}{2}\int\frac{2y}{\sqrt{1+y^2}}dy$$

$$= \frac{-1}{2}2\sqrt{1+y^2} + c \qquad \left(\because \int\frac{f'(x)}{\sqrt{f(x)}}dx = 2\sqrt{f(x)}\right)$$

$$\int\frac{\sqrt{1+x^2}}{x}dx = -\sqrt{1+y^2} + c$$

Consider $\int \frac{\sqrt{1+x^2}}{x}\,dx$

Put $1 + x^2 = t^2$

$\Rightarrow$ $2x\,dx = 2\,t\,d\,t$

$\Rightarrow$ $x\,dx = t\,d\,t$

$$dx = \frac{tdt}{\sqrt{t^2-1}}$$

$$\therefore \int \frac{\sqrt{1+x^2}}{x}\,dx = \int \frac{t}{\sqrt{t^2-1}} \cdot \frac{tdt}{\sqrt{t^2-1}} = \int \frac{t^2}{\left(\sqrt{t^2-1}\right)^2}\,dt$$

$$\int \frac{t^2}{t^2-1}\,dt = \int \left(\frac{t^2-1+1}{t^2-1}\right)dt = \int \left(1+\frac{1}{t^2-1}\right)dt$$

$$= t + \frac{1}{2}\ln\left|\frac{t-1}{t+1}\right|$$

$$\left(\because \int \frac{1}{x^2-a^2}\,dx = \frac{1}{2a}\ln\left|\frac{x-a}{x+a}\right| + c\right)$$

$$= \sqrt{1+x^2} + \frac{1}{2}\ln\left|\frac{\sqrt{1+x^2}-1}{\sqrt{1+x^2}+1}\right| + c$$

$$\therefore \text{ solution is } \quad \sqrt{1+x^2} + \frac{1}{2}\ln\left|\frac{\sqrt{1+x^2}-1}{\sqrt{1+x^2}+1}\right| = -\sqrt{1+y^2} + c = 0$$

$$\therefore \quad \sqrt{1+x^2} + \sqrt{1+y^2} + \frac{1}{2}\ln\left|\frac{\sqrt{1+x^2}-1}{\sqrt{1+x^2}+1}\right| + c$$

9. Solve $(e^x + 1)\,y\,dy + (y + 1)\,dx = 0$

Sol. $(e^x + 1)\,y\,dy = -(y + 1)\,dx$

$$\therefore \quad \frac{ydy}{(y+1)} = -\frac{dx}{(e^x+1)}$$

$$\int \frac{y}{y+1} dy = -\int \frac{1}{e^x+1} dx$$

$$\Rightarrow \quad \int \frac{y+1-1}{y+1} dy = -\int \left(\frac{1+e^x-e^x}{1+e^x}\right) dx$$

$$\Rightarrow \quad \int \left(1-\frac{1}{y+1}\right) dy = -\int \left(-\frac{e^x}{e^x+1}\right) dx$$

$\Rightarrow \quad y - ln(y + 1) = - x + ln\,(e^x + 1) + c$

$\therefore \quad x + y - ln\,(y + 1) = ln\,(e^x + 1) + c$

10. Solve $e^x \cot y\, dx + (1 - e^x) \text{cosec}^2 y\, dy = 0$

Sol. $e^x \cot y\, dx = -(1 - e^x) \text{cosec}^2 y\, dy$

$$\int \frac{e^x}{1-e^x} dx = \int \frac{-\text{cos}ec^2 y}{\cot y} dy$$

$\Rightarrow \quad -ln(1 - e^x) = ln\,(\cot y) + k$

$\Rightarrow \quad ln \cot y + ln\,(1 - e^x) = ln\, c \qquad$ (where $ln\, c = -k$)

$\Rightarrow \quad ln\,(1 - e^x) \cot y) = \ln c$

$\Rightarrow \quad (1 - e^x)(\cot y) = c$

11. Solve $3e^x \cos^2 y\, dx + (1 - e^x) \cot y\, dy = 0$

Sol. $$\int \frac{3e^x .dx}{1-e^x} = -\int \frac{\cot y\, dy}{\cos^2 y}$$

$$-3 \ln(1 - e^x) = -\int \frac{1}{\sin y \cos y} dy$$

$$-3 \ln(1 - e^x) = -2\int \frac{1}{\sin 2y} dy$$

$$\therefore\ 3\, ln\,(1 - e^x) = 2 \int \text{cos}ec\, 2y\, dy = 2\frac{\ln|\text{cos}ec 2y - \cot 2y|}{2} + c$$

$3\, ln\,(1 - e^x) = ln\,|\,\text{cosec}\, 2y - \cot 2y\,| + c$

12. Solve $\frac{dy}{dx}+\frac{y^2+y+1}{x^2+x+1}=0$

Sol. $\frac{dy}{dx} = -\frac{(y^2+y+1)}{x^2+x+1}=0$

$$\therefore \quad \int\frac{dy}{y^2+y+1}=-\int\frac{dx}{x^2+x+1}$$

$$\therefore \quad \int\frac{dy}{\left(y+\frac{1}{2}\right)^2+1-\frac{1}{4}}=-\int\frac{dx}{\left(x+\frac{1}{2}\right)^2+1-\frac{1}{4}}$$

$$\therefore \quad \int\frac{dy}{\left(y+\frac{1}{2}\right)^2+\left(\frac{\sqrt{3}}{2}\right)^2}=-\int\frac{dx}{\left(x+\frac{1}{2}\right)^2+\left(\frac{\sqrt{3}}{2}\right)^2}$$

$$\therefore \quad \frac{1}{\left(\frac{\sqrt{3}}{2}\right)}.\tan^{-1}\left(\frac{y+\frac{1}{2}}{\frac{\sqrt{3}}{2}}\right)=\frac{1}{\left(\frac{\sqrt{3}}{2}\right)}\tan^{-1}\left(\frac{x+\frac{1}{2}}{\frac{\sqrt{3}}{2}}\right)+c$$

$$\left(\because \int\frac{1}{x^2+a^2}dx=\frac{1}{a}tan^{-1}\left(\frac{x}{a}\right)\right)$$

$$\therefore \quad \frac{2}{\sqrt{3}}\tan^{-1}\left(\frac{2y+1}{\sqrt{3}}\right)=-\frac{2}{\sqrt{3}}\tan^{-1}\left(\frac{2x+1}{\sqrt{3}}\right)+c$$

$$\therefore \quad \frac{2}{\sqrt{3}}\tan^{-1}\left(\frac{2x+1}{\sqrt{3}}\right)+\frac{x}{\sqrt{3}}\tan^{-1}\left(\frac{2y+1}{\sqrt{3}}\right)=c$$

13. Solve $\frac{dy}{dx}=\frac{x(2\log x+1)}{\sin y+y\cos y}$

Sol. $\int(\sin y+y\cos y)dy=\int x(2\log x+1)dx$

$$\therefore \quad \int \sin y\, dy + \int y \cos y\, dy = \int 2x \log x\, dx + \int x\, dx$$

$$\Rightarrow \quad -\cos y + y \,.\, \sin y - \int (1) \sin y\, dy = 2\left(\log x . \frac{x^2}{2} - \int \frac{1}{x} . \frac{x^2}{2} dx\right) + \frac{x^2}{2} + c$$

(using biparts)

$$\therefore \quad -\cos y + y \sin y + \cos y = x^2\, ln\, x - \frac{2}{2} \int x.dx + \frac{x^2}{2} + c$$

$$\therefore \quad y \sin y = x^2\, ln\, x - \frac{x^2}{2} + \frac{x^2}{2} + c$$

$$\therefore \quad y \sin y = x^2\, ln\, x + c$$

14. Solve

(i) $\frac{dy}{dx} = (x + y)^2$ (ii) $\frac{dy}{dx} = \tan^2 (x + y)$

Sol. (i) $\frac{dy}{dx} = (x + y)^2$

Put $x + y = t \Rightarrow 1 + \frac{dy}{dx} = \frac{dt}{dx} \Rightarrow \frac{dy}{dx} = \frac{dt}{dx} - 1$

$$\therefore \quad \frac{dy}{dx} = (x + y)^2 \Rightarrow \frac{dt}{dx} - 1 = t^2$$

$$\Rightarrow \frac{dt}{dx} = 1 + t^2 \Rightarrow \frac{dt}{1 + t^2} = dx$$

$$\therefore \quad \int \frac{dt}{1 + t^2} = \int dx \Rightarrow \tan^{-1} (t) = x + c$$

$$\therefore \quad \tan^{-1} (x + y) = x + c$$

(ii) $\frac{dy}{dx} = \tan^2 (x + y)$

Put $x + y = t \Rightarrow 1 + \frac{dy}{dx} = \frac{dt}{dx} \Rightarrow \frac{dy}{dx} = \frac{dt}{dx} - 1$

$$\therefore \quad \frac{dt}{dx} - 1 = \tan^2 t \Rightarrow \frac{dt}{dx} = 1 + \tan^2 t = \sec^2 t$$

$$\therefore \quad \frac{dt}{dx} = \sec^2 t$$

$$\therefore \quad \int \frac{dt}{\sec^2 t} = \int dx$$

$$\Rightarrow \quad \int \cos^2 t \, dt = x + c$$

$$\therefore \quad \int \left(\frac{1 + \cos 2t}{2} \right) dt = x + c$$

$$\therefore \quad \frac{1}{2} t + \frac{1}{2} . \frac{\sin 2t}{2} = x + c$$

$$\therefore \quad \frac{1}{2}(x + y) + \frac{1}{4} \sin (2 (x + y)) = x + c$$

$$\therefore \quad \frac{y}{2} - \frac{x}{2} + \frac{1}{4} \sin (2x + 2y) = c$$

15. Solve

(i) $\frac{dy}{dx} = (3x + y + 4)^2$ (ii) $\frac{dy}{dx} - x \tan (y - x) = 1$

(iii) $\sin^{-1} \left(\frac{dy}{dx} \right) = x + y$

Sol. (i) $\frac{dy}{dx} = (3x + y + 4)^2$

Put $3x + y + 4 = t$

$$\Rightarrow 3 + \frac{dy}{dx} + 0 = \frac{dt}{dx} \quad \Rightarrow \quad \frac{dy}{dx} = \frac{dt}{dx} - 3$$

$$\therefore \quad \frac{dy}{dx} = (3x + y + 4)^2 \text{ becomes } \left(\frac{dt}{dx} - 3 \right) = t^2$$

$$\therefore \quad \frac{dt}{dx} = t^2 + 3 \qquad \Rightarrow \qquad \frac{dt}{t^2+3} = dx$$

$$\therefore \quad \int \frac{dt}{t^2+3} = \int dx \qquad \Rightarrow \qquad \frac{1}{\sqrt{3}} \tan^{-1}\left(\frac{t}{\sqrt{3}}\right) = x + c$$

$$\left(\because \int \frac{dx}{x^2+a^2} = \frac{1}{a} tan^{-1}\left(\frac{x}{a}\right)\right)$$

$$\therefore \quad \frac{1}{\sqrt{3}} \tan^{-1}\left(\frac{3x+y+4}{\sqrt{3}}\right) = x + c$$

(ii) $\dfrac{dy}{dx} - x \tan (y - x) = 1$

Put $y - x = t \quad \Rightarrow \quad \dfrac{dy}{dx} - 1 = \dfrac{dt}{dx}$

$$\Rightarrow \quad \frac{dy}{dx} = 1 + \frac{dt}{dx}$$

$\therefore$ equation becomes

$$\left(1 + \frac{dt}{dx}\right) - x \,.\, \tan(t) = 1$$

$$\therefore \quad \frac{dt}{dx} - x \tan t = 0 \Rightarrow \quad \frac{dt}{dx} = x \tan t$$

cot t . dt = x . dx

$$\int \frac{\cos t}{\sin t} dt = \int x dx \qquad \Rightarrow \qquad ln\,|\sin t| = \frac{x^2}{2} + c$$

(iii) $\sin^{-1}\left(\dfrac{dy}{dx}\right) = x + y$

Sol. $\dfrac{dy}{dx} = \sin(x + y)$

Put $x + y = t$

($\because$ to get variable separable form)

$$\Rightarrow \quad 1+\frac{dy}{dx}=\frac{dt}{dx} \quad \Rightarrow \quad \frac{dy}{dx}=\frac{dt}{dx}-1$$

$\therefore$ Equation becomes

$$\frac{dt}{dx}-1=\sin t \quad \Rightarrow \quad \frac{dt}{dx}=1+\sin t$$

$$\therefore \quad \int\frac{dt}{1+\sin t}=\int dx$$

$$\therefore \quad \int\frac{(1-\sin t)}{1-\sin^2 t}dt=x+c$$

$$\int\frac{1-\sin t}{\cos^2 t}dt=x+c$$

$$\therefore \quad \int(\sec^2 t-\tan t.\sec t)dt=x+c$$

$$\Rightarrow \quad \tan t-\sec t=x+c$$

$$\therefore \quad \tan(x+y)-\sec(x+y)=x+c$$

16. Find the equation of curve which is passing through the origin and whose differential equation is $(y-yx)\,dx+(x+xy)\,dy=0$

Sol. Given $(y-yx)\,dx+(x+xy)\,dy=0$

$$\therefore \quad y(1-x)\,dx=-x(1+y)\,dy$$

$$\therefore \quad \frac{(1-x)dx}{x}=\frac{-(1+y)}{y}dy$$

$$\therefore \quad \int\frac{1-x}{x}dx=-\int\left(\frac{1+y}{y}\right)dy$$

$$\therefore \quad \int\frac{1}{x}dx-\int 1.dx=-\int\frac{1}{y}dy-\int 1.dy$$

$$\therefore \quad \ln x-x=-\ln y-y+c$$

$$\ln xy+y=x+c$$

It is passing through (0, 0) $\Rightarrow$ c = 0

$$\therefore \quad \ln xy+y=x$$

Exercise - 26.2

Solve the following differential equations

1. $x.\dfrac{dy}{dx}=3y$

2. $\dfrac{dy}{dx}=\dfrac{2x}{3y^2}$

3. $\dfrac{dy}{dx}=\dfrac{3y+3}{x-2}$

4. $\dfrac{dy}{dx}+\dfrac{\sqrt{1-y^2}}{\sqrt{1-x^2}}=0$

5. $\dfrac{dy}{dx}=xy+2x+3y+6$

6. $\dfrac{dy}{dx}+xy=xy^2$

7. $x^2\dfrac{dy}{dx}=\sqrt{4-y^2}$

8. $\tan y \,.\, \sec^2 x\, dx + \tan x \sec^2 y\, dy$

9. $3e^x \cos^2 y\, dx + (1-e^x) \cot y\, dy = 0$

10. $\text{cosec}^2 x \,.\, \dfrac{dy}{dx} - \dfrac{1}{y} = 0$

11. $(\sqrt{1-x^2})\sin^{-1} x\, dy + y\, dx = 0$

12. $\cos(x+y)\, dy = dx$

13. $x.e^{x^2+y} = y.\dfrac{dy}{dx}$

14. $ydx - x\,dy + 3x^2 y^2 e^{x^3} dx = 0$

15. Find the equation of curve which passes through (1, 3) and whose slope at any point is $\dfrac{y}{x^2}$.

    (Hint: $\dfrac{dy}{dx}=\dfrac{y}{x^2}$)

16. $\cot y \cdot \frac{dy}{dx} = \cos(x + y) + \cos(x - y)$

17. $(\tan^2 x + 2\tan x + 5)\frac{dy}{dx} = 2(1 + \tan x)\sec^2 x$

18. $\log\left(\frac{dy}{dx}\right) = ax + by$

19. $(x + 1)(y + 1)\,dx + (x - 1)(y + 1)\,dy = 0$

20. $\frac{dy}{dx} = \frac{x + y + 1}{2x + 2y + 3}$

21. $\cos^2(x - 2y) = 1 - 2 \cdot \frac{dy}{dx}$

22. $x + y\frac{dy}{dx} = \sec(x^2 + y^2)$

23. $\frac{dy}{dx} = \sin(x + y) + \cos(x + y)$

Answers

1. $\ln y = 3\ln x + \ln c$ or $y = cx^3$

2. $x^2 = y^3 + c$

3. $\frac{\ln(3y+3)}{3} = \ln(x - 2) + \ln c$ (or) $(y + 1) = k(x - 2)^3$

4. $\sin^{-1} y + \sin^{-1} x = c$

5. $c^{\frac{x^2}{2}+3x} = c(y + 2)$

6. $\ln\left(\frac{y-1}{y}\right) = \frac{x^2}{2} + k$

7. $\sin^{-1}\left(\frac{y}{2}\right) + \frac{1}{x} = c$

8. $\tan x \tan y = c$

9. $\tan y = c(e^x - 1)^3$

10. $2y^2 = 2x - \sin 2x + c$

11. $y \sin^{-1} x = c$

12. $c = \tan \frac{x+y}{2}$

13. $(y+1) e^{-y} + \frac{1}{2} e^{x^2} = c$

14. $\frac{x}{y} + e^{x^3} = c$

(*Hint* : $\int \frac{ydx - xdy}{y^2} + \int 3x^2 . e^{x^3} = c$

and $\left(\frac{ydx - xdy}{y^2}\right) = d\left(\frac{x}{y}\right), \int d\left(\frac{x}{y}\right) = \frac{x}{y}$

15. $y = 3e^{\frac{x-1}{x}}$

16. $ln(\text{cosec } y - \cot y) = 2 \sin x + c$

17. $y = ln (\tan^2 x + 2 \tan x + 5) + c$

18. $\frac{e^{ax}}{a} + \frac{e^{-by}}{b} = c$

19. $(x + y) + 2\, ln\, (x - 1) = c$

20. $\frac{2}{3}(x + y) + \frac{1}{9}\{ln\,(3x + 3y + 4\} = x + c$

21. $\tan(x - 2y) = x + c$

22. $\sin(x^2 + y^2) = 2x + c$

23. $ln\,[1 + \tan\left(\frac{x+y}{2}\right)] = x + c$

26.6 Homogenious Differential Equations

Homogenious function : A function $f(x, y)$ is said to be Homogenious function of deg 'n' if $f(kx, ky) = k^n f(x, y)$. where $k \in R$

Ex: $f(x, y) = \frac{x^3 + y^3}{x + y}$ is a Homogenious function of degree n = 2.

Since $f(kx, ky) = \dfrac{(kx)^3+(ky)^3}{kx+ky} = \dfrac{k^3(x^2+y^2)}{k(x+y)} = k^2.f(x,y)$

$\therefore$ $f(kx, ky) = k^2 f(x, y)$

$\therefore$ f is Homogenious function of degree 2

Homogenious Differential Equations

If f is a Homogenious function of degree zero then $\dfrac{dy}{dx} = f(x,y)$ is called Homogenious Differential Equation of first order first degree.

Ex: (i) $\dfrac{dy}{dx} = \dfrac{x+y}{x-y}$

(ii) $\dfrac{dy}{dx} = \dfrac{x^2 y}{x^3+y^3}$

(iii) $\dfrac{dy}{dx} = \dfrac{x^3 y}{x^4+x^2y^2}$

Method of solving the Homogenious Differential Equation $\dfrac{dy}{dx} = f(x,y)$

Step 1 : take $y = vx$ then $\dfrac{dy}{dx} = v + x.\dfrac{dt}{dx}$

Step 2 : The Differential equation becomes $t + x.\dfrac{dt}{dx} = f(x, kx)$

Step 3 : Separate like cofficients and integration on both sides we get the solution of the Homogeneous Differential Equation.

Ex 1 Solve $\dfrac{dy}{dx} = \dfrac{2xy}{x^2+y^2}$

Sol. Given $\dfrac{dy}{dx} = \dfrac{2xy}{x^2+y^2} = f(x, y)$ is a Homogenious Differential Equation

$\therefore$ Put $y = tx \Rightarrow \dfrac{dy}{dx} = t + x.\dfrac{dt}{dx}$

$\therefore$ the equation becomes

$$t + x\,.\frac{dt}{dx} = \frac{2x\,(tx)}{x^2 + t^2x^2} = \frac{2tx^2}{x^2(1+t^2)} = \frac{2t}{1+t^2}$$

$$\therefore \quad t + x\,.\frac{dt}{dx} = \frac{2t}{1+t^2}$$

$$\Rightarrow \quad x\,.\frac{dt}{dx} = \frac{2t}{1+t^2} - t = \frac{2t - t - t^3}{1+t^2}$$

$$\Rightarrow \quad x\,.\frac{dt}{dx} = \frac{t - t^3}{1+t^2}$$

separate the like coefficients we get

$$\frac{1+t^2}{t-t^3}\,dt = \frac{dx}{x}$$

Integration on both sides we get

$$\int \frac{1+t^2}{t-t^3}\,dt = \int \frac{dx}{x}$$

$$\therefore \quad \int \frac{1+t^2}{t(1-t^2)}\,dt = \ln cx$$

$$\Rightarrow \quad \int \frac{1-t^2+2t^2}{t(1-t^2)}\,dt = \ln cx$$

$$\Rightarrow \quad \int \left(\frac{1}{t} + \frac{2t^2}{t(1-t^2)}\right) dt = \ln cx$$

$$\Rightarrow \quad \int \left(\frac{1}{t} + \frac{2t}{1-t^2}\right) dt = \ln cx$$

$$\Rightarrow \quad \ln t - \ln(1-t^2) = \ln cx$$

$$\Rightarrow \quad \ln\left(\frac{t}{1-t^2}\right) = \ln cx$$

$$\Rightarrow \quad \frac{t}{1-t^2} = cx$$

$$\Rightarrow \quad \frac{\frac{y}{x}}{1-\left(\frac{y}{x}\right)^2} = cx \quad \Rightarrow \quad \frac{xy}{x^2 - y^2} = cx \quad \Rightarrow \quad y = c(x^2 - y^2)$$

$\therefore$ Solution of D.E is $y = c(x^2 - y^2)$

2. Give the solution of $x\sin^2\left(\frac{y}{x}\right)dx = ydx - xdy$ which passes through the point $\left(1, \frac{\pi}{4}\right)$.

Sol. Given equation is $x \,.\, \sin^2\left(\frac{y}{x}\right) dx = ydx - x\,dy$

i.e., $x\,dy = \left[y - x.\sin^2\left(\frac{y}{x}\right)\right] dx$

$$\therefore \quad \frac{dy}{dx} = \frac{y - x.\sin^2\left(\frac{y}{x}\right)}{x}$$

It is Homogenious Differential equation

So take $\quad y = tx$

$$\Rightarrow \quad \frac{dy}{dx} = t + x\frac{dt}{dx}$$

$\therefore$ the equation becomes

$$t + x\frac{dt}{dx} = \frac{tx - x.\sin^2\left(\frac{tx}{x}\right)}{x} = \frac{tx - x\sin^2(t)}{x}$$

$$t + x\frac{dt}{dx} = t - \sin^2(t)$$

$$\Rightarrow \quad x\frac{dt}{dx} = -\sin^2 t$$

$\therefore$ Separate like coefficients we get

$$\frac{dt}{\sin^2 t} = -\frac{dx}{x}$$

i.e., $-\operatorname{cosec}^2 t \, dt = \dfrac{dx}{x}$

Integrating on both sides we get

$$-\int \operatorname{cosec}^2 dt = \int \frac{dx}{x}$$

$$\cot t = ln\,|\,cx\,|$$

i.e., $\cot\left(\dfrac{y}{x}\right) = ln\,|\,cx\,|$ which is the require solution of given Differential Equation

3. Solve $(x - y\log y + y\log x)\,dx + x(\log y - \log x)\,dy = 0$

Sol. Given equation is

$$(x - y\log y + y\log x)\,dx + x(\log y - \log x)\,dy = 0$$

i.e., $(x - y\,[\log y - \log x]\,)\,dx = -x(\log y - \log x)\,dy$

$$[\,x - y\log\left(\frac{y}{x}\right)\,]\,dx = -x\log\left(\frac{y}{x}\right)dy$$

$$\therefore \quad \frac{dy}{dx} = -\frac{\left(x - y\log\left(\frac{y}{x}\right)\right)}{x\log\left(\frac{y}{x}\right)}$$

Put $y = tx$ then

$$t + x\,.\,\frac{dt}{dx} = \frac{-(x - tx\log t)}{x\log t} = \frac{-(1 - t\log t)}{\log t}$$

$$\therefore \quad x\frac{dt}{dx} = \frac{-(1 - t\log t)}{\log t} - t$$

$$\therefore \quad x\,\frac{dt}{dx} = \frac{-(1 - t\log t) - t\log t}{\log t} = \frac{-1 + t\log t - t\log t}{\log t}$$

$$\therefore \quad x\,.\frac{dt}{dx} = \frac{-1}{\log t}$$

now separate like coefficients, we get

$$-\log dt = \frac{dx}{x}$$

Integration on both sides we get

$$-\int \log t\,dt = \int \frac{dx}{x}$$

$$\Rightarrow \quad -\left[(\log t).t - \int \frac{1}{t}.t\,dt\right] = \log cx$$

$$-[t \log t - t] = \log cx$$

$$\Rightarrow \quad t = \log cx + t \log t$$

$$\therefore \quad \frac{y}{x} = \log cx + \frac{y}{x}\log\left(\frac{y}{x}\right)$$

i.e., $y = x \log cx + y \log\left(\frac{y}{x}\right)$ which is the required solution of D.E.

26.7 Linear Differential Equation

The differential equation is of the form $\frac{dy}{dx} + p(x)y = Q(x)$ is called linear differential equation in y of first order and first degree.

Method of solving a linear differential equation

Step 1 : Find Integrating factor $e^{\int p(x)dx}$

Step 2 : Solution of differential equation is

$$y.(\text{I. F}) = \int Q(x).(\text{I.F})dx$$

Note : $\frac{dx}{dy} + P(y)x = Q(y)$ is linear differential equation in x of first order first degree.

1. Solve $(x \log x)\frac{dy}{dx} + y = 2\log x$

Sol. Given equation is

$$(x\log x)\frac{dy}{dx} + y = 2\log x$$

$$\frac{dy}{dx} + \frac{y}{x\log x} = \frac{2\log x}{x\log x} = \frac{2}{x}$$

It is of the form $\frac{dy}{dx} + P(x)\, y = Q(x)$

where $P(x) = \frac{1}{x\log x}$, $Q(x) = \frac{2}{x}$

now $I.F = e^{\int p(x)dx} = e^{\int \frac{1}{x\log x}dx} = e^{\log|\log x|} = \log x$

$\therefore$ Solution of D.E is

$$y\,.\,(I.F) = \int (I.F)\,Q(x)\,dx$$

$$y\,.\log x = \int \log x.\frac{2}{x}dx$$

$$y \log x = 2(\log x)^2 + c$$

2. Solve $(1 + y^2)dx = (\tan^{-1}y - x)\, dy$

Sol. Given equation is $(1 + y^2)\frac{dx}{dy} = (\tan^{-1} y - x)$

$$\Rightarrow \quad (1 + y^2)\frac{dx}{dy} + x = \tan^{-1}y$$

$$\frac{dx}{dy} + \frac{x}{1+y^2} = \frac{\tan^{-1} y}{1+y^2}$$

it is linear Differential equation in x

$$P(y) = \frac{1}{1+y^2},\; Q(y) = \frac{\tan^{-1} y}{1+y^2}$$

$$I.F = e^{\int P(y)dy} = e^{\int \frac{1}{1+y^2}dy} = e^{\tan^{-1} y}$$

$\therefore$ Solution is $\quad x\,.\,I.F = \int (I.F).Q(y)dy$

$$x.e^{\tan^{-1} y} = \int e^{\tan^{-y}} \frac{\tan^{-1} y}{1+y^2}dy$$

Consider $\int e^{\tan^{-1} y}.\frac{\tan^{-1} y}{1+y^2}dy$

Put $\tan^{-1}y = t \Rightarrow \frac{1}{1+y^2}dy = dt$

$\therefore \int e^t . t\, dt$

$= e^t(t-1) + c$

$= e^{\tan^{-1}y}(\tan^{-1}y - 1) + c$

$\therefore$ Solution is $x . e^{\tan^{-1}y} = e^{\tan^{-1}y}(\tan^{-1}y - 1) + c$

3. Solve $x.\frac{dy}{dx} + y = (1+x)e^x$

Sol. Given equation is $x.\frac{dy}{dx} + y = (1+x)e^x$

i.e., $\frac{dy}{dx} + \frac{y}{x} = \frac{(1+x)e^x}{x}$

I.F = $e^{\int \frac{1}{x}dx} = e^{\log x} = x$

$\therefore$ Solution is $y.x = \int \frac{(1+x)e^x}{x}.x.dx$

$= \int (x+1)e^x dx$

$xy = x\, e^x + c$ $\left(\because \int \left(f(x) + f'(n)\right) e^x dx = e^x f(x) + c\right)$

Excercise - 26.3

1. Solve the following differential equations.

(i) $(x^2 + y^2)\, dy = 2xy\, dx$

(ii) $\frac{dy}{dx} = \frac{(x+y)^2}{2x^2}$

(iii) $(y^2 - 2xy)\, dx = (x^2 - 2xy)\, dy$

(iv) $x.\sin\left(\frac{y}{x}\right)\frac{dy}{dx} = y\sin\frac{y}{x} - x$

(v) Find the equation of curve whose gradient is $\frac{dy}{dx} = \frac{y}{x} - \cos^2\frac{y}{x}$ where $x > 0, y > 0$ and which passes through the point $\left(1, \frac{\pi}{4}\right)$

2. Solve the following differential Equations.

(i) $\cos x \cdot \dfrac{dy}{dx} + y \sin x = \tan x$ (ii) $\sin^2 x \cdot \dfrac{dy}{dx} + y = \cot x$

(iii) $\dfrac{dy}{dx} + \dfrac{3x^2 y}{1+x^3} = \dfrac{\sin^2 x}{1+x^3}$ (iv) $(1-x^2)\dfrac{dy}{dx} + 2xy = x\sqrt{1-x^2}$

(v) $x(x-1)\dfrac{dy}{dx} - (x-2)y = x^3(2x-1)$

Answers

1. (i) $k(x^2 - y^2) = y$ (ii) $\log x = 2\tan^{-1}\left(\dfrac{y}{x}\right) + c$

(iii) $xy(y-x) = c$ (iv) $kx = e^{\cos\left(\frac{y}{x}\right)}$

(v) $\tan\left(\dfrac{y}{x}\right) = 1 - \log x$

2. (i) $y \sec x = \dfrac{\tan^2 x}{2} + c$ (ii) $(1 + \cot x)\, e^{-\cot x} + c = ye^{-\cot x}$

(iii) $y(1+x^3) = \dfrac{1}{2}x - \dfrac{\sin 2x}{4} + c$ (iv) $y = \sqrt{1-x^2} + c(1-x^2)$

(v) $y(x-1) = x^2(x^2 - x + c)$

26.8 Exact Differential Equations

Let us consider the differential equation $Mdx + Ndy = 0$ where M, N are functions of x and y

If this equation is to be exact, then it must have been derived by directly diffrentiation some function of x, y.

Hence $Mdx + Ndy = du$ say .....(1)

from differential calculus

$$du = \frac{\partial u}{\partial x}dx + \frac{\partial u}{\partial y}dy \quad .....(2)$$

(1) & (2) $\Rightarrow$

$$Mdx + Ndy = \frac{\partial u}{\partial x}dx + \frac{\partial u}{\partial y}dy$$

$\therefore \quad M = \frac{\partial u}{\partial x} \qquad N = \frac{\partial u}{\partial y}$

$\Rightarrow \quad \frac{\partial M}{\partial y} = \frac{\partial^2 u}{\partial y \partial x} \qquad \frac{\partial N}{\partial x} = \frac{\partial^2 u}{\partial x \partial y}$

$\therefore \quad \frac{\partial M}{\partial y} = \frac{\partial N}{\partial x}$ is the condition for exactness

hence the differential equation $Mdx + Ndy = 0$ is exact of $\frac{\partial M}{\partial y} = \frac{\partial N}{\partial x}$.

$\therefore$ the solution of exact D.E is obtained by

$$\int Mdx \qquad\qquad + \int Ndy = c$$

(treated y as constant integrate wrt x) (integrate wrt y those terms at are independent of x)

1. Solve $(x+2y-3)dy-(2x-y+1)dx=0$

Sol. Consider $(x+2y-3)dy-(2x-y+1)dx=0$ it is of the form $Mdx+Ndy=0$

where $\quad N = x+2y-3 \qquad M = -2x+y-1$

$\frac{\partial M}{\partial y} = 1 \qquad \frac{\partial N}{\partial x} = 1$

$\therefore \quad \frac{\partial M}{\partial y} = \frac{\partial N}{\partial x}$

$\therefore$ given equation is exact

$\therefore \quad \int Mdx = \int(-2x+y-1)dx$

$= \frac{-2x^2}{2} + yx - x$ (by treating y terms as constant)

$\int Ndy = \int(2y-3)dy$

$= \frac{2y^2}{2} - 3y = y^2 - 3y$

(integrating the terms wrt y which are independent of x)

$\therefore$ Solution is

$$\left(-\frac{2x^2}{2}+yx-x\right)+\left(\frac{2y^2}{2}-3y\right)+c$$

i.e., $\quad y^2-x^2+xy-x-3y+c$

2. Solve $\left(x^2+y^2\right)dx+2xy\,dy=0$

Sol. Consider $\left(x^2+y^2\right)dx+2xy\,dy=0$

it is of the form $Mdx+Ndy=0$

where $M=x^2+y^2 \qquad N=2xy$

$$\frac{\partial M}{\partial y}=\frac{\partial}{\partial y}\left(x^2+y^2\right) \qquad \frac{\partial N}{\partial x}=\frac{\partial}{\partial x}(2xy)$$

$$=2y \qquad\qquad =2y$$

$$\therefore \quad \frac{\partial M}{\partial y}=\frac{\partial N}{\partial x}$$

$\therefore$ the given equation is exact D.E.

$\therefore$ Solution is

$$\int Mdx+\int Ndy=C$$

(treat y as constant) (integrate the term of N which are independent of x wrt y)

$$\therefore \quad \int\left(x^2+y^2\right)dx+\int dy=c$$

$$=\frac{x^3}{3}+y^2x+0=c$$

$$=\frac{x^3}{3}+y^2x=c$$

3. $\left(y\cos x+\sin y+y\right)dx+\left(\sin x+x\cos y+x\right)dy=0$

Sol. it is of the form $Mdx+Ndy=0$

$$\frac{\partial M}{\partial y}=\cos x+1 \qquad \frac{\partial N}{\partial x}=\cos x+1$$

$$\therefore \quad \frac{\partial M}{\partial y}=\frac{\partial N}{\partial x}$$

$\therefore$ Solution of D.E is

$$\int (y\cos x + \sin y + y)\, dx + \int (\sin x + x\cos y + x)\, dx = c$$

(treat y as constant) (independent of terms of y)

$$y\sin x + \sin yx + yx + 0 = c$$

$$\therefore \quad y\sin x + \sin yx + yx = c$$

$$y\sin x + x(\sin y + y) = c$$

Excercise - 26.4

1. Solve $\left(1+e^{x/y}\right)dx + e^{x/y}(1-x/y)dy = 0$

2. Solve $\left(e^y+1\right)\cos x\ dx + e^y \sin x\ dy = 0$

3. $\left(x^2 - ay\right)dx = \left(ax - y^2\right)dy$

4. $\left(x^2+y^2-a^2\right)x\,dx + \left(x^2-y^2-b^2\right)y\,dy = 0$

Answers

1. $x + e^{x/y}(y) = c$

2. $\left(e^y+1\right)\sin x = c$

3. $x^3 + y^3 - 3a\,xy = c$

4. $x^4 + 2x^2y^2 - 2a^2x^2 - y^4 - 2b^2y^2 = 4c$

Unit - VI

Exercise Questions

26. Differential Equations

1. Find order and degree of differential equation $1+\left(\frac{d^2y}{dx^2}\right)^2=\left[2+\left(\frac{dy}{dx}\right)^2\right]^{\frac{3}{2}}$

2. Form the differential equation whose solution if y = acos x + b sin x whose a and b are constants.

2. (a) Form the Differential Equation whose solution is $y = a\cos\left(\frac{n}{x}+b\right)$

   (b) Form the Differential Equation of family circles passing through origin and whose centre lies as x-axis.

3. (a) Form the Differential Equation of circles of radius 'a' and the centre at (h, k).
   (b) Define degree and order of Differential Equation and find order and degree

$$\text{of } \frac{\left[1+\left(\frac{dy}{dx}\right)^2\right]^{\frac{3}{2}}}{\frac{d^2y}{dx^2}}=k$$

4. (a) Form the Differential Equation of y = a cos x + b sin x where A and B are arbitrary constants.

   (b) Form the Differential Equation of $y = ae^x + be^{-x}$

5. Form the Differential Equation of $y = ax^3 + bx^2$

6. Form the differential equation y = acos(nx + b)

7. Solve $(e^x + 1)\, y\, dy + (y + 1)dx = 0$

8. Form the Differential Equation which has $y = ax^2 + bx + c$ as a solution where a, b, c are arbitrary constants.

9. Form the differential equation which has y = mx + f(m) its solution where m is the arbitrary constant.

10. Form the Differential Equations from the following equations.

(i) $y = e^x(A \cos x + B \sin x)$

(ii) $xy = Ae^x + Be^{-x}$

11. Form the Differential Equation of $y^2 = 4a\ (x + a)$

12. Form the differential equations of all circles which passes through origin and whose centres on x-axis.

13. Form the Differential Equation by eliminating a, b from $y = ax^2 + \dfrac{b}{x}$

Unit - VI

Answers to Exercise Questions

26. Differential Equations

1. (a) order - 2, degree - 4 (b) $\frac{d^2y}{dx^2} + y = 0$

2. (a) $x^4 \frac{d^2y}{dx} + 2x^3 \frac{dy}{dx} + y = 0$ (b) $y^2 - x^2 - 2xy\ y' = 0$

3. (a) $\left[(1 + \left(\frac{dy}{dx}\right)^2\right]^3 = \left(\frac{d^2y}{dx^2}\right)^2 .r^2$ (b) deg 2, order 2

4. (a) $\frac{d^2y}{dx^2} + y = 0$ (b) $\frac{d^2y}{dx^2} - y = 0$

5. $x^2\left(\frac{d^2y}{dx}\right) - 4x\left(\frac{dy}{dx}\right) + 6y = 0$

6. $\frac{d^2y}{dx^2} + n^2y = 0$

7. $x + y - ln\ (y + 1) - ln(e^x + 1) + c$

8. $\frac{d^3y}{dx^3} = 0$

9. $y = \left(\frac{dy}{dx}\right)x + f\left(\frac{dy}{dx}\right)$

10. $\frac{d^2y}{dx^2} - 2.\frac{dy}{dx} + 2y = 0$

11. $y\left(\frac{dy}{dx}\right)^2 + 2x\left(\frac{dy}{dx}\right) - y = 0$

12. $y^2 - x^2 - 2xy\ \frac{dy}{dx} = 0$

13. $x^2 . \frac{d^2y}{dx^2} - 2y = 0$

Unit - VI

Self Test Questions

26. Differential Equations

1. Define differential equation, order and degree of the differential equation.
2. Write the order and degree of DE

$$\left\{1+\left(\frac{dy}{dx}\right)^2\right\}^{3/2}=\left(\frac{d^2y}{dx^2}\right)^3$$

3. (i) Form the differential equation of $\sin^{-1}x+\sin^{-1}y=c$

   (ii) Form the differential equation of all circles of radius 'a'.

4. (a) Form the differential equation to represent the family of curve y = A cos x + B sin x.

   (b) Form the differential equation from the relation $y = e^x$ (A cos x + B sin x) where A, B are orbitary constants.

5. Form the differential equation of $y = ae^{-x} + b$

6. Solve the D. E $\frac{dy}{dx}=xy+x+y+1$

7. Solve $(2x - y + 1)\,dx + (2y - x - 1)\,dy = 0$

8. Solve $\frac{dy}{dx}=\frac{x[2\log x+1]}{\sin y+y\cos y}$

9. Solve the differential equation $\left(y-x\frac{dy}{dx}\right)x=y$

10. (i) Solve D. E $\frac{dy}{dx}=\tan^2(x+y)$

    (ii) Solve $(x+y)^2\frac{dy}{dx}=a^2$

11. Solve $\frac{dy}{dx}+1=e^{x+y}$

12. Solve $(x+y+1)\frac{dy}{dx}=1$

13. Solve D. E $(1 + x) y\, dx + (1 + y) x\, dy = 0$

14. Define homogeneous differential equations.

15. Solve the differential equation $xdy - ydx = \sqrt{x^2 + y^2}\, dx$.

16. Explain the methods to solve the first order and first degree differential equations.

17. Solve $\frac{dy}{dx} = \frac{y}{x+\sqrt{xy}}$

18. Solve $\left(1+e^{x/y}\right)dx + e^{x/y}\left(1-\frac{x}{y}\right)dy = 0$

UNIT - VII

LAPLACE TRANSFORMS

UNIT - VII

LAPLACE TRANSFORMS

27

Laplace Transforms

27.1 Laplace Transforms

Definition : Let f(t) be a function of t defined for all positive values of t. Then the Laplace transforms of f(t), denoted by L{f(t)} is defined by L {f(t)} = $\int_0^\infty e^{-st} f(t) dt$, Provided that integral exists.

where s is a parameter which may be real or complex number.

L {f(t)} being clearly a function in s. It can be written as $\bar{f}(s)$.

i.e., $L\{f(t)\} = \bar{f}(s)$. Also we can write $f(t) = L^{-1}\{\bar{f}(s)\}$.

The symbol L which transforms f(t) into $\bar{f}(s)$ is called Laplace transformation operator.

27.2 Transforms of Elementary Functions

Theorems :

1. $L(1) = \dfrac{1}{s}$

2. $L(t^n) = \dfrac{n!}{s^{n+1}}$ when n = 0, 1, 2, ...

   $= \dfrac{\Gamma(n+1)}{s^{n+1}}$ otherwise

[The Γ function is defined as $\Gamma(n) = \int_0^\infty e^{-x} x^{n-1}\, dx \; (n > 0)$

Reduction formula for $\Gamma(n)$

$$\Gamma(n+1) = n\Gamma(n) \text{ i.e., } \Gamma(n) = \Gamma(n-1)+1 = (n-1)\Gamma(n-1) \;]$$

3. $L(e^{at}) = \dfrac{1}{s-a}$ $(s > a)$

4. $L(\sin\ at) = \dfrac{a}{s^2+a^2}$ (s>0)

5. $L(\cos at) = \dfrac{s}{s^2+a^2}$ (s>0)

6. $L(\sinh at) = \dfrac{a}{s^2-a^2}$ (s>|a|)

7. $L(\cosh at) = \dfrac{s}{s^2-a^2}$ s>|a|

Theorem : 1

$$L(1) = \frac{1}{s}$$

Proof: We have $L(f(t)) = \int_0^{\infty} e^{-st} f(t)dt$

so $L(1) = \int_0^{\infty} e^{-st}.(1)dt$

$$= \left(\frac{e^{-st}}{-s}\right)_0^{\infty} = \left(\frac{1}{-s.e^{st}}\right)_0^{\infty} = 0 - \left(\frac{1}{-se^0}\right) = \frac{1}{s} \quad (\because \text{as } t \to \infty \Rightarrow st \to \infty \Rightarrow e^{st} \to \infty \Rightarrow \frac{1}{e^{st}} \to 0)$$

$\therefore$ $L(1) = \dfrac{1}{s}$

Theorem: 2

$$L(e^{at}) = \frac{1}{s-a}$$

Proof: Here $f(t) = (e^{at})$

$$L\left(e^{at}\right)=\int_0^\infty e^{-st}.f(t)dt=\int_0^\infty e^{-st}.e^{at}dt$$

$$=\int_0^\infty e^{t(a-s)}dt$$

$$=\left(\frac{e^{-t(a-s)}}{a-s}\right)_0^\infty$$

$$=\left(\frac{e^{-t(s-a)}}{a-s}\right)_0^\infty \qquad \because (s>a)$$

$$=0-\frac{e^{-0}}{a-s}$$

$$=\frac{1}{s-a}$$

$$\therefore \quad L\left(e^{at}\right)=\frac{1}{s-a}$$

Ex: (i) $L\left(e^{5t}\right)=\frac{1}{s-5}$ (ii) $L\left(e^{4t}\right)=\frac{1}{s-4}$ (iii) $L\left(e^{-t}\right)=\frac{1}{s-(-1)}=\frac{1}{s+1}$

Theorem: 3

$$L(t^n)=\frac{n!}{s^{n+1}}$$

Proof: Here $L\left(t^n\right)=\int_0^\infty e^{-st}.t^n dt$

Put st = P, t = P/s

$$\therefore \int_0^\infty e^{-p}.\left(\frac{P}{s}\right)^n\left(\frac{dp}{s}\right)$$

$$=\frac{1}{s^{n+1}}\int_0^\infty e^{-P}p^n dp=\frac{\Gamma(n+1)}{s^{n+1}}$$

in particular $\Gamma\left(t^{-1/2}\right)=\frac{\Gamma(1/2)}{s^{1/2}}=\sqrt{\pi/s}$; $L\left(t^{1/2}\right)=\frac{\sqrt{\pi}}{2s^{3/2}}$

If n is positive integer $L\left(t^{n}\right)=\frac{n!}{s^{n+1}}$

Ex: (i) $L\left(t^{1}\right)=\frac{1!}{s^{1+1}}=\frac{1}{s^{2}}$ (ii) $L\left(t^{5}\right)=\frac{5!}{s^{5+1}}=\frac{120}{s^{6}}$

(iii) $L\left(t^{4/3}\right)=\frac{\Gamma(4/3+1)}{s^{4/3+1}}=\frac{4/3\Gamma 4/3}{s^{7/3}}=\frac{4/3.\frac{1}{3}\Gamma 1/3}{s^{7/3}}$

Theorem: 4

$$L(\sin at)=\frac{a}{s^{2}+a^{2}}$$

Proof

by definition, $L(\sin at)=\int_{0}^{\infty}e^{-st}\sin at dt$

$$=\left[\frac{e^{-st}}{s^{2}+a^{2}}(-s\sin at-a\cos at)\right]_{0}^{\infty}$$

$$\left(\because \int e^{ax}\sin(bx+c)=\frac{e^{ax}}{a^{2}+b^{2}}[a\sin(bx+c)-b\cos(bx+c)]\right)$$

$$=0-\frac{e^{-0}}{s^{2}+a^{2}}\quad(0-a\cos a(0))$$

$$=\frac{a}{s^{2}+a^{2}}$$

Ex. (i) $L(\sin t)=L(\sin 1t)=\frac{1}{s^{2}+1^{2}}=\frac{1}{s^{2}+1}$

(ii) $L(\sin 5t)=\frac{5}{s^{2}+5^{2}}=\frac{5}{s^{2}+25}$

(iii) $L(\sin 8t)=\frac{8}{s^{2}+8^{2}}=\frac{8}{s^{2}+64}$

Theorem: 5

$$L(\cos at) = \frac{s}{s^2+a^2}$$

Proof :

by definition, $L(\cos at) = \int_0^\infty e^{-st}\cos at\, dt$

$$= \left[\frac{e^{-st}}{s^2+a^2}(-s\cos at + a\sin at)\right]_0^\infty$$

$$\left(\because \int e^{ax}\cos(bx+c) = \frac{e^{ax}}{a^2+b^2}[a\cos(bx+c)+b\sin(bx+c)]\right)$$

$$= 0 - \left(\frac{e^{-0}}{s^2+a^2}(-s)\right)$$

$$= \frac{s}{s^2+a^2}$$

Ex. (i) $L(\cos t) = \frac{s}{s^2+1}$

(ii) $L(\cos 2t) = \frac{s}{s^2+2^2} = \frac{s}{s^2+4}$

(iii) $L(\cos 5t) = \frac{s}{s^2+5^2} = \frac{s}{s^2+25}$

Theorem: 6

$$L(\sin hat) = \frac{a}{s^2-a^2}$$

Proof :

by definition, $L(\sinh at) = \int_0^\infty e^{-st}\sinh at\, dt$

$$= \int_0^\infty e^{-st}\left(\frac{e^{at}-e^{-at}}{2}\right)dt$$

$$= \frac{1}{2}\int_0^\infty \left(e^{(a-s)t} - e^{-(a+s)t}\right) dt \quad (s>a)$$

$$= \frac{1}{2}\left[\left(\frac{e^{(a-s)t}}{a-s}\right)_0^\infty - \left(\frac{e^{-(a+s)t}}{-(a+s)}\right)_0^\infty\right]$$

$$= \frac{1}{2}\left[\left(\frac{e^{(a-s)t}}{a-s}\right)_0^\infty + \left(\frac{e^{-(a+s)t}}{a+s}\right)_0^\infty\right]$$

$$= \frac{1}{2}\left[\left(0-\frac{1}{a-s}\right)+\left(0-\frac{1}{a+s}\right)\right]$$

$$= \frac{1}{2}\left[\frac{1}{s-a}-\frac{1}{s+a}\right]$$

$$= \frac{1}{2}\left[\frac{\mathrm{s+a-s+a}}{\mathrm{s}^2-a^2}\right] = \frac{1}{2}\left[\frac{2a}{s^2-a^2}\right]$$

$$= \frac{a}{s^2-a^2}$$

Theorem: 7

Similarly we can do, $L(\cosh at) = \dfrac{s}{s^2-a^2}$

Ex. (i) $L(\sinh 2t) = \dfrac{2}{s^2-2^2} = \dfrac{2}{s^2-4}$

(ii) $L(\cosh 4t) = \dfrac{s}{s^2-4^2} = \dfrac{s}{s^2-16}$

27.3 Linear Property

If a, b, c are constants and f, g, h are any functions of laplace transforms then

$$L(af(t)+bg(t)-ch(t)) = aLf(t)+bLg(t)-cLh(t)$$

Ex : $L\{2+4\sin 3t+5e^{2t}\}$

$$= 2L(1)+4L(\sin 3t)+5.L(e^{2t})$$

$$= 2\left(\frac{1}{s}\right)+4.\left(\frac{3}{s^2+9}\right)+5.\left(\frac{1}{s-2}\right)$$

Some solved examples on transformation of elementary functions

1. Find the laplace transforms of

(i) sin2t sin3t (ii) cost cos3t (iii) sin4t cost

Sol. (i) $\sin 2t \sin 3t = \frac{1}{2}[\cos(3t-2t)-\cos(3t+2t)]$

$(\because \cos(A-B)-\cos(A+B)=2\sin A \sin B)$

$$= \frac{1}{2}[\cos t - \cos 5t]$$

$$\therefore L(\sin 2t \sin 3t) = L\left(\frac{1}{2}(\cos t - \cos 5t)\right) = \frac{1}{2}L(\cos t - \cos 5t)$$

$$= \frac{1}{2}\{L(\cos t) - L(\cos 5t)\}$$

$(\because$ by linear property$)$

$$= \frac{1}{2}\left[\frac{s}{s^2+1^2} - \frac{s}{s^2+5^2}\right]$$

$\left(\because L(\cos at) = \frac{s}{s^2+a^2}\right)$

(ii) cost cos3t] $= \frac{1}{2}[\cos(t+3t)+\cos(t-3t)]$

$$= \frac{1}{2}[\cos 4t + \cos 2t)]$$

$(\because \cos(A+B)+\cos(A-B)) = 2\cos A \cos B$ and $\cos(-\theta) = \cos\theta)$

$$\therefore L(\cos t \cos 3t) = L\left\{\frac{1}{2}(\cos 4t + \cos 2t)\right\}$$

$$= \frac{1}{2}(L\cos 4t) + \frac{1}{2}(L\cos 2t) \quad (\because \text{by linear property})$$

$$= \frac{1}{2}.\frac{s}{s^2+4^2} + \frac{1}{2}.\frac{s}{s^2+2^2}$$

$$= \frac{1}{2}.\left(\frac{s}{s^2+16}\right) + \frac{1}{2}.\left(\frac{s}{s^2+4}\right)$$

(iii) $\sin 4t \cos t = \frac{1}{2}[\sin(4t+t)+\sin(4t-t)] = \frac{1}{2}[\sin 5t + \sin 3t]$

($\because$ sin(A + B) + sin(A – B) = 2 sin A cos B)

$$L\{\sin 4t \cos t\} = L\left\{\frac{1}{2}[\sin 5t + \sin 3t]\right\} = \frac{1}{2}L(\sin 5t) + \frac{1}{2}L(\sin 3t)$$

$$= \frac{1}{2}\left(\frac{5}{s^2+5^2}\right) + \frac{1}{2}\left(\frac{3}{s^2+3^2}\right)$$

$$= \frac{1}{2}\left(\frac{5}{s^2+25}\right) + \frac{1}{2}\left(\frac{3}{s^2-9}\right)$$

2. Find the laplace transforms of

(i) $e^{2t} + 4t^3 - 2\sin t + 3\cos 3t$

(ii) $\cosh at - \cos at$

(iii) $(\sin t - \cos t)^2$

Sol. (i) L{ $e^{2t} + 4t^3 - 2\sin t + 3\cos 3t$ }

$$= L(e^{2t}) + 4L(t^3) - 2L(\sin t) + 3L(\cos 3t)$$

$$= \frac{1}{s-2} + 4.\frac{3!}{s^{3+1}} - 2.\frac{1}{s^2+1} + 3.\frac{s}{s^2+3^2}$$

$$= \frac{1}{s-2} + \frac{24}{s^4} - \frac{2}{s^2+1} + \frac{3s}{s^2+9}$$

(ii) L(coshat – cos at)

= L (coshat) – L(cosat)

$$= L\left(\frac{e^{at}+e^{-at}}{2}\right) - L(\cos at)$$

$$= \frac{1}{2}L(e^{at}) + \frac{1}{2}(e^{-at}) - L(\cos at)$$

$$= \frac{1}{2}.\frac{1}{s-a} + \frac{1}{2}.\frac{1}{s-(-a)} - \frac{s}{s^2+a^2}$$

$$=\frac{1}{2}\left[\frac{1}{s-a}+\frac{1}{s+a}\right]-\frac{s}{s^2+a^2}$$

$$=\frac{1}{2}\left[\frac{2s}{s^2-a^2}\right]-\frac{s}{s^2+a^2}$$

$$=\frac{s}{s^2-a^2}-\frac{s}{s^2+a^2}=\frac{s(s^2+a^2-s^2+a^2)}{s^4-a^4}=\frac{2a^2s}{s^4-a^4}$$

(OR)

$$\frac{s}{s^2-a^2}-\frac{s}{s^2+a^2} \qquad \left(\because L(\cosh at=\frac{s}{s^2-a^2}\right)$$

$$=\frac{s}{s^2-a^2}-\frac{s}{s^2+a^2}$$

$$=\frac{s(s^2+a^2)-s(s^2-a^2)}{(s^2-a^2)(s^2+a^2)}$$

$$=\frac{s^3+a^2s-s^3+a^2s}{s^4-a^4}=\frac{2a^2s}{s^4-a^4}$$

(iii) $(\sin t-\cos t)^2$

$$=\sin^2 t+\cos^2 t-2\sin t\cos t$$

$$=1-2\sin t\cos t=1-\sin 2t$$

$\therefore$ $L\{(\sin t-\cos t)^2\}$

$$=L(1-\sin 2t)$$

$$=L(1)-L(\sin 2t)$$

$$=\frac{1}{s}-\frac{2}{s^2+2^2}=\frac{1}{s}-\frac{2}{s^2+4}$$

3. Find (i) $L(\cos^2 2t)$ (ii) $L(\sin^3 2t)$

Sol. (i) $\cos^2 2t=\frac{1+\cos 2(2t)}{2}$ $\left[\because \cos 2\theta=2\cos^2\theta-1 \text{ i.e., } \cos^2\theta=\frac{1+\cos 2\theta}{2}\right]$

$$L(\cos^2 2t)=L\left(\frac{1+\cos 4t}{2}\right)$$

$$= \frac{1}{2} L(1 + \cos 4t)$$

$$= \frac{1}{2} L(1) + \frac{1}{2} L(\cos 4t) = \frac{1}{2}\left(\frac{1}{s}\right) + \frac{1}{2} \cdot \frac{s}{s^2 + 4^2}$$

(ii) we have $\sin 3\theta = 3\sin\theta - 4\sin^3\theta$

$$\therefore \quad 4\sin^3\theta = 3\sin\theta - \sin 3\theta$$

$$\therefore \quad \sin^3\theta = \frac{1}{4} [3\sin\theta - \sin 3\theta]$$

$$\therefore \quad \sin^3 2t = \frac{1}{4} [3\sin 2t - \sin 3(2t)]$$

$$= \frac{1}{4} [3\sin 2t - \sin 6t]$$

$$L(\sin^3 2t) = L\left(\frac{1}{4} (3\sin 2t - \sin 6t)\right)$$

$$= \frac{3}{4} L(\sin 2t) - \frac{1}{4} L(\sin 6t)$$

$$= \frac{3}{4} \cdot \frac{2}{s^2 + 2^2} - \frac{1}{4} \cdot \frac{6}{s^2 + 6^2} \qquad \left[\because L(\sin at) = \frac{a}{s^2 + a^2}\right]$$

$$= \frac{3}{2(s^2 + 4)} - \frac{3}{2(s^2 + 36)}$$

$$= \frac{3}{2}\left[\frac{(s^2 + 36) - (s^2 + 4)}{(s^2 + 4)(s^2 + 36)}\right] = \frac{3}{2} \cdot \frac{32}{(s^2 + 4)(s^2 + 36)}$$

$$= \frac{96}{2(s^2 + 4)(s^2 + 36)}$$

$$= \frac{48}{(s^2 + 4)(s^2 + 36)}$$

Exercise - 27.1

1. Find the Laplace transforms of
 (i) t^4 (ii) e^{3t} (iii) sin4t
 (iv) cos 7t (v) sin h(3t) (vi) cos h 5t
2. Find the Laplace transforms of
 (i) sin2t cos 3t (ii) sin at sin bt
3. Find the Laplace transforms of
 (i) $\sin^2 3t$ (ii) $\cos^3 2t$
4. Find the Laplace transforms of $1+2\sqrt{t}+\frac{3}{\sqrt{t}}$

Answers

1. (i) $\frac{4}{s^5}$ (ii) $\frac{1}{s-3}$ (iii) $\frac{4}{s^2+16}$
 (iv) $\frac{s}{s^2+49}$ (v) $\frac{3}{s^2-9}$ (vi) $\frac{s}{s^2-25}$.
2. (i) $\frac{1}{2}\left[\frac{5}{s^2+25}-\frac{1}{s^2+1}\right]$ (ii) $\frac{1}{2}\left[\frac{s}{s^2+(a-b)^2}-\frac{s}{s^2+(a+b)^2}\right]$
3. (i) $\frac{1}{2s}-\frac{1}{2}\frac{s}{s^2+36}$ (ii) $\frac{s(s^2+28)}{(s^2+36)(s^2+4)}$
4. $\frac{1}{s}+\frac{\sqrt{\pi}}{s^{\frac{3}{2}}}+3\sqrt{\frac{\pi}{s}}$

27.4(a) First Shifting Property

Theorem : If $L(f(t)) = \bar{f}(s)$ then $L(e^{at} f(t)) = \bar{f}(s-a)$

Proof : Since by definition $L(e^{at} f(t)) = \int_0^\infty e^{-st}e^{at} f(t)dt = \int_0^\infty e^{-(s-a)t} f(t)dt$

$$= \int_0^\infty e^{-rt} f(t)dt \text{ where } r = s-a$$

$$= \bar{f}(r) = \bar{f}(s-a)$$

27.4 (b) Change of Scale Property

Theorem: If L(f(t)) = $\overline{f}(s)$ then L(f(at))

Proof:

$$L(f(at)) = \int_0^\infty e^{-st} f(at)\, dt$$

Lt at = 4 => adt = dt

$$\therefore \quad L(f(at)) = \int_0^\infty e^{-st} \cdot \frac{4}{a} f(4) \frac{dt}{a}$$

$$= \frac{1}{a} \int_0^\infty e^{-s/a^4} \quad f(4)\, dt$$

$$= \frac{1}{a} \cdot \overline{f}\left(\frac{s}{a}\right)$$

$$\therefore \quad Lf(at) = \frac{1}{s} \overline{f}\left(\frac{s}{a}\right)$$

Solved Examples

1. Find Laplace Transforms of

(i) $e^{2t} t^2$ (ii) e^{3t} . sin 4t (iii) e^{4t} cos5t

Sol. (i) We know that $L(t^2) = \frac{2!}{s^{2+1}} = \frac{2}{s^3} = \overline{f}(s)$

by first shifting property

$$L(e^{at} f(t)) = \overline{f}(s-a)$$

$$\therefore \quad L(e^{2t} t^2) = \overline{f}(s-a) = \frac{2}{(s-2)^2} \quad \text{(here a = 2)}$$

(ii) e^{3t} sin 4t

$$L(\sin 4t) = \frac{4}{s^2+4^2} = \frac{4}{s^2+16} = \overline{f}(s)$$

$$\therefore \quad L(e^{3t} \sin 4t) = \overline{f}(s-a) = \frac{4}{(s-3)^2+16}$$

(iii) $e^{4t}\cos 5t$

$$L(\cos 5t) = \frac{s}{s^2+5^2} = \bar{f}(s)$$

$$L(e^{4t}\cos 5t) = \frac{s-4}{(s-4)^2+5^2}$$

2. Find the Laplace transforms of

(i) $e^{-3t}(2\cos 5t - 3\sin 5t)$ (ii) $e^{4t}\sin 2t \cos t$

Sol. (i) $L(e^{-3t}(2\cos 5t - 3\sin 5t))$

$= 2L(e^{-3t}\cos 5t) - 3L(e^{-3t}\sin 5t)$ ..... (1)

we know that $L(\cos 5t) = \dfrac{s}{s^2+5^2}$

$$\therefore\ L(e^{-3t}\cos 5t) = \frac{s-(-3)}{(s-(-3))^2+5^2} = \frac{s+3}{(s+3)^2+25} \quad ..... (2)$$

(by first shifting principle)

again $L(\sin 5t) = \dfrac{5}{s^2+5^2} = \dfrac{5}{s^2+25}$

$$\therefore\ L(e^{-3t}\sin 5t) = \frac{5}{(s+3)^2+5^2} \text{ (by first shinfting principle)} \quad .....(3)$$

$\therefore$ sub (2) & (3) in (1) we get

$$L(e^{-3t}(3\cos 5t - 3\sin 5t) = 2\left(\frac{s+3}{(s+3)^2+25}\right) - 3\left(\frac{5}{(s+3)^2+25}\right)$$

(ii) $e^{4t}(\sin 2t\ \cos t)$

$$= \frac{1}{2}.\lfloor(e^{4t}2\sin 2t\cos t)$$

$$= \frac{1}{2}\lfloor(e^{4t}(\sin(3t)+\sin t)$$

$$= \frac{1}{2}\lfloor(e^{4t}\sin 3t) + \frac{1}{2}\lfloor(e^{4t}\sin t)$$

$$= \frac{1}{2}\left[\frac{3}{(s-4)^2+3^2}\right] + \frac{1}{2}\left[\frac{1}{(s-4)^2+1}\right]$$

3. Find the Laplace transforms of

(i) $e^{3t} \sin^2 t$ (ii) $t^2 e^{-2t}$ (iii) $\sin 3t \cos^2 t\, e^{-t}$

Sol. $e^{3t} \sin^2 t = e^{3t}\left[\frac{1-\cos 2t}{2}\right]$

$$=\frac{1}{2}e^{3t}-\frac{1}{2}(L(e^{3t}\cos 2t))$$

$$L(e^{3t}\sin^2 t)=\frac{1}{2}(L(e^{3t}))-\frac{1}{2}(L(e^{3t}\cos 2t))$$

$$=\frac{1}{2}.\frac{1}{s-3}-\frac{1}{2}\left[\frac{s}{(s-3)^2+2^2}\right]$$

$$=\frac{1}{2(s-3)}-\frac{1}{2}\left[\frac{s}{(s-3)^2+4}\right]$$

(ii) $L(t^2 e^{-2t})$

$$\underline{|e}(t^2)=\frac{2!}{(s)^{2+1}}=\frac{2!}{s^3}$$ (∵ by first shifting property)

$$L(e^{-2t} t^2)=\frac{2!}{(s+2)^3}$$

(iii) $\sin 3t \cos^2 t\, e^{-t}$

$$=\sin 3t\left(\frac{1+\cos 2t}{2}\right)e^{-t}$$

$$=\sin 3t\left(\frac{1}{2}+\frac{1}{2}\cos 2t\right)e^{-t}$$

$$=\left[\frac{1}{2}\sin 3t+\frac{1}{2}\sin 3t\cos 2t\right]e^{-t}$$

$$=\left[\frac{1}{2}\sin 3t+\frac{1}{2}.\frac{1}{2}\sin(5t)+\sin(t)\right]e^{-t}$$

(∵ sin(A + B) + sin (A – B) = 2 sin A cos B)

$$= \left[\frac{1}{2}\sin 3t + \frac{1}{4}\sin 5t + \frac{1}{4}\sin t\right]e^{-t}$$

$\therefore$ L(sin3t cos²t e⁻ᵗ)

$$= \frac{1}{2}L(\sin 3t.e^{-t}) + \frac{1}{4}L(\sin 5t\, e^{-t}) + \frac{1}{4}L(e^{-t}\sin t)$$

$$= \frac{1}{2}\frac{3}{(s+1)^2+3^2} + \frac{1}{4}.\frac{5}{(s+1)^2+5^2} + \frac{1}{4}\left(\frac{1}{(s+1)^2+1^2}\right)$$

4. Find the Laplace transforms of

(i) coshat . sinat (ii) e^{-at} sinhbt

Sol. (i) coshat sinat

$$= \left(\frac{e^{at}+e^{-at}}{2}\right)\sin at$$

$$= \frac{1}{2}\ (e^{at}\ \text{sinat} - e^{-at}\ \text{sin at})$$

$\therefore$ L(cos hat sinat)

$$= \frac{1}{2}L\left(e^{at}\sin at - e^{-at}\sin at\right) = \frac{1}{2}\ \{\ L(e^{at}\ \sin at) + L(e^{-at}\ \sin at)\ \}$$

$$= \frac{1}{2}\left[\frac{a}{(s-a)^2+a^2} + \frac{a}{(s+a)^2+a^2}\right]$$

(ii) $L(\sinh bt) = \dfrac{b}{s^2-b^2}$

$\therefore$ $(e^{-at}\ \sin hbt) = \dfrac{b}{(s+a)^2-b^2}$

Excercise - 27.2

Find Laplace transforms of

1. e^{-2t} sin4t **2.** e^{4t} cos 3t **3.** e^{-t} sin²t

4. e^{3t} t^2 **5.** e^{-2t} . t^3 **6.** e^{-bt} sin h at

Answers

1. $\dfrac{4}{(s+2)^2+16}$

2. $\dfrac{s}{(s-4)^2+9}$

3. $\dfrac{2}{(s+1)(s^2+2s+5)}$

4. $\dfrac{2!}{(s-3)^3}$

5. $\dfrac{3!}{(s+2)^4}$

6. $\dfrac{a}{(s+b)^2-a^2}$

27.5 Transforms of Multiplication by t^n

If $L(f(t)) = \overline{f}(s)$ then

$$L(t^n f(t)) = (-1)^n \frac{d^n}{ds^n}(\overline{f}(s))$$

where n = 1, 2, 3 ....

Ex: **1.** Find the laplace transforms of

(i) t cos at (ii) t^2 sin at (iii) $t^3 e^{-3t}$ (iv) $t.e^{-t}$ sin 3t

Sol. (i) L(t cos at) = ?

we have, $L(\cos at) = \dfrac{s}{s^2+a^2}$

$$\therefore\ L(t^1 \cos at) = (-1)^1 \frac{d^1}{ds^1}\left(\frac{s}{s^2+a^2}\right) \qquad \left[\because L(t^n f(t)) = (-1)^n \frac{d^n}{ds^n}(\overline{f}(s)\right]$$

$$= -\left(\frac{(s^2+a^2)(1)-s(2s)}{(s^2+a^2)^2}\right)$$

$$= -\left(\frac{a^2-s^2}{(s^2+a^2)^2}\right) = \frac{s^2-a^2}{(s^2+a^2)^2}$$

(ii) $L(\sin at) = \dfrac{a}{s^2+a^2}$

$$L(t^2 \sin at) = (-1)^2 \frac{d^2}{ds^2}\left(\frac{a}{s^2+a^2}\right)$$

$$= (+1).\frac{d}{ds}\left[\frac{d}{ds}\left(\frac{a}{s^2+a^2}\right)\right]$$

$$= \frac{d}{ds}\left[\frac{-a}{(s^2+a^2)^2}.2s\right]$$

$$= -2a.\frac{d}{ds}\left[\frac{s}{(s^2+a^2)^2}\right]$$

$$= -2a\left[\frac{(s^2+a^2)^2.(1) - s(2(s^2+a^2).2s}{(s^2+a^2)^2}\right]$$

$$= \frac{2a(3s^2-a^2)}{(s^2+a^2)^3}$$

(iii) $L(e^{-3t}) = \dfrac{1}{s-(-3)} = \dfrac{1}{s+3}$

$$\therefore\ L(t^3 e^{-3t}) = (-1)^3 . \frac{d^3}{ds^3}\left[\frac{1}{s+3}\right]$$

$$= -\frac{d^2}{ds^2}\left[\frac{-1}{(s+3)^2}\right] \qquad \left[\because \frac{d}{dx}\left(\frac{1}{x}\right) = \frac{-1}{x^2}; \frac{d}{dx}\left(\frac{1}{x^2}\right) = \frac{-2}{x^3}\right]$$

$$= +\frac{d}{ds}\left(\frac{-2}{(s+3)^3}\right)$$

$$= \frac{6}{(s+3)^4}$$

(iv) $L(\sin 3t) = \dfrac{3}{s^2+3^2} = \dfrac{3}{s^2+9}$

$L(e^{-t} \sin 3t) = \dfrac{3}{(s+1)^2+9}$ (by first shifting property)

$$\therefore\ L(t.e^{-t}\sin 3t) = (-1)^1 \frac{d^1}{ds^1}\left(\frac{3}{(s+1)^2+9}\right)$$

$$= -\frac{-3}{((s+1)^2+9)^2}\times 2(s+1)$$

$$= \frac{6(s+1)}{(s^2+2s+10)^2}$$

2. Find Laplace transforms of

(i) $t\sin^2 t$ (ii) $t^2 e^{-3t}\sin 2t$

(i) We have $\sin^2 t = \dfrac{1-\cos 2t}{2}$

$$L(\sin^2 t) = \frac{1}{2}L(1) - \frac{1}{2}L(\cos 2t)$$

$$= \frac{1}{2}\cdot\frac{1}{s} - \frac{1}{2}\cdot\frac{s}{s^2+2^2}$$

$$= \frac{1}{2s} - \frac{s}{2(s^2+4)} = \bar{f}(s)$$

$$L(t^1\sin^2 t) = (-1)^1 \frac{d}{ds}(\bar{f}(s))$$

$$= -\frac{d}{ds}\left(\frac{1}{2s} - \frac{s}{2(s^2+4)}\right)$$

$$= -\left[\frac{1}{2}\cdot\frac{-1}{s^2} - \frac{1}{2}\left(\frac{(s^2+4)(1)-s(2s)}{(s^2+4)^2}\right)\right]$$

$$= \frac{1}{2s^2} + \frac{1}{2}\left(\frac{4-s^2}{(s^2+4)^2}\right)$$

(ii) $L(t^2 e^{-3t}\sin 2t)$

$$L(\sin 2t) = \frac{2}{s^2+2^2} = \frac{2}{s^2+4}$$

$$L(e^{-3t}\sin 2t) = \frac{2}{(s+3)^2+4} \qquad \text{(by first shifting property)}$$

$$L(t^2 e^{-3t}\sin 2t) = (-1)^2 \frac{d^2}{ds^2}\left(\frac{2}{(s+3)^2+4}\right)$$

$$= \frac{d}{ds}\left(\frac{-2}{((s+3)^2+4)^2}\times 2(s+3)\right)$$

$$= \frac{d}{ds}\left(\frac{-4(s+3)}{((s+3)^2+4)^2}\right)$$

$$= -4\left(\frac{((s+3)^2+4)^2(1)-(s+3).2\left[(s+3)^2+4\right](2(s+3))}{((s+3)^2+4)^4}\right)$$

$$= \frac{4[3(s+3)^2-4]}{[(s+3)^2+4)]^3}$$

27.6 Transforms of Division by t

If $L(f(t)) = \overline{f}(s)$ then $L(\frac{1}{t}\, f(t)) = \int_s^{\infty} \overline{f}(s)ds$

Ex: Find the laplace transforms of

(i) $\frac{(1-e^t)}{t}$ (ii) $\frac{\cos at - \cos bt}{t}$

(i) $L\left(\frac{1-e^t}{t}\right)$

then $f(t) = 1 - e^t$

$$L(f(t)) = \frac{1}{s} - \frac{1}{s-1} = \overline{f(s)}$$

$$\therefore \quad L\left(\frac{1-e^t}{t}\right) = \int_s^{\infty}\left(\frac{1}{s} - \frac{1}{s-1}\right)dt$$

$$= [lns - ln(s-1)]_s^{\infty}$$

$$= \left(\ln\left(\frac{s}{s-1}\right)\right)_s^{\infty} = -ln\left[\frac{1}{1-\frac{1}{s}}\right]$$

$$= -ln\left(\frac{s-1}{s}\right) = ln\left(\frac{s}{s-1}\right)$$

2. $L(\cos at - \cos bt) = \frac{s}{s^2+a^2} - \frac{s}{s^2+b^2}$

$$\therefore L\frac{\cos at - \cos bt}{t} = \int_s^{\infty}\left(\frac{s}{s^2+a^2} - \frac{s}{s^2+b^2}\right)ds$$

$$= \frac{1}{2}\int_s^{\infty}\left(\frac{2s}{s^2+a^2} - \frac{2s}{s^2+b^2}\right)ds$$

$$= \frac{1}{2}\left[ln(s^2+a^2) - ln(s^2+b^2)\right]_s^{\infty} \qquad \left(\because \int\frac{f'(x)}{f(x)}dx = \ln|f(x)|\right)$$

$$= \frac{1}{2}ln\left[\left(\frac{s^2+a^2}{s^2+b^2}\right)\right]_s^{\infty}$$

$$= \frac{1}{2}\ln\left(\frac{1+\left(\frac{a}{s}\right)^2}{1+\left(\frac{b}{s}\right)^2}\right)_s^{\infty}$$

$$= 0 - \frac{1}{2}ln\left(\frac{s^2+a^2}{s^2+b^2}\right) \qquad (\because \ln 1 = 0)$$

$$= ln\left(\frac{s^2+b^2}{s^2+a^2}\right)^{\frac{1}{2}}$$

3. Find $L\left(\frac{\cos 2t - \cos 3t}{t}\right)$

$$L(\cos 2t - \cos 3t) = \frac{s}{s^2+4} - \frac{s}{s^2+9}$$

$$\therefore\ L\frac{(\cos 2t-\cos 3t)}{t}=\int_s^\infty\left(\frac{s}{s^2+4}-\frac{s}{s^2+9}\right)ds$$

$$=\left[\frac{1}{2}ln(s^2+4)-\frac{1}{2}ln(s^2+9)\right]_s^\infty$$

$$=\left[\frac{1}{2}ln(\frac{s^2+4}{s^2+9})\right]_s^\infty$$

$$=0-\frac{1}{2}ln(\frac{s^2+4}{s^2+9})$$

$$=ln\left(\frac{s^2+4}{s^2+9}\right)^{\frac{-1}{2}}$$

$$=ln\left(\frac{s^2+9}{s^2+4}\right)^{\frac{1}{2}}$$

Exercise - 27.3

1. Find the laplace transforms of

(i) $t^2 \cos at$ (ii) $t \sin hat$ (iii) $te^{2t} \sin 3t$

(iv) $t\, e^{-t} \cos ht$ (v) $t \sin^2 t$

2. Find the laplace transforms of

(i) $\frac{\sin at}{t}$ (ii) $\frac{e^{-at}-e^{-bt}}{t}$ (iii) $\frac{(e^{at}-\cos bt)}{t}$

(iv) $\frac{e^{-t}\sin t}{t}$ (v) $\frac{1-\cos 2t}{t}$

Answers

1. (i) $\frac{2s^3-6a^2s}{(s^2+a^2)^3}$ (ii) $\frac{+2as}{(s^2-a^2)^2}$ (iii) $\frac{6(s-2)}{(s^2-4s+13)^2}$

(iv) $\frac{s^2+2s+2}{(s^2+2s)^2}$ (v) $\frac{2(3s^2+4)}{s^2(s^2+4)^2}$

2. (i) $\cot^{-1}\left(\dfrac{s}{a}\right)$ (ii) $ln\left(\dfrac{s+b}{s+a}\right)$ (iii) $\dfrac{1}{2}ln\left(\dfrac{s^2+b^2}{(s-a)^2}\right)$

(iv) $\cot^{-1}(s+1)$ (v) $\dfrac{1}{2}ln\left(\dfrac{s^2+4}{s^2}\right)$

27.7 Evaluation of Integrals by Laplace Transforms

We have, $\int_0^\infty e^{-st} f(t)dt = L(f(t)) = \overline{f}(s)$

So, If $L(f(t)) = \overline{f}(s)$ then $L\left(\int_0^t f(x)dx\right) = \dfrac{1}{s}\overline{f}(s)$

Ex: (i) Evaluate $\int_0^\infty te^{-2t}\sin 3t dt$

$$= \int_0^\infty e^{-st}(t\sin 3t) \qquad \text{where } s = 2$$

$$= L(t\sin 3t) \qquad \left(\because \int_0^\infty e^{-st} f(t)dt = Lf(t)\right)$$

$$= (-1)1\ \frac{d}{ds}(L(\sin 3t))$$

$$= (-1)\frac{d}{ds}\left(\frac{3}{s^2+9}\right)$$

$$= -\frac{-3(2s)}{(s^2+9)^2} = \frac{3\times 4}{(s^2+9)^2} \qquad (\because s = 2)$$

$$= -\frac{3\times 4}{(4+9)^2} = \frac{3\times 4}{169} = \frac{12}{169}$$

(ii) Evaluate $L\left(\int_0^t \frac{e^t \sin t}{t}\right)dt$

Consider, $L\left(\frac{\sin t}{t}\right) = \int_s^\infty \frac{1}{s^2+1}ds$

$$= \left(\tan^{-1}(s)\right)_s^\infty = \frac{\pi}{2} - \tan^{-1}(s)$$

$$L(e^t \frac{\sin t}{t}) = \frac{\pi}{2} - \tan^{-1}(s-1) = \overline{f}(s)$$

$$\therefore \quad L\left(\int_0^t \frac{et \sin t}{t}\right) = \frac{1}{s}\left[\frac{\pi}{2} - \tan^{-1}(s-1)\right]$$

$$\left(\because\ L\left(\int_0^t f(x)dx\right) = \frac{\overline{f}(s)}{s} \text{ where } \overline{f}(s) = L(f(t))\right)$$

Exercise - 27.4

1. Evaluate $\int_0^\infty te^{-2t}\sin t dt$

2. Evaluate $\int_0^\infty t.e^{-2t}\cos t dt$

3. Evaluate $\int_0^\infty t.e^{-t}\sin^4 t dt$

4. Show that $\int_0^\infty \frac{e^{-t}\sin^2 t}{t} = \frac{1}{4}\log 5$

5. Prove that $\int_0^\infty \frac{e^{-at} - e^{-bt}}{t} = \log\left(\frac{b}{a}\right)$

6. Evaluate $L\left(\int_0^t \frac{\sin t}{t} dt\right)$

7. Evaluate $L\left(\int_0^t e^{-t} \cos t dt\right)$

Answers

1. $\frac{4}{25}$

2. $\frac{3}{25}$

3. $\frac{8(s+1)}{s(s^2+2s+17)}$

6. $\frac{1}{s}\cot^{-1}(s)$

7. $\frac{1}{s}\left(\frac{s+1}{(s+1)^2+1}\right) = \frac{1}{s}\frac{(s+1)}{s^2+2s+2}$

27.8 Inverse Laplace Transforms

If $L(f(t)) = \overline{f}(s)$ then $f(t)$ is called the inverse laplace transformation of $\overline{f}(s)$ and is denoted by $L^{-1}(\overline{f}(s)) = f(t)$ if f_1 and f_2 are continuous functions on $[0, \infty]$ such that $L(f_1(t)) = L(f_2(t))$ or $\overline{f}_1(s) = \overline{f}_2(s)$ then $f_1(t) = f_2(t) \forall\ t > 0\ (\forall\ s > 0)$

Properties of Inverse Laplace Transfermations

1. Linear property

   If k_1, k_2 are any constants and $\overline{f}_1(s)$ and $\overline{f}_2(s)$ are the laplace transforms of $f_1(t)$ and $f_2(t)$ respectively then

$$L^{-1}\left[\left(k_1\overline{f}_1(s)\right) + \left(k_2\overline{f}_2(s)\right)\right] = k_1 f_1(t) + k_2 f_2(t)$$

2. First shifting property

$$L^{-1}\left(e^{-at}\overline{f}(s)\right)=\begin{cases} f(t-a) & for\ t>a \\ 0 & for\ t<a \end{cases}$$

3. Change of scale property

If $L^{-1}\left(\overline{f}(s)\right)=f(t)$ then

then $L^{-1}\left(\overline{f}(as)\right)=\frac{1}{a}f\left(\frac{t}{a}\right)$

4. Inverse laplace transforms of derivations

If $L^{-1}\left(\overline{f}(s)\right)=f(t)$ then

$$L^{-1}\left(\overline{f}^{n}(s)\right)=L^{-1}\left(\frac{d^n}{ds^n}\left(\overline{f}(s)\right)\right)=(-1)^n t^n f(t)$$

5. Inverse laplace transformation of integrals if $L^{-1}\left(\overline{f}(s)\right)=f(t)$ then

$$L^{-1}\left(\int_0^{\infty}\overline{f}(u)\,du\right)=\frac{f(t)}{t}$$

6. Multiplication by s if $L^{-1}\left(F(s)\right)=f(t)$ and $f(0)=0$ then

$$L\left(s\overline{f}(s)\right)=f^{1}(t)$$

7. Division by 's' if $L^{-1}\left(\overline{f}(s)\right)=f(t)$

then $L^{-1}\left(\frac{\overline{f}(s)}{s}\right)=\int_0^t f(u)\,du$

this result can be extended to

$$L^{-1}\left(\frac{\overline{f}(s)}{s^n}\right)=\int_0^t\int_0^t \cdots\cdots\int_0^t f(u)\,du^n$$

Table of inverse transforms

$L(f(t))$	$L^{-1}(\bar{f}(s))$
$L(1)=\frac{1}{s}$	$L^{-1}\left(\frac{1}{s}\right)=1$
$L(e^{-at})=\frac{1}{s+a}$	$L^{-1}\left(\frac{1}{s+a}\right)=e^{-at}$
$L(t^n)=\frac{n!}{s^{n+1}}$	$L^{-1}\left(\frac{1}{s^n+1}\right)=\frac{t^n}{(n+1)!}$
If a is a positive integer $L(\sin at)=\frac{a}{s^2+a^2}$ $L(\cos at)=\frac{s}{s^2+a^2}$ $L(\sinh at)=\frac{a}{s^2-a^2}$ $L(\cosh at)=\frac{s}{s^2-a^2}$	$L^{-1}\left(\frac{1}{s^2+a^2}\right)=\frac{1}{a}\sin at$ $L^{-1}\left(\frac{s}{s^2+a^2}\right)=\cos at$ $L^{-1}\left(\frac{1}{s^2-a^2}\right)=\frac{1}{a}\sinh at$ $L^{-1}\left(\frac{s}{s^2-a^2}\right)=\cosh at$

Solved Examples

1. Find the inverse Laplace transformation of

(i) $\frac{2s+3}{s^2+9}$ (ii) $\frac{1}{4s+5}$

Sol. (i) $L^{-1}\left(\frac{2s+3}{s^2+9}\right)=L^{-1}\left(\frac{2s}{s^2+9}\right)+L^{-1}\left(\frac{3}{s^2+9}\right)$

$$=2L^{-1}\left(\frac{s}{s^2+3^2}\right)+3L^{-1}\left(\frac{1}{s^2+9}\right)$$

$$=2\cos 3t+3\frac{\sin 3t}{3}=2\cos 3t+\sin 3t$$

(ii) $L^{-1}\left(\frac{1}{4s+5}\right)$

$$= \frac{1}{4} L^{-1}\left(\frac{1}{s+\left(\frac{5}{4}\right)}\right) = \frac{1}{4} . e^{-5/4t}$$

2. **Find the inverse laplace transformation of**

(i) $\frac{2s+1}{s+1}$ (ii) $\frac{s+3}{s^2+4}$

Sol. (i) $L^{-1}\left(\frac{2s+1}{s^2+1}\right) = 2L^{-1}\left(\frac{s}{s^2+1}\right) + L^{-1}\left(\frac{1}{s^2+1}\right)$

$$= 2\cos t + \sin t$$

(ii) $L^{-1}\left(\frac{s+3}{s^2+4}\right) = L^{-1}\left(\frac{s}{s^2+4}\right) + 3L^{-1}\left(\frac{1}{s^2+4}\right)$

$$= \cos 2t + \frac{3}{2} . \sin 2t$$

3. **Find the invese laplace transformation of**

(i) $\frac{6s-4}{s^2-4s+20}$ (ii) $\frac{1}{(s-2)^4}$

Sol. (i) $L^{-1}\left(\frac{6s-4}{s^2-4s+20}\right)$

$$= L^{-1}\left(\frac{6s-4}{(s-2)^2+16}\right) = L^{-1}\left(\frac{6(s-2)-4+12}{(s-2)^2+16}\right)$$

$$= 6L^{-1}\left(\frac{(s-2)}{(s-2)^2+4^2}\right) + 8L^{-1}\left(\frac{1}{(s-2)^2+4^2}\right)$$

$$= 6\left(e^{2t} . \cos 4t\right) + 8 . \frac{1}{4} . e^{2t} . \sin 4t$$

$$= 6e^{2t} . \cos 4t + 2e^{2t} . \sin 4t$$

(ii) $L^{-1}\left(\frac{1}{(s-2)^4}\right)=\frac{1}{2}.e^{2t}.t^3$

4. Find the inverse laplace transformation of $\frac{s+4}{s^3+s}$

Sol. $L^{-1}\left(\frac{s+4}{s^3+s}\right)$

Consider $\frac{s+4}{s^3+s}=\frac{s+4}{s\left(s^2+1\right)}=\frac{A}{s}+\frac{Bs+c}{s^2+1}$

$\Rightarrow \quad s+4=A\left(s^2+1\right)+(Bs+c)(s)$

Put s = 0 Comparing s^2 coefficients Comparing s coefficients

$\Rightarrow \quad 4=A(a+1) \qquad 0=A+B$

$A=4 \qquad B=-A \qquad 1=C$

$=-4$

$\therefore \quad \frac{s+4}{s^3+s}=\frac{4}{s}+\frac{-4s+1}{s^2+1}$

$$L^{-1}\left(\frac{s+4}{s^3+s}\right)=4L^{-1}\left(\frac{1}{s}\right)-4L^{-1}\left(\frac{s}{s^2+1}\right)+1\,L^{-1}\left(\frac{1}{s^2+1}\right)$$

$$=4.(1)-4.\cos t+\sin t \;=4-4\cos t+\sin t$$

Exercise - 27.5

1. Find inverse laplace transformation of

(i) $\frac{1}{4s-5}$ (ii) $\frac{3}{s+4}$ (iii) $\frac{3s+5}{9s^2-25}$

2. Find the inverse laplace transformation of

(i) $\frac{\left(s^2-1\right)^2}{s^5}$ (ii) $\frac{2}{s}+\frac{1}{s^3}+\frac{1}{s+4}$

3. Find the inverse laplace transformation of

(i) $\frac{3s+1}{(s-1)\left(s^2+1\right)}$ (ii) $\frac{s}{\left(s^2+1\right)\left(s^2+4\right)}$

Answers

1. (i) $\frac{1}{4}e^{\frac{5}{4}t}$ (ii) $3e^{-4t}$ (iii) $\frac{1}{3}\cosh\left(\frac{5t}{3}\right)+\frac{1}{3}\sinh\left(\frac{5t}{3}\right)$

2. (i) $1+t^2+\frac{t^4}{24}$ (ii) $2+\frac{t^2}{2}+e^{-4t}$

3. (i) $2e^t-2\cos t+\sin t$ (ii) $\frac{1}{3}(\cos t-\cos 2t)$

27.9 Applications to Solve Linear Differential Equations

Working Rule

Step 1: Take the laplace transformation on both sides of equation and use the initial conditions given in the problem

Step 2: Solve the algebric laplace transformation equation which is obtained in step 1.

Step 3: Take inverse laplace transformation on both sides, hence we obtain solution.

Example 1: Solve $y^1+5y=e^{-4x}$ given $y(0)=2$

given $\frac{dy}{dx}+5y=e^{-4x}$

taking laplace transformation on both sides

$$L\left(\frac{dy}{dx}+5y\right)=L\left(e^{-4x}\right)$$

$$\Rightarrow \quad L\left(\frac{dy}{dx}\right)+5L(y)=L\left(e^{-4x}\right)$$

$$\Rightarrow \quad s\bar{f}(s)-\bar{f}(0)+5\bar{f}(s)=\frac{1}{s+4}$$

$$(s+5)\bar{f}(s)-2=\frac{1}{s+4}$$

$$(s+5)\bar{f}(s)=2+\frac{1}{s+4}=\frac{2s+9}{(s+4)}$$

$$\bar{f}(s)=\frac{(2s+9)}{(s+4)(s+5)}$$

$$\therefore \quad L^{-1}\left(\bar{f}(s)\right) = f(t) = L^{-1}\left(\frac{2s+9}{(s+4)(s+5)}\right)$$

$$= L^{-1}\left(\frac{1}{s+4} + \frac{1}{s+5}\right)$$

$$\therefore \quad y = e^{-4x} + e^{-5x} \qquad = e^{-4x} + e^{-5x}$$

Exercise - 27.6

1. Solve $y^1 + y = \sin x$ given $y(0) = 2$

2. Solve $y^1 - 5y = 0$ given $y(\pi) = 2$

3. Solve $\frac{dp}{dt} + 2p = 1$ given $P(0) = 0$

4. $\frac{dP}{dt} = kP$ given $P(0) = 350$ K is constant

Answers

1. $y = \frac{1}{2}e^{-x} - \frac{1}{2}\cos x + \frac{1}{2}\sin x$

2. $y = 2e^{5(x-\pi)}$

3. $y = 5 - 5e^{t/5}$

4. $y = 350\ e^{kt}$

Unit - VII

Exercise Questions

27. Laplace Transforms

1. Find $L(e^{-t} \cos^2 t)$
2. Find $L(\sin^2 t)$
3. Find $L(\sin^4 t)$
4. Find $L(\sin 2t \sin 4t)$
5. Find $L(t \sin 2t)$
6. Find $L(\sin 2t + \cos 3t)$
7. Find $L(e^{-2t} \sin 4t)$
8. Find $L(e^{2t} + 4t^3 - 2 \sin 3t + 3 \cos 3t)$
9. Find $L(\cos^3 2t)$
10. Find $L(\text{sinhat} \cos t)$
11. Find $L(e^{-t} (t + 1)^2)$
12. Find $L(t \cos at)$
13. Find $L(e^{-t} \cos 2t)$
14. Find $L(e^{-3t} \sin 3t)$
15. Find $L(e^{-t} \sin 2t)$
16. Find $L(\sin 2t . \sin t)$
17. Find $L(3t^4 + 4e^{-3t} - 2 \sin 5t)$
18. Find $L(t^3 e^{-2t})$

Unit - VII

Answers to Exercise Questions

27. Laplace Transforms

1. $\frac{1}{2}\left[\frac{1}{s+1}+\frac{s+1}{(s+1)^2+4}\right]$

2. $\frac{1}{2}\left[\frac{1}{s}-\frac{s}{s^2+4}\right]$

3. $\frac{3}{8}\left(\frac{1}{s}\right)+\frac{1}{8}\cdot\left(\frac{s}{s^2+16}\right)-\frac{1}{2}\cdot\left(\frac{s}{s^2+4}\right)$

4. $\frac{1}{2}\left[\frac{s}{s^2+4}-\frac{s}{s^2+36}\right]$

5. $\frac{+4s}{(s^2+4)^2}$

6. $\frac{2}{s^2+4}+\frac{s}{s^2+9}$

7. $\frac{4}{(s+2)^2+16}$

8. $\frac{1}{s-2}+4.\frac{3!}{s^4}-\frac{2.3}{s^2+9}+\frac{3s}{s^2+9}$

9. $\frac{1}{4}\left[\frac{s}{s^2+36}+\frac{3s}{s^2+4}\right]$

10. $\frac{2as^2}{\left((s-a)^2+1\right)+\left((s+a)^2+1\right)}$

11. $\frac{2}{(s+1)^3}+\frac{1}{s+1}+\frac{2}{(s+1)^2}$

12. $\frac{(a^2 - s^2)}{(s^2 + a^2)^2}$

13. $\frac{s}{(s+1)^2 + 4}$

14. $\frac{3}{(s+3)^2 + 9}$

15. $\frac{2}{(s+1)^2 + 4}$

16. $\frac{1}{2}\left[\frac{s}{s^2+1} - \frac{s}{s^2+9}\right]$

17. $3.\frac{4!}{s^5} + \frac{4}{(s+3)} - 2.\frac{5}{s^2+25}$

18. $\frac{3!}{(s+2)^4}$

Unit - VII

Self Test Questions

27. Laplace Transforms

1. Give the statement of Laplace Transformation.
2. Find Laplace Transformation of 1. e^{at} 2. sin at 3. cos at
3. Find L (cosh at)
4. Find $L\left(\frac{e^{-at}-1}{a}\right)$
5. S. T $L(t^n) = \frac{n!}{s^{n+1}}$ where n is positive integer.
6. State sufficient condition for existance of laplace transformation.
7. Find $L\left(e^{-4t}+3e^{-2t}\right)$
8. State linear property of laplace transforms.
9. State and prove first shiftly and change of scale properly.
10. $L\left((t+3)^2 e^t\right)$
11. $L\left(e^{-t}\cos^2 t\right)$
12. Find L (coshat cosbt)
13. Find L (e^{-3t} cos4t + 3 sin4t)
14. Find the Laplace transformation of e^{2t} (sin3t. cos2t)
15. Explain briefly the advantages of Laplace transformation in pharmaceutical sciences.
16. Find L(sin 2t cos 3t)
17. Find $L\left(\frac{1}{\sqrt{t\pi}}\right)$
18. Find L($\cos^3 3t$)
19. Find L($\sin^3 2t$)

UNIT - VIII

UNIT - VIII

28

Applications of Differential Equations of First Order and First Degree

28.1 Newton's Law of Cooling

Definition: The rate of change of temperature of a body is proportional to the difference between the temperature of the body and that of the surrounding medium.

Let θ be the temperature of the body at time t and θ_0 is the temperature of the surrounding medium (usually air)

∴ By definitions of Newton's law of cooling

$$\frac{d\theta}{dt} \propto (\theta - \theta_o)$$

$$\Rightarrow \quad \frac{d\theta}{dt} = -k\,(\theta - \theta_o)$$ [Negative indicates the decreasing of temperature and k is a constant]

Now separate the variables we get

$$\frac{d\theta}{\theta - \theta_o} = -k\,dt$$

Integrating on both sides we get

$$\int \frac{d\theta}{\theta - \theta_o} = \int -k\,dt$$

$$\Rightarrow \quad \log(\theta - \theta_o) = -kt + \log c$$ [log c is an integral constant]

$$\Rightarrow \quad \log(\theta - \theta_o) - \log c = -kt$$

$$\Rightarrow \quad \log\left[\frac{\theta - \theta_o}{c}\right] = -kt$$

$$\Rightarrow \quad \frac{\theta - \theta_o}{c} = e^{-kt}$$

$$\Rightarrow \quad \theta - \theta_o = c.e^{-kt} \qquad .....(1)$$

Suppose at $t = 0$, $\theta = \theta_1$ say then

$$\theta_1 - \theta_0 = c.e^{-k(0)} = c.e^0 = c$$

$$\Rightarrow \quad \theta_1 - \theta_0 = c$$

Substute in (1) we get

$$\theta - \theta_0 = (\theta_1 - \theta_0)\, e^{-kt}$$

$$\Rightarrow \quad \theta = \theta_0 + (\theta_1 - \theta_0)\, e^{-kt} \qquad ....(2)$$

This formula gives the temperature of body at any time 't'.

Hence θ_1 is initial temperature of body sicne t = 0.

Solved Examples

1. A body is originally at 80 °C cools down to 60 °C in 20 minutes. The temperature of air being 40 °C. What will be the temperature of the body after 40 minutes from the original?

Sol. Given intial temperature of body = θ_1 = 80 °C. Temperature of air is θ_0 = 40 °C.

By definition of Newton's law of cooling, the temperature of body at any time 't' is given by

$$\theta = \theta_0 + (\theta_1 - \theta_0)\, e^{-kt}$$

also given when t = 20, θ = 60°

$$\Rightarrow \quad 60 = 40 + (80 - 40)\,.\,e^{-k.20} \Rightarrow 20 = 40\,.\,e^{-20k}$$

$$e^{-20k} = \frac{1}{2} \Rightarrow -20\text{k} = \log_e\left(\frac{1}{2}\right) \qquad .....(1)$$

Now the temperature of body after 40 minutes from the original

$$\theta = \theta_0 + (\theta_1 - \theta_0)\, e^{-kt}$$

$$\theta = \theta_0 + (\theta_1 - \theta_0) \, . \, e^{-k.(40)}$$

$$= 40 + (80 - 40) \, . \, e^{-40k}$$

$$= 40 + 40 \, . \, e^{2(-20k)} = 40 + 40 \, . \, e^{2\left(\log\left(\frac{1}{2}\right)\right)} \qquad (\because \text{ by eq. (1)})$$

$$= 40 + 40 \, . \, e^{\log\left(\frac{1}{4}\right)}$$

$$= 40 + 40 \, . \, \frac{1}{4} = 40 + 10$$

$$= 50 \text{ °C}$$

$\therefore \qquad \theta = 50$ °C

2. If the air is maintained at 30 °C and the temperature of the body cools from 80° to 60 °C in 12 minutes, find the temperature of the body after 24 minutes.

Sol. Given $\theta_0 = 30°$, $\theta_1 = 80°$

and at t = 12 $\qquad \theta = 60°$

We have, by newton's law of cooling the temperature of body at any time 't' is given by

$$\theta = \theta_0 + (\theta_1 - \theta_0) \, e^{-kt}$$

since $\theta = 60$ at $t = 12$

$$\Rightarrow \qquad 60 = 30 + (80 - 30) \, . \, e^{-12k}$$

$$\Rightarrow \qquad 30 = 50 \, e^{-12k} \Rightarrow \left(\frac{3}{5}\right) = e^{-12k}$$

$$\Rightarrow \qquad -12k = \log_e\left(\frac{3}{5}\right) \qquad \text{.....(1)}$$

now the temperature body after 24 minutes is

$$\theta = \theta_0 + (\theta_1 - \theta_0) \, e^{-kt}$$

$$\theta = 30 + (80 - 30) \, . \, e^{-24k}$$

$$\Rightarrow \qquad \theta = 30 + 50 \, . \, e^{-2(-12k)}$$

$$\Rightarrow \qquad \theta = 30 + 50 \, . \, e^{2.\log\left(\frac{3}{5}\right)} \qquad (\because \text{ by eq (1)})$$

$$\Rightarrow \qquad 30 + 50 \, . \, e^{\log\left(\frac{9}{25}\right)}$$

$$\Rightarrow \qquad 30 + 50 \, . \, \frac{9}{25} = 30 + 18$$

$$= 48 \text{ °C}$$

3. If the temperature of the air is 30 °C and the substance cools from 100 °C to 70 °C in 15 minutes. Find the time at which the temperature will be 40 °C.

Sol. Given $\theta_0 = 30^o$, $\theta_1 = 100^oC$

at $t = 15$ min $\theta = 70^o$ C

$t = ?$ when $\theta = 40^oC$

by Newton's law of cooling, the temperature of substance at any time 't' is

$$\theta = \theta_0 + (\theta_1 - \theta_0)\, e^{-kt}$$

given $\theta = 70^o$ C when $t = 15$ min

$$\Rightarrow \quad 70 = 30 + (100 - 30)\,.\, e^{-k(15)}$$

$$\Rightarrow \quad 40 = 70\,.\, e^{-15k} \Rightarrow e^{-15k} = \frac{4}{7} \Rightarrow -15k = \log_e \left(\frac{4}{7}\right)$$

$$\therefore \quad -k = \frac{1}{15}\log\left(\frac{4}{7}\right) \quad .....(1)$$

We have to find 't' when $\theta = 40^o$

So, $$\theta = \theta_0 + (\theta_1 - \theta_0)\,.\, e^{-kt}$$

$$\Rightarrow \quad 40 = 30 + (100 - 30)\,.\, e^{-kt}$$

$$\Rightarrow \quad \frac{10}{70} = e^{-kt} \Rightarrow -kt = \log\left(\frac{1}{7}\right)$$

$$\Rightarrow \frac{1}{15}\log\left(\frac{4}{7}\right).t = \log\left(\frac{1}{7}\right) \quad (\because \text{by eq (1)})$$

$$\Rightarrow t = \frac{15.\log\left(\frac{1}{7}\right)}{\log\left(\frac{4}{7}\right)}$$

$$= \frac{15.\log 7}{\log\left(\frac{7}{4}\right)} = 15 \times 3.48$$

$$= \mathbf{52.20}$$

The temperature will be 40° after 52.2 minutes

28.2 Law of Natural Growth or Decay

Definition: If the rate of chemical change of a quantity y in time t is proportional the quantity at time t.

i.e. $$\frac{dy}{dt} \propto y$$

$$\frac{dy}{dt} = ky$$

For growth k is positive i.e. $\frac{dy}{dt} = ky$, $k > 0$

For decay k is negative i.e. $\frac{dy}{dt} = -ky$, $k < 0$

Case (i)

$$\frac{dy}{dt} = ky$$

$$\Rightarrow \frac{dy}{y} = k.dt$$

$$\Rightarrow \int \frac{dy}{y} = \int k\,dt$$

$$\Rightarrow \log y = kt + \log c$$

$$\Rightarrow \log\left(\frac{y}{c}\right) = kt$$

$$\Rightarrow \frac{y}{c} = e^{kt}$$

$$\Rightarrow \boldsymbol{y = ce^{kt}}$$

Case (ii)

$$\frac{dy}{dt} = -ky$$

$$\Rightarrow \int \frac{dy}{y} = \int -k\,dt$$

$$\Rightarrow \log y = -kt + \log c$$

$$\Rightarrow \log\left(\frac{y}{c}\right) = -kt \quad \text{(where } \log c \text{ is integral constant)}$$

$$\frac{y}{c} = e^{-kt}$$

$$\Rightarrow \boldsymbol{y = c.e^{-kt}}$$

$\therefore$ the quantity at time $t = c.e^{kt}$ for growth
$= ce^{-kt}$ for decay

Solved Examples

1. The number N of bacteria in a culture grew at a rate propirtional to N. The value of N was initially 50 and increase to 150 in one hour. What will be the value of N after 1½ hour.

Sol. Given $\frac{dN}{dt} \propto N \Rightarrow N = c\,e^{+kt}$ for growth

$N = 50$ at $t = 0 \Rightarrow 50 = c\,e^{k(0)} \Rightarrow \mathbf{c = 50}$

$\therefore$ $N = 50 \,.\, e^{kt}$

Given at $t = 1h$ $N = 150 \Rightarrow 150 = 50 . e^k \Rightarrow \mathbf{e^k = 3}$

Now $t = 1\frac{1}{2}h = \frac{3}{2}h$ $N = ?$

$$\Rightarrow \quad N = 50 . e^{kt} = 50 . e^{k.\frac{3}{2}} = 50 . \left(e^k\right)^{\frac{3}{2}}$$

$$= 50. (3)^{\frac{3}{2}}$$

$$\therefore \quad \mathbf{N = 50. (3)^{\frac{3}{2}}}$$

$\therefore$ The value of N after one and half hour is

$$\mathbf{50.(3)^{\frac{3}{2}}}$$

2. The rate at which bacteria multiply is proportional to the instantaneous number present. If the original number doubles in 2 hours. In how many hours will it triple?

Sol. Let N be the no.of bacteria at time 't'.

$$N = ce^{kt}$$

at $t = 0, N = ce^{k.0} \Rightarrow c = N$ .....(1)

now given at $t = 2$ N becomes 2N

$$\therefore \quad 2N = c.e^{k(2)}$$

$$2N = N e^{2k} \Rightarrow 2 = e^{2k} \Rightarrow 2k = \log_e{}^2$$

$$\Rightarrow k = \frac{1}{2} \log_e{}^2 \qquad .....(2)$$

Now t = ? when k becomes 3k.

$$\therefore \quad 3k = c.e^{tk}$$

$$\Rightarrow \quad 3 = e^{tk} \qquad (\because c = k)$$

$$tk = \log_e{}^3 \Rightarrow t . \frac{1}{2}\left(\log_e{}^2\right) = \log_e{}^3 \qquad [\because \text{by eq. (2)}]$$

$$\Rightarrow \quad t = \frac{2\log_e{}^3}{\log_e{}^2} = \frac{2\log 3}{\log 2}$$

3. The number N of bacteria in a culture grew at a rate proportional to N. The value of N was initially 100 and increased to 332 in one hour. What was the value of N after 1½ hours.

Sol. $N = ce^{kt}$

at $t = 0$ $N = 100 \Rightarrow 100 = ce^o$, $\therefore \mathbf{c = 100}$

$N = 332$ when $t = 1h$

$\therefore \quad 332 = 100\, e^{1k}$

$$\Rightarrow \quad e^k = \frac{332}{100} \quad .....(1)$$

Now when $t = \frac{3}{2}h \quad N = ?$

$\therefore \quad N = c\, e^{kt}$

$N = 100 \,.\, e^{k\,3/2}$

$= 100\,(e^k)^{3/2}$ [$\because$ by (1)]

$$= 100.\left(\frac{332}{100}\right)^{\frac{3}{2}}$$

$= 605$

$\therefore \quad N = 605$

4. The rate at a which a substance decompose in a certain solution at any instant proportional to amount in the solution at that instant. Initially there are 27 grams and three hours later it is found that 8 grams are left. How much substance will be left after one more hour.

Sol. Given $\frac{dN}{dt} \propto N \Rightarrow \frac{dN}{dt} = -kt$

$\Rightarrow \quad N = ce^{-kt}$

Given at $t = 0 \quad N = 27 \quad \Rightarrow \quad 27 = c.e^{-0} \quad \Rightarrow \quad \mathbf{c = 27}$ .....(1)

at $t = 3h \quad N = 8 \quad \Rightarrow \quad 8 = ce^{-k(3)}$

$\Rightarrow \quad 8 = 27\, e^{-3k}$

$$\Rightarrow \quad e^{-3k} = \frac{8}{27}. = \left(\frac{2}{3}\right)^3$$

Now at $t = 4h \quad N = ?$

$\therefore \quad N = ce^{-4t}$

$$\Rightarrow \quad N = 27\,.\,\left(e^{-3t}\right)^{\frac{4}{3}} = 27.\left[\left(\frac{2}{3}\right)^3\right]^{\frac{4}{3}}$$

$$= 27.\frac{2^4}{3^4}$$

$$= \frac{16}{3} \text{ grams}$$

Exercise 28.1

1. If the air is maintained at 30 °C and the temperature of body cools from 80 °C to 60 °C in 12 minutes. Find the temperature of body after 36 minutes.
2. The rate of cooling of a body is proportional to the difference between the temperature of body and the surrounding air. If the air temperature is 20 °C and the body cools for 20 minutes from 140 °C to 80 °C, find when the temperature will be 35 °C.
3. A metal ball is heated to temperature of 100 °C and at time t = 0, it it placed in water which is maintained 40 °C. If the temperature of body is reduced to 60 °C in 4 minutes, find the time at which the temperature of ball is 50 °C.
4. Radium decomposes at the rate proportional to the amount present. If p percent of the original amount disappears in l years. How much will remain at the end of $2l$ years.
5. Uranium disintegrates at a rate proportional to the amount then present at any instant. If M_1 and M_2 grams of uranium are present at time T_1 and T_2 respectively find the half life of Uranium.
6. Under certain condition can sugar in water converted into dextrose at a rate which is proportional to the amount unconverted at anytime. If 75 grams was there at time t = 0 and 8 grams are converted during the first 30 minutes, find the amount converted in 1½ hour.

Answers

1. **Ans:** 40.8°
2. **Ans:** 60 minutes
3. **Ans:** $4 \log_3^{6}$
4. **Ans:** $\dfrac{(100-p)^2}{100}\%$
5. **Ans:** $\dfrac{(T_2-T_1)\log 2}{\log\left(\dfrac{M_1}{M_2}\right)}$
6. **Ans:** 21.5 grams

28.3 More Applications of Differential Equations

1. Suppose that a solution initially containing 3 moles/liter of Y and 2 mole/liter of Z is allowed to react. Find an expression for the amount of X at time t.

Sol: by given condition we confirm a differential equation

i.e., $$\frac{dx}{dt} = k(3-x)(2-x) \quad x(0) = 0$$

∴ by separating the variables we get

$$\frac{dx}{(3-x)(2-x)} = k\,dt$$

Integrating on both sides we get

$$\int \frac{dx}{(3-x)(2-x)} = \int k\,dt$$

$$\int \frac{dx}{(3-x)(2-x)} = kt + c \qquad \text{.....(1)}$$

Consider $\dfrac{1}{(3-x)(2-x)} = \dfrac{A}{3-x} + \dfrac{B}{2-x}$

$$\frac{1}{(3-x)(2-x)} = \frac{A(2-x)+B(3-x)}{(3-x)(2-x)}$$

$$\Rightarrow \quad 1 = A(2-x) + B(3-x)$$

Put $x = 2$ $\qquad$ Put $x = 3$

$\Rightarrow 1 = B$ $\qquad \Rightarrow 1 = -A \Rightarrow A = -1$

$$\therefore \quad \frac{-1}{3-x} + \frac{1}{2-x} = \frac{1}{(3-x)(2-x)}$$

$$\therefore \quad \int \frac{1}{(3-x)(2-x)} = \int \left(\frac{-1}{3-x} + \frac{1}{2-x} \right) dx$$

$$= -\frac{ln(3-x)}{-1} + \frac{ln(2-x)}{-1} \qquad \left[\because \int \frac{1}{ax+b}\,dx = \frac{\log(ax+b)}{a} \right]$$

$$= ln(3-x) - ln(2-x)$$

$$= ln\left(\frac{3-x}{2-x} \right)$$

Substitute in (1) we get

$$ln\left(\frac{3-x}{2-x} \right) = kt + c$$

$$\Rightarrow \quad \frac{3-x}{2-x} = e^{(kt+c)}$$

$$\Rightarrow \quad 3-x=(2-x)e^{(kt+c)}$$

$$\left(-1+e^{kt+c}\right)x=2e^{kt+c}-3$$

$$x=\frac{2e^{kt+c}-3}{e^{kt+c}-1}$$

Put $t=0$ we get

$$O=\frac{2e^{c0}-3}{e^{c}-1}\Rightarrow 2e^{c}-3=0\Rightarrow e^{c}=\frac{3}{2}$$

$$\Rightarrow \quad c=\log_e(3/2)$$

$$\therefore \quad x_{(t)}=\frac{2e^{kt+\log_e(3/2)}-3}{e^{kt+\log(3/2)}-1}=\frac{3e^{kt}-3}{\frac{3}{2}e^{kt}-1}$$

2. The time course for which the drug is administered intravenously at constant rate is set into the system of linear D.E $\dfrac{dF(t)}{dt}=-kF(t)+Q_0$ where $F(t)$ is amount of drug present at time t and Q_0 is drug flow rate into the compartment in units of amount/time, then prove that $F(t)=\dfrac{Q_0}{k}\left(1-e^{-kt}\right)$

Sol: Consider $\dfrac{dF(t)}{dt}=-kF(t)+Q_0$

Let $F(t)=y$

$\therefore \quad \dfrac{dy}{dt}+ky=Q_0$ it is linear D.E in y (i.e., $\dfrac{dy}{dt}+P(t)y=Q(t)$)

Integrating factor I.F $=e^{\int pdt}$

$$=e^{\int kdt}=e^{kt}$$

$\therefore$ Solution of D.E is

$$y.(I.F)=\int(I.F)Q(t)\,dt$$

$$\therefore \quad y.e^{kt}=\int e^{kt}.Q_0\,dt$$

$$ye^{kt} = Q_0 \cdot \frac{e^{kt}}{k} + c$$

$$y = \frac{Q_0}{k} + Ce^{-kt}$$

at t = 0

$$y = 0 \Rightarrow 0 = \frac{Q_0}{k} + c.e^0$$

$$\Rightarrow \qquad c = \frac{-Q_0}{k}$$

$$\therefore \qquad y = \frac{Q_0}{k} + \frac{-Q_0}{k}.e^{-kt}$$

$$= \frac{Q_0}{k}\left[1 - e^{-kt}\right]$$

29

Linear Differential Equations of Second and Higher Order

Definition: An equation is of the form

$$\frac{d^n y}{dx^n} + p_1(x)\frac{d^{n-1}x}{dx^{n-1}} + p_2(x).\frac{d^{n-2}y}{dx^{n-2}} + ... + p_n(x) = Q(x) \qquad .....(1)$$

where $p_1(x)$, $p_2(x)$ .... $p_n(x)$ and Q(x) are all real valued and continuous functions of x called linear differential equation of order n.

Ex: $$\frac{d^2 y}{dn} + 2x.\frac{dy}{dx} + y = \sin x$$

29.1 Linear Differential Equation with Constant Coefficients

Def: An equation is of the form

$$\frac{d^n y}{dx^n} + p_1\frac{d^{n-1}y}{dx^{n-1}} + p_2.\frac{d^{n-2}y}{dx^{n-2}} ......p_n.y = Q(x) \qquad .....(1)$$

Where p_1 p_2 ..... p_n are real constants and $Q(x)$ is a continuous function of x is called an ordinary linear differential equation of order n with constant coefficients.

29.2 Operator D

We denote $\frac{d}{dx}, \frac{d^2}{dx^2}, \frac{d^3}{dx^3}$ ... with D, D^2, D^3 .....

$$\therefore \qquad Dy = \frac{dy}{dx}, D^2 y = \frac{d^2}{dx^2}(y) .....$$

The equation (1) can be written as

$$(D^n + p_1 D^{n-1} + p_2 D^{n-2} + \ldots + p_n)\, y = Q(x)$$

i.e. $f(D)\, y = Q(x)$

where $f(D) = D^n + p_1 D^{n-1} + p_2 D^{n-2} + \ldots + p_n$

is polynomial in D. The symbol D stands for operation of differentiation

Ex: $D(\sin x) = \cos x$

$D(x^n) = n.x^{n-1}$

29.3 To Find Complementary Function (C. F) (General Solution) of $f(D)y = 0$

Step 1: Form auxillary equation of $f(D)\, y = 0$

i.e. $f(m) = 0$

i.e. $m^n + p_1 m^{n-1} + p_2 m^{n-2} + \ldots p_n = 0$

Step 2: Since the auxillary equation is polynomial equation of deg n. So it has n roots find them, they are say

$m_1, m_2 \ldots m_n$

Step 3:

Case (i): If $m_1, m_2 \ldots m_n$ are real and distinct then the general solution is

$$\text{C.F.} = c_1 e^{m_1 x} + c_2 e^{m_2 x} + \ldots + c_n e^{m_n x}$$

Case (ii) : If α be a real root of $f(m) = 0$ which is repeated r times

i.e. $f(m) = (m - \alpha)^r\, \theta(m)$. where $\theta(\alpha) \neq 0$

then the corresponding part of the complementary function is $(c_1 + c_2 x + c_3 x^2 + \ldots + c_r x^{r-1})\, e^{\alpha n}$

$$\therefore \quad \text{C.F} = (c_1 + c_2 x + x\, c_3 x^2 + \ldots + c_r x^{r-1})\, e^{\alpha x} + c_{r+1} e^{\alpha_{r+1} x} + \ldots + c_n e^{\alpha_n x}$$

when $\alpha_{r+1}, \alpha_{r+2} \ldots \alpha_n$ are remaining $(n - r)$ different roots of $f(m) = 0$

Case (iii) : If $\alpha + i\beta$ be a non repeated complex roots of $f(m) = 0$ thus $\alpha - i\beta$ is root of $f(m) = 0$.

$\therefore$ the corresponding part of complementary function is $e^{\alpha x}(c_1 \cos\beta x + c_2 \sin\beta x)$

Case (iv): If $\alpha + \sqrt{\beta}$ be real irrational root of $f(m) = 0$ then $\alpha - \sqrt{\beta}$ is also root of $f(m) = 0$. The part of C.F corresponding to these roots is $e^{\alpha x}\, [c_1 \cos h\, \beta x + c_2 \sin h\, \beta x]$.

Examples:

1. If 1, 2, 3 are roots of f(m) = 0

   then $\quad C.F = c_1e^x + c_2e^{2x} + c_3e^{3x}$

2. If 2 + 3i, 2 – 3i are roots of f(m) = 0

   then $\quad C.F = e^{2x}\,[c_1 \cos 3x + c_2 \sin 3x]$

3. If $2 \pm \sqrt{3}$ are roots of f(m) = 0 then $C.F = e^{2x}\,[c_1 \cos h\, \sqrt{3}\, x + c_2 \sin h \sqrt{3}\, x]$

Solved Examples

Solve the following differential equations.

1. $2\dfrac{d^2y}{dx^2} - 13.\dfrac{dy}{dx} + 15y = 0$

Sol. Given D.E is $2.\dfrac{d^2y}{dx^2} - 13.\dfrac{dy}{dx} + 15y = 0$

i.e. $\quad (2D^2 - 13D + 15)\, y = 0 \qquad$ i.e. $f(D)\, y = 0$

∴ the corresponding auxillary equation is $\quad f(m) = 0$

i.e. $\quad 2m^2 - 13m + 15 = 0$

∴ $\quad 2m^2 - 10m - 3m + 15 = 0$

$2m\,(m - 5) - 3\,(m - 5) = 0$

∴ m = 3, 5 are real and distinct

∴ general solution C. F is

$$y = c_1 \,.\, e^{3x} + c_2\, e^{5x}$$

2. $\dfrac{d^3y}{dx^3} - 9.\dfrac{d^2y}{dx^2} + 23.\dfrac{dy}{dx} - 15y = 0$

Sol. Given D.E is $\dfrac{d^3y}{dx^3} - 9.\dfrac{d^2y}{dx^2} + 23.\dfrac{dy}{dx} - 15y = 0$

i.e. $(D^3 - 9D^2 + 23D - 15)\, y = 0 \qquad$ i.e. $f(D)\, y = 0$

∴ the corresponding auxillary equations $f(m) = 0$

i.e. $\quad m^3 - 9m^2 + 23 - 15 = 0$

Since by trile and error method 1 is root of $f(m) = 0$. $\quad (\because 1 - 9 + 23 - 15 = 0)$

Now we find remaining two roots by synthetic division

$$\begin{array}{c|cccc} & 1 & -9 & 23 & -15 \\ 1 & 0 & 1 & -8 & 15 \\ \hline & 1 & -8 & +15 & 0 \end{array}$$

$$f(m) = (m^2 - 8m + 15)(m - 1) = 0$$

$\therefore \quad m^2 - 8m + 15 = 0 \quad \Rightarrow \quad m^2 - 3m - 5m + 15 = 0$

$$m(m-3) - 5(m-3) = 0$$

$$(m-5)(m-3) = 0$$

$$\therefore m = 5, 3$$

$\therefore$ The roots are 1, 3, 5 these are real and distinct.

$\therefore$ The general solution is

$$y = c_1.e^x + c_2\, e^{3x} + c_3 e^{5x}$$

3. $4.\dfrac{d^3y}{dx^3} + 4.\dfrac{d^2y}{dx^2} + \dfrac{dy}{dx} = 0$

Sol. $(4D^3 + 4D^2 + D)\, y = 0$

$\therefore$ the corresponding auxillary equation is

$$4m^3 + 4m^2 + m = 0$$

$$m\,[4m^2 + 4m + 1] = 0$$

$\therefore\ m = 0; \quad 4m^2 + 4m + 1 = 0 \Rightarrow (2m+1)^2 = 0 \Rightarrow m = \dfrac{-1}{2}, \dfrac{-1}{2}$

$\therefore$ the roots are $0, \dfrac{-1}{2}, \dfrac{-1}{2}$ are real and $\dfrac{-1}{2}$ is the root which is repeated, twice

$\therefore$ the general solution is

$$y = c_1.e^{ox} + (c_2 + c_3x)\,.\, e^{\frac{-1}{2}x}$$

4. $D^2 - 6D + 13 = 0$

Sol. The corresponding auxillary equation is

$$m^2 - 6m + 13 = 0$$

$$\therefore \quad m = \frac{+6 \pm \sqrt{36-52}}{2} = \frac{6 \pm \sqrt{-4}}{2} = 3 \pm i2 = 3 \pm 2i$$

$\therefore$ Roots are 3 + 2i, 3 – 2i these are complex

$\therefore$ The general solution is

$$y = e^{3x}[c_1 \cos 2x + c_2 \sin 2x]$$

5. $(D^4 + 18D^2 + 81)\, y = 0$

Sol. The corresponding auxillary equation is

$$m^4 + 18m^2 + 81 = 0$$

$\therefore \quad (m^2 + 9)^2 = 0 \quad \therefore m^2 = -9, -9$

$$\therefore \mathbf{m = \pm 3i \pm 3i}$$

$\therefore$ the roots are –3i, –3i, 3i, 3i

$\therefore$ the roots are complex and repeated.

$$\therefore \quad y = e^{ox}[(C_1 + C_2x) \cos 3x + (C_3 + C_4x) \sin 3x]$$

$$\therefore \quad \mathbf{y = (C_1 + C_2x) \cos 3x + (C_3 + C_4x) \sin 3x}$$

Exercise 29.1

Solve the following differential equations.

1. $\dfrac{d^2y}{dx^2} - 4.\dfrac{dy}{dx} + 5y = 0$
2. $(D^2 - 3D + 4)\, y = 0$
3. $(D^3 + 3D^2 - 4)\, y = 0$
4. $(D^3 - 14D + 8)\, y = 0$
5. $(D^2 + D + 1)\, y = 0$
6. $(D^4 - 2D^3 - 3D^2 + 4D + 4)\, y = 0$

Answers

Ans: $y = C_1 \cos x + C_2 \sin x$

Ans: $y = e^{\frac{3x}{2}}\left[C_1 \cos\dfrac{\sqrt{7}x}{2} + C_2 \sin\dfrac{\sqrt{7}x}{2}\right]$

Ans: $y = C_1e^x + (C_2 + C_3x)\, e^{-2x}$

Ans: $y = C_1e^{-4x} + e^{2x}\,[C_2 \cos h\,(x\sqrt{2}\,) + C_3 \sin h(x\sqrt{2}\,)]$

Ans: $y = e^{\frac{-x}{2}}\left[C_1 \cos\dfrac{x\sqrt{3}}{2} + C_2 \sin\dfrac{x\sqrt{3}}{2}\right]$

Ans: $(C_1 + C_2\, x)\, e^{-x} + (C_3 + C_4x)\, e^{2x}$

29.4 Inverse Operator

To get particular solution of differential equation $D(y) = Q(x)$ we use inverse operator.

The operator D^{-1} is called inverse operator.

$$D^{-1}(y) = \frac{1}{D}\,(y) \text{ i.e. integral of } y.$$

Ex: $$\frac{1}{D}\,(\sin 3x) = \frac{-\cos 3x}{3}$$

Since $$D\left(\frac{-\cos 3x}{3}\right) = +\frac{3\sin 3x}{3} = \sin 3x$$

Note that if $\dfrac{1}{f(D)}\,\theta(x) = R(x)$

Then $$\theta(x) = f(D)\, R(x)$$

For example $$\frac{1}{D^2+4D+3}\,(e^{2x}) = \frac{4}{15}\, e^{2x}$$

Since $$(D^2 + 4D + 3)\left(\frac{4}{15}e^{2x}\right)$$

$$= \frac{4}{15}\left[\frac{e^{2x}}{4} + 4.\frac{e^{2x}}{2} + 3.e^{2x}\right]$$

$$= \frac{4}{15}\left[\frac{1}{4} + \frac{1}{2} + 3\right]e^{2x}$$

$$= \frac{4}{15}\left[\frac{1+2+12}{4}\right]e^{2x} = \frac{4}{15}\times\frac{15}{4}e^{2x} = e^{2x}$$

Theorem: If y is a function x and α is a constant then the particular value of $\frac{1}{D-\alpha}$ (y) is equal to $e^{\alpha x}\int y.e^{-\alpha x}dx$.

Proof: Let $$\frac{1}{D-\alpha}\ y = Q(x) \quad \text{say}$$

$$y = (D - \alpha)\ .\ Q(x)$$

$$y = \frac{d}{dx}.\ Q(x) - \alpha\ Q(x)$$

$$y = Q^1(x) - \alpha\ Q(x)$$

$\therefore$ $Q^1(x) - Q(x)\ \alpha = y$ is linear D.E of first order and first degree

$$\text{I.F} = e^{-\alpha x}$$

Solution is $e^{-\alpha x}\ .\ Q(x) = \int e^{-2x}.\ y.\ dx$

$$\therefore \quad Q(x) = e^{\alpha x}\int e^{-\alpha x}.y\ dx$$

$$\therefore \quad \frac{1}{D-\alpha}(y) = e^{\alpha x}\int y.e^{-2x}.\ dx$$

Ex: Find the particular value (particular integral) (P. I) of $\frac{1}{D+1}$ (x^2)

$$\frac{1}{(D+1)}(x^2) = \frac{1}{D-(-1)}(x^2) = e^{-x}\int e^{+x}.\ x^2dx$$

$$= e^{-x}\left[x^2.e^{+x} - \int 2x.e^x dx\right]$$

$$= e^{-x}.\left[x^2e^x - 2\int x\ e^x dx\right]$$

$$= e^{-x}.\left[x^2e^x - 2\ (x-1)\ e^x\right]$$

$$= x^2 - 2\ (x-1) = x^2 - 2x + 2$$

Verification $(D + 1)\ [x^2 - 2x + 2]$

$$= D(x^2 - 2x + 2) + (x^2 - 2x + 2)$$

$$= 2x - 2 + x^2 - 2x + 2$$

$$= x^2$$

General solution of f(D) y = Q(x).

Let y = y_p is a particular solution (P. I) of f(D) y = Q(x) and

y_c is the general solution (C. F) of f(D)y = 0 than the general solution (complete solution) of f(D)y = Q(x) is

$$y = y_c + y_p \text{ i.e., } y = \text{C. F} + \text{P. I}$$

So to get general solution find C.F through auxillary equation and find particular solution by Inverse operator and addup.

29.5 Particular Integrals of Some Special Cases (Functions)

Type 1: Particular integral of f(D)y = e^{ax}

When f(a) ≠ then P.I is $\frac{1}{f(a)} . e^{ax}$. If f(a) = 0 then (D – a) is a factor of f(D). If a is root repeated k times for f(a) = 0 then f(D) = $(D - a)^k$ g(D) where g(D) ≠ 0.

$$\therefore \qquad \frac{1}{f(D)} e^{ax} = \frac{1}{(D-a)^k g(D)} = \frac{1}{g(a)} . e^{ax} . \frac{x^k}{k!}$$

$\therefore$ P.I of $\qquad f(D)\, y = e^{ax}$ is $\frac{1}{g(a)} . e^{ax} . \frac{x^k}{k!}$

Ex: 1. $\frac{1}{D+2}(e^{3x}) = \frac{e^{3x}}{3+2} = \frac{e^{3x}}{5}$ $\qquad [\because f(D) = D+2 \qquad f(a) = f(3) = 3+2 = 5 \neq 0]$

2. $\frac{1}{(D-2)}(e^{2x}) = \frac{1}{(D-2)\,.1} e^{2x} = \frac{1}{1} . e^{2x} . \frac{x^1}{1!} = x.e^{2x}$

3. $\frac{1}{(D-2)^2.(D-3)}(e^{2x}) = \frac{1}{(2-3)} . e^{2x} . \frac{x^2}{2!}$ $\qquad \left(\because \left(\frac{1}{2-3}\right) . \frac{1}{(D-2)^2} . (e^{2x})\right)$

$$= \frac{e^{2x}.x^2}{2(-1)} = \frac{-1}{2} x^2 e^{2x}$$

4. $\frac{1}{(D^2 - 2D + 1)}(e^x) = \frac{1}{(D-1)^2.1}(e^x)$

$$= \frac{1}{1} . e^x . \frac{x^2}{2!} = \frac{e^x . x^2}{2}$$

So, P.I of $f(D) = e^{ax} = \dfrac{1}{f(D)} e^{ax}$ is

$$\frac{e^{ax}}{f(a)} \qquad f(a) \neq 0$$

$$\frac{e^{ax}}{g(a)} \cdot \frac{x^k}{k!} \qquad f(a) = 0 \text{ and } g(a) \neq 0 \text{ where } f(D) = (D - a)^k g(D)$$

Ex: Solve $\dfrac{d^2y}{dx^2} - 3\dfrac{dy}{dx} + 2y = e^{5x}$

Sol: Given D.E is $D(y) = Q(x)$

Complementary function (y_c)

To find of $D(y) = 0$

Consider $\dfrac{d^2y}{dx^2} - 3\dfrac{dy}{dx} + 2y = 0$

i.e. $(D^2 - 3D + 2)\, y = 0$

its corresponding auxillary equation is

$$m^2 - 3m + 2 = 0 \qquad m = 1, 2$$

$\therefore$ Complementary function $y_c = C_1 e^x + C_2\, e^{2z}$

To find particular solution y_p of $D(y) = D(x)$

$$(D^2 - 3D + 2)\, y = e^{5x}$$

$$y_p = \frac{1}{(D^2 - 3D + 2)} e^{5x}$$

$$= \frac{1}{(D-2)(D-1)} e^{5x}$$

$$= \left(\frac{1}{D-2} - \frac{1}{D-1}\right) e^{5x}$$

$$= \frac{1}{D-2}(e^{5x}) - \frac{1}{D-1}(e^{5x})$$

$$= \frac{e^{5x}}{5-2} - \frac{e^{5x}}{5-1} = \frac{e^{5x}}{3} - \frac{e^{5x}}{4}$$

$$= \frac{1}{12} e^{5x}$$

$$\therefore \qquad y_p = \frac{1}{12} e^{5x}$$

$\therefore$ The general solution of given D.E is

$$y = y_c + y_p = C_1e^x + C_2e^{2x} + \frac{1}{12}e^{5x}$$

Type 2

P.I of f(D) y = ϕ(x) where ϕ(x) = sin bx or cos bx. Where bx is constant.

Let $\qquad f(D) = \sin bx$

$$\Rightarrow \qquad y = \frac{1}{f(D)}\{\sin bx\}$$

$$\therefore \qquad \text{P.I} = \frac{1}{f(D)}\{\sin bx\}$$

Let $f(D) = \phi(D^2)$ then

$$\phi(D^2) \sin bx = \phi(-b^2) \sin bx \text{ and}$$

$$\phi(D^2) \cos bx = \phi(-b^2) \cos bx$$

Case (i) $\qquad$ Let $\phi(-b^2) \neq 0$

then

$$\frac{1}{\phi(D^2)}\left[\phi(D^2)\sin bx\right] = \frac{1}{\phi(D^2)}\left[\phi(-b^2)\sin bx\right]$$

$$= \sin bx = \frac{1}{\phi(D^2)}\left[\phi(-b^2)\sin bx\right]$$

$$\therefore \qquad \frac{\sin bx}{\phi(D^2)} = \frac{\sin bx}{\phi(-b)^2}$$

$$\therefore \qquad \frac{(\sin bx)}{f(D)} = \frac{\sin bx}{\phi(D^2)} = \frac{\sin bx}{\phi(-b^2)} \qquad [\phi(-b^2) \neq 0]$$

by

$$\frac{1}{f(D)}(\cos bx) = \frac{1}{\phi(D^2)}\cos bx = \frac{\cos bx}{\phi(-b)^2}$$

$$\frac{1}{f(D)}\sin bx = \frac{\sin bx}{\phi(-b)^2} \qquad \phi(-b^2) \neq 0$$

$$\frac{1}{f(D)}\cos bx = \frac{\cos bx}{\phi(-b^2)}$$

If $f(-b^2) = 0$ then $D^2 + b^2$ is a factor of $f(D^2)$ and hence it is a factor of $f(D)$.

Let $f(D) = (D^2 + b^2)\,F(D^2)$ when $F(-b^2) \neq 0$

Now
$$\frac{1}{D^2+b^2}(\sin bx) = \frac{-x\cos bx}{2b}$$

$$\frac{1}{D^2+b^2}(\cos bx) = \frac{x\sin bx}{2b}$$

So,

$$P.I = \frac{\sin ax}{f(D^2)} = \frac{\sin ax}{f(-a^2)} \qquad f(-a^2) \neq 0$$

$$P.I = \frac{\cos ax}{f(D^2)} = \frac{\cos ax}{f(-a)^2} \qquad f(-a^2) \neq 0$$

$$P.I - \frac{\cos ax}{D^2+a^2} = \frac{x.\sin 2x}{2a}$$

$$P.I = \frac{\sin ax}{D^2+a^2} = \frac{-x\cos 2x}{2a}$$

Ex: Solve $(D^2 - 3D + 2)\,y = \cos 3x$

Sol: To find y_c:

The auxillary equation is $m^2 - 3m + 2 = 0$

$$m = 1, 2$$

$\therefore$
$$y_c = C_1e^x + C_2\,e^{2x}$$

to get C_p

$$C_p = \frac{1}{(D^2-3D+2)}\,(\cos 3x)$$

$$= \frac{1}{-9-3D+2}\,(\cos 3x) \quad [\text{by put } D^2 = -3^2 = -9]$$

$$= \frac{1}{-3D-7}\,(\cos 3x)$$

$$= -\frac{1}{(3D+7)}\cos 3x = \frac{-(3D-7)}{9D^2-49}(\cos 3x) \qquad \text{(by rationalizing)}$$

$$= (7-3D).\left[\frac{1}{9D^2-49}(\cos 3x)\right]$$

$$= (7-3D)\left[\frac{\cos 3x}{9(-9)-49}\right] = \frac{(7-3D)\cos 3x}{-81-49}$$

$$= (3D-7)\frac{(\cos 3x)}{130}$$

$$= \frac{1}{130}\left[3.(-\sin 3x) - 7.\cos 3x\right]$$

$$= \frac{1}{130}\left[-9\sin 3x - 7.\cos 3x\right]$$

Type 3: P.I (yp) of f(D)y = f(x) where $f(x) = x^k$

Where k is a positive integen

Step 1: Take $\quad f(D)\, y = \phi(x)$

Step 2: Operating $\frac{1}{f(D)}$ on both sides

$$\frac{1}{f(D)}(f(D))y = \frac{1}{f(D)}(\phi(x))$$

$$y = \frac{1}{f(D)}(\phi(x))$$

Step 3: Convert $\frac{1}{f(D)}$ in the form of $\frac{1}{1\pm\phi(D)}$ by taking out lowest degree term from f(D).

Now $\quad \frac{1}{f(D)} = \left[1\pm\phi(D)\right]^{-1}$

And expand it in power of D.

by using binomial theorem

We use,

(i) $\quad \frac{1}{1-D} = \left(1-D^{-1}\right) = 1 + D + D^2 + D^3 + \ldots.$

(ii) $\quad \frac{1}{1+D} = \left(1+D\right)^{-1} = 1 - D + D^2 - D^3 \ldots..$

(iii) $$\frac{1}{(1-D)^2} = (1-D)^{-2} = 1 + 2D + 3D^2 + 4D^3 .....$$

(iv) $$\frac{1}{(1+D)^2} = (1+D)^{-2} = 1 - 2D + 3D^2 - 4D^3 .....$$

(v) $$\frac{1}{(1-D)^3} = (1-D)^{-3} = 1 + 3D + 6D^2 + 10D^3 .....$$

(vi) $$\frac{1}{(1+D)^3} = (1+D)^{-3} = 1 - 3D + 36^2 - 10D^3 .....$$

Ex: Solve $(D^2 - 3D + 2)y = 2x^2$

Sol: To get y_c of D(y) = 0

Corresponding auxiliary equation is

$$m^2 - 3m + 2 = 0 \qquad \Rightarrow m = 1, 2$$

$$\therefore \qquad y_c = C_1e^{2x} + C_2e^{2x}$$

to get y_p of $D(y)$ = Q(x)

$$y_p = \frac{1}{D^2 - 3D + 2}(2x^2)$$

$$= \frac{1}{(D-1)(D-2)}(2x^2)$$

$$= \frac{1}{-2}\left(\frac{1}{1-D/2}\right)(2x^2) + \frac{1}{1-D}(2x^2)$$

$$= \frac{-1}{2}\left(\frac{1}{1-D/2}\right)^{-1}(2x^2) + \frac{1}{1-D}(2x^2)$$

$$= \frac{-1}{2}\left(1 + \frac{D}{2} + \left(\frac{D}{2}\right)^2 + ...\right)(2x^2) + (1-D)^{-1}(2x^2)$$

$$= \frac{-1}{2}\left(2x^2 + \frac{1}{2}.(4x) + \frac{1}{4}.(4)\right) + \left[1 + D + D^2 + ...\right](2x^2)$$

$$= \frac{-1}{2}[2x^2 + 2x + 1] + [2x^2 + 4x + 4]$$

$$= -x^2 - x - \frac{1}{2} + 2x^2 + 4x + 4$$

$$= x^2 + 3x + \frac{7}{2}$$

$\therefore$ the general solution is

$$y = y_c + y_p$$

$$= C_1 e^x + C_2 e^{2x} + x^2 + 3x + \frac{1}{2}$$

Type 4: The P.I (y_p) of $f(D)y = f(x)$ where $f(x) = e^{ax}$ v, where a is constant and v is a function in x.

Step 1: Take f(D), obtain f(D + a) by replacing D by D + a.

Step 2: $$\text{P.I} = \frac{1}{f(D)} (e^{ax} v)$$

$$= e^{ax} . \frac{1}{f(D+a)} . (v)$$

Ex: Solve $(D^2 - 2D + 4)\, y = e^x . \cos x$

To get y_c of D(y) = 0

Consider $(D^2 - 2D + 4)\, y = 0$

The corresponding auxillary equation is

$$m^2 - 2\,m + 4 = 0, \qquad b^2 - 4ac = 4 - 16 = -12 < 0.$$

$$m = \frac{2 \pm \sqrt{4-16}}{2} = \frac{2 \pm 2i\sqrt{3}}{2} = 1 \pm i\sqrt{3}$$

$$\therefore \qquad y_c = e^x \left[c_1 . \cos\sqrt{3}x + c_2 \sin\sqrt{3}x \right]$$

To get y_p of D(y) = Q(x)

Now, $$y_p = \frac{1}{D^2 - 2D + 4}\left(e^x . \cos x\right)$$

$$= e^x \frac{1}{(D+1)^2 - 2(D+1) + 4}(\cos x)$$

$$\left(\because \frac{1}{f(d)} (e^{ax} v) = e^{ax} \frac{1}{f(D+a)} (v) \right)$$

$$= e^{ax} \frac{1}{f(D+a)}(\phi x)$$

$$= e^{x} . \frac{1}{\left(D^2+1+2D-2D+2+4\right)}(\cos x)$$

$$= e^{x} . \frac{1}{D^2+3}(\cos x)$$

$$= e^{x}\left(\frac{1}{-1+3}\right)\cos x\left(D^2 = a^2 = -1\right)$$

$$= \frac{e^x}{2} . \cos x$$

$\therefore$ the general solution of differential equations is $y = y_c + y_p$

$$\therefore \quad y = e^{x}\left[c_1 \cos\sqrt{3}x + c_2 \sin\sqrt{3}x\right]$$

$$+ \frac{e^x}{2} . \cos x$$

Type 5: The P.I (y_p) of

$f(D)\, y = \phi(x)$ where $f(x) = x\,v$ where v is a function of x.

$$\frac{1}{f(D)}(xv) = \left[x - \frac{1}{f(D)} f'(D)\right]\frac{1}{f(D)}(v)$$

Ex: Solve $\dfrac{d^2y}{dx^2} + 9y = x \sin 2x$

Sol: Given D.E is D(y) = Q(x) when D(y) = $(D^2 + 9)$y ; Q(x) = x. sin 2x

To get (y_c) of D(y) = 0

The corresponding Auxillary equation $m^2 + 9 = 0$

$$m^2 = -9$$

$$m = +3i$$

$$\therefore \quad y_c = e^{ox}\left[c_1 . \cos 3x + c_2 \sin 3x\right]$$

To get y_p of D(y) = Q(x)

$$y_p = \frac{1}{f(D)}(x.\sin 2x)$$

$$= \left[x - \frac{1}{f(D)}f'(D)\right]\left(\frac{1}{f(D)}(\sin 2x)\right)$$

where $f(D) = D^2 + 9$

$$= \left(x - \frac{2D}{D^2+9}\right)\left\{\frac{1}{b^2+9}(\sin\ 2x)\right\}$$

$$= \left(x - \frac{2D}{D^2+9}\right)\left\{\frac{\sin 2x}{-2^2+9}\right\}$$

$$= \left(x - \frac{2D}{D^2+9}\right)\left(\frac{\sin 2x}{5}\right)$$

$$= \frac{x\ \sin 2x}{5} - \frac{2D}{5(D^2+9)}(\sin 2x)$$

$$= \frac{x\ \sin 2x}{5} - \frac{2}{5}\frac{1}{D^2+9}(2\cos 2x)$$

$$= \frac{x\ \sin 2x}{5} - \frac{4}{5}\frac{1}{D^2+9}(\cos 2x)$$

$$= \frac{x \sin 2x}{5} - \frac{4}{5}\left[\frac{1}{-2^2+9}(\cos 2x)\right] \quad (\text{put } D^2 = -2^2)$$

$$= \frac{x \sin 2x}{5} - \frac{4}{5}.\frac{1}{5}\cos 2x$$

$$= \frac{x \sin 2x}{5} - \frac{4}{5}\cos 2x$$

$\therefore$ General solution is $= y_c + y_p = (c_1 \cos 3x + c_2 \sin 3x) + \frac{x \sin 2x}{5} - \frac{4}{25}\cos 2x$

Solved Examples

1. Solve $(D^2 + 6D + 9) = 2.e^{-3x}$

Sol: Given DE is D(y) = Q(x), to get y_c of f(D) = 0.

The corresponding auxillary equation is $f(m) = m^2 + 6m + 9 = 0$

$\Rightarrow \quad (m + 3)^2 = 0$

$m = -3, -3$ are real and equal

$\therefore \quad y_c = (c_1 + c_2 x)e^{-3x}$

To get y_p of D(y) = Q(x)

$$y_p = \frac{1}{b^2 + 6D + 9}\left(2e^{-3x}\right)$$

$$= 2\frac{1}{(D+3)^2}\left(e^{-3x}\right)$$

$$= 2.\ e^{-3x}\ .\ \frac{x^2}{2!} \qquad (\because f(a) = f(-3) = 0)$$

$$= x^2\ e^{-3x}$$

$\therefore$ The general solution of given equation is $y = y_c + y_p$

$$y = y_c + y_p$$

$$= (c_1 + c_2 x)\ e^{-3x} + x^2\ e^{-3x}$$

2. Solve $(D^2 - 5D + 6)\ y = 4e^x + 5$

Sol: Consider $(D^2 - 5D + 6)\ y = 0$

The corresponding auxillary equations

$$m^2 - 5m + 6 = 0$$

$$m^2 - 3\ m - 2\ m + 6 = 0$$

$$m\ (m - 3) - 2(m - 3) = 0$$

$$m = 2,\ m = 3$$

$\therefore$ The complementary function is $y_c = c_1\ e^{2x} + c_2\ e^{3x}$

To get y_p : (particular integral)

$$y_p = \frac{1}{(D^2 - 5D + 6)}\ (4e^x + 5)$$

$$= \frac{1}{(D-2)(D-3)}\ (4e^x + 5)$$

$$= \frac{1}{D-3}\left(4e^x + 5\right) - \frac{1}{D-2}\left(4e^x + 5\right)$$

$$= \frac{4.e^{x}}{1-3} + \frac{5.e^{0}}{0-3} - \left(\frac{4.e^{x}}{1-2} + \frac{5e^{o}}{0-2} \right)$$

$$= 2e^{x} - \frac{5}{3} + 4e^{x} + \frac{5}{2} = 2e^{x} + \frac{5}{6}$$

$\therefore$ the general solution is $y = y_c + y_p$

$$y = c_1 e^{2x} + c_2 e^{3x} + 2e^{x} + \frac{5}{6}$$

3. Solve $(D^3 - 5D^2 + 7D - 3)\, y = e^{2x}.\cosh x$

Sol: To get complementary function (y_c)

Consider $(D^3 - 5D^2 + 7D - 3)\, y = 0$

$\therefore$ the corresponding auxillary equation is

$$m^3 - 5m^2 + 7m - 3 = 0$$

By trial and error method $m = 1$ is a roor

$\therefore$ by using synthetic division

	1	–5	7	–3
	0	1	–4	3
$m = 1$	1	–4	3	0
	0	1	–3	
	1	–3	0	

$\therefore \quad (m^2 - 1)(m - 3) = 0$

$\therefore \quad m = 1, 1, 3$

$\therefore \quad y_c = (c_1 + c_2 x)e^{x} + c_3 e^{3x}$

To get particular integral y_p

$$y_p = \frac{1}{D^3 + 5D^2 + 7D - 3}\left(e^{2x} \cosh x\right)$$

$$= \frac{1}{(D-1)^2 (D-3)}\left(e^{2x}.\cosh x\right)$$

Consider $\dfrac{1}{(D-1)^2 (D-3)} = \dfrac{A}{D-1} + \dfrac{B}{(D-1)^2} + \dfrac{C}{D-3}$

$$1 = A(D-1)(D-3) + B(D-3) + C(D-1)^2$$

Put $D = 1 \Rightarrow 1 = B(1-3) \quad \Rightarrow -2B = 1$

$$\Rightarrow \quad B = -\frac{1}{2}$$

Put D = 3 we get $1 = c\,(3-1)^2$

$$\Rightarrow \quad 4c = 1$$

$$\therefore \quad c = \frac{1}{4}$$

Comparing D^2 coefficients an both sides we get

$$0 = A + C \quad \Rightarrow \quad C = -A = +\frac{1}{2}$$

$$\therefore \quad \frac{1}{(D-1)^2(D-3)} = \left(\frac{\frac{1}{2}}{D-1} + \frac{-\frac{1}{2}}{(D-1)^2} + \frac{\frac{1}{4}}{D-3}\right)$$

$$\therefore \quad \frac{1}{(D-1)^2(D-3)}\left(e^x \cosh x\right) = \left(\frac{\frac{1}{2}}{D-1} + \frac{-\frac{1}{2}}{(D-1)^2} + \frac{\frac{1}{4}}{D-3}\right)\left(e^{2x}\cosh x\right)$$

$$= \left(\frac{\frac{1}{2}}{D-1} - \frac{\frac{1}{2}}{(D-1)^2} + \frac{\frac{1}{4}}{D-3}\right)\left(e^{2x}.\frac{e^x + e^{-x}}{2}\right)$$

$$= \left(\frac{\frac{1}{2}}{D-1} - \frac{\frac{1}{2}}{(D-1)^2} + \frac{\frac{1}{4}}{D-3}\right)\left(\frac{e^{3x} + e^x}{2}\right)$$

$$= \left(\frac{1}{2}\frac{1}{D-1} - \frac{1}{2}\frac{1}{(D-1)^2} + \frac{1}{4}\frac{1}{D-3}\right)\left(\frac{e^{3x}}{2}\right)$$

$$+\left(\frac{1}{2}\frac{1}{D-1} - \frac{1}{2}\frac{1}{(D-1)^2} + \frac{1}{4}.\frac{1}{D-3}\right)\left(\frac{e^x}{2}\right)$$

$$= \frac{1}{2}\left\{\frac{1}{2}\frac{1}{3-1} - \frac{1}{2}\cdot\frac{1}{(3-1)^2} + \frac{1}{4}\cdot\frac{e^{3x}}{1}\cdot\frac{x}{1}\right\}$$

$$+\frac{1}{2}\left\{\frac{1}{2}\cdot\frac{e^x}{1}x - \frac{1}{2}.e^x.\frac{x^2}{2!} + \frac{1}{4}\cdot\frac{1}{(1-3)}\right\}$$

$$= \frac{1}{2}\left\{\frac{1}{4} - \frac{1}{8} + \frac{xe^{3x}}{4}\right\} + \frac{1}{2}\left\{\frac{xe^x}{2} - \frac{x^2e^x}{4} - \frac{1}{8}\right\}$$

$$= \frac{1}{8} - \frac{1}{16} + \frac{xe^{3x}}{8} + \frac{xe^x}{4} - \frac{x^2e^x}{8} - \frac{1}{16}$$

$$= \frac{x\,e^{3x}}{8} - \frac{x\,e^x}{4} - \frac{x^2e^x}{8}$$

$\therefore$ the general solution is

$$y = (c_1 + c_2x)e^x + c_3e^{3x} + \frac{x\,e^{3x}}{8} - \frac{x\,e^x}{4} - \frac{x^3e^x}{8}$$

$$y = (c_1 + c_4x)e^x + c_3\,e^{3x} + \frac{x\,e^{3x}}{8} - \frac{x^2e^x}{8}$$

when $c_4 = c_2 - \dfrac{1}{4}$

4. Solve $(D^3 + 1)\,y = 3 + 5\,e^x$

Sol: Given D.E is $D(y) = Q(x)$

when $D(y) = (D^3 + 1)\,y$

$Q(x) = 3 + 5e^x$

to get complementary function y_c of $D(y) = 0$.

Consider $(D^3 + 1)\,y = 0$

The corresponding auxillary equation is

$m^3 + 1 = 0$

Clearly $m = -1$

$$\therefore \quad \begin{array}{r|rrrr} & 1 & 0 & 0 & 1 \\ -1 & 0 & -1 & 1 & -1 \\ \hline & 1 & -1 & 1 & (0) \end{array}$$

$$m^2 - m + 1 = 0$$

$$m = \frac{1 \pm \sqrt{1-4}}{2} = \frac{1 \pm i\sqrt{3}}{2}$$

$\therefore$ roots are $-1, \dfrac{1 \pm i\sqrt{3}}{2}$

$$\therefore y_c = c_1 e^{-x} + e^{x/2}\left[c_2 \cos\frac{\sqrt{3}}{2}x + c_3 \sin\frac{\sqrt{3}}{2}x\right]$$

To get y_p of D(y) = Q(x)

$$y_p = \frac{1}{D^3+1}\left(3+5e^x\right)$$

$$= \frac{1}{(D+1)(D^2+D+1)}\left(3+5e^x\right)$$

Consider $\dfrac{1}{(D+1)(D^2+D+1)} = \dfrac{A}{D+1} + \dfrac{BD+C}{D^2-D+1}$

$$1 = A(D^2 - D + 1) + (BD + C)(D + 1)$$

Put D = –1 we get

$$1 = A(1+1+1) \Rightarrow A = \frac{1}{3}$$

Compare D^2 coefficients on both sides we get

$$0 = A + B \quad \Rightarrow \quad B = -A = -\frac{1}{3}$$

Comparing constant terms on both sides we get

$$1 = A + C \quad \Rightarrow \quad C = 1 - A = 1 - \frac{1}{3} = \frac{2}{3}$$

$$\therefore \quad \frac{1}{(D+1)(D^2-D+1)} = \frac{\frac{1}{3}}{D+1} + \frac{\left(-\frac{1}{3}D + \frac{2}{3}\right)}{D^2-D+1}$$

$$\therefore \quad \frac{1}{(D+1)(D^2-D+1)}\left(3+5e^x\right)$$

$$= \left(\frac{\frac{1}{3}}{D+1} + \frac{-\frac{1}{3}D + \frac{2}{3}}{D^2 - D + 1} \right) \left(3 + 5e^x\right)$$

$$= \frac{1}{3}\left(\frac{1}{D+1}\left(3+5e^x\right)\right) + \left(\frac{-\frac{1}{3}D+\frac{2}{3}}{D^2-D+1}\right)\left(3+5e^x\right)$$

$$= \frac{1}{3}\left(\frac{3}{0+1} + 5.\frac{e^x}{2}\right) + \left(-\frac{1}{3}D + \frac{2}{3}\right)\left(\frac{3}{1} + \frac{5e^x}{1}\right)$$

$$= \frac{1}{3}\left(3 + \frac{5}{2}e^x\right) + \left(\frac{-D}{3} + \frac{2}{3}\right)\left(3 + 5e^x\right)$$

$$= 1 + \frac{5}{6}e^x + -D(0) + \frac{-5}{3}D\left(e^x\right) + 2 + \frac{10}{3}e^x$$

$$= 1 + \frac{5}{6}e^x + (0) - \frac{5}{3}e^x + 2 + \frac{10}{3}e^x$$

$$= 3 + \left(\frac{5}{6} - \frac{5}{3} + \frac{10}{3}\right)e^x$$

$$= 3 + \left(\frac{5 - 10 + 20}{6}\right)e^x$$

$$= 3 + \frac{15}{6}e^x = 3 + \frac{5}{2}e^x$$

$\therefore$ the general solution is $c_1\, e^{-x} + e^{x/2}\left(c_2 \cos\frac{\sqrt{3}}{2}x + c_3 \sin\frac{\sqrt{3}}{2}x\right) + \frac{5}{2}e^x$

5. Solve $(D^2 - 4D + 3)\, y = \sin 3x \cos 2x$

Sol: To get complementary function y_c of $D(y) = 0$ (y_c):

Consider $D^2 - 4D + 3 = 0$

The corresponding auxillary equations

$$m^2 - 4\,m + 3 = 0$$

$$m^2 - 3\,m - m + 3 = 0 \qquad m = 1, 3$$

$$\therefore \qquad y_c = c_1\, e^x + c_2\, e^{3x}$$

to get particular integral (y_p):

$$y_p = \frac{1}{D^2 - 4D - 3}(\sin 3x \cos 2x)$$

$$= \frac{1}{(D-1)(D-1)}\left(\frac{1}{2}(\sin(5x) + \sin(x))\right)$$

$$= \frac{1}{2}\left[\frac{1}{2}\left(\frac{1}{D-3} - \frac{1}{D-1}\right)\right]\{\sin 5x + \sin x\}$$

$$= \frac{1}{4}\left[\frac{1}{D-3}(\sin 5x + \sin x) - \frac{1}{D-1}(\sin 5x + \sin x)\right]$$

$$= \frac{1}{4}\left[\frac{D+3}{D^2-9}(\sin 5x + \sin x) - \frac{(D+1)}{D^2-1}(\sin 5x + \sin x)\right]$$

$$= \frac{1}{4}\left[(D+3)\left(\frac{\sin 5x}{-5^2-9} + \frac{\sin x}{-1^2-9}\right)\right] - (D+1)\left(\frac{\sin 5x}{-5^2-1} + \frac{\sin x}{-1^2-1}\right)$$

($\because$ by put $D^2 = -5^2$, $D^2 = -1^2$)

$$= \frac{1}{4}\left[(D+3)\left(\frac{\sin 5x}{-34} + \frac{\sin x}{-10}\right) - (D+1)\left(\frac{\sin 5x}{-26} + \frac{\sin x}{-2}\right)\right]$$

$$= \frac{1}{4}\begin{bmatrix} \dfrac{-5\cos 5x}{-34} + \dfrac{\cos x}{-10} \dfrac{-3}{34}\sin 5x - \dfrac{3}{10}\sin x \\ + \dfrac{5\cos 5x}{26} - \dfrac{\cos x}{2} + \dfrac{\sin 5x}{26} + \dfrac{\sin x}{2} \end{bmatrix}$$

$$= \frac{10\cos 5x - 11\sin 5x}{4.(221)} + \frac{1}{20}(\sin x + 2\cos x)$$

OR

$$= \frac{1}{D^2 - 4D + 3}(\sin 3x \cos 2x)$$

$$= \frac{1}{2}.\frac{1}{D^2 - 4D + 3}(\sin 5x + \sin x)$$

$$= \frac{1}{2}\left\{\frac{1}{D^2 - 4D + 3}(\sin 5x) + \frac{1}{D^2 - 4D + 3}\sin x\right\}$$

$$= \frac{1}{2} \qquad \{PI_1 \quad + \quad PI_2\}$$

Now, $\quad PI_1 = \dfrac{1}{D^2 - 4D + 3}(\sin 5x)$

Put $\quad D^2 = -5^2 = -25$

$$= \frac{1}{-25 - 4D + 3} = \frac{1}{-22 - 4D}(\sin 5x) = -\frac{1}{2}\left(\frac{1}{11 + 20}\right)(\sin 5x)$$

$$= -\frac{1}{2}\frac{1}{(2D + 11)}(\sin 5x)$$

$$= -\frac{1}{2}\left(\frac{2D - 11}{4D^2 - 121}\right)(\sin 5x)$$

Put $\quad D^2 = -25$

$$= -\frac{1}{2}\left(\frac{2D - 11}{4(-25) - 121}\right)(\sin 5x)$$

$$= -\frac{1}{2}\frac{(2D - 11)(\sin 5x)}{(-221)}$$

$\therefore \quad PI_1 = \dfrac{1}{2(221)}[10\cos 5x - 11\sin 5x]$

Now, $\quad PI_2 = \dfrac{\sin x}{(D^2 - 4D + 3)} \quad$ (put $D^2 = -1$)

$$= \frac{\sin x}{-1 - 4D + 3} = \frac{\sin x}{2 - 4D} = \frac{1}{2(1 - 2D)}\sin x = \frac{1}{2}\frac{(1 + 2D)}{1 - 4D^2}(\sin x)$$

$$= \frac{1}{2}.\frac{1 + 2D}{1 - 4(-1)}(\sin x)$$

$$= \frac{1}{10}.(\sin x + 2\cos x)$$

$\therefore$ the general solution is

$$y = C_1\, e^x + C_2\, e^{3x} + \frac{1}{2}\left[\frac{1}{2(221)}(10 \cos 5x - 11 \sin 5x) + \frac{1}{2}.\frac{1}{10}(\sin x + 2 \cos x)\right]$$

$$= C_1\, e^x + C_2\, e^{3x} + \frac{1}{4(221)}(10 \cos 5x - 11 \sin 5x) + \frac{1}{20}.(\sin x + 2 \cos x)$$

6. Solve $(D^3 - 1)\, y = e^x + \sin 3x + 2$

Sol: To get complementary function y_C.

Consider $D^3 - 1 = 0$

The corresponding auxillary equation is

$$m^3 - 1 = 0 \qquad m = 1, \quad \frac{-1+i\sqrt{3}}{2}, \quad \frac{-1-i\sqrt{3}}{2}$$

∴ the complete integral is

$$y_c = C_1 e^x + e^{-1/2x}\left(C_2 \cos\frac{\sqrt{3}}{2}x + C_3 \sin\frac{\sqrt{3}}{2}x\right)$$

To get particular integral y_P

$$y_P = \frac{1}{D^3 - 1}\left(e^x + \sin 3x + 2\right)$$

$$= \frac{1}{D^3-1}\left(e^x\right) + \frac{1}{D^3-1}(\sin 3x) + \frac{1}{D^3-1}(2)$$

$$= \frac{1}{(D-1)\left(D^2+D+1\right)}\left(e^x\right) + \frac{1}{D(-9)-1}(\sin 3x) + \frac{2}{0-1}$$

(∵ Putting $D^2 = -9$)

$$= \frac{1}{1^2+1+1}.e^x\frac{x^1}{1!} + \frac{1}{-9D-1}(\sin 3x) - 2$$

$$= \frac{1}{3}xe^x - \frac{(9D-1)}{81\,D^2-1}(\sin 3x) - 2$$

$$= \frac{x\,e^x}{3} - (9D-1).\frac{\sin 3x}{(81)(-9)-1} - 2 \qquad (\because \text{ Put } D^2 = -3^2 = -9)$$

$$= \frac{xe^x}{3} - \frac{(9D-1)\ \sin 3x}{-729-1} - 2$$

$$= \frac{xe^x}{3} + \frac{1}{730}(9.3\cos 3x - \sin 3x) - 2$$

$$= \frac{xe^x}{3} + \frac{27}{730}\cos 3x - \frac{1}{730}\sin 3x - 2$$

$\therefore$ the general solution is

$$y = y_c + y_p$$

$$= C_1\, e^{x} + e^{-x/2}\left[C_2 \cos \frac{\sqrt{3}}{2}x + C_3 \sin \frac{\sqrt{3}x}{2}\right]$$

$$+ \frac{1}{730}\left(27 \cos 3x - \sin 3x\right) - 2$$

7. Solve $(D^3 - 7D^2 + 14D - 8)\, y = e^x \cos 2x$

Sol: To get complementary function (y_c):

Consider $D^3 - 7D^2 + 14D - 8 = 0$

The corresponding auxillary equation is

$$f(m) = m^3 - 7\,m^2 + 14\,m - 8 = 0$$

$$f(1) = 1 - 7 + 14 - 8 = 15 - 15 = 0$$

$\therefore$ 1 is root of $f(m) = 0$

now

1	1	–7	14	–8
	0	1	–6	8
	1	–6	8	(0)

$$m^2 - 6\,m + 8 = 0 \quad \Rightarrow \quad m^2 - 4m - 2m + 8 = 0$$

$$m(m-4) - 2\,(m-4) = 0$$

$$\therefore\ m = 2, 4$$

$\therefore$ $m = 1, 2, 4$

$\therefore$ the complementary function is

$$y_c = C_1\, e^x + C_2\, e^{2x} + C_3\, e^{-4x}$$

To get particular integral (y_p)

$$y_p = \frac{1}{D^3 - 7D^2 + 14D - 8}\left(e^x \cos 2x\right)$$

$$= e^x \frac{1}{(D+1)^3 - 7(D+1)^2 + 14(D+1) - 8}(\cos 2x)$$

$$\left(\because \frac{1}{f(d)}\, e^{ax}.\, v = e^{ax}\, \frac{1}{f(D+a)}(v)\right)$$

$$= e^x \left(\frac{1}{D^3 + 3D^2 + 3D + 1 - 7\left(D^2 + 2D + 1\right) + 14D + 14 - 8} \right) (\cos 2x)$$

$$= e^x \left(\frac{1}{D^3 + 3D^2 + 3D + 1 - 7D^2 - 14D - 7 + 14D + 14 - 8} \right) (\cos 2x)$$

$$= e^x \left(\frac{1}{\left(D^3 - 4D^2 + 3D\right)} (\cos 2x) \right)$$

$$= e^x \left(\frac{\cos 2x}{-4D - 4(-4) + 3D} \right) \qquad (\because \text{ put } D^2 = -2^2 = -4)$$

$$= e^x \left(\frac{\cos 2x}{16 - D} \right)$$

$$= e^x \left(\frac{16 + D}{256 - D^2} (\cos 2x) \right)$$

$$= e^x \left[(16 + D) \left(\frac{\cos 2x}{256 - (-4)} \right) \right]$$

$$= e^x \left[(16 + D) \frac{(\cos 2x)}{260} \right]$$

$$= \frac{e^x}{260} [16 \cos 2x - 2 \sin 2x]$$

$\therefore$ general solution is $y = y_c + y_p$

$$= C_1 e^x + C_2 e^{2x} + C_3 e^{4x} + \frac{e^x}{260} \quad [16 \cos 2x - 2 \sin 2x]$$

8. $(D^2 + 4D + 3) y = e^{-x} \sin x + x$

Sol: To get complementary function (y_c)

Consider $(D^2 + 4D + 3) y = 0$

The corresponding auxillary equations

$$f(m) = m^2 + 4m + 3 = 0$$

$\therefore \quad m^2 + 3m + m + 3 = 0 \quad \Rightarrow \quad m(m + 3) + 1(m + 3) = 0$

$\therefore \qquad m = -1, m = -3$

$\therefore$ the complementary function is $y_c = c_1 e^{-x} + c_2 e^{-3x}$

To get particular integral(y_p).

$$y_p = \frac{1}{D^2 + 4D + 3}\left(e^{-x}\sin x + x\right)$$

$$= \frac{1}{D^2 + 4D + 3}\left(e^{-x}\sin x\right) + \frac{1}{D^2 + 4D + 3}(x)$$

$$= e^{-x}\left[\frac{\sin x}{(D-1)^2 + 4(D-1) + 3}\right] + \frac{1}{3\left[1 + \frac{D^2 + 4D}{3}\right]}(x)$$

$$= e^{-x}\left[\frac{\sin x}{D^2 + 1 - 2D + 4D - 4 + 3}\right] + \frac{1}{3}\left(1 + \frac{D^2 + 4D}{3}\right)(x)$$

$$= e^{-x}\left[\frac{\sin x}{D^2 + 2D}\right] + \frac{1}{3}\left(1 - \frac{D^2 + 4D}{3} + \ldots\right)(x)$$

$$= e^{-x}\left(\frac{\sin x}{-1^2 + 2D}\right) + \frac{1}{3}\left[1 - \frac{D^2 + 4D}{3}\right](x)$$

$$= e^{-x}\left(\frac{\sin x}{2D - 1}\right) + \frac{1}{3}\left[x - \frac{1}{3}(0 + 4)\right]$$

$$= e^{-x}\left[\frac{2D + 1}{4D^2 - 1}(\sin x) + \frac{1}{3}\left(x - \frac{4}{3}\right)\right]$$

$$= e^{-x}\left[(2D + 1)\left(\frac{\sin x}{4(-1)^2 - 1}\right) + \frac{1}{3}\left(x - \frac{4}{3}\right)\right]$$

$$= e^{-x}\left[(2D + 1)\left(\frac{\sin x}{-5}\right) + \frac{1}{3}\left(x - \frac{4}{3}\right)\right]$$

$$= e^{-x}\left[\frac{-1}{5}(2\cos x + \sin x)\right] + \frac{1}{3}x - \frac{4}{9}$$

$\therefore$ the general solution by

$$y = y_c + y_p$$

$$\therefore \quad y = c_1 e^{-x} + c_2 e^{-3x} + \frac{1}{3}\left(x - \frac{4}{3}\right) - \frac{e^{-x}}{5}(2\cos x + \sin x)$$

9. Solve $(D^2 - 1)\, y = x \sin x + x^2 e^x$.

Sol: To get complementary function (y_c)

Consider $(D^2 - 1)\, y = 0$

The corresponding auxillary equation is

$$m^2 - 1 = 0 \quad \Rightarrow \quad m = \pm 1$$

$\therefore$ the complementary function is $y_c = c_1 e^x + c_2 e^{-x}$

To get particular integral (y_p):

$$y_p = \frac{1}{D^2 - 1}\left(x \sin x + x^2 e^x\right)$$

$$= \frac{x \sin x}{D^2 - 1} + \frac{x^2 e^x}{D^2 - 1}$$

$$= \left(x - \frac{2D}{D^2 - 1}\right)\frac{1}{D^2 - 1}(\sin x) + e^x\left(\frac{x^2}{(D+1)^2 - 1}\right)$$

$$\left(\because \frac{1}{f(D)}(xv) = \left(x - \frac{f(D)}{f(D)}\frac{1}{f(D)}(v)\right)\right.$$

$$\left.\because \frac{1}{f(D)}\left(e^{ax}v\right) = e^{ax}.\frac{1}{f(D+a)}v\right)$$

$$= \left(x - \frac{2D}{D^2 - 1}\right)\left(\frac{1}{-1^2 - 1}\sin x\right) + e^x\left(\frac{x^2}{D^2 + 2D + 1 - 1}\right)$$

$$= \left(x - \frac{2D}{D^2 - 1}\right)\left(\frac{1}{-2}\sin x\right) + e^x\left(\frac{1}{D^2 + 2D}\left(x^2\right)\right)$$

$$= \frac{-1}{2}x\sin x + \frac{D}{D^2 - 1}(\sin x) + e^x\left[\frac{1}{D(D+2)}\left(x^2\right)\right]$$

$$= \frac{-1}{2}x\sin x + D\left(\frac{\sin x}{-2}\right) + \frac{e^x}{2}\left(\frac{1}{D} - \frac{1}{D+2}\right)(x^2)$$

$$= \frac{-1}{2}x\sin x + \frac{\cos x}{-2} + \frac{e^x}{2}\left[\frac{x^3}{3} - \frac{1}{D+2}(x^2)\right]$$

$$= \frac{-1}{2}x\sin x \frac{-1}{2}\cos x + \frac{x^3e^x}{6} - \frac{e^x}{2}\left(\frac{1}{2\left(1+\frac{D}{2}\right)}x^2\right)$$

$$= \frac{-1}{2}x\sin x \frac{-1}{2}\cos x + \frac{x^3e^x}{6} - \frac{e^x}{4}\left(1+\frac{D}{2}\right)^{-1}(x^2)$$

$$= \frac{-1}{2}x\sin x - \frac{1}{2}\cos x + \frac{x^3e^x}{6} - \frac{e^x}{4}\left(1 - \frac{D}{2} + \left(\frac{D}{2}\right)^2 + \ldots\right)(x^2)$$

$$= \frac{-1}{2}x\sin x - \frac{1}{2}\cos x + \frac{x^3e^x}{6} - \frac{e^x}{4}\left[x^2 - \frac{2x}{2} + \frac{1}{4}.2\right]$$

$$= \frac{-1}{2}x\sin x - \frac{1}{2}\cos x + \frac{x^3e^x}{6} - \frac{x^2e^x}{4} + \frac{xe^x}{4} - \frac{1}{8}e^x$$

$$= \frac{-1}{2}(x\sin x + \cos x) + \frac{x\,e^x}{12}\left(2x^2 - 3x + 3\right) - \frac{1}{8}e^x$$

$\therefore$ The general solution is

$$y = c_3\,e^x + c_2\,e^{-x} - \frac{1}{2}\,(x\sin x + \cos x) + \frac{x\,e^x}{12}\,(2x^2 - 3x + 3)$$

where

$$c_3 = (c_1 - \frac{1}{8})$$

10. Solve $(D^2 - 4D + 4)\,y = x^2\sin x + e^{2x} + 3$

Sol: To get complementary function y_c

Consider $(D^2 - 4D + 4)\,y = 0$

The corresponding auxillary equation is

$$m^2 - 4m = 0 \quad \Rightarrow \quad (m-2)^2 = 0 \quad \Rightarrow \quad m = 2, 2$$

$$\because \quad y_c = (c_1 + c_2 x)\, e^{2x}$$

To get particular integral (y_p)

$$y_p = \frac{1}{(D-2)^2}\left(x^2 \sin x + e^{2x} + 3\right)$$

$$= \frac{1}{(D-2)^2}\left(x^2 \sin x\right) + \frac{1}{(D-2)^2}\left(e^{2x}\right) + \frac{1}{(D-2)^2}(3)$$

$$= \text{IP}_1 + e^{2x}\frac{x^2}{2!} + \frac{3}{(0-2)^2}$$

where

$$\text{IP}_1 = \frac{1}{(D-2)^2}\left(x^2 \sin x\right)$$

$$= \text{Imaginary part of } \frac{1}{(D-2)^2}\left(x^2 . e^{ix}\right)$$

$$= \text{Imaginary part of } e^{ix}\frac{1}{\left[(D+i)-2\right]^2}\left(x^2\right)$$

$$= \text{Imaginary part of } e^{ix}\frac{1}{\left(D^2 + i^2 + 2iD\right) + 4 - 4(D+i)}\left(x^2\right)$$

$$= \frac{1}{625}\left[(220x + 244)\cos x + (40x + 33)\sin x\right]$$

$$\therefore \quad y_p = \frac{1}{625}\left\{(220x + 244)\cos x + (40x + 33)\sin x\right\} + \frac{x^2}{2}e^{2x} + \frac{3}{4}$$

$\therefore$ the general solution is

$$y = y_c + y_p$$

$$= (c_1 + c_2 x)\, e^{2x} + \frac{1}{625}\left\{(220x + 244)\cos x + (40x + 33)\sin x\right\}$$

29.6 Homogenous Linear Equations

An equation of the form $x^n \frac{d^n x}{dx^n} + p_1 x^{n-1} \frac{d^{n-1} y}{dx^{n-1}} + ... + p_n y = \phi(x)$

where $p_1, p_2 ... p_n$ are real constants and $\phi(x)$ is a real valued continuous function of x called a homogenous linear equation or Euler-Cauchy's linear equation of order n.

The equation in the differential operator form is

$$\left(x^n D^n + p_1 x^{n-1} D^{n-1} + ... + p_n\right) y = \phi(x) \text{ where } D = \frac{d}{dx}$$

To solve the Cauchy's linear D.E.

Step 1: To convert Cauchy's linear D.E. in to a linear equation with constant coefficients by change of independent variable with the substitution

$$x = e^z \text{ i.e., } z = \log_e x.$$

$$\Rightarrow \quad \frac{dz}{dx} = \frac{1}{x}$$

$$\therefore \quad \frac{dy}{dx} = \frac{dy}{dz} \cdot \frac{dz}{dx} = \frac{1}{x} \cdot \frac{dy}{dz}$$

$$\Rightarrow \quad x . \frac{dy}{dx} = \frac{dy}{dz}$$

again, $$\frac{d^2 y}{dx^2} = \frac{d}{dx}\left(\frac{dy}{dx}\right) = \frac{d}{dx}\left[\frac{1}{x} \cdot \frac{dy}{dz}\right]$$

$$= \frac{-1}{x^2} \cdot \frac{dy}{dz} + \frac{1}{x} \cdot \frac{d}{dx}\left(\frac{dy}{dz}\right) = \frac{-1}{x^2} \frac{dy}{dz} + \frac{1}{x} \cdot \frac{d}{dz}\left(\frac{dy}{dx}\right)$$

$$= \frac{-1}{x^2} \cdot \frac{dy}{dz} + \frac{1}{x} \cdot \frac{d}{dz}\left(\frac{dy}{dz}\right)\left(\frac{dz}{dx}\right)$$

$$= \frac{-1}{x^2} \cdot \frac{dy}{dz} + \frac{1}{x^2} \frac{d^2 y}{dz^2} \qquad \left(\because \frac{dz}{dx} = \frac{1}{x}\right)$$

$$\therefore \quad x^2 \frac{d^2 y}{dx^2} = \frac{d^2 y}{dz^2} - \frac{dy}{dz}$$

Similarly we can prove $x^3 . \frac{d^3 y}{dx^3} = \frac{d^3 y}{dz^3} - 3 \frac{d^2 y}{dz^2} + 2 . \frac{dy}{dz}$

Step 2: Take $\frac{d}{dz} = \theta$ then

$$x^2 D^2 = \theta(\theta - 1),\ x^3 D^3 = \theta(\theta - 1)(\theta - 2) \text{ etc.}$$

Step 3: Solve the L.D. in θ by above methods

11. Solve $x^2 \frac{d^2y}{dx^2} - x.\frac{dy}{dx} + 2y = x \log x$

Sol: Given differential equations

$$(x^2 D^2 - x. D + 2)\, y = x \log x$$

Put $x = e^z$ then $z = \log x$

$\therefore \quad x^2 D^2 = \theta(\theta - 1),\ xD = \theta \qquad$ where $\theta = \frac{d}{dz}$

$$\therefore \quad [\,\theta(\theta - 1) - \theta + 2]\, y = z.e^z$$

$$[\theta^2 - 2\theta + 2]\, y = ze^z$$

This is linear differential equation with constant coefficients

The corresponding auxillary equation of θ(4) = 0 is

$$m^2 - 2m + 2 = 0 \quad \Rightarrow \quad m = 1 \pm i$$

$$\therefore \quad y_c = e^z (c_1 \cos z + c_2 \sin z)$$

and particular integral is

$$\text{P. I} = y_p = \frac{ze^z}{\theta^2 - 2\theta + 2} = e^z \left(\frac{z}{(\theta+1)^2 - 2(\theta+1) + 2} \right)$$

$$= e^z \frac{z}{(\theta^2 + 1)} = e^z.(1 + \theta^2)^{-1}(z)$$

$$= e^z (1 - \theta^2)(z)$$

$$= e^z (z - 0) = z.e^z$$

∴ the general solution is

$$y = e^z(c_1 \cos z + c_2 \sin z) + ze^z$$

or $\quad y = x[c_1 \cos(\log x) + c_2 \sin(\log x)] + x \log x \qquad (\because e^z - x, \text{ and } z = \log_e x)$

29.7 Legendre's Linear Equation

An equation is of the form

$$(a+bx)^n.\frac{d^n x}{dx^n}+p_1(a+bx)^{n-1}\frac{d^{n-1}y}{dx^{n-1}}+....+p_n y=Q(x)$$

where $p_1, p_2 ..... p_n$ are real constants and Q(x) is a function of x is called legendre's linear equation.

This equation can be solved by using substitution $a + bx = u$ and $u = e^z$.

So that z = log u.

12. Solve $(1+x)^2.\frac{d^2y}{dx^2}+(1+x)\frac{dy}{dx}+y=\sin 2(\log(1+x))$

Sol: Put $x + 1 = u \Rightarrow \quad \frac{dx}{dy}=\frac{du}{dy} \quad \Rightarrow \quad \frac{dy}{dx}=\frac{dy}{du}$

Then $u^2\frac{d^2y}{du}+u\frac{dy}{du}+y=\sin 2(\log u)$ .....(1)

Put $u=e^z \quad \Rightarrow \quad z=\log u$

Then $u^2.\frac{d^2y}{dx^2}=\theta(\theta-1)y$ when $\theta=\frac{d}{dz}$, $u.\frac{dy}{du}=\theta y$

$\therefore$(1) becomes

$$\theta(\theta - 1)y + \theta y + y = \sin 2(z)$$

$$\Rightarrow \quad (\theta^2 - \theta + \theta + 1)\, y = \sin 2z$$

$$\Rightarrow \quad (\theta^2 + 1)y = \sin 2z$$

The auxillary equation is $m^2 + 1 = 0 \Rightarrow m = \pm i$

$\therefore \quad y_c = e^o\,(c_1 \cos z + c_2 \sin z)$

and $\quad \text{P.I} = y_p = \frac{1}{\theta^2+1}(\sin\ 2z)$

$$=\frac{\sin\ 2z}{-2^2+1}=\frac{\sin 2z}{-3}=\frac{\sin 2(\log u)}{-3}$$

$$=\frac{\sin\ 2(\log(1+x))}{-3}$$

$\therefore$ the general solution $y = c_1 \cos z + c_2 \sin z - \frac{1}{3} \sin 2(\log(1+x))$

$$= c_1 \cos \log(x+1) + c_2 \sin(\log(x+1)$$

$$- \frac{1}{3} . \sin 2 (\log(1+x)).$$

29.8 Linear Equation of the Second Order with Variable Coefficients (Method of Variation of Parameters)

An equation is of the form

$$\frac{d^2y}{dx^2} + p(x)\frac{dy}{dx} + Q(x) = R(x)$$

where $p(x)$, $Q(x)$, $R(x)$ are real valued functions of x called linear equation of second order with variable coefficients.

Working rule to solve $\frac{d^2y}{dx^2} + p\frac{dy}{dx} + Qy = R$ by methods of variation of parameters.

Step 1: Reduce the given equation into the standard form if necessary.

Step 2: Find complementary function

$$y_c = c_1 u(x) + c_2 v(x)$$

Step 3: Take P.I $= y_p = Au + Bv$ where A, B, are functions of x obtained by

$$A = -\int \frac{v R\, dx}{u\frac{dv}{dx} - v.\frac{du}{dx}}$$

$$B = \int \frac{u R\, dx}{u\frac{dv}{dx} - v.\frac{du}{dx}}$$

Step 4: Write generation solution by

$$y = c_1 u(x) + c_2 v(x) +$$

$$A(x) . u(x) + B(x). v(x)$$

where c_1, c_2 are constants.

13. Solve $(D^2 + a^2)\, y = \sec ax$ by method of variation of parameters.

Sol: Given equation is $(D^2 + a^2)\, y = \sec ax$.

The auxillary equation is $(m^2 + a^2) = 0$

$\therefore \quad m = \pm ai$

$\therefore$ the complementary function C.F. = e^{ox} ($c_1 \cos(ax) + c_2 \sin(ax)$

$$y = c_1.\cos ax + c_2 \sin ax$$

$\therefore$ i.e., $y = c_1.u(x) + c_2\, v(x)$

where $u(x) = \cos ax,\ v(x) = \sin ax.$

Now $$u.\frac{dv}{dx} - v.\frac{du}{dx} = \cos\ ax.\cos ax\ (a) - \sin ax(-a\ \sin\ ax)$$

$$= a[\cos^2 ax + \sin^2 ax]$$

$$= a$$

Now $$A = -\int \frac{v\,R}{u.\dfrac{dv}{dx} - u.\dfrac{dy}{dn}}dn$$

$$= -\int \frac{\sin\ ax}{a}.\sec ax\ dx$$

$$= -\frac{1}{a}\int \frac{\sin ax}{\cos ax}dx$$

$$= \frac{1}{a^2}\int \frac{-a\sin ax}{\cos ax}dx$$

$$= \frac{1}{a^2}.\ \log(\cos ax)$$

and $$B = \int \frac{u\,R}{u.\dfrac{dv}{dx} - v.\dfrac{du}{dx}}dx$$

$$= \int \frac{\cos ax.\sec ax}{a}dx$$

$$= \int \frac{1}{a}dx = \frac{1}{a}\int dx = \frac{x}{a}$$

$\therefore$ particular integral = P.I = y_p

$$A(x).u(x) + B(x).v(x)$$

$$= \frac{1}{a^2}(\log(\cos ax)(\cos ax) + \frac{x}{a}\ \sin ax$$

∴ the general solution is

$$y = y_c + y_p$$

$$= c_1 \cos ax + c_2 \sin ax + \frac{1}{a^2}\log(\cos ax)\ \cos ax + \frac{x}{a}\sin(ax)$$

Exercise - 29.2

I. Solve the following non homogeneous linear differential equations

1. $\frac{d^2y}{dx^2} + 4.\frac{dy}{dx} + 3y = e^{2x}$
2. $(D^2 + 5D + 6)\ y = e^x$
3. $\frac{d^2y}{dx^2} + \frac{dy}{dx} + y = e^x$
4. $(D^2 + 4)\ y = e^x + \sin 2x + \cos 2x$
5. $(D^3 - 3D^2 + 4) = 6 + 80 \cos 2x$
6. $(D^2 - 3D + 2)\ y = \cos 3x - \cos 2x$
7. $\frac{d^2y}{dx^2} + \frac{dy}{dx} = x^2 + 2x + 4$
8. $(D^2 - 6D + 9)\ y = 54x + 18$
9. $(D^4 - 1).y = e^x \cos x$
10. $(D^3 - 3D^2 + 3D - 1)\ y = x^2 e^x$
11. $(D^2 - 2D + 2)\ y = 1 + x\, e^x$
12. $(D^2 + 4)\ y = x \sin x$
13. $(D^2 + D + 1)\ y = x \cos x$

Ans: $y = c_1\, e^{-x} + c_2\, e^{-3x} + \frac{e^{2x}}{15}$

Ans: $c_1 e^{-3x} + c_2\, e^{-2x} + \frac{e^x}{12}$

Ans: $y = e^{-\frac{x}{2}}\left(c_1 \cos\frac{x\sqrt{3}}{2} + c_2 \sin\frac{x\sqrt{3}}{2}\right) + \frac{e^x}{3}$

Ans: $y = c_1 \cos 2x + c_2 \sin 2x + \frac{1}{5}\, e^x - \frac{x}{4} \cos 2x + \frac{x}{4} \sin 2x$

Ans: $y = c_1 e^{-x} + (c_2 + c_3x)\, e^{2x} + \frac{3}{2} + (4 \cos 2x - 2 \sin 2x).$

Ans: $y = c_1 e^x + c_2 e^{2x} - \frac{15\sin 5x + 23\cos 5x}{1508} + \frac{\cos x - 3\sin x}{20}$

Ans: $y = c_1 + c_2 e^{-x}\, \frac{x^3}{3} + 4x$

Ans: $y = (c_1 + c_2 x)\, e^{3x} + 6x + 6$

Ans: $c_1 e^x + c_2 e^{-x} + c_3 \cos x + 4\sin x - \frac{e^x \cos x}{5}$

Ans: $y = (c_1 + c_2 x + c_3 x^2)\, e^x + e^x .\, \frac{x^5}{60}$

Ans: $y = e^x (c_1 \cos x + c_2 \sin x) + \frac{1}{2} + x.e^x$

Ans: $y = c_1 \cos 2x + c_2 \sin 2x + \frac{x}{3} \sin x - \frac{2}{9} \cos x$

Ans: $(c_1 + c_2 x)\, e^{-x} + \frac{x}{2} \sin + \frac{1}{2} (\cos x - \sin x)$

II Solve the homogeneous linear equations

1. $x^2\frac{d^2y}{dx^2} - x\frac{dy}{dx} + y = \log x$

2. $x^2\frac{d^2y}{dx^2} - 3x\frac{dy}{dx} + 4y = (1+x)^2$

3. $(x^2 D^2 - 2x D - 4)\, y = x^2 + 2\log x$

4. $[(x+1)^2 D^2 + (x+1)D]\, y = (2x - 13)(2x + 4)$

5. $[(1+x)^2 D^2 + (1+x) D + 1]\, y = 4 \cos \log (x+1)$

Ans: $y = (c_1 + c_2 \log x)\, x + \log x + 2$

Ans: $(c_1 + c_2 \log x)\, x^2 + \dfrac{1}{4} + x^2 \dfrac{(\log x)^2}{2} + 2x$

Ans: $y = c_1 x^4 + \dfrac{c_2}{x} - \dfrac{x^2}{6} - \dfrac{1}{2} (\log x - \dfrac{3}{4})$

Ans: $c_1 + c_2 \log (x + 1) + (x + 1)^2 + 6.(x + 1) + [\log (x + 1)]^2$

Ans: $y = c_1 \cos \log (x + 1) + c_2 \log (x + 1) + 2 \log (1 + x) \sin (\log (1 + x))$

III Solve the linear equation by method of variation of parameters

1. $\dfrac{d^2 y}{dx^2} + y = \operatorname{cosec} x$
2. $\dfrac{d^2 y}{dx^2} + 4y = \tan 2x$

Ans: $y = c_1 \cos x + c_2 \sin x - x \cos x + \sin x \log (\sin x)$

Ans: $y = c_1 \cos 2x + c_2 \sin 2x - \dfrac{1}{4} \cos 2x \log|\sec 2x + \tan 2x|$

Questions

1. (a) The three numbers whose sum is 18 are in A.P. If 2,4 and 11 are added to them respectively, the resulting numbers are in G.P. Find the numbers.

   (b) Resolve $\frac{x-1}{x(x+2)(x+6)}$ into partial fractions.

   (c) Solve $4x + y = 7$; $3y + 4z = 5$; $3z + 5x = 2$ by using Cramer's rule.

2. (a) A person standing on the bank of a river observes that the angle of elevation of the top of a tree on the opposite bank is 60^0, when he retires 40 feet from the bank he finds the angle to be 30^0. Find the height of the tree and breadth of the river.

   (b) Show that (i) $\sin 3A = 3 \sin A - 4 \sin^3 A$ (ii) $\cos 3A = 4 \cos^3 A - 3 \cos A$

3. (a) Show that the points (2, – 2), (8, 4), (5, 7) and (–1, 1) are the vertices of the rectangle.

   (b) Find the equation of the locus of the point which moves such that the sum of its distance from (0, 4) and (0, – 4) is 10 units.

   (c) Find the equation of the line which passes through the points (– 5, 4) and is such that the portion of it between the axes is divided by the point in the ratio 2: 1

4. (a) Find $\frac{dy}{dx}$ if (i) $y = x^2. e^x .(\cos x - 4)$ (ii) $y = \sin x . \log x. (e^x + 3)$

   (b) The perimeter of a triangle is 10 cm. If one of the side is 4 cm, what are the other two sides for maximum area of the triangle?

5. (a) Integrate the following w.r.t x

   (i) $4x^2 - 2x + 1$ (ii) $2 \sin x - 4 \sec^2 x + 1$

   (b) Evaluate $\int x \sin x\, dx$ and $\int x^3. e^{2x}\, dx$

6. (a) Evaluate $\int \sec^4 x . \tan x\, dx$ and $\int \cos^3 x . \sin^4 x\, dx$

   (b) Find the area bounded by the curve $y = x^2 - 7x + 10$ and x-axis.

7. (a) Form the Differential Equation, from the relation

   $y = ae^{2x} - be^{-3x}$, where a and b are arbitrary constants.

   (b) Solve $(x^2 + 1) \frac{dy}{dx} + y^2 + 1 = 0$

   (c) Solve $= \frac{dy}{dx} = \frac{(x^2 + y^2)}{2xy}$

8. (a) Define Laplace Transform. Give any two properties of Laplace Transform.

   (b) Find L [sin at] & L [cos at]

Answers

1. (a) Page No. 11 (Direct Model)
   (b) Page No. 43 (Direct Model)
   (c) Page No. 120 (Direct Model)
2. (a) Page No. 258 (Direct Model) (only one numerical change)
   (b) Page No. 229 (Direct Model)
3. (a) Page No. 271 (Direct Model)
   (b) Page No. 296 (Direct Model)
   (c) Page No. 322 (Direct Model)
4. (a) Page No. 418 (Direct Model)
   (b) Page No. 418 (Direct Model)
   (c) Page No. 488 (Model)
5. (a) (i) Page No. 502 (Direct Model) (ii) Page No. 502 (Direct Model)
   (b) (i) Page No. 558 (Direct Model)
6. (a) Page No. 518 (Model)
   (b) Page No. 616 (Direct Model)
7. (a) Page No. 639 (Direct Model)
   (b) Page No. 643 (Direct Model)
   (c) Page No. 663 (Direct Model)
8. (a) Page No. 669, 679 (Direct)
   (b) Page No. 672 (Direct)

1. (a) The three numbers whose sum is [illegible] are [illegible] respectively, the resulting numbers are [illegible]

(b) Resolve [illegible] into partial fractions

(c) Solve $4x + y = 7$; $3y + 4z = 5$; [illegible] by using Cramer's rule.

2. (a) A person standing on the bank of a river observes that the angle of elevation of the top of a tree on the opposite bank is 60^0, when he retires 40 feet from the bank he finds the angle to be 30^0. Find the height of the tree and breadth of the river.

(b) Show that (i) $\sin 3A = 3 \sin A - 4 \sin^3 A$ (ii) $\cos 3A = 4\cos^3 A - 3\cos A$

3. (a) Show that the points (2, − 2), (8, 4), (5, 7) and (−1, 1) are the vertices of the rectangle.

(b) Find the equation of the locus of the point which moves such that the sum of its distances from (0, 4) and (0, − 4) is 10 units

(c) Find the equation of the line which passes through the points (−5, 4) and is such that the portion of it between the axes is divided by the point in the ratio 2 : 1

4. (a) Differentiate: (i) $y = x^2 . e^x (\cos x + 4)$ (ii) $y = \sin x . \log x . (e^x + 3)$

(b) The perimeter of a triangle is 10 cm. If one of the side is 4 cm, what are the other two sides for maximum area of the triangle?

5. (a) Integrate the following w.r.t x
(i) [illegible] (ii) $2 \sin x - 4 \sec^2 x + 1$

(b) Evaluate $\int x \sin x \, dx$ and $\int x^3 e^{2x} dx$

6. (a) Evaluate [illegible] and $\int \cos^3 x \sin^4 x \, dx$

(b) Find the area bounded by the curve $y = x^2 - 7x + 10$ and x-axis.

7. (a) Form a differential equation from the relation [illegible] where a and b are arbitrary constants.

(b) Solve $(x^2 + 1)\frac{dy}{dx} + y^2 + 1 = 0$

(c) Solve [illegible]

8. (a) Define Laplace transform. Give [illegible] properties of Laplace transform.

(b) [illegible]